THESAURUS OF ERIC DESCRIPTORS

ERIC

THESAURUS OF ERIC DESCRIPTORS

with a special chapter on

The Role and Function of the Thesaurus in Education

by

Dr. Frederick Goodman

Department of Education, University of Michigan

New York

CCM Information Corporation

1970

PUBLISHER'S NOTE

The *Thesaurus of ERIC Descriptors* has been developed during the past five years under the auspices of the Educational Resources Information Center of the U.S. Office of Education. The multitude of tasks associated with the project has been guided by James L. Eller, Chief Lexicographer for ERIC and Chairman of the Panel of Educational Terminology of USOE. Mr. Eller has coordinated the assignments of the many contributors to the project, including the ERIC Clearinghouses, North American Rockwell Corporation, and Leasco Systems Corporation.

Previous paperback editions of the *Thesaurus* are superseded by this traditional hard cover edition. All newly assigned descriptors and revised hierarchical displays as of July 1970 are included. CCM Information Corporation has also included "The Role and Function of the Thesaurus in Education" by Dr. Frederick Goodman, Associate Professor of Education at the University of Michigan. This special article will bring to educators and other professionals the insight of one of the leading experts in the field of vocabulary development and communication.

Users are invited to review the *Thesaurus* and to submit comments to James L. Eller, ERIC, National Center for Educational Communication, U.S. Office of Education, 400 Maryland Avenue, S.W., Washington, D.C. 20202.

William E. Burgess
Director, Educational Products
CCM Information Corporation

Library of Congress Catalog Card Number: 78-130347
SBN: 8409-0277-8

CCM Information Corporation
909 Third Avenue
New York, N. Y. 10022

CONTENTS

U.S. Office of Education
Panel on Educational Terminology (PET)

James L. Eller, *Chairman*
ERIC, U.S. Office of
Education

Mary T. Fisher
North American Rockwell
Corp.

Terry L. Gillum
System Development
Corp.

Carter V. Good
ERIC Consultant
University of Cincinnati

Frederick L. Goodman
ERIC Consultant
University of Michigan

Allen R. Lichtenberger
National Center for Educational Statistics

Lawrence S. Papier
ERIC, U.S. Office of
Education

John A. Starkweather
ERIC Consultant
University of California

THE ROLE AND FUNCTION OF THE THESAURUS IN EDUCATION*

Dr. Frederick Goodman

General

A thesaurus developed for information retrieval purposes provides the filing labels which permit information to be stored by one person and retrieved by another. As an information system grows, its thesaurus is systematically built and refined to the point where it represents, in a very special sense, the vocabulary of a subject field. The *Thesaurus of ERIC Descriptors* represents such a vocabulary for the field of education. An understanding of its origins, its function and its limitations, is just as important to the teacher, the student of education or the educational researcher as it is for the indexer or custodian of the information pool it represents. If the *Thesaurus* is understood and used in an appropriate way, it can give all educators not only insight into the ERIC system but also an increased awareness of the language of their field.

Introduction

In his review of the second edition of the *Thesaurus of ERIC Descriptors,* James E. Rush declares that the document is an "authority list" and not, in the best sense of the word, a "thesaurus." He notes, "A Thesaurus is usually used in conjunction with free-vocabulary indexing (and retrieval) while the authority list must be used only with controlled-vocabulary indexing."[1] Although the point may seem a bit pedantic, it does focus attention on a critical aspect of the undertaking. In an area where there is as much confusion over the meaning of words as there is in education, someone must play the role of an authority with respect to terminology. I sincerely doubt that this *Thesaurus* could exist in its present form if it were not the creation of some sponsor with the ability to command considerable authority in one way or another. I shall endeavor in these introductory remarks to clarify the relationship between the "authority"

---

[1] *Journal of Library Automation,* Vol. 2, Number 4 (December 1969), p. 273.

(the Educational Resources Information Center, a division of the United States Office of Education) and the evolution of this "list" which it has authorized. The comments are intended for educators, not for information specialists. It is assumed that many users of the ERIC system may come into contact with this *Thesaurus*. My goal is simply to explain what it is, how it was compiled, and how it is intended that it be used.

Authority may be derived in many ways. A profession or a discipline may be structured in such a fashion that certain experts can clearly be designated as authority figures. In times of relatively stable social conditions, certain institutions may inherit authoritative status. Education, however, does not now appear to be characterized by a singular profession, a singular discipline, or monolithic institutions. Pluralism is the order of the day. Professional organizations proliferate; adherents of one discipline after another appear and argue the advantages of a particular approach, the attractiveness of a different conceptual framework; institutions which until recently seemed quite venerable are attacked from all sides.

Either the documentation system being created had to operate upon a faith that enough people would choose to use terminology in sufficiently similar ways to produce adequate retrieval, or it had to develop a means of controlling the terminology employed in the system. Once the decision was made not to gamble on the former, the issue became that of finding an acceptable, effective way of promoting the latter. Unfortunately, there seemed to be no way of creating a mature terminology control system which would be visibly authoritative from the start. The "authority list" had to grow, and, indeed, in many ways it is still in a stage of adolescence.

A great many terms are necessary to describe the many aspects of education, and the task of relating them in even an approximately consistent way is an enormous one. The undertaking obviously should be managed by people who not only know what they are talking about but who also should be able to predict what people in their field are likely to be talking about in the near future. It should also enlist people who are willing to pay a great deal of attention to the details of relating one term to another within the system. To engage a large number of these two kinds of people over a long period of time is very likely to cost a great deal of money. There is very little proprietary value in producing such a list of terms, for it can very easily be copied, adapted, updated, etc. Thus, because of its high cost and low proprietary value, it becomes a task likely to be funded only by a government.

A government has many ways of spending its money, however. After the decision has been made to spend money to produce an authority list, one must decide how this authority is to be delegated. The history of the development of the ERIC *Thesaurus* is the history of how this authority was delegated. Had the authority been delegated in a way which powerful segments of the educational community had not approved, money could not have bought an accepted "authority list."

If the system was to be acceptable several compromises seemed inevitable. First, enough people should be involved to represent critical expertise, but not so many that a coordinated effort could not be assured. Second, principles which seemed to work for the major documentation efforts in the physical sciences should be employed, but only if they could be relevant in the social science oriented world of education. Third, terminology problems should be solved in conjunction with all the other dimensions of an information system, but they should be separated out for specialized attention.

These became the main contours of the ERIC system. The system operates via many "clearinghouses," each placed in an area of expertise. Retrieval is coordinated through a Washington-based "ERIC Central." The system follows the principles of "coordinate indexing" used, for example, by the Defense Documentation Center and the Engineers Joint Council, two large operating systems. As shall be shown, honoring these principles automatically meant that the terminology in the *Thesaurus* had to come directly from existing educational literature and authorities. Terms are negotiated between individual clearinghouses and lexicographers employed by ERIC Central. Terminology policy is set by a group of people representing various educational and documentation interests (the Panel on Educational Terminology).

The bare bones of this structure were visible in 1964; the details are still being worked out.

Prior to the indexing of the first document selected for entry into the system, there was no *Thesaurus.* When confronted with the first document, the indexer identified the concepts which he felt to be important for purposes of describing (and thus retrieving) it. Each concept was then represented by a term of the indexer's choosing. The term, formally called a "descriptor," was to reflect the language normally used in related literature to describe the concept encountered. The descriptors, fabricated for purposes of describing the first documents to go into the system, became the initial entries in the *Thesaurus.* Obviously, this procedure means that the *Thesaurus* grows as the system grows; each new document entering the system brings with it the potential for at least one new descriptor. Naturally, the indexer is expected to use any descriptors already in the *Thesaurus* rather than add new descriptors which would duplicate existing ones. It is precisely in this sense that the system controls terminology. Differences of opinion on such matters must be negotiated by clearinghouse-based indexers and ERIC Central-employed lexicographers. To the extent that ERIC Central wins out in arguments of this kind the "authority" of the system lies in ERIC Central. To the extent that clearinghouses win the arguments the system's "authority" is decentralized. The growth of the *Thesaurus* is controlled by a constant tug-of-war between the centralizing and decentralizing tendencies built into the system.

But the process is actually more complex than this characterization implies. Most of the detailed ERIC Central lexicographic work has been done on a contract basis by private industry. North American Rockwell was the first large scale contractor. The present contract is with Leasco Systems and Research Corporation. The principle of involving private enterprise in the operation of the ERIC system appears in several other major ways. Distribution of documents, either in microfiche or hard copy form has been done by both Bell and Howell and by National Cash Register. The CCM Information Corporation, a subsidiary of Crowell Collier and Macmillan, is not only involved in the publication of this edition of the *Thesaurus of ERIC Descriptors* but also publishes the monthly *Current Index to Journals in Education,* which consists of items indexed and abstracted by the ERIC clearinghouses.

Thus the concept of "centralization vs. decentralization" is not quite one of a federal agency negotiating with the clearinghouses of academia. There is the additional complexity of the private sector of the economy relating to the public sector.[2] That the contracts have in fact been shifted from one firm to another demonstrates the competitive element built into the system.

Ultimately, however, there is little question about the final nature of the "authority." Clearinghouses may be decentralized, potential contractors may compete with actual contractors, but the Office of Education makes the final decisions as to which university or professional association is the site of a given clearinghouse, which firm is to have the contract, and what the terms will be. The point is that the nature of the federal authority behind the "authority list" is twofold. The U.S. Office of Education serves as both a single party to pluralistic terminology negotiations and as the source of overall power through its role of contract initiator, monitor, and renewer.

Cross-Referencing: Used For and Use Relationship

The basic terminology negotiations are formalized by use of routinized procedures. Candidates for descriptors are to be supported by references from standard dictionaries or textbooks. In addition, each term is to be

---

[2]This three-pronged approach is illustrated quite graphically on the forms used to justify the addition of new terms to the *Thesaurus.* On most of these sheets one can see the comments and initials of personnel from the clearinghouses, the lexicographic contractor, and U. S. Office of Education staff.

related or "cross-referenced" by three basic relationships to other terms already in the *Thesaurus.*

The simplest relationship is the Used For (UF) and Use (U) relationship. To identify which of two terms has won approval as the "preferred" term when a concept is likely to be thought of in two different ways, the Used For phrase is employed. Thus, for example, the approved term **Attendance** is entered along with the reference "used for absenteeism." A reciprocal entry is always required. In other words, at the place where the disallowed term would appear if it were allowed (in this instance, "absenteeism"), it is entered in smaller print to signify that it is not an approved term, and the notation "use **Attendance**" is appended. Another common way in which this relationship is utilized is to specify the use of a spelled-out term instead of an abbreviation. At its appropriate place in the alphabetically arranged list of words appears the abbreviation "CAI," followed by "use **Computer Assisted Instruction.**" The reciprocal entry appears a few pages later.

It should be noted that violations of the principle of using a spelled-out term instead of an abbreviation do occur in the *Thesaurus,* as in the case of **FLES**, which is the descriptor for "foreign language (in) elementary schools." The *Thesaurus* lists **FLES** followed by "UF foreign language elementary school." Then it lists "foreign language elementary school" followed by "use **FLES.**" This is exactly the reverse of the treatment of "CAI" (or of "EEG" for **Electroencephalography**, or "ITA" for **Initial Teaching Alphabet**). This overt discrepancy may be annoying in an abstract way, but it probably does not hinder the functioning of the system at all—at least it does not if one actually uses the *Thesaurus.* If he has checked the term in the *Thesaurus,* anyone conducting a search (or index-ing) will be able to perform his operations just as well by using the abbreviation in the case of **FLES** and the spelled-out version in the case of **Computer Assisted Instruction**. Consistency is desirable, but lapses of this kind are hardly critical.

Actually, the **Computer Assisted Instruction** example already introduced can be used quite well to illustrate the "preferred usage" application of the used for reference as well as the alphabetization or acronym application. Listed under that descriptor are the entries "used for computer aided instruction and computer based instruction."

This illustrates precisely the spirit in which the ERIC *Thesaurus* exercises its "authority." Both "computer *aided* instruction" and "computer *based* instruction" are perfectly reasonable terms, found frequently in educational literature. It is extremely hard to argue that **Computer Assisted Instruction** is intrinsically the best way of describing the concept involved. It is also hard to argue that all three terms should be approved for use, with some documents posted to one term and other documents posted to the other terms. Someone in a position of authority needs to make an arbitrary decision and see to it that, for purposes of indexing and searching within the ERIC system, the decision is followed. It is important that procedures for *arbitration* exist when *arbitrary* decisions must be made, and this is what the system is designed to promote.

Pressing the **Computer Assisted Instruction** example still further, we can illustrate the growing nature of the system, and the basic character of the thesaurus-controlled, coordinate-indexing approach, by noting that another phrase, "computer mediated instruction," may begin to circulate increasingly among educators. When confronted with a particular document which uses that phrase, an indexer working at a clearinghouse devoted to examining such matters must make a decision (1) simply to assign the term **Computer** *Assisted* **Instruction** to it and take no initiative to establish "computer *mediated* instruction" as a cross-reference with **Computer** *Assisted* **Instruction**; or (2) to assign the term **Computer** *Assisted* **Instruction** and take the initiative of recommending that "computer *mediated* instruction" be established as a Use reference in conjunction with **Computer** *Assisted* **Instruction**; or (3) to take the initiative of trying to establish "computer mediated instruction" as a legitimate, new descriptor, in which case the burden of proof falls upon the indexer to demonstrate why such a new term is justified, how the concept behind "computer mediated instruction" differs from the concept behind **Computer Assisted Instruction**. When approved by the ERIC Central lexicographers, the new descriptor could then be assigned to the document.

The theory behind this procedure is that subject-matter oriented people are in the best position to understand when differences in *terminology* involve differences in *concepts*; a centralized lexicography staff should review the implications of recommended new terms to see how they fit with general purpose reference works, the language emerging from other clearinghouses, terms used by other specialized information services, the specific stylistic demands of the ERIC system, and so on.

A significant reason for developing this example in this fashion is to emphasize a point which I hope has become increasingly obvious: deliberations concerning the use of any term (such as "computer mediated instruction") which does *not* now appear in the *Thesaurus* must be initiated by an indexer confronted by a particular document. No lexicographer can add a descriptor merely because he believes it might be useful; no member of the Panel on Educational Terminology can add a descriptor merely because he believes it might be useful; *no one* can ever add a descriptor to the *Thesaurus* unless a document is being filed under it.

This principle is designed to curtail much of the speculative theorizing which is sometimes associated with the elaboration of classification schemes. If he understands this principle, the person examining the

Thesaurus who wonders why he cannot find his favorite term or can find it only as a Use reference may be provided with answers. In the first instance (if he cannot find it at all), the answer is that no indexer has yet been confronted with a document which he believes requires, and which he can prove requires, the use of that term for indexing purposes. An indexer may know full well that he will need a certain term when he begins indexing a certain area of literature, but until he actually starts working on documents which use the concept he may not introduce the term to the *Thesaurus.* In the second instance (if the peruser finds his term in small print and is told to use another term), his term may indeed be a "preferred" term *now.* But documents were posted to another term at an earlier date. When the now favored term emerged, it was linked to the original descriptor as a Use reference because reversing the two terms (preferring the new one and telling people to search with it rather than with the original one) would require going through all of the old documents and changing the outmoded descriptor to the new one. For practical reasons, this has not been done. This kind of difficulty will not inhibit the functioning of the system if the *Thesaurus* is used, even though it may make the system appear inordinately "authoritarian" or "arbitrary."

As a result of this discussion one might conclude that the *Thesaurus of ERIC Descriptors* is a misnomer in another sense than that identified by James Rush. I refer simply to the fact that scattered throughout the alphabetical listing of terms are many words and phrases which are rigorously defined as *not being descriptors.* Such "non-descriptors" (the Use reference) simply appear in small print and are followed immediately by the instruction to turn to the proper descriptor.[3] They should cause no difficulty; indeed, they are entirely necessary as part of the "Thesaurus" of ERIC "Descriptors."

Cross-Referencing: Broader Term and Narrower Term Relationship

The next category of relationships is, perhaps, a more controversial aspect of the indexing approach used by the ERIC system. Descriptors are structured by using the phrases "Broader Term" (BT) and "Narrower Term" (NT). This introduction of hierarchical relationships can lead to both theoretical and practical objections.

Theoretically, one can argue that the idea behind "coordinate indexing" was to avoid building speculative classification schemes and to favor very

---

[3] The non-approved terms which appear in small print may even be entered into the *Thesaurus* in the same way that legitimate descriptors are entered. That is, an idexer fills in the same form that he would for a descriptor, offers the same kind of evidence for his thinking that he would offer a descriptor, initiates the same lexicographic review procedures he would initiate for a descriptor.

pragmatic, "pay-as-you-go" procedures which would stick very close to natural language usage and require a minimum of term "control." Attempts to superimpose "genus-species" type thinking on such an approach can be viewed as a compromise, as admission of defeat, as a "sell-out," or as mere insanity. Before some of the potential difficulties are illustrated, however, the use of the BT, NT notations deserves clarification.

When he fills out a Descriptor Justification Form in defense of a candidate descriptor, an indexer is expected to note which descriptors in the *Thesaurus* are "broader" than the term under consideration and which are "narrower." For example, under the term **Institutes (Training Programs)** are listed two narrower terms: **Science Institutes** and **Summer Institutes.** Obviously, each of these entries is narrower than the main entry, but narrower in quite different senses. One deals with what the institute is about; the other deals with when it is held. That one can immediately think of many other types of institutes—for example, "mathematics institutes," as an elaboration of one sense of narrowness, or perhaps "advanced institutes," to illustrate a still different type of narrowness—illustrates the pitfalls in any departure from the principle of adding descriptors only when forced to do so by the literature: the list might go on and on without any certainty about its completeness or incompleteness. An "NT" denotes simply that terms have gotten into the *Thesaurus* which, at a certain point in time, can be seen as "narrower" in some sense than some other term that happens also to be in the *Thesaurus*. An indexer adding a new term and a lexicographer reviewing a new term examine the *Thesaurus* for such relationships.

The one BT listed under **Institutes (Training Programs)** is **Educational Programs.** About all that can be said of this is that it is clearly moving in the opposite direction from the NT terms. The theoretical issues alluded to now begin to come into focus.

As a form of compromise between an uncontrolled approach and a completely logical, hierarchical system, this BT, NT technique has some advantages. A science teacher entering the *Thesaurus* by looking up **Institutes** would certainly welcome the information that there was a term **Science Institutes.** On the other hand, a person interested in adult education institutes who entered via **Institutes** would find that he could go "up" to the BT **Educational Programs** and, by looking at the entries there, come back "down" to **Adult Education Programs**, one of the narrower terms listed under **Educational Programs.** One obtains some of the theoretical advantages of switching levels of generalization while retaining the advantage of not having to develop logical categories relating different types of "narrowness."

On the negative side of the theoretical concerns, those who point to the after-the-fact nature of attempts to build hierarchies can argue that logic simply cannot prevail in a system which grows with the literature; that one cannot get enough out of the "jerry-built" hierarchies to justify the effort; that the admission that hierarchies are necessary is sufficient evidence to demand that decent, *a priori* hierarchies be built in the first place.

It is not my intention to weigh the relative merits of the theoretical issues; I simply want to identify them.

At the practical level, the BT, NT links allow some very interesting observations. Because the terms in the *Thesaurus* are all available in machine readable form, a computer print-out can be produced to arrange the terms in a hierarchical display, which provides anyone interested in the *Thesaurus* a quick way of seeing its "dynamics"—indeed, the "dynamics" of the ERIC system. One can quickly identify complex clusters of terms that need considerable re-working. In some instances a term will lead upward to a BT which has little or no relationship to it; in other instances obvious BT relationships are omitted. Many new Descriptor Justification Forms, calling for adjustments in the broader and narrower terms, have been prepared as a result of examination of the hierarchies. The impact of such corrections has not yet been fully felt on the *Thesaurus*, for these Descriptor Justification Forms have not been completely processed, but this work should be viewed as one of the potential cures for the *Thesaurus'* present adolescence.

Users of the ERIC system should be aware that only through the BT, NT structure as revealed in the *Thesaurus* can they exploit the hierarchies which have been built into the system. There is no "automatic" posting of documents, so either the indexer or the searcher must associate the term **Institutes (Training Programs)** with the term **Science Institutes.** There is no computer program which automatically lists everything under the narrower term as part of the set of documents posted under the broader term. This is one of the main reasons for using the *Thesaurus* to aid in indexing or, *especially, searching.* The searcher who tries to enter the ERIC system by browsing through the subject headings in *Research in Education* (hereafter referred to as *RIE*), the monthly index to the system, may miss much that he could find if he consulted the *Thesaurus* for suggestions of additional entry points.

Indeed, the importance of the *Thesaurus* becomes even greater when one looks to the future. To date, most users of the ERIC system have had no alternative but to search the system through *RIE*. This announcement journal is arranged in such a way that a document is cross-indexed under several but not all of the descriptors assigned to it by an indexer. The indexer places an asterisk before those terms which are to serve as *RIE* entry points. That is, in the Subject Index portion of the announcement journals, the fact that a document exists is entered only under those descriptors which have been singled out as being of great importance by having an asterisk assigned to them. All descriptors, those with asterisks and those without, are listed along with the abstract of the document in the abstract portion of the publication. But this means that a user who wishes to find a document that has been assigned a non-asterisk descriptor will not find it if he simply looks under that descriptor in the Subject Index. *Thus very few people have ever been in a position to use the depth of indexing that indexers have provided from the beginning of the system.* In this sense the relatively deep indexing has been "wasted" to date, and, by the same reasoning, it might be argued that the relatively complex structuring of terms within the *Thesaurus* has been "wasted" to date.

As ERIC begins to expand its capacity for computer searching, as it is now doing, the deep indexing and the *Thesaurus* are likely to become much more important. If one had the computer tapes on which the citations, descriptors, and abstracts are filed and if he had the computer programs for conducting searches of the tapes, the first step in conducting a search would be to formulate a question composed of the terms on which one wished to search. Only through the *Thesaurus* could one find out about these terms in a comprehensive way.

Cross-Referencing: Related Term Relationship

One basic relationship between descriptors which still remains to be discussed is "Related Term" (RT). When a new term is entered in the *Thesaurus*, this notation is used if indexers and lexicographers agree that future indexers or searchers should be reminded of some interesting, perhaps useful, conceptual relationship between the new descriptor and terms already in the *Thesaurus*. It is reasonable to say that the broader term and narrower term relationships take precedence over the related term relationship; that is, if terms can be characterized as having a "class" relationship of a hierarchical nature, the BT, NT notation should be used. If any other kind of relationship should be specified at all, it should be called an RT relationship.

An extremely heterogeneous list of terms is likely to appear in conjunction with the RT notation. Returning to the **Institutes (Training Programs)** example, one will find: **Conference Reports, Conferences, Inservice Teacher Education, Off The Job Training, Seminars, Speeches,** and **Teacher Education.** Obviously, a conference report need not have very much in common with teacher education. Yet if one is interested in the kind of institutes which are training programs, he might welcome the reminder that he may also want to check conferences or, in particular, the reports summarizing or issuing forth from conferences. Illustrating another use of the relationship, the RT link from **Institutes (Training Programs)** to **Teacher Education** would lead one to the term **Practicums**, one of the Related Terms listed under **Teacher Education**. If the user was not satisfied with the "off the job" connotation of the institute type of training program but was trying to find his way to a specialized program at a fairly advanced level, he might welcome routing to **Practicums**.

To demonstrate the chain-like quality introduced by this policy of structuring, we might note that one of the RT entries listed at **Practicums** is the term **Field Experience Programs**. Far from being a special type of institute, or a broader concept than "institute," it is a term which might be viewed in a very real sense as several steps away from an institute which brings people away from their jobs and into school. It implies a program that gets students out of their schools and into the real world of jobs. I say "several steps" away to illustrate that there is a different conceptual position between these terms, the position represented by the term **Practicums**. Here is a term which conjures up a very specialized existence half-way between the theory of school and the practice of a job. It implies, I think, supervised, perhaps even collective, practice.

This illustration shows how the RT route can lead to a term which is almost an antonym of the original term. Thus an RT pathway may involve anything from a very near synonym **(Conferences)** to an antonym **(Field Experience Programs)**. Since so many different kinds of leads are opened by following RT chains, one must not expect any logical rigor to emerge from the related term structures. The function of RT entries must be viewed as suggestive only. "Logical" difficulties abound.

For example, the scope note for **Institutes (Training Programs)** says, "Programs of training designed to provide advanced study in a subject field, usually more intensive than conventions or conferences but less elaborate than workshops." One of the related terms is **Conferences**, as noted above. **Workshops**, which is a valid descriptor, is not listed here as a related term. The term "conventions" is not listed at all in the *Thesaurus*. Thus the three words used in the scope note to delimit the term **Institutes** are handled in three different ways.

With the final observation that ERIC policy requires at least the very minimum of logical rigor for related terms, that reciprocal relationships must always be listed, we can turn our attention to other features of the *Thesaurus*.

Scope Notes and Parenthetic Qualifiers

As just described in the case of **Institutes (Training Programs)**, other ways than UF, BT and NT, or RT descriptors are used to provide users with information about terms. On occasion, the Scope Notes (SN) mentioned above are utilized to provide additional detail. Policy requires that they be used sparingly, the *Thesaurus* relying primarily on the basic cross-references to define terms. As in the example of **Institutes**, it may be deemed necessary to call attention to the distinctions between an institute, a conference, and a workshop and to add the notation that the word should be used to imply "advanced" training. Here, a scope note is used to attempt to *restrict* the usage of a term.

A scope note can also be used to *explain* a term and in this sense has much in common with another feature of the *Thesaurus*, the "parenthetic qualifier." When a descriptor is ambiguous, in the sense that it might refer to two quite different concepts, clarification might be forthcoming via the use of an additional word or words appended to the main term and enclosed in parentheses. Thus the term "institute" might refer to schools such as Massachusetts *Institute* of Technology rather than to a two-week "institute" held for science teachers during late August on the campus of a small liberal arts college. This ambiguity is handled by appending the words **(Training Programs)** to the word **Institutes.**

But the ambiguity may not be such that it can be resolved with the addition of a word or two. The following example may illustrate the usage: The SN for **Literary Conventions** specifies that the term refers to "accepted elements of technique, such as technical devices, used as recognized means of literary expression." After this explanation it is clear that the descriptor is not to be used to index documents concerning meetings of people to discuss literature. If it were to be so used, it would be easy to use the parenthetic qualifier **(Meetings)**, but there is no single word or two-word phrase that explains the meaning of **Literary Conventions** in the sense in which it is employed. The language of the scope note shows that it is not the intention of the note to *restrict* the usage to just those ideas listed, for the phrase "such as" is an integral part of the note. As with many, perhaps most, scope notes, in retrospect it may be difficult to see how the mature listing of BT, NT, and RT entries can leave the user with very much uncertainty about the meaning of the term. But it must again be recalled that an indexer *is not permitted to make up terms* that will serve to define the descriptor in question. Terms must already exist in the *Thesaurus* to be candidates for cross-referencing. (Questions of timing arise, or course. A "candidate" descriptor for which an indexer is seeking approval may be used as a kind of "tentative" cross-reference, pending its approval. Naturally, much of this tentative behavior occurred during the early days of the system and still has to occur when any new literature area is opened.)

By now it may be quite easy to see why this cardinal principle of thesaurus building exists. If, instead of writing a scope note, an indexer could start on the definition of **Literary Conventions** by fabricating the term **Comedy** to serve as a related term (assuming here that **Comedy** did not already exist as a descriptor), he would then have to consider the structuring of narrower terms, broader terms, and related terms when he entered the term **Comedy** as a descriptor in its own right. Looking at that entry as it now exists, we can see that the indexer should contemplate adding the BT of **Drama**. Doing this should lead him to consider **Tragedy** as an NT for **Drama**, and **Literary Genres** and even the term **Literature** itself as BT entries for **Drama**. At least these are terms which indexers have found useful in the *Thesaurus'* structure built on a pragmatic basis, so there is reason to believe that the indexer would have predicted that such a chain of associations would be useful at a later date. To see the nightmarish character of this approach is to see that the entry of **Literature** should lead to the consideration of at least twenty-two narrower terms, sixteen related terms, and the broader term **Humanities** if the terms that were ultimately to prove useful were to have been structured in "correctly" at that point in time. The minute one allows an indexer to start making up terms that he thinks might be important rather than restricting him to those which have been conceived as "musts" in dealing with actual documents, there is no logical end in sight.

The Multiword Term Problem

Now that the basic relationships which one must understand to use the *Thesaurus* have been introduced, a discussion of the very heart of the "coordinate indexing" approach to documentation is in order. One of the most difficult tasks facing anyone constructing an indexing scheme is to determine just what it is that he will consider to be the basic elements of his work. The control of synonyms or quasi-synonyms, the problems of preferred usage, the questions of hierarchical relationship, and the never-ending mazes of "related terms" are issued conspicuous to anyone who turns the pages of the *Thesaurus*. But at a more basic level than this lies the issue of when to enter a one word descriptor and when to enter a multiword descriptor. Indeed, this is the issue which leads to consideration of the origin of the name "coordinate indexing."

Without going into historical detail, we can reasonably view the approach under consideration as a fundamental departure from the idea of fixing a piece of literature in its place within a logical classification scheme. That is, it is a departure from the slogan "a place for everything, and everything in its place." The "place" for a document under this approach is quite simple: each new piece of literature is simply placed "on top of the pile" in that it is simply given the next available accession number. After it becomes buried in the pile hopes for finding it are pinned on labeling it with an appropriate number of appropriate descriptive terms. Then, either by listing under a descriptor the numbers of all the documents which have been labeled with that particular descriptor, or by arranging for electronically aided high-speed scanning of all documents in such a way that a desired label will be spotted, retrieval is to take place. Chances of finding just what one is looking for rest mainly on being able to "coordinate" two or more labels, descriptors, in the sense that one is presented with the document numbers which are listed under both of two desired terms (or, in the other sense just mentioned, the document numbers which the scanner has spotted as being associated with both of the two desired terms).

Obviously, however, the approach leads to very severe problems. Let us consider just four terms: "college," "students," "teachers," and "part time." If a search were conducted on any two of these, such as "students" and "part time" in order to produce literature on "part time students," the result might involve documents which had been indexed under *"part time"* "teachers" of "college" *"students."* On the other hand, one might search for "college students" and get documents indexed as being about *"college"* "teachers" who taught *"students"* who were "part time." Can literature on "student teachers" be extracted via this scheme? How about "part time colleges"? The problem is just beginning, for any document that has only *three* of the terms could yield the wrong pair. For example, the request for "college students" would yield not only all documents dealing with "college teachers" and *"part time* students," but also all documents dealing with "college teachers" and *any kind of* students as long as the term "students" appeared as a descriptor. Perhaps when one notes that this illustration allowed one "obvious multiword descriptor ("part time") from the start, the incredible nature of a pure one word system begins to emerge. Concepts of "leisure *time,"* television "viewing *time,"* or any kind of *"part,"* could further complicate searches.

A rather wide variety of solutions to such problems have been offered by people interested in retrieving information. Very creative and imaginative approaches have been used to specify the *role* that a term plays in describing a document. Similarly, to avoid false relationships like those just described, efforts have been made to *link* single terms together as they occur as descriptors of a particular document. In fact, work like this on "roles" and "links" at Western Reserve University in the late 1950's and early 1960's contributed to the enthusiasm for specialized information systems that first led to documents proposing that an "ERIC" system be created.

When ERIC was first being developed by the U.S. Office of Education, much of the early thinking about a thesaurus of educational terminology was done at Western Reserve. A publication setting forth the solutions developed there now exists in the form of a book by Gordon C. Barhydt and Charles T. Schmidt, *Information Retrieval Thesaurus of Education Terms* (Press of Case-Western Reserve University, Cleveland, Ohio, 1968). Actually, the Barhydt and Schmidt thesaurus does not utilize the "role and link" approach characteristic of the very early Western Reserve work. It appears to be influenced by another approach to solving the problems that occur when one tries to find documents by assigning them descriptors, namely the "faceted" approach to indexing developed largely at the University of London Institute of Education. Students of information science as well as educators might be very interested in comparing the Barhydt and Schmidt thesaurus with this edition of the ERIC *Thesaurus*.

As suggested at the outset, the approach to coordinating terms which is the basis for the *Thesaurus of ERIC Descriptors* was largely the approach used by several federal agencies and by those developing a retrieval system for engineers. The work done at agencies such as the Department of Defense and the Federal Aviation Agency, as well as that done by the Engineers Joint Council, did not attempt to introduce "roles," "links," "facets," or any other elaboration that went beyond allowing multiword terms to be entered into the thesaurus when deemed necessary. The language used by educators, however, seems to have required far more utilization of multiword terms than is necessary in areas drawing more heavily on the physical sciences. The quickest way to see how few single word terms exist in this *Thesaurus* is to examine them as they appear in the "Rotated Descriptor Display" (the composition of which will be discussed later). There are very, very few indeed.

This proliferation of multiword terms probably did not occur as a matter of policy, although the rules covering multiwords are quite permissive. The rules in question have not changed since October 1966, when they were first presented in the *Rules for Thesaurus Preparation*[4]. The subject is sufficiently important that the relevant passages are shown here (utilizing the system of enumeration employed in the September 1969 version):

> 1.1.1.1   Descriptors should represent important concepts found in the literature rather than concepts derived independently. They should also reflect the language used in the literature to describe such concepts.

> ***********

> 1.1.1.4   Multiword descriptors (bound terms, precoordinated terms, and others) should be used whenever single-word descriptors cannot

---

[4]*Rules for Thesaurus Preparation,* Superintendent of Documents Catalog No. FS 5.212:12047 (U.S. Government Printing Office, Washington, D.C., 1969). $0.20

describe a concept adequately or provide effective retrieval. Many problems of this type can be solved by the careful application of rule 1.1.1.1 above. The following points should also be considered:

1.1.1.4.1   Use of a multiword descriptor is justified if any of the individual words in the multiword descriptor can combine so frequently with other descriptors as to produce many false coordinations.

1.1.1.4.2   Use of a multiword descriptor to represent a unique concept is justified if the individual words of that multiword term are also unique descriptors which, when co-ordinated with each other, represent concepts different from the one intended by the multiword term.
Example: **Students**
            Teachers
            Student Teachers

1.1.1.4.3   If a single-word term (used as a substantive) is so general as to be virtually useless in searching (e.g., **Schools**), consider the use of that term with another term (e.g., **Secondary Schools**).

1.1.1.4.4   Multiword descriptors, like single-word descriptors, must be carefully considered for placement in descriptor hierarchies.

1.1.1.4.5   Do not use inverted entries. (See section 4.0)[5]
Examples: DEVELOPMENT,
             EMOTIONAL EDUCATION,
             ADULT
                 are not valid descriptors;
             Emotional Development
             Adult Education
                 are valid descriptors.

At the present stage in the history of the ERIC system, a definitive statement cannot be made concerning whether there are "too many" multiword descriptors. As pointed out earlier, very little opportunity has existed to search the system utilizing the full depth of indexing provided. As a matter of personal taste, I would judge that indexers and lexicographers could have exercised more restraint and curtailed the number of multiword terms.

---

[5] Section 4.0 simply refers the reader to the "Rotated Descriptor Display" along with the assertion that this makes inverted cross-references in the Descriptor Listing unnecessary.

The proper number of multiword terms is partly a question of the extent to which the *Thesaurus* is used as a searching aid. As in the case of the violation cited earlier concerning consistent application of the "use - used for" rule with respect to an abbreviation (FLES), as long as searchers use the *Thesaurus* to develop a sophisticated search strategy, violations in the form of too many multiword terms may make less difference than one might think.

The extensive proliferation of terms which can occur if multiword terms are made the basic indexing units does seem to mean that documents can be described in more "precise" terms than if only more general, single word, descriptors were used. The cost of this kind of "precision" can be seen in two ways, however. Documents which could have been described by one descriptor may now be described by either or both of two descriptors, or perhaps by even more. For example, it might be dangerous to have the following four descriptors: **Group Tests, Group Intelligence Tests, Group Testing**, and **Group Intelligence Testing**. A searcher might search on one or two of these terms and assume that he had found all the relevant documents. With such a proliferation of multiword terms, the cost can be viewed in terms of relevant documents not found. On the other hand, the cost may be seen in terms of the energy required to perform the more elaborate search made necessary by a level of "precision" necessary so as not to miss relevant documents.

If a searcher makes extensive use of the *Thesaurus* in designing a search strategy, the odds of incurring the "missed document" cost go down, as does the cost of concocting a sophisticated search strategy. Because the *Thesaurus* is extensively cross-referenced, the cost of developing a sophisticated search strategy is less than it would be if one had to exhaustively examine an unstructured list of multiword terms.

At this stage of ERIC's development, the very least that can be said with some certainty about the very large number of multiword descriptors in the system is that they increase the need for searchers to become familiar with and to actually utilize the *Thesaurus*. Of course, the same can be said with respect to the need for indexers to utilize the *Thesaurus* extensively, given the vast number of very similar multiword terms already assigned to documents

Alphabetization and Word Form Conventions

Whether a descriptor be a single word or a multiword term, the user of the *Thesaurus* needs to know two basic conventions which it employs.

First, terms are alphabetized on a "letter by letter" basis, not on a "word by word" basis. This means, for example, that the term **Art**

Expression will be separated from **Art Materials** by terms such as **Articulation, Artificial**, and **Artists**. The term **Art Education** will be followed by **Articulation**, then **Artificial**, then **Artists**, and then back to **Art Materials**. If the convention of "word by word" alphabetizing were followed, all the terms beginning with the word **Art** would precede **Articulation**. In the case of numerals, the convention requires that an Arabic numeral follow the alphabetic element of the descriptor. Thus the convention calls for **Grade 4**, not "4th grade" or "fourth grade." Numerals precede letters for purposes of alphabetization, however. Thus entries move from **Grade 1** to **Grade 14** and then to **Grade A Year Integration**, followed by **Grade Charts**.

Second, choices between singular and plural forms of descriptors are governed by the following rule, again citing the September 1969 *Rules for Thesaurus Preparation*:

1.2.3   Word Form
In choosing between singular and plural noun forms, the precedent long established by major indexing and subject cataloging operations will be followed. Generally, a useful rule of thumb may be applied as follows: use the plural form when the proposed term is a "count noun," that is, a noun about which one should ask "how many?" (e.g., devices such as **Teaching Machines, Projectors**); use the singular form for "mass nouns," that is, those about which one should ask "how much?" (e.g., **Delinquency**); use the singular for specific processes, properties or conditions. Common usage should be followed for term types not covered in the above general rule (e.g., use **Democracy** not **Democracies**).

The Rotated Descriptor Display

Both problems associated with multiword terms and problems raised by efforts to structure terms through either broader term - narrower term relationships or the more general concept of related terms are placed in sharp focus by the presence of a "Rotated Descriptor Display." To those familiar with contemporary documentation techniques, the format of this display will immediately bring "KWIC" indexing to mind. The acronym KWIC stands for Key-Word-In-Context, a technique developed by the late H.P. Luhn, and put to use, with various modifications, in many places.

The first feature of a KWIC index is that it relies, basically, on using the natural language in the title of a document for purposes of retrieval. The second main feature is that, with the exception of a few words selected as unimportant, every word in every title is permitted to serve as an entry point in the index. The third main feature is that most, if not all, of the title is printed at each entry point so that the word that one is "keying" on at a given instance appears "in context." Another interesting dimension of "context" is provided in that normal alphabetization procedures bring titles together into a very interesting larger context. To illustrate these principles, if this document, the *Thesaurus of ERIC Descriptors*, were to appear in a KWIC index it would appear three times. The initial entry would be "Descriptors," the second would be "ERIC," and finally, in the "T" section, would come the term "Thesaurus." The word "of" would not be an entry point since it is obviously one of those words without retrieval value.

A computer usually organizes and prints this sort of index, and Luhn's original work included the preparation of a computer program to handle the chores of blocking out the trivial terms, sorting and re-sorting the titles, and preparing printed copy ready for some form of photographic or multilith reproduction. Early KWIC computer programs positioned the "key-word" in the center of a print column and allowed the rest of the title to be printed on one or the other side, or on both sides, of that word, depending on where the "key-word" occurred in the title.

The "Rotated Descriptor Display" is a list of all the descriptors in the *Thesaurus* with each element of each descriptor entered separately in alphabetical order, but always entered along with the other elements of the descriptor. Thus the "Rotated Descriptor Display" presented with this *Thesaurus* borrows more than just the printing format of the original KWIC idea. It borrows all three of the main assumptions just outlined: the "natural" features of language are exploited; every word of every descriptor is alphabetized separately; and the full descriptor appears as context each time a word is entered in its alphabetical position.

No matter how many artificial constraints are put on words in order to elevate them to the rank of approved descriptors in a thesaurus, the words are still "natural" words. Indeed, they remain *too* natural and not artificial enough, for, as with all natural languages, different people use words in different ways. ERIC, as an authority, does its best to prevent this complication and to promote an artificially constrained use of the approved terms. People trying to find documents in the ERIC system should be reassured to realize that they can look up all the descriptors in the *Thesaurus* in a place which follows the "natural" use of language.

The words "culture," "cultural," and "culturally" illustrate the advantages of having a "Rotated Descriptor Display." If one were to begin by looking up the term **Culturally Disadvantaged** in the *Thesaurus*, he would be presented with three narrower terms, all of which are variations on the "disadvantaged" portion of the term, e.g., **Disadvantaged Youth**. The RT entries lead to the closely related term **Cultural Disadvantagement** and to the word **Culture**, along with concepts like **Acculturation**. All together, there are seven related terms. There is no particular reason to expect that a dense network of terms involving the idea of "cultural" exists in the *Thesaurus*. Yet looking up the term in the "Rotated Descriptor Display" reveals forty-five terms involving either "culture," "cultural," or "culturally." About a dozen of these terms refer to specific cultures, but even some of these specific references, such as **Puerto Rican Culture**, might be of high interest to the searcher. The "Display" reveals such terms as **Cultural Background, Cultural Factors, Culturally Advantaged**, and **Culture Free Tests**. Indeed, many of the terms are likely to be of high interest to the searcher.

The purpose of the "Display," from the searcher's point of view, is to alert him to precisely this kind of situation. The goal is to suggest other descriptors and to provide a perspective of the contents of the *Thesaurus*.

Of course, indexers structuring a new term for entry into the *Thesaurus* also use the "Rotated Descriptor Display." With this "Display," the building of the RT portion of the display at the main entry of a term in the *Thesaurus* is easier and perhaps more complete than it could otherwise be. Not only does it suggest possibilities to the indexer; it also permits him to concentrate on what he might consider the main conceptual cross-references since he knows that a searcher can look in the "Rotated Descriptor Display" and see the same things that he, the indexer, sees. He need not feel compelled to structure in all such terms as BT, NT, or RT entries.

In depending on a natural language, the ERIC approach obviously does not go as far as KWIC indexers do in attempting to retrieve documents solely from the unaltered words in their titles. But the ERIC approach does recognize the associative power of dealing with words in their natural context, in the sense both of their natural order of occurrence in a multiword phrase and of their natural alphabetical order.

Clearly, the ERIC approach is beginning to emerge as one committed to a fairly high degree of redundancy. The duplication or repetition involved in providing the searcher with a "Rotated Descriptor Display," as with all redundancy when used in this sense, would be unnecessary if the main *Thesaurus* were perfectly constructed. Redundancy is a hedge against errors.

The Descriptor Group Display

Another descriptor display serves a similar function. The "Descriptor Group Display" represents an approach which is almost the antithesis of the "Rotated Descriptor Display" hypothesis. Whereas production of the "Rotated Descriptor Display" added an absolute minimum of human interpretation to the association of the descriptors, the words merely being alphabetized repeatedly, the "Descriptor Groups" are solely acts of human interpretation. A study done by ERIC staff had produced enormous clusters of terms which, in one sense or another, seemed to belong to families or groups. These were presented to the Panel on Educational Terminology for further study, the goal being to reduce the number of groups to some kind of workable minimum, and at the same time to leave some logical integrity to each group. The purpose of the effort was, as just mentioned, twofold.

It allowed one to appreciate the broad classes of terms and to find the scope of coverage that the system provided. The main *Thesaurus* display can be very frustrating if one is trying to gain an overview, for each entry takes you only a few steps before you must turn to a narrower term to see what happens next. To some degree the development of this display was a risky thing to do, for the "Descriptor Groups" look suspiciously like a classification scheme, especially after three-digit numbers were assigned to each of the fifty-two groups, leaving a common last digit of zero for each group—leaving, in other words, a column which someone could use to demarcate a further breakdown of groups into smaller classes.

It cannot be emphasized too strongly that the "Descriptor Groups" are *not* to be understood as a classification scheme. If someone tries to find documents by looking for them in association with a single descriptor found in the "Descriptor Group Display," he will find that this approach has very little resolution power. As long as searchers use the groups to suggest a *set of descriptors* rather than to find the one place in the system to look for documents, they will be using the "Descriptor Group Display" as it was intended to be used.

Having stressed the point that the "Descriptor Group Display" is not a classification scheme, I want to demur just a little. There is one part of the ERIC system that does feature an arrangement of *documents* by the principle of descriptor groups. The "abstracts" section of *Research in Education* is arranged by *accession number*; the "abstracts" section of the *Current Index to Journals in Education* is arranged by *descriptor groups.* Both announcement journals feature the "coordinate indexing" approach to searching for references in their "Subject Index" sections, but the journal literature index does actually arrange the document descriptions in what can be called a "classified" manner.

Out of the sorting and shuffling that went on within the Panel on Educational Terminology to produce the fifty-two groups and the lists of descriptors associated with each group, a few principles emerged. Not only do these reflect, to some extent, what went on in the creation of the groups; they now form the guidelines for aiding indexers and lexicographers in the assignment of a new descriptor to a group. These brief suggestions appear in the *Rules for Thesaurus Preparation* (September 1969) in the following form:

2.2   Assigning New Descriptors to Descriptor Groups.
A descriptor is assigned to only one Descriptor Group. Each new descriptor is assigned to a Descriptor Group by an indexer. The following guidelines are designed to assist the indexer in assigning descriptors to the proper Descriptor Group:

2.2.1   The assignment of a descriptor to a group should be considered in relation to the entire field of education rather than to a specialty.

2.2.2   Consult the existing Group Display to determine the disposition of similar, parallel, comparable, and analogous concepts.

2.2.3   Consult the Descriptor Group assignments of terms cross-referenced from the new term.

2.2.4   Where terms appear to be logically related to more than one Group, choose the least abstract Group. (For example, READING ABILITY is assigned to READING rather than ABILITIES.)

2.2.5   Consider the word form of the descriptor since it may suggest a choice among Groups. (For example, **Cosmetology** is assigned to **Occupations; Cosmetologists** is assigned to **Personnel And Groups.**)

After the groups had been formed, a scope note for the name of each group was written to provide a rough definition of the group. These scope notes appear in this publication following the Rotated Descriptor Display.

Identifiers

The user of the *Thesaurus* should be aware that ERIC documents are described by a whole class of terms that do not appear anywhere in any form in the *Thesaurus*. A familiar feature of indexing schemes such as ERIC's, this group of terms is called "identifiers."

Identifiers are the names of very specific phenomena. Unlike descriptors, they are not cross-referenced or structured in any way. They include the names of organizations, geographic locations, tests and testing programs, legislation, and assistance programs. They also include acronyms and "coined terms" that have not been widely recognized, the names of specific methods, theories, and, in some cases, even people. They can be as specific as the names of conferences or projects, but it must be emphasized that in all cases identifiers must be used to describe the *contents* of a document, not the *source* of a document.

The value of using identifiers as they are used by ERIC indexers cannot be reviewed thoroughly yet. The study of this subject will be facilitated greatly by the expansion of opportunities to conduct computerized searches.

Guidelines for developing identifiers are included in the document *Rules for Thesaurus Preparation*, which has been referred to before.

Use of the Thesaurus

Very little is known about the people who have been using the ERIC *Thesaurus*, why and how they have been using it, and what they think of it. Some speculation on these points might, however, be justified.

Throughout my comments I have been alluding to indexers and searchers who would have reason to use the *Thesaurus*. On the indexing side, the matter seems quite simple: those who are attempting to describe a document need recourse to an authority which specifies what agreements have already been made with respect to term usage. They need to know if a suitable term exists for a concept which appears in the document and, if not, how to go about fitting the term they would like to use into the existing structure. They also need to use this *Thesaurus* in the same way they might use *Roget's Thesaurus*: to be reminded of terms which might be more suitable than those they already have in mind.

On the searching side, matters are more complex. It is not clear that a thesaurus is necessary for the typical user of the ERIC system. If he uses *RIE* to search for a document, he can easily and naturally perform some of the functions of the *Thesaurus* by trying several obvious choices of terms as entry points and then examining the other descriptors which have been assigned to the documents found under the initial descriptors. He is very likely to find some related terms and, perhaps, some broader and narrower terms (although they would not be specified as such). He can then turn to one of those terms (much as he would turn to an RT in the *Thesaurus*) and see if there are documents there; if so, he can turn to their abstracts to see what descriptors had been assigned to them, and so on. As pointed out earlier, a severe limitation on this search procedure is that documents are entered in *RIE* only under terms deemed sufficiently important to be marked with an asterisk. Although one may learn about other terms assigned to a document, he need not expect all documents posted to a term to appear in *RIE* under that term *even if they had been indexed in such a way during the time period covered by the particular issue being used.* Thus one would not only be shut off from finding the documents; the terminology trail would be closed off as well. Conceivably a search could be improved if the user would pursue the terminology trail in the *Thesaurus* in conjunction with his use of *RIE*.

The importance of using the *Thesaurus* as a searching aid will probably grow, however, if one is attempting to gain access to the system in a way which permits searching on all terms, not just on terms marked with an asterisk, and which permits searching of a larger portion of the file than that contained in a given issue of *RIE*. Increasingly, it looks as though such searches will be made with the aid of a computer, for not only have experiments of this kind been launched, but arrangements have already been made by ERIC to expand computer search facilities by making tapes and searching programs more available to state departments of education and other public school units.

If a computer is employed, a searcher still might browse through *RIE* to familiarize himself with the descriptors to build into a search question or search strategy. For some users this might be the most efficient approach; whether or not it is probably depends on the user's needs and his experience in using this or similar systems. Factors to be considered in estimating the value of using the *Thesaurus* would be the need to find an exhaustive as opposed to an illustrative list of references; the amount of time and money a person had to invest in the search (especially the extent to which these assets permit sequential searches); the fit between a user's needs and the document coverage provided by the ERIC system; the timing of the input of potentially relevant documents into the system (for if they were scattered in a thin stream over many editions of *RIE*, utilization of those indexes to learn about terms would be much harder); the number of past searches similar to this one a user had performed; and even the general sophistication of the user with respect to the language of the area to be searched.

One of the major questions to be answered about *Thesaurus* use is the extent to which it may be utilized to aid the kind of search performed by a professional searcher acting as an intermediary between the actual user and the system. It may be that a great many future searches of the ERIC system will involve an intermediary person. This possibility should not be viewed simply as an aid to the user; it should also be viewed as a potentially inevitable barrier between the user and the system. In the first instance one can contemplate a highly valuable interface between a naive user and the complex system, an interface in the form of a searcher who translates between the user's natural language and the system's artificially controlled language. In the second instance one can picture a situation in which a user might like to query the system directly, but practical considerations might keep him from doing so. In either instance, it is reasonable to assume that the user might like access to the *Thesaurus* rather than thinking of the *Thesaurus* strictly as an aid to the professional searcher. There seems to be good reason to believe that the dialogue between user and searcher is a very important one, and that the more the user "speaks the searcher's language," the better—at least up to some point and in some cases.

An additional distinction must be made to clarify the relationship of the *Thesaurus* to computer searching.

The role of the *Thesaurus* in computer searching would differ depending on whether one has access to a so-called "on-line" computer system which allows a user to search a file once, modify his question, request another search, and so on, all while sitting at the computer console. The alternative is essentially "batch processing" access to a computer in the sense that a computer operator runs one or more fixed query strategies against a tape (or other kind of) file in one all-encompassing pass.

The need to develop a mature or sophisticated search strategy in the latter case is obvious. It seems quite likely that the *Thesaurus* could play a key role in structuring the question if one had access to a "batch processing" system. The case of the "on-line" computer system is more complex.

One reason for this complexity is that the substance of the *Thesaurus* itself might be displayed via a computer output device, reducing the need for a printed *Thesaurus*. Even this point is not entirely clear, however. Computer displays of a thesaurus might *not* be deemed as useful as browsing through a printed thesaurus by some people. It may not be as easy for some to "become familiar with" a computer as it is to "become familiar with" a book. Offsetting this is the fact that a computer display of a thesaurus can be programed to include the number of items currently posted to a particular descriptor, information which might be perceived as extremely useful by some users.

But apart from the question of computer display *vs.* book format thesauri, it may be that there is little need for searchers to depend heavily on a thesaurus if they have access to an "on-line" computer system. Just as it is not clear that all searchers using *RIE* would profit by using the *Thesaurus*, it is not clear that all users with the capacity of browsing through an "on-line" computing system need to consult a thesaural display at all. Experience with the particular constraints of the ERIC system by its real users seems far more valuable than speculation on such matters at this point, however.

Whereas the concept of *indexer* remains fairly simple, the concept of *searcher* has expanded to cover (1) the user with *RIE*; (2) the user with direct access to an "on-line" or "batch processing" computer system; (3) the user entering a computerized system of one kind or the other through an intermediary; (4) the user in a position to search files in some manual way other than just through *RIE*, with or without the aid of an intermediary. (This last user might, for example, be using an "optical coincidence" or "peek-a-boo" system which consists simply of holes punched into a matrix on a card, where the card is a term in the system and a position on the matrix represents the code number of a document. To search the system, one aligns the cards representing the terms to be searched. If light shows through the stack of cards, the document occupying that position in the matrix has been posted to each term card. This and other manual systems, like the "dual dictionary" prepared for the *ERIC Catalog of Selected Documents on the Disadvantaged*,[6] have been tried by various components of the ERIC system.)

But still another category of person might be interested in utilizing the *Thesaurus*. A nationwide system like ERIC might grow to the point at which the best way to think of "using" it goes beyond "asking it questions." It may be desirable to think of the ERIC system as a facility for developing other systems rather than as a facility for answering questions. In this case, the *Thesaurus* would become less a key for unlocking the system, and more a tool for developing one's own unique approach to solving local, specific documentation problems.

I have seen such an instance, in which the *Thesaurus* was used as a basis for organizing vertical files of information which had been used in answering past questions posed to a local information service. I can foresee utilizations by teachers in colleges of education who would design retrieval systems for something as specific as a single course. In cases like this, the *Thesaurus* might be used not only to help extract documents to go into such a system but also as a point of departure for developing a specialized index to permit students to individualize their approaches to the study of the subject.

Those concerned with in-service training of teachers as well as those involved with pre-service training might think in terms of organizing educational research and related materials for the staff of particular school buildings or systems. In this as in the other examples, the open-ended nature of the *Thesaurus* should be emphasized. If a teacher wishes to enter a document of his own into the system, procedures are now rather well established for adding any descriptors necessary to describe the document.

---

[6] *Catalog of Selected Documents on the Disadvantaged, Number and Author Index,* OE-37001, $0.65; *Subject Index,* OE-37002, $3.00 (Superintendent of Documents, Washington, D.C., 1967)

The addition could be made to the local version of this *Thesaurus*, which might be the entire *Thesaurus* plus locally added terms, or a selected portion of this *Thesaurus* plus locally added terms. There is every reason to hope that for local purposes the authority necessary to maintain a local "authority list" will be delegated to those responsible for local affairs.

Considerations

These introductory comments have been aimed at those who have little familiarity with thesauri or, for that matter, with the use of modern information systems. The comments have been so directed partially because it is too soon in the history of the ERIC system to engage in a factual discussion of the relative strengths or weaknesses of the *Thesaurus* and partially because it seems most important to provide interpretive background to the vast majority of potential users of the *Thesaurus*. As potential users attempt to evaluate the *Thesaurus*, the following considerations might be kept in mind.

At a general level, is one clear in his own mind about what it is that a successful thesaurus and a successful information system are supposed to do? What would one accept as evidence that success is or is not being achieved?

More specifically, is criticism best focused on the descriptors themselves, in the sense that they lack specificity? Are there too many near synonyms? Are terms that one would expect here not included? Is the problem one of getting newer terms into the *Thesaurus* quickly enough? Conversely, is it one of getting archaic terms out of the *Thesaurus* (and the system)? Do the terms reflect the actual questions users ask as well as concepts found in the literature? Are the descriptors appropriate for a wide range of users or only for some sub-groups, such as the very sophisticated—or the very naive?

Should criticism be focused on the way the terms are related to each other? Does this criticism really mean that the relationships are not available, or does it mean that they are not displayed effectively? Or are there too many relationships, displayed in too redundant a fashion?

Are those who criticize the *Thesaurus* really criticizing ERIC's indexing, the ways in which terms in the *Thesaurus* are applied? Does this mean that indexers do not use terms the way users working with the *Thesaurus* would predict they would use them? Or does it mean that indexers use too many or too few of the terms available to them? Is the criticism more accurately leveled at the use of the descriptors in *RIE*, the asterisked descriptors?

Is the reaction to the *Thesaurus* based on extensive familiarity with it and with the ERIC system? Has one's reaction been formed in conjunction with the help one has or has not received from ERIC staff members or anyone else who has been involved in interpreting the *Thesaurus*? Can the reaction to persons, both positive and negative, be separated from reaction to the *Thesaurus*?

Finally, are reactions to the *Thesaurus* colored by one's satisfaction with the contents of the documents actually retrieved and read? Are the problems inherent in doing educational research and making it relevant to the pressing problems of the day influencing one's reaction to the documentation tools involved?

Clearly, the *Thesaurus* must be examined in the context of the entire ERIC system. But then, the whole question of educational information retrieval and dissemination must also be seen in the context of education in general. Documentation enthusiasts must be realistic about the role that articles, microfilm, abstracts, index terms, and computers can play in solving the pressing educational problems of the present or the future.

Scientific research has thrived on efforts to define terms as precisely as possible. It is difficult to say with certainty, however, that solutions to social problems have thrived on a simple diet of scientific research. Contemporary crises seem to demand new and imaginative ways of conceiving problems and talking about them. If this *Thesaurus* or any other scheme for normalizing or controlling language inhibits in the slightest measure the creative use of language, I would warn against its use.

That the *Thesaurus* lags behind the way people are conceptualizing problems, intervention strategies, and solutions must be seen as both a fact and an asset. It is a *fact* because a term must first be found in circulation before it can begin to undergo the review processes which eventually lead to the status of "descriptor." It is an *asset* because no one should be led to believe that any authority has the right to define the terms which individuals use in the discussion of their problems.

Only if the principles and details of the *Thesaurus* are misunderstood can it be used as a constraint on language in a negative sense. Students of education of every kind should see the *Thesaurus* as an opportunity to become increasingly self-conscious about their language and thus about their assumptions and their approaches to educational problems.

SUMMARY OF CONTENTS

Terms and Related Entries

Two types of terms are listed in the *Thesaurus*: descriptors and synonyms or near synonyms. Descriptors, in boldface capital and lower case letters (e.g., **Objectives**) are authoritative terms that are acceptable for indexing and searching the in ERIC system. Synonyms or near synonyms of descriptors are printed in small capital and lower case letters (e.g. Goals). The five notations used to structure and display each type of term are described below. A "Use" entry follows synonyms or near synonyms of descriptors. This entry directs the user to the preferred descriptor for communicating with the system. No documents are indexed by terms appearing in the small print, nor should any attempt be made to use such terms as valid search terms. Synonym entries appear solely to provide as many points of entry to the *Thesaurus* as possible; ideally there should be as many entry points for a given concept as there are ways to describe that concept. The importance of the "Use" entry or relationship extends beyond the clear-cut case of synonymy: the entry can represent the relationship to a descriptor of a near synonym which has a general conceptual similarity, but which is not a true synonym. The user must enter the system with the descriptor denoted under such an entry. Example:

Guidance Goals
USE GUIDANCE OBJECTIVES

The "Used For" (UF) entry is the reverse of the "Use" entry. The UF entry appears only under a descriptor for which there is a synonym or near synonym in the *Thesaurus*. The entry tells the user that the descriptor includes the concept represented by the UF entry. The UF entry adds to the user's understanding of the scope of a descriptor which is "used for" other concepts. From another viewpoint, the UF entry provides the user with negative information in telling him that he cannot attempt his search using the concept listed as UF. (See the section on Descriptor Groups for explanation of the three-digit group code number.) The reverse of the example noted above is as follows:

GUIDANCE OBJECTIVES 090
UF Guidance Goals

"Narrower Term" (NT) denotes a hierarchical relationship between the main descriptor entry and a descriptor which belongs to the same class but is on a lower level of hierarchy, that is, the narrower term is more specific. Example:

GROUPS 380
NT   Audiences
      Choruses
      Clubs
      Disadvantaged Groups
      Discussion Groups
      Ethnic Groups
      Experimental Groups
      Listening Groups
      Low Income Groups
      Matched Groups
      Minority Groups
      Peer Groups

"Broader Term" (BT) is the second hierarchical notation and the reciprocal of the "Narrower Term" notation. A BT entry indicates that the descriptor is of the same class as the main descriptor entry but that it is on a higher level of hierarchy. The following example of a BT entry is the opposite of the example showing the NT entry given above:

DISCUSSION GROUPS 280
BT   Groups

"Related Term" (RT) performs two functions, only one of which is concerned with the scope of the main entry. A term listed as RT clarifies scope, that is, provides further definition of a main descriptor entry. It does this mainly by better describing the context in which the main descriptor entry should be interpreted. The second function of an RT entry is to alert the user to terms other than the main descriptor in which he may be interested, either as an indexer or a searcher. RT entries provide the collateral word relationships in a thesaurus that would not ordinarily be apparent if the user were to think only in terms of the hierarchical scheme.

Two examples of an RT entry are shown here to emphasize that the RT relationship is two-sided:

CHILD WELFARE 480   **CHILD ABUSE** 490
BT   Welfare   BT   Child Care
RT   Adopted Children   RT   Child Rearing
      Child Abuse   Child Welfare

Every hierarchical and collateral entry has a complementary entry elsewhere in the *Thesaurus*. That is, for every "Use" entry, there is a complementary UF entry; for every NT entry, there is a complementary BT entry; conversely, for every BT entry, there is a complementary NT entry; and for every RT entry, there is a complementary RT entry.

The order in which the notations appear under a descriptor, when appropriate, is as follows:

UF	–	Used For
NT	–	Narrower Term
BT	–	Broader Term
RT	–	Related Term

Parenthetical Qualifiers

A number of terms in this *Thesaurus* are followed by a parenthetical word or words. The purpose of these parenthetical qualifying expressions is not to define terms, but rather to clarify homographs and ambiguities in word meaning and usage. Whenever a parenthetical qualifier is used, it appears as an integral part of the descriptor in question, and is carried with that descriptor throughout all of its hierarchical and collateral relationships with other descriptors in the *Thesaurus*. Example:

GRADES (SCHOLASTIC) 180

Scope Notes

Occasionally, descriptors have been selected which, because of their broad usage in the language or because of their special usage in fields other than education, require a brief statement of restricted usage. In such cases, a scope note has been provided directly beneath the main descriptor entry. This is not intended as a formal definition, and is not considered an integral part of the descriptor. Thus it is not carried with the descriptor itself to other locations in the *Thesaurus* where the descriptor is listed in its relationships. The note appears only where the descriptor is a main entry. An example is the term "Acceleration," which has a particular meaning in the field of education, but may have other meanings in the fields of engineering and physics. To prevent ambiguity as to what is meant by the term "Acceleration" in this *Thesaurus*, a scope note has been provided. Example:

ACCELERATION 310
SN The process of progressing through the
school grades at a rate faster than that
of the average child

Rotated Descriptor Display

A multiword term contains two or more words that make up a concept, such as "Rating Scales." In using the *Thesaurus*, the searcher or indexer has no reference point available indicating that "Interest Scales" are types of "Rating Scales," since their filing positions are far apart. When each word of each compound descriptor is "rotated" and filed together, it is a simple matter to match the two words "Scales" to see both of their complete word forms.

Participant	Satisfaction
Behavior Rating	Scales
Grade Equivalent	Scales
Interest	Scales
Rating	Scales
Internal	Scales

Descriptor Groups and Descriptor Group Display

The Descriptor Groups contain a list of all Descriptor Group categories with their respective three-digit group code number and scope note. The Descriptor Group Display is provided for browsing, determining descriptor relationship and usage, and for showing related descriptors to aid in structuring new descriptors. Each Descriptor Group has a list of subject-related descriptors which appear in and are mutually exclusive to that group. Cross references to related Descriptor Groups are given in most scope notes.

DESCRIPTORS

ABBREVIATIONS 080
UF Acronyms
RT Mnemonics
 Orthographic Symbols
 Stenography
 Writing

ABILITY 010
UF Low Ability
NT Academic Ability
 Cognitive Ability
 Creative Ability
 Intelligence
 Language Ability
 Nonverbal Ability
 Predictive Ability (Testing)
 Psychomotor Skills
 Reading Ability
 Student Ability
 Verbal Ability
RT Ability Grouping
 Ability Identification
 Achievement
 Aptitude
 Aspiration
 Complexity Level
 Gifted
 Handicapped
 Mechanical Skills
 Performance
 Productivity
 Slow Learners
 Talent
 Talented Students
 Vocational Aptitude

ABILITY GROUPING 280
BT Student Grouping
RT Ability
 Ability Identification
 Homogeneous Grouping
 Low Ability Students

ABILITY IDENTIFICATION 010
BT Identification
RT Ability
 Ability Grouping
 Critical Incidents Method
 Identification Tests
 Probationary Period

ABLE STUDENTS 380
SN Ability to perform or absorb education at
 a specified level
UF Capable Students
BT Students
RT Academic Ability
 Academic Achievement
 Advanced Students
 Average Students
 Gifted
 Superior Students

Abnormal Psychology
USE PSYCHOPATHOLOGY

Abreaction
USE CATHARSIS

Absenteeism
USE ATTENDANCE

Absolute Humidity
USE HUMIDITY

Absolute Pressure
USE PRESSURE

Abstract Bibliographies
USE ANNOTATED BIBLIOGRAPHIES

ABSTRACTING 330
BT Writing
RT Abstracts
 Annotated Bibliographies
 Documentation
 Indexing

ABSTRACTION LEVELS 420
SN Levels of abstract reasoning reached in
 the process of developing successively
 broader generalizations reflected in
 language usage
UF Levels Of Abstraction
RT Abstraction Tests
 Abstract Reasoning
 Cognitive Processes
 Comprehension
 Conservation (Concept)
 Language Learning Levels
 Learning Processes
 Semantics

ABSTRACTION TESTS 520
BT   Tests
RT   Abstraction Levels
     Cognitive Tests
     Comparative Testing

ABSTRACT REASONING 420
BT   Thought Processes
RT   Abstraction Levels
     Cognitive Processes
     Logical Thinking
     Productive Thinking

ABSTRACTS 320
RT   Abstracting
     Annotated Bibliographies
     Documentation
     Indexes (Locaters)
     Indexing

ACADEMIC ABILITY 010
UF   Scholastic Ability
BT   Ability
RT   Able Students
     Academic Achievement
     Academically Handicapped
     Academic Aptitude
     Academic Aspiration
     Academic Performance
     Average Students
     Cognitive Ability
     Intelligence
     Low Ability Students
     Student Ability
     Students
     Verbal Ability

ACADEMIC ACHIEVEMENT 010
UF   Academic Progress
     Academic Success
     Educational Achievement
     Educational Attainment
     Educational Level
     Scholastic Achievement
     School Achievement
     Student Achievement
BT   Achievement
RT   Able Students
     Academic Ability
     Academic Aptitude
     Academic Aspiration
     Academic Performance
     Academic Probation
     Achievement Rating
     Advanced Placement
     Degree Requirements
     Gifted
     Grades (Scholastic)
     High Achievers
     Intelligence
     Learning Difficulties
     Low Achievers
     Reading Achievement
     Student Evaluation

Student Promotion
     Students
     Superior Students
     Underachievers

Academically Gifted
USE   GIFTED

ACADEMICALLY HANDICAPPED 240
UF   Educationally Handicapped
BT   Handicapped
RT   Academic Ability
     Handicapped Students

Academically Talented
USE   TALENTED STUDENTS

ACADEMIC APTITUDE 010
UF   Low Scholastic Aptitude
     Scholastic Aptitude
     Student Aptitude
BT   Aptitude
RT   Academic Ability
     Academic Achievement
     Academic Aspiration
     Academic Performance
     Intelligence
     Vocational Aptitude

ACADEMIC ASPIRATION 040
BT   Aspiration
RT   Academic Ability
     Academic Achievement
     Academic Aptitude
     Academic Performance
     College Bound Students
     Motivation

Academic Curriculum
USE   ACADEMIC EDUCATION

Academic Deans
USE   COLLEGE DEANS

Academic Departments
USE   DEPARTMENTS

ACADEMIC EDUCATION 140
UF   Academic Curriculum
     Academic Subjects
BT   Education
RT   Academic Enrichment
     College Preparation
     Curriculum
     Residential Colleges

ACADEMIC ENRICHMENT 270
BT   Enrichment
RT   Academic Education

ACADEMIC FAILURE 010
UF   Failure
     Scholastic Failure
     School Failure
NT   Reading Failure
RT   Academic Performance
     Dropouts

Expulsion
Failure Factors
Grade Repetition
Student Promotion

ACADEMIC FREEDOM 140
RT Censorship
College Environment
College Faculty
Freedom Of Speech
School Environment
Teacher Welfare
Teaching Conditions

Academic Games
USE EDUCATIONAL GAMES

ACADEMIC PERFORMANCE 010
UF Scholastic Performance
School Performance
Student Performance
BT Performance
RT Academic Ability
Academic Achievement
Academic Aptitude
Academic Aspiration
Academic Failure
Academic Probation
Academic Standards
Progressive Retardation
Student Promotion

ACADEMIC PROBATION 190
RT Academic Achievement
Academic Performance
Academic Standards
Probationary Period

Academic Progress
USE ACADEMIC ACHIEVEMENT

Academic Promotion
USE STUDENT PROMOTION

ACADEMIC RANK (PROFESSIONAL) 500
RT Doctoral Degrees
Professors
Students
Teacher Interns
Teachers

ACADEMIC RECORDS 020
NT Report Cards
BT Records (Forms)
RT Achievement Rating
Credits
Student Records

ACADEMIC STANDARDS 500
SN Criteria established by an educational institution to determine levels of student achievement
BT Standards
RT Academic Performance
Academic Probation
Accreditation (Institutions)
Admission (School)

Admission Criteria
Pass Fail Grading
Plagiarism
Progressive Retardation

Academic Subjects
USE ACADEMIC EDUCATION

Academic Success
USE ACADEMIC ACHIEVEMENT

ACCELERATED COURSES 110
BT Courses
RT Accelerated Programs
Acceleration
Advanced Placement Programs
Advanced Programs

ACCELERATED PROGRAMS 270
NT Advanced Placement Programs
BT Programs
RT Accelerated Courses
Acceleration
Flexible Progression

ACCELERATION 310
SN The process of progressing through the school grades at a rate faster than that of the average child
RT Accelerated Courses
Accelerated Programs
Advanced Placement
Advanced Students
Flexible Progression
Time Factors (Learning)

Acceptance
USE PEER ACCEPTANCE

ACCIDENT PREVENTION 250
BT Prevention
RT Accidents
Laboratory Safety
Safety
Safety Education
Safety Equipment

ACCIDENTS 250
NT School Accidents
Traffic Accidents
RT Accident Prevention
Emergency Squad Personnel
Injuries
Laboratory Safety
Rescue
Safety
Safety Education

ACCOUNTANTS 380
NT Certified Public Accountants
RT Accounting
Banking Vocabulary
Farm Accounts
Financial Services

ACCOUNTING 220
NT Property Accounting
    School Accounting
RT Accountants
    Bookkeeping
    Budgeting
    Business Subjects
    Certified Public Accountants
    Financial Services

ACCREDITATION (INSTITUTIONS) 500
RT Academic Standards
    Counselor Certification
    State Standards

ACCULTURATION 100
SN Absorption into any group of certain
    features of the culture
UF Assimilation (Cultural)
RT Biculturalism
    Culturally Advantaged
    Culturally Disadvantaged
    Cultural Pluralism
    Culture

Acetylene Welders
USE WELDERS

ACHIEVEMENT 010
UF Achievement Level
    Student Progress
NT Academic Achievement
    Negro Achievement
    Reading Achievement
RT Ability
    Achievement Gains
    Achievement Rating
    Achievement Tests
    Aptitude
    Aspiration
    High Achievers
    Knowledge Level
    Low Achievers
    Overachievers
    Performance
    Productivity
    Progressive Retardation
    Report Cards
    Success Factors
    Teacher Influence
    Underachievers

Achievement Comparison
USE ACHIEVEMENT RATING

ACHIEVEMENT GAINS 180
RT Achievement
    Student Improvement

Achievement Incentives
USE MOTIVATION

Achievement Level
USE ACHIEVEMENT

Achievement Motivation
USE MOTIVATION

ACHIEVEMENT NEED 420
SN Psychological factor providing impetus to
    excel
BT Psychological Needs
RT Affiliation Need
    Goal Orientation
    Learning Motivation
    Status Need

Achievement Prediction
USE ACHIEVEMENT TESTS

ACHIEVEMENT RATING 180
SN The process of comparing achieved
    performance and the ranking assigned
    to compared performances
UF Achievement Comparison
NT Grades (Scholastic)
RT Academic Achievement
    Academic Records
    Achievement
    Achievement Tests
    Grading
    Merit Rating Programs
    Pass Fail Grading
    Progressive Retardation
    Rating Scales
    Report Cards
    Student Evaluation

ACHIEVEMENT TESTS 520
UF Achievement Prediction
BT Tests
RT Achievement
    Achievement Rating
    Essay Tests
    Science Tests
    Timed Tests

ACOUSTICAL ENVIRONMENT 160
UF Sonic Environment
BT Physical Environment
RT Acoustic Insulation
    Acoustics
    Building Design
    Ceilings
    Controlled Environment
    Human Engineering
    Interior Design
    Oral Communication
    School Environment
    Standards
    Theater Arts

Acoustic Barriers
USE ACOUSTIC INSULATION

ACOUSTIC INSULATION 210
UF   Acoustic Barriers
     Acoustic Insulators
     Anechoic Materials
     Sound Absorbing Materials
     Sound Barriers
     Sound Insulation
     Soundproofing
     Sound Reflecting Materials
RT   Acoustical Environment
     Acoustics
     Building Design
     Building Materials
     Construction (Process)
     Controlled Environment

Acoustic Insulators
USE ACOUSTIC INSULATION

ACOUSTIC PHONETICS 290
BT   Phonetics
RT   Artificial Speech
     Consonants
     Distinctive Features
     Force
     Phonology
     Physics
     Spectrograms
     Speech

ACOUSTICS 400
UF   Sound
     Sound Transmission
     Sound Waves
BT   Physics
RT   Acoustical Environment
     Acoustic Insulation
     Architecture
     Audio Equipment
     Audition (Physiology)
     Auditory Discrimination
     Auditory Perception
     Aural Stimuli
     Building Design
     Echolocation
     Environmental Influences
     Psychoacoustics
     Sound Effects

Acronyms
USE ABBREVIATIONS

ACTING 030
BT   Theater Arts
RT   Dramatics
     Films
     Film Study
     Opera
     Outdoor Drama
     Professional Personnel
     Radio
     Television

Action Learning
USE ACTIVITY LEARNING

ACTION PROGRAMS (COMMUNITY) 490
SN   Improvement sponsored by community
UF   Action Projects
BT   Community Programs
RT   Community Action
     Social Action
     State Programs

Action Projects
USE ACTION PROGRAMS (COMMUNITY)

ACTION RESEARCH 450
BT   Research
RT   Evaluation
     Evaluation Methods
     Evaluation Techniques
     Methods Research
     Operations Research
     Program Improvement
     Self Evaluation

ACTIVISM 480
UF   Student Activism
     Student Dissent
     Student Militancy
     Student Protest
     Student Unrest
RT   Civil Disobedience
     Demonstrations (Civil)
     Political Attitudes
     Political Science
     Social Action
     Social Attitudes
     Student Alienation
     Student Attitudes
     Student Behavior
     Student College Relationship
     Student Participation
     Student School Relationship
     Student Teacher Relationship

ACTIVITIES 410
NT   After School Activities
     Art Activities
     Class Activities
     Cocurricular Activities
     Creative Activities
     Cultural Activities
     Enrichment Activities
     Group Activities
     Health Activities
     Individual Activities
     Integrated Activities
     Learning Activities
     Music Activities
     Physical Activities
     Playground Activities
     Recreational Activities
     School Activities
     Science Activities
     Speaking Activities
     Supervisory Activities
RT   Activity Units

ACTIVITY LEARNING 310
SN Learning by doing
UF Action Learning
BT Learning
RT Discovery Processes
    Learning Activities
    Learning Processes
    Work Experience Programs

ACTIVITY UNITS 110
UF Experience Units
BT Units Of Study (Subject Fields)
RT Activities

Adages
USE PROVERBS

ADAPTATION LEVEL THEORY 420
BT Theories
RT Arousal Patterns
    Attention
    Individual Psychology
    Perception
    Personality
    Psychotherapy
    Stimulus Behavior

Adapted Materials
USE INSTRUCTIONAL MATERIALS

ADDITION 340
BT Arithmetic
RT Division
    Multiplication
    Subtraction

Additional Aid
USE EQUALIZATION AID

Addresses
USE SPEECHES

ADHESIVES 460
UF Agglutinants
    Binders (Adhesives)
    Cements (Adhesives)
    Glues
    Mucilages
    Pastes
    Stickers
BT Building Materials
RT Building Design
    Construction (Process)
    Finishing
    Prefabrication
    Sealers

ADJECTIVES 290
BT Form Classes (Languages)
RT Adverbs
    Morphology (Languages)
    Sentence Structure
    Syntax
    Vocabulary

ADJUSTMENT (TO ENVIRONMENT) 420
UF Coping Behavior
NT Emotional Adjustment
    Personal Adjustment
    Social Adjustment
    Student Adjustment
    Vocational Adjustment
RT Adjustment Problems
    Individual Power
    Maladjustment

ADJUSTMENT COUNSELORS 380
BT Counselors
RT Guidance Counseling
    School Social Workers

ADJUSTMENT PROBLEMS 420
BT Problems
RT Adjustment (To Environment)
    Vocational Adjustment

ADMINISTRATION 020
NT Business Administration
    Educational Administration
    Institutional Administration
    Program Administration
    School Administration
    Team Administration
RT Administrative Agencies
    Administrative Change
    Administrative Organization
    Administrative Personnel
    Administrative Policy
    Administrative Principles
    Administrative Problems
    Administrator Attitudes
    Administrator Guides
    Administrator Responsibility
    Administrator Role
    Ancillary Services
    Consortia
    Coordination
    Coordinators
    Management
    Managerial Occupations
    Operations Research
    Organizational Change
    Planning
    Presidents
    Public Administration Education

ADMINISTRATIVE AGENCIES 230
BT Agencies
RT Administration
    Agency Role
    Governance
    Governing Boards
    Voluntary Agencies

ADMINISTRATIVE CHANGE 020
RT Administration
    Administrative Policy

ADMINISTRATIVE ORGANIZATION 020
BT   Organization
RT   Administration
     Centralization
     College Deans
     Consortia
     Decentralization
     Departments
     English Departments
     Governance
     Governing Boards
     Science Departments

ADMINISTRATIVE PERSONNEL 380
UF   Administrative Staff
     Administrators
     Building Officials
     Business Managers
     Business Officials
     Department Chairman
     Management Personnel
     School Administrators
     School Business Officials
NT   Audiovisual Directors
     Chief Administrators
     College Deans
     Community School Directors
     Department Directors (School)
     Personnel Directors
     Research Directors
     Supervisors
     Vocational Directors
BT   Personnel
RT   Administration
     Administrator Attitudes
     Administrator Background
     Administrator Characteristics
     Administrator Evaluation
     Administrator Guides
     Administrator Qualifications
     Administrator Responsibility
     Administrator Role
     Administrator Selection
     Adult Educators
     Business Administration
     Community Coordinators
     Employers
     Industrial Personnel
     Instructor Coordinators
     Managerial Occupations
     Personnel Needs
     Professional Occupations
     Professional Personnel
     School Administration
     School Supervision
     State Foreign Language Supervisors
     State Supervisors
     Trustees

Administrative Planning
USE   PLANNING

ADMINISTRATIVE POLICY 020
UF   University Policy
BT   Policy
RT   Administration
     Administrative Change
     Administrative Principles
     Administrator Guides
     Educational Administration
     Interdistrict Policies
     Official Languages

ADMINISTRATIVE PRINCIPLES 020
RT   Administration
     Administrative Policy
     Administrator Guides
     Administrator Responsibility
     Guidelines
     Management

ADMINISTRATIVE PROBLEMS 020
BT   Problems
RT   Administration

Administrative Secretaries
USE   SECRETARIES

Administrative Staff
USE   ADMINISTRATIVE PERSONNEL

Administrator Appraisal
USE   ADMINISTRATOR EVALUATION

ADMINISTRATOR ATTITUDES 040
UF   Administrator Opinion
BT   Attitudes
RT   Administration
     Administrative Personnel
     Administrator Characteristics
     Administrator Evaluation
     Employers

ADMINISTRATOR BACKGROUND 200
BT   Background
RT   Administrative Personnel
     Administrator Evaluation
     Administrator Qualifications
     Administrator Selection
     Certification
     Credentials
     Cultural Background
     Degrees (Titles)

ADMINISTRATOR CHARACTERISTICS 020
RT   Administrative Personnel
     Administrator Attitudes
     Administrator Evaluation
     Administrator Qualifications
     Administrator Selection
     Individual Characteristics

ADMINISTRATOR EVALUATION 180
UF   Administrator Appraisal
BT   Evaluation
RT   Administrative Personnel
     Administrator Attitudes
     Administrator Background
     Administrator Characteristics
     Administrator Qualifications
     Administrator Selection
     Chief Administrators
     Credentials
     Personnel Evaluation

ADMINISTRATOR GUIDES 020
BT   Guides
RT   Administration
     Administrative Personnel
     Administrative Policy
     Administrative Principles
     Planning
     Responsibility

Administrator Opinion
USE ADMINISTRATOR ATTITUDES

ADMINISTRATOR QUALIFICATIONS 500
BT   Qualifications
RT   Administrative Personnel
     Administrator Background
     Administrator Characteristics
     Administrator Evaluation
     Administrator Selection
     Chief Administrators
     Credentials

ADMINISTRATOR RESPONSIBILITY 040
BT   Responsibility
RT   Administration
     Administrative Personnel
     Administrative Principles
     Child Responsibility
     Educational Responsibility
     Leadership Responsibility
     Parent Responsibility
     Presidents
     Teacher Responsibility

ADMINISTRATOR ROLE 020
RT   Administration
     Administrative Personnel
     College Deans
     Presidents

Administrators
USE ADMINISTRATIVE PERSONNEL

ADMINISTRATOR SELECTION 020
BT   Personnel Selection
RT   Administrative Personnel
     Administrator Background
     Administrator Characteristics
     Administrator Evaluation
     Administrator Qualifications
     Chief Administrators
     Personnel Policy

Administrator Teacher Relationship
USE TEACHER ADMINISTRATOR
     RELATIONSHIP

ADMISSION (SCHOOL) 020
UF   Matriculation
     School Admission
NT   College Admission
     Early Admission
RT   Academic Standards
     Admission Criteria
     Competitive Selection.
     Educational Supply
     Enrollment
     Late School Entrance
     Personnel Selection
     Placement
     School Registration
     Student Application

ADMISSION CRITERIA 500
UF   Student Selection
RT   Academic Standards
     Admission (School)
     Educational Supply
     Nonresident Students
     Resident Students
     School Attendance Laws

ADOLESCENCE 130
RT   Adolescents
     Childhood
     Individual Development

ADOLESCENTS 380
NT   Teenagers
RT   Adolescence

ADOPTED CHILDREN 380
BT   Children
RT   Adoption
     Child Welfare
     Foster Children
     Foster Family

ADOPTION 490
RT   Adopted Children
     Foster Family

ADOPTION (IDEAS) 020
SN   Process of accepting new ideas or
     practices
RT   Changing Attitudes
     Diffusion

ADP
USE ELECTRONIC DATA PROCESSING

ADULT BASIC EDUCATION 140
SN   Instruction of adults in subjects of
     elementary education, social skills, and
     community responsibilities
UF   Fundamental Education
BT   Adult Education
RT   Literacy Education

ADULT CHARACTERISTICS 130
NT Participant Characteristics
RT Background
    Individual Characteristics
    Psychological Characteristics
    Social Characteristics

ADULT COUNSELING 090
BT Counseling
RT Adult Programs
    Counseling Programs
    Counseling Services
    Counselors
    Developmental Tasks
    Manpower Utilization
    Vocational Counseling

ADULT DEVELOPMENT 130
BT Human Development
RT Adult Education
    Adults
    Age Differences
    Developmental Psychology
    Developmental Tasks
    Growth Patterns

ADULT DROPOUTS 380
BT Dropouts
RT Adult Education Programs
    Dropout Rate
    Participant Satisfaction

ADULT EDUCATION 140
UF Continuing Education
    Further Education
NT Adult Basic Education
    Adult Education Programs
    Alumni Education
    Chautauquas
    Labor Education
    Migrant Adult Education
    Professional Continuing Education
    Public School Adult Education
BT Education
RT Adult Development
    Adult Farmer Education
    Adult Programs
    Adults
    Adult Students
    Adult Vocational Education
    Correctional Education
    Parent Education
    Special Degree Programs
    Womens Education

ADULT EDUCATION PROGRAMS 140
BT Adult Education
    Adult Programs
    Educational Programs
RT Adult Dropouts
    Adults
    Alumni Education
    Daytime Programs
    Evening Classes

Illiterate Adults
Program Content
Public School Adult Education
Special Degree Programs

ADULT EDUCATORS 380
BT Instructional Staff
RT Administrative Personnel
    Extension Agents
    Instructor Coordinators
    Teachers
    Trainers

ADULT FARMER EDUCATION 140
SN Education for adults aged 25 or over
    engaged in production agriculture
BT Agricultural Education
RT Adult Education
    Adult Vocational Education
    Farmers
    Farm Visits
    Land Grant Universities
    Young Farmer Education

ADULT LEADERS 380
RT Community Leaders
    Leader Participation
    Leadership
    Leadership Qualities
    Youth Leaders

ADULT LEARNING 310
BT Learning
RT Adults
    Age Differences
    Continuous Learning

ADULT PROGRAMS 410
NT Adult Education Programs
BT Programs
RT Adult Counseling
    Adult Education
    Adult Reading Programs
    Adults
    Alumni Education
    Daytime Programs

ADULT READING PROGRAMS 440
BT Reading Programs
RT Adult Programs
    Alumni Education
    Reading Development
    Reading Instruction
    Sequential Reading Programs

ADULTS 380
NT Illiterate Adults
    Middle Aged
    Older Adults
    Young Adults
BT Age Groups
RT Adult Development
    Adult Education
    Adult Education Programs
    Adult Learning

Adult Programs
Adult Students

ADULT STUDENTS 380
BT   Students
RT   Adult Education
Adults
Evening Students
Single Students
Special Degree Programs

ADULT VOCATIONAL EDUCATION 140
SN   Education for adults or out-of-school
youth aged 16 or over engaged in or
preparing to enter an occupation
BT   Vocational Education
RT   Adult Education
Adult Farmer Education
Industrial Training
Young Farmer Education

Advanced Credit Examinations
USE   EQUIVALENCY TESTS

Advanced Education
USE   HIGHER EDUCATION

Advanced Nations
USE   DEVELOPED NATIONS

ADVANCED PLACEMENT 280
BT   Placement
RT   Academic Achievement
Acceleration
Advanced Placement Programs
Advanced Programs
Advanced Students

ADVANCED PLACEMENT PROGRAMS 410
BT   Accelerated Programs
RT   Accelerated Courses
Advanced Placement
Advanced Students
College Placement
Curriculum Development
Secondary School Students

ADVANCED PROGRAMS 410
BT   Programs
RT   Accelerated Courses
Advanced Placement

Advanced Standing Examinations
USE   EQUIVALENCY TESTS

ADVANCED STUDENTS 380
BT   Students
RT   Able Students
Acceleration
Advanced Placement
Advanced Placement Programs
Superior Students

ADVANCED SYSTEMS 450
RT   Systems Concepts

Advancement
USE   FACULTY PROMOTION

Adverbials
USE   ADVERBS

ADVERBS 290
UF   Adverbials
BT   Form Classes (Languages)
RT   Adjectives
Morphology (Languages)
Sentence Structure
Syntax
Verbs
Vocabulary

Advertising
USE   PUBLICIZE

Advertising Art
USE   COMMERCIAL ART

Advisory Boards
USE   ADVISORY COMMITTEES

ADVISORY COMMITTEES 370
UF   Advisory Boards
BT   Committees
RT   Community Action

Advocates
USE   LAWYERS

A E Mechanics
USE   AVIATION MECHANICS

AEROSPACE INDUSTRY 370
BT   Industry
RT   Aerospace Technology
Aviation Technology
Electromechanical Technology
Engineering

Aerospace Sciences
USE   AEROSPACE TECHNOLOGY

AEROSPACE TECHNOLOGY 400
UF   Aerospace Sciences
Space Sciences
BT   Technology
RT   Aerospace Industry
Aircraft Pilots
Astronomy
Aviation Mechanics
Aviation Technology
Engineering
Industrial Arts
Physical Sciences

Aesthetic Development
USE   CULTURAL ENRICHMENT

AFFECTION 420
BT   Psychological Needs
RT   Affiliation Need
Emotional Experience
Individual Needs

AFFECTIVE BEHAVIOR 060
BT   Behavior
RT   Affective Objectives
      Attitudes
      Behavior Patterns
      Cognitive Development
      Emotional Development
      Interests
      Values

Affective Behavioral Objectives
USE   AFFECTIVE OBJECTIVES

AFFECTIVE OBJECTIVES 060
UF   Affective Behavioral Objectives
BT   Educational Objectives
RT   Affective Behavior
      Behavioral Objectives
      Cognitive Objectives
      Guidance Objectives
      Psychomotor Objectives
      Training Objectives

AFFILIATED SCHOOLS 470
SN   Schools providing experiences for
      student teachers or teacher interns,
      although not integral parts of teacher
      education institutions
UF   Cooperating Schools
BT   Schools
RT   College School Cooperation
      Cooperating Teachers
      Cooperative Education
      Educational Coordination
      Elementary Schools
      Field Experience Programs
      Interinstitutional Cooperation
      Laboratory Schools
      Preservice Education
      Secondary Schools
      Student Teaching
      Teacher Education
      Teacher Experience
      Teaching Experience

AFFILIATION NEED 420
SN   Psychological drive for association with
      others
BT   Psychological Needs
RT   Achievement Need
      Affection
      Status Need

AFFLUENT YOUTH 380
BT   Youth
RT   Socioeconomic Status

AFRICAN AMERICAN STUDIES 110
UF   Afro American Studies
      Black Studies
      Negro Studies
BT   Ethnic Studies
RT   African History
      American History
      Black Community

      Cultural Background
      Cultural Education
      Cultural Images
      Cultural Traits
      Negro Culture
      Negro Education
      Negroes
      Negro History
      Negro Institutions
      Negro Literature
      Negro Role

AFRICAN CULTURE 100
BT   Culture
RT   African History
      African Literature
      Foreign Culture
      Middle Eastern History
      Negro Culture
      Non Western Civilization
      Tribes

AFRICAN HISTORY 260
BT   History
RT   African American Studies
      African Culture
      Middle Eastern History
      Negro Culture
      Negro History
      Negro Literature
      Non Western Civilization

AFRICAN LANGUAGES 300
NT   Akan
      Bantu Languages
      Bemba
      Bini
      Chiluba
      Chinyanja
      Dyula
      Ewe
      Fulani
      Ga
      Gbaya
      Ibo
      Igbo
      Kinyaruanda
      Kirundi
      Kituba
      Lingala
      Mandingo
      Mende
      Mossi
      Nembe
      Sango
      Sara
      Shona
      Susu
      Swahili
      Wolof
      Yoruba
BT   Languages
RT   African Literature
      Language Classification

AFRICAN LITERATURE 260
BT Literature
RT African Culture
African Languages
Ethnic Studies
Negro Literature
World Literature

AFRIKAANS 300
BT Indo European Languages
RT Dutch

Afro American Studies
USE AFRICAN AMERICAN STUDIES

AFRO ASIATIC LANGUAGES 300
NT Berber Languages
Chad Languages
Ganda
Kabyle
Riff
Semitic Languages
BT Languages

AFTER SCHOOL ACTIVITIES 390
BT Activities
RT After School Centers
After School Education
After School Programs
After School Tutoring
Cocurricular Activities
Compensatory Education

AFTER SCHOOL CENTERS 210
RT After School Activities
After School Education
After School Programs
After School Tutoring
Compensatory Education
Study Centers

AFTER SCHOOL EDUCATION 140
BT Education
RT After School Activities
After School Centers
After School Programs
After School Tutoring
Compensatory Education

AFTER SCHOOL PROGRAMS 410
BT Programs
RT After School Activities
After School Centers
After School Education
After School Tutoring
Compensatory Education Programs

AFTER SCHOOL TUTORING 510
BT Tutoring
RT After School Activities
After School Centers
After School Education
After School Programs
Compensatory Education

AGE 070
SN Includes physiological and mental aging processes
UF Age Level
BT Physical Characteristics
RT Age Differences
Age Grade Placement
Age Groups
Middle Aged
Senior Citizens

Aged
USE OLDER ADULTS

AGE DIFFERENCES 070
BT Individual Differences
RT Adult Development
Adult Learning
Age
Middle Aged

AGE GRADE PLACEMENT 280
BT Placement
RT Age
Grouping (Instructional Purposes)
Instructional Program Divisions
Student Promotion

AGE GROUPS 380
NT Adults
RT Age
Middle Aged
Peer Groups
Senior Citizens

Age Level
USE AGE

AGENCIES 230
NT Administrative Agencies
Community Agencies (Public)
Private Agencies
Religious Agencies
State Agencies
Urban Renewal Agencies
Voluntary Agencies
Welfare Agencies
Youth Agencies
RT Agency Role
Government (Administrative Body)
Interagency Coordination
Interagency Planning
Organizations (Groups)

Agency Function
USE AGENCY ROLE

AGENCY ROLE 490
UF Agency Function
BT Institutional Role
RT Administrative Agencies
Agencies
Community Agencies (Public)
Private Agencies
Religious Agencies
Social Agencies

State Agencies
Urban Renewal Agencies
Voluntary Agencies
Welfare Agencies
Youth Agencies

Agglutinants
USE ADHESIVES

AGGRESSION 420
BT Behavior
RT Animal Behavior
Catharsis
Conflict
Crime
Hostility
Violence

AGRICULTURAL CHEMICAL OCCUPATIONS
350
BT Off Farm Agricultural Occupations
RT Agriculture
Farmers
Farm Occupations
Fertilizers
Herbicides
Insecticides
Pesticides
Rodenticides
Vocational Agriculture

AGRICULTURAL COLLEGES 470
BT Colleges
RT Agricultural Education
Agricultural Engineering
Agriculture
Experiment Stations

Agricultural Competencies
USE AGRICULTURAL SKILLS

AGRICULTURAL EDUCATION 140
NT Adult Farmer Education
Vocational Agriculture
Young Farmer Education
BT Vocational Education
RT Agricultural Colleges
Agriculture
Animal Caretakers
Farm Management
Farm Occupations
Food And Drug Inspectors
Land Grant Universities
Off Farm Agricultural Occupations
Technical Occupations
Vocational Agriculture Teachers
Vocational Education Teachers

AGRICULTURAL ENGINEERING 400
UF Agricultural Mechanics (Subject)
Farm Mechanics (Subject Field)
BT Engineering
RT Agricultural Colleges
Agricultural Machinery
Agricultural Machinery Occupations
Agriculture

Assembly (Manufacturing)
Farm Management
Farm Mechanics (Occupation)

Agricultural Extension
USE RURAL EXTENSION

AGRICULTURAL LABOR DISPUTES 150
BT Labor Problems
RT Agriculture

AGRICULTURAL LABORERS 380
UF Agricultural Workers
Farm Laborers
Farm Workers
NT Sharecroppers
BT Laborers
RT Agricultural Occupations
Agricultural Personnel
Agriculture
Crew Leaders
Farmers
Farm Occupations
Migrant Workers
Rural Farm Residents
Seasonal Laborers

AGRICULTURAL MACHINERY 170
BT Mechanical Equipment
RT Agricultural Engineering
Agriculture
Assembly (Manufacturing)
Diesel Engines
Engines
Equipment
Fuels
Hydraulics
Machinery Industry
Tractors

AGRICULTURAL MACHINERY OCCUPATIONS
350
BT Off Farm Agricultural Occupations
RT Agricultural Engineering
Agriculture
Farm Mechanics (Occupation)

Agricultural Mechanics (Subject)
USE AGRICULTURAL ENGINEERING

Agricultural Migrants
USE MIGRANTS

AGRICULTURAL OCCUPATIONS 350
NT Farm Occupations
Off Farm Agricultural Occupations
BT Occupations
RT Agricultural Laborers
Agriculture
Farmers
Farm Labor
Forestry Aides
Part Time Farmers
Vocational Agriculture

AGRICULTURAL PERSONNEL 380
NT   Farmers
BT   Personnel
RT   Agricultural Laborers
      Agriculture
      Extension Agents
      Farm Labor
      Farm Mechanics (Occupation)
      Sharecroppers

AGRICULTURAL PRODUCTION 070
UF   Crop Production
      Livestock Production
RT   Agricultural Supplies
      Agriculture
      Agronomy
      Field Crops
      Harvesting
      Pesticides
      Plant Growth
      Planting
      Transplanting

AGRICULTURAL RESEARCH PROJECTS 450
BT   Research Projects
RT   Agriculture
      Experiment Stations
      Horticulture

AGRICULTURAL SAFETY 250
BT   Safety
RT   Agriculture
      Safety Education

AGRICULTURAL SKILLS 010
UF   Agricultural Competencies
BT   Skills

AGRICULTURAL SUPPLIES 460
UF   Farm Supplies
BT   Supplies
RT   Agricultural Production
      Agricultural Supply Occupations
      Agriculture
      Feed Industry
      Feed Stores
      Fertilizers
      Herbicides
      Insecticides
      Pesticides
      Rodenticides

AGRICULTURAL SUPPLY OCCUPATIONS
350
BT   Off Farm Agricultural Occupations
RT   Agricultural Supplies
      Agriculture
      Feed Industry
      Sales Occupations
      Sales Workers
      Service Occupations
      Service Workers
      Vocational Agriculture

AGRICULTURAL TECHNICIANS 380
BT   Subprofessionals
RT   Agriculture
      Technical Education
      Technical Occupations

AGRICULTURAL TRENDS 070
RT   Agriculture

Agricultural Workers
USE   AGRICULTURAL LABORERS

AGRICULTURE 070
NT   Agronomy
      Forestry
      Horticulture
RT   Agricultural Chemical Occupations
      Agricultural Colleges
      Agricultural Education
      Agricultural Engineering
      Agricultural Labor Disputes
      Agricultural Laborers
      Agricultural Machinery
      Agricultural Machinery Occupations
      Agricultural Occupations
      Agricultural Personnel
      Agricultural Production
      Agricultural Research Projects
      Agricultural Safety
      Agricultural Supplies
      Agricultural Supply Occupations
      Agricultural Technicians
      Agricultural Trends
      Animal Science
      Crop Processing Occupations
      Dairymen
      Entomology
      Farmers
      Farm Management
      Farm Mechanics (Occupation)
      Farm Occupations
      Farm Visits
      Feed Industry
      Fertilizers
      Harvesting
      Herbicides
      Insecticides
      Land Use
      Off Farm Agricultural Occupations
      Pesticides
      Plant Growth
      Planting
      Plant Pathology
      Plant Science
      Rodenticides
      Seasonal Employment
      Soil Conservation
      Soil Science
      Supervised Farm Practice
      Tractors
      Transplanting
      Veterinary Medicine

Vocational Agriculture
Weeds

AGRONOMY 070
BT Agriculture
RT Agricultural Production
    Field Crops
    Grains (Food)
    Harvesting
    Land Use
    Planting
    Soil Science
    Transplanting

Air Bases
USE MILITARY AIR FACILITIES

AIRBORNE FIELD TRIPS 270
UF Flying Classrooms
BT Field Trips
RT Conservation Education
    Field Experience Programs
    Outdoor Education

Airborne Telecasts
USE AIRBORNE TELEVISION

AIRBORNE TELEVISION 050
UF Airborne Telecasts
BT Television
RT Educational Television

AIR CONDITIONING 170
RT Air Conditioning Equipment
    Air Flow
    Building Trades
    Climate Control
    Controlled Environment
    Exhausting
    Heating
    Humidity
    Mechanical Equipment
    Refrigeration
    Refrigeration Mechanics
    Temperature
    Thermal Environment
    Ventilation
    Windowless Rooms

AIR CONDITIONING EQUIPMENT 170
BT Building Equipment
RT Air Conditioning
    Climate Control
    Controlled Environment
    Heating
    Sheet Metal Work
    Temperature
    Thermal Environment
    Ventilation

Air Conditioning Mechanics
USE REFRIGERATION MECHANICS

Aircraft Mechanics
USE AVIATION MECHANICS

AIRCRAFT PILOTS 380
UF Airline Pilots
    Airplane Pilots
    Commercial Pilots
    Copilots
    Helicopter Pilots
BT Personnel
RT Aerospace Technology
    Aviation Technology

AIR FLOW 400
RT Air Conditioning
    Building Design
    Chimneys
    Exhausting
    Heating
    Mechanical Equipment
    Refrigeration
    Temperature
    Ventilation

Air Force Bases
USE MILITARY AIR FACILITIES

Airline Pilots
USE AIRCRAFT PILOTS

Airplane Pilots
USE AIRCRAFT PILOTS

AIR POLLUTION CONTROL 250
UF Atmospheric Pollution Control
RT Chimneys
    Climate Control
    Controlled Environment
    Environmental Education
    Exhausting
    Pollution
    Urban Environment

Air Raid Shelters
USE FALLOUT SHELTERS

AIR STRUCTURES 210
SN Pneumatically inflated structures used as
    buildings or shelters
UF Inflatable Structures
BT Building Design
    Facilities
RT Buildings
    Construction (Process)
    Prefabrication

AKAN 300
UF Twi
BT African Languages

ALBANIAN 300
BT Indo European Languages

ALCOHOL EDUCATION 140
BT Education
RT Alcoholism
    Health Education

ALCOHOLISM 250
UF Drinking
RT Alcohol Education
    Health
    Health Education
    Socially Deviant Behavior

ALGEBRA 340
NT Arithmetic
    Set Theory
BT Mathematics
RT Analytic Geometry
    Topology

Algorisms
USE ALGORITHMS

ALGORITHMS 340
UF Algorisms
BT Mathematics

Alien Culture
USE FOREIGN CULTURE

ALLEGORY 260
BT Figurative Language
RT Ambiguity
    Analytical Criticism
    Epics
    Fables
    Formal Criticism
    Impressionistic Criticism
    Literature
    Metaphors
    Motifs
    Old English Literature
    Poetry
    Prose
    Versification

Allergic Diseases
USE ALLERGY

ALLERGY 250
UF Allergic Diseases
    Hypersensitivity
BT Diseases
RT Asthma
    Physical Health
    Physiology

Allocation Of Resources
USE RESOURCE ALLOCATIONS

ALLOMORPHS 290
BT Morphemes
RT Morphophonemics
    Phonemes

Alphabetic Filing
USE FILING

ALPHABETIZING SKILLS 010
BT Skills
RT Filing

ALPHABETS 290
NT Cyrillic Alphabet
    Initial Teaching Alphabet
    Phonemic Alphabets
RT Phonetic Transcription
    Romanization
    Speech
    Written Language

Altaic Languages
USE URALIC ALTAIC LANGUAGES

ALUMNI 380
NT Graduates
RT Alumni Education

ALUMNI EDUCATION 140
BT Adult Education
RT Adult Education Programs
    Adult Programs
    Adult Reading Programs
    Alumni
    College Programs
    Discussion Programs
    Professional Continuing Education
    Womens Education

Ambient Pressure
USE PRESSURE

AMBIGUITY 260
BT Figurative Language
RT Allegory
    Drama
    Essays
    Fiction
    Literature
    Novels
    Parody
    Poetry
    Prose
    Tales

Ambulance Attendants
USE EMERGENCY SQUAD PERSONNEL

AMERICAN CULTURE 100
UF American Subculture
NT Latin American Culture
BT Culture
RT American Indian Culture
    Anglo Americans
    Jazz
    Revolutionary War (United States)
    Western Civilization

AMERICAN ENGLISH 290
SN English as used in the United States and
    parts of Canada, differing from British or
    other varieties of English principally in
    certain features of vocabulary,
    pronunciation, grammar, and spelling
BT English
RT Dialects
    Etymology
    Idioms

Language Classification
Language Patterns
Language Usage
Linguistics
Regional Dialects
Speech Habits
Standard Spoken Usage

AMERICAN GOVERNMENT (COURSE) 110
BT   Political Science
RT   Civics
Government (Administrative Body)

AMERICAN HISTORY 260
SN   History of the people of South, North,
and Central America
NT   Mexican American History
United States History
BT   History
RT   African American Studies
Civil War (United States)
Reconstruction Era
Revolutionary War (United States)
Science Education History
Science History
Slavery
Western Civilization

AMERICAN INDIAN CULTURE 100
BT   Culture
RT   American Culture
American Indian Languages
American Indians
Ethnic Groups

AMERICAN INDIAN LANGUAGES 300
NT   Apache
Aymara
Cakchiquel
Cherokee
Choctaw
Cree
Navaho
Papago
Pomo
Quechua
Tzeltal
Tzotzil
Uto Aztecan Languages
BT   Languages
RT   American Indian Culture
Language Classification

AMERICAN INDIANS 380
RT   American Indian Culture
Ethnic Groups
Race
Tribes

American Jews
USE   JEWS

AMERICAN LITERATURE 260
BT   Literature
RT   Local Color Writing
Metaphors
Naturalism
Nineteenth Century Literature
Realism
Twentieth Century Literature
World Literature

American Negroes
USE   NEGROES

American Revolutionary War
USE   REVOLUTIONARY WAR (UNITED STATES)

American Subculture
USE   AMERICAN CULTURE

AMETROPIA 240
UF   Error Of Refraction
Ocular Refractive Errors
Refractive Errors
NT   Hyperopia
Myopia
RT   Visual Acuity
Visually Handicapped

AMHARIC 300
BT   Semitic Languages

AMISH 380
BT   Protestants

Amphitheaters
USE   OUTDOOR THEATERS

AMPUTEES 380
BT   Physically Handicapped
RT   Cosmetic Prostheses
Handicapped
Prostheses

ANALOG COMPUTERS 170
BT   Computers
RT   Computer Storage Devices
Digital Computers

Analysis Of Covariance
USE   ANALYSIS OF VARIANCE

ANALYSIS OF VARIANCE 340
UF   Analysis Of Covariance
BT   Statistical Analysis
RT   Discriminant Analysis
Quality Control
Reliability

Analytical Chemistry
USE   CHEMICAL ANALYSIS

ANALYTICAL CRITICISM 260
BT Literature
RT Allegory
Dialogue
Imagery
Italian Literature
Literary Analysis
Literary Conventions
Literary Criticism
Literary Genres
Literary Perspective
Literary Styles
Moral Criticism
Motifs
Odes
Symbols (Literary)
Textual Criticism

ANALYTIC GEOMETRY 340
UF Coordinate Geometry
BT Geometry
RT Algebra

ANATOMY 070
BT Biology
RT Cardiovascular System
Ears
Embryology
Evolution
Eyes
Human Body
Medicine
Neurology
Pathology
Physiology
Scientific Research
Zoology

ANCIENT HISTORY 260
NT Greek Civilization
BT History
RT Archaeology
Biblical Literature

ANCILLARY SERVICES 020
UF Auxiliary Services
Supporting Services
BT School Services
RT Administration
Health Services
Programs
Psychological Services
Special Services
Student Personnel Services
Student Personnel Workers

Anechoic Materials
USE ACOUSTIC INSULATION

ANESTHESIOLOGY 350
RT Health Occupations
Medical Services
Medical Treatment
Professional Occupations

ANGLO AMERICANS 380
UF Anglos
RT American Culture
Cultural Background

Anglos
USE ANGLO AMERICANS

Anglo Saxon
USE OLD ENGLISH

ANIMAL BEHAVIOR 060
BT Behavior
RT Aggression
Animal Facilities
Behavior Development
Behavior Patterns
Psychology
Stimulus Behavior

ANIMAL CARETAKERS 380
UF Animal Keepers
BT Veterinary Assistants
RT Agricultural Education
Animal Facilities
Animal Science
Off Farm Agricultural Occupations
Veterinary Medicine

ANIMAL FACILITIES 210
BT Facilities
RT Animal Behavior
Animal Caretakers
Animal Science
Housing
Laboratory Equipment

Animal Keepers
USE ANIMAL CARETAKERS

Animal Life
USE BIOLOGY

ANIMAL SCIENCE 070
UF Livestock Technology
BT Sciences
RT Agriculture
Animal Caretakers
Animal Facilities
Biochemistry
Biology
Horses
Livestock
Meat
Meat Packing Industry
Microbiology
Rats
Veterinary Assistants
Veterinary Medicine
Wildlife Management
Zoology

Animation
USE MOTION

ANISEIKONIA 240
RT Visual Acuity
    Visually Handicapped

ANNOTATED BIBLIOGRAPHIES 320
UF Abstract Bibliographies
BT Bibliographies
RT Abstracting
    Abstracts
    Literature Reviews
    Publications
    Research Reviews (Publications)

ANNUAL REPORTS 020
SN Includes data on progress, finance,
    material, personnel, instruction, etc.
BT Reports
RT Conference Reports
    Periodicals
    Publications
    Serials
    Yearbooks

Annuals
USE YEARBOOKS

ANOMALIES 070
UF Congenital Anomalies
    Congenital Defects
RT Genetics
    Heredity
    Human Body
    Mongolism
    Pregnancy
    Prenatal Influences

Answer Booklets
USE ANSWER KEYS

ANSWER KEYS 520
SN Device that displays correct answers for
    a test
UF Answer Booklets
    Scoring Keys
RT Evaluation
    Scoring
    Tests
    Test Scoring Machines

ANTHOLOGIES 260
BT Literature
RT French Literature
    German Literature
    Spanish American Literature
    Spanish Literature

ANTHROPOLOGY 480
NT Ethnology
BT Social Sciences
RT Archaeology
    Area Studies
    Componental Analysis
    Cross Cultural Studies
    Museums
    Primatology

Social Studies
Zoology

ANTI INTELLECTUALISM 040
BT Attitudes
RT Class Attitudes

Anti Negro
USE RACIAL DISCRIMINATION

Anti Poverty Programs
USE POVERTY PROGRAMS

ANTI SEGREGATION PROGRAMS 490
BT Programs
RT Civil Rights
    Defacto Segregation
    Racial Integration
    Racial Segregation

ANTI SEMITISM 430
BT Racial Discrimination
RT Jews

ANTI SOCIAL BEHAVIOR 060
BT Behavior
RT Conflict
    Interpersonal Competence
    Socially Deviant Behavior
    Vandalism

ANTITHESIS 260
BT Figurative Language
RT Literature
    Philosophy
    Poetry
    Prose

ANXIETY 420
BT Psychological Patterns
RT Catharsis
    Emotionally Disturbed
    School Phobia

APACHE 300
BT American Indian Languages

APHASIA 240
UF Aphasic Children
BT Learning Disabilities
RT Cerebral Palsy
    Expressive Language
    Language Handicapped
    Speech Education
    Speech Handicapped
    Speech Therapists

Aphasic Children
USE APHASIA

Appetite
USE HUNGER

APPLIANCE REPAIRING 350
BT Skilled Occupations
RT Electrical Appliances
    Electrical Occupations

APPLIANCE SERVICE TECHNICIANS 380
BT Skilled Workers
RT Technical Education
     Technical Occupations

APPLIED LINGUISTICS 290
BT Linguistics
RT English (Second Language)
     Language Instruction
     Nucleation (Language Learning)
     Structural Linguistics
     Substitution Drills
     TENL
     Unwritten Language

APPLIED MUSIC 030
SN Vocal and instrumental music
     performance instruction
BT Music
RT Jazz
     Music Activities
     Music Education
     Orchestras
     Singing

APPLIED READING 440
BT Reading

Applied Research
USE RESEARCH

Apprentice Education
USE APPRENTICESHIPS

Apprentice Programs
USE APPRENTICESHIPS

APPRENTICESHIPS 270
UF Apprentice Education
     Apprentice Programs
     Apprenticeship Training
NT Research Apprenticeships
RT Industrial Training
     Inplant Programs
     On The Job Training
     Trade And Industrial Education
     Trainees
     Vocational Education
     Work Experience Programs

Apprenticeship Training
USE APPRENTICESHIPS

APTITUDE 010
NT Academic Aptitude
     Vocational Aptitude
RT Ability
     Achievement
     Aptitude Tests
     Aspiration
     Cognitive Ability
     Expectation
     Performance
     Students
     Talent

APTITUDE TESTS 520
BT Tests
RT Aptitude
     Occupational Tests

ARABIC 300
BT Semitic Languages
RT Arabs

ARABS 380
RT Arabic
     Ethnic Groups
     Non Western Civilization
     Racial Characteristics

ARBITRATION 150
RT Board Of Education Policy
     Collective Bargaining
     Collective Negotiation
     Employment Problems
     Grievance Procedures
     Labor Demands
     Labor Economics
     Labor Legislation
     Labor Problems
     Negotiation Agreements
     Negotiation Impasses
     Sanctions
     Strikes
     Teacher Associations
     Teacher Militancy
     Teacher Strikes
     Unions

ARCHAEOLOGY 480
BT Social Sciences
RT Ancient History
     Anthropology
     Ethnology
     Paleontology

ARCHITECTS 380
BT Professional Personnel
RT Architectural Education
     Architecture
     Building Design
     Construction Industry
     Professional Occupations

ARCHITECTURAL BARRIERS 210
SN Building elements which become
     obstacles to physically handicapped
     persons
RT Architectural Elements
     Building Design

Architectural Changes
USE BUILDING DESIGN

ARCHITECTURAL CHARACTER 210
SN Stylistic expression of verticality, scale, richness, variety and unity inherent to architectural tradition
UF Architectural Style
Architectural Tradition
RT Architectural Elements
Architecture
Building Design
Campus Planning
Design Preferences

Architectural Design
USE BUILDING DESIGN

ARCHITECTURAL DRAFTING 350
BT Drafting
RT Architectural Education
Architectural Programing
Architecture
Building Plans

ARCHITECTURAL EDUCATION 140
BT Professional Education
RT Architects
Architectural Drafting
Architectural Research
Architecture
Art Education
Building Design
Technical Education

ARCHITECTURAL ELEMENTS 210
SN Building materials that satisfy the architectural requirements of building construction
NT Doors
RT Architectural Barriers
Architectural Character
Architecture
Building Design
Building Materials
Buildings
Construction (Process)
Construction Needs
Masonry
Prefabrication
Prestressed Concrete
School Buildings
School Construction
School Design

ARCHITECTURAL PROGRAMING 210
SN The process of identification and systematic organization of the functional, architectural, structural, mechanical, and esthetic criteria which influence decision making for the design of a functional space, building, or facility
BT Programing
RT Architectural Drafting
Architectural Research
Architecture
Decision Making

Design Needs
Systems Analysis

ARCHITECTURAL RESEARCH 450
BT Research
RT Architectural Education
Architectural Programing
Behavioral Science Research
Building Materials
Component Building Systems
Computers
Design
Environmental Influences
Environmental Research
Mechanical Equipment
Physical Environment
Structural Building Systems

Architectural Style
USE ARCHITECTURAL CHARACTER

Architectural Tradition
USE ARCHITECTURAL CHARACTER

ARCHITECTURE 210
NT School Architecture
RT Acoustics
Architects
Architectural Character
Architectural Drafting
Architectural Education
Architectural Elements
Architectural Programing
Art Education
Building Design
Component Building Systems
Design
Design Needs
Design Preferences
Fine Arts
Interior Design
Lighting Design
Spatial Relationship
Structural Building Systems

ARCHIVES 210
RT College Libraries
Government Libraries
Law Libraries
Libraries
Library Collections
Medical Libraries
National Libraries
Public Libraries
Records (Forms)
State Libraries

Arc Welders
USE WELDERS

Arc Welding
USE WELDING

AREA STUDIES 450
SN Study of political or geographical area
    including history, geography, language
    and general culture
RT Anthropology
    Cross Cultural Studies
    Ecology
    Economics
    Field Instruction
    Field Studies
    Geographic Regions
    Geography
    History
    Language And Area Centers
    Middle Eastern History
    Non Western Civilization
    Political Science
    Regional Dialects
    Relocation
    Social Sciences
    Sociology
    Western Civilization

AREA VOCATIONAL SCHOOLS 470
UF Area Vocational Technical Schools
    Joint Vocational Technical Schools
BT Vocational Schools
RT Secondary Schools
    Vocational High Schools

Area Vocational Technical Schools
USE AREA VOCATIONAL SCHOOLS

ARISTOTELIAN CRITICISM 260
UF Intrinsic Criticism
BT Literary Criticism
RT Drama
    Essays
    Fiction
    Literature
    Novels
    Poetry
    Prose

ARITHMETIC 340
NT Addition
    Division
    Fractions
    Multiplication
    Percentage
    Remedial Arithmetic
    Subtraction
BT Algebra
    Mathematics
RT Integers
    Set Theory

ARITHMETIC CURRICULUM 110
BT Mathematics Curriculum

Arithmetic Deficiencies
USE LEARNING DIFFICULTIES

Arithmetic Systems
USE NUMBER SYSTEMS

ARMED FORCES 370
BT Military Organizations
RT Federal Troops
    Foreign Countries
    Immigration Inspectors
    Military Personnel
    Military Service
    National Defense

ARMENIAN 300
BT Indo European Languages

Army Air Bases
USE MILITARY AIR FACILITIES

AROUSAL PATTERNS 420
BT Behavior Patterns
RT Adaptation Level Theory
    Attention
    Perception
    Stimulus Behavior

ART 030
NT Art Products
    Commercial Art
    Creative Art
    Freehand Drawing
    Graphic Arts
    Handicrafts
    Painting
    Sculpture
    Surrealism
    Visual Arts
BT Fine Arts
RT Art Activities
    Art Appreciation
    Art Education
    Art Expression
    Art Materials
    Art Teachers
    Ceramics
    Existentialism
    Expressionism
    Local Color Writing
    Naturalism
    Nineteenth Century Literature
    Realism

ART ACTIVITIES 030
BT Activities
RT Art
    Art Education
    Art Products
    Freehand Drawing

ART APPRECIATION 030
RT Art

ART EDUCATION 140
BT Education
RT Architectural Education
    Architecture
    Art
    Art Activities

Art Teachers
Commercial Art

ART EXPRESSION 030
NT Art Song
RT Art
Art Products
Color
Freehand Drawing
Surrealism
Symmetry

Arthurian Legends
USE MEDIEVAL ROMANCE

Articles (Grammar)
USE DETERMINERS (LANGUAGES)

ARTICULATION (PROGRAM) 270
RT Program Administration
Program Coordination
Program Development
Program Improvement
Program Planning

ARTICULATION (SPEECH) 290
NT Stuttering
BT Speech
RT Conversational Language Courses
Diction
Language Rhythm
Phonetics
Syllables
Visible Speech
Vowels

ARTIFICIAL SPEECH 290
UF Simulated Speech
Synthetic Speech
BT Speech
RT Acoustic Phonetics
Distinctive Features
Language
Phonology
Spectrograms

ARTISTS 380
RT Art Teachers
Fine Arts
Painting
Surrealism

ART MATERIALS 030
BT Instructional Materials
RT Art
Ceramics
Glass
Paper (Material)
Student Developed Materials
Teacher Developed Materials

ART PRODUCTS 030
NT Sculpture
BT Art
RT Art Activities
Art Expression
Color

ARTS CENTERS 210
UF Fine Arts Centers
RT Auditoriums
Drama Workshops
Educational Facilities
Museums
Resource Centers
Stages
Theaters

ART SONG 030
BT Art Expression
Vocal Music
RT Fine Arts
Singing

ART TEACHERS 380
BT Teachers
RT Art
Art Education
Artists
Faculty

ASIAN HISTORY 260
BT History
RT Middle Eastern History
Non Western Civilization
Science Education History
Science History

Asian Music
USE ORIENTAL MUSIC

ASPHALTS 210
BT Building Materials
RT Flooring
Roofing

ASPIRATION 420
SN Desire to accomplish what one sets out
to do
UF Aspiration Level
Student Aspiration
NT Academic Aspiration
Low Level Aspiration
Occupational Aspiration
Parental Aspiration
RT Ability
Achievement
Aptitude
Career Choice
College Choice
Objectives
Occupational Choice
Performance
Self Concept
Socioeconomic Status

Aspiration Level
USE ASPIRATION

ASSEMBLY (MANUFACTURING) 350
RT   Agricultural Engineering
      Agricultural Machinery
      Equipment
      Manufacturing
      Manufacturing Industry
      Mass Production
      Metal Working Occupations
      Production Technicians
      Sheet Metal Work

ASSEMBLY PROGRAMS 410
BT   Programs
RT   Speeches

ASSESSED VALUATION 220
RT   Building Obsolescence
      Buildings
      Estate Planning
      Property Appraisal
      School Taxes
      Taxes
      Tax Support

ASSIGNMENTS 270
NT   Reading Assignments
      Textbook Assignments
RT   Homework

Assimilation (Cultural)
USE ACCULTURATION

Assistant Grounds Keepers
USE GROUNDS KEEPERS

ASSISTANT SUPERINTENDENT ROLE 020
BT   Superintendent Role

ASSOCIATE DEGREES 140
SN   Two year college degree
BT   Degrees (Titles)
RT   Community Colleges
      Junior Colleges
      Post Secondary Education
      Technical Education

ASSOCIATION (PSYCHOLOGICAL) 420
RT   Association Tests
      Associative Learning
      Connected Discourse
      Identification
      Identification (Psychological)
      Paired Associate Learning
      Serial Learning
      Surrealism
      Thought Processes

ASSOCIATION TESTS 520
BT   Psychological Tests
RT   Association (Psychological)
      Associative Learning
      Patterned Responses
      Psychological Evaluation
      Verbal Stimuli
      Visual Stimuli

ASSOCIATIVE LEARNING 310
UF   Word Associations (Reading)
NT   Paired Associate Learning
BT   Learning
RT   Association (Psychological)
      Association Tests
      Aural Learning
      Behavior
      Conditioned Stimulus
      Nonverbal Learning
      Serial Learning
      Symbolic Learning
      Visual Learning
      Word Recognition

ASTHMA 250
BT   Diseases
RT   Allergy
      Health
      Physical Health
      Physiology
      Special Health Problems

ASTRONOMY 400
BT   Physical Sciences
RT   Aerospace Technology
      Earth Science
      Evolution
      Navigation
      Planetariums
      Scientific Research

ATHLETES 380
RT   Athletic Activities
      Athletics

ATHLETIC ACTIVITIES 390
NT   Tumbling
BT   Physical Activities
RT   Athletes
      Athletic Equipment
      Athletic Programs
      Athletics
      Camp Counselors
      Exercise (Physiology)
      Gymnasiums
      Physical Education
      Physical Fitness
      Physical Recreation Programs
      Playground Activities
      Recreational Activities
      Swimming

ATHLETIC EQUIPMENT 170
BT   Equipment
RT   Athletic Activities
      Athletics
      Gymnasiums
      Physical Education
      Physical Education Facilities
      Physical Fitness
      Physical Recreation Programs

ATHLETIC FIELDS 210
BT   Physical Education Facilities
RT   Athletic Programs
     Athletics
     Educational Parks
     Field Houses
     Gymnasiums
     Parks
     Physical Education
     Physical Recreation Programs
     Playgrounds
     Recreational Activities

ATHLETIC PROGRAMS 390
NT   Extramural Athletic Programs
     Intramural Athletic Programs
BT   Programs
RT   Athletic Activities
     Athletic Fields
     Athletics
     Gymnasiums
     Physical Education
     Physical Fitness
     Physical Recreation Programs

ATHLETICS 390
UF   Sports
RT   Athletes
     Athletic Activities
     Athletic Equipment
     Athletic Fields
     Athletic Programs
     Camp Counselors
     Field Houses
     Gymnasiums
     Locker Rooms
     Physical Education
     Physical Education Facilities
     Physical Fitness
     Physical Recreation Programs
     Swimming Pools

ATLASES 320
BT   Publications
RT   Charts
     Maps

Atmosphere (Social)
USE   ENVIRONMENT

Atmospheric Pollution Control
USE   AIR POLLUTION CONTROL

Atomic Physics
USE   NUCLEAR PHYSICS

ATOMIC STRUCTURE 400
BT   Physics
RT   Atomic Theory
     Chemistry
     Force
     Matter
     Nuclear Physics
     Organic Chemistry
     Physical Sciences

Radioisotopes
Space

ATOMIC THEORY 400
BT   Physics
RT   Atomic Structure
     Force
     Matter
     Nuclear Physics
     Nuclear Warfare
     Radiation Biology
     Radioisotopes
     Space

Atomic Warfare
USE   NUCLEAR WARFARE

ATTENDANCE 020
UF   Absenteeism
     School Attendance
NT   Average Daily Attendance
     Class Attendance
     College Attendance
     Teacher Attendance
RT   Attendance Officers
     Attendance Patterns
     Attendance Records
     Attendance Services
     Leave Of Absence
     School Attendance Laws
     School Holding Power
     Truancy

ATTENDANCE OFFICERS 380
BT   School Personnel
RT   Attendance
     Attendance Patterns
     Attendance Records
     Average Daily Attendance
     Student Personnel Services

ATTENDANCE PATTERNS 060
RT   Attendance
     Attendance Officers
     Attendance Records
     Attendance Services
     Average Daily Attendance
     Behavior Patterns
     Teacher Attendance
     Truancy

ATTENDANCE RECORDS 020
RT   Attendance
     Attendance Officers
     Attendance Patterns
     Attendance Services
     Average Daily Attendance
     Statistical Data

ATTENDANCE SERVICES 020
BT   Pupil Personnel Services
RT   Attendance
     Attendance Patterns
     Attendance Records
     Truancy

ATTENDANTS 380
SN Person who attends or accompanies
    another to give service
BT Personnel
RT Attendant Training
    Domestics
    Nurses Aides
    Residential Care
    Service Occupations

ATTENDANT TRAINING 270
BT Training
RT Attendants
    Day Care Services
    Inservice Programs
    Job Training
    Residential Care

ATTENTION 060
RT Adaptation Level Theory
    Arousal Patterns
    Attention Control
    Attention Span
    Behavior
    Curiosity
    Listening

ATTENTION CONTROL 040
RT Attention
    Motivation

ATTENTION SPAN 060
RT Attention
    Motivation

ATTITUDES 040
NT Administrator Attitudes
    Anti Intellectualism
    Bias
    Changing Attitudes
    Childhood Attitudes
    Class Attitudes
    Community Attitudes
    Counselor Attitudes
    Discriminatory Attitudes (Social)
    Dropout Attitudes
    Educational Attitudes
    Employee Attitudes
    Employer Attitudes
    Family Attitudes
    Majority Attitudes
    Mother Attitudes
    Negative Attitudes
    Negro Attitudes
    Northern Attitudes
    Parent Attitudes
    Political Attitudes
    Program Attitudes
    Racial Attitudes
    Resentment
    School Attitudes
    Scientific Attitudes
    Social Attitudes
    Southern Attitudes

    Student Attitudes
    Teacher Attitudes
    Work Attitudes
RT Affective Behavior
    Attitude Tests
    Behavior
    Beliefs
    Counselor Acceptance
    Forced Choice Technique
    Human Dignity
    Morale
    Opinions
    Organizational Climate
    Press Opinion
    Q Sort
    Readiness (Mental)
    Stereotypes
    Textbook Bias

ATTITUDE TESTS 520
BT Tests
RT Attitudes

Attorneys
USE LAWYERS

AUDIENCE PARTICIPATION 510
BT Participation
RT Group Relations
    Interaction

AUDIENCES 380
BT Groups
RT Communication (Thought Transfer)
    Listening Groups
    Mass Instruction
    Radio
    Television Viewing

AUDIO ACTIVE COMPARE LABORATORIES
210
BT Language Laboratories
RT Audio Active Laboratories
    Audio Passive Laboratories
    Language Laboratory Equipment
    Tape Recorders
    Tape Recordings

AUDIO ACTIVE LABORATORIES 210
UF Listen Respond Laboratories
BT Language Laboratories
RT Audio Active Compare Laboratories
    Audio Passive Laboratories
    Electronic Classrooms
    Language Laboratory Equipment

AUDIO EQUIPMENT 170
UF Sound Equipment
NT Sound Films
    Tape Recorders
BT Equipment
RT Acoustics
    Audio Passive Laboratories
    Dubbing
    Sound Effects
    Spectrograms

Talking Books
Tape Recordings

Audiolingual Approaches
USE AUDIOLINGUAL METHODS

AUDIOLINGUAL METHODS 510
UF Audiolingual Approaches
BT Auditory Training
RT Audition (Physiology)
    Aural Learning
    Aural Stimuli
    Hearing Conservation
    Hearing Therapists
    Hearing Therapy

AUDIOLINGUAL SKILLS 010
UF Aural Oral Skills
NT Listening Skills
    Speech Skills
BT Language Skills
RT Conversational Language Courses
    Language Fluency

AUDIOLOGISTS 380
BT Professional Personnel
RT Audiology
    Audiometrists
    Audition (Physiology)
    Hearing Clinics
    Hearing Therapists
    Hearing Therapy

AUDIOLOGY 070
RT Audiologists
    Audiometrists
    Audition (Physiology)
    Auditory Agnosia
    Hearing Clinics

AUDIOMETRIC TESTS 520
BT Auditory Tests
RT Audition (Physiology)
    Auditory Evaluation
    Aurally Handicapped
    Deaf
    Hard Of Hearing
    Hearing Loss

AUDIOMETRISTS 380
BT Clinic Personnel (School)
RT Audiologists
    Audiology
    Audition (Physiology)
    Auditory Tests
    Hearing Clinics
    Hearing Therapy

AUDIO PASSIVE LABORATORIES 210
UF Listening Laboratories
BT Language Laboratories
RT Audio Active Compare Laboratories
    Audio Active Laboratories
    Audio Equipment
    Aural Stimuli
    Electronic Classrooms

Language Laboratory Equipment
Listening

Audio Tape Recording
USE PHONOTAPE RECORDINGS

AUDIO VIDEO LABORATORIES 210
BT Laboratories
RT Audiovisual Aids
    Audiovisual Instruction
    Autoinstructional Laboratories
    Instructional Television
    Language Laboratories
    Language Laboratory Equipment
    Video Tape Recordings

AUDIOVISUAL AIDS 050
UF Audiovisual Equipment
    Audiovisual Instrumentation
    Audiovisual Materials
    Audiovisual Media
    Visual Aids
    Visual Materials
NT Cartoons
    Central Sound Systems
    Charts
    Display Panels
    Exhibits
    Films
    Graphs
    Illustrations
    Instructional Films
    Language Aids
    Language Laboratories
    Maps
    Microphones
    Overhead Television
    Phonotape Recordings
    Projection Equipment
    Protocol Materials
    Realia
    Slides
    Tachistoscopes
    Tape Recorders
    Transparencies
    Vertical Work Surfaces
BT Instructional Aids
RT Audio Video Laboratories
    Audiovisual Centers
    Audiovisual Communication
    Audiovisual Instruction
    Centers Of Interest
    Chalkboards
    Classroom Materials
    Closed Circuit Television
    Color Presentation
    Diagrams
    Dial Access Information Systems
    Film Study
    Graphic Arts
    Magnification Methods
    Microcounseling
    Microfiche
    Microfilm

Microforms
Microteaching
Open Circuit Television
Single Concept Films
Space Dividers
Teacher Developed Materials
Three Dimensional Aids
Visual Measures

AUDIOVISUAL CENTERS 210
UF Listening Viewing Centers
RT Audiovisual Aids
   Audiovisual Communication
   Demonstration Centers
   Educational Resources
   Instructional Materials Centers

AUDIOVISUAL COMMUNICATION 050
NT Color Presentation
   Educational Television
   Open Circuit Television
   Phonotape Recordings
   Transparencies
BT Mass Media
RT Audiovisual Aids
   Audiovisual Centers
   Audiovisual Instruction
   Audiovisual Programs
   Broadcast Industry
   Facsimile Transmission
   Films
   Film Study
   Information Networks

AUDIOVISUAL COORDINATORS 380
SN A person at the elementary, secondary
   level who has responsibility for
   audiovisual materials and equipment in
   that school unit
BT Media Specialists
RT Audiovisual Instruction
   Audiovisual Programs

AUDIOVISUAL DIRECTORS 380
SN Directors of audiovisual instruction,
   usually at the school district level
BT Administrative Personnel
   School Personnel
RT Audiovisual Instruction
   Audiovisual Programs
   Media Specialists

Audiovisual Education
USE AUDIOVISUAL INSTRUCTION

Audiovisual Equipment
USE AUDIOVISUAL AIDS

AUDIOVISUAL INSTRUCTION 270
UF Audiovisual Education
BT Instruction
RT Audio Video Laboratories
   Audiovisual Aids
   Audiovisual Communication
   Audiovisual Coordinators
   Audiovisual Directors

Audiovisual Programs
Closed Circuit Television
Open Circuit Television
Protocol Materials
Repetitive Film Showings

Audiovisual Instrumentation
USE AUDIOVISUAL AIDS

Audiovisual Materials
USE AUDIOVISUAL AIDS

Audiovisual Media
USE AUDIOVISUAL AIDS

AUDIOVISUAL PROGRAMS 050
UF Coordinated Audiovisual Programs
BT Programs
RT Audiovisual Communication
   Audiovisual Coordinators
   Audiovisual Directors
   Audiovisual Instruction

Audiovisual Television Systems
USE EDUCATIONAL TELEVISION

Audition (Hearing)
USE AUDITION (PHYSIOLOGY)

AUDITION (PHYSIOLOGY) 070
UF Audition (Hearing)
   Hearing
NT Auditory Discrimination
BT Auditory Perception
RT Acoustics
   Audiolingual Methods
   Audiologists
   Audiology
   Audiometric Tests
   Audiometrists
   Auditory Agnosia
   Auditory Evaluation
   Auditory Tests
   Auditory Training
   Auditory Visual Tests
   Aural Learning
   Aurally Handicapped
   Aural Stimuli
   Deaf
   Ears
   Hard Of Hearing
   Hearing Aids
   Hearing Clinics
   Hearing Loss
   Psychoacoustics

AUDITORIUMS 210
BT Educational Facilities
RT Arts Centers
   Music Facilities
   Stages
   Theaters
   Windowless Rooms

AUDITORY AGNOSIA 240
BT Language Handicaps
    Learning Disabilities
RT Audiology
    Audition (Physiology)
    Auditory Perception
    Language Handicapped
    Neurologically Handicapped
    Perceptually Handicapped

Auditory Comprehension
USE LISTENING COMPREHENSION

AUDITORY DISCRIMINATION 070
BT Audition (Physiology)
RT Acoustics
    Auditory Perception
    Aural Learning
    Aural Stimuli
    Psychoacoustics
    Sensory Training

AUDITORY EVALUATION 180
BT Evaluation
RT Audiometric Tests
    Audition (Physiology)
    Auditory Tests
    Aurally Handicapped
    Deaf
    Evaluation Techniques
    Hearing Clinics

AUDITORY PERCEPTION 070
NT Audition (Physiology)
BT Perception
RT Acoustics
    Auditory Agnosia
    Auditory Discrimination
    Aural Learning
    Aural Stimuli
    Echolocation
    Figural Aftereffects
    Psychoacoustics
    Sensory Training

AUDITORY TESTS 520
UF Hearing Tests
    Otological Tests
NT Audiometric Tests
BT Tests
RT Audiometrists
    Audition (Physiology)
    Auditory Evaluation
    Auditory Visual Tests
    Aurally Handicapped
    Evaluation Techniques
    Hard Of Hearing
    Hearing Loss

AUDITORY TRAINING 270
NT Audiolingual Methods
BT Sensory Training
RT Audition (Physiology)
    Hearing Aids
    Hearing Conservation
    Hearing Therapists
    Listening Comprehension
    Psychoacoustics

AUDITORY VISUAL TESTS 520
NT Vision Tests
BT Tests
RT Audition (Physiology)
    Auditory Tests
    Hearing Conservation
    Psychoacoustics
    Tactual Visual Tests
    Vision

Aural Comprehension
USE LISTENING COMPREHENSION

Aural Handicaps
USE AURALLY HANDICAPPED

Aural Language Learning
USE AURAL LEARNING

AURAL LEARNING 310
UF Aural Language Learning
BT Learning
RT Associative Learning
    Audiolingual Methods
    Audition (Physiology)
    Auditory Discrimination
    Auditory Perception
    Hearing Conservation
    Listening Comprehension
    Phonics

AURALLY HANDICAPPED 240
UF Aural Handicaps
    Hearing Impaired Children
NT Deaf
NT Hard Of Hearing
BT Perceptually Handicapped
RT Audiometric Tests
    Audition (Physiology)
    Auditory Evaluation
    Auditory Tests
    Coded Speech
    Cued Speech
    Hearing Aids
    Hearing Clinics
    Hearing Conservation
    Hearing Loss
    Hearing Therapists
    Hearing Therapy
    Loop Induction Systems
    Manual Communication
    Visible Speech

Aural Oral Skills
USE AUDIOLINGUAL SKILLS

AURAL STIMULI 070
BT   Stimuli
RT   Acoustics
     Audiolingual Methods
     Audio Passive Laboratories
     Audition (Physiology)
     Auditory Discrimination
     Auditory Perception
     Echolocation
     Electrical Stimuli
     Hearing Conservation
     Listening Comprehension
     Psychoacoustics

AUSTRALIAN ABORIGINAL LANGUAGES
300
BT   Languages

AUSTRO ASIATIC LANGUAGES 300
BT   Sino Tibetan Languages

Austronesian Languages
USE   MALAYO POLYNESIAN LANGUAGES

AUTHORITARIANISM 480
RT   Dogmatism
     Imperialism
     Political Attitudes
     Political Science
     Sociology

Authority Structure
USE   POWER STRUCTURE

AUTHORS 380
UF   Writers
NT   Poets
RT   Literature
     Publications

AUTISM 240
RT   Behavior Patterns
     Behavior Problems
     Emotionally Disturbed
     Emotional Maladjustment
     Interpersonal Relationship
     Mental Health
     Mental Illness
     Personality Problems
     Psychosis
     Psychotic Children
     Schizophrenia
     Withdrawal Tendencies (Psychology)

AUTOBIOGRAPHIES 260
BT   Literature
RT   Biographies
     Composition (Literary)
     Nineteenth Century Literature

AUTO BODY REPAIRMEN 380
UF   Auto Body Workers
     Body And Fender Repairmen
     Body Men
BT   Skilled Workers
RT   Auto Mechanics (Occupation)
     Motor Vehicles
     Repair
     Skilled Occupations
     Trade And Industrial Education

Auto Body Workers
USE   AUTO BODY REPAIRMEN

AUTOINSTRUCTIONAL AIDS 050
UF   Autoinstructional Devices
     Autoinstructional Materials
     Self Instructional Aids
     Self Instructional Materials
BT   Instructional Aids
RT   Autoinstructional Laboratories
     Autoinstructional Programs
     Computer Assisted Instruction
     Dial Access Information Systems
     Programed Instruction
     Programed Materials
     Teaching Machines

Autoinstructional Devices
USE   AUTOINSTRUCTIONAL AIDS

AUTOINSTRUCTIONAL LABORATORIES 210
RT   Audio Video Laboratories
     Autoinstructional Aids
     Autoinstructional Programs

Autoinstructional Materials
USE   AUTOINSTRUCTIONAL AIDS

AUTOINSTRUCTIONAL METHODS 510
BT   Teaching Methods
RT   Computer Assisted Instruction

AUTOINSTRUCTIONAL PROGRAMS 270
BT   Educational Programs
RT   Autoinstructional Aids
     Autoinstructional Laboratories

Automated Education
USE   AUTOMATION

Automatic Data Processing
USE   ELECTRONIC DATA PROCESSING

Automatic Tracking
USE   TRACKING

AUTOMATION 510
UF   Automated Education
     Library Automation
     Library Mechanization
     Mechanization
RT   Computers
     Computer Science
     Cybernetics
     Dial Access Information Systems
     Electromechanical Technology

Electronic Control
Electronic Data Processing
Information Centers
Information Processing
Instrumentation
Libraries
Library Equipment
Library Technical Processes
Man Machine Systems
Numerical Control
Technological Advancement
Technology

AUTO MECHANICS 400
UF Small Engine Mechanics
RT Auto Mechanics (Occupation)
     Diesel Engines
     Engines
     Industrial Arts
     Mechanics (Process)
     Motor Vehicles
     Power Mechanics

AUTO MECHANICS (OCCUPATION) 350
UF Automobile Mechanics (Occupation)
     Automobile Service Mechanics
     Automotive Service Specialists
     Diesel Mechanics (Occupation)
     Truck Mechanics
BT Skilled Workers
RT Auto Body Repairmen
     Auto Mechanics
     Motor Vehicles
     Skilled Occupations
     Trade And Industrial Education

Automobile Mechanics (Occupation)
USE AUTO MECHANICS (OCCUPATION)

Automobile Service Mechanics
USE AUTO MECHANICS (OCCUPATION)

Automotive Service Specialists
USE AUTO MECHANICS (OCCUPATION)

AUTO PARTS MEN 380
RT Distributive Education
     Merchandising
     Motor Vehicles
     Salesmanship
     Sales Occupations
     Sales Workers
     Trade And Industrial Education

AUXILIARY LABORERS 380
UF Auxiliary Workers
BT Laborers
RT Paraprofessional School Personnel

Auxiliary Services
USE ANCILLARY SERVICES

Auxiliary Workers
USE AUXILIARY LABORERS

AVERAGE DAILY ATTENDANCE 020
BT Attendance
RT Attendance Officers
     Attendance Patterns
     Attendance Records
     Average Daily Enrollment

AVERAGE DAILY ENROLLMENT 020
UF Average Daily Membership
BT Enrollment
RT Average Daily Attendance
     Enrollment Rate
     Student Enrollment

Average Daily Membership
USE AVERAGE DAILY ENROLLMENT

AVERAGE STUDENTS 380
BT Students
RT Able Students
     Academic Ability
     Student Ability
     Student Characteristics
     Student Evaluation
     Student Grouping

AVIATION MECHANICS 380
UF A E Mechanics
     Aircraft Mechanics
BT Personnel
RT Aerospace Technology
     Aviation Technology
     Aviation Vocabulary
     Engines

AVIATION TECHNOLOGY 400
BT Technology
RT Aerospace Industry
     Aerospace Technology
     Aircraft Pilots
     Aviation Mechanics
     Aviation Vocabulary
     Technical Education
     Tracking

AVIATION VOCABULARY 290
BT Vocabulary
RT Aviation Mechanics
     Aviation Technology
     Professional Training

Awareness
USE PERCEPTION

Away From The Job Training
USE OFF THE JOB TRAINING

AYMARA 300
BT American Indian Languages

AZERBAIJANI 300
BT Turkic Languages

Bachelor Of Arts Degrees
USE BACHELORS DEGREES

Bachelor Of Science Degrees
USE BACHELORS DEGREES

BACHELORS DEGREES 140
UF   Bachelor Of Arts Degrees
     Bachelor Of Science Degrees
BT   Degrees (Titles)
RT   Degree Requirements
     Doctoral Degrees
     Masters Degrees
     Special Degree Programs
     Specialist In Education Degrees

BACKGROUND 200
UF   Background Factors
NT   Administrator Background
     Cultural Background
     Experience
     Family Background
     Parental Background
     Socioeconomic Background
     Teacher Background
RT   Adult Characteristics
     Opportunities
     Qualifications

Background Factors
USE BACKGROUND

Bahasa Indonesia
USE INDONESIAN

BALLADS 260
BT   Poetry
RT   Epics
     Lyric Poetry
     Medieval Romance
     Odes
     Sonnets
     Versification

BALLET 030
BT   Dance
RT   Theater Arts

BALUCHI 300
BT   Indo European Languages

BANDS (MUSIC) 030
RT   Jazz
     Music
     Music Activities
     Musical Instruments
     Musicians
     Music Techniques
     Orchestras

BANKING 220
UF   Banking Industry
BT   Business
RT   Banking Vocabulary
     Business Education
     Business Subjects
     Capital
     Economics
     Finance Occupations

     Financial Services
     Investment
     Money Management
     Money Systems
     Risk
     Student Loan Programs

Banking Industry
USE BANKING

BANKING VOCABULARY 290
BT   Vocabulary
RT   Accountants
     Banking
     Economics
     Professional Training

BANTU LANGUAGES 300
NT   Bemba
     Chiluba
     Chinyanja
     Kinyaruanda
     Kirundi
     Kituba
     Lingala
     Shona
     Swahili
BT   African Languages

BARBERS 380
BT   Service Workers
RT   Service Occupations
     Trade And Industrial Education

Barbiturates
USE SEDATIVES

Bards
USE POETS

BAROQUE LITERATURE 260
BT   Literature
RT   English Literature
     French Literature
     German Literature
     Italian Literature
     Prose
     Spanish Literature

Barristers
USE LAWYERS

Basal Reading
USE BASIC READING

BASHKIR 300
BT   Turkic Languages

Basic Language Patterns
USE LANGUAGE PATTERNS

BASIC READING 440
UF   Basal Reading
BT   Reading
     Reading Instruction
RT   Reading Development
     Reading Materials
     Reading Processes

Reading Programs
Sequential Reading Programs
Word Lists

Basic Research
USE RESEARCH

BASIC SKILLS 010
UF Fundamental Skills
BT Skills
RT Basic Vocabulary
Language Skills
Psychomotor Skills
Speech Skills
Study Skills
Verbal Ability
Writing Skills

BASIC VOCABULARY 080
RT Basic Skills
Beginning Reading
Reading Readiness

BASQUE 300
BT Languages

Batteries (Electric)
USE ELECTRIC BATTERIES

Beauticians
USE COSMETOLOGISTS

Beauty Culture
USE COSMETOLOGY

Beginning Farmer Education
USE YOUNG FARMER EDUCATION

BEGINNING READING 440
BT Reading
RT Basic Vocabulary
Language Experience Approach
Phonics
Prereading Experience
Reading Readiness
Sight Method
Sight Vocabulary

BEGINNING TEACHERS 380
BT Teachers
RT Inservice Teaching
Probationary Period
Teacher Certification
Teacher Employment
Teaching Experience

Beginning Workers
USE ENTRY WORKERS

BEHAVIOR 060
NT Affective Behavior
Aggression
Animal Behavior
Anti Social Behavior
Conformity
Covert Response
Delinquent Behavior
Group Behavior

Infant Behavior
Leadership
Misbehavior
Overt Response
Reactive Behavior
Socially Deviant Behavior
Spontaneous Behavior
Stimulus Behavior
Student Behavior
Teacher Behavior
BT Personality
RT Associative Learning
Attention
Attitudes
Behavioral Counseling
Behavioral Objectives
Behavioral Sciences
Behavior Change
Behavior Development
Behavior Patterns
Behavior Problems
Behavior Rating Scales
Behavior Standards
Behavior Theories
Cheating
Conditioned Response
Conditioned Stimulus
Counseling Theories
Curiosity
Emotionally Disturbed
Human Dignity
Individual Power
Motivation
Organizational Climate
Protocol Materials
Psychology
Psychometrics
Psychometrists
Psychomotor Skills
Psychopathology
Self Congruence
Sleep
Sociology
Sociometric Techniques
Sportsmanship

Behavioral Analysis
USE BEHAVIORAL SCIENCE RESEARCH

BEHAVIORAL COUNSELING 090
BT Counseling
RT Behavior
Behavioral Sciences
Behavior Development
Counseling Theories

BEHAVIORAL OBJECTIVES 060
SN Objectives indicating desired changes in
behavior resulting from learning
BT Educational Objectives
RT Affective Objectives
Behavior
Behavior Change
Behavior Patterns

Cognitive Objectives
Continuous Progress Plan
Course Objectives
Protocol Materials
Psychomotor Objectives
Student Behavior

BEHAVIORAL SCIENCE RESEARCH 450
UF Behavioral Analysis
BT Research
RT Architectural Research
Behavioral Sciences
Exceptional Child Research
Experimental Psychology
Language Universals

BEHAVIORAL SCIENCES 480
UF Behavioral Technology
NT Psychiatry
Psychology
Sociology
RT Behavior
Behavioral Counseling
Behavioral Science Research
Operant Conditioning

Behavioral Situation Films
USE PROTOCOL MATERIALS

Behavioral Technology
USE BEHAVIORAL SCIENCES

BEHAVIOR CHANGE 060
SN Complete or partial alteration in the
observable activity or response of a
person as a result of a learning
experience
UF Behavior Modification
RT Behavior
Behavioral Objectives
Behavior Development
Behavior Patterns
Change Agents
Changing Attitudes
Counseling
Habit Formation
Nondirective Counseling
Overt Response
Personality Change
Reactive Behavior
Sensory Deprivation
Teacher Behavior

BEHAVIOR DEVELOPMENT 130
NT Habit Formation
BT Development
RT Animal Behavior
Behavior
Behavioral Counseling
Behavior Change
Bibliotherapy
Probationary Period
Rational Therapy
Self Actualization

Behavior Modification
USE BEHAVIOR CHANGE

BEHAVIOR PATTERNS 060
UF Patterned Behavior
NT Arousal Patterns
Hyperactivity
Inhibition
Withdrawal Tendencies (Psychology)
BT Self Control
RT Affective Behavior
Animal Behavior
Attendance Patterns
Autism
Behavior
Behavioral Objectives
Behavior Change
Empathy
Identification (Psychological)
Imitation
Language Universals
Psychological Patterns
Reactive Behavior
Schizophrenia
Sensory Integration
Sportsmanship
Teacher Behavior

BEHAVIOR PROBLEMS 060
BT Problems
RT Autism
Behavior
Conflict
Conflict Resolution
Emotionally Disturbed
Hyperactivity
Mental Rigidity
Problem Children
Psychopathology
Suicide
Task Analysis

BEHAVIOR RATING SCALES 180
BT Rating Scales
RT Behavior
Personality Assessment
Personality Tests

BEHAVIOR STANDARDS 500
BT Standards
RT Behavior
Group Norms
Probationary Period

BEHAVIOR THEORIES 060
BT Theories
RT Behavior
Counseling Theories
Personality Theories
Social Exchange Theory

BELIEFS 040
RT Attitudes
Values

Belorussian
USE BIELORUSSIAN

BEMBA 300
UF   Chibemba
     Icibemba
BT   African Languages
     Bantu Languages

Benefit Cost Analysis
USE COST EFFECTIVENESS

BENGALI 300
BT   Indo European Languages

BERBER LANGUAGES 300
BT   Afro Asiatic Languages

BIAS 040
UF   Prejudice
     Self Bias
NT   Textbook Bias
BT   Attitudes
RT   Discriminatory Attitudes (Social)
     Social Attitudes
     Social Discrimination

Bibles
USE BIBLICAL LITERATURE

BIBLICAL LITERATURE 260
SN   Derived from the holy bible
UF   Bibles
BT   Literature
RT   Ancient History
     Christianity
     Folk Culture
     Folklore Books
     German Literature
     Judaism
     Legends
     Metaphors
     Mythology
     Poetry
     Prose
     Religion
     Religious Cultural Groups
     Sixteenth Century Literature
     Spanish Literature
     World Literature

BIBLIOGRAPHIC CITATIONS 320
UF   Bibliographic References
     Citations (Bibliographic)
     Literature Citations
     References (Bibliographic)
RT   Bibliographic Coupling
     Bibliographies
     Citation Indexes

Bibliographic Control
USE CATALOGING

BIBLIOGRAPHIC COUPLING 330
SN   Separation of a body of literature into
     small related groups through correlation
     of similar sets of references or
     bibliographies cited
BT   Correlation
RT   Bibliographic Citations
     Bibliographies
     Citation Indexes
     Classification
     Cluster Grouping
     Indexing
     Information Retrieval
     Information Utilization
     Search Strategies

Bibliographic References
USE BIBLIOGRAPHIC CITATIONS

BIBLIOGRAPHIES 320
UF   Literature Search
NT   Annotated Bibliographies
BT   Indexes (Locaters)
     Publications
RT   Bibliographic Citations
     Bibliographic Coupling
     Book Catalogs
     Booklists
     Books
     Catalogs
     Dictionary Catalogs
     Divided Catalogs
     Documentation
     Literature Reviews
     Research Reviews (Publications)
     Union Catalogs

BIBLIOTHERAPY 420
SN   Use of reading to promote mental
     hygiene
BT   Psychotherapy
RT   Behavior Development
     Developmental Reading
     Emotional Adjustment
     Institution Libraries
     Motivation

BICULTURALISM 100
BT   Cultural Pluralism
RT   Acculturation
     Bilingualism
     Cultural Awareness
     Cultural Background
     Cultural Differences
     Cultural Factors
     Cultural Interrelationships
     Culture Conflict
     Culture Contact
     Minority Groups
     Sociocultural Patterns
     Spanish Speaking

Bidding Procedures
USE BIDS

BIDS 220
UF   Bidding Procedures
      Competitive Bidding
      Construction Bidding
RT   Contracts
      Educational Economics
      Educational Finance
      Expenditures
      Purchasing
      School Construction

BIELORUSSIAN 300
UF   Belorussian
      Byelorussian
BT   Slavic Languages

Bigotry
USE SOCIAL DISCRIMINATION

BIKOL 300
BT   Indonesian Languages

Bilingual Children
USE BILINGUAL STUDENTS

BILINGUAL EDUCATION 290
SN   Encouragement of bilingualism through
      the teaching of regular school courses in
      both the national language and a second
      language
BT   Education
RT   Bilingualism
      Bilingual Schools
      Bilingual Students
      Educational Policy
      English (Second Language)
      Language Enrichment
      Language Learning Levels
      Language Programs
      Multilingualism
      Non English Speaking
      Official Languages
      Second Language Learning
      Second Languages

BILINGUALISM 290
BT   Sociolinguistics
RT   Biculturalism
      Bilingual Education
      Bilingual Schools
      Bilingual Students
      Bilingual Teacher Aides
      Bilingual Teachers
      Child Language
      Contrastive Linguistics
      Cultural Pluralism
      English (Second Language)
      Language Handicapped
      Language Research
      Languages
      Modern Languages
      Mutual Intelligibility
      Native Speakers
      Second Languages
      TENL

BILINGUAL SCHOOLS 470
BT   Schools
RT   Bilingual Education
      Bilingualism
      Bilingual Teachers

BILINGUAL STUDENTS 380
UF   Bilingual Children
BT   Students
RT   Bilingual Education
      Bilingualism
      Bilingual Teacher Aides
      Bilingual Teachers
      Spanish Speaking

BILINGUAL TEACHER AIDES 380
BT   Teacher Aides
RT   Bilingualism
      Bilingual Students
      Bilingual Teachers
      English (Second Language)
      Multilingualism
      Non English Speaking
      Nonprofessional Personnel
      School Aides
      Second Languages

BILINGUAL TEACHERS 380
BT   Teachers
RT   Bilingualism
      Bilingual Schools
      Bilingual Students
      Bilingual Teacher Aides
      English (Second Language)
      Multilingualism
      Non English Speaking
      Second Languages

Binders (Adhesives)
USE ADHESIVES

BINI 300
BT   African Languages

Biochemical Effects
USE BIOCHEMISTRY

Biochemical Tests
USE BIOCHEMISTRY

BIOCHEMISTRY 070
UF   Biochemical Effects
      Biochemical Tests
      Physiological Chemistry
NT   Metabolism
BT   Biology
      Chemistry
RT   Animal Science
      Chromatography
      Cytology
      Human Development
      Medicine
      Organic Chemistry
      Physical Sciences
      Physiology

Plant Growth
Plant Science

BIOGRAPHIES 260
BT Literary Genres
Literature
RT Autobiographies
Composition (Literary)
German Literature
Nineteenth Century Literature

BIOLOGICAL INFLUENCES 070
RT Biology
Evolution
Medicine
Prenatal Influences

BIOLOGICAL SCIENCES 070
UF Life Sciences
NT Biology
Medicine
BT Natural Sciences
RT Conservation Education
Environmental Education
Marine Biology

BIOLOGY 070
UF Animal Life
NT Anatomy
Biochemistry
Biophysics
Botany
Cytology
Ecology
Embryology
Entomology
Genetics
Heredity
Human Body
Marine Biology
Microbiology
Physiology
Radiation Biology
Zoology
BT Biological Sciences
RT Animal Science
Biological Influences
Biology Instruction
Chromatography
Evolution
Human Engineering
Livestock
Metabolism
Pregnancy
Primatology
Radioisotopes
Scientific Research
Soil Science

BIOLOGY INSTRUCTION 270
BT Instruction
RT Biology
Marine Biology

BIOMEDICAL EQUIPMENT 170
BT Equipment
RT Electroencephalography
Laboratory Equipment
Medical Laboratory Assistants
Wheel Chairs

Biomedical Equipment Technicians
USE MEDICAL LABORATORY ASSISTANTS

BIOPHYSICS 070
SN Application of physical methods and
principles to biological problems
BT Biology
RT Physics

Biotechnology
USE HUMAN ENGINEERING

BIRACIAL COMMITTEES 370
BT Committees
RT Community Cooperation
Race Relations
Racial Integration

BIRACIAL ELEMENTARY SCHOOLS 470
BT Biracial Schools
Elementary Schools

BIRACIAL GOVERNMENT 230
BT Government (Administrative Body)
RT Community Agencies (Public)
Race Relations
Racial Integration

BIRACIAL SCHOOLS 470
NT Biracial Elementary Schools
Biracial Secondary Schools
BT Schools
RT Race Relations
School Integration

BIRACIAL SECONDARY SCHOOLS 470
BT Biracial Schools
Secondary Schools

Birth Control
USE CONTRACEPTION

BIRTH ORDER 070
RT Family (Sociological Unit)
Siblings

Black And White Films
USE FILMS

Blackboards
USE CHALKBOARDS

BLACK COMMUNITY 490
UF Negro Community
BT Community
RT African American Studies
Black Power
Community Influence
Ethnic Groups
Identification (Psychological)
Negro Attitudes

Negroes
Socioeconomic Influences

Black Literature
USE NEGRO LITERATURE

Black Nationalism
USE BLACK POWER

BLACK POWER 430
UF Black Nationalism
RT Black Community
Civil Rights
Identification (Psychological)
Individual Power
Nationalism
Negro Attitudes
Negro Leadership
Negro Organizations
Negro Role
Political Power
Power Structure
Racism
Self Concept

Black Studies
USE AFRICAN AMERICAN STUDIES

BLIND 240
NT Blind Children
BT Visually Handicapped
RT Braille
Deaf Blind
Echolocation
Partially Sighted
Raised Line Drawings
Sensory Aids
Tactile Adaptation
Travel Training
Visually Handicapped Mobility
Visually Handicapped Orientation

BLIND CHILDREN 380
BT Blind
Children
RT Partially Sighted

Block Time Teaching
USE TIME BLOCKS

BLOOD CIRCULATION 070
UF Hemodynamics
BT Physiology
RT Cardiovascular System
Heart Rate

BLUE COLLAR OCCUPATIONS 350
BT Occupations
RT Semiskilled Occupations
Semiskilled Workers
Unskilled Labor
Unskilled Occupations
Unskilled Workers

BLUEPRINTS 210
RT Building Design
Building Plans
Drafting

BOARD ADMINISTRATOR RELATIONSHIP
020
BT Relationship
RT Federal State Relationship
Governing Boards
State School District Relationship
Student School Relationship
Teacher Administrator Relationship

BOARD CANDIDATES 380
RT Boards Of Education
Trustees

BOARDING HOMES 210
RT Boarding Schools
College Housing
Foster Homes
Regional Schools
Special Education

BOARDING SCHOOLS 470
BT Schools
RT Boarding Homes
Child Development Centers
College Housing
Housing
Institutional Environment
Rehabilitation Centers
Residential Schools
Special Education

BOARD OF EDUCATION POLICY 020
UF School Board Policy
School District Policy
BT Policy
RT Arbitration
Boards Of Education
Interdistrict Policies
Negotiation Agreements
Negotiation Impasses
School Closing
School District Autonomy

BOARD OF EDUCATION ROLE 020
UF School Board Role
RT Boards Of Education
School District Autonomy
Trustees

Board Of Regents
USE GOVERNING BOARDS

Board Of Trustees
USE GOVERNING BOARDS

BOARDS OF EDUCATION 020
UF   School Boards
BT   Governing Boards
RT   Board Candidates
     Board Of Education Policy
     Board Of Education Role
     County School Systems
     Intermediate Administrative Units
     Loyalty Oaths
     Public School Teachers
     School Administration
     School District Autonomy
     State Boards Of Education

BOATMEN 380
UF   Boat Operators
     Motorboat Operators
BT   Semiskilled Workers
RT   Navigation
     Seamen
     Semiskilled Occupations
     Trade And Industrial Education

Boat Operators
USE   BOATMEN

Body And Fender Repairmen
USE   AUTO BODY REPAIRMEN

Body Attitude
USE   HUMAN POSTURE

Body Care
USE   HYGIENE

BODY HEIGHT 070
BT   Physical Characteristics
RT   Growth Patterns
     Physical Development

BODY IMAGE 420
SN   Conceptual representation of one's own
     body derived from internal and external
     sensations, emotions, and fantasies
     related to orientation, movement, and
     behavior
UF   Body Schema
BT   Self Concept
RT   Human Body
     Kinesthetic Perception
     Space Orientation

Body Men
USE   AUTO BODY REPAIRMEN

Body Schema
USE   BODY IMAGE

BODY WEIGHT 070
BT   Physical Characteristics
RT   Growth Patterns
     Physical Development

Bomb Shelters
USE   FALLOUT SHELTERS

BOND ISSUES 220
RT   Educational Finance

Book Buying
USE   LIBRARY ACQUISITION

BOOK CATALOGS 320
SN   Library catalog entries printed page by
     page and bound together in book form
BT   Catalogs
RT   Bibliographies
     Booklists
     Cataloging
     Check Lists
     Indexes (Locaters)
     Information Processing
     Libraries

Book Industry
USE   PUBLISHING INDUSTRY

BOOKKEEPING 110
BT   Business Subjects
RT   Accounting
     Business Education
     Financial Services
     Recordkeeping

Book Lending
USE   LIBRARY CIRCULATION

BOOKLISTS 320
BT   Indexes (Locaters)
     Publications
RT   Bibliographies
     Book Catalogs
     Books
     Catalogs
     Check Lists
     Dictionary Catalogs
     Divided Catalogs
     Periodicals
     Research Reviews (Publications)
     Union Catalogs

BOOKMOBILES 170
BT   Motor Vehicles
RT   Branch Libraries
     Library Extension
     Library Facilities
     Library Services

BOOK REVIEWS 320
BT   Publications
RT   Books
     Historical Reviews
     Literature Reviews

BOOKS 320
NT   Childrens Books
     Folklore Books
     Foreign Language Books
     Health Books
     Paperback Books
     Reference Books
     Textbooks

BT   Publications
RT   Bibliographies
     Booklists
     Book Reviews
     German Literature
     High Interest Low Vocabulary Books
     Library Collections
     Library Material Selection
     Literature
     Newsletters
     Novels
     Periodicals
     Serials
     Short Stories

BOOK THEFTS 060
BT   Stealing
RT   Discipline Problems
     Misbehavior

Border Guards
USE IMMIGRATION INSPECTORS

Border Patrol Officers
USE IMMIGRATION INSPECTORS

BOTANY 070
BT   Biology
RT   Culturing Techniques
     Embryology
     Forestry
     Microbiology
     Plant Growth
     Plant Identification
     Plant Pathology
     Plant Propagation
     Plant Science
     Radiation Biology
     Radioisotopes
     Weeds

Boys
USE MALES

BRACERO PROGRAMS 490
BT   Programs
RT   Braceros

BRACEROS 380
BT   Foreign Workers
RT   Bracero Programs
     Migrant Workers
     Seasonal Employment
     Seasonal Laborers

BRAHMINS 300
BT   Dravidian Languages

BRAILLE 080
BT   Reading
     Writing
RT   Blind
     Raised Line Drawings
     Reading Instruction
     Sensory Aids
     Special Education

     Tactile Adaptation
     Talking Books

BRANCHING 270
NT   Optional Branching
RT   Computer Assisted Instruction
     Linear Programing
     Programed Instruction

BRANCH LIBRARIES 210
BT   Libraries
RT   Bookmobiles
     County Libraries
     Public Libraries
     Regional Libraries

Breadwinners
USE HEADS OF HOUSEHOLDS

BREAKFAST PROGRAMS 250
BT   Programs
RT   Food Standards
     Hunger
     Nutrition

BRICKLAYERS 380
UF   Brick Masons
     Masons
BT   Skilled Workers
RT   Building Trades
     Skilled Occupations
     Trade And Industrial Education

BRICKLAYING 350
BT   Building Trades
RT   Masonry
     Skilled Occupations

Brick Masons
USE BRICKLAYERS

BROADCAST INDUSTRY 370
BT   Industry
RT   Audiovisual Communication
     Commercial Television
     Educational Radio
     Educational Television
     Instructional Television
     Radio
     Telecommunication
     Television

BROADCAST RECEPTION EQUIPMENT 170
BT   Equipment
RT   Broadcast Television

BROADCAST TELEVISION 050
BT   Television
RT   Broadcast Reception Equipment
     Commercial Television
     Educational Television
     Fixed Service Television
     Viewing Time

Bucolic Literature
USE PASTORAL LITERATURE

Budget Allocations
USE BUDGETING

BUDGETING 220
UF Budget Allocations
NT Program Budgeting
RT Accounting
　　Budgets
　　Educational Administration
　　Educational Finance
　　Expenditures
　　Money Management

BUDGETS 220
RT Budgeting
　　Educational Finance
　　Expenditures
　　School Budget Elections

BUILDING CONVERSION 210
SN Change in use or purpose
RT Building Design
　　Building Improvement
　　Building Innovation
　　Building Obsolescence
　　Buildings
　　Construction Costs
　　Construction Needs
　　Facility Expansion
　　Space Utilization

BUILDING DESIGN 030
UF Architectural Changes
　　Architectural Design
NT Air Structures
BT Design
RT Acoustical Environment
　　Acoustic Insulation
　　Acoustics
　　Adhesives
　　Air Flow
　　Architects
　　Architectural Barriers
　　Architectural Character
　　Architectural Education
　　Architectural Elements
　　Architecture
　　Blueprints
　　Building Conversion
　　Building Materials
　　Building Obsolescence
　　Building Plans
　　Campus Planning
　　Chimneys
　　College Buildings
　　Color Planning
　　Construction (Process)
　　Construction Costs
　　Corridors
　　Design Needs
　　Design Preferences
　　Doors
　　Electrical Systems
　　Facility Guidelines

　　Facility Requirements
　　Fire Protection
　　Flexible Classrooms
　　Flexible Facilities
　　Flexible Lighting Design
　　Fuel Consumption
　　Glass Walls
　　Health Facilities
　　Heating
　　Interior Design
　　Interior Space
　　Lighting
　　Lighting Design
　　Modular Building Design
　　Open Plan Schools
　　Physical Design Needs
　　Prefabrication
　　Psychological Design Needs
　　School Buildings
　　School Design
　　Sealers
　　Space Utilization
　　Spatial Relationship
　　Structural Building Systems
　　Thermal Environment
　　Windows

BUILDING EQUIPMENT 170
NT Air Conditioning Equipment
　　Furniture
BT Equipment
RT Buildings
　　Chimneys
　　Educational Equipment
　　Equipment Manufacturers
　　Mechanical Equipment
　　Sanitary Facilities
　　Sheet Metal Work
　　Storage

BUILDING IMPROVEMENT 210
BT Improvement
RT Building Conversion
　　Building Obsolescence
　　Buildings
　　Building Trades
　　Facility Improvement

BUILDING INNOVATION 210
BT Innovation
RT Building Conversion
　　Buildings

BUILDING MATERIALS 460
UF Construction Materials
NT Adhesives
　　Asphalts
　　Masonry
　　Prestressed Concrete
　　Sealers
RT Acoustic Insulation
　　Architectural Elements
　　Architectural Research
　　Building Design

Buildings
Carpeting
Cement Industry
Construction (Process)
Construction Costs
Construction Needs
Doors
Facilities
Flooring
Prefabrication
Roofing

BUILDING OBSOLESCENCE 210
SN Decline of functional utility due to changes in style, practice, and technology, not including physical deterioration
BT Obsolescence
RT Assessed Valuation
Building Conversion
Building Design
Building Improvement
Facility Improvement
Property Appraisal
Technological Advancement

Building Officials
USE ADMINISTRATIVE PERSONNEL

BUILDING OPERATION 210
NT Climate Control
RT Buildings
Building Trades
School Maintenance

BUILDING PLANS 210
NT Studio Floor Plans
RT Architectural Drafting
Blueprints
Building Design
Campus Planning
College Planning
Design
Facility Requirements
House Plan
Library Planning
Master Plans
Planning
School Design
School Planning
Space Classification
Space Utilization
Spatial Relationship

Building Programs
USE CONSTRUCTION PROGRAMS

BUILDINGS 210
NT College Buildings
School Buildings
BT Facilities
RT Air Structures
Architectural Elements
Assessed Valuation
Building Conversion

Building Equipment
Building Improvement
Building Innovation
Building Materials
Building Operation
Bus Garages
Ceilings
Construction Costs
Construction Industry
Educational Complexes
Facility Improvement
Flooring
Hotels
Maintenance
Prefabrication
Real Estate Occupations
Repair
Resources
Roofing
School Construction
Structural Building Systems
Visual Arts

BUILDING TRADES 350
UF Construction Occupations
Structural Work Occupations
NT Bricklaying
BT Occupations
RT Air Conditioning
Bricklayers
Building Improvement
Building Operation
Cabinetmaking
Carpenters
Construction (Process)
Construction Industry
Electricians
Flooring
Industrial Arts
Painting
Plumbing
Roofing
Semiskilled Occupations
Skilled Occupations
Trade And Industrial Education
Woodworking

BULGARIAN 300
BT Slavic Languages

BULLETIN BOARDS 170
UF Tackboards
RT Centers Of Interest
Chalkboards
Vertical Work Surfaces

BULLETINS 320
BT Serials
RT Manuals
Newsletters
Newspapers
Periodicals

BUREAUCRACY 230
RT Organization

BURIAT 300
BT Mongolian Languages
    Uralic Altaic Languages

BURMESE 300
BT Sino Tibetan Languages
RT Burmese Culture

BURMESE CULTURE 100
BT Culture
RT Burmese
    Non Western Civilization

BURUSHASKI 300
BT Languages

Buses
USE SERVICE VEHICLES

BUS GARAGES 210
BT Facilities
    Parking Facilities
RT Buildings
    Maintenance
    Motor Vehicles
    Repair

BUSINESS 370
SN A commercial enterprise
NT Banking
RT Business Correspondence
    Business Cycles
    Business Education
    Business Responsibility
    Exports
    Industry
    Insurance Companies
    Mergers
    Office Machines
    Office Occupations
    Organization Size (Groups)
    Producer Services

BUSINESS ADMINISTRATION 110
SN Subject dealing with the organization
    and management of business enterprises
BT Administration
RT Administrative Personnel
    Business Subjects
    Curriculum
    Law Schools
    Management Development
    Managerial Occupations
    Medical Schools
    Professional Training
    Public Administration Education

Business Competencies
USE BUSINESS SKILLS

BUSINESS CORRESPONDENCE 080
UF Business Letters
BT Letters (Correspondence)
RT Business
    Business English
    Business Subjects
    Communication (Thought Transfer)
    Writing

BUSINESS CYCLES 220
UF Business Fluctuations
    Economic Cycles
    Economic Fluctuations
RT Business
    Economic Climate
    Economic Factors
    Economic Progress
    Economics
    Labor Economics

BUSINESS EDUCATION 140
UF Commercial Education
NT Office Occupations Education
BT Vocational Education
RT Banking
    Bookkeeping
    Business
    Business Education Teachers
    Business Skills
    Business Subjects
    Clerical Workers
    Court Reporters
    Data Processing Occupations
    Distributive Education
    File Clerks
    Merchandising
    Office Occupations
    Office Practice
    Recordkeeping
    Salesmanship
    Vocational Education Teachers

BUSINESS EDUCATION FACILITIES 210
BT Educational Facilities
RT Classrooms
    School Planning

BUSINESS EDUCATION TEACHERS 380
UF Business Teachers
BT Vocational Education Teachers
RT Business Education
    Office Occupations Education

BUSINESS ENGLISH 110
BT Business Subjects
    English
RT Business Correspondence

Business Fluctuations
USE BUSINESS CYCLES

Business Games
USE MANAGEMENT GAMES

Business Letters
USE BUSINESS CORRESPONDENCE

Business Machines
USE OFFICE MACHINES

Business Managers
USE ADMINISTRATIVE PERSONNEL

Business Officials
USE ADMINISTRATIVE PERSONNEL

BUSINESS RESPONSIBILITY 040
SN Reflects the obligations of the commercial business community
BT Responsibility
RT Business
Fire Insurance

BUSINESS SKILLS 010
UF Business Competencies
BT Skills
RT Business Education
Employment Qualifications
Job Skills

BUSINESS SUBJECTS 110
UF Commercial Subjects
NT Bookkeeping
Business English
Office Practice
Typewriting
BT Units Of Study (Subject Fields)
RT Accounting
Banking
Business Administration
Business Correspondence
Business Education
Distributive Education
Farm Accounts
Office Occupations Education
Recordkeeping
Salesmanship
Stenography

Business Teachers
USE BUSINESS EDUCATION TEACHERS

Busing
USE BUS TRANSPORTATION

BUS TRANSPORTATION 020
UF Busing
BT Transportation
RT School Buses
Student Loading Areas

Bus Trips
USE FIELD TRIPS

Byelorussian
USE BIELORUSSIAN

CABINETMAKING 350
UF Millwork
RT Building Trades
Carpenters
Industrial Arts
Woodworking

CABINET TYPE PROJECTORS 170
BT Projection Equipment

CABLE TELEVISION 080
SN Distant television signals brought to subscribers in a community via coaxial cable
BT Television
RT Community Antennas

Cafeterias
USE DINING FACILITIES

CAI
USE COMPUTER ASSISTED INSTRUCTION

CAKCHIQUEL 300
BT American Indian Languages

CALCULATION 340
SN The act or process of computing or estimating through the use of numbers and/or other mathematical symbols
RT Measurement
Statistical Data
Statistics
Subtraction
Tests Of Significance

CALCULUS 340
BT Mathematics

CALISTHENICS 390
BT Exercise (Physiology)
RT Muscular Strength
Physical Fitness

Calligraphy
USE MANUSCRIPT WRITING (HANDLETTERING)

CALORIMETERS 170
UF Microcalorimeters
BT Measurement Instruments
RT Heat

CAMBODIAN 300
BT Sino Tibetan Languages

CAMP COUNSELORS 380
BT Counselors
RT Athletic Activities
Athletics
Camping
Outdoor Education
Recreational Programs

CAMPING 390
BT Recreational Activities
RT Camp Counselors
Outdoor Education
Resident Camp Programs
Tourism
Trails

CAMPUSES 210
RT   Campus Planning
     College Buildings
     Educational Complexes
     Educational Parks
     School Buildings

CAMPUS PLANNING 210
BT   Planning
RT   Architectural Character
     Building Design
     Building Plans
     Campuses
     College Planning
     Construction Programs
     Educational Complexes
     Educational Environment
     Educational Facilities
     Facility Expansion
     Facility Guidelines
     Facility Requirements
     Master Plans
     Parking Facilities
     Residential Colleges
     School Architecture
     School Buildings
     School Location
     School Planning
     Site Analysis
     Space Utilization
     Vehicular Traffic

Campus Schools
USE LABORATORY SCHOOLS

Cannabis Indica
USE MARIHUANA

Cannabis Sativa
USE MARIHUANA

CANTONESE 300
BT   Chinese

Capable Students
USE ABLE STUDENTS

CAPITAL 220
BT   Financial Support
RT   Banking
     Capital Outlay (For Fixed Assets)
     Educational Finance
     Estate Planning
     Organization Size (Groups)
     Private Financial Support
     Trusts (Financial)

CAPITALIZATION (ALPHABETIC) 290
RT   Composition Skills (Literary)
     Punctuation
     Sentence Structure
     Spelling
     Writing Skills

CAPITAL OUTLAY (FOR FIXED ASSETS)
220
BT   Costs
RT   Capital
     Educational Finance
     Organization Size (Groups)

CARDIAC (PERSON) 380
BT   Physically Handicapped
RT   Handicapped
     Health
     Physical Characteristics
     Physical Development

CARDIOVASCULAR SYSTEM 070
UF   Circulatory System
     Vascular System
BT   Physiology
RT   Anatomy
     Blood Circulation
     Heart Rate
     Human Body
     Zoology

CAREER CHANGE 150
UF   Employment Change
     Job Change
     Vocational Change
     Work Change
RT   Career Choice
     Career Opportunities
     Career Planning
     Careers
     Employment Opportunities
     Job Satisfaction
     Labor Turnover
     Occupational Choice
     Occupational Mobility
     Promotion (Occupational)
     Vocational Adjustment

CAREER CHOICE 150
RT   Aspiration
     Career Change
     Career Planning
     Careers
     Employment Opportunities
     Occupational Aspiration
     Occupational Choice
     Occupations
     Personal Interests
     Vocational Interests

Career Objectives
USE OCCUPATIONAL CHOICE

CAREER OPPORTUNITIES 360
BT   Opportunities
RT   Career Change
     Career Planning
     Careers
     Demand Occupations
     Employment Counselors
     Employment Opportunities

Recruitment
Vocational Development

Career Orientation
USE CAREER PLANNING

CAREER PLANNING 090
UF Career Orientation
BT Planning
RT Career Change
Career Choice
Career Opportunities
Careers
Goal Orientation
Guidance
Occupational Choice
Vocational Counseling
Vocational Development

CAREERS 150
NT Science Careers
RT Career Change
Career Choice
Career Opportunities
Career Planning
Employment
Negro Businesses
Occupations

CARPENTERS 380
BT Skilled Workers
RT Building Trades
Cabinetmaking
Trade And Industrial Education
Woodworking

CARPETING 210
UF Carpets
RT Building Materials
Flooring
Maintenance
Physical Design Needs
Psychological Design Needs

Carpet Layers
USE FLOOR LAYERS

Carpets
USE CARPETING

CARRELS 170
BT Library Equipment
Study Facilities

CARTOONS 050
BT Audiovisual Aids
RT Color Presentation
Film Study
Freehand Drawing

CASE (GRAMMAR) 290
RT Form Classes (Languages)
Grammar
Language Patterns
Language Universals
Syntax

CASE RECORDS 020
BT Records (Forms)
RT Case Studies
Case Studies (Education)
Confidential Records
Data Collection
Medical Case Histories
Student Records

CASE STUDIES 450
NT Case Studies (Education)
Cross Sectional Studies
Facility Case Studies
Longitudinal Studies
BT Research
RT Case Records
Counseling

CASE STUDIES (EDUCATION) 450
SN Collections of available evidence, such as
social, biological, environmental, etc.,
related to educational guidance and as
an aid to teachers for instructional
planning
BT Case Studies
RT Case Records
Counseling
Evaluation
Research

CASEWORKER APPROACH 490
BT Social Work
RT Caseworkers
Field Interviews

CASEWORKERS 380
NT Client Caseworkers
BT Social Workers
RT Caseworker Approach
School Social Workers
Social Work

CATALOGING 330
UF Bibliographic Control
BT Library Technical Processes
RT Book Catalogs
Catalogs
Classification
Codification
Dictionary Catalogs
Divided Catalogs
Documentation
Indexes (Locaters)
Indexing
Information Processing
Libraries
Subject Index Terms
Union Catalogs

CATALOGS 320
NT Book Catalogs
    Dictionary Catalogs
    Divided Catalogs
    Union Catalogs
BT Publications
RT Bibliographies
    Booklists
    Cataloging
    Check Lists
    Directories
    Documentation
    Filing
    Indexes (Locaters)
    Libraries
    Program Descriptions
    Subject Index Terms

Categorization
USE CLASSIFICATION

CATHARSIS 060
SN Relaxation of emotional tension by
    expressive reaction
UF Abreaction
    Psychocatharsis
BT Emotional Experience
RT Aggression
    Anxiety
    Emotional Development
    Hostility
    Psychological Patterns
    Psychotherapy
    Reactive Behavior
    Self Expression

CATHOLIC EDUCATORS 380
BT Instructional Staff
RT Catholics
    Catholic Schools
    Church Related Colleges
    Church Workers
    Nun Teachers
    Religious Education

CATHOLIC ELEMENTARY SCHOOLS 470
BT Catholic Schools
    Elementary Schools

CATHOLIC HIGH SCHOOLS 470
BT Catholic Schools
    High Schools

CATHOLIC PARENTS 380
BT Catholics
    Parents

CATHOLICS 380
NT Catholic Parents
BT Religious Cultural Groups
RT Catholic Educators
    Nuns
    Priests

CATHOLIC SCHOOLS 470
NT Catholic Elementary Schools
    Catholic High Schools
BT Parochial Schools
RT Catholic Educators
    Church Related Colleges
    Nun Teachers

CAUCASIAN LANGUAGES 300
BT Languages

CAUCASIAN RACE 380
UF White Race
BT Race
RT Caucasians
    Caucasian Students

CAUCASIANS 380
SN Members of the white race not limited to
    a geographic area
UF Whites
RT Caucasian Race
    Caucasian Students
    Racial Characteristics

CAUCASIAN STUDENTS 380
UF White Students
BT Students
RT Caucasian Race
    Caucasians

CCTV
USE CLOSED CIRCUIT TELEVISION

CEBUANO 300
BT Visayan
RT Dialects

CEILINGS 210
RT Acoustical Environment
    Buildings
    Construction (Process)

CELL THEORY 070
BT Cytology
RT Evolution

CEMENT INDUSTRY 370
UF Cement Manufacturing Industry
    Concrete Industry
BT Industry
RT Building Materials
    Construction Industry
    Prestressed Concrete

Cement Manufacturing Industry
USE CEMENT INDUSTRY

Cements (Adhesives)
USE ADHESIVES

CENSORSHIP 500
RT Academic Freedom
    Moral Issues
    Moral Values
    Sanctions

CENSUS FIGURES 120
BT Statistical Data
RT Community Size
    Demography
    Incidence

CENTERS OF INTEREST 510
BT Teaching Techniques
RT Audiovisual Aids
    Bulletin Boards

CENTRALIZATION 020
RT Administrative Organization
    Decentralization
    Mergers
    Organization
    School Organization

Centralized Schools
USE CONSOLIDATED SCHOOLS

CENTRAL SOUND SYSTEMS 170
BT Audiovisual Aids

Ceramic Materials
USE CERAMICS

Ceramic Processes
USE CERAMICS

CERAMICS 030
UF Ceramic Materials
    Ceramic Processes
RT Art
    Art Materials
    Glass
    Handicrafts
    Industrial Arts

CEREBRAL DOMINANCE 420
BT Physical Characteristics
RT Human Development
    Lateral Dominance
    Neurological Organization
    Perceptual Development

CEREBRAL PALSY 240
BT Neurologically Handicapped
RT Aphasia
    Exceptional (Atypical)
    Mentally Handicapped
    Physically Handicapped
    Speech Handicaps

CERTIFICATION 500
UF Licensing
NT Counselor Certification
    Student Certification
    Teacher Certification
RT Administrator Background
    Credentials
    Educational Certificates
    Proprietary Schools
    State Licensing Boards
    Teacher Background

Teacher Certificates
Teacher Qualifications

CERTIFIED PUBLIC ACCOUNTANTS 380
BT Accountants
RT Accounting
    Financial Services

CHAD LANGUAGES 300
NT Hausa
BT Afro Asiatic Languages
RT Language Classification

CHALKBOARDS 170
UF Blackboards
BT Vertical Work Surfaces
RT Audiovisual Aids
    Bulletin Boards
    Display Panels

CHANGE AGENTS 490
UF Village Workers
RT Behavior Change
    Changing Attitudes
    Educational Innovation
    Social Change

CHANGING ATTITUDES 040
BT Attitudes
RT Adoption (Ideas)
    Behavior Change
    Change Agents

Chanson De Geste
USE MEDIEVAL ROMANCE

Characteristics (Individual)
USE INDIVIDUAL CHARACTERISTICS

CHARACTERIZATION (LITERATURE) 260
UF Character Portrayal
BT Literature
RT Classical Literature
    Comedy
    Composition (Literary)
    Drama
    English Literature
    Fiction
    Literary Analysis
    Literary Conventions
    Literary Criticism
    Novels
    Platonism
    Playwriting
    Poetry
    Prose
    Short Stories
    Tragedy
    Twentieth Century Literature

Character Portrayal
USE CHARACTERIZATION (LITERATURE)

CHARACTER RECOGNITION 080
UF   Magnetic Ink Character Recognition
BT   Pattern Recognition
RT   Information Processing
     Perception
     Reading

CHARTS 050
NT   Grade Charts
BT   Audiovisual Aids
RT   Atlases
     Color Presentation
     Diagrams
     Graphs

CHAUTAUQUAS 270
BT   Adult Education
RT   Concerts
     Dramatics
     Lecture

CHEATING 060
BT   Conduct
     Misbehavior
RT   Behavior

CHECK LISTS 190
RT   Book Catalogs
     Booklists
     Catalogs

Chefs
USE   COOKS

CHEMICAL ANALYSIS 400
UF   Analytical Chemistry
     Chemical Determination
     Composition Measurement
     Determination (Chemical)
RT   Chemical Reactions
     Chemistry
     Chromatography
     Metallurgy

CHEMICAL BONDING 400
RT   Chemical Reactions
     Chemistry
     Organic Chemistry
     Physical Sciences

Chemical Determination
USE   CHEMICAL ANALYSIS

CHEMICAL EQUILIBRIUM 400
UF   Equilibrium Constants
RT   Chemical Reactions
     Chemistry
     Thermodynamics

CHEMICAL INDUSTRY 370
BT   Industry
RT   Chemical Technicians
     Manufacturing Industry

CHEMICAL REACTIONS 400
UF   Chemical Synthesis
NT   Oxidation
     Photochemical Reactions
RT   Chemical Analysis
     Chemical Bonding
     Chemical Equilibrium
     Chemistry
     Organic Chemistry

Chemical Synthesis
USE   CHEMICAL REACTIONS

CHEMICAL TECHNICIANS 380
BT   Subprofessionals
RT   Chemical Industry
     Chemistry
     Organic Chemistry
     Technical Education
     Technical Occupations

CHEMISTRY 400
NT   Biochemistry
     Organic Chemistry
BT   Physical Sciences
RT   Atomic Structure
     Chemical Analysis
     Chemical Bonding
     Chemical Equilibrium
     Chemical Reactions
     Chemical Technicians
     Chromatography
     Coordination Compounds
     Earth Science
     Metallurgical Technicians
     Metallurgy
     Meteorology
     Oxidation
     Photochemical Reactions
     Physics Teachers
     Radiation Biology
     Radioisotopes
     Scientific Research
     Soil Science

CHEMISTRY INSTRUCTION 270
BT   Science Instruction
RT   Physics Instruction
     Science Courses
     Science Education

CHEMISTRY TEACHERS 380
BT   Teachers
RT   Physics Teachers

Chemotherapy
USE   DRUG THERAPY

CHEREMIS 300
BT   Uralic Altaic Languages

CHEROKEE 300
BT   American Indian Languages

Chibemba
USE   BEMBA

CHIEF ADMINISTRATORS 380
NT Presidents
    Principals
    Superintendents
BT Administrative Personnel
RT Administrator Evaluation
    Administrator Qualifications
    Administrator Selection
    College Administration
    School Administration

Chief Cooks
USE COOKS

CHILD ABUSE 490
BT Child Care
RT Child Rearing
    Child Welfare
    Family Problems
    Hunger
    Parent Child Relationship
    Social Problems
    Welfare Problems

CHILD CARE 490
NT Child Abuse
RT Child Care Centers
    Child Care Occupations
    Child Care Workers
    Child Rearing
    Children
    Immunization Programs
    Pediatrics Training
    Self Care Skills

CHILD CARE CENTERS 210
NT Migrant Child Care Centers
RT Child Care
    Child Care Occupations
    Child Care Workers
    Welfare Services

CHILD CARE OCCUPATIONS 350
BT Service Occupations
RT Child Care
    Child Care Centers
    Child Care Workers
    Child Rearing
    Day Care Services
    Occupational Home Economics

CHILD CARE WORKERS 380
RT Child Care
    Child Care Centers
    Child Care Occupations
    Child Rearing
    Children
    Nursery Schools
    Service Occupations

CHILD DEVELOPMENT 130
BT Development
RT Child Development Centers
    Child Development Specialists
    Child Language
    Child Rearing
    Children
    Echolalia
    Growth Patterns
    Human Posture
    Individual Development
    Maturation
    Motor Development
    Neurological Organization
    Retarded Speech Development

CHILD DEVELOPMENT CENTERS 210
RT Boarding Schools
    Child Development
    Disadvantaged Youth
    Preschool Children
    Preschool Education

CHILD DEVELOPMENT SPECIALISTS 380
BT Specialists
RT Child Development
    Consultation Programs
    Professional Services

CHILDHOOD 130
NT Early Childhood
RT Adolescence
    Childhood Attitudes
    Childhood Friendship
    Childhood Interests
    Children
    Early Experience
    Individual Development
    Infancy

CHILDHOOD ATTITUDES 040
UF Childrens Attitudes
BT Attitudes
RT Childhood

CHILDHOOD FRIENDSHIP 490
BT Friendship
RT Childhood

CHILDHOOD INTERESTS 040
BT Interests
RT Childhood

CHILDHOOD NEEDS 420
BT Individual Needs
RT Children

CHILD LABOR 150
BT Labor
RT Child Labor Laws
    Children

Child Labor Bills
USE CHILD LABOR LAWS

CHILD LABOR LAWS 230
UF   Child Labor Bills
BT   Labor Laws
RT   Child Labor
     Children
     Child Welfare

CHILD LANGUAGE 290
BT   Language
RT   Bilingualism
     Child Development
     Language Ability
     Language Arts
     Language Development
     Language Handicaps
     Language Patterns
     Language Research
     Pronunciation
     Psycholinguistics
     Speech
     Speech Habits
     Verbal Communication
     Verbal Development

Child Parent Relationship
USE   PARENT CHILD RELATIONSHIP

CHILD PSYCHOLOGY 420
BT   Individual Psychology
RT   Children

CHILD REARING 130
RT   Child Abuse
     Child Care
     Child Care Occupations
     Child Care Workers
     Child Development
     Children
     Family Relationship

CHILDREN 380
NT   Adopted Children
     Blind Children
     Crippled Children
     Deaf Children
     Emotionally Disturbed Children
     Exceptional Children
     Foster Children
     Handicapped Children
     Homebound Children
     Hospitalized Children
     Kindergarten Children
     Migrant Children
     Minority Group Children
     Neurotic Children
     Preschool Children
     Problem Children
     Psychotic Children
     Retarded Children
     Transient Children
RT   Child Care
     Child Care Workers
     Child Development
     Childhood

     Childhood Needs
     Child Labor
     Child Labor Laws
     Child Psychology
     Child Rearing
     Childrens Books
     Childrens Games
     Child Responsibility
     Child Role
     Child Welfare
     Dependents
     Family Life
     Family Problems
     Parent Child Relationship
     Siblings
     Twins

Childrens Attitudes
USE   CHILDHOOD ATTITUDES

CHILDRENS BOOKS 320
BT   Books
RT   Children

Childrens Courts
USE   JUVENILE COURTS

CHILDRENS GAMES 390
BT   Games
RT   Children
     Educational Games

Childrens Theater
USE   THEATER ARTS

CHILD RESPONSIBILITY 040
BT   Responsibility
RT   Administrator Responsibility
     Children
     Educational Responsibility
     Parent Responsibility
     Teacher Responsibility

CHILD ROLE 490
RT   Children
     Family Role

CHILD WELFARE 480
BT   Welfare
RT   Adopted Children
     Child Abuse
     Child Labor Laws
     Children
     Foster Children
     Foster Family

CHILUBA 300
BT   African Languages
     Bantu Languages

CHIMNEYS 210
UF   Exhaust Stacks
     Smokestacks
     Stacks (Exhaust)
RT   Air Flow
     Air Pollution Control
     Building Design

Building Equipment
Exhausting
Heat
Heating
Pollution
Ventilation

CHINESE 300
NT Cantonese
     Foochow
     Mandarin Chinese
BT Sino Tibetan Languages
RT Chinese Americans
     Chinese Culture

CHINESE AMERICANS 380
BT Ethnic Groups
RT Chinese
     Ethnic Origins
     Minority Groups
     Racial Characteristics

CHINESE CULTURE 100
BT Culture
RT Chinese
     Foreign Culture
     Non Western Civilization

CHINYANJA 300
UF Cinyanja
     Nyanja
BT African Languages
     Bantu Languages

Chivalric Novels
USE MEDIEVAL ROMANCE

CHOCTAW 300
BT American Indian Languages

Choirs
USE CHORUSES

Choral Literature
USE CHORAL MUSIC

CHORAL MUSIC 030
UF Choral Literature
BT Vocal Music
RT Choruses
     Music Activities
     Musical Composition
     Music Education
     Music Techniques
     Singing

CHORAL SPEAKING 030
BT Speaking
RT Choruses
     Literature
     Literature Appreciation
     Poetry
     Speech

CHORUSES 380
UF Choirs
     Glee Clubs
     Vocal Ensembles
BT Groups
RT Choral Music
     Choral Speaking
     Music Activities
     Music Education
     Music Techniques
     Singing
     Vocal Music

CHRISTIANITY 480
BT Religion
RT Biblical Literature
     History
     Humanities
     Literature
     Philosophy
     Religious Cultural Groups

CHROMATOGRAPHY 400
UF Electrochromatography
BT Laboratory Techniques
RT Biochemistry
     Biology
     Chemical Analysis
     Chemistry

Chronically Ill
USE SPECIAL HEALTH PROBLEMS

CHRONICLES 260
BT Literature
RT History
     Medieval Literature
     Old English Literature
     Poetry
     Prose
     Textual Criticism

Chronic Medical Problems
USE SPECIAL HEALTH PROBLEMS

Church Action
USE CHURCH ROLE

CHURCHES 210
BT Institutions
RT Church Migrant Projects
     Church Programs
     Church Responsibility
     Church Role
     Church Workers
     Clergymen
     Mergers
     Priests
     Religion
     State Church Separation
     Theological Education

CHURCH MIGRANT PROJECTS 490
BT   Migrant Worker Projects
RT   Churches
      Church Programs
      Community Migrant Projects
      Migrant Welfare Services
      Religious Education

CHURCH PROGRAMS 490
UF   Church Projects
BT   Church Role
      Programs
RT   Churches
      Church Migrant Projects
      Church Related Colleges
      Church Workers
      Religion
      Religious Education

Church Projects
USE   CHURCH PROGRAMS

CHURCH RELATED COLLEGES 470
UF   Denominational Colleges
      Sectarian Colleges
      Seminaries
BT   Colleges
RT   Catholic Educators
      Catholic Schools
      Church Programs
      Parochial Schools
      Private Colleges
      Religious Education
      Religious Organizations
      Theological Education

CHURCH RESPONSIBILITY 040
BT   Responsibility
RT   Churches

CHURCH ROLE 490
UF   Church Action
NT   Church Programs
BT   Institutional Role
RT   Churches
      Religion
      State Church Separation

CHURCH WORKERS 380
UF   Parish Workers
RT   Catholic Educators
      Churches
      Church Programs
      Clergymen
      Laymen
      Lay Teachers
      Nuns
      Priests
      Religion
      Religious Education

CHUVASH 300
BT   Turkic Languages

Cinyanja
USE   CHINYANJA

Circuitry
USE   ELECTRIC CIRCUITS

Circuits (Electronic)
USE   ELECTRIC CIRCUITS

Circuit Teachers
USE   ITINERANT TEACHERS

Circulation (Libraries)
USE   LIBRARY CIRCULATION

Circulation Patterns
USE   TRAFFIC PATTERNS

Circulatory System
USE   CARDIOVASCULAR SYSTEM

CITATION INDEXES 320
BT   Indexes (Locaters)
RT   Bibliographic Citations
      Bibliographic Coupling
      Documentation
      Indexing
      Information Retrieval
      Reference Materials

Citations (Bibliographic)
USE   BIBLIOGRAPHIC CITATIONS

Citizen Involvement
USE   CITIZEN PARTICIPATION

CITIZEN PARTICIPATION 490
UF   Citizen Involvement
      Civic Involvement
BT   Citizenship
RT   Citizens Councils
      Citizenship Responsibility
      Civil Disobedience
      Community Action
      Community Attitudes
      Community Organizations
      Community Role
      Community Support
      Public Affairs Education
      Social Action

Citizen Responsibility
USE   CITIZENSHIP RESPONSIBILITY

CITIZEN ROLE 490
RT   Citizenship
      Senior Citizens

CITIZENS COUNCILS 370
BT   Community Organizations
RT   Citizen Participation

CITIZENSHIP 230
UF   Good Citizenship
NT   Citizen Participation
      Citizenship Responsibility
RT   Citizen Role
      Civic Belief
      Civics
      Community Attitudes
      Public Affairs Education

CITIZENSHIP RESPONSIBILITY 490
UF   Citizen Responsibility
     Civic Responsibility
BT   Citizenship
     Social Responsibility
RT   Citizen Participation
     Community Responsibility
     Voting

CITY DEMOGRAPHY 120
NT   Residential Patterns
BT   Demography
RT   Community

CITY GOVERNMENT 230
UF   Local Government
NT   City Officials
     City Wide Commissions
BT   Government (Administrative Body)
RT   City Improvement
     City Planning
     City Problems
     City Wide Programs
     Community Agencies (Public)
     Depository Libraries
     Government Publications
     School District Autonomy

CITY IMPROVEMENT 160
BT   Improvement
RT   City Government
     City Wide Programs
     Community
     Community Change
     Community Responsibility
     Neighborhood Improvement
     Social Responsibility
     Urban Renewal

CITY OFFICIALS 380
UF   Elected City Officials
     Local Officials
BT   City Government
RT   County Officials
     Legislators
     Public Officials

CITY PLANNING 230
UF   Urban Planning
BT   Planning
RT   City Government
     City Wide Programs
     Community Planning
     Land Use
     Regional Planning
     Road Construction
     Social Planning
     Urban Renewal

CITY PROBLEMS 230
UF   Urban Problems
BT   Problems
RT   City Government

City Schools
USE   URBAN SCHOOLS

CITY WIDE COMMISSIONS 230
BT   City Government

CITY WIDE PROGRAMS 490
BT   Programs
RT   City Government
     City Improvement
     City Planning
     Community

CIVIC BELIEF 040
RT   Citizenship

Civic Groups
USE   COMMUNITY ORGANIZATIONS

Civic Involvement
USE   CITIZEN PARTICIPATION

Civic Organizations
USE   COMMUNITY ORGANIZATIONS

Civic Programs
USE   COMMUNITY PROGRAMS

Civic Relations
USE   COMMUNITY RELATIONS

Civic Responsibility
USE   CITIZENSHIP RESPONSIBILITY

CIVICS 480
BT   Political Science
RT   American Government (Course)
     Citizenship
     Constitutional History
     Public Affairs Education

CIVIL DEFENSE 490
RT   Community Programs
     Emergency Programs
     Military Science
     National Defense
     Nuclear Warfare

CIVIL DISOBEDIENCE 490
RT   Activism
     Citizen Participation
     Civil Rights
     Civil Rights Legislation
     Demonstrations (Civil)
     Segregationist Organizations

CIVIL ENGINEERING 400
UF   Highway Engineering
BT   Engineering
RT   Engineering Drawing
     Engineering Graphics
     Highway Engineering Aides
     Road Construction
     Structural Building Systems

CIVIL LIBERTIES 230
UF Human Rights
    Individual Rights
    Personal Liberty
NT Civil Rights
    Freedom Of Speech
RT Civil Rights Legislation
    Democracy
    Equal Protection
    Federal Laws
    United States History
    Voting Rights

CIVIL RIGHTS 230
SN Rights of minority groups in the United
    States
UF Minority Rights
NT Equal Education
    Equal Opportunities (Jobs)
    Equal Protection
    Voting Rights
BT Civil Liberties
RT Anti Segregation Programs
    Black Power
    Civil Disobedience
    Civil Rights Legislation
    Democracy
    Demonstrations (Civil)
    Discriminatory Legislation
    Equal Facilities
    Federal State Relationship
    Freedom Of Speech
    Freedom Organizations
    Freedom Schools
    Intergroup Education
    Minority Groups
    Negro Leadership
    Negro Organizations
    Racial Integration
    Racial Segregation
    Segregationist Organizations
    Social Discrimination

CIVIL RIGHTS LEGISLATION 230
BT Legislation
RT Civil Disobedience
    Civil Liberties
    Civil Rights

Civil Service Employees
USE GOVERNMENT EMPLOYEES

CIVIL WAR (UNITED STATES) 260
RT American History
    Reconstruction Era
    United States History

CLASS ACTIVITIES 140
UF Class Projects
BT Activities
RT Classes (Groups Of Students)
    Class Newspapers

CLASS ATTENDANCE 020
BT Attendance
RT Classes (Groups Of Students)

CLASS ATTITUDES 040
BT Attitudes
RT Anti Intellectualism
    Classes (Groups Of Students)
    Program Attitudes

CLASS AVERAGE 500
UF Grade Average
RT Classes (Groups Of Students)
    Grades (Scholastic)
    Grading
    Measurement

Class Discipline
USE DISCIPLINE

Class Discussion
USE DISCUSSION (TEACHING TECHNIQUE)

CLASSES (GROUPS OF STUDENTS) 280
NT Class Size
    Evening Classes
    Literacy Classes
    Multigraded Classes
    Nonauthoritarian Classes
    Nongraded Classes
    Opportunity Classes
    Small Classes
    Special Classes
    Transitional Classes
    Ungraded Classes
RT Class Activities
    Class Attendance
    Class Attitudes
    Class Average
    Class Management
    Class Organization
    Classroom Integration
    Student Grouping

Classical Greek
USE GREEK

CLASSICAL LANGUAGES 300
NT Greek
BT Languages
RT Classical Literature
    College Language Programs

CLASSICAL LITERATURE 260
SN Literature of Ancient Greece and Rome
UF Classicism
BT Literature
RT Characterization (Literature)
    Classical Languages
    Drama
    Dramatic Unities
    Epics
    Fables
    Greek
    Humanism
    Latin

Legends
Metaphors
Mythology
Platonism
Spanish Literature
World Literature

Classicism
USE CLASSICAL LITERATURE

CLASSIFICATION 330
UF Categorization
NT Language Classification
Space Classification
Taxonomy
Typology
RT Bibliographic Coupling
Cataloging
Documentation
Facility Inventory
Filing
Grouping (Instructional Purposes)
Indexes (Locaters)
Indexing
Language Typology
Library Technical Processes
Search Strategies
Subject Index Terms

Classification Clerks
USE FILE CLERKS

Class Integration
USE CLASSROOM INTEGRATION

CLASS MANAGEMENT 270
BT Management
RT Classes (Groups Of Students)
Class Organization
Classroom Techniques
Discipline

CLASS NEWSPAPERS 080
BT School Publications
RT Class Activities
School Newspapers

CLASS ORGANIZATION 370
RT Classes (Groups Of Students)
Class Management
Classroom Arrangement
Cluster Grouping
Furniture Arrangement
Grouping (Instructional Purposes)

Class Projects
USE CLASS ACTIVITIES

CLASSROOM ARRANGEMENT 160
RT Class Organization
Classroom Design
Classrooms
Class Size
Corridors
Flexible Classrooms
Flexible Facilities
Flexible Lighting Design

Furniture Arrangement
Space Dividers
Space Utilization

CLASSROOM COMMUNICATION 080
BT Communication (Thought Transfer)
RT Classrooms
Nonverbal Communication
Student Teacher Relationship
Verbal Communication

CLASSROOM DESIGN 030
BT Design
RT Classroom Arrangement
Classroom Environment
Classroom Research
Design Needs
Flexible Classrooms
Glass Walls
Interior Design
Multipurpose Classrooms
Open Plan Schools
Space Utilization

CLASSROOM ENVIRONMENT 160
UF Classroom Situation
BT Environment
RT Classroom Design
Classroom Guidance Programs
Classrooms
College Environment
Permissive Environment
Physical Environment
Teacher Welfare
Teaching Conditions
Temperature

Classroom Equipment
USE EDUCATIONAL EQUIPMENT

CLASSROOM FURNITURE 170
UF Furniture (Classroom)
BT Furniture
RT Classrooms
Furniture Arrangement
Furniture Design
Storage

CLASSROOM GAMES 510
BT Educational Games
RT Classrooms

CLASSROOM GUIDANCE PROGRAMS 410
BT Guidance Programs
RT Classroom Environment
Classrooms
Group Guidance
Guidance Services

CLASSROOM INTEGRATION 430
UF Class Integration
Integrated Classes
RT Classes (Groups Of Students)
Racial Integration
School Integration
Social Integration

CLASSROOM LIBRARIES 210
BT Libraries
RT Classrooms

CLASSROOM MATERIALS 050
BT Instructional Materials
RT Audiovisual Aids
Classrooms
Color Presentation
Manipulative Materials
Resource Materials
Science Materials
Student Developed Materials
Teacher Developed Materials

CLASSROOM OBSERVATION TECHNIQUES
510
SN Procedures which use systematic
observation to measure classroom
behavior
UF Observed Classroom Behaviors
BT Measurement Techniques
RT Classroom Research
Interaction Process Analysis
Observation
Student Behavior
Teacher Behavior
Teaching Experience

CLASSROOM PARTICIPATION 270
BT Participation

CLASSROOM RESEARCH 450
BT Educational Research
R1 Classroom Design
Classroom Observation Techniques
Classrooms

CLASSROOMS 210
NT Electronic Classrooms
Flexible Classrooms
Mobile Classrooms
Multipurpose Classrooms
Self Contained Classrooms
Self Directed Classrooms
BT Educational Facilities
RT Business Education Facilities
Classroom Arrangement
Classroom Communication
Classroom Environment
Classroom Furniture
Classroom Games
Classroom Guidance Programs
Classroom Libraries
Classroom Materials
Classroom Research
Classroom Techniques
Corridors
Music Facilities
School Shops
Stages

Classroom Situation
USE CLASSROOM ENVIRONMENT

CLASSROOM TECHNIQUES 510
BT Teaching Techniques
RT Class Management
Classrooms
Individualized Instruction

CLASS SIZE 280
BT Classes (Groups Of Students)
RT Classroom Arrangement
Facility Utilization Research
Flexible Schedules
Flexible Scheduling
Small Classes
Student Teacher Ratio

Class Status
USE SOCIAL STATUS

CLEANING 250
NT Dishwashing
BT Sanitation
RT Disease Control
Equipment Maintenance
Health
Hygiene
Maintenance
Physical Design Needs
Preservation
Public Health
Repair
Sanitation Improvement
School Maintenance
School Safety

CLEARINGHOUSES 210
RT Resource Centers

CLEFT LIP 240
BT Speech Handicaps
RT Cleft Palate
Handicapped
Speech
Speech Handicapped
Speech Therapy

CLEFT PALATE 240
BT Speech Handicaps
RT Cleft Lip
Handicapped
Speech
Speech Handicapped
Speech Therapy

CLERGYMEN 380
UF Ministers
Parsons
Preachers
BT Professional Personnel
RT Churches
Church Workers
Priests
Religion
Religious Education
Religious Organizations

CLERICAL OCCUPATIONS 350
BT Occupations
RT Clerical Workers
    Court Reporters
    File Clerks
    Office Occupations
    Secretaries
    Stenographers
    Typists

CLERICAL WORKERS 380
NT Court Reporters
    File Clerks
    Secretaries
    Stenographers
    Typists
BT Nonprofessional Personnel
RT Business Education
    Clerical Occupations
    Employees
    Office Occupations
    Office Occupations Education

Clerk Stenographers
USE STENOGRAPHERS

Clerk Typists
USE TYPISTS

CLIENT CASEWORKERS 380
BT Caseworkers
RT Nondirective Counseling

Client Centered Counseling
USE NONDIRECTIVE COUNSELING

CLIMATE CONTROL 160
BT Building Operation
RT Air Conditioning
    Air Conditioning Equipment
    Air Pollution Control
    Climatic Factors
    Controlled Environment
    Heating
    Humidity
    Instrumentation
    Lighting
    Physical Design Needs
    Solar Radiation
    Temperature
    Thermal Environment
    Ventilation
    Windowless Rooms
    Windows

CLIMATIC FACTORS 160
BT Physical Environment
RT Climate Control
    Earth Science
    Environmental Influences
    Geographic Location
    Heat
    Humidity
    Light
    Meteorology

Ocean Engineering
Solar Radiation
Temperature
Thermal Environment

CLINICAL DIAGNOSIS 180
SN Identification of conditions requiring
    treatment
RT Educational Diagnosis
    Electroencephalography
    Etiology
    Medical Case Histories
    Medical Evaluation
    Psychoeducational Clinics
    Tests

CLINICAL EXPERIENCE 200
SN Practical experience in patient and
    patient related services which occur as
    part of an educational program
UF Clinical Learning Experience
BT Learning Experience
RT Clinics
    Field Experience Programs
    Health Occupations Education
    Internship Programs
    Practicums
    Practicum Supervision
    Student Experience

Clinical Learning Experience
USE CLINICAL EXPERIENCE

CLINICAL PROFESSORS 380
BT Professors
RT College Supervisors
    Cooperating Teachers
    Differentiated Staffs
    Practicum Supervision
    Teacher Education
    Teacher Educator Education
    Teacher Educators

Clinical Services
USE CLINICS

Clinical Teaching
USE INDIVIDUALIZED INSTRUCTION

CLINIC PERSONNEL (SCHOOL) 380
UF Clinic Staff
NT Audiometrists
BT School Personnel
RT Clinics
    Consultants
    Health Personnel
    Health Services
    Medical Evaluation
    Medical Services
    Nurses
    Paramedical Occupations

CLINICS 210
UF Clinical Services
     Treatment Centers
NT Dental Clinics
     Hearing Clinics
     Itinerant Clinics
     Mental Health Clinics
     Preschool Clinics
     Psychoeducational Clinics
     Reading Clinics
     Rural Clinics
     Speech Clinics
BT Health Services
RT Clinical Experience
     Clinic Personnel (School)
     Health Facilities
     Hospitals

Clinic Staff
USE CLINIC PERSONNEL (SCHOOL)

Clockmakers
USE WATCHMAKERS

CLOSED CIRCUIT TELEVISION 050
UF CCTV
BT Telecommunication
     Television
RT Audiovisual Aids
     Audiovisual Instruction
     Educational Television
     Viewing Time

Closed Schools
USE SCHOOL CLOSING

CLOTHING 250
RT Clothing Design
     Clothing Instruction
     Clothing Maintenance Specialists
     Needle Trades
     Patternmaking

CLOTHING DESIGN 350
UF Costume Design
     Dress Design
BT Design
RT Clothing
     Clothing Instruction
     Needle Trades
     Patternmaking

CLOTHING INSTRUCTION 270
BT Instruction
RT Clothing
     Clothing Design
     Clothing Maintenance Specialists
     Consumer Science
     Home Economics Education
     Needle Trades
     Patternmaking
     Seamstresses
     Textiles Instruction

CLOTHING MAINTENANCE SPECIALISTS 380
BT Service Workers
RT Clothing
     Clothing Instruction
     Distributive Education
     Occupational Home Economics
     Service Occupations
     Textiles Instruction

Clothing Service Workers
USE SEAMSTRESSES

Cloze Materials
USE CLOZE PROCEDURE

CLOZE PROCEDURE 520
UF Cloze Materials
     Cloze Technique
BT Study Skills
RT Language Ability
     Reading
     Reading Ability
     Reading Comprehension
     Reading Skills
     Writing Skills

Cloze Technique
USE CLOZE PROCEDURE

CLUBS 370
NT Girls Clubs
     Science Clubs
BT Groups
     Organizations (Groups)

Clues
USE CUES

CLUSTER GROUPING 280
SN Clustering of related items within any given collection of persons or things
RT Bibliographic Coupling
     Class Organization
     Correlation
     Grouping Procedures
     Group Structure
     Matched Groups
     Occupational Clusters
     Student Grouping

COACHING TEACHERS 380
BT Teachers
RT Remedial Instruction
     Remedial Programs
     Remedial Teachers
     Tutorial Programs
     Tutoring

Coast Guard Air Stations
USE MILITARY AIR FACILITIES

COLLEGE TEACHERS 380
NT Counselor Educators
    Teacher Educators
BT Teachers
RT Colleges
    College Supervisors
    Mathematics Teachers
    Professors
    Sabbatical Leaves

College Unions
USE STUDENT UNIONS

Colloquial Standard Usage
USE STANDARD SPOKEN USAGE

COLONIAL HISTORY (UNITED STATES) 260
BT United States History
RT Colonialism
    Puritans
    Revolutionary War (United States)

COLONIALISM 230
BT Foreign Policy
RT Colonial History (United States)
    Foreign Relations
    Imperialism
    Nationalism
    Political Attitudes
    Political Divisions (Geographic)
    Revolutionary War (United States)

Colonization
USE LAND SETTLEMENT

COLOR 030
UF Hue
RT Art Expressio.i
    Art Products
    Color Planning
    Color Presentation
    Contrast
    Light
    Painting
    Perception
    Visual Perception

Color Films
USE FILMS

COLOR PLANNING 030
BT Planning
RT Building Design
    Color
    Design Needs
    Environmental Influences
    Illumination Levels
    Interior Design
    Physical Environment
    School Planning
    Space Utilization
    Visual Arts
    Visual Perception

COLOR PRESENTATION 050
BT Audiovisual Communication
RT Audiovisual Aids
    Cartoons
    Charts
    Classroom Materials
    Color
    Color Television
    Films
    Filmstrips
    Instructional Aids
    Slides
    Transparencies

COLOR TELEVISION 050
BT Television
RT Color Presentation
    Pictorial Stimuli
    Television Lighting
    Television Viewing
    Video Tape Recordings

COM
USE COMPUTER OUTPUT MICROFILM

COMEDY 260
UF Comedy Of Manners
BT Drama
RT Characterization (Literature)
    Composition (Literary)
    English Neoclassic Literary Period
    French Literature
    Literary Analysis
    Literary Conventions
    Poetry
    Prose
    Scripts
    Spanish American Literature
    Spanish Literature

Comedy Of Manners
USE COMEDY

COMMERCIAL ART 030
UF Advertising Art
BT Art
RT Art Education
    Graphic Arts
    Merchandising
    Publicize
    Vocational Education

Commercial Correspondence Schools
USE CORRESPONDENCE SCHOOLS

Commercial Education
USE BUSINESS EDUCATION

Commercial Fisheries
USE FISHERIES

Commercial Pilots
USE AIRCRAFT PILOTS

Commercial Subjects
USE BUSINESS SUBJECTS

COCOUNSELING 090
UF Team Counseling
BT Counseling
RT Teamwork
Therapy

COCURRICULAR ACTIVITIES 390
UF Extracurricular Activities
School Related Activities
Student Activities (Not Classwork)
BT Activities
RT After School Activities
Curriculum
Debate
Recreational Activities
School Newspapers
Science Clubs
Science Fairs
Student Interests
Student Organizations
Student Projects
Students
Student Unions

CODED SPEECH 290
SN Representation of high frequency sounds
in low frequency range
BT Speech
RT Aurally Handicapped
Deaf Education
Hearing Therapy

CODIFICATION 330
RT Cataloging
Indexes (Locaters)
Information Retrieval
Laws
Standards

COEDUCATION 140
BT Education
RT Womens Education

COGNITIVE ABILITY 010
BT Ability
RT Academic Ability
Aptitude
Cognitive Development
Intelligence
Productive Thinking

Cognitive Behavioral Objectives
USE COGNITIVE OBJECTIVES

COGNITIVE DEVELOPMENT 130
BT Development
RT Affective Behavior
Cognitive Ability
Cognitive Objectives
Conservation (Concept)
Intellectual Development
Learning Disabilities
Preschool Learning

COGNITIVE MEASUREMENT 180
BT Measurement
RT Cognitive Tests
Learning Plateaus

COGNITIVE OBJECTIVES 060
UF Cognitive Behavioral Objectives
BT Educational Objectives
RT Affective Objectives
Behavioral Objectives
Cognitive Development
Guidance Objectives
Psychomotor Objectives
Training Objectives

COGNITIVE PROCESSES 310
NT Memorizing
Memory
RT Abstraction Levels
Abstract Reasoning
Comprehension
Conservation (Concept)
Convergent Thinking
Decision Making Skills
Divergent Thinking
Inquiry Training
Learning Processes
Linguistic Competence
Logic
Logical Thinking
Mediation Theory
Questioning Techniques
Risk
Sensory Deprivation
Thought Processes
Visualization

COGNITIVE TESTS 520
BT Tests
RT Abstraction Tests
Cognitive Measurement
Essay Tests
Intelligence Tests
Projective Tests
Science Tests

COLLECTIVE BARGAINING 150
BT Employer Employee Relationship
RT Arbitration
Collective Negotiation
Employment Problems
Grievance Procedures
Industrial Relations
Negotiation Impasses
Strikes
Teacher Militancy
Teacher Strikes
Unions
Wages

COLLECTIVE NEGOTIATION 150
UF Professional Negotiation
RT Arbitration
Collective Bargaining
Grievance Procedures
Industrial Relations
Negotiation Agreements
Negotiation Impasses
Sanctions
Strikes
Teacher Militancy
Teacher Strikes

COLLECTIVE SETTLEMENTS 370
SN Communities practicing common
ownership and cooperative living
UF Communistic Settlements
BT Community
RT Communism
Cooperatives
Municipalities
Neighborhood
Rural Areas
Settlement Houses

COLLEGE ADMINISTRATION 020
BT Educational Administration
RT Chief Administrators
College Deans
Colleges
Governance
Governing Boards
University Administration

COLLEGE ADMISSION 020
BT Admission (School)
RT College Bound Students
College Choice
College Entrance Examinations
College Freshmen
College Placement
Colleges
Post High School Guidance

COLLEGE ATTENDANCE 020
BT Attendance
RT College Bound Students
Colleges

COLLEGE BOUND STUDENTS 380
BT Secondary School Students
RT Academic Aspiration
College Admission
College Attendance
College Day
College High School Cooperation
College Preparation

COLLEGE BUILDINGS 210
BT Buildings
Educational Facilities
RT Building Design
Campuses
Colleges
Educational Equipment
School Design
Universities

COLLEGE CHOICE 140
RT Aspiration
College Admission
College Placement
College Preparation
Competitive Selection
Decision Making
Objectives
Personal Interests
Student Placement
Students

COLLEGE COOPERATION 020
NT College School Cooperation
BT Interinstitutional Cooperation
RT Colleges
Intercollegiate Programs

COLLEGE CREDITS 180
BT Credits
RT College Curriculum
Credit Courses
Grades (Scholastic)
Pass Fail Grading
Special Degree Programs
Student Evaluation
Transfer Policy

COLLEGE CURRICULUM 110
BT Curriculum
RT College Credits
College Language Programs
Colleges

COLLEGE DAY 090
SN Day set aside to aid secondary school
students to select a college
BT College High School Cooperation
RT College Bound Students
Colleges

COLLEGE DEANS 380
UF Academic Deans
Deans Of Men
Deans Of Students
Deans Of Women
BT Administrative Personnel
Student Personnel Workers
RT Administrative Organization
Administrator Role
College Administration
Student Personnel Services
University Administration

COLLEGE ENTRANCE EXAMINATIONS 520
UF   Entrance Examinations
BT   Tests
RT   College Admission
     Colleges

COLLEGE ENVIRONMENT 160
BT   Educational Environment
RT   Academic Freedom
     Classroom Environment
     Colleges
     Institutional Environment
     Residential Colleges
     School Environment

COLLEGE FACULTY 380
BT   Faculty
RT   Academic Freedom
     Colleges
     Counselor Educators
     Professors
     Teacher Educators
     Teaching Assistants

COLLEGE FRESHMEN 380
BT   Freshmen
RT   College Admission
     College Placement
     Colleges
     College Students

College Grades (Scholastic)
USE GRADES (SCHOLASTIC)

COLLEGE GRADUATES 380
BT   Graduates
RT   Colleges
     College Students
     Degrees (Titles)
     Graduate Students
     Graduate Study
     Graduate Surveys

COLLEGE HIGH SCHOOL COOPERATION 090
UF   High School College Cooperation
NT   College Day
BT   College School Cooperation
RT   College Bound Students
     College Preparation
     Colleges
     High Schools

COLLEGE HOUSING 210
UF   Student Housing
NT   Dormitories
BT   Housing
RT   Boarding Homes
     Boarding Schools
     Design Needs
     Housing Needs
     Residential Colleges
     Residential Schools
     Students

COLLEGE INSTRUCTION 270
BT   Instruction
RT   Colleges

COLLEGE INTEGRATION 430
UF   Integrated Colleges
RT   Colleges
     Racial Integration
     Social Integration

COLLEGE LANGUAGE PROGRAMS 290
BT   Language Programs
RT   Classical Languages
     College Curriculum
     Language Instruction
     Modern Languages

COLLEGE LIBRARIES 210
NT   Junior College Libraries
BT   Libraries
RT   Archives
     Colleges
     Medical Libraries
     University Libraries

COLLEGE MAJORS 140
UF   Departmental Majors
NT   Education Majors
     Liberal Arts Majors
RT   Degree Requirements
     Degrees (Titles)
     Departments
     Specialization
     Units Of Study (Subject Fields)

COLLEGE MATHEMATICS 340
BT   Mathematics
RT   Elementary School Mathematics
     Mathematics Curriculum
     Mathematics Education
     Mathematics Instruction
     Secondary School Mathematics

COLLEGE PLACEMENT 090
BT   Placement
RT   Advanced Placement Programs
     College Admission
     College Choice
     College Freshmen
     Colleges

COLLEGE PLANNING 020
BT   Planning
RT   Building Plans
     Campus Planning
     Colleges
     Construction Programs
     Educational Specifications
     Facility Case Studies
     Facility Guidelines
     Facility Inventory
     Facility Requirements
     Facility Utilization Research
     House Plan

Residential Colleges
Space Classification

COLLEGE PREPARATION 140
RT Academic Education
  College Bound Students
  College Choice
  College High School Cooperation
  Colleges
  Higher Education
  Post High School Guidance

COLLEGE PROGRAMS 410
NT Intercollegiate Programs
  Student Personnel Work
BT Programs
RT Alumni Education
  Colleges
  Doctoral Programs
  Student Personnel Workers

COLLEGE ROLE 470
SN Functions expected of or carried out by
  the college in society
BT Institutional Role
RT Colleges
  Educational Objectives
  Educational Responsibility
  Training Objectives

COLLEGES 470
UF Senior Colleges
NT Agricultural Colleges
  Church Related Colleges
  Community Colleges
  Evening Colleges
  Experimental Colleges
  Junior Colleges
  Negro Colleges
  Private Colleges
  Residential Colleges
  State Colleges
  Teachers Colleges
BT Institutions
RT College Administration
  College Admission
  College Attendance
  College Buildings
  College Cooperation
  College Curriculum
  College Day
  College Entrance Examinations
  College Environment
  College Faculty
  College Freshmen
  College Graduates
  College High School Cooperation
  College Instruction
  College Integration
  College Libraries
  College Placement
  College Planning
  College Preparation
  College Programs

College Role
College School Cooperation
College Segregation
College Students
College Teachers
Extension Education
higher Education
State Universities
Undergraduate Study
Universities
Urban Universities

COLLEGE SCHOOL COOPERATION 020
UF School College Cooperation
NT College High School Cooperation
BT College Cooperation
RT Affiliated Schools
  Colleges
  Schools

COLLEGE SCIENCE 110
BT Science Education
RT Elementary School Science
  Secondary School Science

COLLEGE SEGREGATION 430
BT Racial Segregation
RT Colleges

College Student Relationship
USE STUDENT COLLEGE RELATIONSHIP

COLLEGE STUDENTS 380
NT Junior College Students
  Liberal Arts Majors
  Middle Class College Students
  Terminal Students
BT Students
RT College Freshmen
  College Graduates
  Colleges
  Degree Requirements
  Education Majors
  Foreign Student Advisers
  Freshmen
  Graduate Students
  Seniors
  Single Students
  Student College Relationship

COLLEGE SUPERVISORS 380
SN Staff member of a college who observes
  student teachers
UF Student Teacher Supervisors
BT Supervisors
RT Clinical Professors
  College Teachers
  Cooperating Teachers
  Practicum Supervision
  Student Teachers
  Student Teaching
  Teacher Educator Education
  Teacher Educators

COMMERCIAL TELEVISION 050
BT   Television
RT   Broadcast Industry
     Broadcast Television
     Mass Media
     Television Commercials
     Viewing Time

COMMITTEES 370
NT   Advisory Committees
     Biracial Committees
     Farm Committees
     Research Committees
RT   Faculty Organizations
     Organizations (Groups)

COMMON FRACTIONS 340
UF   Simple Fractions
     Vulgar Fractions
BT   Fractions

COMMUNICABLE DISEASES 250
UF   Contagious Diseases
BT   Diseases
RT   Community Health
     Disease Control
     Infectious Diseases
     Rubella

COMMUNICATION (THOUGHT TRANSFER)
080
NT   Classroom Communication
     Intercommunication
     Interschool Communication
     Manual Communication
     Nonverbal Communication
     Semiotics
     Verbal Communication
RT   Audiences
     Business Correspondence
     Communication Problems
     Communication Skills
     Content Analysis
     Deaf Interpreting
     Diffusion
     Informal Organization
     Information Seeking
     Information Theory
     Interpreters
     Language Arts
     Letters (Correspondence)
     Paralinguistics
     Persuasive Discourse
     Receptive Language
     Visible Speech

Communication Networks
USE   TELECOMMUNICATION

COMMUNICATION PROBLEMS 080
BT   Problems
RT   Communication (Thought Transfer)
     Nonverbal Communication

COMMUNICATIONS 080
NT   Fixed Service Television
     Telecommunication
RT   Communication Satellites
     Industrial Arts
     Information Networks
     Input Output
     Mass Media
     Publicize
     Publishing Industry
     Radar
     Telephone Communications Industry
     Utilities

COMMUNICATION SATELLITES 080
RT   Communications
     Mass Media
     Networks
     Telecommunication
     Telephone Communications Industry

Communication Services
USE   TELECOMMUNICATION

COMMUNICATION SKILLS 010
BT   Skills
RT   Communication (Thought Transfer)
     Deaf Interpreting
     Finger Spelling
     Nonverbal Communication
     Receptive Language
     Teaching Skills
     Verbal Ability

Communications Media
USE   MASS MEDIA

Communication Systems
USE   TELECOMMUNICATION

Communication Theory
USE   INFORMATION THEORY

COMMUNISM 480
BT   Economics
RT   Collective Settlements
     Democracy
     Government (Administrative Body)
     Imperialism
     Political Science

Communistic Settlements
USE   COLLECTIVE SETTLEMENTS

COMMUNITY 230
UF   Community Factors
NT   Black Community
     Collective Settlements
     Municipalities
     Neighborhood
     Planned Community
     Southern Community
RT   City Demography
     City Improvement
     City Wide Programs
     Community Action

Community Agencies (Public)
Community Attitudes
Community Benefits
Community Characteristics
Community Colleges
Community Consultants
Community Cooperation
Community Coordination
Community Coordinators
Community Development
Community Education
Community Health
Community Influence
Community Involvement
Community Leaders
Community Migrant Projects
Community Organizations
Community Planning
Community Problems
Community Programs
Community Recreation Legislation
Community Recreation Programs
Community Relations
Community Resources
Community Responsibility
Community Role
Community Schools
Community Services
Community Study
Community Support
Local Issues
Metropolitan Areas
Police Community Relationship
School Community Cooperation
School Community Programs
School Community Relationship

COMMUNITY ACTION 160
UF Community Effort
BT Social Action
RT Action Programs (Community)
    Advisory Committees
    Citizen Participation
    Community
    Community Control
    Community Cooperation
    Community Involvement
    Community Role
    Community Services
    Community Support

COMMUNITY AGENCIES (PUBLIC) 230
UF Public Agencies
NT Local Housing Authorities
    Planning Commissions
BT Agencies
RT Agency Role
    Biracial Government
    City Government
    Community
    Community Benefits
    Corrective Institutions

Welfare Agencies
Youth Agencies

Community Analysis
USE COMMUNITY STUDY

COMMUNITY ANTENNAS 170
RT Cable Television
    Television

COMMUNITY ATTITUDES 040
BT Attitudes
RT Citizen Participation
    Citizenship
    Community
    Community Characteristics

COMMUNITY BENEFITS 360
RT Community
    Community Agencies (Public)
    Community Cooperation
    Community Development
    Community Organizations
    Community Programs

COMMUNITY CHANGE 160
RT City Improvement
    Social Action
    Social Change
    Urban Renewal

COMMUNITY CHARACTERISTICS 490
UF Community Traits
NT Community Size
RT Community
    Community Attitudes
    Community Cooperation
    Community Development
    Local Issues
    Urban Environment

Community College Libraries
USE JUNIOR COLLEGE LIBRARIES

COMMUNITY COLLEGES 470
BT Colleges
RT Associate Degrees
    Community
    Junior College Libraries
    Junior Colleges
    Junior College Students
    Post Secondary Education
    State Colleges
    Technical Institutes
    Undergraduate Study

Community Committees
USE COMMUNITY ORGANIZATIONS

Community Compliance
USE COMMUNITY COOPERATION

COMMUNITY CONSULTANT PROGRAMS
090
BT Community Programs
RT Community Consultants

COMMUNITY CONSULTANTS 380
BT Consultants
RT Community
    Community Consultant Programs

COMMUNITY CONTROL 020
RT Community Action
    Community Involvement
    Decentralization
    Governance
    School Community Relationship
    School District Autonomy

COMMUNITY COOPERATION 160
UF Community Compliance
RT Biracial Committees
    Community
    Community Action
    Community Benefits
    Community Characteristics
    Community Coordination
    Community Involvement
    Community Relations
    Community Role
    Community Services
    Community Support

COMMUNITY COORDINATION 160
BT Coordination
RT Community
    Community Cooperation
    Community Coordinators

COMMUNITY COORDINATORS 380
BT Coordinators
RT Administrative Personnel
    Community
    Community Coordination

COMMUNITY DEVELOPMENT 130
SN Educational processes and activities in a
    community which embody the principle
    of self help
BT Development
RT Community
    Community Benefits
    Community Characteristics
    Extension Education
    Rural Development
    Rural Extension
    Technical Assistance

COMMUNITY EDUCATION 140
BT Education
RT Community

Community Effort
USE COMMUNITY ACTION

Community Enterprises
USE COMMUNITY PROGRAMS

Community Experiences
USE FIELD EXPERIENCE PROGRAMS

Community Factors
USE COMMUNITY

COMMUNITY HEALTH 250
BT Public Health
RT Communicable Diseases
    Community
    Community Health Services
    Disease Control
    Preventive Medicine
    Sanitation

COMMUNITY HEALTH SERVICES 250
BT Health Services
RT Community Health
    Home Visits
    Immunization Programs

COMMUNITY INFLUENCE 160
UF Community Power
RT Black Community
    Community
    Social Factors

COMMUNITY INVOLVEMENT 160
UF Community Participation
RT Community
    Community Action
    Community Control
    Community Cooperation
    Community Role
    Community Services
    Community Support

COMMUNITY LEADERS 380
RT Adult Leaders
    Community
    Leadership

COMMUNITY MIGRANT PROJECTS 490
BT Migrant Worker Projects
RT Church Migrant Projects
    Community
    Migrant Adult Education
    Migrant Child Care Centers
    Migrant Child Education
    Migrant Housing
    Migrant Problems
    Migrant Welfare Services

COMMUNITY ORGANIZATIONS 370
UF Civic Groups
    Civic Organizations
    Community Committees
    Community Workers
NT Citizens Councils
BT Organizations (Groups)
RT Citizen Participation
    Community
    Community Benefits
    Community Programs
    Human Relations Organizations
    National Organizations
    Public Affairs Education
    Social Organizations

Community Participation
USE COMMUNITY INVOLVEMENT

COMMUNITY PLANNING 230
BT Planning
RT City Planning
  Community
  Community Programs
  Community Zoning

Community Police Relationship
USE POLICE COMMUNITY RELATIONSHIP

Community Power
USE COMMUNITY INFLUENCE

COMMUNITY PROBLEMS 230
UF Community Tensions
NT Local Issues
BT Problems
RT Community

COMMUNITY PROGRAMS 490
UF Civic Programs
  Community Enterprises
  Community Projects
NT Action Programs (Community)
  Community Consultant Programs
  Community Recreation Programs
  Community Service Programs
BT Programs
RT Civil Defense
  Community
  Community Benefits
  Community Organizations
  Community Planning
  Settlement Houses
  Social Responsibility
  Youth Programs

Community Projects
USE COMMUNITY PROGRAMS

COMMUNITY RECREATION LEGISLATION
230
BT Recreation Legislation
RT Community
  Community Recreation Programs

COMMUNITY RECREATION PROGRAMS
390
BT Community Programs
  Recreational Programs
RT Community
  Community Recreation Legislation

COMMUNITY RELATIONS 490
UF Civic Relations
BT Relationship
RT Community
  Community Cooperation

COMMUNITY RESOURCES 460
NT Public Libraries
  Zoos
BT Resources
RT Community
  Recreational Facilities

COMMUNITY RESPONSIBILITY 490
BT Social Responsibility
RT Citizenship Responsibility
  City Improvement
  Community
  Community Role
  Community Service Programs
  Community Services
  Neighborhood Improvement

COMMUNITY ROLE 490
RT Citizen Participation
  Community
  Community Action
  Community Cooperation
  Community Involvement
  Community Responsibility
  Community Services
  Community Support

COMMUNITY ROOMS 210
BT Recreational Facilities

COMMUNITY SCHOOL DIRECTORS 380
BT Administrative Personnel
RT Community Schools

Community School Programs
USE SCHOOL COMMUNITY PROGRAMS

Community School Relationship
USE SCHOOL COMMUNITY RELATIONSHIP

COMMUNITY SCHOOLS 470
BT Schools
RT Community
  Community School Directors
  Compensatory Education
  Public School Adult Education

COMMUNITY SERVICE PROGRAMS 490
BT Community Programs
  Community Services
RT Community Responsibility
  Recreational Programs
  Social Responsibility

COMMUNITY SERVICES 230
NT Community Service Programs
BT Services
RT Community
  Community Action
  Community Cooperation
  Community Involvement
  Community Responsibility
  Community Role
  Community Support
  Exceptional Child Services
  Neighborhood Centers

Public Health
Public Housing
Social Responsibility
Social Services

COMMUNITY SIZE 120
BT Community Characteristics
RT Census Figures
Demography
Geographic Distribution
Overpopulation
Population Distribution
Population Growth
Urban Population

COMMUNITY STUDY 490
UF Community Analysis
BT Research
RT Community

COMMUNITY SUPPORT 160
RT Citizen Participation
Community
Community Action
Community Cooperation
Community Involvement
Community Role
Community Services
Public Support

COMMUNITY SURVEYS 180
BT Surveys
RT Occupational Surveys
Research

Community Tensions
USE COMMUNITY PROBLEMS

Community Traits
USE COMMUNITY CHARACTERISTICS

Community Workers
USE COMMUNITY ORGANIZATIONS

COMMUNITY ZONING 120
BT Zoning
RT Community Planning

Commuter Schools
USE NONRESIDENTIAL SCHOOLS

COMMUTING STUDENTS 380
BT Students
RT Nonresidential Schools
Parking Controls
Student Transportation
Traffic Circulation

COMPANIONS (OCCUPATION) 380
UF Home Attendants
Home Health Aides
BT Service Workers
RT Handicapped
Health Occupations
Health Occupations Education
Health Personnel
Maids

Nurses
Nurses Aides
Occupational Home Economics
Older Adults
Patients (Persons)
Practical Nurses
Public Health
Residential Care
Service Occupations

Company Size (Industry)
USE ORGANIZATION SIZE (GROUPS)

COMPARATIVE ANALYSIS 510
UF Comparative Evaluation
Comparative Study
BT Educational Research
RT Comparative Statistics
Comparative Testing
Correlation
Cross Cultural Studies
Etymology
Evaluation Methods
Glottochronology
Group Norms
Language Classification
Lexicology
National Norms
Surveys
Synthesis

COMPARATIVE EDUCATION 140
SN Study of the comparison of current
educational theory in practice in different
countries
BT Education
RT International Education

Comparative Evaluation
USE COMPARATIVE ANALYSIS

COMPARATIVE STATISTICS 340
BT Statistical Data
RT Comparative Analysis
Correlation
Equated Scores

Comparative Study
USE COMPARATIVE ANALYSIS

COMPARATIVE TESTING 190
BT Testing
RT Abstraction Tests
Comparative Analysis
National Norms

Compatibility
USE RELATIONSHIP

Compensatory Development
USE COMPENSATORY EDUCATION

COMPENSATORY EDUCATION 140
UF   Compensatory Development
       Compensatory Opportunity
BT   Education
RT   After School Activities
       After School Centers
       After School Education
       After School Tutoring
       Community Schools
       Compensatory Education Programs
       Cultural Enrichment
       Educationally Disadvantaged
       Extended School Day
       Neighborhood Schools
       Remedial Programs
       Study Centers

COMPENSATORY EDUCATION PROGRAMS
140
UF   Educationally Deprived Programs
BT   Educational Programs
RT   After School Programs
       Compensatory Education
       Program Content

Compensatory Opportunity
USE   COMPENSATORY EDUCATION

Compensatory Tracking
USE   TRACKING

Competitive Bidding
USE   BIDS

COMPETITIVE SELECTION 020
BT   Selection
RT   Admission (School)
       College Choice
       Educational Supply
       Personnel Selection
       Students

COMPLEXITY LEVEL 310
UF   Intricacy
       Levels Of Complexity
       Levels Of Difficulty
RT   Ability
       Comprehension
       Performance
       Problems
       Skill Development
       Task Analysis

COMPONENT BUILDING SYSTEMS 030
SN   Interacting or interdependent structural
       or mechanical building elements
       designed and constructed in terms of
       flexibility and economics
UF   Component Systems
       System Components
RT   Architectural Research
       Architecture
       Construction Costs
       Construction Needs
       Facility Guidelines

Flexible Classrooms
Flexible Facilities
Master Plans
Modular Building Design
Planning
Prefabrication
Prestressed Concrete
School Construction
School Design
School Planning
Standards
Structural Building Systems

COMPONENTIAL ANALYSIS 290
RT   Anthropology
       Distinctive Features
       Lexicology
       Linguistic Patterns
       Linguistic Theory
       Phonological Units
       Phonology
       Scientific Methodology
       Semantics
       Structural Analysis

Component Systems
USE   COMPONENT BUILDING SYSTEMS

Composition (Language)
USE   COMPOSITION (LITERARY)

COMPOSITION (LITERARY) 080
UF   Composition (Language)
       Theme Writing
       Written Expression
NT   Paragraph Composition
BT   Writing
RT   Autobiographies
       Biographies
       Characterization (Literature)
       Comedy
       Composition Skills (Literary)
       Descriptive Writing
       Diaries
       Drama
       Epics
       Essays
       Expository Writing
       Fables
       French Literature
       Journalism
       Legends
       Letters (Correspondence)
       Literary Analysis
       Literary Conventions
       Medieval Romance
       Modernism
       Novels
       Parallelism (Literary)
       Plagiarism
       Poetry
       Rhetoric
       Satire
       Scripts

Short Stories
Spanish American Literature
Spanish Literature
Student Writing Models
Surrealism
Symbols (Literary)
Tragedy
Written Language

Composition (Music)
USE MUSICAL COMPOSITION

Composition Measurement
USE CHEMICAL ANALYSIS

COMPOSITION SKILLS (LITERARY) 010
BT Writing Skills
RT Capitalization (Alphabetic)
Composition (Literary)
Descriptive Writing
Expository Writing
Persuasive Discourse
Punctuation
Technical Writing

COMPREHENSION 010
NT Listening Comprehension
Reading Comprehension
BT Intelligence
RT Abstraction Levels
Cognitive Processes
Complexity Level
Comprehension Development
Interpretive Reading
Linguistic Competence
Perception
Scientific Literacy

COMPREHENSION DEVELOPMENT 130
BT Development
RT Comprehension

COMPREHENSIVE DISTRICTS 120
BT School Districts
RT Comprehensive Programs

Comprehensive Four Year High Schools
USE COMPREHENSIVE HIGH SCHOOLS

Comprehensive General Shops
USE SCHOOL SHOPS

COMPREHENSIVE HIGH SCHOOLS 470
UF Comprehensive Four Year High Schools
BT High Schools
RT Comprehensive Programs

COMPREHENSIVE PROGRAMS 410
BT Programs
RT Comprehensive Districts
Comprehensive High Schools

COMPUTATIONAL LINGUISTICS 290
BT Linguistics
RT Information Processing
Information Retrieval
Linguistic Theory
Machine Translation
Mathematical Linguistics
Mathematical Logic
Programing Languages
Semantics
Statistics
Word Frequency

Computer Aided Instruction
USE COMPUTER ASSISTED INSTRUCTION

COMPUTER ASSISTED INSTRUCTION 270
UF CAI
Computer Aided Instruction
Computer Based Instruction
BT Instruction
RT Autoinstructional Aids
Autoinstructional Methods
Branching
Computer Graphics
Computer Oriented Programs
Computers
Dial Access Information Systems
Educational Technology
Instructional Media
Man Machine Systems
Programed Instruction
Programed Materials
Programing
Teaching Machines
Time Sharing

Computer Based Instruction
USE COMPUTER ASSISTED INSTRUCTION

COMPUTER BASED LABORATORIES 210
BT Laboratories
RT Computers

COMPUTER GRAPHICS 510
SN Computer techniques for the display of graphic information on output devices.
RT Computer Assisted Instruction
Graphic Arts
Photocomposition

Computer Languages
USE PROGRAMING LANGUAGES

COMPUTER ORIENTED PROGRAMS 270
SN The application of computer technology to education for both instructional and business application
BT Computer Programs
RT Computer Assisted Instruction
Computers
Computer Science
Computer Science Education
Educational Technology
Electronic Data Processing

Programed Instruction
Time Sharing

COMPUTER OUTPUT MICROFILM 050
UF COM
BT Microforms
RT Computers
Information Storage
Input Output Devices

Computer Programing
USE PROGRAMING

COMPUTER PROGRAMS 080
NT Computer Oriented Programs
Sequential Programs
BT Programs
RT Computers
Numerical Control
Programers
Programing Languages

COMPUTERS 170
NT Analog Computers
Digital Computers
BT Electronic Equipment
RT Architectural Research
Automation
Computer Assisted Instruction
Computer Based Laboratories
Computer Oriented Programs
Computer Output Microfilm
Computer Programs
Computer Science
Computer Science Education
Cybernetics
Data Bases
Data Processing
Display Systems
Electromechanical Aids
Electronic Data Processing
Information Processing
Input Output Devices
Linear Programing
Office Machines
Optical Scanners
Programed Instruction
Technological Advancement
Telecommunication
Time Sharing

COMPUTER SCIENCE 080
UF Computer Technology
BT Sciences
RT Automation
Computer Oriented Programs
Computers
Computer Science Education
Cybernetics
Data Processing
Electronic Data Processing
Information Processing
Information Science
Information Theory
Input Output

Programing
Programing Languages

COMPUTER SCIENCE EDUCATION 140
BT Education
RT Computer Oriented Programs
Computers
Computer Science
Data Processing
Data Processing Occupations
Electronic Data Processing
Programing
Technical Education

COMPUTER STORAGE DEVICES 170
UF Machine Storage Devices
Memory Devices (Electronic)
BT Electronic Equipment
RT Analog Computers
Data Processing
Digital Computers
Electronic Data Processing
Information Storage
Input Output Devices
Magnetic Tapes

Computer Technology
USE COMPUTER SCIENCE

Concept Development
USE CONCEPT FORMATION

CONCEPT FORMATION 310
UF Concept Development
Conceptual Distinctions
Number Concept Development
BT Learning Processes
RT Concept Teaching
Conceptual Schemes
Conservation (Concept)
Creative Thinking
Creativity
Definitions
Fundamental Concepts
Generalization
Information Seeking
Intellectualization

Concept Of Conservation
USE CONSERVATION (CONCEPT)

CONCEPT TEACHING 510
BT Teaching
RT Concept Formation
Generalization

Conceptual Distinctions
USE CONCEPT FORMATION

Conceptual Frameworks
USE MODELS

CONCEPTUAL SCHEMES 310
BT Models
RT Concept Formation
Theories

CONCERTS 030
BT   Music
RT   Chautauquas
     Jazz
     Musicians
     Orchestras
     Singing

CONCORDANCES 320
RT   Indexes (Locaters)
     Structural Analysis

Concrete Industry
USE CEMENT INDUSTRY

Concurrent Validity
USE TEST VALIDITY

Conditioned Reflex
USE CONDITIONED RESPONSE

CONDITIONED RESPONSE 060
UF   Conditioned Reflex
     Psychological Conditioning
NT   Operant Conditioning
BT   Psychology
RT   Behavior
     Conditioned Stimulus
     Discrimination Learning
     Extinction (Psychology)
     Learning
     Stimulus Behavior
     Stimulus Generalization
     Verbal Operant Conditioning

CONDITIONED STIMULUS 060
RT   Associative Learning
     Behavior
     Conditioned Response
     Electrical Stimuli
     Extinction (Psychology)
     Stimuli
     Stimulus Behavior

CONDUCT 060
NT   Cheating
BT   Student Behavior
RT   Misbehavior
     Student Adjustment

CONFERENCE REPORTS 080
BT   Reports
RT   Annual Reports
     Conferences
     Institutes (Training Programs)
     Meetings
     Symposia

CONFERENCES 510
NT   Parent Conferences
     Parent Student Conferences
RT   Conference Reports
     Institutes (Training Programs)
     Meetings
     Speeches
     Symposia

CONFIDENTIAL RECORDS 020
BT   Records (Forms)
RT   Case Records
     Student Records

CONFLICT 420
NT   Culture Conflict
     Role Conflict
RT   Aggression
     Anti Social Behavior
     Behavior Problems
     Conflict Resolution

CONFLICT RESOLUTION 420
RT   Behavior Problems
     Conflict
     Decision Making
     Problem Solving

CONFORMITY 060
BT   Behavior
RT   Identification (Psychological)
     Peer Groups

Congenital Anomalies
USE ANOMALIES

Congenital Defects
USE ANOMALIES

Congressmen
USE LEGISLATORS

Congress Role
USE GOVERNMENT ROLE

CONGRUENCE 340
BT   Mathematical Concepts
RT   Geometry
     Integers
     Number Concepts

CONNECTED DISCOURSE 290
RT   Association (Psychological)
     Discourse Analysis
     Language Patterns
     Language Tests
     Paragraphs
     Prose
     Psycholinguistics
     Recall (Psychological)
     Semantics
     Syntax
     Word Frequency

CONSERVATION (CONCEPT) 310
SN   The concept that a factor such as
     quantity, weight, or volume remains
     constant despite other related changes
UF   Concept Of Conservation
     Conservation Of Number
     Conservation Of Quantity
     Conservation Of Substance
     Conservation Of Volume
     Conservation Of Weight
RT   Abstraction Levels

Cognitive Development
Cognitive Processes
Concept Formation
Learning Processes
Mathematical Concepts
Retention
Scientific Concepts

CONSERVATION EDUCATION 140
BT   Environmental Education
RT   Airborne Field Trips
     Biological Sciences
     Fire Science Education
     Forestry
     Geography
     Natural Resources
     Outdoor Education
     Physical Sciences
     Soil Conservation
     Trails

Conservation Of Number
USE   CONSERVATION (CONCEPT)

Conservation Of Quantity
USE   CONSERVATION (CONCEPT)

Conservation Of Substance
USE   CONSERVATION (CONCEPT)

Conservation Of Volume
USE   CONSERVATION (CONCEPT)

Conservation Of Weight
USE   CONSERVATION (CONCEPT)

CONSOLIDATED SCHOOLS 470
UF   Centralized Schools
     School Consolidation
BT   Schools
RT   Regional Schools
     School Administration
     School Districts
     School Redistricting
     School Systems
     School Zoning

CONSONANTS 290
BT   Phonemes
RT   Acoustic Phonetics
     Distinctive Features
     Phonemic Alphabets
     Phonetics
     Syllables
     Vowels

CONSORTIA 020
UF   Consortiums
RT   Administration
     Administrative Organization
     Cooperative Planning
     Cooperative Programs
     Coordination
     Dual Enrollment
     Educational Coordination
     Facility Expansion
     Facility Improvement

Interinstitutional Cooperation
Management
Organization
Resources
Shared Services

Consortiums
USE   CONSORTIA

Constituent Structure
USE   PHRASE STRUCTURE

CONSTITUTIONAL HISTORY 260
BT   History
RT   Civics
     Government (Administrative Body)
     Governmental Structure
     Government Role
     Political Science
     World History

CONSTRUCTED RESPONSE 060
BT   Response Mode
RT   Intermode Differences
     Programed Instruction

CONSTRUCTION (PROCESS) 210
SN   Act of putting parts together
NT   Road Construction
     School Construction
     Test Construction
RT   Acoustic Insulation
     Adhesives
     Air Structures
     Architectural Elements
     Building Design
     Building Materials
     Building Trades
     Ceilings
     Construction Industry
     Flooring
     Industrial Arts
     Masonry
     Prefabrication
     Roofing
     Sealers
     Structural Building Systems

Construction Bidding
USE   BIDS

CONSTRUCTION COSTS 220
BT   Costs
RT   Building Conversion
     Building Design
     Building Materials
     Buildings
     Component Building Systems
     Construction Industry
     Construction Needs
     Construction Programs
     Performance Specifications
     Prefabrication
     Road Construction
     Specifications
     Structural Building Systems

CONSTRUCTION INDUSTRY 370
BT   Industry
RT   Architects
      Buildings
      Building Trades
      Cement Industry
      Construction (Process)
      Construction Costs
      Housing Industry
      Prefabrication
      Road Construction
      School Construction

Construction Materials
USE BUILDING MATERIALS

CONSTRUCTION NEEDS 210
BT   Needs
RT   Architectural Elements
      Building Conversion
      Building Materials
      Component Building Systems
      Construction Costs
      Construction Programs
      Facility Guidelines
      Facility Requirements
      Prefabrication
      Road Construction
      School Construction

Construction Occupations
USE BUILDING TRADES

CONSTRUCTION PROGRAMS 210
UF   Building Programs
BT   Programs
RT   Campus Planning
      College Planning
      Construction Costs
      Construction Needs
      Educational Specifications
      Facility Expansion
      Facility Inventory
      Facility Utilization Research
      Master Plans
      Road Construction
      School Planning
      Site Development

CONSULTANTS 380
NT   Community Consultants
      Medical Consultants
      Reading Consultants
      Science Consultants
BT   Human Resources
RT   Clinic Personnel (School)
      Consultation Programs
      Counselor Functions
      Elementary School Counselors
      Faculty
      Professional Services
      Referral
      Resource Teachers
      School Psychologists

Specialists
Technical Assistance

CONSULTATION PROGRAMS 090
BT   Programs
RT   Child Development Specialists
      Consultants
      Elementary School Counseling
      Elementary School Guidance
      Intermediate Administrative Units
      Referral

Consumer Behavior
USE CONSUMER ECONOMICS

CONSUMER ECONOMICS 480
SN   Economic principles and forces that
      affect the consumer and the
      interpretation of economic theories in
      terms of consumer interest as
      distinguished from producer interest
UF   Consumer Behavior
      Consumer Expenditures
      Family Economics
BT   Economics
RT   Consumer Education
      Consumer Science
      Educational Demand
      Educational Economics
      Educational Supply
      Home Economics
      Home Management
      Merchandise Information
      Purchasing

CONSUMER EDUCATION 110
SN   Study of intelligent and effective
      methods of buying and using goods and
      services, competent money
      management, and relationship of
      consumer to the economic system
NT   Consumer Science
BT   Education
RT   Consumer Economics
      Consumer Science
      Family Life Education
      Health Education
      Home Economics
      Home Economics Education
      Homemaking Education
      Home Management
      Money Management
      Purchasing
      Vocational Education

Consumer Expenditures
USE CONSUMER ECONOMICS

CONSUMER SCIENCE 110
SN   Instruction in those phases of science
      needed by or useful to the consumer
      including operation and repair of simple
      household equipment, effects of cleaning
      and other products, and preservation
      and care of food and clothing

UF   Household Science
BT   Consumer Education
      Sciences
RT   Clothing Instruction
      Consumer Economics
      Consumer Education
      Foods Instruction
      Home Economics
      Home Economics Education
      Maintenance
      Repair

Contagious Diseases
USE COMMUNICABLE DISEASES

CONTENT ANALYSIS 190
BT   Evaluation Methods
RT   Communication (Thought Transfer)
      Course Content
      Critical Reading
      Data Analysis
      Item Analysis
      Literary Analysis
      Literary Criticism
      Literature Reviews
      Textbook Content

CONTENT READING 440
BT   Reading
RT   Interpretive Reading
      Reading Comprehension
      Reading Instruction

CONTEXT CLUES 310
RT   Reading
      Reading Comprehension
      Structural Analysis
      Vocabulary Skills
      Word Recognition

CONTEXT FREE GRAMMAR 290
BT   Transformation Theory (Language)
RT   Grammar
      Machine Translation
      Phrase Structure
      Transformation Generative Grammar
      Transformations (Language)

CONTINUATION EDUCATION 140
SN   A special program to meet the needs of
      potential learners who have rejected
      conventional schooling
UF   Continuation Programs
BT   Education
RT   Continuation High Schools
      Continuation Students
      Delinquent Rehabilitation
      Dropout Prevention
      Dropout Programs
      Dropout Rehabilitation
      Rehabilitation Programs
      Remedial Programs
      Terminal Education
      Vocational Education

CONTINUATION HIGH SCHOOLS 470
SN   School with specialized curriculum and
      services to meet the needs of students
      who have rejected conventional schooling
BT   High Schools
RT   Continuation Education
      Continuation Students
      Vocational High Schools

Continuation Programs
USE CONTINUATION EDUCATION

CONTINUATION STUDENTS 380
SN   Students who have rejected conventional
      schooling who are provided with special
      continuation educational programs
BT   Students
RT   Continuation Education
      Continuation High Schools
      Delinquent Rehabilitation
      Dropout Prevention
      Dropouts
      Low Achievers
      Part Time Students
      Student Adjustment
      Student Rehabilitation
      Truancy
      Underachievers

Continuing Education
USE ADULT EDUCATION

CONTINUING EDUCATION CENTERS 210
BT   Educational Facilities
RT   Residential Centers
      University Extension

CONTINUOUS GUIDANCE 090
SN   The continuous counseling of students
      by the same counselor from grades 7
      through 12
BT   Guidance

CONTINUOUS LEARNING 310
UF   Education Permanente
      Lifelong Education
      Permanent Education
BT   Learning
RT   Adult Learning
      Discovery Processes
      Education
      Experience
      Information Seeking
      Learning Experience
      Learning Processes

CONTINUOUS PROGRESS PLAN 270
SN   Organized curriculum using a sequence
      of courses to provide individual study
      and progress
RT   Behavioral Objectives
      Flexible Progression
      Flexible Schedules
      Individual Study

Nongraded System
Quarter System

CONTRACEPTION 250
UF Birth Control
RT Family Planning
Illegitimate Births
Pregnancy
Sex Education

Contractor Vehicles
USE SERVICE VEHICLES

CONTRACTS 220
RT Bids
Contract Salaries
Fire Insurance
Negotiation Agreements
Performance Specifications
Probationary Period
Specifications
Teaching Load
Tenure

CONTRACT SALARIES 220
BT Salaries
RT Contracts
Salary Differentials
Tenure

CONTRAST 030
SN The perceived diversity of adjacent
elements in the visual field.
UF Contrast Ratios
RT Color
Illumination Levels
Light
Lighting
Lighting Design
Visual Discrimination

Contrastive Language Analysis
USE CONTRASTIVE LINGUISTICS

CONTRASTIVE LINGUISTICS 290
UF Contrastive Language Analysis
BT Synchronic Linguistics
RT Bilingualism
Cross Cultural Studies
Diachronic Linguistics
Interference (Language Learning)
Language Instruction
Lexicology
Machine Translation
Mutual Intelligibility
Phonemics
Second Language Learning

Contrast Ratios
USE CONTRAST

CONTROL GROUPS 450
RT Experimental Groups
Research Methodology

CONTROLLED ENVIRONMENT 160
SN Temperature, humidity, and light
BT Environment
RT Acoustical Environment
Acoustic Insulation
Air Conditioning
Air Conditioning Equipment
Air Pollution Control
Climate Control
Exhausting
Greenhouses
Heating
Humidity
Psychological Design Needs
Solar Radiation
Thermal Environment
Ventilation

Convalescent Homes
USE NURSING HOMES

CONVENTIONAL INSTRUCTION 270
BT Instruction
RT Traditional Schools

CONVERGENT THINKING 310
NT Evaluative Thinking
BT Critical Thinking
RT Cognitive Processes
Deductive Methods
Logical Thinking
Problem Solving

CONVERSATIONAL LANGUAGE COURSES
110
BT Courses
RT Articulation (Speech)
Audiolingual Skills
Language Fluency
Language Instruction
Oral Communication
Standard Spoken Usage

Conversational Spanish
USE SPANISH

Convicts
USE CRIMINALS

COOKING INSTRUCTION 270
BT Instruction
RT Cooks
Foods Instruction
Home Economics Education
Nutrition Instruction

COOKS 380
UF Chefs
Chief Cooks
Family Dinner Service Specialists
BT Service Workers
RT Cooking Instruction
Dietitians
Food
Food Service
Food Service Industry

Food Service Occupations
Food Service Workers
Foods Instruction
Nutrition Instruction
Occupational Home Economics
Trade And Industrial Education

Cooperating Schools
USE AFFILIATED SCHOOLS

COOPERATING TEACHERS 380
BT Teachers
RT Affiliated Schools
Clinical Professors
College Supervisors
Episode Teaching
Mathematics Teachers
Practicum Supervision
Preservice Education
Student Teachers
Student Teaching
Teacher Education
Teacher Educator Education

Cooperative Activities
USE GROUP ACTIVITIES

COOPERATIVE EDUCATION 140
SN Work and school experiences under the
direction of a vocational teacher
coordinator designed to complement
each other toward an occupational goal
UF Cooperative Training
Vocational Work Experience
BT Education
RT Affiliated Schools
Cooperative Programs
Coordinators
Distributive Education
Project Training Methods
Vocational Education
Work Experience Programs
Work Study Programs

COOPERATIVE PLANNING 020
BT Planning
RT Consortia
School Industry Relationship
Shared Services
Team Administration
Teamwork

COOPERATIVE PROGRAMS 410
UF Co Op Programs
BT Programs
RT Consortia
Cooperative Education
Dual Enrollment
Interdisciplinary Approach
Library Cooperation
Off The Job Training
School Industry Relationship
Shared Services
Work Study Programs

COOPERATIVES 370
SN Economic enterprise wholly owned by its
users
BT Organizations (Groups)
RT Collective Settlements

COOPERATIVE TEACHING 510
BT Teaching Methods
RT Departmental Teaching Plans

Cooperative Training
USE COOPERATIVE EDUCATION

Co Op Programs
USE COOPERATIVE PROGRAMS

Coordinated Audiovisual Programs
USE AUDIOVISUAL PROGRAMS

Coordinate Geometry
USE ANALYTIC GEOMETRY

COORDINATE INDEXES 320
UF Post Coordinate Indexes
Uniterm Indexes
BT Indexes (Locaters)
RT Correlation
Documentation
Indexing
Information Retrieval
Permuted Indexes
Subject Index Terms
Thesauri

Coordinate Indexing
USE INDEXING

COORDINATION 020
NT Community Coordination
Educational Coordination
Interagency Coordination
Perceptual Motor Coordination
Program Coordination
RT Administration
Consortia
Coordinators
Management
Managerial Occupations
Organization
Research Coordinating Units

COORDINATION COMPOUNDS 400
RT Chemistry
Organic Chemistry

COORDINATORS 380
NT Community Coordinators
Instructor Coordinators
RT Administration
Cooperative Education
Coordination
Educational Programs
Industry
Organization

Coordinator Trainers
USE INSTRUCTOR COORDINATORS

Copilots
USE AIRCRAFT PILOTS

Coping Behavior
USE ADJUSTMENT (TO ENVIRONMENT)

COPYRIGHTS 230
RT Laws
Plagiarism
Printing
Publishing Industry
Standards
Textbook Publications

CORE COURSES 110
UF Required Courses
BT Courses
RT Degree Requirements

CORE CURRICULUM 110
UF Hard Core Curriculum
Teaching Core
BT Curriculum
RT Interdisciplinary Approach

CORN (FIELD CROP) 070
BT Field Crops
Grains (Food)
RT Crop Processing Occupations
Food
Plant Science

CORRECTIONAL EDUCATION 140
UF Prison Education
BT Education
RT Adult Education
Correctional Rehabilitation
Corrective Institutions
Criminals
Criminology
Delinquent Rehabilitation
Human Services
Institutionalized (Persons)
Prisoners
Recreational Activities
Rehabilitation
Rehabilitation Counseling
Rehabilitation Programs
Vocational Rehabilitation

CORRECTIONAL REHABILITATION 090
UF Correctional Systems
Corrections (Rehabilitation)
NT Delinquent Rehabilitation
BT Rehabilitation
RT Correctional Education
Corrective Institutions
Crime
Criminals
Criminology
Human Services
Institutionalized (Persons)
Prisoners
Probationary Period
Rehabilitation Programs

Correctional Systems
USE CORRECTIONAL REHABILITATION

Corrections (Rehabilitation)
USE CORRECTIONAL REHABILITATION

CORRECTIVE INSTITUTIONS 210
BT Institutions
RT Community Agencies (Public)
Correctional Education
Correctional Rehabilitation
Crime
Criminals
Criminology
Delinquent Rehabilitation
Institutionalized (Persons)
Institution Libraries
Prisoners
Rehabilitation

CORRECTIVE READING 440
SN Reading instruction for retarded readers
within a regular class. For handicapped
readers see remedial reading
BT Remedial Reading

CORRELATION 340
UF Correlation Studies
Statistical Association Methods
NT Bibliographic Coupling
BT Statistical Analysis
RT Cluster Grouping
Comparative Analysis
Comparative Statistics
Coordinate Indexes
Evaluation Methods
Measurement Techniques
Validity

Correlation Studies
USE CORRELATION

Correspondence (Letters)
USE LETTERS (CORRESPONDENCE)

CORRESPONDENCE COURSES 110
BT Courses
RT Correspondence Schools
Correspondence Study
Extension Education
Home Study
Refresher Courses

CORRESPONDENCE SCHOOLS 470
UF Commercial Correspondence Schools
BT Schools
RT Correspondence Courses
Correspondence Study
Extension Education
Home Study
Independent Study
Private Schools
Proprietary Schools

CORRESPONDENCE STUDY 270
SN Method of instruction with teacher
     student interaction by mail
BT Study
RT Correspondence Courses
     Correspondence Schools
     Home Study
     Independent Study
     Part Time Students

CORRIDORS 210
UF Hallways
BT Facilities
RT Building Design
     Classroom Arrangement
     Classrooms
     School Space
     Space Utilization
     Windowless Rooms

COSMETIC PROSTHESES 250
BT Prostheses
RT Amputees
     Physically Handicapped
     Sensory Aids

Cosmetics Inspectors
USE FOOD AND DRUG INSPECTORS

COSMETOLOGISTS 380
UF Beauticians
     Beauty Operators
BT Service Workers
RT Service Occupations
     Trade And Industrial Education
     Vocational Education

COSMETOLOGY 350
UF Beauty Culture
RT Hygiene

Cost Analysis
USE COST EFFECTIVENESS

Cost Benefit Analysis
USE COST EFFECTIVENESS

COST EFFECTIVENESS 190
UF Benefit Cost Analysis
     Cost Analysis
     Cost Benefit Analysis
     Cost Effectiveness Analysis
     Cost Utility Analysis
BT Evaluation Methods
RT Costs
     Critical Path Method
     Expenditures
     Operations Research
     Program Budgeting
     Program Costs
     Program Effectiveness
     Program Evaluation
     Program Planning
     Resource Allocations
     Systems Analysis

Cost Effectiveness Analysis
USE COST EFFECTIVENESS

COSTS 220
NT Capital Outlay (For Fixed Assets)
     Construction Costs
     Estimated Costs
     Legal Costs
     Police Costs
     Program Costs
     Student Costs
     Unit Costs
BT Expenditures
RT Cost Effectiveness
     Educational Finance
     Expenditure Per Student
     Fees
     Private Financial Support

Costume Design
USE CLOTHING DESIGN

Cost Utility Analysis
USE COST EFFECTIVENESS

COUNSELING 090
UF Counseling Process
     Counseling Techniques
NT Adult Counseling
     Behavioral Counseling
     Cocounseling
     Educational Counseling
     Elementary School Counseling
     Family Counseling
     Group Counseling
     Guidance Counseling
     Individual Counseling
     Marriage Counseling
     Microcounseling
     Nondirective Counseling
     Parent Counseling
     Rehabilitation Counseling
     Vocational Counseling
RT Behavior Change
     Case Studies
     Case Studies (Education)
     Counseling Centers
     Counseling Effectiveness
     Counseling Goals
     Counseling Instructional Programs
     Counseling Programs
     Counseling Services
     Counseling Theories
     Counselor Acceptance
     Counselors
     Crisis Therapy
     Educational Therapy
     Guidance
     Juvenile Courts
     Manpower Utilization
     Milieu Therapy
     Ombudsmen
     Pupil Personnel Services
     Pupil Personnel Workers

Rational Therapy
Social Workers

COUNSELING CENTERS 210
RT Counseling
    Counseling Services
    Guidance Facilities
    Student Personnel Work

COUNSELING EFFECTIVENESS 180
RT Counseling
    Counseling Goals
    Counselor Functions
    Counselor Performance
    Counselor Role
    Evaluation

COUNSELING GOALS 090
RT Counseling
    Counseling Effectiveness
    Counseling Instructional Programs
    Counselor Evaluation
    Guidance Objectives

COUNSELING INSTRUCTIONAL PROGRAMS
410
SN Program for counselor and teacher interaction to determine classroom activities
BT Programs
RT Counseling
    Counseling Goals
    Counseling Programs
    Instructional Programs

Counseling Process
USE COUNSELING

COUNSELING PROGRAMS 090
NT Evening Counseling Programs
BT Programs
RT Adult Counseling
    Counseling
    Counseling Instructional Programs
    Elementary School Counselors
    Elementary School Guidance
    Student Personnel Programs

COUNSELING SERVICES 090
BT Human Services
RT Adult Counseling
    Counseling
    Counseling Centers
    Counselor Characteristics
    Counselor Functions
    Elementary School Counselors
    Parent Counseling
    Psychiatric Services
    Student Personnel Services
    Student Personnel Work
    Student Personnel Workers

Counseling Techniques
USE COUNSELING

COUNSELING THEORIES 090
BT Theories
RT Behavior
    Behavioral Counseling
    Behavior Theories
    Counseling
    Nondirective Counseling

COUNSELOR ACCEPTANCE 420
SN The counselors attitude toward the client as expressed in the counseling relationship
BT Counselor Attitudes
RT Attitudes
    Counseling
    Counselors
    Therapeutic Environment

COUNSELOR ATTITUDES 040
UF Counselor Opinion
    Counselor Reaction
NT Counselor Acceptance
BT Attitudes
RT Counselor Characteristics
    Counselor Performance
    Counselors

COUNSELOR CERTIFICATION 500
BT Certification
RT Accreditation (Institutions)
    Counselor Evaluation
    Standards

COUNSELOR CHARACTERISTICS 090
RT Counseling Services
    Counselor Attitudes
    Counselor Performance
    Counselor Role
    Counselors
    Counselor Selection
    Individual Characteristics

COUNSELOR CLIENT RATIO 420
RT Counselors
    Student Distribution

COUNSELOR EDUCATORS 380
SN Members of a college or university faculty who are primarily concerned with the preparation of counselors
BT College Teachers
RT College Faculty
    Counselor Evaluation
    Counselor Training
    Professional Education
    Professors
    Teachers

COUNSELOR EVALUATION 180
SN Process of judging counselor performance as related to established criteria
BT Evaluation
RT Counseling Goals
    Counselor Certification

114

Counselor Educators
Counselor Performance
Counselors
Counselor Selection
Evaluation Methods
Evaluation Techniques
Measurement Techniques
Personnel Evaluation

COUNSELOR FUNCTIONS 090
BT   Counselor Role
RT   Consultants
     Counseling Effectiveness
     Counseling Services
     Counselor Performance
     Counselors
     Guidance Functions
     Role Theory

Counselor Opinion
USE COUNSELOR ATTITUDES

COUNSELOR PERFORMANCE 090
BT   Performance
RT   Counseling Effectiveness
     Counselor Attitudes
     Counselor Characteristics
     Counselor Evaluation
     Counselor Functions
     Counselor Qualifications
     Counselor Role
     Counselors
     Performance Factors

Counselor Preparation
USE COUNSELOR TRAINING

COUNSELOR QUALIFICATIONS 500
BT   Qualifications
RT   Counselor Performance
     Counselors
     Standards

Counselor Reaction
USE COUNSELOR ATTITUDES

COUNSELOR ROLE 490
NT   Counselor Functions
RT   Counseling Effectiveness
     Counselor Characteristics
     Counselor Performance
     Counselors
     Role Theory

COUNSELORS 380
UF   Guidance Counselors
     Guidance Workers
NT   Adjustment Counselors
     Camp Counselors
     Elementary School Counselors
     Employment Counselors
     Secondary School Counselors
     Special Counselors
BT   Guidance Personnel
RT   Adult Counseling
     Counseling

Counselor Acceptance
Counselor Attitudes
Counselor Characteristics
Counselor Client Ratio
Counselor Evaluation
Counselor Functions
Counselor Performance
Counselor Qualifications
Counselor Role
Counselor Selection
Counselor Training
Faculty Advisors
Guidance
Guidance Counseling
Student Personnel Workers

COUNSELOR SELECTION 150
BT   Personnel Selection
RT   Counselor Characteristics
     Counselor Evaluation
     Counselors
     Counselor Training
     Guidance Personnel

COUNSELOR TRAINING 270
UF   Counselor Preparation
BT   Training
RT   Counselor Educators
     Counselors
     Counselor Selection
     Microcounseling
     Practicums

COUNTY LIBRARIES 210
BT   Public Libraries
RT   Branch Libraries
     Library Cooperation
     Library Networks
     Regional Libraries

COUNTY OFFICIALS 380
BT   Public Officials
RT   City Officials
     Government Employees
     Legislators
     State Officials

COUNTY SCHOOL SYSTEMS 230
BT   School Systems
RT   Boards Of Education
     Public School Systems
     Rural School Systems
     School Districts

COURSE CONTENT 110
BT   Course Organization
RT   Content Analysis
     Course Descriptions
     Course Objectives
     Curriculum Development
     Curriculum Guides
     Program Content

COURSE DESCRIPTIONS 110
RT   Course Content
     Course Objectives
     Course Organization
     Courses
     Curriculum Guides

Course Enrichment
USE CURRICULUM ENRICHMENT

COURSE EVALUATION 180
BT   Evaluation
RT   Course Objectives
     Curriculum Evaluation
     Evaluation Methods
     Faculty Evaluation
     Program Evaluation
     Student Evaluation
     Teacher Evaluation
     Textbook Evaluation

COURSE OBJECTIVES 110
BT   Educational Objectives
RT   Behavioral Objectives
     Course Content
     Course Descriptions
     Course Evaluation
     Courses

COURSE ORGANIZATION 280
NT   Course Content
BT   Organization
RT   Course Descriptions
     Courses
     Flexible Schedules
     Flexible Scheduling
     Units Of Study (Subject Fields)

Course Outlines
USE CURRICULUM GUIDES

COURSES 110
NT   Accelerated Courses
     Conversational Language Courses
     Core Courses
     Correspondence Courses
     Credit Courses
     Education Courses
     Inservice Courses
     Institute Type Courses
     Intensive Language Courses
     Methods Courses
     Noncredit Courses
     Refresher Courses
     Remedial Courses
     Science Courses
     Short Courses
     Units Of Study (Subject Fields)
BT   Curriculum
RT   Course Descriptions
     Course Objectives
     Course Organization
     Credits
     Grade Charts
     Intellectual Disciplines

Journalism
Science Institutes
Summer Institutes

Court Action
USE COURT LITIGATION

COURT CASES 230
RT   Courts

Court Decisions
USE COURT LITIGATION

COURT DOCTRINE 230
RT   Courts

COURT LITIGATION 230
UF   Court Action
     Court Decisions
     Judicial Action
     Legal Decisions
     Litigation
NT   Federal Court Litigation
     Supreme Court Litigation
RT   Juvenile Courts
     Lawyers
     Legal Problems

COURT REPORTERS 380
BT   Clerical Workers
RT   Business Education
     Clerical Occupations
     Stenographers
     Typists

COURT ROLE 230
RT   Courts

COURTS 230
NT   Federal Courts
     Juvenile Courts
     Supreme Courts
BT   Institutions
RT   Court Cases
     Court Doctrine
     Court Role
     Equal Protection

COVERT RESPONSE 060
BT   Behavior

Crafts
USE HANDICRAFTS

CRAFTS ROOMS 210
BT   Educational Facilities
RT   Handicrafts
     School Shops

CREATIVE ABILITY 010
BT   Ability
RT   Creative Activities
     Creative Development
     Creativity
     Creativity Research
     Imagination
     Originality

CREATIVE ACTIVITIES 510
NT Creative Art
    Creative Dramatics
    Creative Expression
    Creative Reading
    Creative Teaching
    Creative Thinking
    Creative Writing
BT Activities
    Creativity
RT Creative Ability
    Playwriting
    Surrealism

CREATIVE ART 030
BT Art
    Creative Activities
RT Freehand Drawing
    Surrealism

CREATIVE DEVELOPMENT 130
BT Development
RT Creative Ability
    Creativity
    Surrealism
    Talent Development

CREATIVE DRAMATICS 030
BT Creative Activities
    Dramatics

CREATIVE EXPRESSION 080
BT Creative Activities
RT Creativity
    Surrealism

CREATIVE READING 510
BT Creative Activities
    Reading

CREATIVE TEACHING 510
BT Creative Activities
    Teaching

CREATIVE THINKING 310
NT Divergent Thinking
BT Creative Activities
    Thought Processes
RT Concept Formation
    Nucleation (Language Learning)
    Productive Thinking
    Surrealism

CREATIVE WRITING 080
BT Creative Activities
    Writing
RT Descriptive Writing
    Expository Writing
    Figurative Language
    Haiku
    Literary Conventions
    Metaphors
    Playwriting
    Scripts
    Student Writing Models

CREATIVITY 310
UF Individual Creativity
    Student Creativity
NT Creative Activities
    Originality
RT Concept Formation
    Creative Ability
    Creative Development
    Creative Expression
    Creativity Research
    Imagination
    Individualism
    Self Expression
    Surrealism

CREATIVITY RESEARCH 450
BT Research
RT Creative Ability
    Creativity

CREDENTIALS 500
BT Qualifications
RT Administrator Background
    Administrator Evaluation
    Administrator Qualifications
    Certification
    Degrees (Titles)
    Educational Certificates
    Special Degree Programs
    Standards
    Student Certification
    Student Evaluation
    Student Records
    Teacher Certification
    Teacher Evaluation
    Teacher Experience
    Teacher Qualifications
    Teaching Experience

CREDIT (FINANCE) 220
RT Economics
    Financial Needs
    Financial Services
    Investment
    Merchandising
    Money Management

Credit By Examination
USE EQUIVALENCY TESTS

CREDIT COURSES 110
BT Courses
RT College Credits
    Credits
    Grades (Scholastic)
    Noncredit Courses

CREDITS 180
UF Student Credit Hours
NT College Credits
RT Academic Records
    Courses
    Credit Courses
    Grades (Scholastic)
    Transfers

CREE 300
BT   American Indian Languages

CREOLES 300
SN   A language developing from a pidgin and
     having native speakers
NT   Gullah
     Haitian Creole
     Sierra Leone Creole
BT   Languages

Crew Boss
USE   CREW LEADERS

CREW LEADERS 380
UF   Crew Boss
     Farm Foremen
     Leadmen
     Row Boss
     Straw Boss
RT   Agricultural Laborers
     Migrant Workers
     Supervisors

CRIME 060
BT   Socially Deviant Behavior
RT   Aggression
     Correctional Rehabilitation
     Corrective Institutions
     Criminals
     Criminology
     Delinquency
     Drug Addiction
     Juvenile Courts
     Parole Officers
     Police
     Probation Officers
     Vandalism
     Violence

CRIMINALS 380
UF   Convicts
RT   Correctional Education
     Correctional Rehabilitation
     Corrective Institutions
     Crime
     Delinquents
     Prisoners

CRIMINOLOGY 490
RT   Correctional Education
     Correctional Rehabilitation
     Corrective Institutions
     Crime
     Delinquents
     Prisoners

CRIPPLED CHILDREN 240
BT   Children
     Physically Handicapped

CRISIS THERAPY 420
BT   Therapy
RT   Counseling
     Family Counseling
     Marriage Counseling
     Psychiatric Services
     Rehabilitation

CRITERIA 500
NT   Environmental Criteria
     Evaluation Criteria
     Performance Criteria
     Research Criteria
RT   Educational Specifications
     Performance Specifications
     Specifications
     Standards

CRITICAL INCIDENTS METHOD 180
SN   Method for determining needed abilities
     for a particular task in order to establish
     standards or make inferences
UF   Critical Incidents Technique
BT   Methods
RT   Ability Identification
     Job Analysis
     Measurement Techniques
     Observation
     Problem Solving
     Research Methodology
     Simulation
     Skill Analysis
     Task Analysis

Critical Incidents Technique
USE   CRITICAL INCIDENTS METHOD

CRITICAL PATH METHOD 020
UF   Path Analysis
     Pert
BT   Methods
RT   Cost Effectiveness
     Management Systems
     Networks
     Operations Research
     Planning
     Program Evaluation
     Scheduling
     Sequential Approach
     Systems Analysis

CRITICAL READING 440
BT   Reading Skills
RT   Content Analysis
     Interpretive Reading
     Literary Analysis
     Literary Criticism
     Literary Discrimination

CRITICAL THINKING 310
NT   Convergent Thinking
BT   Thought Processes
RT   Evaluative Thinking
     Logic
     Productive Thinking

Crop Harvesting
USE HARVESTING

Crop Planting
USE PLANTING

CROP PROCESSING OCCUPATIONS 350
UF Grain Elevator Occupations
BT Off Farm Agricultural Occupations
RT Agriculture
     Corn (Field Crop)
     Field Crops
     Vocational Agriculture

Crop Production
USE AGRICULTURAL PRODUCTION

Cross Age Helping
USE CROSS AGE TEACHING

CROSS AGE TEACHING 270
SN Utilization of older students from higher
     grade levels to provide increased help
     and attention for younger students at
     lower grade levels
UF Cross Age Helping
BT Teaching Techniques
RT Interpersonal Relationship
     Peer Teaching
     Remedial Instruction
     Social Experience
     Socialization
     Student Projects
     Tutoring

CROSS CULTURAL STUDIES 100
UF Cultural Comparisons
BT Culture
RT Anthropology
     Area Studies
     Comparative Analysis
     Contrastive Linguistics
     Cross Cultural Training
     Cultural Differences
     Cultural Education
     Cultural Interrelationships
     Culture Conflict
     Culture Contact
     Culture Free Tests
     Ethnology
     Foreign Culture
     Intercultural Programs
     Sociocultural Patterns
     Sociology

CROSS CULTURAL TRAINING 270
BT Training
RT Cross Cultural Studies
     Culture Contact
     Intercultural Programs
     International Education

Cross Culture Tests
USE CULTURE FREE TESTS

Cross Eyes
USE HETEROTROPIA

CROSS SECTIONAL STUDIES 450
BT Case Studies
RT Longitudinal Studies

Cue Cards
USE CUES

CUED SPEECH 290
SN Method of language learning for the deaf
     utilizing manual configurations as a
     supplement to lipreading
BT Speech
RT Aurally Handicapped
     Deaf Education
     Deaf Interpreting
     Finger Spelling
     Lipreading
     Manual Communication

Cueing
USE PROMPTING

CUES 310
UF Clues
     Cue Cards
     Prompts
RT Memory
     Prompting
     Recall (Psychological)
     Retention
     Stimulus Devices

CULTURAL ACTIVITIES 100
BT Activities
RT Cultural Interrelationships
     Culture

CULTURAL AWARENESS 040
UF Cultural Understanding
RT Biculturalism
     Cultural Background
     Cultural Factors
     Cultural Opportunities
     Cultural Pluralism
     Culture
     Culture Conflict
     Culture Contact
     Nationalism
     Second Language Learning

CULTURAL BACKGROUND 100
SN The cumulative intellectual, artistic, and
     social heritage and experience of an
     individual or group, including institutions,
     folkways, literature, mores, and
     communal experiences
UF Cultural Heritage
NT Economic Status
     Educational Background
     Social Background
BT Background
RT Administrator Background
     African American Studies

Anglo Americans
Biculturalism
Cultural Awareness
Cultural Pluralism
Cultural Traits
Culture
Ethnic Groups
Ethnology
Non Western Civilization
Western Civilization

CULTURAL CENTERS 210
RT   Cultural Enrichment
Culture
Educational Complexes

Cultural Comparisons
USE CROSS CULTURAL STUDIES

CULTURAL CONTEXT 100
BT   Culture
RT   Cultural Environment
Cultural Factors
Cultural Traits
Proverbs
Social Characteristics
Social Structure
Social Values

Cultural Deprivation
USE CULTURAL DISADVANTAGEMENT

CULTURAL DIFFERENCES 100
UF   Cultural Diversity
RT   Biculturalism
Cross Cultural Studies
Cultural Interrelationships
Cultural Pluralism
Culture
Racial Characteristics

CULTURAL DISADVANTAGEMENT 100
UF   Cultural Deprivation
Deprivation
Disadvantagement
Limited Background
NT   Economic Disadvantagement
Educational Disadvantagement
RT   Cultural Isolation
Culturally Disadvantaged
Culture
Delinquency Causes
Disadvantaged Environment
Functional Illiteracy
Limited Experience
Sensory Deprivation
Slums
Social Disadvantagement

Cultural Diversity
USE CULTURAL DIFFERENCES

CULTURAL EDUCATION 140
BT   Education
RT   African American Studies
Cross Cultural Studies
Cultural Enrichment
Culture
Folk Schools
Intercultural Programs

CULTURAL ENRICHMENT 100
UF   Aesthetic Development
BT   Enrichment
RT   Compensatory Education
Cultural Centers
Cultural Education
Cultural Exchange
Culture
Fine Arts
Intercultural Programs

CULTURAL ENVIRONMENT 160
BT   Environment
RT   Cultural Context
Culture
Culture Contact
Ethnology
Native Speakers
Non Western Civilization
Western Civilization

CULTURAL EVENTS 100
RT   Culture

CULTURAL EXCHANGE 100
UF   Cultural Interaction
RT   Cultural Enrichment
Culture
Culture Contact
Exchange Programs
Intercultural Programs

CULTURAL FACTORS 100
UF   Cultural Influences
Ethnic Factors
RT   Biculturalism
Cultural Awareness
Cultural Context
Cultural Interrelationships
Cultural Pluralism
Culture
Dutch Culture
Educational Sociology
Ethnic Studies
Folk Culture
Individual Power
Language Role
Non Western Civilization
Social Factors
Social Influences
Student Subcultures
Subculture
Urban Language
Western Civilization

Cultural Heritage
USE CULTURAL BACKGROUND

CULTURAL IMAGES 100
RT African American Studies
Culture
Ethnology

Cultural Influences
USE CULTURAL FACTORS

Cultural Interaction
USE CULTURAL EXCHANGE

CULTURAL INTERRELATIONSHIPS 100
BT Relationship
RT Biculturalism
Cross Cultural Studies
Cultural Activities
Cultural Differences
Cultural Factors
Cultural Pluralism
Cultural Traits
Ethnology
Multicultural Textbooks
. Social Influences
Social Integration
Sociocultural Patterns

CULTURAL ISOLATION 100
RT Cultural Disadvantagement
Culture Conflict
Social Isolation

Cultural Lag
USE CULTURE LAG

CULTURALLY ADVANTAGED 380
RT Acculturation
Culture
Middle Class
Upper Class

Culturally Deprived
USE CULTURALLY DISADVANTAGED

Culturally Deprived Children
USE DISADVANTAGED YOUTH

CULTURALLY DISADVANTAGED 380
UF Culturally Deprived
Deprived
Disadvantaged
Underprivileged
NT Disadvantaged Youth
Educationally Disadvantaged
Socially Disadvantaged
RT Acculturation
Cultural Disadvantagement
Culture
Disadvantaged Groups
Economically Disadvantaged
Lower Class
TENL

CULTURAL OPPORTUNITIES 360
NT Economic Opportunities
Social Opportunities
BT Opportunities
RT Cultural Awareness
Culture

CULTURAL PLURALISM 100
NT Biculturalism
RT Acculturation
Bilingualism
Cultural Awareness
Cultural Background
Cultural Differences
Cultural Factors
Cultural Interrelationships
Culture
Culture Conflict
Culture Contact
Minority Groups
Sociocultural Patterns

CULTURAL TRAITS 100
RT African American Studies
Cultural Background
Cultural Context
Cultural Interrelationships
Student Subcultures
Subculture

Cultural Understanding
USE CULTURAL AWARENESS

CULTURE 100
NT African Culture
American Culture
American Indian Culture
Burmese Culture
Chinese Culture
Cross Cultural Studies
Cultural Context
Dutch Culture
Folk Culture
Foreign Culture
Islamic Culture
Japanese American Culture
Korean Culture
Luso Brazilian Culture
Middle Class Culture
Negro Culture
Spanish Culture
Subculture
Urban Culture
RT Acculturation
Cultural Activities
Cultural Awareness
Cultural Background
Cultural Centers
Cultural Differences
Cultural Disadvantagement
Cultural Education
Cultural Enrichment
Cultural Environment
Cultural Events

Cultural Exchange
Cultural Factors
Cultural Images
Culturally Advantaged
Culturally Disadvantaged
Cultural Opportunities
Cultural Pluralism
Culture Lag
Ethnic Groups
Intercultural Programs
Minority Groups
Nineteenth Century Literature
Non Western Civilization
Power Structure
Religious Cultural Groups
Sociocultural Patterns
Western Civilization

CULTURE CONFLICT 100
UF Culture Shock
BT Conflict
RT Biculturalism
Cross Cultural Studies
Cultural Awareness
Cultural Isolation
Cultural Pluralism
Family School Relationship
School Role
Social Class
Social Differences
Social Environment
Social Influences
Social Problems
Values

CULTURE CONTACT 100
RT Biculturalism
Cross Cultural Studies
Cross Cultural Training
Cultural Awareness
Cultural Environment
Cultural Exchange
Cultural Pluralism
Intercultural Programs

CULTURE FREE TESTS 520
UF Cross Culture Tests
BT Tests
RT Cross Cultural Studies
Intelligence Tests

CULTURE LAG 100
UF Cultural Lag
RT Culture

Culture Shock
USE CULTURE CONFLICT

CULTURING TECHNIQUES 510
BT Laboratory Techniques
RT Botany
Cytology
Microbiology
Physiology
Zoology

Cumulative Records
USE STUDENT RECORDS

CURIOSITY 420
BT Individual Characteristics
RT Attention
Behavior
Personality
Student Interests
Student Motivation

CURRENT EVENTS 480
BT Social Studies
RT World Affairs

CURRICULUM 110
UF Curriculum Content
Teaching Areas
NT College Curriculum
Core Curriculum
Courses
Elementary School Curriculum
English Curriculum
Ethnic Studies
Experimental Curriculum
Fused Curriculum
High School Curriculum
Honors Curriculum
Individualized Curriculum
Integrated Curriculum
Mathematics Curriculum
Modern Language Curriculum
Physics Curriculum
Preschool Curriculum
Science Curriculum
Shop Curriculum
Social Studies
Speech Curriculum
Spiral Curriculum
Teacher Education Curriculum
Television Curriculum
Ungraded Curriculum
RT Academic Education
Business Administration
Cocurricular Activities
Curriculum Development
Curriculum Enrichment
Curriculum Evaluation
Curriculum Guides
Curriculum Planning
Curriculum Research
Education
Elective Subjects
English (Second Language)
English Programs
FLES Programs
Grade Charts
Independent Study
Instruction
Intellectual Disciplines
School Activities
Science Course Improvement Project
Specialization

State Curriculum Guides
Teaching Programs

Curriculum Adaptation
USE CURRICULUM DEVELOPMENT

Curriculum Changes
USE CURRICULUM DEVELOPMENT

Curriculum Content
USE CURRICULUM

CURRICULUM DESIGN 110
UF Curriculum Plan
BT Design
RT Curriculum Development
Curriculum Planning
Curriculum Research

CURRICULUM DEVELOPMENT 130
UF Curriculum Adaptation
Curriculum Changes
Curriculum Development Projects
Curriculum Improvement
Curriculum Materials Development
Curriculum Reorganization
Curriculum Revisions
BT Educational Development
RT Advanced Placement Programs
Course Content
Curriculum
Curriculum Design
Curriculum Planning
Curriculum Problems
Curriculum Research
Curriculum Study Centers
Experimental Colleges
Flexible Scheduling
Relevance (Education)
Science Course Improvement Project
Spiral Curriculum
State Curriculum Guides
Unified Studies Programs

Curriculum Development Projects
USE CURRICULUM DEVELOPMENT

CURRICULUM ENRICHMENT 110
UF Course Enrichment
BT Enrichment
RT Curriculum

CURRICULUM EVALUATION 180
UF Curriculum Reevaluation
BT Evaluation
RT Course Evaluation
Curriculum
Faculty Evaluation
Program Evaluation

CURRICULUM GUIDES 110
UF Course Outlines
Syllabus
NT Language Guides
State Curriculum Guides
BT Guides
RT Course Content
Course Descriptions
Curriculum
Curriculum Planning
Curriculum Problems
Lesson Plans
Library Guides
Literature Guides
Teaching Guides

Curriculum Improvement
USE CURRICULUM DEVELOPMENT

Curriculum Materials
USE INSTRUCTIONAL MATERIALS

Curriculum Materials Development
USE CURRICULUM DEVELOPMENT

Curriculum Plan
USE CURRICULUM DESIGN

CURRICULUM PLANNING 020
BT Planning
RT Curriculum
Curriculum Design
Curriculum Development
Curriculum Guides
Curriculum Problems
Curriculum Research
Spiral Curriculum
State Curriculum Guides

CURRICULUM PROBLEMS 110
BT Problems
RT Curriculum Development
Curriculum Guides
Curriculum Planning

Curriculum Reevaluation
USE CURRICULUM EVALUATION

Curriculum Relevance
USE RELEVANCE (EDUCATION)

Curriculum Reorganization
USE CURRICULUM DEVELOPMENT

CURRICULUM RESEARCH 450
BT Educational Research
RT Curriculum
Curriculum Design
Curriculum Development
Curriculum Planning
Curriculum Study Centers
Institutional Research

Curriculum Resources
USE EDUCATIONAL RESOURCES

Curriculum Revisions
USE CURRICULUM DEVELOPMENT

CURRICULUM STUDY CENTERS 210
BT Study Centers
RT Curriculum Development
Curriculum Research
Instructional Materials Centers
Research And Development Centers

CURSIVE WRITING 080
UF Running Writing
BT Handwriting
RT Handwriting Skills
Writing Exercises

CUSTODIAL MENTALLY HANDICAPPED
240
BT Mentally Handicapped
RT Mental Retardation
Residential Care
Residential Schools
Self Care Skills

CUSTODIAN TRAINING 270
BT Job Training
RT Jobs
Job Skills
School Maintenance
Vocational Education

Customs Inspectors
USE IMMIGRATION INSPECTORS

Customs Officials
USE IMMIGRATION INSPECTORS

CUTANEOUS SENSE 070
UF Dermal Sense
RT Haptic Perception
Perception
Physiology
Sensory Experience
Tactual Perception

CYBERNETICS 080
RT Automation
Computers
Computer Science
Electromechanical Technology
Feedback
Game Theory
Human Engineering
Information Theory
Input Output
Instrumentation
Man Machine Systems
Numerical Control
Pattern Recognition
Technological Advancement

Cyclophoria
USE HETEROPHORIA

Cyesis
USE PREGNANCY

CYRILLIC ALPHABET 290
BT Alphabets
RT Slavic Languages
Written Language

CYTOLOGY 070
NT Cell Theory
BT Biology
RT Biochemistry
Culturing Techniques
Embryology
Physiology

CZECH 300
BT Slavic Languages

CZECH LITERATURE 260
BT Literature
RT Drama
Essays
Fiction
Films
Novels
Poetry
Prose
Theater Arts
World Literature

Dactylology
USE FINGER SPELLING

DAGUR 300
BT Mongolian Languages

Dairy Farmers
USE DAIRYMEN

Dairy Farm Operators
USE DAIRYMEN

DAIRYMEN 380
UF Dairy Farmers
Dairy Farm Operators
RT Agriculture
Farmers
Farm Occupations

Dairy Product Inspectors
USE FOOD AND DRUG INSPECTORS

DANCE 030
NT Ballet
BT Fine Arts
RT Dramatics
Music
Outdoor Drama
Theater Arts

DATA 080
NT Personnel Data
Statistical Data
Tables (Data)
RT Data Analysis
Data Bases
Data Collection
Data Processing
Data Sheets

Diagrams
Measurement
Taxonomy

Data Accumulation
USE DATA COLLECTION

DATA ANALYSIS 180
RT Content Analysis
Data
Data Collection
Data Processing
Taxonomy

Data Banks
USE DATA BASES

DATA BASES 330
UF Data Banks
RT Computers
Data
Data Processing
Electronic Data Processing
Information Processing
Information Sources
Information Storage

DATA COLLECTION 450
UF Data Accumulation
RT Case Records
Data
Data Analysis
Data Processing
Data Sheets
Information Storage
Medical Record Technicians
Recordkeeping
Reports
Sampling

DATA PROCESSING 080
UF Data Tabulation
NT Electronic Data Processing
RT Computers
Computer Science
Computer Science Education
Computer Storage Devices
Data
Data Analysis
Data Bases
Data Collection
Data Processing Occupations
Electronic Equipment
Information Processing
Information Retrieval
Information Storage
Information Systems
Input Output Analysis
Machine Translation
Office Management
Programing
Q Sort

DATA PROCESSING OCCUPATIONS 350
BT Occupations
RT Business Education
Computer Science Education
Data Processing
Electronic Data Processing
Electronic Technicians
Office Occupations
Semiskilled Occupations
Skilled Occupations
Trade And Industrial Education

DATA SHEETS 080
BT Records (Forms)
RT Data
Data Collection

Data Tabulation
USE DATA PROCESSING

DATING (SOCIAL) 490
BT Social Development
Social Relations
RT Social Life

DAY CAMP PROGRAMS 390
UF Day Camps
BT Programs
Recreational Programs
Summer Programs
RT Day Care Services
Exceptional Child Services
Resident Camp Programs

Day Camps
USE DAY CAMP PROGRAMS

Day Care Centers
USE DAY CARE SERVICES

DAY CARE PROGRAMS 490
BT Programs
RT Day Care Services
Exceptional Child Services

DAY CARE SERVICES 490
UF Day Care Centers
RT Attendant Training
Child Care Occupations
Day Camp Programs
Day Care Programs
Residential Care

DAYLIGHT 210
UF Natural Light
Sunlight
BT Light
RT Illumination Levels
Solar Radiation
Windows

DAY PROGRAMS 410
BT Programs
RT Day Schools
    Day Students
    Evening Classes
    Evening Programs

Day Release
USE RELEASED TIME

DAY SCHOOLS 470
BT Schools
RT Day Programs
    Day Students
    Nonresidential Schools

DAY STUDENTS 380
BT Students
RT Day Programs
    Day Schools

DAYTIME PROGRAMS 410
SN Adult education courses for adults whc
    attend class during the day
BT Programs
RT Adult Education Programs
    Adult Programs
    Evening Classes
    Evening Programs

DEAF 240
NT Deaf Children
BT Aurally Handicapped
RT Audiometric Tests
    Audition (Physiology)
    Auditory Evaluation
    Deaf Blind
    Deaf Education
    Deaf Interpreting
    Deaf Research
    Hard Of Hearing
    Hearing Aids
    Hearing Conservation
    Hearing Loss
    Hearing Therapists
    Hearing Therapy
    Loop Induction Systems

DEAF BLIND 240
BT Multiply Handicapped
RT Blind
    Deaf
    Exceptional (Atypical)

DEAF CHILDREN 380
BT Children
    Deaf

DEAF EDUCATION 140
BT Special Education
RT Coded Speech
    Cued Speech
    Deaf
    Deaf Research
    Lipreading

Manual Communication
    Visible Speech

DEAF INTERPRETING 080
SN Process of acting as interpreter to
    facilitate communications between deaf
    and hearing persons
UF Interpreting For The Deaf
RT Communication (Thought Transfer)
    Communication Skills
    Cued Speech
    Deaf
    Finger Spelling
    Interpreters
    Interpretive Skills
    Lipreading
    Manual Communication
    Sign Language

DEAF RESEARCH 450
BT Research
RT Deaf
    Deaf Education
    Exceptional Child Research
    Medical Research

Dealers
USE MERCHANTS

Deans Of Men
USE COLLEGE DEANS

Deans Of Students
USE COLLEGE DEANS

Deans Of Women
USE COLLEGE DEANS

DEATH 070
UF Decease
NT Suicide
BT Physiology
RT Pathology

DEBATE 080
RT Cocurricular Activities
    Persuasive Discourse
    Public Speaking
    Social Problems

Decease
USE DEATH

DECENTRALIZATION 020
RT Administrative Organization
    Centralization
    Community Control
    Dial Access Information Systems
    Organization
    School Organization

DECENTRALIZED LIBRARY SYSTEMS 330
BT Libraries
RT Information Centers

DECENTRALIZED SCHOOL DESIGN 030
BT School Design

DECIMAL FRACTIONS 340
UF   Decimals
BT   Fractions

Decimals
USE   DECIMAL FRACTIONS

DECISION MAKING 310
RT   Architectural Programing
      College Choice
      Conflict Resolution
      Decision Making Skills
      Game Theory
      Individual Power
      Management Games
      Management Systems
      Problem Solving
      Productive Thinking
      Psychology
      Risk

DECISION MAKING SKILLS 010
BT   Skills
RT   Cognitive Processes
      Decision Making
      Problem Solving

Deductive Logic
USE   LOGIC

DEDUCTIVE METHODS 270
BT   Methods
RT   Convergent Thinking
      Inductive Methods
      Intellectualization
      Learning Processes
      Logic
      Teaching Methods
      Thought Processes

DEEP STRUCTURE 290
UF   Depth Grammar
BT   Transformation Theory (Language)
RT   Generative Grammar
      Grammar
      Phrase Structure
      Semantics
      Sentence Diagraming
      Sentence Structure
      Surface Structure
      Syntax
      Transformation Generative Grammar
      Transformations (Language)

DEFACTO SEGREGATION 430
BT   Racial Segregation
RT   Anti Segregation Programs
      Token Integration

DEFINITIONS 080
RT   Concept Formation
      Dictionaries
      Linguistics
      Vocabulary

Degree Curriculums
USE   DEGREES (TITLES)

DEGREE REQUIREMENTS 500
BT   Graduation Requirements
RT   Academic Achievement
      Bachelors Degrees
      College Majors
      College Students
      Core Courses
      Degrees (Titles)
      Doctoral Degrees
      Doctoral Programs
      Graduate Students
      Graduate Study
      Masters Degrees
      Special Degree Programs

DEGREES (TITLES) 140
UF   Degree Curriculums
NT   Associate Degrees
      Bachelors Degrees
      Doctoral Degrees
      Masters Degrees
      Specialist In Education Degrees
RT   Administrator Background
      College Graduates
      College Majors
      Credentials
      Degree Requirements
      Doctoral Theses
      Masters Theses
      Special Degree Programs

DEJURE SEGREGATION 430
BT   Racial Segregation

Delayed Speech
USE   RETARDED SPEECH DEVELOPMENT

DELINQUENCY 060
UF   Juvenile Delinquency
NT   Vandalism
RT   Crime
      Delinquency Causes
      Delinquency Prevention
      Delinquent Behavior
      Delinquent Identification
      Delinquent Rehabilitation
      Delinquents
      Juvenile Gangs
      Police School Relationship
      Prisoners
      Socially Deviant Behavior
      Violence

DELINQUENCY CAUSES 490
UF   Delinquenogenic Causes
RT   Cultural Disadvantagement
      Delinquency
      Delinquents
      Etiology

Delinquency Prediction
USE   DELINQUENT IDENTIFICATION

DELINQUENCY PREVENTION 490
UF Juvenile Delinquency Prevention
BT Prevention
RT Delinquency
    Delinquent Rehabilitation
    Delinquents

Delinquenogenic Causes
USE DELINQUENCY CAUSES

DELINQUENT BEHAVIOR 060
BT Behavior
RT Delinquency
    Delinquents

Delinquent Detection
USE DELINQUENT IDENTIFICATION

DELINQUENT IDENTIFICATION 420
UF Delinquency Prediction
    Delinquent Detection
BT Identification
RT Delinquency
    Delinquents

DELINQUENT REHABILITATION 090
BT Correctional Rehabilitation
RT Continuation Education
    Continuation Students
    Correctional Education
    Corrective Institutions
    Delinquency
    Delinquency Prevention
    Delinquents
    Juvenile Courts
    Probationary Period
    Rehabilitation Programs

DELINQUENT ROLE 490
RT Delinquents

DELINQUENTS 380
UF Delinquent Students
RT Criminals
    Criminology
    Delinquency
    Delinquency Causes
    Delinquency Prevention
    Delinquent Behavior
    Delinquent Identification
    Delinquent Rehabilitation
    Delinquent Role
    Juvenile Courts
    Juvenile Gangs
    Prisoners
    Probation Officers
    School Vandalism

Delinquent Students
USE DELINQUENTS

Demand For Education
USE EDUCATIONAL DEMAND

DEMAND OCCUPATIONS 350
BT Occupations
RT Career Opportunities
    Employment Opportunities
    Occupational Information

Dementia Praecox
USE SCHIZOPHRENIA

DEMOCRACY 230
RT Civil Liberties
    Civil Rights
    Communism
    Democratic Values
    Freedom Of Speech

DEMOCRATIC VALUES 040
BT Values
RT Democracy
    Political Attitudes

Demographic Factors
USE DEMOGRAPHY

DEMOGRAPHY 120
UF Demographic Factors
NT City Demography
    National Demography
    Population Distribution
    Population Growth
    Population Trends
    School Demography
BT Statistical Data
RT Census Figures
    Community Size
    Feeder Patterns
    Geographic Distribution
    Land Settlement
    Overpopulation
    Rural Population
    Social Distribution
    Urban Population

DEMONSTRATION CENTERS 210
BT Educational Facilities
RT Audiovisual Centers
    Demonstrations (Educational)
    Instructional Materials Centers
    Science Equipment
    Stages
    Theaters

DEMONSTRATION PROGRAMS 270
UF Model Programs
BT Programs
RT Demonstrations (Educational)

DEMONSTRATION PROJECTS 270
BT Projects
RT Demonstrations (Educational)
    Pilot Projects

DEMONSTRATIONS (CIVIL) 490
UF Public Demonstrations
RT Activism
    Civil Disobedience
    Civil Rights
    School Boycotts
    Violence

DEMONSTRATIONS (EDUCATIONAL) 510
BT Teaching Techniques
RT Demonstration Centers
    Demonstration Programs
    Demonstration Projects
    Laboratory Procedures
    Microcounseling
    Microteaching

Denominational Colleges
USE CHURCH RELATED COLLEGES

Dental Assessment
USE DENTAL EVALUATION

DENTAL ASSISTANTS 380
BT Paramedical Occupations
RT Dental Clinics
    Dental Hygienists
    Dental Technicians
    Dentistry
    Health Personnel
    Health Services

DENTAL ASSOCIATIONS 370
BT Professional Associations
RT National Organizations

DENTAL CLINICS 210
BT Clinics
RT Dental Assistants
    Dental Evaluation
    Dental Health
    Dental Hygienists
    Dental Schools
    Dental Technicians
    Dentistry
    Dentists

DENTAL EVALUATION 180
UF Dental Assessment
BT Dental Health
    Evaluation
RT Dental Clinics
    Dentistry

DENTAL HEALTH 250
NT Dental Evaluation
BT Health
RT Dental Clinics
    Dental Hygienists
    Dentistry
    Hygiene

DENTAL HYGIENISTS 380
UF Oral Hygienists
BT Health Personnel
RT Dental Assistants
    Dental Clinics
    Dental Health
    Dental Technicians
    Dentistry
    Health Occupations
    Health Occupations Education
    Health Services
    Hygiene
    Paramedical Occupations

Dental Laboratory Technicians
USE DENTAL TECHNICIANS

Dental Practice
USE DENTISTRY

DENTAL SCHOOLS 470
UF Schools Of Dentistry
BT Schools
RT Dental Clinics
    Dentistry
    Higher Education
    Medical Schools
    Professional Education

Dental Science
USE DENTISTRY

Dental Surgeons
USE DENTISTS

DENTAL TECHNICIANS 380
UF Dental Laboratory Technicians
    Orthodontic Technicians
BT Health Personnel
RT Dental Assistants
    Dental Clinics
    Dental Hygienists
    Dentistry
    Health Occupations Education
    Health Services
    Laboratory Technology
    Paramedical Occupations
    Subprofessionals
    Technical Education
    Technical Occupations

DENTISTRY 350
UF Dental Practice
    Dental Science
    Orthodontics
RT Dental Assistants
    Dental Clinics
    Dental Evaluation
    Dental Health
    Dental Hygienists
    Dental Schools
    Dental Technicians
    Dentists
    Health Personnel

DENTISTS 380
UF Dental Surgeons
     Doctors Of Dentistry
     Orthodontists
BT Professional Personnel
RT Dental Clinics
     Dentistry
     Health Occupations
     Health Personnel
     Professional Occupations

Departmentalization
USE DEPARTMENTAL TEACHING PLANS

Departmental Majors
USE COLLEGE MAJORS

DEPARTMENTAL TEACHING PLANS 020
SN Plan under which each teacher teaches
     one subject or one group of closely
     related subjects
UF Departmentalization
BT Teaching Methods
RT Cooperative Teaching
     Departments
     English Departments
     School Organization
     Team Teaching

Department Chairman
USE ADMINISTRATIVE PERSONNEL

DEPARTMENT DIRECTORS (SCHOOL) 380
BT Administrative Personnel
RT English Departments

DEPARTMENTS 020
UF Academic Departments
NT English Departments
     Science Departments
BT School Organization
RT Administrative Organization
     College Majors
     Departmental Teaching Plans
     Intellectual Disciplines
     Units Of Study (Subject Fields)

DEPENDENTS 380
NT Welfare Recipients
RT Children
     Family Structure
     Older Adults

DEPLETED RESOURCES 460
BT Resources
RT Natural Resources
     Soil Conservation

DEPOSITORY LIBRARIES 210
BT Libraries
RT City Government
     Federal Government
     Government Publications
     Public Libraries
     Special Libraries
     State Government
     University Libraries

DEPRESSED AREAS (GEOGRAPHIC) 120
UF Economically Depressed Areas
     Poverty Areas
     Poverty Pockets
NT Ghettos
     Slums
RT Economic Disadvantagement
     Low Income Counties
     Relocation
     Socioeconomic Status

Deprivation
USE CULTURAL DISADVANTAGEMENT

Deprived
USE CULTURALLY DISADVANTAGED

Deprived Children
USE DISADVANTAGED YOUTH

Deprived Environment
USE DISADVANTAGED ENVIRONMENT

Depth Grammar
USE DEEP STRUCTURE

Depth Perception
USE STEREOPSIS

Dermal Sense
USE CUTANEOUS SENSE

Descriptive Geometry
USE ORTHOGONAL PROJECTION

DESCRIPTIVE LINGUISTICS 290
BT Synchronic Linguistics
RT Linguistic Theory
     Phonemics
     Structural Grammar
     Tone Languages

Descriptive Reports
USE PROGRAM DESCRIPTIONS

DESCRIPTIVE WRITING 080
BT Writing
RT Composition (Literary)
     Composition Skills (Literary)
     Creative Writing
     Expository Writing
     Figurative Language
     Literary Conventions
     Metaphors
     Poetry
     Prose
     Student Writing Models
     Writing Exercises
     Writing Skills

Descriptors
USE SUBJECT INDEX TERMS

Desegregated Public Facilities
USE INTEGRATED PUBLIC FACILITIES

Desegregated Schools
USE SCHOOL INTEGRATION

Desegregation
USE RACIAL INTEGRATION

Desegregation Litigation
USE INTEGRATION LITIGATION

Desegregation Methods
USE INTEGRATION METHODS

Desegregation Motivation
USE INTEGRATION METHODS

Desegregation Trends
USE INTEGRATION METHODS

DESIGN 030
NT Building Design
     Classroom Design
     Clothing Design
     Curriculum Design
     Flexible Lighting Design
     Furniture Design
     Instructional Design
     Interior Design
     Lighting Design
     Modular Building Design
     Park Design
     Program Design
     Research Design
     School Design
RT Architectural Research
     Architecture
     Building Plans
     Design Crafts
     Designers
     Design Needs
     Design Preferences
     Draftsmen
     Mechanical Design Technicians
     Sign Painters
     Studio Floor Plans

DESIGN CRAFTS 030
RT Design
     Handicrafts

DESIGNERS 380
BT Professional Personnel
RT Design
     Drafting

DESIGN NEEDS 500
SN Human requirements supplied or relieved
     by the physical environment
UF Design Requirements
NT Physical Design Needs
     Psychological Design Needs
BT Needs
RT Architectural Programing
     Architecture
     Building Design
     Classroom Design
     College Housing
     Color Planning
     Design
     Design Preferences
     Facilities
     Fire Protection
     Flexible Facilities
     Furniture Design
     Heating
     Human Engineering
     Interior Design
     Interior Space
     Lighting
     Lighting Design
     Space Classification
     Space Utilization
     Spatial Relationship
     Storage
     Ventilation

DESIGN PREFERENCES 040
RT Architectural Character
     Architecture
     Building Design
     Design
     Design Needs
     Furniture Design
     Individual Needs
     Interior Design
     Physical Design Needs
     Physical Environment
     Psychological Design Needs
     Storage

Design Requirements
USE DESIGN NEEDS

Destiny Control
USE INDIVIDUAL POWER

Determination (Chemical)
USE CHEMICAL ANALYSIS

DETERMINERS (LANGUAGES) 290
UF Articles (Grammar)
BT Form Classes (Languages)
RT Function Words
     Grammar
     Morphology (Languages)
     Syntax

DEVELOPED NATIONS 120
UF Advanced Nations
     Economically Advanced Nations
     Industrial Nations
     Richer Nations
RT Employment
     Human Resources
     Income
     Industrial Personnel
     Industrial Structure
     Labor Economics
     Labor Force
     Manpower Utilization
     Productivity
     Scientific Concepts

Scientific Enterprise
Scientific Methodology
Scientific Principles
Scientific Research
Services
Technological Advancement
Technology

DEVELOPING NATIONS 120
UF Emerging Nations
Underdeveloped Nations
RT Development
Economic Development
Foreign Relations
Nationalism
National Programs
Technical Assistance
World Affairs
World Problems

DEVELOPMENT 130
NT Behavior Development
Child Development
Cognitive Development
Community Development
Comprehension Development
Creative Development
Economic Development
Educational Development
Emotional Development
Handwriting Development
Human Development
Individual Development
Intellectual Development
Language Development
Manpower Development
Material Development
Maturation
Mental Development
Motor Development
Perceptual Development
Personality Development
Physical Development
Program Development
Reading Development
Retarded Speech Development
Rural Development
Site Development
Skill Development
Social Development
Student Development
Systems Development
Talent Development
Verbal Development
Vocabulary Development
Vocational Development
RT Developing Nations
Developmental Programs
Developmental Reading
Developmental Tasks
Research And Development Centers

DEVELOPMENTAL GUIDANCE 090
BT Guidance
RT Developmental Psychology
Developmental Tasks
Human Development

DEVELOPMENTAL PROGRAMS 270
BT Programs
RT Development

DEVELOPMENTAL PSYCHOLOGY 420
BT Individual Psychology
RT Adult Development
Developmental Guidance
Developmental Tasks
Maturation

DEVELOPMENTAL READING 440
BT Reading
RT Bibliotherapy
Development

DEVELOPMENTAL TASKS 130
RT Adult Counseling
Adult Development
Development
Developmental Guidance
Developmental Psychology
Maturation
Motor Development
Vocational Development

DEVELOPMENTAL VOCABULARY 080
BT Vocabulary
RT Vocabulary Development

DIABETES 250
UF Diabetes Insipidus
Diabetes Mellitus
BT Diseases
RT Health
Physical Health
Physiology
Special Health Problems

Diabetes Insipidus
USE DIABETES

Diabetes Mellitus
USE DIABETES

DIACHRONIC LINGUISTICS 290
UF Historical Linguistics
History Of Language
Language History
NT Etymology
Glottochronology
BT Linguistics
RT Contrastive Linguistics
Language Classification
Language Research
Language Universals
Lexicology
Middle English
Morphology (Languages)
Old English

Onomastics
Phonemics
Phonology
Structural Analysis
Structural Linguistics
Synchronic Linguistics

DIACRITICAL MARKING 290
UF Diacritical Marks
BT Phonetics
RT Orthographic Symbols
    Phonetic Transcription
    Pronunciation
    Reading
    Spelling

Diacritical Marks
USE DIACRITICAL MARKING

Diagnosis
USE EDUCATIONAL DIAGNOSIS

DIAGNOSTIC TEACHING 270
UF Prescriptive Teaching
BT Teaching
RT Diagnostic Tests
    Educational Diagnosis
    Learning Difficulties
    Psychoeducational Processes
    Remedial Instruction
    Special Education
    Teaching Procedures

DIAGNOSTIC TESTS 520
BT Tests
RT Diagnostic Teaching
    Educational Diagnosis
    Educational Therapy
    Etiology
    Prognostic Tests
    Projective Tests
    Psychoeducational Clinics

DIAGRAMS 050
RT Audiovisual Aids
    Charts
    Data
    Geometric Concepts
    Graphic Arts
    Illustrations
    Mathematical Models
    Measurement
    Sentence Diagraming

Dial Access Information Retrieval
USE DIAL ACCESS INFORMATION SYSTEMS

DIAL ACCESS INFORMATION SYSTEMS
050
UF Dial Access Information Retrieval
BT Information Systems
RT Audiovisual Aids
    Autoinstructional Aids
    Automation
    Computer Assisted Instruction
    Decentralization

Facsimile Transmission
Information Networks
Information Retrieval
Instructional Technology
Instructional Television
Language Laboratories
Language Laboratory Equipment
Man Machine Systems
Telephone Communication Systems

DIALECTS 290
NT Nonstandard Dialects
    Regional Dialects
    Social Dialects
BT Languages
RT American English
    Cebuano
    Dialect Studies
    Diglossia
    Foochow
    Idioms
    Language
    Language Classification
    Language Standardization
    Linguistics
    Mutual Intelligibility
    Native Speakers

DIALECT STUDIES 290
BT Language Research
RT Dialects
    Diglossia
    Etymology
    Regional Dialects
    Social Dialects
    Sociolinguistics

DIALOGUE 260
BT Literature
RT Analytical Criticism
    Formal Criticism
    Literary Conventions
    Literary Criticism
    Literary Genres
    Local Color Writing
    Realism
    Scripts

DIARIES 260
UF Minutes (Records)
BT Records (Forms)
RT Composition (Literary)
    Prose
    Writing

DICTION 290
BT Speech
RT Articulation (Speech)
    Enunciation Improvement
    Figurative Language
    Language Fluency
    Language Patterns
    Pronunciation
    Speaking

DICTIONARIES 320
UF Lexicons
BT Reference Materials
RT Definitions
    Lexicography
    Lexicology
    Syntax
    Thesauri
    Word Lists

DICTIONARY CATALOGS 320
SN Catalogs in which entries and related
    references are arranged in one
    alphabetic sequence
BT Catalogs
RT Bibliographies
    Booklists
    Cataloging
    Divided Catalogs
    Indexes (Locaters)
    Information Storage
    Libraries

DIDACTICISM 260
BT Literature
RT Drama
    Epics
    Essays
    Fables
    Fiction
    Poetry
    Prose
    Short Stories
    Tales

DIESEL ENGINES 170
BT Engines
RT Agricultural Machinery
    Auto Mechanics
    Locomotive Engineers
    Motor Vehicles

Diesel Mechanics (Occupation)
USE AUTO MECHANICS (OCCUPATION)

DIETETICS 250
UF Diets
RT Dietitians
    Eating Habits
    Food
    Food Standards
    Health
    Nutrition

DIETITIANS 380
BT Health Personnel
RT Cooks
    Dietetics
    Food
    Food Service
    Food Service Industry
    Food Service Occupations
    Food Service Workers
    Foods Instruction
    Food Standards

    Nutrition
    Occupational Home Economics

Diets
USE DIETETICS

Differentiated Staffing
USE DIFFERENTIATED STAFFS

DIFFERENTIATED STAFFS 380
SN Staffs utilizing various levels of
    professional and semiprofessional
    personnel
UF Differentiated Staffing
    Differentiated Teaching Staffs
RT Clinical Professors
    Instructional Staff
    Master Teachers
    Paraprofessional School Personnel
    Staff Utilization
    Subprofessionals
    Teacher Aides
    Teacher Interns
    Teachers

Differentiated Teaching Staffs
USE DIFFERENTIATED STAFFS

DIFFUSION 140
RT Adoption (Ideas)
    Communication (Thought Transfer)
    Educational Innovation
    Information Dissemination
    Innovation
    Transfer Of Training

DIGITAL COMPUTERS 170
BT Computers
RT Analog Computers
    Computer Storage Devices

DIGLOSSIA 290
SN A particular kind of language
    standardization where two varieties of a
    language exist side by side in a
    community
BT Language
RT Dialects
    Dialect Studies
    Language Classification
    Mutual Intelligibility
    Nonstandard Dialects
    Official Languages
    Social Dialects
    Sociolinguistics

DINING FACILITIES 210
UF Cafeterias
    Dining Rooms
    Snack Bars
BT Facilities
RT Dishwashing
    Food Handling Facilities
    Food Service

Dining Rooms
USE DINING FACILITIES

DIRECTED READING ACTIVITY 440
BT Reading
RT Learning Activities
    Reading Development
    Reading Instruction
    Reading Readiness
    Reading Skills

DIRECTION WRITING 080
BT Writing
RT Expository Writing
    Student Writing Models

DIRECTORIES 320
SN Systematically arranged list of persons
    or organizations
BT Publications
RT Catalogs
    Guides
    Indexes (Locaters)
    Reference Materials

Directors Of Research
USE RESEARCH DIRECTORS

Disabled
USE PHYSICALLY HANDICAPPED

Disadvantaged
USE CULTURALLY DISADVANTAGED

Disadvantaged Children
USE DISADVANTAGED YOUTH

DISADVANTAGED ENVIRONMENT 160
UF Deprived Environment
BT Environment
RT Cultural Disadvantagement

DISADVANTAGED GROUPS 380
BT Groups
RT Culturally Disadvantaged
    Subemployment

DISADVANTAGED SCHOOLS 470
BT Schools

Disadvantaged Students
USE DISADVANTAGED YOUTH

DISADVANTAGED YOUTH 380
UF Culturally Deprived Children
    Deprived Children
    Disadvantaged Children
    Disadvantaged Students
    Inner City Children
    Slum Children
BT Culturally Disadvantaged
    Youth
RT Child Development Centers
    Study Centers

Disadvantagement
USE CULTURAL DISADVANTAGEMENT

Disaster Readiness
USE EMERGENCY PROGRAMS

Disciplinary Action
USE DISCIPLINE

DISCIPLINE 060
UF Class Discipline
    Disciplinary Action
NT Expulsion
    Suspension
RT Class Management
    Discipline Policy
    Discipline Problems
    Self Control

DISCIPLINE POLICY 020
BT School Policy
RT Discipline
    Plagiarism
    Suspension

DISCIPLINE PROBLEMS 060
BT Problems
RT Book Thefts
    Discipline
    Misbehavior
    Stealing
    Suspension

DISCOURSE ANALYSIS 290
BT Structural Analysis
RT Connected Discourse
    Grammar
    Language Research
    Morphology (Languages)
    Paragraph Composition
    Semantics
    Sentences
    Syntax

Discovery
USE DISCOVERY PROCESSES

DISCOVERY LEARNING 310
BT Learning
RT Discovery Processes
    Learning Processes

DISCOVERY PROCESSES 310
UF Discovery
RT Activity Learning
    Continuous Learning
    Discovery Learning
    Inductive Methods
    Learning
    Learning Activities
    Learning Processes
    Learning Readiness
    Learning Theories

DISCRIMINANT ANALYSIS 340
UF Discriminant Function
    Discriminant Function Analysis
    Discriminatory Analysis
BT Statistical Analysis
RT Analysis Of Variance
    Factor Analysis

Item Analysis
Mathematical Models

Discriminant Function
USE DISCRIMINANT ANALYSIS

Discriminant Function Analysis
USE DISCRIMINANT ANALYSIS

Discrimination (Social)
USE SOCIAL DISCRIMINATION

Discrimination Attitudes
USE DISCRIMINATORY ATTITUDES (SOCIAL)

DISCRIMINATION LEARNING 310
BT Learning
RT Conditioned Response
Perception
Reinforcement
Sensory Training

Discriminatory Analysis
USE DISCRIMINANT ANALYSIS

DISCRIMINATORY ATTITUDES (SOCIAL)
040
UF Discrimination Attitudes
BT Attitudes
RT Bias
Social Discrimination

DISCRIMINATORY LEGISLATION 230
BT Legislation
RT Civil Rights
Social Discrimination

DISCUSSION (TEACHING TECHNIQUE) 510
UF Class Discussion
NT Group Discussion
BT Teaching Techniques
RT Discussion Experience
Discussion Groups
Discussion Programs

DISCUSSION EXPERIENCE 200
BT Experience
RT Discussion (Teaching Technique)
Discussion Groups
Discussion Programs

DISCUSSION GROUPS 280
UF Study Circles
BT Groups
RT Discussion (Teaching Technique)
Discussion Experience
Discussion Programs
Group Discussion
Listening Groups
T Groups

DISCUSSION PROGRAMS 270
BT Programs
RT Alumni Education
Discussion (Teaching Technique)
Discussion Experience
Discussion Groups
Speeches

DISEASE CONTROL 250
RT Cleaning
Communicable Diseases
Community Health
Diseases
Dishwashing
Pesticides
Sanitation

Disease Incidence
USE DISEASE RATE

DISEASE RATE 250
UF Disease Incidence
BT Statistical Data
RT Diseases

DISEASES 250
NT Allergy
Asthma
Communicable Diseases
Diabetes
Epilepsy
Infectious Diseases
Occupational Diseases
Psychosomatic Diseases
RT Disease Control
Disease Rate
Health
Hygiene
Pollution
Prenatal Influences

DISHWASHING 250
BT Cleaning
RT Dining Facilities
Disease Control
Food Handling Facilities
Food Service
Health
Health Needs
Hygiene
Infectious Diseases
Public Health
Sanitary Facilities
Sanitation
Sanitation Improvement

Dismissal
USE DISQUALIFICATION

Disordered Behavior
USE MALADJUSTMENT

DISPLAY PANELS 170
BT Audiovisual Aids
RT Chalkboards
Educational Equipment
Exhibits
Merchandising
Three Dimensional Aids
Vertical Work Surfaces

DISPLAY SYSTEMS 050
RT   Computers
      Electronic Data Processing
      Electronic Equipment
      Information Processing
      Input Output
      Man Machine Systems

DISQUALIFICATION 500
UF   Dismissal
RT   Withdrawal

Dissemination
USE   INFORMATION DISSEMINATION

DISTANCE 160
UF   Proximity
      Range (Distance)
RT   Geographic Location
      Height
      Instructional Trips
      Intervals
      School Location
      Topology
      Transportation

DISTINCTIVE FEATURES 290
RT   Acoustic Phonetics
      Artificial Speech
      Componential Analysis
      Consonants
      Language Universals
      Linguistics
      Phonemes
      Phonetics
      Phonology
      Physics

Distribution (Economics)
USE   MARKETING

DISTRIBUTIVE EDUCATION 140
UF   Retail Training
BT   Vocational Education
RT   Auto Parts Men
      Business Education
      Business Subjects
      Clothing Maintenance Specialists
      Cooperative Education
      Distributive Education Teachers
      Food Service Occupations
      Marketing
      Merchandising
      Office Occupations
      Office Practice
      Retailing
      Salesmanship
      Sales Occupations
      Sales Workers
      Vocational Education Teachers
      Wholesaling

DISTRIBUTIVE EDUCATION TEACHERS 380
BT   Vocational Education Teachers
RT   Distributive Education

District Libraries
USE   REGIONAL LIBRARIES

DIVERGENT THINKING 310
BT   Creative Thinking
RT   Cognitive Processes
      Inductive Methods
      Problem Solving
      Productive Thinking

DIVIDED CATALOGS 320
SN   Catalogs in which entries are separated
      into two or more filing sequences
BT   Catalogs
RT   Bibliographies
      Booklists
      Cataloging
      Dictionary Catalogs
      Indexes (Locaters)
      Information Storage
      Libraries

DIVISION 340
BT   Arithmetic
RT   Addition
      Multiplication

DOCTORAL DEGREES 140
BT   Degrees (Titles)
RT   Academic Rank (Professional)
      Bachelors Degrees
      Degree Requirements
      Doctoral Programs
      Doctoral Theses
      Masters Degrees
      Specialist In Education Degrees
      Teacher Educator Education

Doctoral Dissertations
USE   DOCTORAL THESES

DOCTORAL PROGRAMS 410
BT   Programs
RT   College Programs
      Degree Requirements
      Doctoral Degrees
      Graduate Study
      Higher Education
      Teacher Educator Education

DOCTORAL THESES 460
UF   Doctoral Dissertations
BT   Publications
RT   Degrees (Titles)
      Doctoral Degrees
      Research

Doctors Of Dentistry
USE   DENTISTS

DOCUMENTATION 330
SN Document generation, processing, and use
NT Information Processing
BT Information Science
RT Abstracting
    Abstracts
    Bibliographies
    Cataloging
    Catalogs
    Citation Indexes
    Classification
    Coordinate Indexes
    Indexes (Locaters)
    Indexing
    Information Dissemination
    Information Retrieval
    Information Storage
    Information Systems
    Libraries
    Library Research
    Library Science
    Permuted Indexes
    Reports
    Subject Index Terms
    Symposia
    Use Studies

Document Readers
USE OPTICAL SCANNERS

DOGMATISM 040
RT Authoritarianism
    Opinions

DOMESTICS 380
SN Any female household employee working in a private home
NT Maids
BT Service Workers
RT Attendants
    Service Occupations

DOORS 210
BT Architectural Elements
RT Building Design
    Building Materials

DORMITORIES 210
UF Residence Halls
BT College Housing
RT House Plan
    Housing
    Resident Assistants

Double Employment
USE MULTIPLE EMPLOYMENT

DOUBLE SESSIONS 020
RT Flexible Schedules
    Scheduling
    School Administration
    School Organization
    School Schedules
    Student Enrollment

Downs Anomaly
USE MONGOLISM
Downs Syndrome
USE MONGOLISM

DRAFTING 350
NT Architectural Drafting
    Engineering Drawing
    Technical Illustration
RT Blueprints
    Designers
    Draftsmen
    Engineering Graphics
    Industrial Arts
    Orthogonal Projection

DRAFTSMEN 380
BT Subprofessionals
RT Design
RT Drafting
RT Technical Occupations
RT Trade And Industrial Education

DRAMA 260
NT Comedy
    Folk Drama
    Tragedy
BT Literary Genres
RT Ambiguity
    Aristotelian Criticism
    Characterization (Literature)
    Classical Literature
    Composition (Literary)
    Czech Literature
    Didacticism
    Dramatics
    Dramatic Unities
    English Neoclassic Literary Period
    Expressionism
    French Literature
    German Literature
    Humanism
    Irony
    Italian Literature
    Literary Analysis
    Literary Conventions
    Literary Perspective
    Local Color Writing
    Medieval Literature
    Metaphors
    Mythic Criticism
    Narration
    Nineteenth Century Literature
    Outdoor Drama
    Pastoral Literature
    Platonism
    Poetry
    Polish Literature
    Prose
    Realism
    Renaissance Literature
    Romanticism
    Russian Literature

Satire
Scripts
Seventeenth Century Literature
Sixteenth Century Literature
Spanish American Literature
Spanish Literature
Symbols (Literary)
Theoretical Criticism

Dramatic Arts
USE DRAMATICS

DRAMATIC PLAY 030
RT Teaching Techniques

DRAMATICS 030
SN Activities in the creation, preparation, and production of plays
UF Dramatic Arts
NT Creative Dramatics
Outdoor Drama
BT Theater Arts
RT Acting
Chautauquas
Dance
Drama
Drama Workshops
Outdoor Theaters
Playwriting
Prompting
Skits
Theaters

DRAMATIC UNITIES 260
RT Classical Literature
Drama
Literary Criticism
Prose
Theater Arts

DRAMA WORKSHOPS 270
BT Workshops
RT Arts Centers
Dramatics
Theaters

DRAVIDIAN LANGUAGES 300
NT Brahmins
Kannada
Malayalam
Tamil
Telugu
BT Languages
RT Language Classification
Native Speakers

Dress Design
USE CLOTHING DESIGN

Drill Presses
USE MACHINE TOOLS

Drinking
USE ALCOHOLISM

DRIVER EDUCATION 140
UF Driver Training
BT Education
RT Traffic Safety

Driver Training
USE DRIVER EDUCATION

DRIVEWAYS 210
RT Parking Areas
Parking Facilities
Traffic Circulation
Vehicular Traffic

DROPOUT ATTITUDES 040
BT Attitudes
RT Dropouts
Student Alienation

DROPOUT CHARACTERISTICS 490
RT Dropouts
Individual Characteristics

Dropout Employability
USE EMPLOYMENT

Dropout Employment
USE DROPOUT PROGRAMS

DROPOUT IDENTIFICATION 500
UF Identifying Dropouts
BT Identification
RT Dropout Prevention
Dropout Research
Dropouts
Potential Dropouts

DROPOUT PREVENTION 510
RT Continuation Education
Continuation Students
Dropout Identification
Dropout Programs
Dropout Research
Dropouts

DROPOUT PROBLEMS 490
BT Problems
RT Dropouts

DROPOUT PROGRAMS 490
UF Dropout Employment
BT Programs
RT Continuation Education
Dropout Prevention
Dropout Rehabilitation
Dropouts
Dropout Teaching

DROPOUT RATE 120
BT Statistical Data
RT Adult Dropouts
Dropout Research
Dropouts

DROPOUT REHABILITATION 090
BT   Rehabilitation
RT   Continuation Education
      Dropout Programs
      Dropouts
      Rehabilitation Programs

DROPOUT RESEARCH 450
BT   Educational Research
RT   Dropout Identification
      Dropout Prevention
      Dropout Rate
      Dropouts

DROPOUT ROLE 490
RT   Dropouts

DROPOUTS 380
UF   High School Dropouts
      School Dropouts
NT   Adult Dropouts
      Potential Dropouts
      Rural Dropouts
      Urban Dropouts
RT   Academic Failure
      Continuation Students
      Dropout Attitudes
      Dropout Characteristics
      Dropout Identification
      Dropout Prevention
      Dropout Problems
      Dropout Programs
      Dropout Rate
      Dropout Rehabilitation
      Dropout Research
      Dropout Role
      Dropout Teaching
      Expulsion
      Out Of School Youth
      Persistence
      Retraining
      School Holding Power
      Students
      Unemployed
      Unemployment
      Youth

DROPOUT TEACHING 270
BT   Teaching
RT   Dropout Programs
      Dropouts

Drowsiness
USE SLEEP

DRUG ABUSE 060
BT   Socially Deviant Behavior
RT   Drug Legislation
      Health Education
      Lysergic Acid Diethylamide
      Marihuana
      Narcotics
      Prenatal Influences

DRUG ADDICTION 060
UF   Narcotics Addiction
BT   Drug Abuse
RT   Crime
      Drug Legislation
      Health
      Health Education
      Lysergic Acid Diethylamide
      Marihuana
      Narcotics
      Socially Deviant Behavior

Druggists
USE PHARMACISTS

Drug Inspectors
USE FOOD AND DRUG INSPECTORS

DRUG LEGISLATION 230
BT   Legislation
RT   Drug Abuse
      Drug Addiction
      Federal Legislation
      Health
      Laws
      Marihuana
      Narcotics

DRUG THERAPY 250
UF   Chemotherapy
BT   Therapy
RT   Medical Treatment

DUAL ENROLLMENT 020
SN   Enrollment of students in two schools at
      the same time
UF   Dual School Enrollment
      Shared Time
      Split Time
BT   Student Enrollment
RT   Consortia
      Cooperative Programs
      School Registration
      Shared Services

Dual School Enrollment
USE DUAL ENROLLMENT

DUBBING 050
SN   Combining two or more signals into a
      single recording
UF   Duplicating Tapes
RT   Audio Equipment
      Language Laboratories
      Material Development
      Tape Recorders
      Tape Recordings

Dues
USE FEES

Duplicating Tapes
USE DUBBING

DUSUN 300
BT   Indonesian Languages

DUTCH 300
BT   Indo European Languages
RT   Afrikaans

DUTCH CULTURE 100
BT   Culture
RT   Cultural Factors

DYSLEXIA 440
BT   Language Handicaps
     Learning Disabilities
RT   Reading Difficulty

DYULA 300
BT   African Languages

EARLY ADMISSION 020
BT   Admission (School)
RT   Enrollment

EARLY CHILDHOOD 130
BT   Childhood
RT   Early Childhood Education
     Early Experience

EARLY CHILDHOOD EDUCATION 140
BT   Education
RT   Early Childhood
     Kindergarten
     Preschool Education
     Preschool Programs
     Primary Grades

Early Detection
USE IDENTIFICATION

EARLY EXPERIENCE 200
UF   Preschool Experience
BT   Experience
RT   Childhood
     Early Childhood

EARLY READING 440
BT   Reading
RT   Reading Achievement
     Reading Instruction

EARS 070
RT   Anatomy
     Audition (Physiology)
     Hard Of Hearing
     Hearing Loss
     Hearing Therapy

EARTH SCIENCE 400
NT   Geology
     Geophysics
     Meteorology
     Oceanology
     Seismology
     Soil Science
BT   Physical Sciences
RT   Astronomy
     Chemistry
     Climatic Factors
     Paleontology
     Physical Geography

     Physics
     Planetariums

Eastern Civilization
USE NON WESTERN CIVILIZATION

EATING HABITS 060
RT   Dietetics
     Health
     Nutrition

ECHOLALIA 060
SN   Involuntary and senseless repetition of
     words heard spoken by another person
UF   Echophasia
RT   Child Development
     Language Development
     Language Handicaps
     Language Patterns
     Languages
     Mental Illness

ECHOLOCATION 070
RT   Acoustics
     Auditory Perception
     Aural Stimuli
     Blind
     Travel Training
     Visually Handicapped
     Visually Handicapped Mobility
     Visually Handicapped Orientation

Echophasia
USE ECHOLALIA

ECOLOGICAL FACTORS 070
BT   Ecology
RT   Pollution

ECOLOGY 070
NT   Ecological Factors
BT   Biology
RT   Area Studies
     Environment
     Environmental Education
     Evolution
     Marine Biology
     Ocean Engineering
     Radiation Biology
     Scientific Research
     Zoology

Economically Advanced Nations
USE DEVELOPED NATIONS

Economically Depressed Areas
USE DEPRESSED AREAS (GEOGRAPHIC)

Economically Deprived
USE ECONOMICALLY DISADVANTAGED

ECONOMICALLY DISADVANTAGED 490
UF   Economically Deprived
      Poverty Stricken
RT   Culturally Disadvantaged
      Economic Disadvantagement
      Low Income Groups
      Welfare Recipients

Economic Analysis
USE ECONOMIC RESEARCH

ECONOMIC CHANGE 220
BT   Economics
RT   Economic Climate
      Economic Development
      Economic Factors
      Economic Opportunities
      Economic Progress
      Economic Status

ECONOMIC CLIMATE 220
RT   Business Cycles
      Economic Change
      Economics

Economic Cycles
USE BUSINESS CYCLES

ECONOMIC DEVELOPMENT 130
BT   Development
RT   Developing Nations
      Economic Change
      Economic Progress
      Economics
      Educational Economics

ECONOMIC DISADVANTAGEMENT 200
UF   Economic Insecurity
      Economic Plight
      Poverty
      Poverty Conditions
      Rural Poverty
      Urban Poverty
BT   Cultural Disadvantagement
RT   Depressed Areas (Geographic)
      Economically Disadvantaged
      Functional Illiteracy
      Hunger
      Low Income
      Poverty Programs
      Subemployment

ECONOMIC FACTORS 480
UF   Poverty Factors
NT   Income
RT   Business Cycles
      Economic Change
      Living Standards

Economic Fluctuations
USE BUSINESS CYCLES

Economic Insecurity
USE ECONOMIC DISADVANTAGEMENT

ECONOMIC OPPORTUNITIES 360
BT   Cultural Opportunities
RT   Economic Change

Economic Plight
USE ECONOMIC DISADVANTAGEMENT

ECONOMIC PROGRESS 480
RT   Business Cycles
      Economic Change
      Economic Development
      Economics

ECONOMIC RESEARCH 450
UF   Economic Analysis
BT   Research
RT   Economics
      Input Output Analysis
      Labor Economics

ECONOMICS 480
UF   Economy
NT   Communism
      Consumer Economics
      Economic Change
      Educational Economics
      Home Economics
      Labor Economics
      Money Systems
      Rural Economics
BT   Social Sciences
      Social Studies
RT   Area Studies
      Banking
      Banking Vocabulary
      Business Cycles
      Credit (Finance)
      Economic Climate
      Economic Development
      Economic Progress
      Economic Research
      Economic Status
      Exports
      Finance Occupations
      Human Capital
      Interest
      International Trade Vocabulary
      Investment
      Productivity
      Socioeconomic Status

Economics Of Education
USE EDUCATIONAL ECONOMICS

ECONOMIC STATUS 480
BT   Cultural Background
      Status
RT   Economic Change
      Economics
      Socioeconomic Status

Economic Support
USE FINANCIAL SUPPORT

Economy
USE ECONOMICS

EDP
USE ELECTRONIC DATA PROCESSING

EDUCABLE MENTALLY HANDICAPPED 240
BT Mentally Handicapped
RT Mental Retardation
Prevocational Education
Trainable Mentally Handicapped

Educated Colloquial Usage
USE STANDARD SPOKEN USAGE

EDUCATION 140
UF Education Factors
NT Academic Education
Adult Education
After School Education
Alcohol Education
Art Education
Bilingual Education
Coeducation
Community Education
Comparative Education
Compensatory Education
Computer Science Education
Consumer Education
Continuation Education
Cooperative Education
Correctional Education
Cultural Education
Driver Education
Early Childhood Education
Elementary Education
Engineering Education
English Education
Environmental Education
Equal Education
Exceptional Child Education
Extension Education
Family Life Education
General Education
Health Education
Higher Education
Industrial Education
Inservice Education
Intergroup Education
International Education
Library Education
Literacy Education
Mathematics Education
Migrant Education
Music Education
Negro Education
Nondiscriminatory Education
Outdoor Education
Parent Education
Physical Education
Post Secondary Education
Preschool Education
Professional Education
Public Administration Education
Public Affairs Education
Public Education
Religious Education
Rural Education

RT Continuous Learning
Curriculum
Educational Attitudes
Educational Background
Educational Change
Educational Complexes
Educational Counseling
Educational Demand
Educational Disadvantagement
Educational Discrimination
Educational Environment
Educational Equality
Educational Equipment
Educational Experience
Educational Experiments
Educational Facilities
Educational Finance
Educational Guidance
Educational Improvement
Educational Legislation
Educationally Disadvantaged
Educational Methods
Educational Mobility
Educational Needs
Educational Objectives
Educational Opportunities
Educational Philosophy
Educational Planning
Educational Policy
Educational Practice
Educational Principles
Educational Problems
Educational Programs
Educational Psychology
Educational Quality
Educational Research
Educational Resources
Educational Responsibility
Educational Retardation
Educational Status Comparison
Educational Strategies
Educational Supply
Educational Television
Educational Testing
Educational Theories
Educational Trends
Education Service Centers
Learning
Teaching Programs
Training

Educational Achievement
USE ACADEMIC ACHIEVEMENT

EDUCATIONAL ADMINISTRATION 020
NT College Administration
School Administration
University Administration
BT Administration
RT Administrative Policy
Budgeting
Educational Finance
Educational Policy
Financial Policy

Management
Planning
Project Applications
School Accounting

Educational Advantages
USE EDUCATIONAL OPPORTUNITIES

Educational Attainment
USE ACADEMIC ACHIEVEMENT

EDUCATIONAL ATTITUDES 040
BT Attitudes
RT Education
Educational Interest

EDUCATIONAL BACKGROUND 200
NT Educational Experience
BT Cultural Background
RT Education
Educational Environment
Educational Opportunities
Knowledge Level
Participant Characteristics

EDUCATIONAL BENEFITS 140
SN Individual benefits obtained from
acquisition of advanced education
RT Professional Recognition
Rewards
Social Mobility
Social Opportunities
Socioeconomic Status

EDUCATIONAL CERTIFICATES 500
RT Certification
Credentials
Equivalency Tests
Student Certification
Teacher Certificates

EDUCATIONAL CHANGE 130
UF Educational Reform
RT Education
Educational Innovation

EDUCATIONAL COMPLEXES 210
RT Buildings
Campuses
Campus Planning
Cultural Centers
Education
Educational Parks
School Systems

EDUCATIONAL COORDINATION 020
BT Coordination
RT Affiliated Schools
Consortia
Educational Planning
Interagency Coordination
Program Coordination

EDUCATIONAL COUNSELING 090
BT Counseling
RT Education
Educational Guidance
Educational Psychology
Faculty Advisors

EDUCATIONAL DEMAND 140
SN Consumer demand for education
UF Demand For Education
RT Consumer Economics
Education
Educational Economics
Educational Supply
Educational Trends
Enrollment
Enrollment Influences

Educational Deprivation
USE EDUCATIONAL DISADVANTAGEMENT

EDUCATIONAL DEVELOPMENT 130
SN Developmental change of one or more
characteristics of the educational
systems variables in a positive direction
in terms of some valued criterion
UF Educational Systems Development
NT Curriculum Development
BT Development
RT Educational Improvement
Educational Innovation
Educational Research
Educational Technology
Experimental Teaching
Instructional Innovation
Instructional Technology
Program Development
Relevance (Education)
Research And Development Centers
Systems Development

EDUCATIONAL DIAGNOSIS 180
SN Identification of the nature or level of
student ability or skill
UF Diagnosis
NT Reading Diagnosis
RT Clinical Diagnosis
Diagnostic Teaching
Diagnostic Tests
Educational Therapy
Error Patterns
Identification
Learning Difficulties
Psychoeducational Clinics
Psychological Evaluation
Student Evaluation

EDUCATIONAL DISADVANTAGEMENT 200
UF Educational Deprivation
Unequal Education
BT Cultural Disadvantagement
RT Education
Educationally Disadvantaged
Functional Illiteracy

EDUCATIONAL DISCRIMINATION 490
BT   Social Discrimination
RT   Education

EDUCATIONAL ECONOMICS 480
UF   Economics Of Education
BT   Economics
RT   Bids
     Consumer Economics
     Economic Development
     Educational Demand
     Educational Finance
     Educational Supply
     Financial Policy
     Financial Support
     Fiscal Capacity
     Human Capital
     Investment
     Private Financial Support
     Productivity
     School Support

EDUCATIONAL ENVIRONMENT 160
UF   School Climate
NT   College Environment
     School Environment
BT   Environment
RT   Campus Planning
     Education
     Educational Background

EDUCATIONAL EQUALITY 140
RT   Education
     Universal Education

EDUCATIONAL EQUIPMENT 170
UF   Classroom Equipment
NT   Teaching Machines
BT   Educational Facilities
     Equipment
RT   Building Equipment
     College Buildings
     Display Panels
     Education
     Educational Resources
     Electromechanical Aids
     Equipment Maintenance
     Equipment Manufacturers
     Instructional Materials
     School Buildings
     Science Equipment
     Wheel Chairs

EDUCATIONAL EXPERIENCE 200
UF   School Experience
     Educational Background
     Experience
RT   Education

EDUCATIONAL EXPERIMENTS 450
BT   Experiments
RT   Education

EDUCATIONAL FACILITIES 210
UF   School Facilities
     School Plant
     Teaching Facilities
NT   Auditoriums
     Business Education Facilities
     Classrooms
     College Buildings
     Continuing Education Centers
     Crafts Rooms
     Demonstration Centers
     Educational Equipment
     Educational Parks
     Guidance Centers
     Guidance Facilities
     Health Occupations Centers
     Instructional Materials Centers
     Library Facilities
     Museums
     Off Campus Facilities
     Physical Education Facilities
     Reading Centers
     Residential Centers
     Resource Centers
     School Buildings
     School Shops
     Skill Centers
     Study Facilities
BT   Facilities
RT   Arts Centers
     Campus Planning
     Education
     Educational Resources
     Facility Guidelines
     Facility Inventory
     Facility Requirements
     Facility Utilization Research
     House Plan
     Information Centers
     Music Facilities
     Residential Colleges
     State Colleges
     State Universities
     Studio Floor Plans

EDUCATIONAL FINANCE 220
UF   Educational Support
     Finance
     School Finance
RT   Bids
     Bond Issues
     Budgeting
     Budgets
     Capital
     Capital Outlay (For Fixed Assets)
     Costs
     Education
     Educational Administration
     Educational Economics
     Equalization Aid
     Expenditure Per Student
     Expenditures

Federal Aid
Fellowships
Financial Needs
Financial Policy
Financial Problems
Financial Services
Financial Support
Fiscal Capacity
Foundation Programs
Grants
Incentive Grants
Program Budgeting
Proprietary Schools
Purchasing
Salary Differentials
Scholarships
School Accounting
School Budget Elections
School District Spending
School Funds
State Aid
Student Loan Programs

EDUCATIONAL GAMES 270
UF   Academic Games
      Heuristic Games
NT   Classroom Games
      Reading Games
BT   Games
RT   Childrens Games
      Instructional Materials
      Puzzles

Educational Goals
USE   EDUCATIONAL OBJECTIVES

EDUCATIONAL GUIDANCE 090
BT   Guidance
RT   Education
      Educational Counseling
      Faculty Advisors
      Group Guidance

EDUCATIONAL HISTORY 140
UF   History Of Education
NT   Science Education History
BT   History
RT   Educational Practice
      Educational Theories

EDUCATIONAL IMPROVEMENT 140
NT   Instructional Improvement
BT   Improvement
RT   Education
      Educational Development
      Educational Quality
      Educational Technology
      Experimental Colleges
      Relevance (Education)
      Research And Instruction Units

Educational Inequality
USE   EQUAL EDUCATION

EDUCATIONAL INNOVATION 140
BT   Innovation
RT   Change Agents
      Diffusion
      Educational Change
      Educational Development
      Educational Research
      Educational Technology
      Instructional Innovation

EDUCATIONAL INTEREST 040
SN   Interest in continuing ones education
RT   Educational Attitudes
      Motivation
      Student Interests

Educational Intervention
USE   INTERVENTION

EDUCATIONAL LEGISLATION 230
BT   Legislation
RT   Education
      Educationally Disadvantaged
      Federal Legislation
      Legislators
      State Legislation

Educational Level
USE   ACADEMIC ACHIEVEMENT

Educationally Deprived
USE   EDUCATIONALLY DISADVANTAGED

Educationally Deprived Programs
USE   COMPENSATORY EDUCATION
      PROGRAMS

EDUCATIONALLY DISADVANTAGED 380
UF   Educationally Deprived
BT   Culturally Disadvantaged
RT   Compensatory Education
      Education
      Educational Disadvantagement
      Educational Legislation
      Educational Opportunities
      Low Ability Students
      Low Achievers
      Mentally Handicapped
      Rehabilitation
      Remedial Programs
      Slow Learners

Educationally Handicapped
USE   ACADEMICALLY HANDICAPPED

Educational Materials
USE   INSTRUCTIONAL MATERIALS

Educational Media
USE   INSTRUCTIONAL MATERIALS

EDUCATIONAL METHODS 510
NT   Project Training Methods
      Teaching Methods
BT   Methods
RT   Education
      Progressive Education

EDUCATIONAL MOBILITY 120
BT Mobility
RT Education
Migrant Education
Transfers

EDUCATIONAL NEEDS 140
UF Training Needs
BT Needs
RT Education
Educational Objectives
Educational Planning
Information Needs
Research Needs

EDUCATIONAL OBJECTIVES 140
UF Educational Goals
Educational Purposes
NT Affective Objectives
Behavioral Objectives
Cognitive Objectives
Course Objectives
Psychomotor Objectives
BT Objectives
RT College Role
Education
Educational Needs
Educational Philosophy
Educational Theories
Institutional Role
Residential Colleges
Training Objectives

EDUCATIONAL OPPORTUNITIES 360
UF Educational Advantages
Training Opportunities
BT Opportunities
RT Education
Educational Background
Educationally Disadvantaged
Universal Education

EDUCATIONAL PARKS 210
UF School Parks
BT Educational Facilities
RT Athletic Fields
Campuses
Educational Complexes

EDUCATIONAL PHILOSOPHY 140
UF School Philosophy
NT Educational Principles
Progressive Education
BT Philosophy
RT Education
Educational Objectives
Educational Theories
Experimental Colleges
Logic

EDUCATIONAL PLANNING 020
UF Educational Plans
BT Planning
RT Education
Educational Coordination
Educational Needs
Educational Strategies
Faculty Advisors

Educational Plans
USE EDUCATIONAL PLANNING

EDUCATIONAL POLICY 020
BT Policy
RT Bilingual Education
Education
Educational Administration
Language Planning
Official Languages
School District Autonomy

EDUCATIONAL PRACTICE 140
RT Education
Educational History
Educational Research
Progressive Education

EDUCATIONAL PRINCIPLES 140
BT Educational Philosophy
RT Education
Educational Psychology
Educational Research
Educational Theories

EDUCATIONAL PROBLEMS 140
BT Problems
RT Education

Educational Processes
USE LEARNING PROCESSES

EDUCATIONAL PROGRAMS 140
UF Training Programs
NT Adult Education Programs
Autoinstructional Programs
Compensatory Education Programs
Field Experience Programs
Institutes (Training Programs)
Internship Programs
Language And Area Centers
Preschool Programs
Unified Studies Programs
BT Programs
RT Coordinators
Education
International Programs
Itinerant Teachers
Program Content

EDUCATIONAL PSYCHOLOGY 420
BT Psychology
RT Education
   Educational Counseling
   Educational Principles
   Educational Sociology
   Educational Theories
   Intervention

Educational Purposes
USE EDUCATIONAL OBJECTIVES

EDUCATIONAL QUALITY 140
UF Quality Education
RT Education
   Educational Improvement

EDUCATIONAL RADIO 050
BT Radio
RT Broadcast Industry
   Educational Television
   Listening Groups
   Mass Media
   Radio Technology

Educational Reform
USE EDUCATIONAL CHANGE

Educational Relevance
USE RELEVANCE (EDUCATION)

EDUCATIONAL RESEARCH 450
NT Classroom Research
   Comparative Analysis
   Curriculum Research
   Dropout Research
   Experimental Teaching
   Reading Research
   Retention Studies
BT Research
RT Education
   Educational Development
   Educational Innovation
   Educational Practice
   Educational Principles
   Educational Researchers
   Educational Status Comparison
   Educational Technology
   Educational Testing
   Exceptional Child Research
   Field Studies
   Graduate Surveys
   Institutional Research
   Laboratory Schools
   Program Effectiveness
   Relevance (Education)
   Research And Instruction Units
   Research Coordinating Units
   Researchers
   Research Utilization
   School Surveys

EDUCATIONAL RESEARCHERS 380
UF Research Specialists (Education)
BT Researchers
RT Educational Research
   Research Skills

EDUCATIONAL RESOURCES 460
UF Curriculum Resources
   Learning Resources
   Teaching Resources
NT Instructional Materials
BT Resources
RT Audiovisual Centers
   Education
   Educational Equipment
   Educational Facilities

EDUCATIONAL RESPONSIBILITY 490
BT Social Responsibility
RT Administrator Responsibility
   Child Responsibility
   College Role
   Education
   Institutional Role
   Noninstructional Responsibility
   Parent Responsibility
   Teacher Responsibility

EDUCATIONAL RETARDATION 310
UF Grade Retardation
NT Progressive Retardation
BT Retardation
RT Education

Educational Service Centers
USE SUPPLEMENTARY EDUCATIONAL
   CENTERS

EDUCATIONAL SOCIOLOGY 490
BT Sociology
RT Cultural Factors
   Educational Psychology
   School Community Relationship
   Social Change
   Social Influences
   Social Psychology

EDUCATIONAL SPECIFICATIONS 500
SN Detailed, precise, expert presentation of
   a plan or proposal for educational
   facilities including equipment,
   classrooms, laboratories, curriculum, etc.
BT Specifications
RT College Planning
   Construction Programs
   Criteria
   Equipment Evaluation
   Equipment Maintenance
   Facilities
   Facility Guidelines
   Facility Requirements
   Facility Utilization Research
   Field Check
   Performance Criteria
   Performance Specifications

Planning
Purchasing
Science Facilities

EDUCATIONAL STATUS COMPARISON 190
RT   Education
     Educational Research

EDUCATIONAL STRATEGIES 140
SN   Overall plans for implementing
     instructional goals, methods or
     techniques
BT   Instruction
RT   Education
     Educational Planning
     Instructional Design
     Motivation Techniques
     Teaching Procedures

EDUCATIONAL SUPPLY 140
SN   Education provided to meet consumer
     demand
UF   Supply Of Education
RT   Admission (School)
     Admission Criteria
     Competitive Selection
     Consumer Economics
     Education
     Educational Demand
     Educational Economics
     Educational Trends
     Enrollment
     Enrollment Influences

Educational Support
USE   EDUCATIONAL FINANCE

Educational Surveys
USE   SCHOOL SURVEYS

Educational Systems Development
USE   EDUCATIONAL DEVELOPMENT

EDUCATIONAL TECHNOLOGY 140
BT   Technology
RT   Computer Assisted Instruction
     Computer Oriented Programs
     Educational Development
     Educational Improvement
     Educational Innovation
     Educational Research
     Instructional Technology
     Language Laboratories
     Programed Instruction

EDUCATIONAL TELEVISION 050
UF   Audiovisual Television Systems
     ETV
NT   Public Television
BT   Audiovisual Communication
     Television
RT   Airborne Television
     Broadcast Industry
     Broadcast Television
     Closed Circuit Television
     Education

Educational Radio
Listening Groups
Multichannel Programing
Open Circuit Television
Telecourses
Televised Instruction
Viewing Time

EDUCATIONAL TESTING 180
BT   Testing
RT   Education
     Educational Research
     Prognostic Tests
     Psychological Testing

EDUCATIONAL THEORIES 140
BT   Theories
RT   Education
     Educational History
     Educational Objectives
     Educational Philosophy
     Educational Principles
     Educational Psychology
     Progressive Education

EDUCATIONAL THERAPY 090
BT   Therapy
RT   Counseling
     Diagnostic Tests
     Educational Diagnosis
     Emotional Adjustment
     Evaluation
     Guidance
     Intervention
     Medical Treatment
     Mental Health
     Psychoeducational Clinics
     Rehabilitation
     Remedial Programs
     Speech Therapy
     Therapeutic Environment

EDUCATIONAL TRENDS 140
RT   Education
     Educational Demand
     Educational Supply

Educational Trips
USE   INSTRUCTIONAL TRIPS

EDUCATION COURSES 110
BT   Courses
RT   Inservice Courses
     Methods Courses
     Teacher Education Curriculum

Education Factors
USE   EDUCATION

Education For Librarianship
USE   LIBRARY EDUCATION

EDUCATION MAJORS 140
BT   College Majors
RT   College Students
     Liberal Arts Majors
     Student Teachers
     Teacher Education
     Teacher Education Curriculum

Education Permanente
USE   CONTINUOUS LEARNING

EDUCATION SERVICE CENTERS 210
RT   Education
     Nature Centers
     Science Teaching Centers

EEG
USE   ELECTROENCEPHALOGRAPHY

EFFECTIVE TEACHING 270
UF   Teacher Effectiveness
BT   Teaching
RT   Relevance (Education)
     Teacher Evaluation

EFL
USE   ENGLISH (SECOND LANGUAGE)

Egg Inspectors
USE   FOOD AND DRUG INSPECTORS

Ego Strength
USE   SELF CONCEPT

EIDETIC IMAGES 070
RT   Thought Processes
     Vision

EIGHTEENTH CENTURY LITERATURE 260
BT   Literature
RT   English Literature
     French Literature
     Italian Literature
     Literary Criticism
     Romanticism
     Spanish Literature
     World Literature

Elected City Officials
USE   CITY OFFICIALS

ELECTIONS 230
NT   School Budget Elections
BT   Political Science
RT   Political Issues
     Voter Registration
     Voting
     Voting Rights

ELECTIVE READING 440
UF   Optional Reading
BT   Reading
RT   Recreational Reading

ELECTIVE SUBJECTS 110
RT   Curriculum
     Honors Curriculum
     Independent Study

Electrical Appliance Repairmen
USE   ELECTRICAL APPLIANCE SERVICEMEN

ELECTRICAL APPLIANCES 170
BT   Equipment
RT   Appliance Repairing
     Electrical Appliance Servicemen
     Electricity
     Electric Motors
     Home Furnishings

ELECTRICAL APPLIANCE SERVICEMEN 380
UF   Electrical Appliance Repairmen
     Home Appliance Servicemen
BT   Service Workers
RT   Electrical Appliances
     Electricians
     Repair
     Service Occupations
     Trade And Industrial Education

Electrical Communication Systems
USE   TELECOMMUNICATION

Electrical Controls
USE   ELECTRONIC CONTROL

ELECTRICAL OCCUPATIONS 350
UF   Electromechanical Occupations
     Electromechanical Technicians
BT   Occupations
RT   Appliance Repairing
     Electricians
     Electricity
     Electromechanical Technology
     Electronics
     Equipment Maintenance
     Semiskilled Occupations
     Skilled Occupations
     Trade And Industrial Education

ELECTRICAL STIMULI 070
BT   Stimuli
RT   Aural Stimuli
     Conditioned Stimulus
     Medical Treatment
     Pictorial Stimuli
     Stimulus Devices
     Verbal Stimuli
     Visual Stimuli

ELECTRICAL SYSTEMS 210
UF   Electric Systems
RT   Building Design
     Electricians
     Electricity
     Electronic Control
     Electronics
     Lighting
     Utilities

Electrical Technicians
USE   ELECTRONIC TECHNICIANS

ELECTRIC BATTERIES 170
UF   Batteries (Electric)
     Storage Batteries
RT   Electric Circuits
     Electricity
     Electronics

ELECTRIC CIRCUITS 170
UF   Circuitry
     Circuits (Electronic)
     Electronic Circuits
RT   Electric Batteries
     Electricity
     Electronics

ELECTRICIANS 380
BT   Skilled Workers
RT   Building Trades
     Electrical Appliance Servicemen
     Electrical Occupations
     Electrical Systems
     Electricity
     Electronics
     Electronic Technicians
     Skilled Occupations
     Trade And Industrial Education

ELECTRICITY 400
BT   Physics
RT   Electrical Appliances
     Electrical Occupations
     Electrical Systems
     Electric Batteries
     Electric Circuits
     Electricians
     Electric Motors
     Electromechanical Technology
     Electronics
     Electronic Technicians
     Electrooptics
     Force
     Magnets
     Potentiometers (Instruments)
     Transistors

ELECTRIC MOTORS 170
BT   Engines
RT   Electrical Appliances
     Electricity

Electric Systems
USE   ELECTRICAL SYSTEMS

Electric Utilities
USE   UTILITIES

Electrochromatography
USE   CHROMATOGRAPHY

ELECTROENCEPHALOGRAPHY 510
UF   EEG
RT   Biomedical Equipment
     Clinical Diagnosis
     Measurement Techniques
     Medical Evaluation
     Neurology

ELECTROMECHANICAL AIDS 050
BT   Instructional Aids
RT   Computers
     Educational Equipment
     Electromechanical Technology
     Electronic Classrooms
     Electronic Equipment
     Mechanical Teaching Aids

Electromechanical Occupations
USE   ELECTRICAL OCCUPATIONS

Electromechanical Technicians
USE   ELECTRICAL OCCUPATIONS

ELECTROMECHANICAL TECHNOLOGY 400
BT   Technology
RT   Aerospace Industry
     Automation
     Cybernetics
     Electrical Occupations
     Electricity
     Electromechanical Aids
     Electronic Control
     Electronics
     Electronics Industry
     Engineering
     Horology
     Mechanical Design Technicians

Electronic Aids
USE   ELECTRONIC EQUIPMENT

Electronic Circuits
USE   ELECTRIC CIRCUITS

ELECTRONIC CLASSROOMS 210
NT   Electronic Classroom Use
BT   Classrooms
RT   Audio Active Laboratories
     Audio Passive Laboratories
     Electromechanical Aids
     Electronic Equipment

ELECTRONIC CLASSROOM USE 210
BT   Electronic Classrooms

Electronic Communication Systems
USE   TELECOMMUNICATION

ELECTRONIC CONTROL 170
UF   Electrical Controls
     Magnetic Amplifiers
     Static Controls
RT   Automation
     Electrical Systems
     Electromechanical Technology
     Electronic Equipment
     Electronics
     Instrumentation
     Kinetics
     Numerical Control

ELECTRONIC DATA PROCESSING 080
SN Data processing by means of computers
UF ADP
    Automatic Data Processing
    EDP
BT Data Processing
RT Automation
    Computer Oriented Programs
    Computers
    Computer Science
    Computer Science Education
    Computer Storage Devices
    Data Bases
    Data Processing Occupations
    Display Systems
    Information Systems
    Input Output Devices
    Optical Scanners
    Programing
    Programing Languages

ELECTRONIC EQUIPMENT 170
UF Electronic Aids
NT Computers
    Computer Storage Devices
BT Equipment
RT Data Processing
    Display Systems
    Electromechanical Aids
    Electronic Classrooms
    Electronic Control
    Electronics
    Electronics Industry
    Facsimile Transmission
    Input Output Devices
    Instrumentation
    Instrumentation Technicians
    Loop Induction Systems
    Optical Scanners
    Radar
    Television
    Tracking
    Visible Speech

ELECTRONICS 400
BT Physics
RT Electrical Occupations
    Electrical Systems
    Electric Batteries
    Electric Circuits
    Electricians
    Electricity
    Electromechanical Technology
    Electronic Control
    Electronic Equipment
    Electronics Industry
    Electronic Technicians
    Industrial Arts
    Instrumentation Technicians
    Lasers
    Magnets
    Optics
    Radar

Trade And Industrial Education
Transistors

ELECTRONICS INDUSTRY 370
BT Industry
RT Electromechanical Technology
    Electronic Equipment
    Electronics
    Manufacturing Industry

ELECTRONIC TECHNICIANS 380
UF Electrical Technicians
BT Subprofessionals
RT Data Processing Occupations
    Electricians
    Electricity
    Electronics
    Engineering Technicians
    Medical Laboratory Assistants
    Technical Education
    Technical Occupations
    Trade And Industrial Education

Electrooptical Effects
USE ELECTROOPTICS

ELECTROOPTICS 400
UF Electrooptical Effects
BT Optics
RT Electricity
    Lasers
    Light

Electroplating
USE FINISHING

Elementary Curriculum
USE ELEMENTARY SCHOOL CURRICULUM

ELEMENTARY EDUCATION 140
NT Primary Education
BT Education
RT Elementary Grades
    Elementary Schools
    Elementary School Students
    Elementary School Teachers
    FLES
    Laboratory Schools

ELEMENTARY GRADES 280
UF Elementary Instructional Level
    Elementary Level
BT Instructional Program Divisions
RT Elementary Education
    Elementary School Curriculum

Elementary Instructional Level
USE ELEMENTARY GRADES

Elementary Level
USE ELEMENTARY GRADES

ELEMENTARY SCHOOL COUNSELING 090
BT Counseling
RT Consultation Programs
    Elementary School Guidance
    Elementary Schools

ELEMENTARY SCHOOL COUNSELORS 380
BT   Counselors
     Pupil Personnel Workers
RT   Consultants
     Counseling Programs
     Counseling Services
     Elementary Schools
     Guidance Personnel
     Guidance Services

ELEMENTARY SCHOOL CURRICULUM 110
UF   Elementary Curriculum
BT   Curriculum
RT   Elementary Grades
     Elementary Schools
     Ungraded Curriculum

ELEMENTARY SCHOOL GUIDANCE 090
BT   Guidance
RT   Consultation Programs
     Counseling Programs
     Elementary School Counseling
     Elementary Schools
     Guidance Personnel
     Guidance Programs
     Guidance Services

ELEMENTARY SCHOOL LIBRARIES 210
BT   School Libraries

ELEMENTARY SCHOOL MATHEMATICS 340
BT   Mathematics
RT   College Mathematics
     Mathematics Curriculum
     Mathematics Education
     Mathematics Instruction
     Secondary School Mathematics

ELEMENTARY SCHOOL ROLE 140
BT   School Role

ELEMENTARY SCHOOLS 470
NT   Biracial Elementary Schools
     Catholic Elementary Schools
BT   Schools
RT   Affiliated Schools
     Elementary Education
     Elementary School Counseling
     Elementary School Counselors
     Elementary School Curriculum
     Elementary School Guidance
     Elementary School Students
     Elementary School Supervisors
     Elementary School Teachers
     FLES Materials
     FLES Programs
     FLES Teachers

ELEMENTARY SCHOOL SCIENCE 110
BT   Science Education
RT   College Science
     Secondary School Science

ELEMENTARY SCHOOL STUDENTS 380
BT   Students
RT   Elementary Education
     Elementary Schools

ELEMENTARY SCHOOL SUPERVISORS 380
BT   Supervisors
RT   Elementary Schools
     School Administration

ELEMENTARY SCHOOL TEACHERS 380
BT   Teachers
RT   Elementary Education
     Elementary Schools
     Mathematics Teachers
     Public School Teachers

ELEMENTARY SCIENCE 110
BT   Science Curriculum

EMBRYOLOGY 070
BT   Biology
RT   Anatomy
     Botany
     Cytology
     Evolution
     Genetics
     Medicine
     Pathology
     Physiology
     Plant Growth
     Zoology

EMERGENCY PROGRAMS 020
UF   Disaster Readiness
     Emergency Readiness
BT   Programs
RT   Civil Defense
     School Safety

Emergency Readiness
USE   EMERGENCY PROGRAMS

EMERGENCY SQUAD PERSONNEL 380
UF   Ambulance Attendants
     Rescue Squad Personnel
BT   Service Workers
RT   Accidents
     Fire Fighters
     Fire Science Education
     First Aid
     Health Occupations
     Medical Services
     Police
     Rescue
     Service Occupations

Emerging Nations
USE   DEVELOPING NATIONS

EMOTIONAL ADJUSTMENT 420
BT   Adjustment (To Environment)
RT   Bibliotherapy
       Educational Therapy
       Emotionally Disturbed
       Emotional Maladjustment
       Emotional Problems
       Vocational Adjustment

EMOTIONAL DEVELOPMENT 130
BT   Development
RT   Affective Behavior
       Catharsis
       Empathy
       Progressive Retardation
       Psychological Patterns

EMOTIONAL EXPERIENCE 200
NT   Catharsis
BT   Experience
RT   Affection
       Psychological Patterns

Emotional Health
USE   MENTAL HEALTH

EMOTIONALLY DISTURBED 420
UF   Emotionally Handicapped
NT   Emotionally Disturbed Children
BT   Exceptional (Atypical)
RT   Anxiety
       Autism
       Behavior
       Behavior Problems
       Emotional Adjustment
       Emotional Maladjustment
       Hyperactivity
       Mental Illness
       Play Therapy
       Psychiatrists
       Schizophrenia
       Special Health Problems

EMOTIONALLY DISTURBED CHILDREN 380
UF   Emotionally Disturbed Pupils
BT   Children
       Emotionally Disturbed
RT   School Phobia

Emotionally Disturbed Pupils
USE   EMOTIONALLY DISTURBED CHILDREN

Emotionally Handicapped
USE   EMOTIONALLY DISTURBED

EMOTIONAL MALADJUSTMENT 420
BT   Maladjustment
RT   Autism
       Emotional Adjustment
       Emotionally Disturbed
       Psychiatrists
       Psychiatry

Emotional Patterns
USE   PSYCHOLOGICAL PATTERNS

EMOTIONAL PROBLEMS 420
BT   Problems
RT   Emotional Adjustment
       Psychological Patterns

EMPATHY 040
BT   Identification (Psychological)
RT   Behavior Patterns
       Emotional Development
       Imitation
       Psychological Characteristics
       Social Development

Employable Skills
USE   JOB SKILLS

EMPLOYEE ATTITUDES 040
SN   Attitude of employees on any subject
       other than work attitudes
UF   Employee Opinion
BT   Attitudes
RT   Employees
       Employer Employee Relationship
       Employment
       Work Attitudes

Employee Evaluation
USE   PERSONNEL EVALUATION

Employee Opinion
USE   EMPLOYEE ATTITUDES

Employee Relations
USE   INDUSTRIAL RELATIONS

EMPLOYEE RESPONSIBILITY 040
BT   Responsibility
RT   Employees
       Employer Employee Relationship
       Employment
       Indemnity Bonds
       Probationary Period

EMPLOYEES 380
NT   Entry Workers
       Government Employees
BT   Personnel
RT   Clerical Workers
       Employee Attitudes
       Employee Responsibility
       Employer Attitudes
       Employer Employee Relationship
       Employers
       Employment
       Employment Interviews
       Industrial Personnel
       Laborers
       Personnel Needs
       Professional Personnel
       Sales Workers
       Service Workers
       Skilled Workers
       Subprofessionals
       Teachers
       Unskilled Workers

EMPLOYER ATTITUDES 040
UF Employer Opinion
BT Attitudes
RT Employees
    Employer Employee Relationship
    Employers
    Employment

EMPLOYER EMPLOYEE RELATIONSHIP 150
NT Collective Bargaining
BT Relationship
RT Employee Attitudes
    Employee Responsibility
    Employees
    Employer Attitudes
    Employers
    Employment
    Industrial Relations
    Leave Of Absence
    Probationary Period
    Released Time
    Teacher Administrator Relationship
    Vocational Adjustment

Employer Opinion
USE EMPLOYER ATTITUDES

EMPLOYERS 380
RT Administrative Personnel
    Administrator Attitudes
    Employees
    Employer Attitudes
    Employer Employee Relationship
    Employment
    Employment Interviews
    Industrial Personnel

EMPLOYMENT 150
UF Dropout Employability
    Work
NT Migrant Employment
    Multiple Employment
    Negro Employment
    Overseas Employment
    Seasonal Employment
    Student Employment
    Teacher Employment
    Youth Employment
RT Careers
    Developed Nations
    Employee Attitudes
    Employee Responsibility
    Employees
    Employer Attitudes
    Employer Employee Relationship
    Employers
    Employment Experience
    Employment Interviews
    Employment Level
    Employment Opportunities
    Employment Patterns
    Employment Potential
    Employment Practices
    Employment Problems

    Employment Programs
    Employment Qualifications
    Employment Services
    Employment Trends
    Industrial Relations
    Job Applicants
    Labor Economics
    Man Days
    Manpower Utilization
    Occupational Surveys
    Occupational Therapists
    Occupations
    Persistence
    Personnel
    Personnel Directors
    Skilled Occupations
    Unemployed
    Unemployment
    Work Environment
    Working Hours
    Working Women

Employment Adjustment
USE VOCATIONAL ADJUSTMENT

Employment Change
USE CAREER CHANGE

EMPLOYMENT COUNSELORS 380
BT Counselors
RT Career Opportunities
    Employment Services
    Occupational Guidance
    Personnel

EMPLOYMENT EXPERIENCE 200
BT Experience
RT Employment
    Entry Workers
    Occupational Mobility
    Personnel Data
    Work Experience

Employment Forecasts
USE EMPLOYMENT PROJECTIONS

EMPLOYMENT INTERVIEWS 150
UF Job Interviews
BT Interviews
RT Employees
    Employers
    Employment
    Employment Qualifications
    Employment Services
    Job Application
    Personnel Selection

EMPLOYMENT LEVEL 150
RT Employment
    Promotion (Occupational)
    Unemployment

Employment Market
USE LABOR MARKET

EMPLOYMENT OPPORTUNITIES 360
UF Job Opportunities
     Job Vacancies
     Youth Work Opportunities
BT Opportunities
RT Career Change
     Career Choice
     Career Opportunities
     Demand Occupations
     Employment
     Employment Programs
     Employment Projections
     Employment Services
     Equal Opportunities (Jobs)
     Job Applicants
     Job Application
     Job Development
     Job Market
     Jobs
     Job Skills
     Labor Market
     Manpower Needs
     Occupational Choice
     Occupational Guidance
     Occupational Mobility
     Occupational Surveys
     Occupations
     Promotion (Occupational)
     Recruitment

EMPLOYMENT PATTERNS 150
RT Employment
     Employment Projections
     Employment Statistics
     Labor Economics
     Labor Turnover
     Occupational Surveys

EMPLOYMENT POTENTIAL 150
RT Employment
     Employment Qualifications
     Job Satisfaction
     Skill Obsolescence

EMPLOYMENT PRACTICES 150
RT Employment
     Job Layoff
     Loyalty Oaths

Employment Preparation
USE JOB TRAINING

EMPLOYMENT PROBLEMS 150
BT Problems
RT Arbitration
     Collective Bargaining
     Employment
     Job Development
     Negotiation Impasses
     Persistence
     Subemployment
     Unemployed

EMPLOYMENT PROGRAMS 490
BT Programs
RT Employment
     Employment Opportunities
     Employment Services

EMPLOYMENT PROJECTIONS 150
UF Employment Forecasts
RT Employment Opportunities
     Employment Patterns
     Employment Trends

EMPLOYMENT QUALIFICATIONS 500
BT Qualifications
RT Business Skills
     Employment
     Employment Interviews
     Employment Potential
     Entry Workers
     Home Economics Skills
     Job Analysis
     Job Applicants
     Job Application
     Job Skills
     Job Tenure
     Loyalty Oaths
     Mechanical Skills
     Occupational Information
     Office Occupations
     Personnel Data
     Personnel Evaluation
     Promotion (Occupational)
     Skill Obsolescence
     Task Analysis
     Vocational Aptitude
     Work Experience

Employment Referral Services
USE EMPLOYMENT SERVICES

Employment Satisfaction
USE JOB SATISFACTION

EMPLOYMENT SERVICES 150
UF Employment Referral Services
NT Job Placement
BT Human Services
RT Employment
     Employment Counselors
     Employment Interviews
     Employment Opportunities
     Employment Programs
     Exceptional Child Services
     Job Analysis
     Job Applicants
     Job Application
     Student Personnel Services

EMPLOYMENT STATISTICS 150
NT Man Days
BT Statistical Data
RT Employment Patterns
     Labor Market

156

Employment Surveys
USE OCCUPATIONAL SURVEYS

EMPLOYMENT TRENDS 150
RT Employment
Employment Projections
Labor Economics
Labor Turnover
Occupational Surveys

ENCYCLOPEDIAS 320
BT Reference Materials
RT Literature
Publications
Reference Books

ENERGY 400
BT Physics
RT Fatigue (Biology)
Force
Heat
Kinetics
Lasers
Light
Motion
Optics
Quantum Mechanics
Radiation
Relativity

Engine Development Technicians
USE MECHANICAL DESIGN TECHNICIANS

ENGINEERING 400
NT Agricultural Engineering
Civil Engineering
Human Engineering
Ocean Engineering
Operating Engineering
RT Aerospace Industry
Aerospace Technology
Electromechanical Technology
Engineering Technicians
Engineering Technology
Engineers
Highway Engineering Aides
Sciences
Site Development
Technology

ENGINEERING DRAWING 350
BT Drafting
RT Civil Engineering
Engineering Graphics
Graphic Arts

ENGINEERING EDUCATION 140
BT Education
RT Engineering Technology
Land Grant Universities
Science Education
Technical Education
Vocational Education

ENGINEERING GRAPHICS 350
BT Graphic Arts
RT Civil Engineering
Drafting
Engineering Drawing
Signs

Engineering Secretaries
USE SECRETARIES

Engineering Stenographers
USE STENOGRAPHERS

ENGINEERING TECHNICIANS 380
NT Highway Engineering Aides
BT Subprofessionals
RT Electronic Technicians
Engineering
Engineering Technology
Mechanical Design Technicians
Metallurgical Technicians
Production Technicians
Seamen
Technical Education
Technical Occupations

ENGINEERING TECHNOLOGY 400
BT Technology
RT Engineering
Engineering Education
Engineering Technicians
Technical Education

ENGINEERS 380
BT Personnel
Scientific Personnel
RT Engineering
Mathematicians
Professional Occupations
Scientists

ENGINES 170
NT Diesel Engines
Electric Motors
RT Agricultural Machinery
Auto Mechanics
Aviation Mechanics
Fuels
Hydraulics
Kinetics
Locomotive Engineers
Lubricants

ENGLISH 300
NT American English
Business English
English (Second Language)
Middle English
Old English
Oral English
BT Languages
Modern Languages
RT English Curriculum
English Education
English Instruction

English Programs
Linguistics

ENGLISH (SECOND LANGUAGE) 300
SN Non-English speaking students learning
    English as a second or foreign language
UF EFL
    ESL
    ESOL
    TEFL
    TENES
    TESL
    TESOL
BT English
RT Applied Linguistics
    Bilingual Education
    Bilingualism
    Bilingual Teacher Aides
    Bilingual Teachers
    Curriculum
    Instructional Materials Centers
    Language Programs
    Language Skills
    Linguistics
    Multilingualism
    Second Language Learning
    Second Languages
    Spanish Speaking
    Teaching Methods
    Teaching Techniques

ENGLISH CURRICULUM 110
BT Curriculum
RT English
    English Programs
    Essays

ENGLISH DEPARTMENTS 370
BT Departments
RT Administrative Organization
    Departmental Teaching Plans
    Department Directors (School)
    High School Organization
    Science Departments
    Universities

ENGLISH EDUCATION 140
BT Education
RT English
    Language
    Language Arts
    Language Development
    Language Instruction
    Language Laboratories
    Language Skills

ENGLISH INSTRUCTION 270
NT TENL
BT Instruction
RT English
    English Programs
    Student Writing Models

ENGLISH LITERATURE 260
NT Old English Literature
BT Literature
RT Baroque Literature
    Characterization (Literature)
    Eighteenth Century Literature
    English Neoclassic Literary Period
    Local Color Writing
    Metaphors
    Naturalism
    Nineteenth Century Literature
    Realism
    Twentieth Century Literature
    World Literature

ENGLISH NEOCLASSIC LITERARY PERIOD 260
SN The period in English literature between
    the years 1660 and 1798
UF Neoclassic English Literary Period
BT Literary History
RT Comedy
    Drama
    English Literature
    German Literature
    Literary Conventions
    Literary Criticism
    Literature
    Novels
    Poetry
    Prose
    Satire
    Tragedy

ENGLISH PROGRAMS 260
BT Programs
RT Curriculum
    English
    English Curriculum
    English Instruction
    Language Programs
    Languages
    Modern Languages

ENLISTED MEN 380
BT Military Personnel
RT Military Science
    Military Service
    Military Training
    Veterans

Enriching Experience
USE ENRICHMENT

ENRICHMENT 510
UF Enriching Experience
NT Academic Enrichment
    Cultural Enrichment
    Curriculum Enrichment
    Language Enrichment
    Mathematical Enrichment
RT Enrichment Activities
    Enrichment Experience
    Enrichment Programs

ENRICHMENT ACTIVITIES 510
BT   Activities
RT   Enrichment
     Enrichment Experience
     Enrichment Programs

ENRICHMENT EXPERIENCE 200
BT   Experience
RT   Enrichment
     Enrichment Activities
     Enrichment Programs

ENRICHMENT PROGRAMS 110
BT   Programs
RT   Enrichment
     Enrichment Activities
     Enrichment Experience

ENROLLMENT 020
NT   Average Daily Enrollment
     Language Enrollment
     Late School Entrance
     Open Enrollment
     Student Enrollment
RT   Admission (School)
     Early Admission
     Educational Demand
     Educational Supply
     Enrollment Influences
     Enrollment Projections
     Enrollment Rate
     Enrollment Trends

ENROLLMENT INFLUENCES 490
SN   Factors affecting enrollment
RT   Educational Demand
     Educational Supply
     Enrollment
     Enrollment Rate
     Enrollment Trends

ENROLLMENT PROJECTIONS 020
RT   Enrollment
     Enrollment Rate
     Enrollment Trends

ENROLLMENT RATE 020
RT   Average Daily Enrollment
     Enrollment
     Enrollment Influences
     Enrollment Projections
     Language Enrollment

ENROLLMENT TRENDS 020
RT   Enrollment
     Enrollment Influences
     Enrollment Projections
     Language Enrollment

ENTOMOLOGY 070
UF   Insects
BT   Biology
RT   Agriculture
     Evolution
     Horticulture
     Insecticides

Entrance Examinations
USE   COLLEGE ENTRANCE EXAMINATIONS

ENTRY WORKERS 380
UF   Beginning Workers
BT   Employees
RT   Employment Experience
     Employment Qualifications

ENUNCIATION IMPROVEMENT 290
RT   Diction
     Speech Improvement

ENVIRONMENT 160
UF   Atmosphere (Social)
NT   Classroom Environment
     Controlled Environment
     Cultural Environment
     Disadvantaged Environment
     Educational Environment
     Family Environment
     Institutional Environment
     Permissive Environment
     Physical Environment
     Rural Environment
     Slum Environment
     Social Environment
     Suburban Environment
     Therapeutic Environment
     Urban Environment
     Work Environment
RT   Ecology
     Environmental Criteria
     Environmental Education
     Environmental Influences
     Environmental Research
     Human Engineering
     Organizational Climate
     Pollution
     Pressure
     Temperature

ENVIRONMENTAL CRITERIA 500
SN   Standards by which to judge the effects
     of the physical environment on the
     human being
BT   Criteria
RT   Environment
     Environmental Research
     Environmental Technicians
     Research Criteria
     Standards

ENVIRONMENTAL EDUCATION 140
NT   Conservation Education
BT   Education
RT   Air Pollution Control
     Biological Sciences
     Ecology
     Environment
     Forestry
     Natural Resources
     Outdoor Education
     Pollution

Soil Conservation
Water Pollution Control

Environmental Factors
USE ENVIRONMENTAL INFLUENCES

ENVIRONMENTAL INFLUENCES 160
UF   Environmental Factors
RT   Acoustics
     Architectural Research
     Climatic Factors
     Color Planning
     Environment
     Environmental Research
     Humidity
     Individual Power
     Physical Environment
     Prenatal Influences
     Social Factors
     Social Responsibility
     Solar Radiation
     Thermal Environment

Environmental Learning
USE LEARNING

ENVIRONMENTAL RESEARCH 450
SN   Study of the relationship between the
     physical environment and the human
     subject
BT   Research
RT   Architectural Research
     Environment
     Environmental Criteria
     Environmental Influences
     Physical Environment

Environmental Sanitarian Assistant
USE ENVIRONMENTAL TECHNICIANS

ENVIRONMENTAL TECHNICIANS 380
UF   Environmental Sanitarian Assistant
     Sanitarian Technicians
     Sanitary Engineering Technicians
     Sanitary Inspectors
BT   Health Personnel
RT   Environmental Criteria
     Quality Control
     Sanitation Improvement

Epic Characteristics
USE EPICS

EPICS 260
UF   Epic Characteristics
BT   Poetry
RT   Allegory
     Ballads
     Classical Literature
     Composition (Literary)
     Didacticism
     Fables
     French Literature
     Legends
     Literary Analysis
     Lyric Poetry

Medieval Literature
Medieval Romance
Mythology
Old English Literature
Poets
Sonnets
Spanish American Literature
Spanish Literature
Versification

Epidemic Roseola
USE RUBELLA

EPILEPSY 240
BT   Diseases
RT   Handicapped
     Neurologically Handicapped
     Physically Handicapped
     Seizures
     Special Health Problems

EPISODE TEACHING 270
BT   Student Teaching
RT   Cooperating Teachers
     Microteaching
     Student Teachers
     Teacher Interns
     Teaching Techniques
     Team Teaching

EQUAL EDUCATION 230
UF   Educational Inequality
     Equal Educational Opportunities
     Equality Of Education
BT   Civil Rights
     Education

Equal Educational Opportunities
USE EQUAL EDUCATION

Equal Employment
USE EQUAL OPPORTUNITIES (JOBS)

EQUAL FACILITIES 210
UF   Equalized Facilities
BT   Facilities
RT   Civil Rights
     Public Facilities

Equality Of Education
USE EQUAL EDUCATION

EQUALIZATION AID 220
UF   Additional Aid
RT   Educational Finance
     Federal Aid
     Financial Policy
     Financial Support
     Fiscal Capacity
     Grants
     Resource Allocations
     State Aid
     State Federal Aid
     State Federal Support
     Tax Effort

Equalized Facilities
USE EQUAL FACILITIES

EQUAL OPPORTUNITIES (JOBS) 230
UF Equal Employment
BT Civil Rights
Opportunities
RT Employment Opportunities
Equal Protection
Job Development

EQUAL PROTECTION 230
BT Civil Rights
RT Civil Liberties
Courts
Equal Opportunities (Jobs)
Laws

EQUATED SCORES 190
BT Statistical Data
RT Comparative Statistics
Statistical Analysis
Testing
Test Interpretation
Test Results

Equilibrium Constants
USE CHEMICAL EQUILIBRIUM

EQUIPMENT 170
NT Athletic Equipment
Audio Equipment
Biomedical Equipment
Broadcast Reception Equipment
Building Equipment
Educational Equipment
Electrical Appliances
Electronic Equipment
Hand Tools
Laboratory Equipment
Measurement Instruments
Mechanical Equipment
Safety Equipment
RT Agricultural Machinery
Assembly (Manufacturing)
Equipment Maintenance
Equipment Manufacturers
Equipment Standards
Equipment Storage
Equipment Utilization
Facilities
Facility Inventory
Machinery Industry
Maintenance
Repair
Resources
Sanitary Facilities
School Buses
Storage
Supplies
Wheel Chairs

EQUIPMENT EVALUATION 180
BT Evaluation
RT Educational Specifications
Equipment Standards
Field Check
Inspection
Quality Control
School Visitation

Equipment Inventory
USE FACILITY INVENTORY

EQUIPMENT MAINTENANCE 170
UF Equipment Repair
Equipment Upkeep
BT Maintenance
RT Cleaning
Educational Equipment
Educational Specifications
Electrical Occupations
Equipment
Equipment Storage
Language Laboratory Equipment
Machine Repairmen
Mechanical Equipment
School Maintenance

EQUIPMENT MANUFACTURERS 370
BT Manufacturing Industry
RT Building Equipment
Educational Equipment
Equipment
Equipment Standards
Furniture Industry
Industry
Laboratory Equipment
Manufacturing
Mechanical Equipment
Science Equipment

Equipment Purchasing
USE PURCHASING

Equipment Repair
USE EQUIPMENT MAINTENANCE

EQUIPMENT STANDARDS 500
BT Standards
RT Equipment
Equipment Evaluation
Equipment Manufacturers
Field Check
Mechanical Equipment
Performance Specifications
Purchasing
Specifications

EQUIPMENT STORAGE 210
BT Storage
RT Equipment
Equipment Maintenance
Locker Rooms
Space Utilization
Warehouses

Equipment Upkeep
USE EQUIPMENT MAINTENANCE

EQUIPMENT UTILIZATION 170
RT Equipment
Facility Inventory
Mechanical Equipment
Operating Engineering

EQUIVALENCY TESTS 520
SN Tests to measure the extent to which
previous schooling or knowledge satisfies
course requirements
UF Advanced Credit Examinations
Advanced Standing Examinations
Credit By Examination
Ged Tests
Proficiency Examinations
BT Tests
RT Educational Certificates
Evaluation Techniques
Grade Equivalent Scales
Measurement Instruments
Measurement Techniques
Special Degree Programs
Student Certification
Student Evaluation

Ergonomics
USE HUMAN ENGINEERING

Error Of Refraction
USE AMETROPIA

ERROR PATTERNS 190
SN Systematically recurring errors affecting
all of a set of observations in same
manner
RT Educational Diagnosis
Evaluation Techniques
Testing

Escapees
USE REFUGEES

ESKIMOS 380
RT Ethnic Groups
Race
Racial Characteristics

ESL
USE ENGLISH (SECOND LANGUAGE)

ESOL
USE ENGLISH (SECOND LANGUAGE)

Esophoria
USE HETEROPHORIA

Esotropia
USE HETEROTROPIA

ESSAYS 260
BT Literary Genres
Literature
RT Ambiguity
Aristotelian Criticism
Composition (Literary)
Czech Literature
Didacticism
English Curriculum
Expository Writing
French Literature
Humor
Irony
Italian Literature
Local Color Writing
Metaphors
Narration
Parody
Polish Literature
Realism
Renaissance Literature
Romanticism
Satire
Seventeenth Century Literature
Spanish American Literature
Spanish Literature
Theoretical Criticism

ESSAY TESTS 520
BT Tests
RT Achievement Tests
Cognitive Tests
Interest Tests
Measurement Instruments
Test Construction
Verbal Tests

ESTATE PLANNING 220
BT Planning
RT Assessed Valuation
Capital
Finance Occupations
Investment
Money Management
Property Accounting
Property Appraisal
Taxes
Tax Rates
Trustees
Trusts (Financial)
Wills

ESTIMATED COSTS 220
BT Costs
RT Unit Costs

ESTONIAN 300
BT Finno Ugric Languages

ETHICAL INSTRUCTION 270
UF Moral Instruction
BT Instruction
RT Ethical Values
Ethics
Moral Values
Religious Education
Sex Education

ETHICAL VALUES 040
BT Values
RT Ethical Instruction
Ethics

ETHICS 490
UF Morals
RT Ethical Instruction
Ethical Values
Moral Values
Religious Education
Sex Education

Ethnic Community
USE ETHNIC GROUPS

Ethnic Cultural Groups
USE ETHNIC GROUPS

ETHNIC DISTRIBUTION 120
RT Ethnic Groups

Ethnic Factors
USE CULTURAL FACTORS

ETHNIC GROUPING 100
RT Ethnic Groups
Heterogeneous Grouping

ETHNIC GROUPS 100
UF Ethnic Community
Ethnic Cultural Groups
Racial Groups
NT Chinese Americans
Filipino Americans
Italian Americans
Japanese Americans
Korean Americans
Mexican Americans
Native Speakers
Spanish Americans
BT Groups
RT American Indian Culture
American Indians
Arabs
Black Community
Cultural Background
Culture
Eskimos
Ethnic Distribution
Ethnic Grouping
Ethnic Origins
Ethnic Status
Ethnic Stereotypes
Ethnic Studies
Ethnology
Foreign Culture

Ghettos
Indians
Jews
Minority Groups
Nationalism
Negroes
Puerto Rican Culture
Puerto Ricans
Race
Subculture
Tribes

Ethnic Group Studies
USE ETHNIC STUDIES

ETHNIC ORIGINS 100
RT Chinese Americans
Ethnic Groups
Ethnic Studies
Filipino Americans
Japanese Americans
Korean Americans
Regional Dialects

ETHNIC RELATIONS 490
BT Relationship
RT Ethnic Status
Ethnology
Group Relations

ETHNIC STATUS 100
RT Ethnic Groups
Ethnic Relations

ETHNIC STEREOTYPES 100
RT Ethnic Groups
Ethnic Studies

ETHNIC STUDIES 110
UF Ethnic Group Studies
NT African American Studies
BT Curriculum
RT African Literature
Cultural Factors
Ethnic Groups
Ethnic Origins
Ethnic Stereotypes
Minority Groups

Ethnic Unity
USE GROUP UNITY

ETHNOLOGY 480
BT Anthropology
RT Archaeology
Cross Cultural Studies
Cultural Background
Cultural Environment
Cultural Images
Cultural Interrelationships
Ethnic Groups
Ethnic Relations
Race Relations
Racial Recognition
Social Studies

Sociocultural Patterns
Sociology

ETIOLOGY 250
RT   Clinical Diagnosis
Delinquency Causes
Diagnostic Tests
Reading Diagnosis

ETV
USE EDUCATIONAL TELEVISION

ETYMOLOGY 290
NT   Onomastics
BT   Diachronic Linguistics
RT   American English
Comparative Analysis
Dialect Studies
Glottochronology
Language Classification
Language Research
Languages
Language Typology
Lexicography
Linguistic Patterns
Semantics
Statistical Analysis

EUROPEAN HISTORY 260
BT   History
RT   Science Education History
Science History
Western Civilization

EVALUATION 180
NT   Administrator Evaluation
Auditory Evaluation
Counselor Evaluation
Course Evaluation
Curriculum Evaluation
Dental Evaluation
Equipment Evaluation
Faculty Evaluation
Field Check
Medical Evaluation
Personnel Evaluation
Preschool Evaluation
Profile Evaluation
Program Evaluation
Property Appraisal
Psychological Evaluation
Relevance (Education)
Relevance (Information Retrieval)
Self Evaluation
Speech Evaluation
Student Evaluation
Teacher Evaluation
Textbook Evaluation
BT   Measurement
RT   Action Research
Answer Keys
Case Studies (Education)
Counseling Effectiveness
Educational Therapy
Evaluation Methods

Evaluation Needs
Evaluation Techniques
Evaluative Thinking
Expectation
Inspection
Measurement Techniques
Medical Treatment
Merit Rating Programs
National Competency Tests
Observation
Participant Satisfaction
Performance Criteria
Performance Specifications
School Visitation
Success Factors
Synthesis
Testing
Test Results
Tests
Validity

EVALUATION CRITERIA 500
BT   Criteria
RT   Evaluation Methods
Evaluation Techniques
Research Problems
Standards

Evaluation Designs
USE EVALUATION TECHNIQUES

EVALUATION METHODS 190
NT   Content Analysis
Cost Effectiveness
Followup Studies
Graduate Surveys
BT   Methods
RT   Action Research
Comparative Analysis
Correlation
Counselor Evaluation
Course Evaluation
Evaluation
Evaluation Criteria
Evaluation Techniques
Quality Control
Relevance (Information Retrieval)

EVALUATION NEEDS 180
BT   Needs
RT   Evaluation

Evaluation Procedures
USE EVALUATION TECHNIQUES

EVALUATION TECHNIQUES 190
UF   Evaluation Designs
Evaluation Procedures
BT   Techniques
RT   Action Research
Auditory Evaluation
Auditory Tests
Counselor Evaluation
Equivalency Tests
Error Patterns

Evaluation
Evaluation Criteria
Evaluation Methods
Grade Equivalent Scales

EVALUATIVE THINKING 310
BT Convergent Thinking
RT Critical Thinking
Evaluation
Productive Thinking
Validity

EVENING CLASSES 280
BT Classes (Groups Of Students)
RT Adult Education Programs
Day Programs
Daytime Programs
Evening Programs
Evening Students
Part Time Students

EVENING COLLEGES 470
BT Colleges
RT Evening Programs
Evening Students
Night Schools
Part Time Students
University Extension

EVENING COUNSELING PROGRAMS 090
BT Counseling Programs
RT Evening Programs

EVENING PROGRAMS 410
BT Programs
RT Day Programs
Daytime Programs
Evening Classes
Evening Colleges
Evening Counseling Programs
Evening Students
Extension Education
Night Schools
Part Time Students

EVENING STUDENTS 380
BT Students
RT Adult Students
Evening Classes
Evening Colleges
Evening Programs
Extension Education
Night Schools
Part Time Students

EVOLUTION 130
RT Anatomy
Astronomy
Biological Influences
Biology
Cell Theory
Ecology
Embryology
Entomology
Genetics
Heredity

Paleontology
Physiology
Zoology

EWE 300
BT African Languages

Examinations
USE TESTS

EXAMINERS 380
UF Test Examiners
BT Personnel
RT Testing
Tests

EXCEPTIONAL (ATYPICAL) 380
NT Emotionally Disturbed
Exceptional Children
Exceptional Students
Gifted
Handicapped
Homebound
RT Cerebral Palsy
Deaf Blind
Exceptional Child Research
Hard Of Hearing
Hearing Therapy
Hospitalized Children
Intervention
Mentally Handicapped
Multiply Handicapped
Partially Sighted
Retarded Children
Special Education Teachers
Special Health Problems
Talent

EXCEPTIONAL CHILD EDUCATION 140
BT Education
RT Individual Instruction
Learning Disabilities
Self Care Skills
Special Classes
Special Education
Special Programs
Special Schools
Special Services
Telephone Instruction

EXCEPTIONAL CHILDREN 380
BT Children
Exceptional (Atypical)
RT Itinerant Teachers

EXCEPTIONAL CHILD RESEARCH 450
BT Research
RT Behavioral Science Research
Deaf Research
Educational Research
Exceptional (Atypical)
Gifted
Handicapped
Medical Research
Personality Studies
Psychological Studies

EXCEPTIONAL CHILD SERVICES 090
BT   Human Services
RT   Community Services
     Day Camp Programs
     Day Care Programs
     Employment Services
     Professional Services
     Recreational Programs
     Rehabilitation
     School Services
     Special Services

EXCEPTIONAL STUDENTS 380
NT   Talented Students
BT   Exceptional (Atypical)
     Students
RT   Handicapped Students

EXCHANGE PROGRAMS 490
NT   Student Exchange Programs
     Teacher Exchange Programs
BT   Programs
RT   Cultural Exchange
     Interinstitutional Cooperation

Excursions
USE INSTRUCTIONAL TRIPS

Executive Development
USE MANAGEMENT DEVELOPMENT

Executive Secretaries
USE SECRETARIES

EXERCISE (PHYSIOLOGY) 390
UF   Gymnastics
     Muscular Exercise
     Physical Exercise
NT   Calisthenics
BT   Physical Activities
RT   Athletic Activities
     Fatigue (Biology)
     Lifting
     Muscular Strength
     Physical Fitness
     Running
     Tumbling

EXHAUSTING 210
RT   Air Conditioning
     Air Flow
     Air Pollution Control
     Chimneys
     Controlled Environment
     Fuel Consumption
     Heating
     Mechanical Equipment
     Ventilation

Exhaustion
USE FATIGUE (BIOLOGY)

Exhaust Stacks
USE CHIMNEYS

EXHIBITS 050
BT   Audiovisual Aids
RT   Display Panels
     Realia

Exiles
USE REFUGEES

EXISTENTIALISM 260
BT   Philosophy
RT   Art
     Fiction
     Individualism
     Literary Criticism
     Literature
     Novels
     Prose
     Short Stories
     Twentieth Century Literature

Exophoria
USE HETEROPHORIA

Exotropia
USE HETEROTROPIA

Expansion
USE SCHOOL EXPANSION

Expectancy
USE EXPECTATION

EXPECTANCY TABLES 340
BT   Tables (Data)
RT   Expectation
     Prediction
     Probability
     Statistical Analysis
     Statistics

EXPECTATION 180
UF   Expectancy
NT   Work Life Expectancy
RT   Aptitude
     Evaluation
     Expectancy Tables
     Observation
     Performance
     Prediction
     Predictive Validity
     Probability
     Probability Theory
     Reliability

Expenditure Per Pupil
USE EXPENDITURE PER STUDENT

EXPENDITURE PER STUDENT 220
UF   Expenditure Per Pupil
BT   Expenditures
RT   Costs
     Educational Finance
     School District Spending

EXPENDITURES 220
UF Expenses
NT Costs
   Expenditure Per Student
   Initial Expenses
   Library Expenditures
   Operating Expenses
   Salaries
   School District Spending
RT Bids
   Budgeting
   Budgets
   Cost Effectiveness
   Educational Finance
   Tax Rates

Expenses
USE EXPENDITURES

EXPERIENCE 200
NT Discussion Experience
   Early Experience
   Educational Experience
   Emotional Experience
   Employment Experience
   Enrichment Experience
   Group Experience
   Intellectual Experience
   Learning Experience
   Limited Experience
   Mathematical Experience
   Prereading Experience
   Sensory Experience
   Social Experience
   Student Experience
   Teacher Experience
   Teaching Experience
   Work Experience
BT Background
   Continuous Learning

EXPERIENCE CHARTS 170
BT Teaching Techniques
RT Reading Instruction

EXPERIENCED LABORERS 380
UF Experienced Workers
BT Laborers
RT Job Skills

Experienced Workers
USE EXPERIENCED LABORERS

Experience Units
USE ACTIVITY UNITS

EXPERIMENTAL COLLEGES 470
UF Free Universities
BT Colleges
RT Curriculum Development
   Educational Improvement
   Educational Philosophy
   Experimental Curriculum
   Experimental Groups
   Experimental Programs

   Experimental Schools
   Experimental Teaching
   Innovation
   Learning Processes
   Relevance (Education)
   Self Directed Groups
   Student Interests
   Student Participation
   Student School Relationship
   Universities

EXPERIMENTAL CURRICULUM 110
BT Curriculum
RT Experimental Colleges
   Experimental Teaching

Experimental Extinction
USE EXTINCTION (PSYCHOLOGY)

EXPERIMENTAL GROUPS 450
BT Groups
RT Control Groups
   Experimental Colleges
   Research Methodology

EXPERIMENTAL PROGRAMS 450
BT Programs
RT Experimental Colleges
   Experimental Teaching
   Experiments
   Institutional Research
   Research
   Research Needs

EXPERIMENTAL PSYCHOLOGY 420
BT Psychology
RT Behavioral Science Research
   Experiments
   Extinction (Psychology)
   Laboratory Experiments
   Psychological Studies
   Research

EXPERIMENTAL SCHOOLS 470
UF Project Schools
BT Schools
RT Experimental Colleges
   Laboratory Schools
   Teaching Experience

Experimental Studies
USE RESEARCH

EXPERIMENTAL TEACHING 270
BT Educational Research
   Teaching
RT Educational Development
   Experimental Colleges
   Experimental Curriculum
   Experimental Programs
   Teaching Methods

Experimentation
USE EXPERIMENTS

EXPERIMENTS 510
UF Experimentation
NT Educational Experiments
    Laboratory Experiments
    Science Experiments
RT Experimental Programs
    Experimental Psychology
    Experiment Stations
    Research

EXPERIMENT STATIONS 210
UF Field Stations
RT Agricultural Colleges
    Agricultural Research Projects
    Experiments
    Research And Development Centers
    Scientific Research

Exploratory Studies
USE RESEARCH

EXPORTS 460
UF Export Trade
RT Business
    Economics
    Foreign Relations
    International Trade Vocabulary

Export Trade
USE EXPORTS

Exposition (Literary)
USE EXPOSITORY WRITING

EXPOSITORY WRITING 080
SN Form of written prose that deals with
    definitions, processes, generalizations,
    and the clarification of ideas and
    principles, with the intent of presenting
    meanings in readily communicable and
    unemotive language
UF Exposition (Literary)
BT Writing
RT Composition (Literary)
    Composition Skills (Literary)
    Creative Writing
    Descriptive Writing
    Direction Writing
    Essays
    Prose
    Rhetoric
    Student Writing Models
    Technical Writing
    Writing Exercises
    Writing Skills

EXPRESSIONISM 260
BT Philosophy
RT Art
    Drama
    Fiction
    Literature
    Music
    Novels
    Poetry

Prose
Twentieth Century Literature

EXPRESSIVE LANGUAGE 290
BT Language
RT Aphasia
    Idioms
    Language Development
    Language Fluency
    Language Handicapped
    Language Skills
    Language Styles
    Paralinguistics
    Proverbs
    Receptive Language
    Speaking

EXPULSION 020
SN Forced withdrawal from school
BT Discipline
RT Academic Failure
    Dropouts
    School Attendance Laws
    Suspension
    Withdrawal

Extended Day Programs
USE EXTENDED SCHOOL DAY

EXTENDED SCHOOL DAY 020
UF Extended Day Programs
RT Compensatory Education

EXTENDED SCHOOL YEAR 020
UF Lengthened School Year
RT Quarter System
    School Calendars
    School Schedules
    Semester Division
    Summer Schools
    Trimester Schedules
    Year Round Schools

EXTENSION AGENTS 380
RT Adult Educators
    Agricultural Personnel
    Instructional Staff

EXTENSION EDUCATION 140
SN Instructional activities of educational
    institutions directed to clientele outside
    immediate student body
UF Extension Services
NT Library Extension
    Rural Extension
    University Extension
    Urban Extension
BT Education
RT Colleges
    Community Development
    Correspondence Courses
    Correspondence Schools
    Evening Programs
    Evening Students
    Home Study
    Mobile Educational Services

Night Schools
Part Time Students
Rural Education
Universities
Urban Education

Extension Services
USE EXTENSION EDUCATION

EXTINCTION (PSYCHOLOGY) 420
SN Progressive reduction in conditioned
response after prolonged repetition of
the eliciting stimulus without
reinforcement
UF Experimental Extinction
RT Conditioned Response
Conditioned Stimulus
Experimental Psychology
Reinforcement
Retention
Stimulus Behavior

Extracurricular Activities
USE COCURRICULAR ACTIVITIES

Extrainstructional Duties
USE NONINSTRUCTIONAL RESPONSIBILITY

EXTRAMURAL ATHLETIC PROGRAMS 390
UF Extramural Sports
BT Athletic Programs
RT Intramural Athletic Programs

Extramural Departments
USE UNIVERSITY EXTENSION

Extramural Sports
USE EXTRAMURAL ATHLETIC PROGRAMS

Extrateaching Duties
USE NONINSTRUCTIONAL RESPONSIBILITY

EYE FIXATIONS 070
BT Eye Movements

EYE HAND COORDINATION 070
BT Psychomotor Skills
RT Eye Movements
Motor Development
Object Manipulation
Tracking

EYE MOVEMENTS 070
NT Eye Fixations
Eye Regressions
RT Eye Hand Coordination
Eyes
Eye Voice Span
Pupillary Dilation
Reading Skills

EYE REGRESSIONS 070
BT Eye Movements

EYES 070
RT Anatomy
Eye Movements
Ophthalmology
Optometrists
Pupillary Dilation
Vision
Visual Discrimination
Visually Handicapped
Visual Perception

EYE VOICE SPAN 010
BT Oral Reading
RT Eye Movements
Perceptual Motor Coordination
Reading Skills
Speech Skills
Visual Perception

FABLES 260
BT Literary Genres
Literature
RT Allegory
Classical Literature
Composition (Literary)
Didacticism
Epics
French Literature
Medieval Literature
Metaphors
Mythology
Russian Literature
Satire
Seventeenth Century Literature
Spanish American Literature
Spanish Literature
Versification

Fabrication
USE MANUFACTURING

FACILITIES 210
NT Air Structures
Animal Facilities
Buildings
Bus Garages
Corridors
Dining Facilities
Educational Facilities
Equal Facilities
Fallout Shelters
Flexible Facilities
Greenhouses
Health Facilities
Institutional Facilities
Military Air Facilities
Music Facilities
Nurseries (Horticulture)
Offices (Facilities)
Parking Areas
Parking Facilities
Personal Care Homes
Physical Facilities
Public Facilities

Recreational Facilities
Sanitary Facilities
Science Facilities
Student Unions
Theaters
Warehouses
Windowless Rooms
RT   Building Materials
Design Needs
Educational Specifications
Equipment
Facility Expansion
Facility Guidelines
Facility Improvement
Facility Inventory
Facility Requirements
Interior Space
Landlords
Research And Development Centers
Resources
Space Utilization

Facilities Needs
USE   FACILITY REQUIREMENTS

FACILITY CASE STUDIES 450
SN   Gathering and organizing of all relevant
material to enable analysis and
explication of facilities
BT   Case Studies
Research
RT   College Planning
Facility Guidelines
Facility Inventory
Facility Requirements
Facility Utilization Research
Site Analysis

FACILITY EXPANSION 210
RT   Building Conversion
Campus Planning
Consortia
Construction Programs
Facilities
Facility Guidelines
Facility Improvement
Facility Requirements
Purchasing
Site Analysis
Space Utilization

FACILITY GUIDELINES 210
SN   Written guidelines, specifications,
standards, or criteria used in assessing
physical facility requirements
UF   Facility Specifications
Facility Standards
BT   Guidelines
RT   Building Design
Campus Planning
College Planning
Component Building Systems
Construction Needs
Educational Facilities

Educational Specifications
Facilities
Facility Case Studies
Facility Expansion
Facility Inventory
Facility Requirements
Facility Utilization Research
Master Plans
School Planning
Site Analysis
Space Utilization

FACILITY IMPROVEMENT 210
BT   Improvement
RT   Building Improvement
Building Obsolescence
Buildings
Consortia
Facilities
Facility Expansion

FACILITY INVENTORY 210
UF   Equipment Inventory
Materials Inventory
Property Inventory
RT   Classification
College Planning
Construction Programs
Educational Facilities
Equipment
Equipment Utilization
Facilities
Facility Case Studies
Facility Guidelines
Facility Requirements
Facility Utilization Research
Property Accounting
Resources
Space Classification
Supplies

FACILITY REQUIREMENTS 500
SN   Any aspect of the physical plant
determined necessary to accommodate
various functions
UF   Facilities Needs
BT   Needs
RT   Building Design
Building Plans
Campus Planning
College Planning
Construction Needs
Educational Facilities
Educational Specifications
Facilities
Facility Case Studies
Facility Expansion
Facility Guidelines
Facility Inventory
Facility Utilization Research
Master Plans
School Planning
Space Utilization
Storage

Facility Specifications
USE FACILITY GUIDELINES

Facility Standards
USE FACILITY GUIDELINES

FACILITY UTILIZATION RESEARCH 210
BT Study
RT Class Size
College Planning
Construction Programs
Educational Facilities
Educational Specifications
Facility Case Studies
Facility Guidelines
Facility Inventory
Facility Requirements
Scheduling
Space Classification
Space Utilization

FACSIMILE COMMUNICATION SYSTEMS 080
NT Facsimile Transmission
BT Telecommunication
RT Information Networks
Telephone Communication Systems

FACSIMILE TRANSMISSION 050
UF Fax
Telefacsimile
Telefax
BT Facsimile Communication Systems
RT Audiovisual Communication
Dial Access Information Systems
Electronic Equipment
Information Dissemination
Input Output Devices
Telephone Communication Systems

FACTOR ANALYSIS 340
BT Statistical Analysis
RT Discriminant Analysis
Factor Structure
Item Analysis
Q Sort
Testing

FACTOR STRUCTURE 450
RT Factor Analysis

FACTUAL READING 440
BT Reading
RT Reading Comprehension
Reading Development
Reading Skills

FACULTY 380
NT College Faculty
Faculty Advisors
Instructional Staff
Ombudsmen
BT School Personnel
RT Art Teachers
Consultants
Faculty Evaluation
Faculty Fellowships
Faculty Integration
Faculty Mobility
Faculty Recruitment
Public School Teachers
Science Consultants
Science Teachers

FACULTY ADVISORS 380
UF Faculty Counselor
BT Faculty
RT Counselors
Educational Counseling
Educational Guidance
Educational Planning
Foreign Student Advisers
Ombudsmen

Faculty Counselor
USE FACULTY ADVISORS

FACULTY EVALUATION 180
BT Evaluation
RT Course Evaluation
Curriculum Evaluation
Faculty
Personnel Evaluation
Program Evaluation

FACULTY FELLOWSHIPS 220
BT Fellowships
RT Faculty

FACULTY INTEGRATION 430
UF Integrated Faculty
Integrated School Faculty
NT Teacher Integration
RT Faculty
Racial Integration
Social Integration

Faculty Load
USE TEACHING LOAD

FACULTY MOBILITY 120
BT Mobility
RT Faculty
Occupational Mobility

Faculty Offices
USE OFFICES (FACILITIES)

FACULTY ORGANIZATIONS 370
BT Organizations (Groups)
RT Committees
Groups

FACULTY PROMOTION 020
UF Advancement
Rank Upgrading
Salary Raise
NT Teacher Promotion
BT Promotion (Occupational)
RT Salaries

FACULTY RECRUITMENT 150
NT   Teacher Recruitment
BT   Recruitment
RT   Faculty
     Loyalty Oaths

Failure
USE   ACADEMIC FAILURE

FAILURE FACTORS 180
RT   Academic Failure
     Plagiarism
     Success Factors

FALLOUT SHELTERS 210
UF   Air Raid Shelters
     Bomb Shelters
BT   Facilities
RT   Safety
     Windowless Rooms

Familial Culture
USE   FAMILY LIFE

FAMILY (SOCIOLOGICAL UNIT) 490
UF   Family Factors
     Households
NT   Foster Family
     Heads Of Households
     One Parent Family
     Rural Family
RT   Birth Order
     Family Attitudes
     Family Background
     Family Characteristics
     Family Environment
     Family Health
     Family Income
     Family Influence
     Family Involvement
     Family Life
     Family Management
     Family Mobility
     Family Planning
     Family Problems
     Family Programs
     Family Projects
     Family Relationship
     Family Resources
     Family Role
     Family School Relationship
     Family Status
     Family Structure
     Housewives
     Marriage
     Parents
     Siblings
     Twins

FAMILY ATTITUDES 040
BT   Attitudes
RT   Family (Sociological Unit)
     Family Counseling

FAMILY BACKGROUND 200
BT   Background
RT   Family (Sociological Unit)

Family Breadwinners
USE   HEADS OF HOUSEHOLDS

FAMILY CHARACTERISTICS 490
RT   Family (Sociological Unit)
     Heads Of Households
     One Parent Family
     Student Characteristics

FAMILY COUNSELING 090
BT   Counseling
RT   Crisis Therapy
     Family Attitudes
     Family Influence
     Family Problems
     Family Relationship
     Group Counseling
     Group Dynamics
     Group Therapy
     Marriage Counseling
     Parent Child Relationship
     Therapy

Family Dinner Service Specialists
USE   COOKS

Family Economics
USE   CONSUMER ECONOMICS

FAMILY ENVIRONMENT 160
UF   Home
     Home Conditions
     Home Environment
BT   Environment
RT   Family (Sociological Unit)
     Family Influence
     One Parent Family
     Permissive Environment

Family Factors
USE   FAMILY (SOCIOLOGICAL UNIT)

FAMILY HEALTH 250
BT   Health
RT   Family (Sociological Unit)
     Homemaking Education

FAMILY INCOME 220
BT   Income
RT   Family (Sociological Unit)
     Family Resources
     Family Status

FAMILY INFLUENCE 490
UF   Home Influence
NT   Fatherless Family
RT   Family (Sociological Unit)
     Family Counseling
     Family Environment
     Family Status
     Fatherless Family
     Motherless Family

One Parent Family
Parental Aspiration
Parent Attitudes
Parent Participation
Parent Reaction
Parent Role

FAMILY INVOLVEMENT 490
RT   Family (Sociological Unit)
     Family Life Education

FAMILY LIFE 490
UF   Familial Culture
     Family Living
     Home Life
RT   Children
     Family (Sociological Unit)
     Family Life Education
     Family Programs
     Family Projects
     Homemaking Education
     Housewives
     Marital Instability
     Marriage
     Marriage Counseling
     Parents

FAMILY LIFE EDUCATION 140
UF   Home And Family Life Education
BT   Education
RT   Consumer Education
     Family Involvement
     Family Life
     Family Management
     Family Relationship
     Homemaking Education

Family Living
USE   FAMILY LIFE

FAMILY MANAGEMENT 490
BT   Management
RT   Family (Sociological Unit)
     Family Life Education
     Homemaking Education
     Home Management
     Housewives
     Money Management

FAMILY MOBILITY 120
BT   Mobility
RT   Family (Sociological Unit)

FAMILY PLANNING 490
BT   Planning
RT   Contraception
     Family (Sociological Unit)
     Population Trends

FAMILY PROBLEMS 490
BT   Problems
RT   Child Abuse
     Children
     Family (Sociological Unit)
     Family Counseling
     Marital Instability

Marriage Counseling
Parents
Visiting Homemakers

FAMILY PROGRAMS 410
BT   Programs
RT   Family (Sociological Unit)
     Family Life

FAMILY PROJECTS 490
BT   Projects
RT   Family (Sociological Unit)
     Family Life

FAMILY RELATIONSHIP 490
NT   Parent Child Relationship
     Parent Student Relationship
BT   Relationship
RT   Child Rearing
     Family (Sociological Unit)
     Family Counseling
     Family Life Education
     Family Status
     Homemaking Education
     Housewives

FAMILY RESOURCES 460
BT   Resources
RT   Family (Sociological Unit)
     Family Income
     Family Status

FAMILY ROLE 490
RT   Child Role
     Family (Sociological Unit)
     Housewives
     Parent Role
     Student Role

FAMILY SCHOOL RELATIONSHIP 490
UF   Home School Relationship
     School Family Relationship
     School Home Relationship
BT   Relationship
RT   Culture Conflict
     Family (Sociological Unit)
     Parental Grievances
     Parent School Relationship
     Parent Student Relationship
     Schools
     Student School Relationship

FAMILY STATUS 490
BT   Status
RT   Family (Sociological Unit)
     Family Income
     Family Influence
     Family Relationship
     Family Resources

FAMILY STRUCTURE 490
RT   Dependents
     Family (Sociological Unit)
     Housewives

Family Unity
USE   GROUP UNITY

FANTASY 420
BT Psychological Patterns
RT Fiction
  Imagination
  Science Fiction

FARM ACCOUNTS 020
RT Accountants
  Business Subjects
  Farm Management
  Records (Forms)

Farm Animals
USE LIVESTOCK

FARM COMMITTEES 370
BT Committees
RT Farmers
  Farm Labor Problems
  Rural Farm Residents

FARMERS 380
UF Farm Operators
NT Part Time Farmers
BT Agricultural Personnel
RT Adult Farmer Education
  Agricultural Chemical Occupations
  Agricultural Laborers
  Agricultural Occupations
  Agriculture
  Dairymen
  Farm Committees
  Farm Management
  Farm Occupations
  Farm Visits
  Rural Farm Residents
  Young Farmer Education

Farm Foremen
USE CREW LEADERS

FARM LABOR 150
BT Labor
RT Agricultural Occupations
  Agricultural Personnel
  Farm Labor Legislation
  Farm Labor Problems
  Farm Labor Supply
  Farm Occupations
  Part Time Farmers

Farm Laborers
USE AGRICULTURAL LABORERS

FARM LABOR LEGISLATION 230
BT Labor Legislation
RT Farm Labor

FARM LABOR PROBLEMS 150
BT Labor Problems
RT Farm Committees
  Farm Labor

FARM LABOR SUPPLY 150
BT Labor Supply
RT Farm Labor

FARM MANAGEMENT 020
BT Management
RT Agricultural Education
  Agricultural Engineering
  Agriculture
  Farm Accounts
  Farmers
  Farm Visits
  Part Time Farmers

FARM MECHANICS (OCCUPATION) 380
BT Skilled Workers
RT Agricultural Engineering
  Agricultural Machinery Occupations
  Agricultural Personnel
  Agriculture

Farm Mechanics (Subject Field)
USE AGRICULTURAL ENGINEERING

Farm Mechanics Shops
USE SCHOOL SHOPS

FARM OCCUPATIONS 350
BT Agricultural Occupations
RT Agricultural Chemical Occupations
  Agricultural Education
  Agricultural Laborers
  Agriculture
  Dairymen
  Farmers
  Farm Labor
  Off Farm Agricultural Occupations
  Part Time Farmers
  Vocational Agriculture

Farm Operators
USE FARMERS

Farm Related Occupations
USE OFF FARM AGRICULTURAL
  OCCUPATIONS

Farm Shops
USE SCHOOL SHOPS

Farm Supplies
USE AGRICULTURAL SUPPLIES

FARM VISITS 510
RT Adult Farmer Education
  Agriculture
  Farmers
  Farm Management
  Instructional Trips
  Supervised Farm Practice
  Young Farmer Education

Farm Workers
USE AGRICULTURAL LABORERS

Farm Youth
USE RURAL YOUTH

Farsightedness
USE HYPEROPIA

174

FATHERLESS FAMILY 490
UF Fatherless Home
BT Family Influence
     One Parent Family
RT Family Influence
     Heads Of Households
     Illegitimate Births

Fatherless Home
USE FATHERLESS FAMILY

Father Role
USE PARENT ROLE

FATHERS 380
NT Middle Class Fathers
BT Parents
RT Parent Associations

FATIGUE (BIOLOGY) 250
UF Exhaustion
     Weariness
RT Energy
     Exercise (Physiology)
     Health
     Physical Fitness
     Sensory Deprivation

Fax
USE FACSIMILE TRANSMISSION

FEAR 420
BT Psychological Patterns
RT School Phobia

FEASIBILITY STUDIES 450
BT Research
RT Surveys

FEDERAL AID 220
UF Federal Grants
RT Educational Finance
     Equalization Aid
     Federal Government
     Federal Programs
     Financial Support
     Foundation Programs
     Incentive Grants
     Land Grant Universities
     State Federal Aid
     State Federal Support
     Training Allowances
     Veterans Education

Federal Court Action
USE FEDERAL COURT LITIGATION

Federal Court Decisions
USE FEDERAL COURT LITIGATION

FEDERAL COURT LITIGATION 230
UF Federal Court Action
     Federal Court Decisions
BT Court Litigation
RT Federal Courts

FEDERAL COURTS 230
BT Courts
RT Federal Court Litigation
     Federal Government
     Federal Legislation

FEDERAL GOVERNMENT 230
BT Government (Administrative Body)
RT Depository Libraries
     Federal Aid
     Federal Courts
     Federal Laws
     Federal Legislation
     Federal Programs
     Federal State Relationship
     Federal Troops
     Government Publications
     Immigration Inspectors
     Military Organizations
     National Libraries
     State Church Separation

Federal Grants
USE FEDERAL AID

FEDERAL LAWS 230
BT Laws
RT Civil Liberties
     Federal Government
     Immigration Inspectors
     Legislators
     Loyalty Oaths
     Patents

FEDERAL LEGISLATION 230
BT Legislation
RT Drug Legislation
     Educational Legislation
     Federal Courts
     Federal Government
     Federal Programs
     Federal Recreation Legislation
     Legislators
     Loyalty Oaths
     State Legislation

Federal Libraries
USE GOVERNMENT LIBRARIES

FEDERAL PROGRAMS 230
BT Programs
RT Federal Aid
     Federal Government
     Federal Legislation
     Student Loan Programs

FEDERAL RECREATION LEGISLATION 230
BT Recreation Legislation
RT Federal Legislation

FEDERAL STATE RELATIONSHIP 230
BT   Relationship
RT   Board Administrator Relationship
Civil Rights
Federal Government
State Government
State School District Relationship
States Powers

FEDERAL TROOPS 370
RT   Armed Forces
Federal Government
Immigration Inspectors
Military Personnel
Military Service

FEEDBACK 080
UF   Knowledge Of Results
BT   Learning Processes
RT   Cybernetics
Grades (Scholastic)
Information Processing
Man Machine Systems
Programed Instruction
Reinforcement

FEEDER PATTERNS 120
RT   Demography
Feeder Programs
School Redistricting

FEEDER PROGRAMS 410
BT   Programs
RT   Feeder Patterns
School Integration

FEED INDUSTRY 370
BT   Industry
RT   Agricultural Supplies
Agricultural Supply Occupations
Agriculture
Feed Stores
Food
Food Processing Occupations
Grains (Food)
Off Farm Agricultural Occupations

FEED STORES 210
UF   Livestock Feed Stores
RT   Agricultural Supplies
Feed Industry
Merchandising

FEES 220
UF   Dues
NT   Tuition
RT   Costs
Financial Support
Fines (Penalties)

FELLOWSHIPS 110
NT   Faculty Fellowships
BT   Private Financial Support
RT   Educational Finance

FEMALES 070
UF   Girls
Women
NT   Housewives
Working Women
BT   Sex (Characteristics)
RT   Women Teachers

Fenestration
USE   WINDOWS

Fenno Ugric Languages
USE   FINNO UGRIC LANGUAGES

FERTILIZERS 070
RT   Agricultural Chemical Occupations
Agricultural Supplies
Agriculture
Plant Growth
Plant Science
Soil Science

FICTION 260
NT   Science Fiction
BT   Literary Genres
Literature
RT   Ambiguity
Aristotelian Criticism
Characterization (Literature)
Czech Literature
Didacticism
Existentialism
Expressionism
Fantasy
French Literature
German Literature
Humor
Impressionistic Criticism
Literary Conventions
Literary Influences
Literary Perspective
Local Color Writing
Metaphors
Mythic Criticism
Narration
Naturalism
Parody
Pastoral Literature
Polish Literature
Realism
Romanticism
Russian Literature
Satire
Sociological Novels
Spanish American Literature
Spanish Literature
Surrealism
Symbols (Literary)
Theoretical Criticism

FIELD CHECK 180
SN Examination, inspection, and
     investigation of equipment
BT Evaluation
RT Educational Specifications
     Equipment Evaluation
     Equipment Standards
     Inspection

FIELD CROPS 070
NT Corn (Field Crop)
     Grains (Food)
RT Agricultural Production
     Agronomy
     Crop Processing Occupations
     Harvesting
     Planting
     Plant Science
     Transplanting

FIELD EXPERIENCE PROGRAMS 410
UF Community Experiences
     Home Experiences
     Home Projects
BT Educational Programs
RT Affiliated Schools
     Airborne Field Trips
     Clinical Experience
     Field Trips
     Internship Programs
     Practicums
     Practicum Supervision
     Student Experience
     Student Projects
     Supervised Farm Practice
     Teaching Experience

FIELD HOUSES 210
BT Physical Education Facilities
RT Athletic Fields
     Athletics
     Recreational Facilities

FIELD INSTRUCTION 270
BT Instruction
RT Area Studies
     Teaching Methods
     Unwritten Language

FIELD INTERVIEWS 190
BT Interviews
RT Caseworker Approach

Field Stations
USE EXPERIMENT STATIONS

FIELD STUDIES 450
BT Research
RT Area Studies
     Educational Research
     Research Methodology

FIELD TRIPS 510
UF Bus Trips
NT Airborne Field Trips
BT Instructional Trips
RT Field Experience Programs

FIFTEENTH CENTURY LITERATURE 260
BT Literature
RT Literary Analysis
     Literary Criticism
     Literary Genres
     Prose
     World Literature

FIGURAL AFTEREFFECTS 070
RT Auditory Perception
     Kinesthetic Perception
     Perception
     Perceptual Development
     Psychophysiology
     Sensory Experience
     Stimulus Behavior
     Tactual Perception
     Vision
     Visual Perception

FIGURATIVE LANGUAGE 260
NT Allegory
     Ambiguity
     Antithesis
     Imagery
     Irony
     Metaphors
BT Language
RT Creative Writing
     Descriptive Writing
     Diction
     Haiku
     Literary Analysis
     Literary Conventions
     Poetry
     Prose
     Proverbs
     Satire
     Symbols (Literary)

FILE CLERKS 380
UF Classification Clerks
     Record Clerks
BT Clerical Workers
RT Business Education
     Clerical Occupations
     Filing
     Information Storage
     Medical Record Technicians
     Office Occupations
     Office Occupations Education

FILING 330
SN Systematic arrangement
UF Alphabetic Filing
    Numeric Filing
RT Alphabetizing Skills
    Catalogs
    Classification
    File Clerks
    Indexing
    Information Processing
    Information Storage

Filing Systems
USE INFORMATION STORAGE

FILIPINO AMERICANS 380
BT Ethnic Groups
RT Ethnic Origins
    Minority Groups
    Racial Characteristics

Film Clips
USE FILMSTRIPS

Film Loops
USE FILMSTRIPS

FILM PRODUCTION 050
RT Film Production Specialists
    Films
    Film Study

FILM PRODUCTION SPECIALISTS 380
BT Specialists
RT Film Production

FILMS 050
UF Black And White Films
    Color Films
    Motion Pictures
NT Foreign Language Films
    Instructional Films
    Single Concept Films
    Sound Films
BT Audiovisual Aids
    Mass Media
RT Acting
    Audiovisual Communication
    Color Presentation
    Czech Literature
    Film Production
    Filmstrips
    Film Study
    Kinescope Recordings
    Photographs
    Repetitive Film Showings

FILMSTRIP PROJECTORS 170
BT Projection Equipment
RT Filmstrips

FILMSTRIPS 050
UF Film Clips
    Film Loops
RT Color Presentation
    Films
    Filmstrip Projectors
    Microfilm
    Single Concept Films
    Slides

FILM STUDY 050
UF Screen Education
BT Study
RT Acting
    Audiovisual Aids
    Audiovisual Communication
    Cartoons
    Film Production
    Films
    Foreign Language Films
    Instructional Films
    Mass Media
    Photography
    Production Techniques
    Repetitive Film Showings
    Single Concept Films
    Sound Effects
    Sound Films

Finance
USE EDUCATIONAL FINANCE

FINANCE OCCUPATIONS 350
BT Occupations
RT Banking
    Economics
    Estate Planning
    Financial Services
    Investment
    Money Management
    Office Occupations
    Trusts (Financial)

Financial Barriers
USE FINANCIAL PROBLEMS

FINANCIAL NEEDS 220
BT Needs
RT Credit (Finance)
    Educational Finance
    Financial Support
    Purchasing
    Student Loan Programs

FINANCIAL POLICY 220
UF Fiscal Policy
RT Educational Administration
    Educational Economics
    Educational Finance
    Equalization Aid
    Fire Insurance
    Fiscal Capacity
    Money Management

FINANCIAL PROBLEMS 220
UF Financial Barriers
BT Problems
RT Educational Finance

FINANCIAL SERVICES 220
BT Services
RT Accountants
    Accounting
    Banking
    Bookkeeping
    Certified Public Accountants
    Credit (Finance)
    Educational Finance
    Finance Occupations
    Fire Insurance
    Interest
    Trusts (Financial)

FINANCIAL SUPPORT 220
UF Economic Support
    Financing
    Fund Raising
NT Capital
    Grants
    Private Financial Support
    Recreation Finances
    School Funds
    School Support
    School Taxes
    Tax Support
RT Educational Economics
    Educational Finance
    Equalization Aid
    Federal Aid
    Fees
    Financial Needs
    Foundation Programs
    Project Applications
    Public Support
    State Aid
    Student Loan Programs
    Tax Allocation
    Training Allowances

Financing
USE FINANCIAL SUPPORT

FINE ARTS 030
NT Art
    Dance
    Music
    Theater Arts
BT Humanities
RT Architecture
    Artists
    Art Song
    Cultural Enrichment
    Musicians

Fine Arts Centers
USE ARTS CENTERS

FINES (PENALTIES) 220
UF Library Fines
RT Fees

FINGER SPELLING 290
SN Spelling by finger movements
UF Dactylology
BT Spelling
RT Communication Skills
    Cued Speech
    Deaf Interpreting
    Manual Communication
    Sign Language

FINISHING 350
UF Electroplating
    Metal Finishing
    Surface Finishing
    Textile Finishing
    Wood Finishing
RT Adhesives
    Welding
    Woodworking

FINNISH 300
BT Finno Ugric Languages

FINNO UGRIC LANGUAGES 300
UF Fenno Ugric Languages
NT Estonian
    Finnish
    Hungarian
    Ostyak
BT Uralic Altaic Languages

FIRE FIGHTERS 380
UF Firemen
BT Service Workers
RT Emergency Squad Personnel
    Fire Science Education
    Service Occupations
    Trade And Industrial Education

FIRE INSURANCE 220
RT Business Responsibility
    Contracts
    Financial Policy
    Financial Services
    Health Insurance
    Risk

Firemen
USE FIRE FIGHTERS

Fire Prevention
USE FIRE PROTECTION

FIRE PROTECTION 250
UF Fire Prevention
BT Safety
RT Building Design
    Design Needs
    Fire Science Education
    Health Needs
    Preservation
    Prevention

Safety Education
School Safety

FIRE SCIENCE EDUCATION 140
BT Technical Education
RT Conservation Education
Emergency Squad Personnel
Fire Fighters
Fire Protection
Safety Education

FIRST AID 250
BT Medical Services
RT Emergency Squad Personnel
Health Education
Health Facilities
Health Services
Injuries
Rescue

FISCAL CAPACITY 220
SN Ability of government to manage
financial matters
RT Educational Economics
Educational Finance
Equalization Aid
Financial Policy
Resource Allocations
Tax Effort

Fiscal Policy
USE FINANCIAL POLICY

FISHERIES 210
UF Commercial Fisheries
RT Seafood

Fish Inspectors
USE FOOD AND DRUG INSPECTORS

FIXED SEQUENCE 020
BT Sequential Programs

FIXED SERVICE TELEVISION 050
SN Instruction television in 2500-2690 MHz
portion of the spectrum authorized by
FCC
UF ITFS
BT Communications
Instructional Television
RT Broadcast Television

FLES 110
UF Foreign Language Elementary School
RT Elementary Education
FLES Guides
FLES Materials
FLES Programs
FLES Teachers
Language Development
Language Instruction
Language Programs

FLES GUIDES 290
BT Language Guides
RT FLES
FLES Programs
FLES Teachers

FLES MATERIALS 050
BT Instructional Materials
RT Elementary Schools
FLES
Language Instruction
Languages

FLES PROGRAMS 290
BT Language Programs
RT Curriculum
Elementary Schools
FLES
FLES Guides
FLES Teachers
Languages
Second Languages

FLES TEACHERS 380
BT Teachers
RT Elementary Schools
FLES
FLES Guides
FLES Programs
Language Instruction

FLEXIBLE CLASSROOMS 210
SN Classrooms with easily changed
dimensions
BT Classrooms
RT Building Design
Classroom Arrangement
Classroom Design
Component Building Systems
Flexible Facilities
Interior Space
Movable Partitions
Multipurpose Classrooms
Open Plan Schools
School Design
School Planning
School Space
Space Dividers
Space Utilization

FLEXIBLE FACILITIES 210
BT Facilities
RT Building Design
Classroom Arrangement
Component Building Systems
Design Needs
Flexible Classrooms
Flexible Lighting Design
Furniture Arrangement
Mobile Classrooms
Movable Partitions
Multipurpose Classrooms
Open Plan Schools
School Planning

Space Utilization
Spatial Relationship

FLEXIBLE LIGHTING DESIGN 210
SN   Lighting unit arrangement as well as
     lighting fixture design that allows for
     flexible lighting requirements
BT   Design
     Lighting Design
RT   Building Design
     Classroom Arrangement
     Flexible Facilities
     Illumination Levels
     Lighting
     Lights
     Multipurpose Classrooms

FLEXIBLE PROGRESSION 510
UF   Track System
RT   Accelerated Programs
     Acceleration
     Continuous Progress Plan
     Student Promotion
     Ungraded Classes

FLEXIBLE SCHEDULES 020
BT   School Schedules
RT   Class Size
     Continuous Progress Plan
     Course Organization
     Double Sessions
     Flexible Scheduling
     Grouping (Instructional Purposes)
     Schedule Modules
     Small Group Instruction
     Team Teaching
     Time Blocks

FLEXIBLE SCHEDULING 020
BT   Scheduling
RT   Class Size
     Course Organization
     Curriculum Development
     Flexible Schedules
     Grouping (Instructional Purposes)
     Schedule Modules
     School Schedules
     Team Teaching
     Time Blocks

FLIGHT TRAINING 110
SN   Training of military or civilian aircraft
     personnel
UF   Pilot Training
BT   Training
RT   Job Training
     Military Training

Floor Covering
USE   FLOORING

FLOORING 210
UF   Floor Covering
     Floor Installation
     Floors
     Resilient Floor Covering
RT   Asphalts
     Building Materials
     Buildings
     Building Trades
     Carpeting
     Construction (Process)
     Floor Layers

Floor Installation
USE   FLOORING

FLOOR LAYERS 380
UF   Carpet Layers
BT   Skilled Workers
RT   Flooring
     Skilled Occupations
     Trade And Industrial Education

Floors
USE   FLOORING

FLORICULTURE 070
BT   Ornamental Horticulture
RT   Landscaping
     Plant Identification

FLUID POWER EDUCATION 400
BT   Physical Sciences
RT   Hydraulics
     Industrial Education
     Industry
     Kinetics
     Power Mechanics
     Vocational Education

Flying Classrooms
USE   AIRBORNE FIELD TRIPS

Folding Partitions
USE   MOVABLE PARTITIONS

FOLK CULTURE 100
BT   Culture
RT   Biblical Literature
     Cultural Factors
     Folk Drama
     Legends
     Mythology
     Oriental Music
     Proverbs

FOLK DRAMA 260
BT   Drama
RT   Folk Culture
     Literature
     Poetry
     Prose

FOLKLORE BOOKS 320
BT Books
RT Biblical Literature
    Literature

FOLK SCHOOLS 470
BT Schools
RT Cultural Education
    Recreational Programs
    Residential Centers

Followup Programs
USE FOLLOWUP STUDIES

FOLLOWUP STUDIES 190
UF Followup Programs
NT Graduate Surveys
BT Evaluation Methods
RT Vocational Followup

FOOCHOW 300
BT Chinese
RT Dialects

FOOD 250
NT Seafood
RT Cooks
    Corn (Field Crop)
    Dietetics
    Dietitians
    Feed Industry
    Food And Drug Inspectors
    Food Processing Occupations
    Food Service
    Foods Instruction
    Food Standards
    Food Stores
    Grains (Food)
    Meat
    Meat Packing Industry
    Nutrition

FOOD AND DRUG INSPECTORS 380
UF Cosmetics Inspectors
    Dairy Product Inspectors
    Drug Inspectors
    Egg Inspectors
    Fish Inspectors
    Food Inspectors
    Fruit And Vegetable Inspectors
    Meat Inspectors
    Peanut Inspectors
    Processed Foods Inspectors
BT Professional Personnel
RT Agricultural Education
    Food
    Food Processing Occupations
    Meat Packing Industry

FOOD HANDLING FACILITIES 210
SN Equipment and space for storing,
    preparing, and serving food
RT Dining Facilities
    Dishwashing
    Food Service
    Lunch Programs

Food Inspectors
USE FOOD AND DRUG INSPECTORS

Food Markets
USE FOOD STORES

FOOD PROCESSING OCCUPATIONS 350
BT Off Farm Agricultural Occupations
RT Feed Industry
    Food
    Food And Drug Inspectors
    Meat Packing Industry

FOOD SERVICE 250
RT Cooks
    Dietitians
    Dining Facilities
    Dishwashing
    Food
    Food Handling Facilities
    Food Service Industry
    Food Service Occupations
    Food Service Workers
    Foods Instruction
    Food Standards
    Seafood

FOOD SERVICE INDUSTRY 370
BT Industry
RT Cooks
    Dietitians
    Food Service
    Food Service Occupations
    Food Service Workers
    Food Stores
    Seafood
    Service Occupations

FOOD SERVICE OCCUPATIONS 350
BT Service Occupations
RT Cooks
    Dietitians
    Distributive Education
    Food Service
    Food Service Industry
    Food Service Workers
    Foods Instruction
    Occupational Home Economics
    Trade And Industrial Education

FOOD SERVICE WORKERS 380
UF Supervised Food Service Workers
BT Service Workers
RT Cooks
    Dietitians
    Food Service
    Food Service Industry

Food Service Occupations
Occupational Home Economics

FOODS INSTRUCTION 270
BT Instruction
RT Consumer Science
Cooking Instruction
Cooks
Dietitians
Food
Food Service
Food Service Occupations
Food Standards
Home Economics Education
Nutrition Instruction

FOOD STANDARDS 500
BT Standards
RT Breakfast Programs
Dietetics
Dietitians
Food
Food Service
Foods Instruction
Lunch Programs
Meat Packing Industry
Nutrition

FOOD STORES 210
SN Retail markets selling foodstuffs
UF Food Markets
Grocery Stores
Supermarkets
RT Food
Food Service Industry
Meat
Merchandising
Retailing

Foot Candles
USE ILLUMINATION LEVELS

FORCE 400
UF Force (Physical)
BT Physics
RT Acoustic Phonetics
Atomic Structure
Atomic Theory
Electricity
Energy
Kinetic Molecular Theory
Kinetics
Motion
Nuclear Physics
Pressure
Quantum Mechanics
Weight

Force (Physical)
USE FORCE

FORCED CHOICE TECHNIQUE 190
RT Attitudes
Measurement Techniques
Rating Scales
Techniques

FORCE FIELD ANALYSIS 420
SN Method of distinguishing factors in the
psychological environment of individuals
or groups, based on Lewins theory
RT Interdisciplinary Approach
Psychological Studies
Research Methodology
Statistical Analysis

FOREIGN COUNTRIES 230
RT Armed Forces
Foreign Diplomats
Foreign Relations
Overseas Employment

FOREIGN CULTURE 100
UF Alien Culture
BT Culture
RT African Culture
Chinese Culture
Cross Cultural Studies
Ethnic Groups
International Education
Native Speakers
Puerto Rican Culture

FOREIGN DIPLOMATS 380
RT Foreign Countries
Foreign Relations

FOREIGN LANGUAGE BOOKS 320
BT Books
RT Foreign Language Films
Foreign Language Periodicals
Languages
Library Collections

Foreign Language Elementary School
USE FLES

FOREIGN LANGUAGE FILMS 050
BT Films
RT Film Study
Foreign Language Books
Foreign Language Periodicals
Languages

Foreign Language Learning
USE SECOND LANGUAGE LEARNING

FOREIGN LANGUAGE PERIODICALS 320
BT Periodicals
RT Foreign Language Books
Foreign Language Films
Languages
Library Collections

Foreign Languages
USE LANGUAGES

Foreign Language Speakers
USE NATIVE SPEAKERS

Foreign Language Stenographers
USE STENOGRAPHERS

Foreign Language Teaching
USE LANGUAGE INSTRUCTION

FOREIGN POLICY 230
NT Colonialism
BT Political Science
RT Foreign Relations
Policy
Social Sciences
World Affairs

FOREIGN RELATIONS 480
UF International Relations
BT Political Science
RT Colonialism
Developing Nations
Exports
Foreign Countries
Foreign Diplomats
Foreign Policy
International Education
International Organizations
International Trade Vocabulary
World Affairs

FOREIGN STUDENT ADVISERS 380
BT Student Personnel Workers
RT College Students
Faculty Advisors
Foreign Students
Student Exchange Programs
Student Personnel Services
Student Personnel Work

FOREIGN STUDENTS 380
BT Students
RT Foreign Student Advisers
Student Exchange Programs

FOREIGN WORKERS 380
NT Braceros
BT Laborers

Foreman
USE SUPERVISORS

Forester Aids
USE FORESTRY AIDES

FORESTRY 070
BT Agriculture
RT Botany
Conservation Education
Environmental Education
Forestry Aides
Forestry Occupations
Natural Resources
Nurseries (Horticulture)
Plant Science
Soil Conservation
Transplanting
Trees
Wildlife Management

FORESTRY AIDES 380
UF Forester Aids
RT Agricultural Occupations
Forestry
Forestry Occupations
Off Farm Agricultural Occupations
Trees
Vocational Agriculture

FORESTRY OCCUPATIONS 350
BT Off Farm Agricultural Occupations
RT Forestry
Forestry Aides
Lumber Industry
Vocational Agriculture

FORMAL CRITICISM 260
BT Literature
RT Allegory
Dialogue
Imagery
Impressionistic Criticism
Italian Literature
Literary Analysis
Literary Conventions
Literary Criticism
Literary Genres
Literary Perspective
Literary Styles
Moral Criticism
Motifs
Symbols (Literary)
Tales
Textual Criticism

Formal Organizations
USE ORGANIZATIONS (GROUPS)

FORM CLASSES (LANGUAGES) 290
UF Parts Of Speech
NT Adjectives
Adverbs
Determiners (Languages)
Function Words
Nominals
Pronouns
Verbs
BT Grammar
RT Case (Grammar)
Language Patterns
Morphology (Languages)
Phrase Structure
Plurals
Structural Grammar
Suffixes
Syntax
Traditional Grammar

FORMER TEACHERS 380
SN Teachers who have left the profession
BT Teachers
RT Substitute Teachers

Fossils
USE PALEONTOLOGY

FOSTER CHILDREN 380
BT Children
RT Adopted Children
    Child Welfare
    Foster Family
    Foster Homes

FOSTER FAMILY 490
BT Family (Sociological Unit)
RT Adopted Children
    Adoption
    Child Welfare
    Foster Children

FOSTER HOMES 210
SN Private homes provided by other than
    natural parents, with or without adoption
BT Residential Care
RT Boarding Homes
    Foster Children
    Nursing Homes
    Older Adults
    Personal Care Homes

FOUNDATION PROGRAMS 410
BT Programs
RT Educational Finance
    Federal Aid
    Financial Support
    Incentive Grants
    Private Financial Support
    State Aid
    Trusts (Financial)

FOUNDRIES 210
UF Iron Foundries
    Steel Foundries
RT Industrial Arts
    Metal Industry

FRACTIONS 340
NT Common Fractions
    Decimal Fractions
BT Arithmetic
    Numbers

FRATERNITIES 370
BT Organizations (Groups)

FREE CHOICE TRANSFER PROGRAMS 020
BT Transfer Programs
RT Open Enrollment
    Transfer Policy
    Transfers
    Transfer Students

FREEDOM OF SPEECH 230
BT Civil Liberties
RT Academic Freedom
    Civil Rights
    Democracy
    Freedom Organizations

FREEDOM ORGANIZATIONS 370
BT Organizations (Groups)
RT Civil Rights
    Freedom Of Speech

FREEDOM SCHOOLS 470
BT Schools
RT Civil Rights

FREEHAND DRAWING 030
BT Art
RT Art Activities
    Art Expression
    Cartoons
    Creative Art
    Painting
    Visual Arts

Free Universities
USE EXPERIMENTAL COLLEGES

FRENCH 300
BT Romance Languages
RT Modernism
    Surrealism

FRENCH LITERATURE 260
BT Literature
RT Anthologies
    Baroque Literature
    Comedy
    Composition (Literary)
    Drama
    Eighteenth Century Literature
    Epics
    Essays
    Fables
    Fiction
    Journalism
    Legends
    Letters (Correspondence)
    Literary Analysis
    Literary Conventions
    Literary Criticism
    Literary Genres
    Novels
    Poetry
    Prose
    Russian Literature
    Satire
    Short Stories
    Symbolism
    Tragedy
    Twentieth Century Literature
    World Literature

FRESHMEN 380
NT College Freshmen
BT Students
RT College Students
    High School Students

FRIENDSHIP 490
NT Childhood Friendship
BT Social Development
    Social Relations
RT Peer Relationship

FRINGE BENEFITS 150
RT Health Insurance
    Industrial Relations
    Salaries
    Unemployment Insurance
    Wages

Fruit And Vegetable Inspectors
USE FOOD AND DRUG INSPECTORS

FUEL CONSUMPTION 210
RT Building Design
    Exhausting
    Fuels
    Heating
    Temperature
    Thermal Environment
    Ventilation

Fuel Oil
USE FUELS

FUELS 460
UF Fuel Oil
    Gasoline
    Heating Oils
    Natural Gases
RT Agricultural Machinery
    Engines
    Fuel Consumption
    Heat
    Heating
    Kinetics
    Motor Vehicles
    Utilities

Fula
USE FULANI

FULANI 300
UF Fula
BT African Languages

FUNCTIONAL ILLITERACY 440
BT Illiteracy
RT Cultural Disadvantagement
    Economic Disadvantagement
    Educational Disadvantagement
    Illiterate Adults
    Language Handicaps
    Social Disadvantagement

FUNCTIONAL READING 440
BT Reading

Functional Systems Theory
USE SYSTEMS ANALYSIS

FUNCTION WORDS 290
UF Functors
BT Form Classes (Languages)
RT Determiners (Languages)
    Grammar
    Morphology (Languages)
    Sentence Structure
    Structural Grammar
    Surface Structure
    Syntax
    Tagmemic Analysis

Functors
USE FUNCTION WORDS

FUNDAMENTAL CONCEPTS 310
NT Generalization
RT Concept Formation

Fundamental Education
USE ADULT BASIC EDUCATION

Fundamental Skills
USE BASIC SKILLS

Fund Raising
USE FINANCIAL SUPPORT

FURNITURE 170
NT Classroom Furniture
BT Building Equipment
RT Furniture Arrangement
    Furniture Design
    Furniture Industry
    Home Furnishings
    Storage

Furniture (Classroom)
USE CLASSROOM FURNITURE

FURNITURE ARRANGEMENT 210
RT Class Organization
    Classroom Arrangement
    Classroom Furniture
    Flexible Facilities
    Furniture
    Furniture Design
    Interior Design
    Interior Space
    Space Utilization
    Storage

FURNITURE DESIGN 030
BT Design
RT Classroom Furniture
    Design Needs
    Design Preferences
    Furniture
    Furniture Arrangement
    Furniture Industry
    Lumber Industry
    Physical Design Needs
    Psychological Design Needs
    Storage

FURNITURE INDUSTRY 370
BT Industry
RT Equipment Manufacturers
Furniture
Furniture Design
Lumber Industry
Manufacturing Industry

Further Education
USE ADULT EDUCATION

FUSED CURRICULUM 110
BT Curriculum
RT Unified Studies Programs

GA 300
BT African Languages

Gages
USE MEASUREMENT INSTRUMENTS

Gamekeeping
USE WILDLIFE MANAGEMENT

GAMES 390
NT Childrens Games
Educational Games
Management Games
RT Puzzles
Recreational Activities
Toys

GAME THEORY 510
BT Operations Research
RT Cybernetics
Decision Making
Management Games
Mathematical Models
Mathematics
Probability Theory
Problem Solving
Risk
Simulation

GANDA 300
UF Luganda
BT Afro Asiatic Languages

Gardeners
USE GROUNDS KEEPERS

Gasoline
USE FUELS

Gas Utilities
USE UTILITIES

Gas Welders
USE WELDERS

Gas Welding
USE WELDING

Gauges
USE MEASUREMENT INSTRUMENTS

GBAYA 300
UF Gbeya
BT African Languages

Gbeya
USE GBAYA

Ged Tests
USE EQUIVALENCY TESTS

GENERAL EDUCATION 140
UF Liberal Education
BT Education
RT General High Schools
Liberal Arts

GENERAL HIGH SCHOOLS 470
BT High Schools
RT General Education

GENERALIZATION 310
NT Stimulus Generalization
BT Fundamental Concepts
RT Concept Formation
Concept Teaching

General Mechanics
USE MECHANICS (PROCESS)

General Methods Courses
USE METHODS COURSES

GENERAL SCIENCE 110
BT Science Curriculum

General Shop
USE SHOP CURRICULUM

General Unit Shops
USE SCHOOL SHOPS

GENERATION GAP 040
RT Student Alienation
Youth Problems

GENERATIVE GRAMMAR 290
NT Transformation Generative Grammar
BT Grammar
RT Deep Structure
Linguistic Theory
Sentence Structure
Surface Structure
Syntax

Generative Transformation Grammar
USE TRANSFORMATION GENERATIVE
GRAMMAR

GENETICS 070
BT Biology
RT Anomalies
Embryology
Evolution
Heredity
Medicine
Mongolism
Prenatal Influences
Radiation Biology
Radioisotopes
Zoology

Geographical Dialects
USE REGIONAL DIALECTS

GEOGRAPHIC CONCEPTS 480
RT Geography
Geography Instruction
Northern Attitudes
Physical Geography

GEOGRAPHIC DISTRIBUTION 120
RT Community Size
Demography
Geography
Incidence
Physical Geography

Geographic Factors
USE GEOGRAPHY

GEOGRAPHIC LOCATION 120
RT Climatic Factors
Distance
Geography
Physical Geography
Relocation
Site Analysis

GEOGRAPHIC REGIONS 120
NT Southern States
RT Area Studies
Geography
Physical Geography
Regional Dialects

GEOGRAPHY 480
UF Geographic Factors
NT Physical Geography
World Geography
BT Social Sciences
Social Studies
RT Area Studies
Conservation Education
Geographic Concepts
Geographic Distribution
Geographic Location
Geographic Regions
Geography Instruction
Maps
Map Skills
Oceanology
Physical Divisions (Geographic)
Political Divisions (Geographic)

GEOGRAPHY INSTRUCTION 270
BT Instruction
RT Geographic Concepts
Geography

GEOLOGY 400
NT Paleontology
BT Earth Science
RT Geophysics
Oceanology
Physical Geography
Scientific Research

Seismology
Soil Science

Geometrical Optics
USE OPTICS

GEOMETRIC CONCEPTS 340
RT Diagrams
Geometry

Geometrodynamics
USE RELATIVITY

GEOMETRY 340
NT Analytic Geometry
Plane Geometry
Solid Geometry
Topology
BT Mathematics
RT Congruence
Geometric Concepts
Symmetry

GEOPHYSICS 400
BT Earth Science
RT Geology
Physics
Seismology

GERIATRICS 250
BT Medicine
RT Health
Medical Services
Older Adults
Senior Citizens

GERMAN 300
NT Yiddish
BT Indo European Languages

GERMAN LITERATURE 260
BT Literature
RT Anthologies
Baroque Literature
Biblical Literature
Biographies
Books
Drama
English Neoclassic Literary Period
Fiction
Legends
Letters (Correspondence)
Literary Analysis
Literary Criticism
Literary Genres
Literary History
Literature Appreciation
Mythology
Novels
Poetry
Poets
Prose
Satire
Short Stories
Twentieth Century Literature
World Literature

German Measles
USE RUBELLA

Gestation
USE PREGNANCY

GHETTOS 490
BT Depressed Areas (Geographic)
RT Ethnic Groups
    Racial Discrimination
    Slums
    Social Mobility
    Urban Environment

GIFTED 380
UF Academically Gifted
    Gifted Children
    Gifted Students
    Gifted Teachers
    Gifted Youth
    Mentally Advanced Children
BT Exceptional (Atypical)
RT Ability
    Able Students
    Academic Achievement
    Exceptional Child Research
    High Achievers
    Regular Class Placement
    Special Education Teachers
    Superior Students
    Talented Students

Gifted Children
USE GIFTED

Gifted Students
USE GIFTED

Gifted Teachers
USE GIFTED

Gifted Youth
USE GIFTED

Girls
USE FEMALES

GIRLS CLUBS 370
BT Clubs

GLARE 210
RT Illumination Levels
    Light
    Lighting
    Lighting Design
    Lights
    Luminescence
    Task Performance
    Visual Acuity
    Visual Discrimination
    Visual Environment
    Visual Perception
    Windows

GLASS 170
RT Art Materials
    Ceramics
    Glaziers

Glass Installers
USE GLAZIERS

GLASS WALLS 210
SN Walls consisting largely of windows
UF Window Walls
RT Building Design
    Classroom Design
    School Design
    Windows

GLAZIERS 380
UF Glass Installers
BT Skilled Workers
RT Glass
    Skilled Occupations
    Trade And Industrial Education

Glee Clubs
USE CHORUSES

GLOSSARIES 320
BT Reference Materials
RT Reference Books
    Thesauri
    Vocabulary
    Word Lists

GLOTTOCHRONOLOGY 290
SN A technique for estimating by statistical
    comparison of vocabulary samples the
    time during which two or more
    languages have evolved separately from
    a common source
BT Diachronic Linguistics
RT Comparative Analysis
    Etymology
    Language Classification
    Language Research
    Languages
    Lexicography
    Lexicology
    Linguistics
    Statistical Analysis
    Vocabulary

Glues
USE ADHESIVES

GOAL ORIENTATION 270
SN Psychological disposition toward
    achieving ones objectives
BT Orientation
RT Achievement Need
    Career Planning
    Need Gratification
    Objectives
    Personality Assessment
    Personal Values
    Psychological Characteristics

Goals
USE OBJECTIVES

Good Citizenship
USE CITIZENSHIP

GOVERNANCE 020
RT Administrative Agencies
Administrative Organization
College Administration
Community Control
Governing Boards
Government (Administrative Body)
Institutional Administration
Policy Formation
Private Colleges
Trustees
University Administration

GOVERNING BOARDS 020
SN Group charged with the responsibility for
some degree of control over managing
the affairs of public or private
institutions
UF Board Of Regents
Board Of Trustees
NT Boards Of Education
State Boards Of Education
State Licensing Boards
RT Administrative Agencies
Administrative Organization
Board Administrator Relationship
College Administration
Governance
Institutional Administration
Policy Formation
School Administration
Trustees
University Administration

GOVERNMENT (ADMINISTRATIVE BODY)
230
NT Biracial Government
City Government
Federal Government
Governmental Structure
State Government
RT Agencies
American Government (Course)
Communism
Constitutional History
Governance
Government Role
Immigration Inspectors
Legislation
Police
Political Affiliation
Producer Services
Public Administration Education

Governmental Functions
USE GOVERNMENT ROLE

GOVERNMENTAL STRUCTURE 230
BT Government (Administrative Body)
RT Constitutional History
Public Administration Education
School District Autonomy

Government Documents
USE GOVERNMENT PUBLICATIONS

GOVERNMENT EMPLOYEES 380
UF Civil Service Employees
Public Employees
NT Immigration Inspectors
Public School Teachers
BT Employees
RT County Officials
Laborers
Personnel
Public Officials

GOVERNMENT LIBRARIES 210
UF Federal Libraries
BT Special Libraries
RT Archives
Legislative Reference Libraries
National Libraries
State Libraries

GOVERNMENT PUBLICATIONS 320
UF Government Documents
Public Documents
BT Publications
RT City Government
Depository Libraries
Federal Government
State Government

GOVERNMENT ROLE 230
UF Congress Role
Governmental Functions
RT Constitutional History
Government (Administrative Body)

GRADE 1 280
BT Instructional Program Divisions

GRADE 2 280
BT Instructional Program Divisions

GRADE 3 280
BT Instructional Program Divisions

GRADE 4 280
BT Instructional Program Divisions

GRADE 5 280
BT Instructional Program Divisions

GRADE 6 280
BT Instructional Program Divisions

GRADE 7 280
BT Instructional Program Divisions

GRADE 8 280
BT Instructional Program Divisions

GRADE 9 280
BT Instructional Program Divisions

GRADE 10 280
BT Instructional Program Divisions

GRADE 11 280
BT Instructional Program Divisions

GRADE 12 280
BT Instructional Program Divisions

GRADE 13 280
BT Instructional Program Divisions

GRADE 14 280
BT Instructional Program Divisions

Grade Average
USE CLASS AVERAGE

Grade A Year Desegregation
USE GRADE A YEAR INTEGRATION

GRADE A YEAR INTEGRATION 430
UF Grade A Year Desegregation
RT Racial Integration

GRADE CHARTS 170
BT Charts
RT Courses
    Curriculum

GRADE EQUIVALENT SCALES 190
RT Equivalency Tests
    Evaluation Techniques
    Measurement Techniques
    Rating Scales
    Testing
    Test Interpretation

Grade Levels
USE INSTRUCTIONAL PROGRAM DIVISIONS

GRADE ORGANIZATION 280
BT Organization
RT Instructional Program Divisions
    Middle Schools

GRADE POINT AVERAGE 180
UF Quality Point Ratio
    School Grade Average
BT Grades (Scholastic)
RT Grade Prediction

GRADE PREDICTION 190
BT Prediction
RT Grade Point Average
    Grades (Scholastic)
    Grading
    Predictive Ability (Testing)
    Predictive Measurement

GRADE REPETITION 510
RT Academic Failure
    Student Promotion

Grade Retardation
USE EDUCATIONAL RETARDATION

Grades (Program Divisions)
USE INSTRUCTIONAL PROGRAM DIVISIONS

GRADES (SCHOLASTIC) 180
UF College Grades (Scholastic)
    High School Grades (Scholastic)
NT Grade Point Average
BT Achievement Rating
RT Academic Achievement
    Class Average
    College Credits
    Credit Courses
    Credits
    Feedback
    Grade Prediction
    Grading
    Pass Fail Grading
    Report Cards
    Scoring
    Student Evaluation

GRADING 190
UF Marking (School Mark)
NT Pass Fail Grading
BT Measurement
RT Achievement Rating
    Class Average
    Grade Prediction
    Grades (Scholastic)
    Scoring

Graduate Education
USE GRADUATE STUDY

GRADUATE PROFESSORS 380
BT Professors
RT Graduate Study

GRADUATES 380
NT College Graduates
    High School Graduates
BT Alumni
RT Graduate Students
    Graduate Surveys

GRADUATE STUDENTS 380
BT Students
RT College Graduates
    College Students
    Degree Requirements
    Graduates
    Graduate Study
    Higher Education
    Teaching Assistants

GRADUATE STUDY 140
UF Graduate Education
    Graduate Training
RT College Graduates
    Degree Requirements
    Doctoral Programs
    Graduate Professors
    Graduate Students
    Higher Education
    Inservice Education

Professional Education
Universities
Urban Universities

GRADUATE SURVEYS 180
SN Followup studies of students who have
been graduated
BT Evaluation Methods
Followup Studies
Surveys
RT College Graduates
Educational Research
Graduates
School Surveys
Vocational Followup

Graduate Training
USE GRADUATE STUDY

GRADUATION 140
RT Graduation Requirements

GRADUATION REQUIREMENTS 500
NT Degree Requirements
RT Graduation

Grain Elevator Occupations
USE CROP PROCESSING OCCUPATIONS

Grain Marketing
USE GRAINS (FOOD)

Grain Processing
USE GRAINS (FOOD)

Grain Production
USE GRAINS (FOOD)

GRAINS (FOOD) 460
UF Grain Marketing
Grain Processing
Grain Production
NT Corn (Field Crop)
BT Field Crops
RT Agronomy
Feed Industry
Food

GRAMMAR 290
NT Form Classes (Languages)
Generative Grammar
Morphology (Languages)
Structural Grammar
Traditional Grammar
BT Linguistics
RT Case (Grammar)
Context Free Grammar
Deep Structure
Determiners (Languages)
Discourse Analysis
Function Words
Grammar Translation Method
Idioms
Kernel Sentences
Morphemes
Negative Forms (Language)
Plurals

Sentence Diagraming
Sentences
Sentence Structure
Surface Structure
Tagmemic Analysis
Transformation Theory (Language)

GRAMMAR TRANSLATION METHOD 270
BT Teaching Methods
RT Grammar
Language Instruction
Translation

GRANTS 220
NT Incentive Grants
Tuition Grants
BT Financial Support
RT Educational Finance
Equalization Aid

GRAPHEMES 290
BT Linguistics
RT Orthographic Symbols
Phonetics
Romanization
Spelling
Structural Analysis

GRAPHIC ARTS 030
NT Engineering Graphics
Printing
Technical Illustration
BT Art
RT Audiovisual Aids
Commercial Art
Computer Graphics
Diagrams
Engineering Drawing
Photocomposition
Sign Painters
Signs

GRAPHS 050
BT Audiovisual Aids
RT Charts
Topology

Grass (Drug)
USE MARIHUANA

Grease
USE LUBRICANTS

GREEK 300
UF Classical Greek
Modern Greek
BT Classical Languages
Indo European Languages
RT Classical Literature
Greek Civilization

GREEK CIVILIZATION 260
BT Ancient History
RT Greek
Western Civilization

GREENHOUSES 210
UF   Hothouses
BT   Facilities
RT   Controlled Environment
     Nurseries (Horticulture)
     Ornamental Horticulture
     Plant Growth

Greenhouse Workers
USE NURSERY WORKERS (HORTICULTURE)

Gregariousness
USE INTERPERSONAL COMPETENCE

GRIEVANCE PROCEDURES 150
RT   Arbitration
     Collective Bargaining
     Collective Negotiation
     Labor Demands
     Negotiation Impasses
     Ombudsmen

Grinding Machines
USE MACHINE TOOLS

Grocery Stores
USE FOOD STORES

Grounds Caretakers
USE GROUNDS KEEPERS

GROUNDS KEEPERS 380
UF   Assistant Grounds Keepers
     Gardeners
     Grounds Caretakers
     Sports Grounds Keepers
     Yard Laborers
BT   Ornamental Horticulture Occupation
RT   Landscaping
     Ornamental Horticulture
     Plant Propagation
     Turf Management
     Vocational Agriculture

GROUP ACTIVITIES 140
UF   Cooperative Activities
BT   Activities
RT   Group Guidance
     Groups
     Self Directed Groups

GROUP BEHAVIOR 060
BT   Behavior
RT   Group Dynamics
     Group Guidance
     Groups
     Interaction Process Analysis
     Teamwork

Group Cohesiveness
USE GROUP UNITY

GROUP COUNSELING 090
BT   Counseling
RT   Family Counseling
     Group Guidance
     Groups

GROUP DISCUSSION 080
SN   Method of learning through interaction in
     peer groups
BT   Discussion (Teaching Technique)
RT   Discussion Groups
     Sensitivity Training

GROUP DYNAMICS 490
UF   Group Pressures
     Group Processes
BT   Social Psychology
RT   Family Counseling
     Group Behavior
     Group Experience
     Group Guidance
     Group Instruction
     Group Living
     Group Membership
     Group Relations
     Groups
     Group Status
     Group Structure
     Interaction Process Analysis
     Self Directed Groups
     Sociometric Techniques
     T Groups
     Training Laboratories

GROUP EXPERIENCE 200
BT   Experience
RT   Group Dynamics
     Groups
     Self Directed Groups

GROUP GUIDANCE 090
BT   Guidance
RT   Classroom Guidance Programs
     Educational Guidance
     Group Activities
     Group Behavior
     Group Counseling
     Group Dynamics
     Group Instruction
     Groups
     Group Status
     Group Structure
     Guidance Services
     Occupational Guidance

GROUPING (INSTRUCTIONAL PURPOSES)
280
NT   Student Grouping
RT   Age Grade Placement
     Classification
     Class Organization
     Flexible Schedules
     Flexible Scheduling
     Grouping Procedures
     Group Instruction
     Group Membership
     Group Reading
     Groups
     Matched Groups

Psychological Design Needs
Tutorial Programs

Grouping Practices
USE GROUPING PROCEDURES

GROUPING PROCEDURES 510
UF Grouping Practices
RT Cluster Grouping
Grouping (Instructional Purposes)

GROUP INSTRUCTION 270
BT Instruction
RT Group Dynamics
Group Guidance
Grouping (Instructional Purposes)
Groups
Listening Groups

GROUP INTELLIGENCE TESTING 190
BT Testing
RT Group Intelligence Tests
Groups

GROUP INTELLIGENCE TESTS 520
BT Group Tests
Intelligence Tests
RT Group Intelligence Testing
Groups

Group Interaction
USE GROUP RELATIONS

GROUP LIVING 490
RT Group Dynamics
Group Norms
Group Relations
Groups
Human Relations

GROUP MEMBERSHIP 490
RT Group Dynamics
Grouping (Instructional Purposes)
Group Norms
Groups

GROUP NORMS 500
BT Standards
RT Behavior Standards
Comparative Analysis
Group Living
Group Membership
Measurement
National Norms
Social Values
Tests
Values

Group Pressures
USE GROUP DYNAMICS

Group Processes
USE GROUP DYNAMICS

GROUP READING 440
BT Reading
RT Grouping (Instructional Purposes)
Groups

GROUP RELATIONS 490
UF Group Interaction
NT Group Unity
Intergroup Relations
BT Relationship
RT Audience Participation
Ethnic Relations
Group Dynamics
Group Living
Groups
Group Status
Human Relations
Interpersonal Competence
Interpersonal Relationship
Self Directed Groups
Sociometric Techniques

GROUPS 380
NT Audiences
Choruses
Clubs
Disadvantaged Groups
Discussion Groups
Ethnic Groups
Experimental Groups
Listening Groups
Low Income Groups
Matched Groups
Minority Groups
Peer Groups
Religious Cultural Groups
Self Directed Groups
T Groups
Tribes
RT Faculty Organizations
Group Activities
Group Behavior
Group Counseling
Group Dynamics
Group Experience
Group Guidance
Grouping (Instructional Purposes)
Group Instruction
Group Intelligence Testing
Group Intelligence Tests
Group Living
Group Membership
Group Reading
Group Relations
Group Status
Group Structure
Group Tests
Group Therapy
Organizations (Groups)
Social Psychology

GROUP STATUS 490
BT Status
RT Group Dynamics
Group Guidance
Group Relations
Groups
Group Structure

Peer Relationship
Sociometric Techniques

GROUP STRUCTURE 490
RT Cluster Grouping
Group Dynamics
Group Guidance
Groups
Group Status
Interaction Process Analysis
Social Systems
Sociometric Techniques

GROUP TESTS 520
NT Group Intelligence Tests
BT Tests
RT Groups
Objective Tests

GROUP THERAPY 420
BT Psychotherapy
RT Family Counseling
Groups
Milieu Therapy
Sensitivity Training

GROUP UNITY 490
SN Cohesiveness of groups of people,
families, tribes and nations
UF Ethnic Unity
Family Unity
Group Cohesiveness
Unification
BT Group Relations
RT Nationalism

Group Values
USE SOCIAL VALUES

Growth Motivation
USE SELF ACTUALIZATION

GROWTH PATTERNS 130
BT Human Development
RT Adult Development
Body Height
Body Weight
Child Development
Individual Development
Maturation
Neurological Organization
Personal Growth
Physiology
Self Actualization

Guaranteed Annual Wage
USE GUARANTEED INCOME

GUARANTEED INCOME 220
UF Guaranteed Annual Wage
Guaranteed Wage
Negative Income Tax
BT Income
RT Minimum Wage
Salaries
Security
Wages

Guaranteed Wage
USE GUARANTEED INCOME

GUIDANCE 090
NT Continuous Guidance
Developmental Guidance
Educational Guidance
Elementary School Guidance
Group Guidance
Occupational Guidance
Post High School Guidance
Teacher Guidance
RT Career Planning
Counseling
Counselors
Educational Therapy
Guidance Centers
Guidance Counseling
Guidance Functions
Guidance Personnel
Guidance Programs
Guidance Services
Interviews

GUIDANCE CENTERS 210
BT Educational Facilities
RT Guidance
Guidance Facilities

GUIDANCE COUNSELING 090
BT Counseling
RT Adjustment Counselors
Counselors
Guidance
Guidance Functions
Guidance Services
Pupil Personnel Services

Guidance Counselors
USE COUNSELORS

GUIDANCE FACILITIES 210
BT Educational Facilities
RT Counseling Centers
Guidance Centers
Guidance Services

GUIDANCE FUNCTIONS 090
RT Counselor Functions
Guidance
Guidance Counseling
Guidance Programs
Guidance Services

Guidance Goals
USE GUIDANCE OBJECTIVES

GUIDANCE OBJECTIVES 090
UF Guidance Goals
BT Objectives
RT Affective Objectives
Cognitive Objectives
Counseling Goals
Guidance Programs
Guidance Services
Psychomotor Objectives

GUIDANCE PERSONNEL 380
UF   Guidance Specialists
NT   Counselors
BT   Personnel
RT   Counselor Selection
      Elementary School Counselors
      Elementary School Guidance
      Guidance
      Instructor Coordinators
      Pupil Personnel Workers
      School Psychologists
      School Social Workers
      Secondary School Counselors
      Student Personnel Workers

GUIDANCE PROGRAMS 090
NT   Classroom Guidance Programs
BT   Programs
RT   Elementary School Guidance
      Guidance
      Guidance Functions
      Guidance Objectives
      Guidance Services
      Pupil Personnel Services
      Secondary School Counselors
      Student Personnel Services

GUIDANCE SERVICES 090
BT   Services
RT   Classroom Guidance Programs
      Elementary School Counselors
      Elementary School Guidance
      Group Guidance
      Guidance
      Guidance Counseling
      Guidance Facilities
      Guidance Functions
      Guidance Objectives
      Guidance Programs
      Pupil Personnel Services
      Pupil Personnel Workers
      Secondary School Counselors
      Student Personnel Services
      Student Personnel Work
      Student Placement

Guidance Specialists
USE   GUIDANCE PERSONNEL

Guidance Workers
USE   COUNSELORS

GUIDELINES 020
NT   Facility Guidelines
RT   Administrative Principles
      Guides
      Objectives

GUIDES 320
NT   Administrator Guides
      Curriculum Guides
      Leaders Guides
      Library Guides
      Literature Guides
      Program Guides
      Resource Guides
      Study Guides
      Teaching Guides
RT   Directories
      Guidelines
      Laboratory Manuals
      Manuals

GUJARATI 300
UF   Gujerati
BT   Indo European Languages

Gujerati
USE   GUJARATI

GULLAH 300
BT   Creoles

GYMNASIUMS 210
BT   Physical Education Facilities
RT   Athletic Activities
      Athletic Equipment
      Athletic Fields
      Athletic Programs
      Athletics

Gymnastics
USE   EXERCISE (PHYSIOLOGY)

HABIT FORMATION 420
BT   Behavior Development
RT   Behavior Change
      Listening Habits
      Personality
      Reading Habits
      Self Care Skills
      Speech Habits

HAIKU 260
UF   Hokku
BT   Poetry
RT   Creative Writing
      Figurative Language
      Imagery
      Literary Genres
      Symbolism

HAITIAN CREOLE 300
BT   Creoles

Halfway Houses
USE   REHABILITATION CENTERS

Hallways
USE   CORRIDORS

HANDICAP-DETECTION 240
RT   Handicapped

HANDICAPPED 240
NT Academically Handicapped
Language Handicapped
Mentally Handicapped
Multiply Handicapped
Neurologically Handicapped
Perceptually Handicapped
Physically Handicapped
Speech Handicapped
BT Exceptional (Atypical)
RT Ability
Amputees
Cardiac (Person)
Cleft Lip
Cleft Palate
Companions (Occupation)
Epilepsy
Exceptional Child Research
Handicap Detection
Handicapped Children
Handicapped Students
Language Handicaps
Learning Disabilities
Occupational Therapy
Residential Care
Sensory Deprivation
Special Education Teachers
Wheel Chairs

HANDICAPPED CHILDREN 240
BT Children
RT Handicapped
Handicapped Students
Homebound
Hospitalized Children
Itinerant Teachers
Multiply Handicapped
Regular Class Placement

HANDICAPPED STUDENTS 240
BT Students
RT Academically Handicapped
Exceptional Students
Handicapped
Handicapped Children
Language Handicaps
Mentally Handicapped
Physically Handicapped

HANDICRAFTS 030
UF Crafts
Leather Crafts
BT Art
RT Ceramics
Crafts Rooms
Design Crafts

HAND TOOLS 170
BT Equipment
RT Machine Tools
Shop Curriculum
Vocational Education
Woodworking

HANDWRITING 080
NT Cursive Writing
Manuscript Writing (Handlettering)
BT Writing
RT Handwriting Development
Handwriting Instruction
Handwriting Materials
Handwriting Readiness
Handwriting Skills
Left Handed Writer

HANDWRITING DEVELOPMENT 130
BT Development
RT Handwriting

HANDWRITING INSTRUCTION 270
UF Handwriting Teaching
BT Instruction
RT Handwriting

HANDWRITING MATERIALS 050
BT Instructional Materials
RT Handwriting
Paper (Material)

HANDWRITING READINESS 180
BT Readiness
RT Handwriting

HANDWRITING SKILLS 010
BT Skills
RT Cursive Writing
Handwriting
Manuscript Writing (Handlettering)

Handwriting Teaching
USE HANDWRITING INSTRUCTION

HAPTIC PERCEPTION 070
BT Perception
RT Cutaneous Sense
Kinesthetic Perception
Sensory Experience
Sensory Training
Tactual Perception

Hard Core Curriculum
USE CORE CURRICULUM

HARD OF HEARING 240
BT Aurally Handicapped
RT Audiometric Tests
Audition (Physiology)
Auditory Tests
Deaf
Ears
Exceptional (Atypical)
Hearing Aids
Hearing Conservation
Hearing Loss
Hearing Therapists
Hearing Therapy
Loop Induction Systems

HARVESTING 350
UF   Crop Harvesting
RT   Agricultural Production
     Agriculture
     Agronomy
     Field Crops
     Horticulture
     Plant Science

Hashish
USE MARIHUANA

HAUSA 300
BT   Chad Languages

HAWAIIAN 300
BT   Malayo Polynesian Languages

HEADS OF HOUSEHOLDS 380
UF   Breadwinners
     Family Breadwinners
     Household Heads
BT   Family (Sociological Unit)
RT   Family Characteristics
     Fatherless Family
     Motherless Family
     One Parent Family
     Parents

HEALTH 250
NT   Dental Health
     Family Health
     Mental Health
     Physical Health
     Public Health
RT   Alcoholism
     Asthma
     Cardiac (Person)
     Cleaning
     Diabetes
     Dietetics
     Diseases
     Dishwashing
     Drug Addiction
     Drug Legislation
     Eating Habits
     Fatigue (Biology)
     Geriatrics
     Health Activities
     Health Books
     Health Conditions
     Health Education
     Health Insurance
     Health Needs
     Health Occupations Education
     Health Programs
     Health Services
     Human Body
     Hygiene
     Infectious Diseases
     Injuries
     Nutrition
     Prenatal Influences
     Psychosomatic Diseases
     Sanitation Improvement
     Sedatives
     Smoking
     Special Health Problems
     Stimulants
     Tobacco

HEALTH ACTIVITIES 250
BT   Activities
RT   Health
     Health Activities Handbooks
     Health Education

HEALTH ACTIVITIES HANDBOOKS 050
BT   Health Books
RT   Health Activities
     Health Guides

HEALTH BOOKS 050
NT   Health Activities Handbooks
BT   Books
RT   Health

HEALTH CONDITIONS 250
RT   Health
     Sanitary Facilities
     Sanitation Improvement

HEALTH EDUCATION 140
BT   Education
RT   Alcohol Education
     Alcoholism
     Consumer Education
     Drug Abuse
     Drug Addiction
     First Aid
     Health
     Health Activities
     Health Guides
     Health Occupations Education
     Health Programs
     Human Body
     Hygiene
     Nutrition Instruction
     Sanitation Improvement
     Smoking
     Tobacco

HEALTH FACILITIES 210
UF   Infirmaries
NT   Hospitals
     Nursing Homes
BT   Facilities
RT   Building Design
     Clinics
     First Aid
     Health Needs
     Health Occupations Centers
     Health Services
     Medical Services
     Medical Treatment
     Sanitary Facilities
     Toilet Facilities

HEALTH GUIDES 250
RT Health Activities Handbooks
    Health Education

Health Impaired
USE SPECIAL HEALTH PROBLEMS

HEALTH INSURANCE 250
RT Fire Insurance
    Fringe Benefits
    Health
    Health Services
    Insurance Occupations
    Insurance Programs
    Unemployment Insurance
    Workmans Compensation

Health Manpower
USE HEALTH PERSONNEL

HEALTH NEEDS 250
BT Needs
RT Dishwashing
    Fire Protection
    Health
    Health Facilities

HEALTH OCCUPATIONS 350
NT Paramedical Occupations
    Surgical Technicians
BT Occupations
RT Anesthesiology
    Companions (Occupation)
    Dental Hygienists
    Dentists
    Emergency Squad Personnel
    Health Occupations Education
    Health Services
    Hospital Personnel
    Inhalation Therapists
    Medical Associations
    Medical Consultants
    Medical Laboratory Assistants
    Medical Schools
    Nurses
    Nurses Aides
    Occupational Therapy Assistants
    Pharmacists
    Physical Therapists
    Physical Therapy Aides
    Physicians
    Psychiatric Aides

HEALTH OCCUPATIONS CENTERS 210
BT Educational Facilities
RT Health Facilities
    Health Occupations Education

HEALTH OCCUPATIONS EDUCATION 140
BT Vocational Education
RT Clinical Experience
    Companions (Occupation)
    Dental Hygienists
    Dental Technicians
    Health

    Health Education
    Health Occupations
    Health Occupations Centers
    Health Personnel
    Health Services
    Inhalation Therapists
    Medical Laboratory Assistants
    Medical Record Technicians
    Medical Technologists
    Nurses Aides
    Occupational Therapy Assistants
    Paramedical Occupations
    Surgical Technicians

Health Occupations Personnel
USE HEALTH PERSONNEL

HEALTH PERSONNEL 380
UF Health Manpower
    Health Occupations Personnel
    Health Service Personnel
    Health Service Workers
    Health Workers
NT Dental Hygienists
    Dental Technicians
    Dietitians
    Environmental Technicians
    Inhalation Therapists
    Medical Assistants
    Medical Laboratory Assistants
    Medical Record Technicians
    Medical Technologists
    Nurses
    Nurses Aides
    Occupational Therapy Assistants
    Physical Therapy Aides
    Psychiatric Aides
    Radiologic Technologists
    Veterinary Assistants
BT Personnel
RT Clinic Personnel (School)
    Companions (Occupation)
    Dental Assistants
    Dentistry
    Dentists
    Health Occupations Education
    Health Services
    Hospital Personnel
    Medical Laboratory Assistants
    Medical Record Librarians
    Occupational Therapists
    Paramedical Occupations
    Pharmacists
    Physical Therapists
    Physicians
    Psychiatrists
    Pupil Personnel Workers

HEALTH PROGRAMS 250
NT   Immunization Programs
     Mental Health Programs
BT   Programs
RT   Health
     Health Education
     Student Personnel Programs

Health Related Professions
USE PARAMEDICAL OCCUPATIONS

Health Service Personnel
USE HEALTH PERSONNEL

HEALTH SERVICES 250
NT   Clinics
     Community Health Services
     Medical Services
     Migrant Health Services
     School Health Services
BT   Human Services
RT   Ancillary Services
     Clinic Personnel (School)
     Dental Assistants
     Dental Hygienists
     Dental Technicians
     First Aid
     Health
     Health Facilities
     Health Insurance
     Health Occupations
     Health Occupations Education
     Health Personnel
     Hospitals
     Medical Laboratory Assistants
     Medical Treatment
     Nurses
     Paramedical Occupations
     Pharmacists
     Psychiatric Hospitals
     Sanitation Improvement
     Teacher Nurses

Health Service Workers
USE HEALTH PERSONNEL

Health Workers
USE HEALTH PERSONNEL

Hearing
USE AUDITION (PHYSIOLOGY)

HEARING AIDS 250
RT   Audition (Physiology)
     Auditory Training
     Aurally Handicapped
     Deaf
     Hard Of Hearing
     Loop Induction Systems
     Sensory Aids

HEARING CLINICS 210
BT   Clinics
RT   Audiologists
     Audiology
     Audiometrists
     Audition (Physiology)
     Auditory Evaluation
     Aurally Handicapped
     Hearing Therapists
     Hearing Therapy

HEARING CONSERVATION 250
RT   Audiolingual Methods
     Auditory Training
     Auditory Visual Tests
     Aural Learning
     Aurally Handicapped
     Aural Stimuli
     Deaf
     Hard Of Hearing

Hearing Impaired Children
USE AURALLY HANDICAPPED

HEARING LOSS 240
RT   Audiometric Tests
     Audition (Physiology)
     Auditory Tests
     Aurally Handicapped
     Deaf
     Ears
     Hard Of Hearing

Hearing Tests
USE AUDITORY TESTS

HEARING THERAPISTS 380
BT   Therapists
RT   Audiolingual Methods
     Audiologists
     Auditory Training
     Aurally Handicapped
     Deaf
     Hard Of Hearing
     Hearing Clinics
     Hearing Therapy
     Lipreading
     Speech Therapists

HEARING THERAPY 250
BT   Therapy
RT   Audiolingual Methods
     Audiologists
     Audiometrists
     Aurally Handicapped
     Coded Speech
     Deaf
     Ears
     Exceptional (Atypical)
     Hard Of Hearing
     Hearing Clinics
     Hearing Therapists
     Language Development
     Lipreading

HEART RATE 070
UF   Pulse Rate
BT   Physiology
RT   Blood Circulation
     Cardiovascular System
     Physical Fitness
     Physical Health

HEAT 400
RT   Calorimeters
     Chimneys
     Climatic Factors
     Energy
     Fuels
     Kinetic Molecular Theory
     Kinetics
     Solar Radiation
     Temperature
     Thermodynamics

Heat Equations
USE   THERMODYNAMICS

HEATING 170
RT   Air Conditioning
     Air Conditioning Equipment
     Air Flow
     Building Design
     Chimneys
     Climate Control
     Controlled Environment
     Design Needs
     Exhausting
     Fuel Consumption
     Fuels
     Humidity
     Lighting
     Mechanical Equipment
     Physical Environment
     Temperature
     Thermal Environment
     Utilities
     Ventilation

Heating Oils
USE   FUELS

HEBREW 300
BT   Semitic Languages

HEIGHT 400
BT   Scientific Concepts
RT   Distance
     Mathematics
     Measurement

Helicopter Pilots
USE   AIRCRAFT PILOTS

Hemodynamics
USE   BLOOD CIRCULATION

HERBICIDES 070
BT   Pesticides
RT   Agricultural Chemical Occupations
     Agricultural Supplies
     Agriculture
     Horticulture
     Insecticides
     Plant Growth
     Plant Pathology
     Plant Science
     Pollution
     Weeds

HEREDITY 070
BT   Biology
RT   Anomalies
     Evolution
     Genetics
     Prenatal Influences

Heroic Epics
USE   MEDIEVAL ROMANCE

Heterogeneous Classes
USE   HETEROGENEOUS GROUPING

HETEROGENEOUS GROUPING 280
UF   Heterogeneous Classes
BT   Student Grouping
RT   Ethnic Grouping
     T Groups

HETEROPHORIA 240
UF   Cyclophoria
     Esophoria
     Exophoria
     Hyperphoria
     Hypophoria
RT   Heterotropia
     Visual Acuity

HETEROTROPIA 240
UF   Cross Eyes
     Esotropia
     Exotropia
     Hypertropia
     Hypotropia
     Strabismus
     Walleyes
RT   Heterophoria
     Visual Acuity
     Visually Handicapped

Heuristic Games
USE   EDUCATIONAL GAMES

Hierarchy
USE   ORGANIZATION

HIGH ACHIEVERS 380
BT   Students
RT   Academic Achievement
     Achievement
     Gifted
     Overachievers

Superior Students
Talented Students

HIGHER EDUCATION 140
UF Advanced Education
NT Post Doctoral Education
BT Education
RT College Preparation
Colleges
Dental Schools
Doctoral Programs
Graduate Students
Graduate Study
Junior Colleges
Junior College Students
Library Schools
Medical Schools
Medical Students
Negro Colleges
Private Colleges
Professors
State Colleges
State Universities
Undergraduate Study
Universities
Urban Universities
Womens Education

HIGH INTEREST LOW VOCABULARY BOOKS 050
BT Textbooks
RT Books
Instructional Materials
Reading Materials
Special Education

High School College Cooperation
USE COLLEGE HIGH SCHOOL COOPERATION

HIGH SCHOOL CURRICULUM 110
BT Curriculum
RT High Schools

HIGH SCHOOL DESIGN 030
BT School Design
RT High Schools

High School Dropouts
USE DROPOUTS

High School Grades (Scholastic)
USE GRADES (SCHOLASTIC)

HIGH SCHOOL GRADUATES 380
BT Graduates
RT High Schools
Post High School Guidance

HIGH SCHOOL ORGANIZATION 020
BT School Organization
RT English Departments

HIGH SCHOOL ROLE 490
NT Junior High School Role
BT School Role

HIGH SCHOOLS 470
UF Precollege Level
NT Catholic High Schools
Comprehensive High Schools
Continuation High Schools
General High Schools
Junior High Schools
Senior High Schools
Vocational High Schools
BT Schools
RT College High School Cooperation
High School Curriculum
High School Design
High School Graduates
High School Students
High School Supervisors
Middle Schools
Post High School Guidance
Secondary Grades
Secondary Schools

HIGH SCHOOL STUDENTS 380
BT Secondary School Students
RT Freshmen
High Schools
Junior High School Students
Seniors

HIGH SCHOOL SUPERVISORS 380
BT Supervisors
RT High Schools
School Administration

High School Teachers
USE SECONDARY SCHOOL TEACHERS

Highway Construction
USE ROAD CONSTRUCTION

Highway Engineering
USE CIVIL ENGINEERING

HIGHWAY ENGINEERING AIDES 380
BT Engineering Technicians
RT Civil Engineering
Engineering
Technical Occupations

HINDI 300
BT Indo European Languages
RT Urdu

HISTORICAL CRITICISM 260
BT Literature
RT Literary Analysis
Literary Conventions
Literary Criticism
Literary Genres
Moral Criticism
Symbols (Literary)
Textual Criticism

Historical Linguistics
USE DIACHRONIC LINGUISTICS

HISTORICAL REVIEWS 320
BT Publications
RT Book Reviews
    History
    Literature Reviews

HISTORY 260
NT African History
    American History
    Ancient History
    Asian History
    Constitutional History
    Educational History
    European History
    Literary History
    Medieval History
    Middle Eastern History
    Modern History
    Negro History
    Science History
    World History
BT Social Sciences
    Social Studies
RT Area Studies
    Christianity
    Chronicles
    Historical Reviews
    History Instruction
    History Textbooks
    Judaism
    Language And Area Centers
    Museums
    Non Western Civilization
    Western Civilization

HISTORY INSTRUCTION 270
BT Instruction
RT History
    Modern History

History Of Education
USE EDUCATIONAL HISTORY

History Of Language
USE DIACHRONIC LINGUISTICS

HISTORY TEXTBOOKS 050
BT Textbooks
RT History

HOBBIES 390
BT Recreational Activities
RT Personal Interests

Hokku
USE HAIKU

Holding Power (Of Schools)
USE SCHOOL HOLDING POWER

Home
USE FAMILY ENVIRONMENT

Home And Family Life Education
USE FAMILY LIFE EDUCATION

Home Appliance Servicemen
USE ELECTRICAL APPLIANCE SERVICEMEN

Home Attendants
USE COMPANIONS (OCCUPATION)

HOMEBOUND 240
SN Status of person receiving instruction
    confined to domicile
BT Exceptional (Atypical)
RT Handicapped Children
    Homebound Children
    Homebound Teachers
    Home Instruction
    Special Education

HOMEBOUND CHILDREN 380
SN Physically or mentally disabled children
    confined to their homes
BT Children
RT Homebound
    Home Instruction
    Residential Care

HOMEBOUND TEACHERS 380
BT Itinerant Teachers
    Special Education Teachers
    Teachers
RT Homebound
    Home Instruction

Home Conditions
USE FAMILY ENVIRONMENT

HOME ECONOMICS 110
BT Economics
RT Consumer Economics
    Consumer Education
    Consumer Science
    Home Economics Education
    Home Economics Teachers
    Homemaking Skills
    Home Management
    Housewives
    Nutrition

Home Economics Competencies
USE HOME ECONOMICS SKILLS

HOME ECONOMICS EDUCATION 140
NT Homemaking Education
    Occupational Home Economics
BT Vocational Education
RT Clothing Instruction
    Consumer Education
    Consumer Science
    Cooking Instruction
    Foods Instruction
    Home Economics
    Home Economics Skills
    Home Economics Teachers
    Homemakers Clubs
    Homemaking Skills
    Home Management
    Home Visits
    Money Management

Nutrition Instruction
Sewing Instruction
Textiles Instruction

Home Economics Gainful Employment
USE OCCUPATIONAL HOME ECONOMICS

HOME ECONOMICS SKILLS 010
UF   Home Economics Competencies
BT   Skills
RT   Employment Qualifications
      Home Economics Education
      Homemaking Skills
      Job Skills

HOME ECONOMICS TEACHERS 380
BT   Vocational Education Teachers
RT   Home Economics
      Home Economics Education
      Homemaking Education
      Occupational Home Economics

Home Economics Wage Earning
USE OCCUPATIONAL HOME ECONOMICS

Home Environment
USE FAMILY ENVIRONMENT

Home Experiences
USE FIELD EXPERIENCE PROGRAMS

HOME FURNISHINGS 170
RT   Electrical Appliances
      Furniture
      Housing
      Storage

Home Health Aides
USE COMPANIONS (OCCUPATION)

Home Influence
USE FAMILY INFLUENCE

HOME INSTRUCTION 270
BT   Instruction
RT   Homebound
      Homebound Children
      Homebound Teachers

Home Life
USE FAMILY LIFE

Homemakers Assistants
USE MAIDS

HOMEMAKERS CLUBS 370
RT   Home Economics Education
      Homemaking Skills

HOMEMAKING EDUCATION 140
BT   Home Economics Education
RT   Consumer Education
      Family Health
      Family Life
      Family Life Education
      Family Management
      Family Relationship
      Home Economics Teachers

HOMEMAKING SKILLS 010
BT   Skills
RT   Home Economics
      Home Economics Education
      Home Economics Skills
      Homemakers Clubs
      Housewives
      Maids
      Practical Arts

HOME MANAGEMENT 490
RT   Consumer Economics
      Consumer Education
      Family Management
      Home Economics
      Home Economics Education
      Housewives
      Housing Management Aides
      Money Management
      Visiting Homemakers

HOME PROGRAMS 410
BT   Programs

Home Projects
USE FIELD EXPERIENCE PROGRAMS

Home School Relationship
USE FAMILY SCHOOL RELATIONSHIP

Homes For The Aged
USE PERSONAL CARE HOMES

HOME STUDY 270
BT   Study
RT   Correspondence Courses
      Correspondence Schools
      Correspondence Study
      Extension Education
      Homework
      Independent Study

HOME VISITS 270
RT   Community Health Services
      Home Economics Education
      Parents
      Parent School Relationship
      Parent Teacher Cooperation
      Students
      Student Teacher Relationship
      Teachers

HOMEWORK 270
UF   Homework Assignments
RT   Assignments
      Home Study

Homework Assignments
USE HOMEWORK

Homogeneous Classes
USE HOMOGENEOUS GROUPING

HOMOGENEOUS GROUPING 280
UF   Homogeneous Classes
BT   Student Grouping
RT   Ability Grouping

HONORS CLASSES 280
BT   Honors Curriculum

Honors Courses
USE   HONORS CURRICULUM

HONORS CURRICULUM 110
UF   Honors Courses
     Honors Programs
NT   Honors Classes
BT   Curriculum
RT   Elective Subjects
     Honor Societies
     Independent Study

HONOR SOCIETIES 370
RT   Honors Curriculum
     International Organizations
     National Organizations

Honors Programs
USE   HONORS CURRICULUM

HORIZONTAL ORGANIZATION 020
BT   Organization
RT   Pyramid Organization
     Vertical Organization

HORIZONTAL TEXTS 050
BT   Programed Texts

Horologists
USE   WATCHMAKERS

HOROLOGY 350
RT   Electromechanical Technology
     Instrumentation
     Kinetics
     Motion
     Technical Education
     Time
     Watchmakers

HORSES 070
BT   Livestock
RT   Animal Science
     Veterinary Medicine

HORTICULTURE 070
NT   Ornamental Horticulture
BT   Agriculture
RT   Agricultural Research Projects
     Entomology
     Harvesting
     Herbicides
     Nurseries (Horticulture)
     Plant Growth
     Plant Identification
     Planting
     Plant Propagation
     Plant Science
     Transplanting

Hospital Attendants
USE   NURSES AIDES

HOSPITALIZED CHILDREN 380
BT   Children
RT   Exceptional (Atypical)
     Handicapped Children
     Hospital Schools

Hospital Libraries
USE   MEDICAL LIBRARIES

HOSPITAL PERSONNEL 380
BT   Personnel
RT   Health Occupations
     Health Personnel
     Institutional Personnel
     Nurses
     Physicians
     Professional Occupations

Hospital Record Librarians
USE   MEDICAL RECORD LIBRARIANS

HOSPITALS 210
UF   Sanatoriums
NT   Psychiatric Hospitals
BT   Health Facilities
RT   Clinics
     Health Services
     Hospital Schools
     Institution Libraries
     Medical Services
     Nursing Homes

HOSPITAL SCHOOLS 470
BT   Schools
RT   Hospitalized Children
     Hospitals

HOSTILITY 420
BT   Psychological Patterns
RT   Aggression
     Catharsis

HOTELS 210
UF   Inns
     Motels
     Tourist Courts
RT   Buildings
     Tourism

Hothouses
USE   GREENHOUSES

Hours Of Work
USE   WORKING HOURS

Household Heads
USE   HEADS OF HOUSEHOLDS

Households
USE   FAMILY (SOCIOLOGICAL UNIT)

Household Science
USE   CONSUMER SCIENCE

Housekeepers
USE   MAIDS

Housekeeping Aides
USE MAIDS

HOUSE PLAN 210
SN The organization of a large college or
     university into smaller communities,
     each having its own residence hall, etc.
BT School Organization
RT Building Plans
     College Planning
     Dormitories
     Educational Facilities
     Housing
     Master Plans

HOUSEWIVES 380
BT Females
RT Family (Sociological Unit)
     Family Life
     Family Management
     Family Relationship
     Family Role
     Family Structure
     Home Economics
     Homemaking Skills
     Home Management
     Labor Force Nonparticipants
     Marital Status
     Marriage

HOUSING 210
NT College Housing
     Low Rent Housing
     Middle Income Housing
     Migrant Housing
     Negro Housing
     Public Housing
     Suburban Housing
     Teacher Housing
RT Animal Facilities
     Boarding Schools
     Dormitories
     Home Furnishings
     House Plan
     Housing Deficiencies
     Housing Discrimination
     Housing Industry
     Housing Management Aides
     Housing Needs
     Housing Opportunities
     Housing Patterns
     Human Services
     Landlords
     Local Housing Authorities
     Planned Community
     Real Estate Occupations
     Urban Renewal Agencies

HOUSING DEFICIENCIES 490
RT Housing

HOUSING DISCRIMINATION 490
BT Social Discrimination
RT Housing
     Housing Opportunities

HOUSING INDUSTRY 370
BT Industry
RT Construction Industry
     Housing
     Housing Opportunities
     Real Estate Occupations

HOUSING MANAGEMENT AIDES 380
SN Persons who aid public or private
     housing residents concerning
     regulations, relocations, etc. in addition
     to providing records for owners or
     managers
BT Subprofessionals
RT Home Management
     Housing
     Occupational Home Economics
     Public Housing
     Public Housing Residents
     Real Estate Occupations
     Welfare Services

HOUSING NEEDS 210
BT Needs
RT College Housing
     Housing

HOUSING OPPORTUNITIES 360
BT Opportunities
RT Housing
     Housing Discrimination
     Housing Industry

HOUSING PATTERNS 120
RT Housing

Hue
USE COLOR

HUMAN BODY 070
BT Biology
RT Anatomy
     Anomalies
     Body Image
     Cardiovascular System
     Health
     Health Education
     Human Development
     Human Posture
     Hygiene
     Medicine
     Space Orientation

HUMAN CAPITAL 460
SN Investment in the education and skills of
     a nations population
RT Economics
     Educational Economics
     Human Development
     Individual Development
     Investment

Labor Supply
Productivity

HUMAN DEVELOPMENT 130
UF Human Growth
NT Adult Development
Growth Patterns
Management Development
BT Development
RT Biochemistry
Cerebral Dominance
Developmental Guidance
Human Body
Human Capital
Human Posture
Maturation
Motor Development
Neurological Organization
Self Actualization

HUMAN DIGNITY 490
UF Individual Dignity
BT Sociology
RT Attitudes
Behavior
Individualism
Self Esteem

HUMAN ENGINEERING 420
SN Activity or science of designing, building,
or equipping environments or mechanical
devices to anthropometric, physiological,
or psychological requirements of human
operators
UF Biotechnology
Ergonomics
Human Factors Engineering
BT Engineering
Technology
RT Acoustical Environment
Biology
Cybernetics
Design Needs
Environment
Lighting
Man Machine Systems
Medicine
Physical Design Needs
Physical Environment
Pollution
Psychological Design Needs
Thermal Environment
Work Environment

Human Factors Engineering
USE HUMAN ENGINEERING

Human Growth
USE HUMAN DEVELOPMENT

HUMANISM 260
UF Humanitarianism
BT Philosophy
RT Classical Literature
Drama
Individualism
Literature
Poetry
Prose
Renaissance Literature

Humanitarianism
USE HUMANISM

HUMANITIES 260
NT Fine Arts
Languages
Literature
Philosophy
BT Liberal Arts
RT Christianity
Humanities Instruction
Judaism
Language And Area Centers
Nineteenth Century Literature
Religion

HUMANITIES INSTRUCTION 270
BT Instruction
RT Humanities

HUMAN LIVING 490
BT Sociocultural Patterns

HUMAN POSTURE 250
UF Body Attitude
Posture Development
Posture Patterns
RT Child Development
Human Body
Human Development

HUMAN RELATIONS 490
NT Race Relations
BT Relationship
RT Group Living
Group Relations
Human Relations Organizations
Human Relations Programs
Human Relations Units
Interfaith Relations
Intergroup Education
Intergroup Relations
Interpersonal Relationship
Rapport
Social Integration
Social Relations

Human Relations Commissions
USE HUMAN RELATIONS ORGANIZATIONS

Human Relations Committees
USE HUMAN RELATIONS ORGANIZATIONS

HUMAN RELATIONS ORGANIZATIONS 370
UF   Human Relations Commissions
      Human Relations Committees
BT   Organizations (Groups)
RT   Community Organizations
      Human Relations

HUMAN RELATIONS PROGRAMS 490
BT   Programs
RT   Human Relations

Human Relations Training
USE SENSITIVITY TRAINING

HUMAN RELATIONS UNITS 110
BT   Units Of Study (Subject Fields)
RT   Human Relations

HUMAN RESOURCES 460
NT   Consultants
BT   Resources
RT   Developed Nations
      Resource Teachers

Human Rights
USE CIVIL LIBERTIES

HUMAN SERVICES 490
SN   Fields of public service in which a
      person-to-person relationship, crucial to
      the provision of services, exists between
      the receivers and the providers of the
      services
NT   Counseling Services
      Employment Services
      Exceptional Child Services
      Health Services
      Psychological Services
      School Services
      Social Services
      Sociopsychological Services
      Welfare Services
BT   Services
RT   Correctional Education
      Correctional Rehabilitation
      Housing
      Law Enforcement
      Public Relations
      Recreation
      Rehabilitation

Humid Areas
USE HUMIDITY

HUMIDITY 160
UF   Absolute Humidity
      Humid Areas
      Relative Humidity
RT   Air Conditioning
      Climate Control
      Climatic Factors
      Controlled Environment
      Environmental Influences
      Heating
      Meteorology
      Physical Design Needs

      Temperature
      Thermal Environment

HUMOR 260
BT   Literature
RT   Essays
      Fiction
      Legends
      Novels
      Poetry
      Prose
      Tales

HUNGARIAN 300
BT   Finno Ugric Languages

HUNGER 250
UF   Appetite
RT   Breakfast Programs
      Child Abuse
      Economic Disadvantagement
      Lunch Programs
      Nutrition
      Welfare Problems

HYDRAULICS 400
RT   Agricultural Machinery
      Engines
      Fluid Power Education
      Kinetics

HYGIENE 250
UF   Body Care
      Personal Grooming
      Personal Health
RT   Cleaning
      Cosmetology
      Dental Health
      Dental Hygienists
      Diseases
      Dishwashing
      Health
      Health Education
      Human Body
      Infectious Diseases
      Locker Rooms
      Physical Health
      Sanitary Facilities
      Sanitation
      Self Care Skills

HYPERACTIVITY 060
BT   Behavior Patterns
RT   Behavior Problems
      Emotionally Disturbed
      Neurologically Handicapped

HYPEROPIA 240
UF   Farsightedness
BT   Ametropia
RT   Myopia

Hyperphoria
USE HETEROPHORIA

Hypersensitivity
USE ALLERGY

Hypertropia
USE HETEROTROPIA

HYPNOSIS 420
RT Psychotherapy

Hypnotics
USE SEDATIVES

Hypophoria
USE HETEROPHORIA

HYPOTHESIS TESTING 180
BT Statistical Analysis
RT Mathematical Models
Statistics
Tests Of Significance

Hypotropia
USE HETEROTROPIA

IBO 300
BT African Languages

Icibemba
USE BEMBA

IDENTIFICATION 180
UF Early Detection
NT Ability Identification
Delinquent Identification
Dropout Identification
Talent Identification
RT Association (Psychological)
Educational Diagnosis
Identification Tests

IDENTIFICATION (PSYCHOLOGICAL) 420
SN Process or state of imitating or merging
emotionally with someone or something
UF Introjection
NT Empathy
Imitation
BT Psychological Patterns
RT Association (Psychological)
Behavior Patterns
Black Community
Black Power
Conformity
Psychological Characteristics
Role Perception
Role Theory
Self Actualization
Self Concept

IDENTIFICATION TESTS 520
BT Tests
RT Ability Identification
Identification
Talent Identification

Identifying Dropouts
USE DROPOUT IDENTIFICATION

Idiomatic Expressions
USE IDIOMS

IDIOMS 290
UF Idiomatic Expressions
BT Language Patterns
RT American English
Dialects
Expressive Language
Grammar
Languages
Proverbs
Psycholinguistics
Regional Dialects
Sociolinguistics
Structural Analysis
Synchronic Linguistics
Verbal Communication

IGBO 300
BT African Languages

Illegitimacy
USE ILLEGITIMATE BIRTHS

ILLEGITIMATE BIRTHS 490
UF Illegitimacy
Illicit Birth
RT Contraception
Fatherless Family
Marital Instability
One Parent Family
Pregnancy

Illicit Birth
USE ILLEGITIMATE BIRTHS

ILLITERACY 440
NT Functional Illiteracy
RT Illiterate Adults

ILLITERATE ADULTS 380
BT Adults
RT Adult Education Programs
Functional Illiteracy
Illiteracy

Illumination
USE LIGHTING

ILLUMINATION LEVELS 500
SN Lighting requirements primarily
measured in foot candles
UF Foot Candles
RT Color Planning
Contrast
Daylight
Flexible Lighting Design
Glare
Light
Lighting
Lighting Design
Lights
Luminescence
Optics
Physical Environment
Task Performance
Visual Discrimination

Visual Perception
Windows

ILLUSTRATIONS 050
BT Audiovisual Aids
RT Diagrams
    Technical Illustration

IMAGERY 260
BT Figurative Language
RT Analytical Criticism
    Formal Criticism
    Haiku
    Impressionistic Criticism
    Literary Criticism
    Literature
    Metaphors
    Motifs
    Poetry
    Prose
    Symbols (Literary)

IMAGINATION 420
RT Creative Ability
    Creativity
    Fantasy
    Surrealism
    Thought Processes

IMITATION 420
BT Identification (Psychological)
RT Behavior Patterns
    Empathy
    Socialization

IMMATURITY 060
NT Social Immaturity
BT Psychological Patterns

IMMIGRANTS 380
RT Migrants
    Refugees
    Transient Children

IMMIGRATION INSPECTORS 380
UF Border Guards
    Border Patrol Officers
    Customs Inspectors
    Customs Officials
BT Government Employees
RT Armed Forces
    Federal Government
    Federal Laws
    Federal Troops
    Government (Administrative Body)
    Law Enforcement
    Military Personnel
    National Defense
    Officer Personnel
    Public Officials
    State Officials
    State Police

IMMUNIZATION PROGRAMS 250
BT Health Programs
RT Child Care
    Community Health Services
    Preventive Medicine

Impasse Resolution
USE NEGOTIATION IMPASSES

Imperative Mood
USE VERBS

IMPERIALISM 230
BT Policy
RT Authoritarianism
    Colonialism
    Communism
    Nationalism
    Political Attitudes
    Political Divisions (Geographic)
    Political Power
    World Problems

IMPRESSIONISTIC CRITICISM 260
BT Literary Criticism
RT Allegory
    Fiction
    Formal Criticism
    Imagery
    Literature
    Novels
    Poetry
    Prose

IMPROVEMENT 130
UF Upgrading
NT Building Improvement
    City Improvement
    Educational Improvement
    Facility Improvement
    Neighborhood Improvement
    Program Improvement
    Reading Improvement
    Sanitation Improvement
    School Improvement
    Staff Improvement
    Student Improvement
    Teacher Improvement
RT Improvement Programs
    Refresher Courses

IMPROVEMENT PROGRAMS 410
NT Self Help Programs
BT Programs
RT Improvement
    Refresher Courses

Impulse Control
USE SELF CONTROL

INCENTIVE GRANTS 220
BT Grants
RT Educational Finance
    Federal Aid
    Foundation Programs
    Private Financial Support

Incentives
USE MOTIVATION

INCENTIVE SYSTEMS 020
RT Teacher Motivation
RT Teaching Quality

INCIDENCE 120
SN Rate or range of occurrance or influence
of a condition
RT Census Figures
Geographic Distribution
Population Distribution
Racial Distribution
Social Distribution
Student Distribution
Teacher Distribution

INCIDENTAL LEARNING 310
BT Learning

INCOME 220
UF Income Patterns
Revenue
Salary Income
NT Family Income
Guaranteed Income
Low Income
Premium Pay
Salaries
Wages
BT Economic Factors
RT Developed Nations
Middle Income Housing
Money Management
Overtime
Socioeconomic Status
Trusts (Financial)

Income Patterns
USE INCOME

Incoming Transfer Students
USE TRANSFER STUDENTS

INDEMNITY BONDS 220
RT Employee Responsibility
Insurance Programs
Legal Responsibility
Risk

Independent Learning
USE INDEPENDENT STUDY

INDEPENDENT READING 440
BT Reading
RT Independent Study

INDEPENDENT STUDY 510
SN Study carried on with a minimum or a
complete absence of external guidance
UF Independent Learning
Self Teaching
BT Study
RT Correspondence Schools
Correspondence Study

Curriculum
Elective Subjects
Home Study
Honors Curriculum
Independent Reading
Individual Instruction
Individual Study

INDEXES (LOCATERS) 370
NT Bibliographies
Booklists
Citation Indexes
Coordinate Indexes
Permuted Indexes
BT Reference Materials
RT Abstracts
Book Catalogs
Cataloging
Catalogs
Classification
Codification
Concordances
Dictionary Catalogs
Directories
Divided Catalogs
Documentation
Indexing
Information Retrieval
Information Utilization
Library Science
Publications
Subject Index Terms
Taxonomy
Thesauri
Union Catalogs

INDEXING 330
UF Coordinate Indexing
BT Library Technical Processes
RT Abstracting
Abstracts
Bibliographic Coupling
Cataloging
Citation Indexes
Classification
Coordinate Indexes
Documentation
Filing
Indexes (Locaters)
Information Retrieval
Library Science
Permuted Indexes
Search Strategies
Subject Index Terms

INDIANS 380
SN Natives of India or of the East Indies
RT Ethnic Groups
Race

Indicative Mood
USE VERBS

INDIGENOUS PERSONNEL 380
BT Personnel

INDIVIDUAL ACTIVITIES 510
BT Activities

Individual Approach
USE INDIVIDUAL INSTRUCTION

INDIVIDUAL CHARACTERISTICS 380
UF Characteristics (Individual)
    Personality Traits
NT Curiosity
    Individual Differences
    Integrity
    Learning Characteristics
    Physical Characteristics
RT Administrator Characteristics
    Adult Characteristics
    Counselor Characteristics
    Dropout Characteristics
    Participant Characteristics
    Personality
    Personality Tests
    Psychological Characteristics
    Student Characteristics
    Teacher Characteristics

INDIVIDUAL COUNSELING 090
BT Counseling
RT Parent Counseling

Individual Creativity
USE CREATIVITY

INDIVIDUAL DEVELOPMENT 130
UF Personal Development
    Self Growth
BT Development
RT Adolescence
    Child Development
    Childhood
    Growth Patterns
    Human Capital
    Individual Differences
    Infancy
    Learning Readiness
    Maturation
    Motor Development
    Personal Growth
    Personality Development
    Self Actualization
    Self Congruence
    Self Control
    Sportsmanship
    Student Development

INDIVIDUAL DIFFERENCES 420
NT Age Differences
    Sex Differences
BT Individual Characteristics
RT Individual Development
    Individual Instruction
    Social Differences

Individual Dignity
USE HUMAN DIGNITY

INDIVIDUAL INSTRUCTION 270
UF Individual Approach
BT Instruction
RT Exceptional Child Education
    Independent Study
    Individual Differences
    Individualized Curriculum
    Individualized Instruction
    Individualized Programs
    Individual Needs
    Itinerant Teachers
    Large Group Instruction
    Multimedia Instruction
    Special Education
    Telephone Instruction
    Tutorial Programs
    Tutoring

Individual Inventory
USE STUDENT RECORDS

INDIVIDUALISM 260
BT Philosophy
RT Creativity
    Existentialism
    Human Dignity
    Humanism
    Individual Power
    Self Actualization
    Self Expression
    Social Development
    Social Values

Individuality
USE PERSONALITY

INDIVIDUALIZED CURRICULUM 110
NT Individual Reading
BT Curriculum
RT Individual Instruction
    Individualized Instruction
    Individualized Programs

Individualized Education
USE INDIVIDUALIZED INSTRUCTION

INDIVIDUALIZED INSTRUCTION 270
UF Clinical Teaching
    Individualized Education
BT Instruction
RT Classroom Techniques
    Individual Instruction
    Individualized Curriculum
    Individualized Programs
    Individualized Reading
    Mass Instruction

INDIVIDUALIZED PROGRAMS 410
BT Programs
RT Individual Instruction
    Individualized Curriculum
    Individualized Instruction
    Individualized Reading
    Tutorial Programs

212

INDIVIDUALIZED READING 440
SN   Technique concerned with the overall
     development of a persons reading skills
     and interests attempting to follow
     concept of self selection
BT   Reading
RT   Individualized Instruction
     Individualized Programs
     Reading Instruction
     Reading Programs
     Teaching Methods

INDIVIDUAL NEEDS 420
NT   Childhood Needs
BT   Needs
RT   Affection
     Design Preferences
     Individual Instruction
     Psychological Needs
     Storage

INDIVIDUAL POWER 010
SN   Feeling of power to effect changes in
     ones social and physical surroundings by
     decision making
UF   Destiny Control
     Individual Volition
     Self Determination
     Volition
RT   Adjustment (To Environment)
     Behavior
     Black Power
     Cultural Factors
     Decision Making
     Environmental Influences
     Individualism
     Personal Growth
     Self Concept
     Self Control

Individual Projects
USE   STUDENT PROJECTS

INDIVIDUAL PSYCHOLOGY 420
UF   Psychology (Individual)
NT   Child Psychology
     Developmental Psychology
     Psychological Patterns
BT   Psychology
RT   Adaptation Level Theory
     Personality
     Projective Tests
     Psychoeducational Processes
     Psychological Characteristics
     Psychological Needs
     Psychotherapy
     Rational Therapy
     Self Actualization

INDIVIDUAL READING 440
BT   Individualized Curriculum
     Reading
RT   Individual Study

Individual Rights
USE   CIVIL LIBERTIES

INDIVIDUAL STUDY 510
BT   Study
RT   Continuous Progress Plan
     Independent Study
     Individual Reading

INDIVIDUAL TESTS 520
BT   Tests
RT   Performance Tests
     Projective Tests

Individual Volition
USE   INDIVIDUAL POWER

INDO EUROPEAN LANGUAGES 300
NT   Afrikaans
     Albanian
     Armenian
     Baluchi
     Bengali
     Dutch
     German
     Greek
     Gujarati
     Hindi
     Kashmiri
     Kurdish
     Marathi
     Nepali
     Norwegian
     Ossetic
     Panjabi
     Pashto
     Persian
     Romance Languages
     Sanskrit
     Singhalese
     Tajik
     Urdu
BT   Languages
RT   Language Classification
     Middle English
     Native Speakers
     Old English

INDONESIAN 300
UF   Bahasa Indonesia
BT   Indonesian Languages

INDONESIAN LANGUAGES 300
NT   Bikol
     Dusun
     Indonesian
     Malagasy
     Malay
     Maranao
     Tagalog
     Visayan
BT   Malayo Polynesian Languages

INDUCTIVE METHODS 510
BT Methods
RT Deductive Methods
Discovery Processes
Divergent Thinking
Intellectualization
Learning Processes
Teaching Methods
Thought Processes

INDUSTRIAL ARTS 030
UF Industrial Crafts
Practical Skills
RT Aerospace Technology
Auto Mechanics
Building Trades
Cabinetmaking
Ceramics
Communications
Construction (Process)
Drafting
Electronics
Foundries
Industrial Arts Teachers
Industrial Education
Industry
Laboratory Technology
Metals
Operating Engineering
Orthogonal Projection
Plastics
Power Mechanics
Practical Arts
Printing
School Shops
Service Education
Service Occupations
Shop Curriculum
Trade And Industrial Education
Vocational Education
Woodworking

Industrial Arts Laboratories
USE SCHOOL SHOPS

Industrial Arts Shops
USE SCHOOL SHOPS

INDUSTRIAL ARTS TEACHERS 380
BT Teachers
RT Industrial Arts

Industrial Crafts
USE INDUSTRIAL ARTS

INDUSTRIAL EDUCATION 140
SN All types of education related to industry
including industrial arts and education
for occupations in industry at all levels
UF Industrial Instruction
BT Education
RT Fluid Power Education
Industrial Arts
Industrial Technology
Industrial Training

Trade And Industrial Education
Trade And Industrial Teachers
Vocational Education
Vocational Schools

Industrial Instruction
USE INDUSTRIAL EDUCATION

INDUSTRIALIZATION 490
RT Industrial Structure
Industry
Socioeconomic Influences
Steel Industry
Technological Advancement
Technology

Industrial Nations
USE DEVELOPED NATIONS

INDUSTRIAL PERSONNEL 380
BT Personnel
RT Administrative Personnel
Developed Nations
Employees
Employers
Industrial Relations
Industry
Laborers
Mechanical Design Technicians
Production Technicians
Supervisors

INDUSTRIAL RELATIONS 150
UF Employee Relations
Labor Relations
BT Relationship
RT Collective Bargaining
Collective Negotiation
Employer Employee Relationship
Employment
Fringe Benefits
Industrial Personnel
Industrial Training
Labor Unions
Public Relations

INDUSTRIAL STRUCTURE 490
RT Developed Nations
Industrialization
Industry
Mergers
Organization Size (Groups)

INDUSTRIAL TECHNOLOGY 400
BT Technology
RT Industrial Education
Industry
Technical Education

INDUSTRIAL TRAINING 270
SN Training for employees conducted by
industrial organizations
BT Training
RT Adult Vocational Education
Apprenticeships
Industrial Education

Industrial Relations
Inplant Programs
Job Training
Off The Job Training
On The Job Training
Released Time
Trade And Industrial Education
Trainees
Trainers

Industrial X Ray Operators
USE RADIOGRAPHERS

INDUSTRY 370
NT Aerospace Industry
Broadcast Industry
Cement Industry
Chemical Industry
Construction Industry
Electronics Industry
Feed Industry
Food Service Industry
Furniture Industry
Housing Industry
Lumber Industry
Manufacturing Industry
Meat Packing Industry
Metal Industry
Publishing Industry
Telephone Communications Industry
Tourism
RT Business
Coordinators
Equipment Manufacturers
Fluid Power Education
Industrial Arts
Industrialization
Industrial Personnel
Industrial Structure
Industrial Technology
Instrumentation
Mergers
Needle Trades
Office Machines
Organizations (Groups)
Organization Size (Groups)
Producer Services
School Industry Relationship

Industry School Relationship
USE SCHOOL INDUSTRY RELATIONSHIP

INEQUALITIES 340
BT Mathematical Concepts

INFANCY 130
RT Childhood
Individual Development
Infants
Pediatrics Training
Premature Infants

INFANT BEHAVIOR 060
BT Behavior
RT Infants

INFANTS 380
NT Premature Infants
RT Infancy
Infant Behavior

INFECTIOUS DISEASES 250
NT Rubella
BT Diseases
RT Communicable Diseases
Dishwashing
Health
Hygiene

Infirmaries
USE HEALTH FACILITIES

Inflatable Structures
USE AIR STRUCTURES

Informal Conversational Usage
USE STANDARD SPOKEN USAGE

INFORMAL LEADERSHIP 060
BT Leadership

INFORMAL ORGANIZATION 020
BT Organization
RT Communication (Thought Transfer)
Organizational Climate
Organizations (Groups)
Power Structure

INFORMAL READING INVENTORY 520
BT Reading Tests
RT Reading Ability
Reading Comprehension
Reading Materials
Word Recognition

INFORMATION CENTERS 210
BT Information Sources
RT Automation
Decentralized Library Systems
Educational Facilities
Information Science
Information Storage
Instructional Materials Centers
Libraries
Library Facilities
Library Technicians

INFORMATION DISSEMINATION 330
UF Dissemination
BT Information Processing
RT Diffusion
Documentation
Facsimile Transmission
Information Networks
Information Science
Information Services
Information Systems
Information Theory
Mass Media
Microfiche
Microfilm

Publicize
Publishing Industry

INFORMATION NEEDS 330
BT Needs
RT Educational Needs
    Information Retrieval
    Information Science
    Information Seeking
    Information Sources
    Library Reference Services
    Use Studies

INFORMATION NETWORKS 080
SN Information systems linked for
    information exchange through formal
    communications
BT Networks
RT Audiovisual Communication
    Communications
    Dial Access Information Systems
    Facsimile Communication Systems
    Information Dissemination
    Information Services
    Information Systems
    Intercommunication
    Library Networks
    Telephone Communication Systems

INFORMATION PROCESSING 080
NT Information Dissemination
    Information Retrieval
    Information Storage
BT Documentation
RT Automation
    Book Catalogs
    Cataloging
    Character Recognition
    Computational Linguistics
    Computers
    Computer Science
    Data Bases
    Data Processing
    Display Systems
    Feedback
    Filing
    Information Science
    Information Services
    Information Systems
    Information Theory
    Information Utilization
    Input Output
    Input Output Analysis
    Input Output Devices
    Library Research
    Library Technical Processes
    Machine Translation
    Optical Scanners
    Pattern Recognition
    Programing Languages

INFORMATION RETRIEVAL 330
NT Search Strategies
BT Information Processing
RT Bibliographic Coupling
    Citation Indexes
    Codification
    Computational Linguistics
    Coordinate Indexes
    Data Processing
    Dial Access Information Systems
    Documentation
    Indexes (Locaters)
    Indexing
    Information Needs
    Information Science
    Information Seeking
    Information Services
    Information Systems
    Information Theory
    Library Reference Services
    Library Science
    Permuted Indexes
    Programing Languages
    Relevance (Information Retrieval)
    Thesauri

Information Retrieval Precision
USE RELEVANCE (INFORMATION RETRIEVAL)

INFORMATION SCIENCE 330
SN Generation, transformation,
    communication, storage, retrieval, and
    use of information
NT Documentation
RT Computer Science
    Information Centers
    Information Dissemination
    Information Needs
    Information Processing
    Information Retrieval
    Information Services
    Information Storage
    Information Systems
    Information Utilization
    Library Education
    Library Research
    Library Schools
    Library Science
    Search Strategies
    Use Studies

INFORMATION SEEKING 310
BT Learning Processes
RT Communication (Thought Transfer)
    Concept Formation
    Continuous Learning
    Information Needs
    Information Retrieval
    Information Sources
    Information Theory
    Information Utilization
    Problem Solving

Search Strategies
Use Studies

INFORMATION SERVICES 330
RT Information Dissemination
Information Networks
Information Processing
Information Retrieval
Information Science
Information Storage
Information Systems
Information Utilization
Interlibrary Loans
Library Reference Services
Library Services

INFORMATION SOURCES 460
NT Information Centers
RT Data Bases
Information Needs
Information Seeking
Information Storage
Information Utilization
Instructional Materials Centers
Libraries
Library Reference Services
Resources
Use Studies

INFORMATION STORAGE 330
UF Filing Systems
BT Information Processing
Storage
RT Computer Output Microfilm
Computer Storage Devices
Data Bases
Data Collection
Data Processing
Dictionary Catalogs
Divided Catalogs
Documentation
File Clerks
Filing
Information Centers
Information Science
Information Services
Information Sources
Information Systems
Information Theory
Magnetic Tapes
Medical Record Technicians
Microforms
Programing Languages
Recordkeeping
Search Strategies
Union Catalogs

INFORMATION SYSTEMS 330
NT Dial Access Information Systems
RT Data Processing
Documentation
Electronic Data Processing
Information Dissemination
Information Networks

Information Processing
Information Retrieval
Information Science
Information Services
Information Storage
Information Theory
Information Utilization
Interlibrary Loans
Management Systems
Man Machine Systems
Relevance (Information Retrieval)
Telecommunication

INFORMATION THEORY 080
UF Communication Theory
BT Theories
RT Communication (Thought Transfer)
Computer Science
Cybernetics
Information Dissemination
Information Processing
Information Retrieval
Information Seeking
Information Storage
Information Systems
Information Utilization
Input Output
Linguistics
Models
Operations Research
Speech Compression
Telecommunication

INFORMATION UTILIZATION 330
RT Bibliographic Coupling
Indexes (Locaters)
Information Processing
Information Science
Information Seeking
Information Services
Information Sources
Information Systems
Information Theory
Library Research
Research Utilization
Use Studies

INHALATION THERAPISTS 380
UF Inhalation Therapy Technicians
Oxygen Therapists
Oxygen Therapy Technicians
BT Health Personnel
RT Health Occupations
Health Occupations Education

Inhalation Therapy Technicians
USE INHALATION THERAPISTS

INHIBITION 420
UF Proactive Inhibition
Reactive Inhibition
Retroactive Inhibition
BT Behavior Patterns
RT Psychological Patterns
Socialization

INITIAL EXPENSES 220
UF   Minimum Initial Expenses
BT   Expenditures

INITIAL TEACHING ALPHABET 440
UF   ITA
BT   Alphabets
RT   Orthographic Symbols
     Phonics
     Reading
     Reading Instruction

INJURIES 250
RT   Accidents
     First Aid
     Health
     Medical Services
     Safety

nmates
USE   PRISONERS

INNER CITY 490
RT   Slums
     Urban Environment
     Urban Renewal Agencies

Inner City Children
USE   DISADVANTAGED YOUTH

Inner City Education
USE   URBAN EDUCATION

INNER SPEECH (SUBVOCAL) 290
BT   Speech
RT   Reading

INNOVATION 140
NT   Building Innovation
     Educational Innovation
     Instructional Innovation
RT   Diffusion
     Experimental Colleges
     Research

Inns
USE   HOTELS

INPLANT PROGRAMS 410
SN   Educational or training programs carried
     on within business or industrial
     establishments
BT   Programs
RT   Apprenticeships
     Industrial Training
     Labor Education
     Off The Job Training
     On The Job Training

Input Devices
USE   INPUT OUTPUT DEVICES

INPUT OUTPUT 080
UF   I O
RT   Communications
     Computer Science
     Cybernetics
     Display Systems
     Information Processing
     Information Theory
     Input Output Analysis
     Input Output Devices
     Optical Scanners

INPUT OUTPUT ANALYSIS 080
UF   Input Output Relationship
RT   Data Processing
     Economic Research
     Information Processing
     Input Output
     Systems Analysis

INPUT OUTPUT DEVICES 170
UF   Input Devices
     Output Devices
RT   Computer Output Microfilm
     Computers
     Computer Storage Devices
     Electronic Data Processing
     Electronic Equipment
     Facsimile Transmission
     Information Processing
     Input Output
     Magnetic Tapes
     Optical Scanners
     Telecommunication

Input Output Relationship
USE   INPUT OUTPUT ANALYSIS

Inquiry
USE   QUESTIONING TECHNIQUES

INQUIRY TRAINING 270
BT   Training
RT   Cognitive Processes
     Laboratory Procedures
     Learning
     Questioning Techniques
     Teaching Techniques

INSECTICIDES 070
BT   Pesticides
RT   Agricultural Chemical Occupations
     Agricultural Supplies
     Agriculture
     Entomology
     Herbicides
     Plant Growth
     Plant Science
     Rodenticides

Insects
USE   ENTOMOLOGY

INSECURITY 420
UF   Insecurity Factors
BT   Psychological Patterns

Insecurity Factors
USE INSECURITY

INSERVICE COURSES 110
BT Courses
RT Education Courses
    Inservice Education
    Inservice Programs
    Inservice Teacher Education
    Professional Training
    Refresher Courses
    Science Institutes
    Summer Institutes

INSERVICE EDUCATION 140
SN Educational courses or programs to
    provide advanced study to professional
    persons in fields other than teaching
UF Inservice Training
BT Education
RT Graduate Study
    Inservice Courses
    Inservice Programs
    Inservice Teacher Education
    Professional Training

Inservice Education Programs
USE INSERVICE PROGRAMS

INSERVICE PROGRAMS 020
UF Inservice Education Programs
BT Programs
RT Attendant Training
    Inservice Courses
    Inservice Education
    Inservice Teacher Education
    Science Institutes
    Summer Institutes

INSERVICE TEACHER EDUCATION 140
UF Inservice Teacher Training
BT Teacher Education
RT Inservice Courses
    Inservice Education
    Inservice Programs
    Inservice Teaching
    Institutes (Training Programs)
    Professional Training
    School Visitation
    Teacher Educator Education
    Teacher Interns
    Teacher Workshops

Inservice Teacher Training
USE INSERVICE TEACHER EDUCATION

INSERVICE TEACHING 270
BT Teaching
RT Beginning Teachers
    Inservice Teacher Education
    Lesson Observation Criteria
    Microteaching
    Teaching Experience

Inservice Teaching Experience
USE TEACHING EXPERIENCE

Inservice Training
USE INSERVICE EDUCATION

INSPECTION 180
RT Equipment Evaluation
    Evaluation
    Field Check
    Measurement
    Observation
    Radiographers

In State Students
USE RESIDENT STUDENTS

INSTITUTES (TRAINING PROGRAMS) 410
SN Programs of training designed to provide
    advanced study in a subject field, usually
    more intensive than conventions or
    conferences but less elaborate than
    workshops
NT Science Institutes
    Summer Institutes
BT Educational Programs
RT Conference Reports
    Conferences
    Inservice Teacher Education
    Off The Job Training
    Seminars
    Speeches
    Teacher Education

INSTITUTE TYPE COURSES 110
BT Courses
RT Post Doctoral Education
    Science Institutes
    Seminars
    Summer Institutes
    Symposia

INSTITUTIONAL ADMINISTRATION 020
BT Administration
RT Governance
    Governing Boards
    Institutional Schools
    Institutions
    Special Education

INSTITUTIONAL ENVIRONMENT 160
BT Environment
RT Boarding Schools
    College Environment
    Institutions

INSTITUTIONAL FACILITIES 210
BT Facilities
RT Institutions

Institutional Function
USE INSTITUTIONAL ROLE

INSTITUTIONALIZED (PERSONS) 380
UF Institutionalized Youth
NT Prisoners
RT Correctional Education
    Correctional Rehabilitation
    Corrective Institutions
    Mental Illness
    Patients (Persons)
    Retarded Children
    Self Care Skills

Institutionalized Youth
USE INSTITUTIONALIZED (PERSONS)

Institutional Mission
USE INSTITUTIONAL ROLE

INSTITUTIONAL PERSONNEL 380
BT Personnel
RT Hospital Personnel
    Institutions
    Special Education

INSTITUTIONAL RESEARCH 450
SN Research conducted by an institution for
    its own use
BT Research
RT Curriculum Research
    Educational Research
    Experimental Programs
    Institutions
    Media Research
    Researchers

INSTITUTIONAL ROLE 490
UF Institutional Function
    Institutional Mission
NT Agency Role
    Church Role
    College Role
    School Role
RT Educational Objectives
    Educational Responsibility
    Leadership Responsibility
    Objectives
    Research
    Residential Colleges
    Responsibility
    Teaching
    Training
    Training Objectives

INSTITUTIONAL SCHOOLS 470
BT Schools
RT Institutional Administration
    Institutions
    Residential Care
    Residential Schools

INSTITUTION LIBRARIES 210
UF Prison Libraries
    Reformatory Libraries
BT Special Libraries
RT Bibliotherapy
    Corrective Institutions
    Hospitals
    Medical Libraries
    Nursing Homes
    Psychiatric Hospitals
    Rehabilitation Centers
    Residential Schools

INSTITUTIONS 210
NT Churches
    Colleges
    Corrective Institutions
    Courts
    Libraries
    Negro Institutions
    Rehabilitation Centers
    Schools
    Universities
RT Institutional Administration
    Institutional Environment
    Institutional Facilities
    Institutional Personnel
    Institutional Research
    Institutional Schools
    Interinstitutional Cooperation
    Producer Services

INSTRUCTION 270
NT Audiovisual Instruction
    Biology Instruction
    Clothing Instruction
    College Instruction
    Computer Assisted Instruction
    Conventional Instruction
    Cooking Instruction
    Educational Strategies
    English Instruction
    Ethical Instruction
    Field Instruction
    Foods Instruction
    Geography Instruction
    Group Instruction
    Handwriting Instruction
    History Instruction
    Home Instruction
    Humanities Instruction
    Individual Instruction
    Individualized Instruction
    Language Instruction
    Large Group Instruction
    Law Instruction
    Library Instruction
    Mass Instruction
    Mathematics Instruction
    Multimedia Instruction
    Nutrition Instruction
    Physics Instruction
    Programed Instruction

Reading Instruction
Remedial Instruction
Science Instruction
Sewing Instruction
Small Group Instruction
Speech Instruction
Spelling Instruction
Telephone Instruction
Televised Instruction
Textiles Instruction
RT Curriculum
Instructional Design
Instructional Films
Instructional Improvement
Instructional Materials
Instructional Programs
Instructional Technology
Instructional Trips
Laboratory Procedures
Lead Lecture Plan
Learning
Orientation
School Supervision
Teaching
Teaching Methods
Teaching Models
Teaching Techniques

INSTRUCTIONAL AIDS 050
UF Teaching Aids
NT Audiovisual Aids
Autoinstructional Aids
Electromechanical Aids
Mechanical Teaching Aids
Sensory Aids
Teaching Machines
Three Dimensional Aids
BT Instructional Materials
RT Color Presentation
Instructional Television
Large Type Materials
Loop Induction Systems
Science Materials
Slides
Student Developed Materials
Talking Books
Teacher Developed Materials

INSTRUCTIONAL DESIGN 270
BT Design
RT Educational Strategies
Instruction
Instructional Innovation
Instructional Technology
Multimedia Instruction
Research Design

INSTRUCTIONAL FILMS 050
BT Audiovisual Aids
Films
RT Film Study
Instruction
Protocol Materials
Single Concept Films

INSTRUCTIONAL IMPROVEMENT 270
BT Educational Improvement
RT Instruction
Instructional Media
Instructional Technology

INSTRUCTIONAL INNOVATION 270
BT Innovation
RT Educational Development
Educational Innovation
Instructional Design
Instructional Materials
Instructional Media
Instructional Technology
Multimedia Instruction
Research And Instruction Units

Instructional Interaction
USE INTERACTION

INSTRUCTIONAL MATERIALS 050
UF Adapted Materials
Curriculum Materials
Educational Materials
Educational Media
Materials
Multimedia Materials
Special Materials
Teaching Materials
NT Art Materials
Classroom Materials
Fles Materials
Handwriting Materials
Instructional Aids
Large Type Materials
Manipulative Materials
Manuals
Mathematics Materials
Orientation Materials
Programed Materials
Readability
Reading Materials
Resource Materials
Science Materials
Student Developed Materials
Teacher Developed Materials
Telegraphic Materials
Workbooks
Worksheets
BT Educational Resources
RT Educational Equipment
Educational Games
High Interest Low Vocabulary Books
Instruction
Instructional Innovation
Instructional Materials Centers
Instructional Media
Instructional Technology
Magnification Methods
Master Tapes (Audio)
Material Development
Multimedia Instruction
Programers

Protocol Materials
Reading Material Selection
Student Writing Models
Supplementary Textbooks
Supplies
Talking Books
Textbooks
Toys
Unwritten Language

INSTRUCTIONAL MATERIALS CENTERS 210
UF   Learning Resources Centers
Media Centers
BT   Educational Facilities
RT   Audiovisual Centers
Curriculum Study Centers
Demonstration Centers
English (Second Language)
Information Centers
Information Sources
Instructional Materials
Instructional Media
Libraries
School Libraries

INSTRUCTIONAL MEDIA 050
BT   Mass Media
RT   Computer Assisted Instruction
Instructional Improvement
Instructional Innovation
Instructional Materials
Instructional Materials Centers
Instructional Technology
Teaching Techniques
Telephone Communication Systems
Telephone Instruction
Televised Instruction

Instructional Procedures
USE   TEACHING PROCEDURES

INSTRUCTIONAL PROGRAM DIVISIONS 280
UF   Grade Levels
Grades (Program Divisions)
Six Three Three Organization
NT   Elementary Grades
Grade 1
Grade 2
Grade 3
Grade 4
Grade 5
Grade 6
Grade 7
Grade 8
Grade 9
Grade 10
Grade 11
Grade 12
Grade 13
Grade 14
Intermediate Grades
Kindergarten

Primary Grades
Secondary Grades
RT   Age Grade Placement
Grade Organization
Multigraded Classes
Student Promotion

INSTRUCTIONAL PROGRAMS 270
BT   Programs
RT   Counseling Instructional Programs
Instruction
International Programs
Programers

INSTRUCTIONAL STAFF 380
UF   Professional Staff
Staff (Instructional)
Teaching Staff
NT   Adult Educators
Catholic Educators
Teachers
Trainers
BT   Faculty
School Personnel
RT   Differentiated Staffs
Extension Agents
Staff Improvement
Staff Meetings
Staff Orientation
Staff Role
Staff Utilization

INSTRUCTIONAL TECHNOLOGY 270
BT   Technology
RT   Dial Access Information Systems
Educational Development
Educational Technology
Instruction
Instructional Design
Instructional Improvement
Instructional Innovation
Instructional Materials
Instructional Media
Loop Induction Systems
Media Technology
Multimedia Instruction
Programed Materials
Programers

INSTRUCTIONAL TELEVISION 050
NT   Fixed Service Television
Instructor Centered Television
BT   Television
RT   Audio Video Laboratories
Broadcast Industry
Dial Access Information Systems
Instructional Aids
Public Television

INSTRUCTIONAL TRIPS 510
UF Educational Trips
    Excursions
    School Excursions
NT Field Trips
RT Distance
    Farm Visits
    Instruction
    Tourism
    Transportation
    Travel

INSTRUCTOR CENTERED TELEVISION 050
BT Instructional Television

INSTRUCTOR COORDINATORS 380
SN Teachers responsible for coordinating
    education and on the job activities of the
    students
UF Coordinator Trainers
    Teacher Coordinators
BT Coordinators
RT Administrative Personnel
    Adult Educators
    Guidance Personnel
    Program Coordination
    Special Counselors
    Supervisors
    Teachers

Instructor Role
USE TEACHER ROLE

Instructors
USE TEACHERS

Instrumental Conditioning
USE OPERANT CONDITIONING

INSTRUMENTATION 170
SN Use of or operation with instruments for
    observing, measuring, or controlling
    performance
NT Measurement Instruments
    Measurement Techniques
RT Automation
    Climate Control
    Cybernetics
    Electronic Control
    Electronic Equipment
    Horology
    Industry
    Instrumentation Technicians
    Measurement
    Polygraphs
    Testing
    Test Scoring Machines
    Transistors

INSTRUMENTATION TECHNICIANS 380
BT Subprofessionals
RT Electronic Equipment
    Electronics
    Instrumentation
    Technical Education
    Technical Occupations

Instrumented Laboratories
USE TRAINING LABORATORIES

INSURANCE COMPANIES 370
UF Insurance Industry
RT Business
    Insurance Occupations
    Insurance Programs

Insurance Industry
USE INSURANCE COMPANIES

INSURANCE OCCUPATIONS 350
BT Occupations
RT Health Insurance
    Insurance Companies
    Insurance Programs
    Unemployment Insurance

INSURANCE PROGRAMS 410
SN Device for the reduction of economic risk
BT Programs
RT Health Insurance
    Indemnity Bonds
    Insurance Companies
    Insurance Occupations
    Property Appraisal
    Risk
    Unemployment Insurance
    Workmans Compensation

INTEGERS 340
NT Prime Numbers
BT Rational Numbers
RT Arithmetic
    Congruence

INTEGRATED ACTIVITIES 140
SN Systematic organization of units into a
    meaningful pattern
UF Integrated Teaching Approach
BT Activities
RT Integrated Curriculum
    Interdisciplinary Approach
    Teaching Techniques

Integrated Classes
USE CLASSROOM INTEGRATION

Integrated Colleges
USE COLLEGE INTEGRATION

INTEGRATED CURRICULUM 110
SN Systematic organization of curriculum content and parts into a meaningful pattern
UF Integrated Education
    Integrated Learning
BT Curriculum
RT Integrated Activities

Integrated Education
USE INTEGRATED CURRICULUM

Integrated Faculty
USE FACULTY INTEGRATION

Integrated Learning
USE INTEGRATED CURRICULUM

Integrated Neighborhoods
USE NEIGHBORHOOD INTEGRATION

INTEGRATED PUBLIC FACILITIES 210
UF Desegregated Public Facilities
BT Public Facilities
RT Racial Integration

Integrated School Faculty
USE FACULTY INTEGRATION

Integrated Schools
USE SCHOOL INTEGRATION

Integrated Teaching Approach
USE INTEGRATED ACTIVITIES

Integration (Racial)
USE RACIAL INTEGRATION

Integration (Social)
USE SOCIAL INTEGRATION

INTEGRATION EFFECTS 430
UF Integration Impact
RT Racial Integration
    Social Integration

Integration Impact
USE INTEGRATION EFFECTS

INTEGRATION LITIGATION 430
UF Desegregation Litigation
RT Racial Integration

INTEGRATION METHODS 430
UF Desegregation Methods
    Desegregation Motivation
    Desegregation Trends
RT Multicultural Textbooks
    Racial Integration

INTEGRATION PLANS 430
RT Racial Integration

INTEGRATION READINESS 430
BT Readiness
RT Racial Integration

INTEGRATION STUDIES 430
BT Research
RT Racial Integration

INTEGRITY 060
BT Individual Characteristics

INTELLECTUAL DEVELOPMENT 130
BT Development
RT Cognitive Development
    Intellectual Experience
    Intelligence
    Mental Development
    Mental Rigidity
    Task Analysis

INTELLECTUAL DISCIPLINES 110
UF Subject Disciplines
NT Units Of Study (Subject Fields)
RT Courses
    Curriculum
    Departments

INTELLECTUAL EXPERIENCE 200
BT Experience
RT Intellectual Development
    Intelligence

INTELLECTUALIZATION 510
SN Process of reasoning abstractly
RT Concept Formation
    Deductive Methods
    Inductive Methods
    Thought Processes

INTELLIGENCE 010
UF Mental Ability
NT Comprehension
    Intelligence Factors
BT Ability
RT Academic Ability
    Academic Achievement
    Academic Aptitude
    Cognitive Ability
    Intellectual Development
    Intellectual Experience
    Intelligence Differences
    Intelligence Level
    Intelligence Quotient
    Intelligence Tests
    Literacy
    Logical Thinking
    Mental Development
    Mental Retardation
    Thought Processes

INTELLIGENCE DIFFERENCES 010
RT Intelligence
    Intelligence Tests

INTELLIGENCE FACTORS 420
BT Intelligence

INTELLIGENCE LEVEL 010
RT Intelligence
    Intelligence Quotient
    Learning Plateaus

Intelligence Measures
USE INTELLIGENCE TESTS

INTELLIGENCE QUOTIENT 010
RT Intelligence
   Intelligence Level
   Intelligence Tests
   National Intelligence Norm

INTELLIGENCE TESTS 520
UF Intelligence Measures
NT Group Intelligence Tests
BT Tests
RT Cognitive Tests
   Culture Free Tests
   Intelligence
   Intelligence Differences
   Intelligence Quotient
   Performance Tests

INTENSIVE LANGUAGE COURSES 110
BT Courses
RT Language Instruction
   Languages
   Second Language Learning

INTERACTION 490
UF Instructional Interaction
BT Relationship
RT Audience Participation
   Interaction Process Analysis
   Intergroup Relations
   Intermode Differences
   Interpersonal Competence
   Man Machine Systems
   Statistical Analysis

Interaction Analysis
USE INTERACTION PROCESS ANALYSIS

INTERACTION PROCESS ANALYSIS 510
UF Interaction Analysis
RT Classroom Observation Techniques
   Group Behavior
   Group Dynamics
   Group Structure
   Interaction
   Laboratory Training
   Self Directed Groups
   Sensitivity Training
   Social Integration
   Social Relations
   Social Systems
   T Groups

INTERAGENCY COOPERATION 020
RT Interagency Coordination
   Interdistrict Policies
   Interinstitutional Cooperation
   Library Cooperation
   Networks
   Regional Cooperation
   School Community Cooperation

INTERAGENCY COORDINATION 020
BT Coordination
RT Agencies
   Educational Coordination
   Interagency Cooperation
   Interagency Planning
   Intercollegiate Programs
   Interdistrict Policies
   Networks

INTERAGENCY PLANNING 020
BT Planning
RT Agencies
   Interagency Coordination
   Intercollegiate Programs

INTERCOLLEGIATE PROGRAMS 410
BT College Programs
RT College Cooperation
   Interagency Coordination
   Interagency Planning
   Interdistrict Policies

INTERCOMMUNICATION 080
BT Communication (Thought Transfer)
RT Information Networks
   Networks

INTERCULTURAL PROGRAMS 100
BT Programs
RT Cross Cultural Studies
   Cross Cultural Training
   Cultural Education
   Cultural Enrichment
   Cultural Exchange
   Culture
   Culture Contact
   Teacher Exchange Programs

INTERDISCIPLINARY APPROACH 510
SN Participation or cooperation of two or
   more disciplines
BT Methodology
RT Cooperative Programs
   Core Curriculum
   Force Field Analysis
   Integrated Activities
   Thematic Approach

INTERDISTRICT POLICIES 020
BT Policy
RT Administrative Policy
   Board Of Education Policy
   Interagency Cooperation
   Interagency Coordination
   Intercollegiate Programs
   Policy Formation
   School Policy

INTEREST 220
SN The price paid for the use of money over time
RT Economics
Financial Services
Investment
Money Systems
Productivity

Interest Lack
USE LOW MOTIVATION

Interest Measurement
USE INTEREST TESTS

INTEREST RESEARCH 450
BT Research
RT Interests
Student Science Interests

INTERESTS 040
NT Childhood Interests
Personal Interests
Reading Interests
Student Interests
Vocational Interests
RT Affective Behavior
Interest Research
Interest Scales
Interest Tests

INTEREST SCALES 180
BT Rating Scales
RT Interests
Student Science Interests

Interest Testing
USE INTEREST TESTS

INTEREST TESTS 520
UF Interest Measurement
Interest Testing
BT Tests
RT Essay Tests
Interests
Science Tests
Student Science Interests

INTERFAITH RELATIONS 480
BT Relationship
RT Human Relations
Intergroup Education
Intergroup Relations
Religion

INTERFERENCE (LANGUAGE LEARNING) 310
RT Contrastive Linguistics
Learning Processes
Second Language Learning

INTERGROUP EDUCATION 140
BT Education
RT Civil Rights
Human Relations
Interfaith Relations
Intergroup Relations
Social Discrimination

INTERGROUP RELATIONS 490
BT Group Relations
RT Human Relations
Interaction
Interfaith Relations
Intergroup Education
Intermarriage
Social Integration
Social Relations

INTERINSTITUTIONAL COOPERATION 020
NT College Cooperation
Library Cooperation
RT Affiliated Schools
Consortia
Exchange Programs
Institutions
Interagency Cooperation

Interior Decorating
USE INTERIOR DESIGN

Interior Decoration
USE INTERIOR DESIGN

INTERIOR DESIGN 030
UF Interior Decorating
Interior Decoration
BT Design
RT Acoustical Environment
Architecture
Building Design
Classroom Design
Color Planning
Design Needs
Design Preferences
Furniture Arrangement
Interior Space
Lighting
Lighting Design
Offices (Facilities)
Physical Design Needs
Physical Environment
Psychological Design Needs
Space Classification
Space Utilization
Spatial Relationship
Thermal Environment

INTERIOR SPACE 210
SN Area available within a building
RT Building Design
Design Needs
Facilities
Flexible Classrooms
Furniture Arrangement
Interior Design

Offices (Facilities)
Open Plan Schools
Physical Environment
School Size
School Space
Space Classification
Space Utilization
Storage

INTERLIBRARY LOANS 330
BT   Library Cooperation
RT   Information Services
     Information Systems
     Libraries
     Library Circulation
     Library Collections
     Library Materials
     Library Programs
     Library Services
     Union Catalogs

INTERMARRIAGE 490
BT   Marriage
RT   Intergroup Relations

INTERMEDIATE ADMINISTRATIVE UNITS
020
SN   Administering to districts rather than
     students
UF   Intermediate School Districts
     Intermediate School Units
     Intermediate Service Units
RT   Boards Of Education
     Consultation Programs
     Professional Services
     Regional Cooperation
     School Districts
     State School District Relationship

INTERMEDIATE GRADES 280
BT   Instructional Program Divisions
RT   Middle Schools

Intermediate School Districts
USE   INTERMEDIATE ADMINISTRATIVE UNITS

Intermediate School Units
USE   INTERMEDIATE ADMINISTRATIVE UNITS

Intermediate Service Units
USE   INTERMEDIATE ADMINISTRATIVE UNITS

INTERMODE DIFFERENCES 510
SN   Variations among instruction
     presentation modes
RT   Constructed Response
     Interaction
     Programed Instruction
     Response Mode
     Teaching Methods.

Internal Immigrants
USE   MIGRANTS

INTERNAL SCALING 190
BT   Test Construction

INTERNATIONAL EDUCATION 140
SN   Study of the educational, social, political,
     and economic forces in international
     relations
BT   Education
RT   Comparative Education
     Cross Cultural Training
     Foreign Culture
     Foreign Relations
     International Organizations
     International Programs
     International Trade Vocabulary

INTERNATIONAL ORGANIZATIONS 370
BT   Organizations (Groups)
RT   Foreign Relations
     Honor Societies
     International Education
     International Programs
     Library Associations
     National Organizations

INTERNATIONAL PROGRAMS 410
BT   Programs
RT   Educational Programs
     Instructional Programs
     International Education
     International Organizations

International Relations
USE   FOREIGN RELATIONS

INTERNATIONAL TRADE VOCABULARY 290
BT   Vocabulary
RT   Economics
     Exports
     Foreign Relations
     International Education
     Professional Training

INTERNSHIP PROGRAMS 410
BT   Educational Programs
RT   Clinical Experience
     Field Experience Programs
     Practicums
     Practicum Supervision
     Teaching Experience
     Trainees

Intern Teachers
USE   TEACHER INTERNS

INTERPERSONAL COMPETENCE 010
UF   Gregariousness
     Sociability
     Social Awareness
     Social Competence
     Social Skills
BT   Skills
RT   Anti Social Behavior
     Group Relations
     Interaction
     Interpersonal Relationship
     Laboratory Training
     Sensitivity Training

Social Adjustment
Social Attitudes
Social Characteristics
Social Development
Social Experience
Socialization
Social Maturity
Social Relations
Teamwork

INTERPERSONAL PROBLEMS 420
BT   Problems
RT   Interpersonal Relationship
Parental Grievances
Social Problems

INTERPERSONAL RELATIONSHIP 480
NT   Rapport
BT   Relationship
RT   Autism
Cross Age Teaching
Group Relations
Human Relations
Interpersonal Competence
Interpersonal Problems
Marriage Counseling
Social Integration
Social Life
Social Relations
Sociometric Techniques
Teamwork

INTERPRETERS 380
UF   Oral Language Translators
RT   Communication (Thought Transfer)
Deaf Interpreting
Language Ability
Language Skills
Speech Skills
Translation
Verbal Communication

Interpreting For The Deaf
USE   DEAF INTERPRETING

INTERPRETIVE READING 440
UF   Oral Interpretation
BT   Reading
RT   Comprehension
Content Reading
Critical Reading

INTERPRETIVE SKILLS 010
BT   Skills
RT   Deaf Interpreting

INTERPROFESSIONAL RELATIONSHIP 150
BT   Relationship
RT   Professional Services

Interracial Experience
USE   RACE RELATIONS

Interracial Primers
USE   MULTICULTURAL TEXTBOOKS

Interracial Relations
USE   RACE RELATIONS

INTERSCHOOL COMMUNICATION 080
BT   Communication (Thought Transfer)

Interschool Visits
USE   SCHOOL VISITATION

Intersensory Integration
USE   SENSORY INTEGRATION

INTERSTATE PROGRAMS 410
BT   Programs
RT   State Programs

INTERSTATE WORKERS 380
BT   Laborers

INTERVAL PACING 510
BT   Pacing
RT   Intervals
Teaching Techniques
Time Factors (Learning)

INTERVALS 400
BT   Scientific Concepts
RT   Distance
Interval Pacing
Scheduling
Semester Division
Space
Spatial Relationship

INTERVENTION 090
SN   Action performed to direct or influence behavior
UF   Educational Intervention
Medical Intervention
Psychoeducational Intervention
RT   Educational Psychology
Educational Therapy
Exceptional (Atypical)
Medical Services
Psychoeducational Processes
Psychology
Special Education

INTERVIEWS 150
NT   Employment Interviews
Field Interviews
Question Answer Interviews
RT   Guidance
Personnel Selection
Surveys

INTONATION 290
UF   Intonation Contours
BT   Suprasegmentals
RT   Linguistics
Morphology (Languages)
Phonemes
Phonology
Sentences
Syllables

Intonation Contours
USE INTONATION

INTRAMURAL ATHLETIC PROGRAMS 390
UF Intramural Sports
BT Athletic Programs
RT Extramural Athletic Programs
    Physical Activities
    Physical Fitness

Intramural Sports
USE INTRAMURAL ATHLETIC PROGRAMS

Intricacy
USE COMPLEXITY LEVEL

Intrinsic Criticism
USE ARISTOTELIAN CRITICISM

Introjection
USE IDENTIFICATION (PSYCHOLOGICAL)

Invalids
USE PATIENTS (PERSONS)

INVESTIGATIONS 180
RT Research

INVESTMENT 220
RT Banking
    Credit (Finance)
    Economics
    Educational Economics
    Estate Planning
    Finance Occupations
    Human Capital
    Interest
    Productivity
    Trusts (Financial)

I O
USE INPUT OUTPUT

Iris Reflex
USE PUPILLARY DILATION

Iron Foundries
USE FOUNDRIES

IRONY 260
UF Sarcasm
BT Figurative Language
RT Drama
    Essays
    Literature
    Poetry
    Prose

ISLAMIC CULTURE 100
BT Culture
RT Religion

Isolation (Perceptual)
USE SENSORY DEPRIVATION

ITA
USE INITIAL TEACHING ALPHABET

ITALIAN 300
BT Romance Languages

ITALIAN AMERICANS 380
BT Ethnic Groups
RT Minority Groups
    Racial Characteristics

ITALIAN LITERATURE 260
BT Literature
RT Analytical Criticism
    Baroque Literature
    Drama
    Eighteenth Century Literature
    Essays
    Formal Criticism
    Poetry
    Prose
    Textual Criticism
    World Literature

ITEM ANALYSIS 190
BT Test Construction
    Test Validity
RT Content Analysis
    Discriminant Analysis
    Factor Analysis
    Testing
    Tests

ITFS
USE FIXED SERVICE TELEVISION

ITINERANT CLINICS 210
BT Clinics
RT Itinerant Teachers
    Mobile Laboratories

ITINERANT TEACHERS 380
UF Circuit Teachers
    Traveling Teachers
NT Homebound Teachers
BT Teachers
RT Educational Programs
    Exceptional Children
    Handicapped Children
    Individual Instruction
    Itinerant Clinics
    Mobile Educational Services
    Regular Class Placement
    Resource Teachers
    Special Education
    Special Education Teachers
    Specialists

Jail Inmates
USE PRISONERS

JAPANESE 300
NT Okinawan
BT Languages

JAPANESE AMERICAN CULTURE 100
BT Culture
RT Japanese Americans

JAPANESE AMERICANS 380
BT   Ethnic Groups
RT   Ethnic Origins
     Japanese American Culture
     Minority Groups
     Racial Characteristics

JAVANESE 300
BT   Malayo Polynesian Languages

JAZZ 030
UF   Ragtime Music
     Swing Music
BT   Music
RT   American Culture
     Applied Music
     Bands (Music)
     Concerts
     Musical Composition
     Music Techniques

JEWISH STEREOTYPES 100
BT   Stereotypes
RT   Jews

JEWS 380
UF   American Jews
BT   Religious Cultural Groups
RT   Anti Semitism
     Ethnic Groups
     Jewish Stereotypes
     Judaism
     Minority Groups

Job Adjustment
USE   VOCATIONAL ADJUSTMENT

JOB ANALYSIS 150
NT   Task Analysis
RT   Critical Incidents Method
     Employment Qualifications
     Employment Services
     Jobs
     Occupational Information
     Skill Analysis
     Task Performance
     Work Simplification

JOB APPLICANTS 380
UF   Job Seekers
BT   Personnel
RT   Employment
     Employment Opportunities
     Employment Qualifications
     Employment Services
     Job Application
     Job Placement
     Jobs
     Labor Market
     Underemployed
     Unemployed
     Unemployment

JOB APPLICATION 150
RT   Employment Interviews
     Employment Opportunities
     Employment Qualifications
     Employment Services
     Job Applicants
     Jobs

Job Behaviors
USE   JOB SKILLS

Job Change
USE   CAREER CHANGE

Job Clusters
USE   OCCUPATIONAL CLUSTERS

Job Creation
USE   JOB DEVELOPMENT

Job Descriptions
USE   OCCUPATIONAL INFORMATION

Job Design
USE   JOB DEVELOPMENT

JOB DEVELOPMENT 150
UF   Job Creation
     Job Design
RT   Employment Opportunities
     Employment Problems
     Equal Opportunities (Jobs)
     Jobs
     Manpower Development
     Promotion (Occupational)
     Work Simplification

Job Experience
USE   WORK EXPERIENCE

Job Families
USE   OCCUPATIONAL CLUSTERS

Job Interviews
USE   EMPLOYMENT INTERVIEWS

JOB LAYOFF 150
UF   Reduction In Force
RT   Employment Practices
     Job Market
     Job Tenure
     Personnel Policy
     Unemployed
     Unemployment

JOB MARKET 150
RT   Employment Opportunities
     Job Layoff
     Jobs
     Labor Market
     Labor Supply
     Manpower Needs
     Occupational Surveys
     Unemployment

Job Mobility
USE   OCCUPATIONAL MOBILITY

Journals
USE PERIODICALS

Journeymen
USE SKILLED LABOR

JUDAISM 480
BT Religion
RT Biblical Literature
History
Humanities
Jews
Literature
Philosophy
Religious Cultural Groups

Judicial Action
USE COURT LITIGATION

JUNIOR COLLEGE LIBRARIES 210
UF Community College Libraries
BT College Libraries
RT Community Colleges
Junior Colleges

JUNIOR COLLEGES 470
BT Colleges
RT Associate Degrees
Community Colleges
Higher Education
Junior College Libraries
Junior College Students
Post Secondary Education
State Colleges
Technical Institutes
Undergraduate Study

JUNIOR COLLEGE STUDENTS 380
BT College Students
RT Community Colleges
Higher Education
Junior Colleges
Post Secondary Education

JUNIOR HIGH SCHOOL ROLE 140
BT High School Role

JUNIOR HIGH SCHOOLS 470
BT High Schools
RT Junior High School Students
Middle Schools
Senior High Schools

JUNIOR HIGH SCHOOL STUDENTS 380
BT Secondary School Students
RT High School Students
Junior High Schools

Junior High School Teachers
USE SECONDARY SCHOOL TEACHERS

JUVENILE COURTS 230
UF Childrens Courts
BT Courts
RT Counseling
Court Litigation
Crime
Delinquent Rehabilitation
Delinquents
Socially Deviant Behavior
Youth Problems

Juvenile Delinquency
USE DELINQUENCY

Juvenile Delinquency Prevention
USE DELINQUENCY PREVENTION

JUVENILE GANGS 380
RT Delinquency
Delinquents

KABYLE 300
BT Afro Asiatic Languages

KANNADA 300
BT Dravidian Languages

KASHMIRI 300
BT Indo European Languages

Kechua
USE QUECHUA

KERNEL SENTENCES 290
BT Transformation Theory (Language)
RT Grammar
Phonology
Phrase Structure
Sentence Structure
Syntax
Transformations (Language)

Key Word In Context
USE PERMUTED INDEXES

Khalkha
USE MONGOLIAN

Kikongo Ya Leta
USE KITUBA

KINDERGARTEN 280
BT Instructional Program Divisions
RT Early Childhood Education
Kindergarten Children

KINDERGARTEN CHILDREN 380
BT Children
RT Kindergarten

Kindergarten Teachers
USE PRESCHOOL TEACHERS

KINESCOPE RECORDINGS 050
UF Kinescopes
BT Phonotape Recordings
RT Films
Television

Kinescopes
USE KINESCOPE RECORDINGS

Kinesthesia
USE KINESTHETIC PERCEPTION

Kinesthesis
USE KINESTHETIC PERCEPTION

Kinesthetic Memory
USE KINESTHETIC PERCEPTION

KINESTHETIC METHODS 510
UF Kinesthetic Techniques
BT Methods
RT Kinesthetic Perception
    Paralinguistics
    Reading Instruction
    Speech Instruction

KINESTHETIC PERCEPTION 070
SN Sense perception of movement, weight,
    resistance, and position
UF Kinesthesia
    Kinesthesis
    Kinesthetic Memory
    Muscle Sense
BT Perception
RT Body Image
    Figural Aftereffects
    Haptic Perception
    Kinesthetic Methods
    Space Orientation
    Tactual Perception

Kinesthetic Techniques
USE KINESTHETIC METHODS

KINETIC MOLECULAR THEORY 400
BT Physics
RT Force
    Heat
    Kinetics
    Motion

KINETICS 400
UF Power Transfer Systems
BT Physics
RT Electronic Control
    Energy
    Engines
    Fluid Power Education
    Force
    Fuels
    Heat
    Horology
    Hydraulics
    Kinetic Molecular Theory
    Mechanics (Process)
    Motion
    Relativity
    Utilities

KINYARUANDA 300
BT African Languages
    Bantu Languages

KIRGHIZ 300
UF Kirgiz
BT Turkic Languages

Kirgiz
USE KIRGHIZ

KIRUNDI 300
BT African Languages
    Bantu Languages

KITUBA 300
UF Kikongo Ya Leta
    Munukutaba
BT African Languages
    Bantu Languages

KNOWLEDGE LEVEL 010
SN Extent of knowledge gained
RT Achievement
    Educational Background

Knowledge Of Results
USE FEEDBACK

KOREAN 300
BT Languages

KOREAN AMERICANS 380
BT Ethnic Groups
RT Ethnic Origins
    Korean Culture
    Minority Groups
    Racial Characteristics

KOREAN CULTURE 100
BT Culture
RT Korean Americans
    Non Western Civilization

Krio
USE SIERRA LEONE CREOLE

KURDISH 300
BT Indo European Languages

Kwic Indexes
USE PERMUTED INDEXES

Kwoc Indexes
USE PERMUTED INDEXES

LABOR 150
NT Child Labor
    Farm Labor
    Seasonal Labor
    Skilled Labor
    Unskilled Labor
RT Labor Camps
    Labor Conditions
    Labor Demands
    Labor Economics
    Laborers
    Labor Force
    Labor Laws
    Labor Legislation
    Labor Market
    Labor Problems

Labor Standards
Labor Supply
Labor Unions

LABORATORIES 210
NT Audio Video Laboratories
Computer Based Laboratories
Language Laboratories
Learning Laboratories
Mobile Laboratories
Regional Laboratories
Satellite Laboratories
Science Laboratories
Training Laboratories
RT Laboratory Equipment
Laboratory Experiments
Laboratory Manuals
Laboratory Technology

LABORATORY EQUIPMENT 170
NT Language Laboratory Equipment
Microscopes
BT Equipment
RT Animal Facilities
Biomedical Equipment
Equipment Manufacturers
Laboratories
Laboratory Techniques

LABORATORY EXPERIMENTS 510
BT Experiments
RT Experimental Psychology
Laboratories
Laboratory Techniques
Rats

LABORATORY MANUALS 050
BT Manuals
RT Guides
Laboratories
Publications

LABORATORY PROCEDURES 510
SN Teaching procedures used in the
laboratory phase of instruction
BT Teaching Procedures
RT Demonstrations (Educational)
Inquiry Training
Instruction
Laboratory Techniques
Science Activities
Science Experiments
Science Projects
Small Group Instruction
Teaching Methods

LABORATORY SAFETY 250
BT Safety
RT Accident Prevention
Accidents
Radiation
Radiation Effects

LABORATORY SCHOOLS 470
SN School of elementary and secondary
grades attached to a university for
purposes of research and teacher
training
UF Campus Schools
University Schools
BT Schools
RT Affiliated Schools
Educational Research
Elementary Education
Experimental Schools
Laboratory Training
Secondary Education
Teacher Education
Teaching Experience

LABORATORY TECHNIQUES 510
NT Chromatography
Culturing Techniques
BT Techniques
RT Laboratory Equipment
Laboratory Experiments
Laboratory Procedures
Teaching Techniques

LABORATORY TECHNOLOGY 110
BT Technology
RT Dental Technicians
Industrial Arts
Laboratories
Medical Laboratory Assistants

LABORATORY TRAINING 270
SN Method of training designed to facilitate
self insight, process awareness,
interpersonal competence, and dynamics
of change
BT Training
RT Interaction Process Analysis
Interpersonal Competence
Laboratory Schools
Microteaching
Practicums
Practicum Supervision
Protocol Materials
Self Directed Groups
Sensitivity Training
Simulation
Teacher Education
Teaching Experience
T Groups
Trainers
Training Laboratories

LABOR CAMP COMMISSARIES 210
BT Labor Camps

LABOR CAMPS 210
NT Labor Camp Commissaries
RT Labor
Laborers

LABOR CONDITIONS 150
RT Labor
    Labor Demands
    Labor Economics
    Laborers
    Labor Legislation
    Labor Problems
    Labor Unions
    Manpower Needs

LABOR DEMANDS 150
RT Arbitration
    Grievance Procedures
    Labor
    Labor Conditions
    Labor Economics
    Laborers
    Labor Legislation
    Labor Problems
    Labor Unions
    Manpower Needs
    Negotiation Impasses
    Sanctions
    Strikes

LABOR ECONOMICS 480
BT Economics
RT Arbitration
    Business Cycles
    Developed Nations
    Economic Research
    Employment
    Employment Patterns
    Employment Trends
    Labor
    Labor Conditions
    Labor Demands
    Labor Force
    Labor Market
    Labor Supply
    Manpower Utilization
    Negotiation Impasses
    Unemployment

LABOR EDUCATION 140
SN Education and training of labor union
    members sponsored by unions
    sometimes in cooperation with
    educational institutions
UF Workers Education
BT Adult Education
RT Inplant Programs
    Labor Force
    Labor Unions
    Off The Job Training

LABORERS 380
UF Work Force
NT Agricultural Laborers
    Auxiliary Laborers
    Experienced Laborers
    Foreign Workers
    Interstate Workers
    Migrant Workers

    Seasonal Laborers
RT Employees
    Government Employees
    Industrial Personnel
    Labor
    Labor Camps
    Labor Conditions
    Labor Demands
    Labor Force
    Labor Laws
    Labor Legislation
    Labor Market
    Labor Problems
    Labor Standards
    Labor Unions
    Unemployed

LABOR FORCE 150
RT Developed Nations
    Labor
    Labor Economics
    Labor Education
    Laborers
    Labor Force Nonparticipants
    Labor Market
    Labor Supply
    Labor Turnover
    Man Days
    Manpower Needs
    Occupational Surveys
    Organization Size (Groups)
    Strikes
    Working Women

LABOR FORCE NONPARTICIPANTS 380
SN Persons neither working nor looking for
    work
UF Voluntarily Idle
BT Unemployed
RT Housewives
    Labor Force
    Labor Supply
    Manpower Utilization
    Mentally Handicapped
    Physically Handicapped
    Retirement
    Students
    Work Attitudes

Labor Force Surveys
USE OCCUPATIONAL SURVEYS

LABOR LAWS 230
NT Child Labor Laws
BT Laws
RT Labor
    Laborers
    Labor Legislation
    Labor Standards

LABOR LEGISLATION 230
NT   Farm Labor Legislation
BT   Legislation
RT   Arbitration
     Labor
     Labor Conditions
     Labor Demands
     Laborers
     Labor Laws
     Labor Unions
     Negotiation Impasses

LABOR MARKET 150
UF   Employment Market
NT   Labor Supply
     Teacher Supply And Demand
RT   Employment Opportunities
     Employment Statistics
     Job Applicants
     Job Market
     Labor
     Labor Economics
     Laborers
     Labor Force
     Labor Turnover
     Manpower Needs
     Occupational Surveys
     Personnel Selection
     Unemployment

Labor Mobility
USE   OCCUPATIONAL MOBILITY

LABOR PROBLEMS 150
NT   Agricultural Labor Disputes
     Farm Labor Problems
     Labor Turnover
BT   Problems
RT   Arbitration
     Labor
     Labor Conditions
     Labor Demands
     Laborers
     Negotiation Impasses
     Relocation
     Strikes
     Teacher Strikes

Labor Relations
USE   INDUSTRIAL RELATIONS

LABOR STANDARDS 500
BT   Standards
RT   Labor
     Laborers
     Labor Laws

LABOR SUPPLY 150
UF   Supply Of Labor
NT   Farm Labor Supply
BT   Labor Market
RT   Human Capital
     Job Market
     Labor
     Labor Economics

     Labor Force
     Labor Force Nonparticipants
     Labor Turnover
     Manpower Utilization
     Occupational Surveys

LABOR TURNOVER 150
BT   Labor Problems
RT   Career Change
     Employment Patterns
     Employment Trends
     Labor Force
     Labor Market
     Labor Supply
     Mobility
     Relocation

LABOR UNIONS 150
UF   Trade Unions
BT   Unions
RT   Industrial Relations
     Labor
     Labor Conditions
     Labor Demands
     Labor Education
     Laborers
     Labor Legislation
     Local Unions

Land Colonization
USE   LAND SETTLEMENT

Land Grant Colleges
USE   LAND GRANT UNIVERSITIES

LAND GRANT UNIVERSITIES 470
UF   Land Grant Colleges
BT   Universities
RT   Adult Farmer Education
     Agricultural Education
     Engineering Education
     Federal Aid
     Professional Education
     Rural Extension
     Science Education
     Technical Education

LANDLORDS 380
BT   Personnel
RT   Facilities
     Housing
     Land Use
     Real Estate
     Real Estate Occupations

LANDSCAPING 350
BT   Ornamental Horticulture
RT   Floriculture
     Grounds Keepers
     Plant Identification
     Plant Science
     Site Development
     Trails
     Turf Management

LAND SETTLEMENT 460
UF Colonization
     Land Colonization
     Resettlement
     Settlement Patterns
RT Demography
     Nomads
     Population Trends
     Refugees
     Relocation

LAND USE 460
RT Agriculture
     Agronomy
     City Planning
     Landlords
     Real Estate
     Road Construction
     Soil Conservation
     Soil Science
     Turf Management

LANGUAGE 290
NT Child Language
     Diglossia
     Expressive Language
     Figurative Language
     Language Universals
     Official Languages
     Programing Languages
     Receptive Language
     Rhetoric
     Second Languages
     Symbolic Language
     Tone Languages
     Uncommonly Taught Languages
     Unwritten Language
     Urban Language
     Written Language
RT Artificial Speech
     Dialects
     English Education
     Language And Area Centers
     Language Arts
     Language Development
     Language Enrichment
     Language Handicapped
     Language Handicaps
     Language Instruction
     Language Patterns
     Language Programs
     Language Records (Phonograph)
     Language Research
     Language Rhythm
     Language Role
     Languages
     Language Skills
     Language Styles
     Language Tests
     Linguistics
     Nucleation (Language Learning)
     Onomastics
     Semiotics

     Sign Language
     Social Dialects
     Speech
     Word Frequency

LANGUAGE ABILITY 290
BT Ability
RT Child Language
     Cloze Procedure
     Interpreters
     Language Learning Levels
     Languages
     Language Skills
     Linguistic Competence
     Linguistics
     Second Language Learning
     Translation

LANGUAGE AIDS 050
NT Language Records (Phonograph)
BT Audiovisual Aids
RT Language Instruction

LANGUAGE AND AREA CENTERS 210
SN Centers staffed jointly by humanists,
     social scientists, and historians
BT Educational Programs
RT Area Studies
     History
     Humanities
     Language
     Middle Eastern History
     Social Sciences
     Social Studies

LANGUAGE ARTS 290
NT Journalism
     Listening
     Reading
     Speaking
     Translation
     Writing
RT Child Language
     Communication (Thought Transfer)
     English Education
     Language
     Speech Curriculum
     Speech Education
     Vocabulary

Language Barriers
USE LANGUAGE HANDICAPS

LANGUAGE CLASSIFICATION 290
BT Classification
RT African Languages
     American English
     American Indian Languages
     Chad Languages
     Comparative Analysis
     Diachronic Linguistics
     Dialects
     Diglossia
     Dravidian Languages
     Etymology

Glottochronology
Indo European Languages
Language Research
Languages
Language Styles
Language Typology
Malayo Polynesian Languages
Mutual Intelligibility
Regional Dialects
Sino Tibetan Languages
Slavic Languages
Urban Language
Uto Aztecan Languages

LANGUAGE DEVELOPMENT 130
BT   Development
RT   Child Language
     Echolalia
     English Education
     Expressive Language
     FLES
     Hearing Therapy
     Language
     Language Enrichment
     Language Fluency
     Language Handicaps
     Language Instruction
     Language Universals
     Nucleation (Language Learning)
     Psycholinguistics
     Retarded Speech Development
     Second Language Learning
     Speech Habits
     Verbal Development

Language Difficulties
USE LANGUAGE HANDICAPS

LANGUAGE ENRICHMENT 290
UF   Language Experiences
BT   Enrichment
RT   Bilingual Education
     Language
     Language Development
     Language Instruction
     Languages
     Second Language Learning

LANGUAGE ENROLLMENT 290
BT   Enrollment
RT   Enrollment Rate
     Enrollment Trends
     Languages

LANGUAGE EXPERIENCE APPROACH 270
BT   Reading Instruction
RT   Beginning Reading
     Reading Programs

Language Experiences
USE LANGUAGE ENRICHMENT

LANGUAGE FLUENCY 290
BT   Language Skills
RT   Audiolingual Skills
     Conversational Language Courses
     Diction
     Expressive Language
     Language Development
     Languages
     Second Language Learning
     Speech Skills

Language Guidebooks
USE LANGUAGE GUIDES

LANGUAGE GUIDES 290
UF   Language Guidebooks
NT   FLES Guides
BT   Curriculum Guides
RT   Language Instruction

LANGUAGE HANDICAPPED 240
SN   A person with a receptive or expressive language defect which is not caused by defects of peripherical speech mechanisms
BT   Handicapped
RT   Aphasia
     Auditory Agnosia
     Bilingualism
     Expressive Language
     Language
     Neurologically Handicapped

LANGUAGE HANDICAPS 240
UF   Language Barriers
     Language Difficulties
     Language Problems
NT   Auditory Agnosia
     Dyslexia
     Speech Handicaps
RT   Child Language
     Echolalia
     Functional Illiteracy
     Handicapped
     Handicapped Students
     Language
     Language Development
     Non English Speaking
     TENL

Language History
USE DIACHRONIC LINGUISTICS

LANGUAGE INSTRUCTION 270
UF   Foreign Language Teaching
     Language Teaching
NT   Pattern Drills (Language)
BT   Instruction
RT   Applied Linguistics
     College Language Programs
     Contrastive Linguistics
     Conversational Language Courses
     English Education
     FLES
     FLES Materials

FLES Teachers
Grammar Translation Method
Intensive Language Courses
Language
Language Aids
Language Development
Language Enrichment
Language Guides
Language Laboratories
Language Learning Levels
Language Proficiency
Language Programs
Language Records (Phonograph)
Languages
Language Teachers
Language Usage
Second Language Learning
Second Languages
Speech Instruction
Substitution Drills
TENL
Unwritten Language

Language Interrelationship
USE LANGUAGES

LANGUAGE LABORATORIES 210
NT Audio Active Compare Laboratories
 Audio Active Laboratories
 Audio Passive Laboratories
BT Audiovisual Aids
 Laboratories
RT Audio Video Laboratories
 Dial Access Information Systems
 Dubbing
 Educational Technology
 English Education
 Language Instruction
 Language Laboratory Equipment
 Language Laboratory Use
 Language Programs
 Languages
 Master Tapes (Audio)
 Programed Instruction

LANGUAGE LABORATORY EQUIPMENT 170
BT Laboratory Equipment
RT Audio Active Compare Laboratories
 Audio Active Laboratories
 Audio Passive Laboratories
 Audio Video Laboratories
 Dial Access Information Systems
 Equipment Maintenance
 Language Laboratories

LANGUAGE LABORATORY USE 290
RT Language Laboratories

Language Learning
USE SECOND LANGUAGE LEARNING

LANGUAGE LEARNING LEVELS 310
UF Levels Of Language Learning
RT Abstraction Levels
 Bilingual Education
 Language Ability
 Language Instruction
 Language Patterns
 Language Skills
 Learning

LANGUAGE PATTERNS 290
UF Basic Language Patterns
NT Idioms
 Language Rhythm
 Morphemes
 Negative Forms (Language)
 Paragraphs
 Plurals
 Suprasegmentals
RT American English
 Case (Grammar)
 Child Language
 Connected Discourse
 Diction
 Echolalia
 Form Classes (Languages)
 Language
 Language Learning Levels
 Language Styles
 Language Typology
 Language Universals
 Language Usage
 Lexicology
 Literary Conventions
 Morphology (Languages)
 Native Speakers
 Nominals
 Phonemics
 Pronouns
 Semiotics
 Sentence Diagraming
 Speech
 Speech Habits
 Speech Skills
 Standard Spoken Usage
 Syntax
 Tagmemic Analysis
 Urban Language

LANGUAGE PLANNING 290
NT Language Standardization
BT Planning
 Sociolinguistics
RT Educational Policy
 Language Usage
 National Norms
 National Programs
 Official Languages
 Policy Formation
 Public Policy
 Second Languages
 Social Planning

Sociocultural Patterns
Standard Spoken Usage

Language Problems
USE LANGUAGE HANDICAPS

LANGUAGE PROFICIENCY 290
RT Language Instruction
Language Skills
Language Tests
Nucleation (Language Learning)
Second Language Learning

LANGUAGE PROGRAMS 110
NT College Language Programs
Fles Programs
BT Programs
RT Bilingual Education
English (Second Language)
English Programs
FLES
Language
Language Instruction
Language Laboratories
Languages
Language Standardization
Modern Language Curriculum
Second Languages

LANGUAGE RECORDS (PHONOGRAPH)
050
BT Language Aids
Phonograph Records
RT Language
Language Instruction
Languages

LANGUAGE RESEARCH 450
NT Dialect Studies
Lexicography
Lexicology
BT Research
RT Bilingualism
Child Language
Diachronic Linguistics
Discourse Analysis
Etymology
Glottochronology
Language
Language Classification
Language Role
Languages
Language Universals
Onomastics
Speech Compression
Unwritten Language
Urban Language

LANGUAGE RHYTHM 290
SN Regular or intermittent pattern in the
flow of spoken or written language
BT Language Patterns
RT Articulation (Speech)
Language
Language Styles

Literary Conventions
Oral Communication
Oral Expression
Poetry
Prose
Speech
Speech Habits
Speech Skills
Written Language

LANGUAGE ROLE 290
RT Cultural Factors
Language
Language Research
Social Dialects
Social Influences
Sociolinguistics

LANGUAGES 300
SN Use a more specific term if possible
UF Foreign Languages
Language Interrelationship
NT African Languages
Afro Asiatic Languages
American Indian Languages
Australian Aboriginal Languages
Basque
Burushaski
Caucasian Languages
Classical Languages
Creoles
Dialects
Dravidian Languages
English
Indo European Languages
Japanese
Korean
Malayo Polynesian Languages
Modern Languages
Pidgins
Sino Tibetan Languages
Slavic Languages
Somali
Uralic Altaic Languages
BT Humanities
RT Bilingualism
Echolalia
English Programs
Etymology
FLES Materials
FLES Programs
Foreign Language Books
Foreign Language Films
Foreign Language Periodicals
Glottochronology
Idioms
Intensive Language Courses
Language
Language Ability
Language Classification
Language Enrichment
Language Enrollment
Language Fluency

Language Instruction
Language Laboratories
Language Programs
Language Records (Phonograph)
Language Research
Language Skills
Language Tests
Language Typology
Language Usage
Middle English
Multilingualism
Mutual Intelligibility
Old English
Word Frequency

LANGUAGE SKILLS 010
NT Audiolingual Skills
    Language Fluency
BT Skills
RT Basic Skills
    English (Second Language)
    English Education
    Expressive Language
    Interpreters
    Language
    Language Ability
    Language Learning Levels
    Language Proficiency
    Languages
    Listening Comprehension
    Nucleation (Language Learning)
    Second Language Learning
    Speech Skills
    TENL
    Translation
    Verbal Ability
    Word Study Skills

LANGUAGE STANDARDIZATION 500
BT Language Planning
RT Dialects
    Language Programs
    Multilingualism
    National Norms
    National Programs
    Official Languages
    Romanization
    Sociolinguistics
    Standard Spoken Usage
    TENL

LANGUAGE STYLES 290
RT Expressive Language
    Language
    Language Classification
    Language Patterns
    Language Rhythm
    Literary Conventions
    Native Speakers
    Speech Skills
    Standard Spoken Usage
    Writing Skills

Language Tapes
USE PHONOTAPE RECORDINGS

LANGUAGE TEACHERS 380
BT Teachers
RT Language Instruction

Language Teaching
USE LANGUAGE INSTRUCTION

LANGUAGE TESTS 520
BT Tests
RT Connected Discourse
    Language
    Language Proficiency
    Languages

Language Therapy
USE SPEECH THERAPY

LANGUAGE TYPOLOGY 290
BT Typology
RT Classification
    Etymology
    Language Classification
    Language Patterns
    Languages
    Language Universals
    Morphology (Languages)
    Phonemes
    Phonology
    Synchronic Linguistics
    Syntax
    Tone Languages

LANGUAGE UNIVERSALS 290
SN Characteristics assumed to be common
    to all languages
UF Linguistic Universals
BT Language
RT Behavioral Science Research
    Behavior Patterns
    Case (Grammar)
    Diachronic Linguistics
    Distinctive Features
    Language Development
    Language Patterns
    Language Research
    Language Typology
    Linguistic Theory
    Negative Forms (Language)
    Structural Analysis
    Synchronic Linguistics

LANGUAGE USAGE 290
NT Standard Spoken Usage
RT American English
    Language Instruction
    Language Patterns
    Language Planning
    Languages
    Linguistics
    Native Speakers
    Oral Communication
    Regional Dialects

Speech
Speech Habits
Verbal Communication
Written Language

LAO 300
UF Laotian
BT Sino Tibetan Languages

Laotian
USE LAO

Large Cities
USE URBAN AREAS

LARGE GROUP INSTRUCTION 270
BT Instruction
RT Individual Instruction
Mass Instruction
Small Group Instruction

Large Scale Production
USE MASS PRODUCTION

Large Type Books
USE LARGE TYPE MATERIALS

LARGE TYPE MATERIALS 050
UF Large Type Books
BT Instructional Materials
RT Instructional Aids
Partially Sighted
Reading Instruction
Reading Materials
Special Education
Visually Handicapped

Laser Oscillators
USE LASERS

LASERS 400
UF Laser Oscillators
Light Amplifiers (Lasers)
Optical Masers
RT Electronics
Electrooptics
Energy
Light
Optics
Physics
Radiation
Science Equipment
Semiconductor Devices
Solar Radiation

LATERAL DOMINANCE 420
BT Physical Characteristics
RT Cerebral Dominance
Left Handed Writer
Neurological Organization
Physical Development
Psychomotor Skills

LATE SCHOOL ENTRANCE 020
SN Enrollment after the school semester has
begun
BT Enrollment
RT Admission (School)

Lathes
USE MACHINE TOOLS

LATIN 300
BT Romance Languages
RT Classical Literature

LATIN AMERICAN CULTURE 100
NT Puerto Rican Culture
BT American Culture
RT Luso Brazilian Culture
Modernism
Spanish American Literature
Spanish Culture
Western Civilization

LAW ENFORCEMENT 230
RT Human Services
Immigration Inspectors
Laws
Police

Law Enforcement Officers
USE POLICE

LAW INSTRUCTION 270
NT School Law
BT Instruction
RT Laws
Law Schools
Lawyers

LAW LIBRARIES 210
BT Special Libraries
RT Archives
Laws
Legislation
Legislative Reference Libraries

Lawmakers
USE LEGISLATORS

Lawn Maintenance
USE TURF MANAGEMENT

LAWS 230
NT Federal Laws
Labor Laws
Loyalty Oaths
Minimum Wage Laws
Public Health Laws
State Laws
RT Codification
Copyrights
Drug Legislation
Equal Protection
Law Enforcement
Law Instruction
Law Libraries
Lawyers

Legal Responsibility
Legislation
Legislative Reference Libraries
Sanctions

LAW SCHOOLS 470
BT   Schools
RT   Business Administration
Law Instruction
Lawyers

LAWYERS 380
UF   Advocates
Attorneys
Barristers
Solicitors
BT   Professional Personnel
RT   Court Litigation
Law Instruction
Laws
Law Schools
Legal Aid
Legal Aid Projects
Legal Problems
Legal Responsibility
Professional Occupations

LAYMEN 380
NT   Lay Teachers
RT   Church Workers

LAY TEACHERS 380
BT   Laymen
Teachers
RT   Church Workers
Programed Tutoring

LEADER PARTICIPATION 060
BT   Participation
RT   Adult Leaders
Leadership

LEADERS GUIDES 020
BT   Guides
RT   Leadership
Leadership Training

LEADERSHIP 060
NT   Informal Leadership
Negro Leadership
Student Leadership
BT   Behavior
RT   Adult Leaders
Community Leaders
Leader Participation
Leaders Guides
Leadership Qualities
Leadership Responsibility
Leadership Training
Nonauthoritarian Classes
Supervisors
Youth Leaders

LEADERSHIP QUALITIES 010
RT   Adult Leaders
Leadership
Leadership Responsibility
Leadership Training

LEADERSHIP RESPONSIBILITY 020
BT   Social Responsibility
RT   Administrator Responsibility
Institutional Role
Leadership
Leadership Qualities
Teacher Responsibility

LEADERSHIP STYLES 510
RT   Teaching Styles

LEADERSHIP TRAINING 270
BT   Training
RT   Leaders Guides
Leadership
Leadership Qualities
Management Development
Management Education
Supervisory Methods
Supervisory Training
Trainers
Youth Leaders

LEAD LECTURE PLAN 510
BT   Teaching Techniques
RT   Instruction
Lecture
Team Teaching

Leadmen
USE   CREW LEADERS

Leaflets
USE   PAMPHLETS

LEARNING 310
UF   Environmental Learning
Learning Experiments
NT   Activity Learning
Adult Learning
Associative Learning
Aural Learning
Continuous Learning
Discovery Learning
Discrimination Learning
Incidental Learning
Learning Difficulties
Multisensory Learning
Nonverbal Learning
Perceptual Motor Learning
Preschool Learning
Rote Learning
Second Language Learning
Sequential Learning
Serial Learning
Symbolic Learning
Verbal Learning
Visual Learning
RT   Conditioned Response

Discovery Processes
Education
Inquiry Training
Instruction
Language Learning Levels
Learning Activities
Learning Characteristics
Learning Experience
Learning Laboratories
Learning Motivation
Learning Processes
Learning Readiness
Learning Theories
Mnemonics
Recall (Psychological)
Teaching
Time Factors (Learning)

LEARNING ACTIVITIES 310
BT Activities
RT Activity Learning
Directed Reading Activity
Discovery Processes
Learning
Learning Experience
Learning Readiness
Mnemonics
Rote Learning

LEARNING CHARACTERISTICS 310
BT Individual Characteristics
RT Learning
Learning Difficulties
Learning Experience
Learning Motivation
Learning Processes
Learning Readiness

Learning Cycles
USE LEARNING PROCESSES

LEARNING DIFFICULTIES 310
UF Arithmetic Deficiencies
BT Learning
RT Academic Achievement
Diagnostic Teaching
Educational Diagnosis
Learning Characteristics
Learning Disabilities
Nonverbal Learning
Remedial Instruction
Symbolic Learning

LEARNING DISABILITIES 240
SN Distinguished by sharp imbalance within
the students cognitive development and
by marked underachievement
NT Aphasia
Auditory Agnosia
Dyslexia
RT Cognitive Development
Exceptional Child Education
Handicapped
Learning Difficulties
Minimally Brain Injured

Neurologically Handicapped
Perceptually Handicapped
Reading Difficulty
Underachievers

LEARNING EXPERIENCE 200
NT Clinical Experience
BT Experience
RT Continuous Learning
Learning
Learning Activities
Learning Characteristics
Learning Readiness
Mnemonics

Learning Experiments
USE LEARNING

LEARNING LABORATORIES 210
BT Laboratories
RT Learning
Project Training Methods
Regional Laboratories
Training Laboratories

LEARNING MOTIVATION 040
BT Motivation
RT Achievement Need
Learning
Learning Characteristics
Learning Readiness

LEARNING PLATEAUS 310
RT Cognitive Measurement
Intelligence Level
Learning Processes
Learning Theories
Psychological Characteristics

LEARNING PROCESSES 310
UF Educational Processes
Learning Cycles
NT Concept Formation
Feedback
Information Seeking
Mnemonics
Retention
Review (Reexamination)
Stimulus Generalization
RT Abstraction Levels
Activity Learning
Cognitive Processes
Conservation (Concept)
Continuous Learning
Deductive Methods
Discovery Learning
Discovery Processes
Experimental Colleges
Inductive Methods
Interference (Language Learning)
Learning
Learning Characteristics
Learning Plateaus
Learning Specialists
Learning Theories

Mediation Theory
Memory
Perceptual Motor Learning
Progressive Education
Recall (Psychological)
Rote Learning
Thought Processes
Transfer Of Training

LEARNING READINESS 180
BT Readiness
RT Discovery Processes
Individual Development
Learning
Learning Activities
Learning Characteristics
Learning Experience
Learning Motivation
Readiness (Mental)

Learning Reinforcement
USE REINFORCEMENT

Learning Resources
USE EDUCATIONAL RESOURCES

Learning Resources Centers
USE INSTRUCTIONAL MATERIALS CENTERS

LEARNING SPECIALISTS 380
SN Person who assumes leadership of an
instruction unit and is responsible for the
learning efficiency of the students
BT Specialists
RT Learning Processes

LEARNING THEORIES 310
NT Transfer Of Training
BT Theories
RT Discovery Processes
Learning
Learning Plateaus
Learning Processes
Mnemonics
Paired Associate Learning
Reinforcement
Rote Learning
Serial Learning
Stimulus Generalization

Leather Crafts
USE HANDICRAFTS

LEAVE OF ABSENCE 150
SN Authorized absence or vacation from
duty or employment
UF Maternity Leave
Sick Leave
Vacations
NT Sabbatical Leaves
RT Attendance
Employer Employee Relationship
Personnel Policy
Teacher Welfare

LECTURE 510
UF Lecture Method
BT Teaching Techniques
RT Chautauquas
Lead Lecture Plan
Speeches

Lecture Method
USE LECTURE

LEFT HANDED WRITER 380
RT Handwriting
Lateral Dominance

LEGAL AID 230
RT Lawyers
Legal Aid Projects
Legal Costs
Legal Problems

LEGAL AID PROJECTS 230
BT Projects
RT Lawyers
Legal Aid
Legal Costs
Legal Problems

LEGAL COSTS 220
BT Costs
RT Legal Aid
Legal Aid Projects

Legal Decisions
USE COURT LITIGATION

LEGAL PROBLEMS 230
BT Problems
RT Court Litigation
Lawyers
Legal Aid
Legal Aid Projects
Legal Responsibility

LEGAL RESPONSIBILITY 020
BT Responsibility
RT Indemnity Bonds
Laws
Lawyers
Legal Problems

Legal Secretaries
USE SECRETARIES

LEGAL SEGREGATION 430
BT Racial Segregation

Legal Stenographers
USE STENOGRAPHERS

LEGENDS 260
BT Literature
RT Biblical Literature
Classical Literature
Composition (Literary)
Epics
Folk Culture
French Literature

German Literature
Humor
Medieval Literature
Medieval Romance
Metaphors
Mythology
Old English Literature
Polish Literature
Russian Literature
Spanish American Literature
Spanish Literature

LEGISLATION 230
NT Civil Rights Legislation
Discriminatory Legislation
Drug Legislation
Educational Legislation
Federal Legislation
Labor Legislation
Minimum Wage Legislation
Recreation Legislation
State Legislation
RT Government (Administrative Body)
Law Libraries
Laws
Legislative Reference Libraries
Legislators
Political Issues
State Programs

LEGISLATIVE REFERENCE LIBRARIES 210
BT Special Libraries
RT Government Libraries
Law Libraries
Laws
Legislation

LEGISLATORS 380
UF Congressmen
Lawmakers
Representatives
Senators
BT Public Officials
RT City Officials
County Officials
Educational Legislation
Federal Laws
Federal Legislation
Legislation
State Laws
State Officials

Leisure
USE LEISURE TIME

LEISURE TIME 390
UF Leisure
RT Recreational Activities

Leisure Time Reading
USE RECREATIONAL READING

Leitmotifs
USE MOTIFS

Leitmotivs
USE MOTIFS

Lending Of Books
USE LIBRARY CIRCULATION

Lengthened School Year
USE EXTENDED SCHOOL YEAR

Less Commonly Taught Languages
USE UNCOMMONLY TAUGHT LANGUAGES

Lesson Notes
USE LESSON PLANS

LESSON OBSERVATION CRITERIA 500
RT Inservice Teaching
Lesson Plans
Observation
Reliability
Student Teaching
Teacher Evaluation
Teacher Rating

LESSON PLANS 510
UF Lesson Notes
RT Curriculum Guides
Lesson Observation Criteria
Master Plans
Planning

Letters
USE LETTERS (CORRESPONDENCE)

LETTERS (CORRESPONDENCE) 080
UF Correspondence (Letters)
Letters
NT Business Correspondence
RT Communication (Thought Transfer)
Composition (Literary)
French Literature
German Literature
Literature
Nineteenth Century Literature
Spanish American Literature
Spanish Literature
Writing

Levels Of Abstraction
USE ABSTRACTION LEVELS

Levels Of Complexity
USE COMPLEXITY LEVEL

Levels Of Difficulty
USE COMPLEXITY LEVEL

Levels Of Language Learning
USE LANGUAGE LEARNING LEVELS

LEXICOGRAPHY 290
BT Language Research
RT Dictionaries
Etymology
Glottochronology
Lexicology
Thesauri

LEXICOLOGY 290
BT Language Research
RT Comparative Analysis
    Componential Analysis
    Contrastive Linguistics
    Diachronic Linguistics
    Dictionaries
    Glottochronology
    Language Patterns
    Lexicography
    Morphology (Languages)
    Onomastics
    Semantics
    Vocabulary

Lexicons
USE DICTIONARIES

LIBERAL ARTS 110
NT Humanities
    Sciences
RT General Education
    Liberal Arts Majors
    Special Degree Programs

LIBERAL ARTS MAJORS 140
BT College Majors
    College Students
RT Education Majors
    Liberal Arts

Liberal Education
USE GENERAL EDUCATION

LIBRARIANS 380
UF Library Specialists
NT Medical Record Librarians
BT Professional Personnel
RT Libraries
    Library Associations
    Library Schools
    Library Science
    Professional Occupations

LIBRARIES 210
NT Branch Libraries
    Classroom Libraries
    College Libraries
    Decentralized Library Systems
    Depository Libraries
    National Libraries
    Public Libraries
    Regional Libraries
    Research Libraries
    School Libraries
    Special Libraries
    University Libraries
BT Institutions
RT Archives
    Automation
    Book Catalogs
    Cataloging
    Catalogs
    Dictionary Catalogs
    Divided Catalogs

Documentation
Information Centers
Information Sources
Instructional Materials Centers
Interlibrary Loans
Librarians
Library Cooperation
Library Equipment
Library Expenditures
Library Facilities
Library Guides
Library Instruction
Library Materials
Library Networks
Library Planning
Library Programs
Library Reference Services
Library Research
Library Science
Library Services
Library Skills
Library Standards
Library Surveys
Library Technicians
Study Facilities
Union Catalogs
Use Studies

LIBRARY ACQUISITION 330
SN Process of acquiring library materials
UF Book Buying
BT Library Technical Processes
RT Library Collections
    Library Materials
    Library Material Selection
    Purchasing

Library Aides
USE LIBRARY TECHNICIANS

Library Aids
USE LIBRARY FACILITIES

LIBRARY ASSOCIATIONS 370
UF Library Organizations
    Library Societies
BT Professional Associations
RT International Organizations
    Librarians
    National Organizations

Library Automation
USE AUTOMATION

LIBRARY CIRCULATION 330
UF Book Lending
    Circulation (Libraries)
    Lending Of Books
    Library Loans
BT Library Services
RT Interlibrary Loans
    Library Collections
    Library Materials

LIBRARY COLLECTIONS 320
UF Library Holdings
RT Archives
     Books
     Foreign Language Books
     Foreign Language Periodicals
     Interlibrary Loans
     Library Acquisition
     Library Circulation
     Library Materials
     Library Material Selection
     Paperback Books
     Periodicals
     Reference Materials
     Serials

LIBRARY COOPERATION 020
NT Interlibrary Loans
BT Interinstitutional Cooperation
RT Cooperative Programs
     County Libraries
     Interagency Cooperation
     Libraries
     Library Networks
     Library Programs
     Library Services
     Regional Libraries
     Union Catalogs

LIBRARY EDUCATION 140
SN Education or training of professional and
     non professional library personnel
UF Education For Librarianship
     Library Training
BT Education
RT Information Science
     Library Instruction
     Library Schools
     Library Science
     Library Skills
     Professional Education

LIBRARY EQUIPMENT 170
NT Carrels
BT Library Facilities
RT Automation
     Libraries

LIBRARY EXPENDITURES 220
BT Expenditures
RT Libraries
     Library Technical Processes

LIBRARY EXTENSION 330
SN Educational activities of public libraries
BT Extension Education
RT Bookmobiles
     Library Services

LIBRARY FACILITIES 210
UF Library Aids
NT Library Equipment
BT Educational Facilities
RT Bookmobiles
     Information Centers
     Libraries
     Library Planning

Library Fines
USE FINES (PENALTIES)

Library Goals
USE LIBRARY INSTRUCTION

LIBRARY GUIDES 320
BT Guides
RT Curriculum Guides
     Libraries

Library Holdings
USE LIBRARY COLLECTIONS

LIBRARY INSTRUCTION 270
UF Library Goals
BT Instruction
RT Libraries
     Library Education
     Library Science

Library Loans
USE LIBRARY CIRCULATION

LIBRARY MATERIALS 320
RT Interlibrary Loans
     Libraries
     Library Acquisition
     Library Circulation
     Library Collections
     Library Material Selection
     Library Technical Processes
     Publications
     Reference Materials

LIBRARY MATERIAL SELECTION 330
UF Selection Of Library Materials
RT Books
     Library Acquisition
     Library Collections
     Library Materials
     Library Technical Processes
     Reading Material Selection

Library Mechanization
USE AUTOMATION

LIBRARY NETWORKS 330
UF Library Systems
BT Networks
RT County Libraries
     Information Networks
     Libraries
     Library Cooperation
     Library Programs
     Library Services
     Regional Libraries

Library Organizations
USE LIBRARY ASSOCIATIONS

LIBRARY PLANNING 020
SN Formulation of plans for library objectives
BT Planning
RT Building Plans
  Libraries
  Library Facilities
  Library Programs
  Library Services
  Library Surveys

LIBRARY PROGRAMS 330
BT Library Science
  Programs
RT Interlibrary Loans
  Libraries
  Library Cooperation
  Library Networks
  Library Planning
  Library Services

LIBRARY REFERENCE SERVICES 330
UF Reference Work
BT Library Services
RT Information Needs
  Information Retrieval
  Information Services
  Information Sources
  Libraries
  Reference Books
  Reference Materials
  Research Libraries

LIBRARY RESEARCH 450
BT Research
RT Documentation
  Information Processing
  Information Science
  Information Utilization
  Libraries
  Library Science
  Use Studies

LIBRARY SCHOOLS 470
BT Schools
RT Higher Education
  Information Science
  Librarians
  Library Education
  Library Science
  Professional Education

LIBRARY SCIENCE 330
NT Library Programs
  Library Services
RT Documentation
  Indexes (Locaters)
  Indexing
  Information Retrieval
  Information Science
  Librarians
  Libraries

  Library Education
  Library Instruction
  Library Research
  Library Schools
  Search Strategies
  Use Studies

LIBRARY SERVICES 330
NT Library Circulation
  Library Reference Services
BT Library Science
RT Bookmobiles
  Information Services
  Interlibrary Loans
  Libraries
  Library Cooperation
  Library Extension
  Library Networks
  Library Planning
  Library Programs
  Library Technical Processes

LIBRARY SKILLS 010
BT Skills
RT Libraries
  Library Education

Library Societies
USE LIBRARY ASSOCIATIONS

Library Specialists
USE LIBRARIANS

LIBRARY STANDARDS 500
BT Standards
RT Libraries
  Library Surveys

LIBRARY SURVEYS 330
BT Surveys
RT Libraries
  Library Planning
  Library Standards
  Use Studies

Library Systems
USE LIBRARY NETWORKS

Library Technical Assistants
USE LIBRARY TECHNICIANS

LIBRARY TECHNICAL PROCESSES 330
SN Acquisition, organization, and preparation of library materials for use
UF Technical Processes (Libraries)
  Technical Services (Libraries)
NT Cataloging
  Indexing
  Library Acquisition
RT Automation
  Classification
  Information Processing
  Library Expenditures
  Library Materials
  Library Material Selection
  Library Services

LINGUISTIC COMPETENCE 290
RT Cognitive Processes
    Comprehension
    Language Ability
    Linguistic Performance
    Linguistics

LINGUISTIC PATTERNS 290
RT Componential Analysis
    Etymology
    Linguistics
    Paralinguistics
    Phonemics
    Suffixes

LINGUISTIC PERFORMANCE 290
BT Performance
RT Linguistic Competence
    Linguistics
    Oral Communication
    Oral Expression
    Speech

LINGUISTICS 290
NT Applied Linguistics
    Computational Linguistics
    Diachronic Linguistics
    Grammar
    Graphemes
    Mathematical Linguistics
    Paralinguistics
    Phonetics
    Psycholinguistics
    Semantics
    Sociolinguistics
    Structural Linguistics
    Synchronic Linguistics
    Syntax
RT American English
    Definitions
    Dialects
    Distinctive Features
    English
    English (Second Language)
    Glottochronology
    Information Theory
    Intonation
    Language
    Language Ability
    Language Usage
    Linguistic Competence
    Linguistic Patterns
    Linguistic Performance
    Middle English
    Old English
    Onomastics
    Phonemics
    Semiotics
    Sentence Diagraming
    Social Dialects
    Speech
    Speech Education

    Structural Analysis
    Traditional Grammar

LINGUISTIC THEORY 290
NT Transformation Theory (Language)
BT Theories
RT Componential Analysis
    Computational Linguistics
    Descriptive Linguistics
    Generative Grammar
    Language Universals
    Nucleation (Language Learning)
    Psycholinguistics
    Sociolinguistics

Linguistic Universals
USE LANGUAGE UNIVERSALS

LIPREADING 080
UF Speech Reading
BT Reading
RT Cued Speech
    Deaf Education
    Deaf Interpreting
    Hearing Therapists
    Hearing Therapy
    Speech Education

LISTENING 080
BT Language Arts
RT Attention
    Audio Passive Laboratories
    Listening Comprehension
    Listening Habits
    Listening Skills

LISTENING COMPREHENSION 310
UF Auditory Comprehension
    Aural Comprehension
BT Comprehension
RT Auditory Training
    Aural Learning
    Aural Stimuli
    Language Skills
    Listening
    Listening Habits
    Listening Skills

LISTENING GROUPS 380
BT Groups
RT Audiences
    Discussion Groups
    Educational Radio
    Educational Television
    Group Instruction
    Listening Habits
    Mass Instruction

LISTENING HABITS 420
RT Habit Formation
    Listening
    Listening Comprehension
    Listening Groups
    Listening Skills

Listening Laboratories
USE AUDIO PASSIVE LABORATORIES

LISTENING SKILLS 010
BT Audiolingual Skills
RT Listening
Listening Comprehension
Listening Habits

Listening Viewing Centers
USE AUDIOVISUAL CENTERS

Listen Respond Laboratories
USE AUDIO ACTIVE LABORATORIES

LITERACY 440
UF Literacy Skills
NT Reading
Scientific Literacy
Writing
RT Intelligence
Literacy Classes
Readability

LITERACY CLASSES 440
BT Classes (Groups Of Students)
RT Literacy

LITERACY EDUCATION 140
SN Teaching of reading, writing and social
skills to prepare persons to function at
the fifth grade level
BT Education
RT Adult Basic Education

Literacy Skills
USE LITERACY

LITERARY ANALYSIS 260
BT Literature
RT Analytical Criticism
Characterization (Literature)
Comedy
Composition (Literary)
Content Analysis
Critical Reading
Drama
Epics
Fifteenth Century Literature
Figurative Language
Formal Criticism
French Literature
German Literature
Historical Criticism
Literary Conventions
Literary Criticism
Literary Discrimination
Literary Genres
Literary Styles
Local Color Writing
Medieval Romance
Metaphors
Modernism
Moral Criticism
Mythic Criticism
Naturalism

Nineteenth Century Literature
Realism
Satire
Spanish American Literature
Spanish Literature
Symbols (Literary)
Textual Criticism
Tragedy
Victorian Literature

LITERARY CONVENTIONS 080
SN Accepted elements of technique, such as
technical devices, used as recognized
means of literary expression
UF Literary Devices
Literary Modes
NT Motifs
RT Analytical Criticism
Characterization (Literature)
Comedy
Composition (Literary)
Creative Writing
Descriptive Writing
Dialogue
Drama
English Neoclassic Literary Period
Fiction
Figurative Language
Formal Criticism
French Literature
Historical Criticism
Language Patterns
Language Rhythm
Language Styles
Literary Analysis
Literary Criticism
Literary Genres
Literary Styles
Modernism
Pastoral Literature
Poetry
Prose
Rhetoric
Satire
Spanish American Literature
Spanish Literature
Symbols (Literary)
Textual Criticism
Tragedy
Victorian Literature

LITERARY CRITICISM 260
NT Aristotelian Criticism
Impressionistic Criticism
Literary Styles
Moral Criticism
Textual Criticism
Theoretical Criticism
RT Analytical Criticism
Characterization (Literature)
Content Analysis
Critical Reading
Dialogue

Dramatic Unities
Eighteenth Century Literature
English Neoclassic Literary Period
Existentialism
Fifteenth Century Literature
Formal Criticism
French Literature
German Literature
Historical Criticism
Imagery
Literary Analysis
Literary Conventions
Literary Discrimination
Literary History
Literary Influences
Literary Perspective
Literature
Local Color Writing
Metaphors
Modernism
Motifs
Mythic Criticism
Naturalism
Nineteenth Century Literature
Pastoral Literature
Platonism
Realism
Spanish American Literature
Spanish Literature
Victorian Literature

Literary Devices
USE LITERARY CONVENTIONS

LITERARY DISCRIMINATION 310
RT   Critical Reading
     Literary Analysis
     Literary Criticism
     Literature
     Reading Comprehension
     Reading Skills

LITERARY GENRES 260
SN   Divisions of literature into categories or
     classes which group works by form or
     type, such as biographies, drama,
     essays, fiction, or poetry, rather than by
     movements such as naturalism, realism,
     romanticism or by subject matter as in
     legends, myths, etc.
NT   Biographies
     Drama
     Essays
     Fables
     Fiction
     Novels
     Poetry
     Satire
     Short Stories
BT   Literature
RT   Analytical Criticism
     Dialogue
     Fifteenth Century Literature
     Formal Criticism

French Literature
German Literature
Haiku
Historical Criticism
Literary Analysis
Literary Conventions
Local Color Writing
Medieval Romance
Modernism
Moral Criticism
Naturalism
Nineteenth Century Literature
Realism
Spanish American Literature
Spanish Literature
Textual Criticism
Typology
Victorian Literature

LITERARY HISTORY 260
SN   The study of literature in its historical
     context
NT   English Neoclassic Literary Period
BT   History
RT   German Literature
     Literary Criticism
     Literature
     Medieval Romance

LITERARY INFLUENCES 260
BT   Literature
RT   Fiction
     Literary Criticism
     Mythic Criticism
     Novels
     Poetry
     Prose

Literary Modes
USE LITERARY CONVENTIONS

LITERARY PERSPECTIVE 260
UF   Point Of View (Literature)
BT   Literature
RT   Analytical Criticism
     Drama
     Fiction
     Formal Criticism
     Literary Criticism
     Novels
     Poetry
     Prose

LITERARY STYLES 260
BT   Literary Criticism
RT   Analytical Criticism
     Formal Criticism
     Literary Analysis
     Literary Conventions
     Literature
     Platonism
     Poetry
     Prose

LITERATURE 260
NT African Literature
American Literature
Analytical Criticism
Anthologies
Autobiographies
Baroque Literature
Biblical Literature
Biographies
Characterization (Literature)
Chronicles
Classical Literature
Czech Literature
Dialogue
Didacticism
Eighteenth Century Literature
English Literature
Essays
Fables
Fiction
Fifteenth Century Literature
Formal Criticism
French Literature
German Literature
Historical Criticism
Humor
Italian Literature
Legends
Literary Analysis
Literary Genres
Literary Influences
Literary Perspective
Medieval Literature
Medieval Romance
Modernism
Mythic Criticism
Mythology
Naturalism
Negro Literature
Nineteenth Century Literature
Novels
Parody
Pastoral Literature
Poetry
Polish Literature
Prose
Realism
Renaissance Literature
Romanticism
Russian Literature
Satire
Scripts
Seventeenth Century Literature
Short Stories
Sixteenth Century Literature
Spanish American Literature
Spanish Literature
Symbolism

Tales
Twentieth Century Literature
Victorian Literature
World Literature
BT Humanities
RT Allegory
Ambiguity
Antithesis
Aristotelian Criticism
Authors
Books
Choral Speaking
Christianity
Encyclopedias
English Neoclassic Literary Period
Existentialism
Expressionism
Folk Drama
Folklore Books
Humanism
Imagery
Impressionistic Criticism
Irony
Judaism
Letters (Correspondence)
Literary Criticism
Literary Discrimination
Literary History
Literary Styles
Literature Appreciation
Literature Guides
Literature Programs
Literature Reviews
Lyric Poetry
Metaphors
Moral criticism
Motifs
Narration
Odes
Paperback Books
Parallelism (Literary)
Platonism
Poets
Proverbs
Science Fiction
Sociological Novels
Surrealism
Symbols (Literary)
Textual Criticism
Thematic Approach
Versification

LITERATURE APPRECIATION 260
UF Reading Enjoyment
RT Choral Speaking
German Literature
Literature
Literature Guides
Nineteenth Century Literature

Literature Citations
USE BIBLIOGRAPHIC CITATIONS

LITERATURE GUIDES 320
BT   Guides
RT   Curriculum Guides
     Literature
     Literature Appreciation

LITERATURE PROGRAMS 270
BT   Programs
RT   Literature

LITERATURE REVIEWS 320
UF   Reviews Of Literature
BT   Surveys
RT   Annotated Bibliographies
     Bibliographies
     Book Reviews
     Content Analysis
     Historical Reviews
     Literature
     Research
     Research Reviews (Publications)
     Review (Reexamination)

Literature Search
USE   BIBLIOGRAPHIES

Litigation
USE   COURT LITIGATION

I.IVESTOCK 070
UF   Farm Animals
NT   Horses
RT   Animal Science
     Biology

Livestock Feed Stores
USE   FEED STORES

Livestock Production
USE   AGRICULTURAL PRODUCTION

Livestock Technology
USE   ANIMAL SCIENCE

LIVING STANDARDS 500
BT   Standards
RT   Economic Factors

Local Autonomy
USE   SCHOOL DISTRICT AUTONOMY

LOCAL COLOR WRITING 260
BT   Realism
RT   American Literature
     Art
     Dialogue
     Drama
     English Literature
     Essays
     Fiction
     Literary Analysis
     Literary Criticism
     Literary Genres
     Novels
     Poetry
     Prose

     Short Stories
     Twentieth Century Literature

Local Control
USE   SCHOOL DISTRICT AUTONOMY

Local Government
USE   CITY GOVERNMENT

LOCAL HOUSING AUTHORITIES 230
BT   Community Agencies (Public)
RT   Housing

LOCAL ISSUES 230
BT   Community Problems
RT   Community
     Community Characteristics
     School District Autonomy

Local Officials
USE   CITY OFFICIALS

LOCAL RECREATION LEGISLATION 230
BT   Recreation Legislation

LOCAL UNIONS 150
BT   Unions
RT   Labor Unions

LOCATIONAL SKILLS (SOCIAL STUDIES)
010
BT   Skills
RT   Social Studies
     Study Skills

LOCKER ROOMS 210
RT   Athletics
     Equipment Storage
     Hygiene
     Physical Education Facilities
     Sanitary Facilities
     Sanitation

LOCOMOTIVE ENGINEERS 380
BT   Skilled Workers
RT   Diesel Engines
     Engines
     Mechanical Skills
     Skilled Occupations

LOGIC 310
UF   Deductive Logic
NT   Mathematical Logic
RT   Cognitive Processes
     Critical Thinking
     Deductive Methods
     Educational Philosophy
     Logical Thinking
     Persuasive Discourse
     Philosophy
     Productive Thinking
     Thought Processes
     Validity

LOGICAL THINKING 310
BT Thought Processes
RT Abstract Reasoning
    Cognitive Processes
    Convergent Thinking
    Intelligence
    Logic
    Productive Thinking

LONGITUDINAL STUDIES 190
BT Case Studies
RT Cross Sectional Studies

Look Guess Method
USE SIGHT METHOD

Look Say Method
USE SIGHT METHOD

LOOP INDUCTION SYSTEMS 170
SN Electronic system consisting of
    microphone, amplifier, and a loop of wire
    circling the room. Sound is transmitted
    to students through coils in their hearing
    aids
RT Aurally Handicapped
    Deaf
    Electronic Equipment
    Hard Of Hearing
    Hearing Aids
    Instructional Aids
    Instructional Technology

Low Ability
USE ABILITY

LOW ABILITY STUDENTS 380
BT Students
RT Ability Grouping
    Academic Ability
    Educationally Disadvantaged
    Low Achievers
    Mentally Handicapped
    Retarded Children
    Slow Learners
    Student Ability
    Student Characteristics
    Underachievers

Low Achievement
USE LOW ACHIEVERS

LOW ACHIEVEMENT FACTORS 010
RT Low Achievers

LOW ACHIEVERS 380
UF Low Achievement
BT Students
RT Academic Achievement
    Achievement
    Continuation Students
    Educationally Disadvantaged
    Low Ability Students
    Low Achievement Factors
    Progressive Retardation

LOWER CLASS 490
BT Social Class
RT Culturally Disadvantaged
    Lower Class Males
    Lower Class Parents
    Lower Class Students
    Lower Middle Class
    Low Income
    Low Income Groups

Lower Class Boys
USE LOWER CLASS MALES

LOWER CLASS MALES 380
UF Lower Class Boys
BT Males
RT Lower Class

LOWER CLASS PARENTS 380
BT Parents
RT Lower Class

LOWER CLASS STUDENTS 380
BT Students
RT Lower Class

LOWER MIDDLE CLASS 380
BT Middle Class
RT Lower Class
    Socioeconomic Status
    Upper Class

LOW INCOME 220
BT Income
RT Economic Disadvantagement
    Lower Class
    Low Income Counties
    Low Income Groups
    Low Income States
    Poverty Programs
    Subemployment

LOW INCOME COUNTIES 230
BT Low Income States
RT Depressed Areas (Geographic)
    Low Income
    Low Income Groups

LOW INCOME GROUPS 380
BT Groups
RT Economically Disadvantaged
    Lower Class
    Low Income
    Low Income Counties
    Low Income States
    Welfare Recipients

LOW INCOME STATES 230
NT Low Income Counties
RT Low Income
    Low Income Groups

LOW LEVEL ASPIRATION 420
BT Aspiration

LOW MOTIVATION 040
UF   Interest Lack
BT   Motivation

LOW RENT HOUSING 210
BT   Housing
RT   Public Housing

Low Scholastic Aptitude
USE   ACADEMIC APTITUDE

LOYALTY OATHS 230
BT   Laws
RT   Boards Of Education
     Employment Practices
     Employment Qualifications
     Faculty Recruitment
     Federal Laws
     Federal Legislation
     State Laws
     State Legislation
     Student Loan Programs
     Teacher Employment
     Teaching Conditions

LSD
USE   LYSERGIC ACID DIETHYLAMIDE

LUBRICANTS 460
UF   Grease
     Oil
RT   Engines

Luganda
USE   GANDA

LUMBER INDUSTRY 370
UF   Lumbering
     Timber Based Industry
BT   Industry
RT   Forestry Occupations
     Furniture Design
     Furniture Industry
     Woodworking

Lumbering
USE   LUMBER INDUSTRY

LUMINESCENCE 400
UF   Photometric Brightness
RT   Glare
     Illumination Levels
     Light
     Lighting
     Lights
     Physics
     Radiation

LUNCH PROGRAMS 250
BT   Programs
RT   Food Handling Facilities
     Food Standards
     Hunger
     Nutrition

LUSO BRAZILIAN CULTURE 100
BT   Culture
RT   Latin American Culture

LYRIC POETRY 260
NT   Odes
BT   Poetry
RT   Ballads
     Epics
     Literature
     Medieval Romance
     Versification

Lyric Poets
USE   POETS

LYSERGIC ACID DIETHYLAMIDE 250
UF   Lsd
RT   Drug Abuse
     Drug Addiction

Machine Maintenance Men
USE   MACHINE REPAIRMEN

Machine Maintenance Repairmen
USE   MACHINE REPAIRMEN

MACHINE REPAIRMEN 380
UF   Machine Maintenance Men
     Machine Maintenance Repairmen
     Machinery Maintenance Repairmen
     Maintenance Machinists
     Repair Mechanics
     Shop Mechanics
BT   Skilled Workers
RT   Equipment Maintenance
     Mechanics (Process)
     Repair
     Skilled Occupations
     Trade And Industrial Education

MACHINERY INDUSTRY 370
SN   Manufacturers of machinery and
     equipment other than electrical or
     transportation eqipment
UF   Machinery Manufacturing Industry
BT   Manufacturing Industry
RT   Agricultural Machinery
     Equipment
     Machine Tools
     Tool And Die Makers

Machinery Maintenance Repairmen
USE   MACHINE REPAIRMEN

Machinery Manufacturing Industry
USE   MACHINERY INDUSTRY

Machine Storage Devices
USE   COMPUTER STORAGE DEVICES

MACHINE TOOL OPERATORS 380
UF Production Machine Operators
BT Semiskilled Workers
RT Machine Tools
    Machinists
    Metal Working Occupations
    Semiskilled Occupations
    Sheet Metal Workers
    Skilled Occupations
    Skilled Workers
    Tool And Die Makers
    Trade And Industrial Education

MACHINE TOOLS 170
UF Drill Presses
    Grinding Machines
    Lathes
    Milling Machines
    Punch Presses
    Shapers
BT Mechanical Equipment
RT Hand Tools
    Machinery Industry
    Machine Tool Operators
    Machinists
    Manufacturing Industry
    Mechanics (Process)
    Numerical Control
    Tool And Die Makers

MACHINE TRANSLATION 290
UF Mechanical Translation
BT Translation
RT Computational Linguistics
    Context Free Grammar
    Contrastive Linguistics
    Data Processing
    Information Processing

MACHINISTS 380
BT Skilled Workers
RT Machine Tool Operators
    Machine Tools
    Mechanics (Process)
    Metal Working Occupations
    Skilled Occupations
    Tool And Die Makers
    Trade And Industrial Education

Magazines
USE PERIODICALS

Magnetic Amplifiers
USE ELECTRONIC CONTROL

Magnetic Ink Character Recognition
USE CHARACTER RECOGNITION

MAGNETIC TAPES 170
RT Computer Storage Devices
    Information Storage
    Input Output Devices
    Tape Recorders
    Tape Recordings

MAGNETS 400
UF Permanent Magnets
BT Physics
RT Electricity
    Electronics

MAGNIFICATION METHODS 510
BT Methods
RT Audiovisual Aids
    Instructional Materials
    Tactile Adaptation

MAIDS 380
UF Homemakers Assistants
    Housekeepers
    Housekeeping Aides
BT Domestics
    Service Workers
RT Companions (Occupation)
    Homemaking Skills
    Occupational Home Economics
    Service Occupations
    Visiting Homemakers

MAINTENANCE 020
SN Preservation or continuance of a
    condition
NT Equipment Maintenance
    School Maintenance
RT Buildings
    Bus Garages
    Carpeting
    Cleaning
    Consumer Science
    Equipment
    Obsolescence
    Preservation
    Repair

Maintenance Machinists
USE MACHINE REPAIRMEN

Maintenance Vehicles
USE SERVICE VEHICLES

MAJORITY ATTITUDES 040
BT Attitudes
RT Minority Groups
    Public Opinion

Majority Culture
USE MIDDLE CLASS CULTURE

Maladjusted Children
USE MALADJUSTMENT

Maladjusted Students
USE MALADJUSTMENT

Maladjustive Behavior
USE MALADJUSTMENT

MALADJUSTMENT 420
UF Disordered Behavior
    Maladjusted Children
    Maladjusted Students
    Maladjustive Behavior
NT Emotional Maladjustment
BT Psychological Patterns
RT Adjustment (To Environment)
    School Phobia
    Social Isolation
    Socially Maladjusted
    Teacher Alienation

MALAGASY 300
BT Indonesian Languages

MALAY 300
BT Indonesian Languages

MALAYALAM 300
BT Dravidian Languages

MALAYO POLYNESIAN LANGUAGES 300
UF Austronesian Languages
NT Hawaiian
    Indonesian Languages
    Javanese
    Melanesian Languages
    Samoan
BT Languages
RT Language Classification
    Native Speakers

MALES 070
UF Boys
NT Lower Class Males
BT Sex (Characteristics)

MANAGEMENT 020
NT Class Management
    Family Management
    Farm Management
    Money Management
    Office Management
    Personnel Management
RT Administration
    Administrative Principles
    Consortia
    Coordination
    Educational Administration
    Managerial Occupations

MANAGEMENT DEVELOPMENT 130
SN Broad educational program to increase
    personal, interpersonal, managerial, and
    technical competencies of managers
UF Executive Development
NT Management Education
BT Human Development
RT Business Administration
    Leadership Training
    Management Systems
    Manpower Development
    Off The Job Training
    Professional Continuing Education

Professional Training
Supervisory Training

MANAGEMENT EDUCATION 140
SN Educational program to increase
    managerial and supervisory skills of
    managers and management trainees
UF Management Training
BT Management Development
RT Leadership Training
    Manpower Development

MANAGEMENT GAMES 270
UF Business Games
BT Games
RT Decision Making
    Game Theory
    Management Systems
    Problem Solving
    Simulated Environment
    Simulation
    Training Techniques

Management Personnel
USE ADMINISTRATIVE PERSONNEL

MANAGEMENT SYSTEMS 020
RT Critical Path Method
    Decision Making
    Information Systems
    Management Development
    Management Games
    Operations Research
    Problem Solving
    Systems Analysis
    Systems Approach
    Systems Concepts
    Systems Development

Management Training
USE MANAGEMENT EDUCATION

MANAGERIAL OCCUPATIONS 350
BT Occupations
RT Administration
    Administrative Personnel
    Business Administration
    Coordination
    Management
    White Collar Occupations

MANDARIN CHINESE 300
BT Chinese

MAN DAYS 150
SN Unit consisting of one hypothetical
    average man day
BT Employment Statistics
RT Employment
    Labor Force
    Time Blocks
    Working Hours

MANDINGO 300
BT African Languages

Mangala
USE LINGALA

MANIPULATIVE MATERIALS 050
BT Instructional Materials
RT Classroom Materials
Resource Materials
Student Developed Materials
Teacher Developed Materials

Man Machine Communication
USE MAN MACHINE SYSTEMS

Man Machine Interaction
USE MAN MACHINE SYSTEMS

Man Machine Interface
USE MAN MACHINE SYSTEMS

MAN MACHINE SYSTEMS 080
SN Men and machines interacting to form
single systems
UF Man Machine Communication
Man Machine Interaction
Man Machine Interface
RT Automation
Computer Assisted Instruction
Cybernetics
Dial Access Information Systems
Display Systems
Feedback
Human Engineering
Information Systems
Interaction

MANPOWER DEVELOPMENT 130
BT Development
RT Job Development
Management Development
Management Education
Manpower Needs
Manpower Utilization
Off The Job Training
Scientific Manpower
Trade And Industrial Education
Training
Vocational Education

MANPOWER NEEDS 150
RT Employment Opportunities
Job Market
Labor Conditions
Labor Demands
Labor Force
Labor Market
Manpower Development
Manpower Utilization
Promotion (Occupational)

MANPOWER UTILIZATION 150
RT Adult Counseling
Counseling
Developed Nations
Employment
Labor Economics
Labor Force Nonparticipants
Labor Supply
Manpower Development
Manpower Needs
Persistence
Relocation
Scientific Manpower
Subemployment
Unemployment
Work Simplification

MANUAL COMMUNICATION 080
NT Sign Language
BT Communication (Thought Transfer)
RT Aurally Handicapped
Cued Speech
Deaf Education
Deaf Interpreting
Finger Spelling

MANUALS 320
NT Laboratory Manuals
BT Instructional Materials
RT Bulletins
Guides
Supplementary Textbooks

MANUFACTURING 510
UF Fabrication
Manufacturing Methods
Manufacturing Techniques
NT Mass Production
RT Assembly (Manufacturing)
Equipment Manufacturers
Manufacturing Industry
Production Technicians

MANUFACTURING INDUSTRY 370
NT Equipment Manufacturers
Machinery Industry
BT Industry
RT Assembly (Manufacturing)
Chemical Industry
Electronics Industry
Furniture Industry
Machine Tools
Manufacturing
Mechanical Design Technicians
Production Technicians

Manufacturing Methods
USE MANUFACTURING

Manufacturing Techniques
USE MANUFACTURING

MANUSCRIPT WRITING (HANDLETTERING) 080
SN Handwriting based on adaptations of the printed letter forms
UF Calligraphy
Printscript
Uncial Script
BT Handwriting
RT Handwriting Skills
Writing Exercises

Map Reading Skills
USE MAP SKILLS

MAPS 050
BT Audiovisual Aids
RT Atlases
Geography
Map Skills

MAP SKILLS 010
UF Map Reading Skills
BT Skills
RT Geography
Maps

MARANAO 300
BT Indonesian Languages

MARATHI 300
BT Indo European Languages

MARIHUANA 250
UF Cannabis Indica
Cannabis Sativa
Grass (Drug)
Hashish
Marijuana
Mary Jane (Drug)
Pot (Drug)
Weed (Drug)
BT Narcotics
RT Drug Abuse
Drug Addiction
Drug Legislation

Marijuana
USE MARIHUANA

MARINE BIOLOGY 070
BT Biology
RT Biological Sciences
Biology Instruction
Ecology
Marine Technicians
Natural Sciences
Ocean Engineering
Radiation Biology

Marine Corps Air Stations
USE MILITARY AIR FACILITIES

MARINE TECHNICIANS 380
BT Subprofessionals
RT Marine Biology
Oceanology
Seamen
Technical Education
Technical Occupations

Marital Counseling
USE MARRIAGE COUNSELING

MARITAL INSTABILITY 490
RT Family Life
Family Problems
Illegitimate Births
Marriage
Marriage Counseling
One Parent Family

MARITAL STATUS 490
UF Married Students
BT Status
RT Housewives
Marriage
Single Students

MARKETING 110
SN An aggregate of functions involved in the transfer of goods from producer to consumer
UF Distribution (Economics)
NT Merchandising
Retailing
Wholesaling
RT Distributive Education
Merchandise Information
Merchants
Rail Transportation

Marking (School Mark)
USE GRADING

MARKSMANSHIP 010
BT Psychomotor Skills
RT Military Science

MARRIAGE 490
NT Intermarriage
BT Social Development
Social Relations
RT Family (Sociological Unit)
Family Life
Housewives
Marital Instability
Marital Status

MARRIAGE COUNSELING 090
UF Marital Counseling
BT Counseling
RT Crisis Therapy
Family Counseling
Family Life
Family Problems
Interpersonal Relationship
Marital Instability

Married Students
USE MARITAL STATUS

Mary Jane (Drug)
USE MARIHUANA

MASONRY 210
BT Building Materials
RT Architectural Elements
    Bricklaying
    Construction (Process)
    Prefabrication
    Prestressed Concrete
    Structural Building Systems

Masons
USE BRICKLAYERS

Mass Communications
USE MASS MEDIA

Massed Negative Reinforcement
USE NEGATIVE REINFORCEMENT

MASS INSTRUCTION 270
BT Instruction
    Teaching Techniques
RT Audiences
    Individualized Instruction
    Large Group Instruction
    Listening Groups
    Public Television

MASS MEDIA 050
UF Communications Media
    Mass Communications
    Media
NT Audiovisual Communication
    Films
    Instructional Media
    News Media
    Phonotape Recordings
    Publications
    Radio
    Television
RT Commercial Television
    Communications
    Communication Satellites
    Educational Radio
    Film Study
    Information Dissemination
    Media Technology
    Publicize
    Publishing Industry
    Telecommunication
    Telephone Communications Industry

MASS PRODUCTION 510
UF Large Scale Production
BT Manufacturing
RT Assembly (Manufacturing)

Master Of Arts Degrees
USE MASTERS DEGREES

Master Of Arts In College Teaching
USE MASTERS DEGREES

Master Of Arts In Teaching
USE MASTERS DEGREES

Master Of Science Degrees
USE MASTERS DEGREES

Master Of Science In Teaching
USE MASTERS DEGREES

MASTER PLANS 020
RT Building Plans
    Campus Planning
    Component Building Systems
    Construction Programs
    Facility Guidelines
    Facility Requirements
    House Plan
    Lesson Plans
    Planning
    Vehicular Traffic

MASTERS DEGREES 140
UF Master Of Arts Degrees
    Master Of Arts In College Teaching
    Master Of Arts In Teaching
    Master Of Science Degrees
    Master Of Science In Teaching
BT Degrees (Titles)
RT Bachelors Degrees
    Degree Requirements
    Doctoral Degrees
    Masters Theses
    Special Degree Programs
    Specialist In Education Degrees
    Teacher Educator Education

MASTERS THESES 460
BT Publications
RT Degrees (Titles)
    Masters Degrees
    Research

MASTER TAPES (AUDIO) 050
BT Tape Recordings
RT Instructional Materials
    Language Laboratories
    Tape Recorders

MASTER TEACHERS 380
BT Teachers
RT Differentiated Staffs

MATCHED GROUPS 190
BT Groups
RT Cluster Grouping
    Grouping (Instructional Purposes)
    Testing

MATERIAL DEVELOPMENT 130
UF Material Research
BT Development
RT Dubbing
    Instructional Materials
    Student Developed Materials
    Tactile Adaptation
    Teacher Developed Materials

Material Research
USE MATERIAL DEVELOPMENT

Materials
USE INSTRUCTIONAL MATERIALS

Materials Inventory
USE FACILITY INVENTORY

Material Sources
USE RESOURCE MATERIALS

Maternity Leave
USE LEAVE OF ABSENCE

MATHEMATICAL APPLICATIONS 340
RT Mathematical Experience
    Mathematical Models
    Mathematics
    Numerical Control
    Trigonometry

MATHEMATICAL CONCEPTS 340
NT Congruence
    Inequalities
    Number Concepts
RT Conservation (Concept)
    Mathematical Models
    Mathematics
    Percentage
    Probability Theory
    Ratios (Mathematics)
    Reciprocals (Mathematics)
    Trigonometry

MATHEMATICAL ENRICHMENT 340
BT Enrichment
RT Mathematics
    Trigonometry

MATHEMATICAL EXPERIENCE 200
BT Experience
RT Mathematical Applications
    Mathematics
    Trigonometry

MATHEMATICAL LINGUISTICS 290
BT Linguistics
RT Computational Linguistics
    Mathematics

MATHEMATICAL LOGIC 340
BT Logic
RT Computational Linguistics
    Mathematics
    Statistics

MATHEMATICAL MODELS 340
BT Mathematics
    Models
RT Diagrams
    Discriminant Analysis
    Game Theory
    Hypothesis Testing
    Linear Programing
    Mathematical Applications
    Mathematical Concepts
    Operations Research
    Statistics

Mathematical Statistics
USE STATISTICAL ANALYSIS

MATHEMATICAL VOCABULARY 340
BT Vocabulary
RT Mathematics
    Trigonometry

MATHEMATICIANS 380
BT Scientific Personnel
RT Engineers
    Mathematics Teachers
    Professional Occupations

MATHEMATICS 340
NT Algebra
    Algorithms
    Arithmetic
    Calculus
    College Mathematics
    Elementary School Mathematics
    Geometry
    Mathematical Models
    Modern Mathematics
    Operations Research
    Practical mathematics
    Remedial Mathematics
    Secondary School Mathematics
    Set Theory
    Statistics
    Symbols (Mathematics)
    Technical Mathematics
    Trigonometry
BT Sciences
RT Game Theory
    Height
    Mathematical Applications
    Mathematical Concepts
    Mathematical Enrichment
    Mathematical Experience
    Mathematical Linguistics
    Mathematical Logic
    Mathematical Vocabulary
    Mathematics Curriculum
    Mathematics Education
    Mathematics Instruction
    Mathematics Materials
    Mathematics Teachers
    Numbers
    Number Systems

MATHEMATICS CURRICULUM 110
NT   Arithmetic Curriculum
BT   Curriculum
RT   College Mathematics
      Elementary School Mathematics
      Mathematics

MATHEMATICS EDUCATION 140
BT   Education
RT   College Mathematics
      Elementary School Mathematics
      Mathematics
      Secondary School Mathematics

MATHEMATICS INSTRUCTION 270
BT   Instruction
RT   College Mathematics
      Elementary School Mathematics
      Mathematics
      Mathematics Materials
      Mathematics Teachers
      Secondary School Mathematics

MATHEMATICS MATERIALS 050
BT   Instructional Materials
RT   Mathematics
      Mathematics Instruction
      Science Materials
      Student Developed Materials
      Teacher Developed Materials

MATHEMATICS TEACHERS 380
BT   Teachers
RT   College Teachers
      Cooperating Teachers
      Elementary School Teachers
      Mathematicians
      Mathematics
      Mathematics Instruction
      Resource Teachers
      Secondary School Teachers
      Television Teachers

Matriculation
USE   ADMISSION (SCHOOL)

MATTER 400
BT   Physics
RT   Atomic Structure
      Atomic Theory
      Nuclear Physics
      Quantum Mechanics
      Radioisotopes
      Relativity
      Weight

MATURATION 130
BT   Development
RT   Child Development
      Developmental Psychology
      Developmental Tasks
      Growth Patterns
      Human Development
      Individual Development
      Maturity Tests

      Motor Development
      Personal Growth
      Physical Development
      Readiness
      Readiness (Mental)
      Retarded Speech Development
      Social Maturity

MATURITY TESTS 520
BT   Tests
RT   Maturation

MEASUREMENT 180
NT   Cognitive Measurement
      Evaluation
      Grading
      National Intelligence Norm
      National Norms
      Predictive Measurement
      Psychometrics
RT   Calculation
      Class Average
      Data
      Diagrams
      Group Norms
      Height
      Inspection
      Instrumentation
      Measurement Goals
      Measurement Instruments
      Measurement Techniques
      Operations Research
      Participant Satisfaction
      Rating Scales
      Readiness
      Readiness (Mental)
      Research Criteria
      Scoring
      Statistical Data
      Surveys
      Testing
      Tests Of Significance

Measurement Aids
USE   MEASUREMENT INSTRUMENTS

MEASUREMENT GOALS 180
BT   Objectives
RT   Measurement

MEASUREMENT INSTRUMENTS 170
UF   Gages
      Gauges
      Measurement Aids
      Measuring Instruments
      Meters
NT   Calorimeters
      Polygraphs
      Potentiometers (Instruments)
BT   Equipment
      Instrumentation
RT   Equivalency Tests
      Essay Tests
      Measurement
      National Competency Tests

264

Tests
Timed Tests

MEASUREMENT TECHNIQUES 190
NT Classroom Observation Techniques
    Q Sort
    Sociometric Techniques
BT Instrumentation
    Techniques
RT Correlation
    Counselor Evaluation
    Critical Incidents Method
    Electroencephalography
    Equivalency Tests
    Evaluation
    Forced Choice Technique
    Grade Equivalent Scales
    Measurement
    Research Criteria
    Sampling
    Testing

Measuring Instruments
USE MEASUREMENT INSTRUMENTS

MEAT 460
RT Animal Science
    Food
    Food Stores
    Meat Packing Industry

Meat Inspectors
USE FOOD AND DRUG INSPECTORS

MEAT PACKING INDUSTRY 370
BT Industry
RT Animal Science
    Food
    Food And Drug Inspectors
    Food Processing Occupations
    Food Standards
    Meat

Mechanical Competencies
USE MECHANICAL SKILLS

MECHANICAL DESIGN TECHNICIANS 380
UF Engine Development Technicians
    Mechanical Engineering Assistants
    Propulsion Development Technicians
BT Subprofessionals
RT Design
    Electromechanical Technology
    Engineering Technicians
    Industrial Personnel
    Manufacturing Industry
    Mechanics (Process)
    Technical Education
    Technical Occupations
    Trade And Industrial Education

Mechanical Devices
USE MECHANICAL EQUIPMENT

Mechanical Engineering Assistants
USE MECHANICAL DESIGN TECHNICIANS

MECHANICAL EQUIPMENT 170
SN Machinery or tools which automatically
    perform operations in controlling or
    producing a physical change in
    environment or in accomplishment of a
    given task
UF Mechanical Devices
NT Agricultural Machinery
    Machine Tools
    Mechanical Teaching Aids
    Projection Equipment
    Vending Machines
BT Equipment
RT Air Conditioning
    Air Flow
    Architectural Research
    Building Equipment
    Equipment Maintenance
    Equipment Manufacturers
    Equipment Standards
    Equipment Utilization
    Exhausting
    Heating
    Ventilation
    Wheel Chairs

MECHANICAL SKILLS 010
UF Mechanical Competencies
BT Skills
RT Ability
    Employment Qualifications
    Job Skills
    Locomotive Engineers
    Mechanics (Process)
    Trade And Industrial Education

MECHANICAL TEACHING AIDS 050
BT Instructional Aids
    Mechanical Equipment
RT Electromechanical Aids

Mechanical Translation
USE MACHINE TRANSLATION

MECHANICS (PROCESS) 400
UF General Mechanics
RT Auto Mechanics
    Kinetics
    Machine Repairmen
    Machine Tools
    Machinists
    Mechanical Design Technicians
    Mechanical Skills

Mechanization
USE AUTOMATION

Media
USE MASS MEDIA

Media Centers
USE INSTRUCTIONAL MATERIALS CENTERS

MEDIA RESEARCH 450
BT Research
RT Institutional Research
      Media Specialists

MEDIA SPECIALISTS 380
NT Audiovisual Coordinators
BT Specialists
RT Audiovisual Directors
      Media Research
      Media Technology

MEDIA TECHNOLOGY 080
UF Television Technology
BT Technology
RT Instructional Technology
      Mass Media
      Media Specialists
      Radio Technology

MEDIATION THEORY 420
BT Theories
RT Cognitive Processes
      Learning Processes
      Memorizing
      Recall (Psychological)
      Retention
      Stimulus Behavior
      Stimulus Generalization
      Thought Processes
      Verbal Learning

Medical Assistance
USE MEDICAL SERVICES

MEDICAL ASSISTANTS 380
BT Health Personnel
RT Medical Laboratory Assistants
      Medical Services
      Nonprofessional Personnel
      Nurses Aides
      Secretaries

MEDICAL ASSOCIATIONS 370
BT Professional Associations
RT Health Occupations
      National Organizations

Medical Care
USE MEDICAL SERVICES

MEDICAL CASE HISTORIES 250
BT Records (Forms)
RT Case Records
      Clinical Diagnosis
      Medical Evaluation
      Medical Record Librarians
      Medical Record Technicians
      Medical Research
      Medical Services
      Patients (Persons)

MEDICAL CONSULTANTS 380
BT Consultants
RT Health Occupations
      Medical Services
      Ophthalmology
      Physicians
      Psychiatrists

Medical Disadvantagement
USE WELFARE PROBLEMS

Medical Doctors
USE PHYSICIANS

MEDICAL EDUCATION 140
BT Professional Education
RT Medical Schools
      Medical Students
      Medicine
      Nursing

MEDICAL EVALUATION 180
BT Evaluation
RT Clinical Diagnosis
      Clinic Personnel (School)
      Electroencephalography
      Medical Case Histories
      Medical Research
      Medical Services
      Medical Treatment
      Psychoeducational Clinics

Medical Intervention
USE INTERVENTION

MEDICAL LABORATORY ASSISTANTS 380
UF Biomedical Equipment Technicians
      Medical Technicians
BT Health Personnel
RT Biomedical Equipment
      Electronic Technicians
      Health Occupations
      Health Occupations Education
      Health Personnel
      Health Services
      Laboratory Technology
      Medical Assistants
      Medical Technologists
      Subprofessionals
      Technical Education
      Technical Occupations

Medical Laboratory Technologists
USE MEDICAL TECHNOLOGISTS

MEDICAL LIBRARIES 210
UF Hospital Libraries
BT Special Libraries
RT Archives
      College Libraries
      Institution Libraries
      Medical Record Technicians
      Medical Research

Medical Record Clerks
USE MEDICAL RECORD TECHNICIANS

MEDICAL RECORD LIBRARIANS 380
UF Hospital Record Librarians
    Registered Record Librarians
BT Librarians
RT Health Personnel
    Medical Case Histories
    Medical Record Technicians

MEDICAL RECORD TECHNICIANS 380
UF Medical Record Clerks
BT Health Personnel
    Library Technicians
RT Data Collection
    File Clerks
    Health Occupations Education
    Information Storage
    Medical Case Histories
    Medical Libraries
    Medical Record Librarians
    Recordkeeping
    Subprofessionals
    Technical Education
    Technical Occupations

MEDICAL RESEARCH 450
BT Research
RT Deaf Research
    Exceptional Child Research
    Medical Case Histories
    Medical Evaluation
    Medical Libraries
    Medical Services

MEDICAL SCHOOLS 470
UF Schools Of Medicine
BT Schools
RT Business Administration
    Dental Schools
    Health Occupations
    Higher Education
    Medical Education
    Medical Students
    Professional Education

Medical Secretaries
USE SECRETARIES

MEDICAL SERVICES 250
UF Medical Assistance
    Medical Care
NT First Aid
    Nursing
    Psychiatric Services
BT Health Services
RT Anesthesiology
    Clinic Personnel (School)
    Emergency Squad Personnel
    Geriatrics
    Health Facilities
    Hospitals
    Injuries
    Intervention
    Medical Assistants
    Medical Case Histories

    Medical Consultants
    Medical Evaluation
    Medical Research
    Medical Treatment
    Nursing Homes
    Occupational Therapy
    Ophthalmology
    Paramedical Occupations
    Patients (Persons)
    Physical Therapy
    Practical Nursing
    Preventive Medicine
    Psychiatrists
    Rescue
    Surgical Technicians
    Therapy
    Veterinary Medicine

Medical Stenographers
USE STENOGRAPHERS

MEDICAL STUDENTS 380
BT Students
RT Higher Education
    Medical Education
    Medical Schools
    Medical Vocabulary
    Professional Education

Medical Technicians
USE MEDICAL LABORATORY ASSISTANTS

MEDICAL TECHNOLOGISTS 380
UF Medical Laboratory Technologists
BT Health Personnel
RT Health Occupations Education
    Medical Laboratory Assistants

MEDICAL TREATMENT 250
RT Anesthesiology
    Drug Therapy
    Educational Therapy
    Electrical Stimuli
    Evaluation
    Health Facilities
    Health Services
    Medical Evaluation
    Medical Services
    Nursing Homes
    Occupational Therapy
    Physical Therapy
    Psychiatry
    Sedatives
    Speech Therapy

MEDICAL VOCABULARY 290
BT Vocabulary
RT Medical Students
    Physicians
    Professional Training

MEDICINE 070
NT Geriatrics
    Neurology
    Ophthalmology
    Pathology
    Preventive Medicine
    Veterinary Medicine
BT Biological Sciences
RT Anatomy
    Biochemistry
    Biological Influences
    Embryology
    Genetics
    Human Body
    Human Engineering
    Medical Education
    Microbiology
    Physiology
    Radiation Biology

MEDIEVAL HISTORY 260
BT History

MEDIEVAL LITERATURE 260
BT Literature
RT Chronicles
    Drama
    Epics
    Fables
    Legends
    Medieval Romance
    Mythology
    Poetry
    Poets
    Prose
    World Literature

MEDIEVAL ROMANCE 260
UF Arthurian Legends
    Chanson De Geste
    Chivalric Novels
    Heroic Epics
    Middle English Romance
    Romance
    Vulgate Romance
BT Literature
RT Ballads
    Composition (Literary)
    Epics
    Legends
    Literary Analysis
    Literary Genres
    Literary History
    Lyric Poetry
    Medieval Literature
    Mythology
    Poetry
    Poets

MEETINGS 510
NT Planning Meetings
    Staff Meetings
RT Conference Reports
    Conferences
    Speeches
    Symposia

MELANESIAN LANGUAGES 300
BT Malayo Polynesian Languages

Memorization
USE MEMORIZING

MEMORIZING 310
UF Memorization
BT Cognitive Processes
RT Mediation Theory
    Memory
    Psychomotor Skills
    Recall (Psychological)
    Retention
    Rote Learning
    Verbal Learning
    Visualization

MEMORY 310
BT Cognitive Processes
RT Cues
    Learning Processes
    Memorizing
    Recall (Psychological)
    Recognition
    Retention
    Visualization

Memory Devices (Electronic)
USE COMPUTER STORAGE DEVICES

MENDE 300
BT African Languages

Mental Ability
USE INTELLIGENCE

MENTAL DEVELOPMENT 310
BT Development
RT Intellectual Development
    Intelligence
    Mental Retardation
    Mental Rigidity
    Task Analysis

MENTAL HEALTH 250
UF Emotional Health
    Mental Hygiene
BT Health
RT Autism
    Educational Therapy
    Mental Health Clinics
    Mental Health Programs
    Mental Illness
    Milieu Therapy
    Morale
    Psychiatric Hospitals
    Psychiatric Services

Psychiatry
Schizophrenia

MENTAL HEALTH CLINICS 210
BT Clinics
RT Mental Health
Psychiatric Hospitals
Psychoeducational Clinics
Rehabilitation

MENTAL HEALTH PROGRAMS 250
UF Mental Health Resources
BT Health Programs
RT Mental Health
Psychiatric Services

Mental Health Resources
USE MENTAL HEALTH PROGRAMS

Mental Hygiene
USE MENTAL HEALTH

MENTAL ILLNESS 250
UF Psychological Defects
NT Neurosis
Psychosis
RT Autism
Echolalia
Emotionally Disturbed
Institutionalized (Persons)
Mental Health
Psychiatric Aides
Psychiatric Hospitals
Psychiatric Services
Psychiatry
Psychology
Psychopathology
Schizophrenia

Mentally Advanced Children
USE GIFTED

MENTALLY HANDICAPPED 240
NT Custodial Mentally Handicapped
Educable Mentally Handicapped
Trainable Mentally Handicapped
BT Handicapped
RT Cerebral Palsy
Educationally Disadvantaged
Exceptional (Atypical)
Handicapped Students
Labor Force Nonparticipants
Low Ability Students
Mental Retardation
Minimally Brain Injured
Mongolism
Neurologically Handicapped
Patients (Persons)
Retarded Children
Slow Learners
Special Health Problems

MENTAL RETARDATION 240
BT Retardation
RT Custodial Mentally Handicapped
Educable Mentally Handicapped
Intelligence
Mental Development
Mentally Handicapped
Mongolism
Trainable Mentally Handicapped

MENTAL RIGIDITY 420
RT Behavior Problems
Intellectual Development
Mental Development

MENTAL TESTS 520
BT Tests
RT Projective Tests

MERCHANDISE INFORMATION 080
SN Literature or labels identifying product
value, regulation, service, and care for
the consumer and the trade
UF Product Information
Product Labels
Product Literature
RT Consumer Economics
Marketing
Merchandising
Salesmanship

MERCHANDISING 110
SN Sales promotion as a comprehensive
function including market research,
advertising, and selling
UF Sales Promotion
BT Marketing
RT Auto Parts Men
Business Education
Commercial Art
Credit (Finance)
Display Panels
Distributive Education
Feed Stores
Food Stores
Merchandise Information
Merchants
Occupations
Retailing
Salesmanship
Sales Occupations

MERCHANTS 380
UF Dealers
BT Nonprofessional Personnel
RT Marketing
Merchandising
Sales Occupations
Sales Workers

MERGERS 020
RT Business
   Centralization
   Churches
   Industrial Structure
   Industry
   Organization
   Organizational Change
   Organizations (Groups)
   Organization Size (Groups)

MERIT RATING PROGRAMS 180
BT Programs
RT Achievement Rating
   Evaluation
   Job Skills
   Rewards
   Teacher Rating

METABOLISM 070
BT Biochemistry
RT Biology
   Physiology

Metal Finishing
USE FINISHING

Metal Forming Occupations
USE METAL WORKING OCCUPATIONS

METAL INDUSTRY 370
NT Steel Industry
BT Industry
RT Foundries
   Metallurgical Technicians
   Metallurgy
   Metals
   Metal Working Occupations

METALLURGICAL TECHNICIANS 380
BT Subprofessionals
RT Chemistry
   Engineering Technicians
   Metal Industry
   Metallurgy
   Physics
   Radiographers
   Technical Education
   Technical Occupations

METALLURGY 400
RT Chemical Analysis
   Chemistry
   Metal Industry
   Metallurgical Technicians
   Metals
   Physics

METALS 460
RT Industrial Arts
   Metal Industry
   Metallurgy
   Metalworking Occupations

Metal Trades
USE METAL WORKING OCCUPATIONS

METAL WORKING OCCUPATIONS 350
UF Metal Forming Occupations
   Metal Trades
NT Sheet Metal Work
BT Occupations
RT Assembly (Manufacturing)
   Machine Tool Operators
   Machinists
   Metal Industry
   Metals
   Semiskilled Occupations
   Semiskilled Workers
   Sheet Metal Workers
   Skilled Occupations
   Skilled Workers
   Tool And Die Makers
   Trade And Industrial Education
   Welding

METAPHORS 260
BT Figurative Language
RT Allegory
   American Literature
   Biblical Literature
   Classical Literature
   Creative Writing
   Descriptive Writing
   Drama
   English Literature
   Essays
   Fables
   Fiction
   Imagery
   Legends
   Literary Analysis
   Literary Criticism
   Literature
   Mythology
   Novels
   Poetry
   Prose
   Satire
   Short Stories
   Symbols (Literary)
   Twentieth Century Literature

METEOROLOGY 400
BT Earth Science
RT Chemistry
   Climatic Factors
   Humidity
   Natural Sciences
   Physics

Meters
USE MEASUREMENT INSTRUMENTS

METHODOLOGY 510
NT Interdisciplinary Approach
   Scientific Methodology
RT Methods
   Techniques

METHODS 510
NT Critical Incidents Method
Critical Path Method
Deductive Methods
Educational Methods
Evaluation Methods
Inductive Methods
Kinesthetic Methods
Magnification Methods
RT Methodology
Methods Courses
Methods Research
Methods Teachers

METHODS COURSES 270
UF General Methods Courses
Special Methods Courses
BT Courses
RT Education Courses
Methods
Methods Teachers
Student Teaching
Teacher Education
Teacher Programs

METHODS RESEARCH 450
BT Research
RT Action Research
Methods
Program Effectiveness

METHODS TEACHERS 380
BT Teachers
RT Methods
Methods Courses
Teacher Education

METROPOLITAN AREAS 120
BT Urban Areas
RT Community
Municipalities
Neighborhood
Suburban Environment
Suburbs

MEXICAN AMERICAN HISTORY 260
BT American History
RT Mexican Americans

MEXICAN AMERICANS 380
BT Ethnic Groups
RT Mexican American History
Racial Characteristics
Spanish Americans

MICROBIOLOGY 070
BT Biology
RT Animal Science
Botany
Culturing Techniques
Medicine
Physiology
Plant Science
Zoology

Microcalorimeters
USE CALORIMETERS

MICROCOUNSELING 090
BT Counseling
RT Audiovisual Aids
Counselor Training
Demonstrations (Educational)
Microteaching
Practicums
Video Tape Recordings

MICROFICHE 050
BT Microforms
RT Audiovisual Aids
Information Dissemination
Records (Forms)

MICROFILM 050
BT Microforms
RT Audiovisual Aids
Filmstrips
Information Dissemination
Records (Forms)

MICROFORMS 050
UF Microtexts
NT Computer Output Microfilm
Microfiche
Microfilm
RT Audiovisual Aids
Information Storage
Publications

MICROPHONES 170
BT Audiovisual Aids

MICROSCOPES 170
BT Laboratory Equipment

MICROTEACHING 270
UF Miniature Teaching
BT Teaching
Training Techniques
RT Audiovisual Aids
Demonstrations (Educational)
Episode Teaching
Inservice Teaching
Laboratory Training
Microcounseling
Protocol Materials
Student Teachers
Student Teaching
Teacher Education
Teacher Experience
Teaching Experience
Teaching Skills
Teaching Techniques
Video Tape Recordings

Microtexts
USE MICROFORMS

MIDDLE AGED 380
SN   Age 45-65
BT   Adults
RT   Age
     Age Differences
     Age Groups

MIDDLE CLASS 490
NT   Lower Middle Class
BT   Social Class
RT   Culturally Advantaged
     Middle Class College Students
     Middle Class Culture
     Middle Class Norm
     Middle Class Parents
     Middle Class Values

MIDDLE CLASS COLLEGE STUDENTS 380
BT   College Students
RT   Middle Class

MIDDLE CLASS CULTURE 100
UF   Majority Culture
BT   Culture
RT   Middle Class
     Middle Class Norm

MIDDLE CLASS FATHERS 380
BT   Fathers
     Middle Class Parents

MIDDLE CLASS MOTHERS 380
BT   Middle Class Parents
     Mothers

MIDDLE CLASS NORM 500
BT   Standards
RT   Middle Class
     Middle Class Culture

MIDDLE CLASS PARENTS 380
NT   Middle Class Fathers
     Middle Class Mothers
BT   Parents
RT   Middle Class

MIDDLE CLASS VALUES 040
BT   Values
RT   Middle Class

MIDDLE EASTERN HISTORY 260
UF   Near Eastern History
BT   History
RT   African Culture
     African History
     Area Studies
     Asian History
     Language And Area Centers
     Non Western Civilization
     Social Sciences
     World History

MIDDLE ENGLISH 300
BT   English
RT   Diachronic Linguistics
     Indo European Languages
     Languages
     Linguistics

Middle English Romance
USE   MEDIEVAL ROMANCE

MIDDLE INCOME HOUSING 210
BT   Housing
RT   Income

MIDDLE SCHOOLS 470
BT   Schools
RT   Grade Organization
     High Schools
     Intermediate Grades
     Junior High Schools
     Primary Grades

Midtwentieth Century Literature
USE   TWENTIETH CENTURY LITERATURE

MIGRANT ADULT EDUCATION 140
BT   Adult Education
     Migrant Education
RT   Community Migrant Projects
     Migrant Child Education

Migrant Adults
USE   MIGRANTS

MIGRANT CHILD CARE CENTERS 210
BT   Child Care Centers
RT   Community Migrant Projects
     Migrant Children
     Migrant Welfare Services

MIGRANT CHILD EDUCATION 140
BT   Migrant Education
RT   Community Migrant Projects
     Migrant Adult Education
     Migrant Children
     Migrant Schools
     Migration

MIGRANT CHILDREN 380
UF   Migratory Children
BT   Children
     Migrants
RT   Migrant Child Care Centers
     Migrant Child Education
     Migrant Youth

MIGRANT EDUCATION 140
NT   Migrant Adult Education
     Migrant Child Education
BT   Education
RT   Educational Mobility
     Migrants
     Mobile Educational Services

MIGRANT EMPLOYMENT 150
BT Employment
RT Migrants
    Migrant Transportation
    Seasonal Employment

MIGRANT HEALTH SERVICES 250
BT Health Services
RT Migrants

MIGRANT HOUSING 210
UF Migrant Housing Bills
BT Housing
RT Community Migrant Projects
    Migrants

Migrant Housing Bills
USE MIGRANT HOUSING

Migrant Population
USE MIGRANTS

MIGRANT PROBLEMS 490
BT Problems
RT Community Migrant Projects
    Migrants

MIGRANTS 380
UF Agricultural Migrants
    Internal Immigrants
    Migrant Adults
    Migrant Population
    Native Migrants
NT Migrant Children
    Migrant Workers
    Migrant Youth
    Nomads
RT Immigrants
    Migrant Education
    Migrant Employment
    Migrant Health Services
    Migrant Housing
    Migrant Problems
    Migrant Schools
    Migrant Welfare Services
    Migration
    Migration Patterns
    Mobility
    Occupational Mobility
    Refugees
    Relocation
    Transient Children

MIGRANT SCHOOLS 470
BT Schools
RT Migrant Child Education
    Migrants
    Migrant Transportation

MIGRANT TRANSPORTATION 020
BT Transportation
RT Migrant Employment
    Migrant Schools

MIGRANT WELFARE SERVICES 230
BT Welfare Services
RT Church Migrant Projects
    Community Migrant Projects
    Migrant Child Care Centers
    Migrants

MIGRANT WORKER PROJECTS 490
NT Church Migrant Projects
    Community Migrant Projects
BT Projects
RT Migrant Workers

MIGRANT WORKERS 380
UF Migratory Agricultural Workers
BT Laborers
    Migrants
RT Agricultural Laborers
    Braceros
    Crew Leaders
    Migrant Worker Projects
    Seasonal Laborers

MIGRANT YOUTH 380
BT Migrants
    Youth
RT Migrant Children

MIGRATION 120
UF Northward Movement
NT Relocation
RT Migrant Child Education
    Migrants
    Migration Patterns
    Nomads
    Transient Children

MIGRATION PATTERNS 120
UF Migration Trends
RT Migrants
    Migration
    Nomads
    Relocation

Migration Trends
USE MIGRATION PATTERNS

Migratory Agricultural Workers
USE MIGRANT WORKERS

Migratory Children
USE MIGRANT CHILDREN

MILIEU THERAPY 420
BT Therapy
RT Counseling
    Group Therapy
    Mental Health
    Play Therapy
    Therapeutic Environment
    Therapists

MILITARY AIR FACILITIES 210
UF Air Bases
     Air Force Bases
     Army Air Bases
     Coast Guard Air Stations
     Marine Corps Air Stations
     Naval Air Stations
BT Facilities
RT Military Science
     Military Service
     Military Training
     Physical Facilities

MILITARY ORGANIZATIONS 370
NT Armed Forces
BT Organizations (Groups)
RT Federal Government
     Military Personnel
     National Defense

MILITARY PERSONNEL 380
NT Enlisted Men
     Officer Personnel
BT Personnel
RT Armed Forces
     Federal Troops
     Immigration Inspectors
     Military Organizations
     Military Science
     Military Service
     Military Training
     National Defense
     Veterans
     Veterans Education

MILITARY SCHOOLS 470
BT Schools
RT Military Science
     Military Training

MILITARY SCIENCE 110
BT Sciences
RT Civil Defense
     Enlisted Men
     Marksmanship
     Military Air Facilities
     Military Personnel
     Military Schools
     Military Service
     Military Training
     National Defense
     Nuclear Warfare
     Political Science

MILITARY SERVICE 350
RT Armed Forces
     Enlisted Men
     Federal Troops
     Military Air Facilities
     Military Personnel
     Military Science
     Military Training
     Veterans

MILITARY TRAINING 110
BT Training
RT Enlisted Men
     Flight Training
     Military Air Facilities
     Military Personnel
     Military Schools
     Military Science
     Military Service
     National Defense
     Officer Personnel

Milling Machines
USE MACHINE TOOLS

Millwork
USE CABINETMAKING

Miniature Teaching
USE MICROTEACHING

MINIMALLY BRAIN INJURED 240
RT Learning Disabilities
     Mentally Handicapped
     Neurologically Handicapped

Minimum Initial Expenses
USE INITIAL EXPENSES

Minimum Operating Expenses
USE OPERATING EXPENSES

MINIMUM WAGE 220
BT Wages
RT Guaranteed Income
     Minimum Wage Laws
     Minimum Wage Legislation

Minimum Wage Bills
USE MINIMUM WAGE LAWS

MINIMUM WAGE LAWS 230
UF Minimum Wage Bills
BT Laws
RT Minimum Wage
     Minimum Wage Legislation

MINIMUM WAGE LEGISLATION 230
BT Legislation
RT Minimum Wage
     Minimum Wage Laws

Ministers
USE CLERGYMEN

Minnesingers
USE POETS

Minority Culture
USE MINORITY GROUPS

MINORITY GROUP CHILDREN 380
BT Children
RT Minority Groups

MINORITY GROUPS 380
UF   Minority Culture
     Population Minorities
BT   Groups
RT   Biculturalism
     Chinese Americans
     Civil Rights
     Cultural Pluralism
     Culture
     Ethnic Groups
     Ethnic Studies
     Filipino Americans
     Italian Americans
     Japanese Americans
     Jews
     Korean Americans
     Majority Attitudes
     Minority Group Children
     Minority Group Teachers
     Minority Role
     Tribes

MINORITY GROUP TEACHERS 380
NT   Negro Teachers
BT   Teachers
RT   Minority Groups

Minority Rights
USE   CIVIL RIGHTS

MINORITY ROLE 490
RT   Minority Groups

Minutes (Records)
USE   DIARIES

Miosis
USE   MYOPIA

MISBEHAVIOR 060
NT   Cheating
     Stealing
BT   Behavior
RT   Book Thefts
     Conduct
     Discipline Problems
     Suspension
     Vandalism

MNEMONICS 310
BT   Learning Processes
RT   Abbreviations
     Learning
     Learning Activities
     Learning Experience
     Learning Theories
     Reinforcement
     Retention
     Retention Studies

MOBILE CLASSROOMS 210
UF   Mobile Classroom Units
BT   Classrooms
RT   Flexible Facilities
     Mobile Educational Services
     School Design
     School Expansion
     Transportation

Mobile Classroom Units
USE   MOBILE CLASSROOMS

MOBILE EDUCATIONAL SERVICES 140
RT   Extension Education
     Itinerant Teachers
     Migrant Education
     Mobile Classrooms
     Special Education
     Special Services

MOBILE LABORATORIES 210
BT   Laboratories
RT   Itinerant Clinics

MOBILITY 120
NT   Educational Mobility
     Faculty Mobility
     Family Mobility
     Occupational Mobility
     Social Mobility
     Student Mobility
     Visually Handicapped Mobility
RT   Labor Turnover
     Migrants
     Nomads
     Relocation
     Transient Children
     Wheel Chairs

MOBILITY AIDS 240
SN   Devices or materials which assist
     primarily visually handicapped persons
     to move freely within their environment
NT   Wheel Chairs
BT   Sensory Aids
RT   Travel Training
     Visually Handicapped
     Visually Handicapped Mobility
     Visually Handicapped Orientation

Model Programs
USE   DEMONSTRATION PROGRAMS

MODELS 510
SN   Representation of an object, principle, or
     idea
UF   Conceptual Frameworks
     Theoretical Models
NT   Conceptual Schemes
     Mathematical Models
     Teaching Models
RT   Information Theory
     Operations Research
     Research Methodology
     Research Tools

Simulators
Student Writing Models
Systems Analysis
Systems Approach
Theories

Modern Greek
USE GREEK

MODERN HISTORY 260
BT History
RT History Instruction
Nuclear Warfare

MODERNISM 260
BT Literature
RT Composition (Literary)
French
Latin American Culture
Literary Analysis
Literary Conventions
Literary Criticism
Literary Genres
Poetry
Spanish
Symbols (Literary)
Twentieth Century Literature

MODERN LANGUAGE CURRICULUM 110
BT Curriculum
RT Language Programs
Modern Languages

MODERN LANGUAGES 300
NT English
BT Languages
RT Bilingualism
College Language Programs
English Programs
Modern Language Curriculum
Multilingualism
Second Language Learning

MODERN MATHEMATICS 340
BT Mathematics

MODERN SCIENCE 110
BT Science Curriculum

MODULAR BUILDING DESIGN 030
SN Orderly planning so arranged as to make logical and extensive use of a repetitive module or dimension of one foot or more
UF Modular Coordination
Modular Drafting
Modular Planning
BT Design
RT Building Design
Component Building Systems
School Architecture
School Construction
School Design

Modular Coordination
USE MODULAR BUILDING DESIGN

Modular Drafting
USE MODULAR BUILDING DESIGN

Modular Planning
USE MODULAR BUILDING DESIGN

Modular Scheduling
USE SCHEDULE MODULES

Mole
USE MOSSI

MONEY MANAGEMENT 220
BT Management
RT Banking
Budgeting
Consumer Education
Credit (Finance)
Estate Planning
Family Management
Finance Occupations
Financial Policy
Home Economics Education
Home Management
Income

MONEY SYSTEMS 220
BT Economics
RT Banking
Interest

Mongol
USE MONGOLIAN

MONGOLIAN 300
UF Khalkha
Mongol
BT Mongolian Languages

Mongolian Idiocy
USE MONGOLISM

Mongolian Imbecility
USE MONGOLISM

MONGOLIAN LANGUAGES 300
NT Buriat
Dagur
Mongolian
BT Uralic Altaic Languages

MONGOLISM 240
UF Downs Anomaly
Downs Syndrome
Mongolian Idiocy
Mongolian Imbecility
RT Anomalies
Genetics
Mentally Handicapped
Mental Retardation
Physical Characteristics

Moonlighting
USE MULTIPLE EMPLOYMENT

MORAL CRITICISM 260
BT Literary Criticism
RT Analytical Criticism
    Formal Criticism
    Historical Criticism
    Literary Analysis
    Literary Genres
    Literature
    Odes

MORALE 040
BT Psychological Patterns
RT Attitudes
    Mental Health
    Motivation
    Need Gratification
    Peer Acceptance
    Personal Adjustment
    Rewards
    Self Actualization
    Self Concept
    Sportsmanship
    Teamwork

Moral Instruction
USE ETHICAL INSTRUCTION

MORAL ISSUES 490
RT Censorship
    Moral Values
    Plagiarism

Morals
USE ETHICS

MORAL VALUES 040
BT Values
RT Censorship
    Ethical Instruction
    Ethics
    Moral Issues
    Sanctions

More
USE MOSSI

MORPHEMES 290
NT Allomorphs
    Phonemes
    Suffixes
    Syllables
BT Language Patterns
RT Grammar
    Morphology (Languages)
    Morphophonemics
    Phonemes
    Syntax

Morphemics
USE MORPHOLOGY (LANGUAGES)

MORPHOLOGY (LANGUAGES) 290
UF Morphemics
NT Morphophonemics
BT Grammar
RT Adjectives
    Adverbs
    Determiners (Languages)
    Diachronic Linguistics
    Discourse Analysis
    Form Classes (Languages)
    Function Words
    Intonation
    Language Patterns
    Language Typology
    Lexicology
    Morphemes
    Nominals
    Phonemes
    Phonemics
    Phonology
    Plurals
    Pronouns
    Suffixes
    Suprasegmentals
    Surface Structure
    Synchronic Linguistics
    Syntax
    Traditional Grammar
    Verbs

MORPHOPHONEMICS 290
NT Phonology
BT Morphology (Languages)
RT Allomorphs
    Morphemes
    Negative Forms (Language)
    Phonemes
    Phonemics
    Phonetics
    Suffixes
    Surface Structure
    Tone Languages

MOSSI 300
UF Mole
    More
BT African Languages

Motels
USE HOTELS

MOTHER ATTITUDES 040
BT Attitudes
RT Mothers

Mother Child Interaction
USE PARENT CHILD RELATIONSHIP

Motherhood
USE MOTHERS

MOTHERLESS FAMILY 490
UF   Motherless Home
BT   One Parent Family
RT   Family Influence
     Heads Of Households

Motherless Home
USE MOTHERLESS FAMILY

Mother Role
USE PARENT ROLE

MOTHERS 380
UF   Motherhood
NT   Middle Class Mothers
     Negro Mothers
     Unwed Mothers
BT   Parents
RT   Mother Attitudes
     Parent Associations

MOTIFS 260
UF   Leitmotifs
     Leitmotivs
BT   Literary Conventions
RT   Allegory
     Analytical Criticism
     Formal Criticism
     Imagery
     Literary Criticism
     Literature
     Symbols (Literary)

MOTION 400
UF   Animation
     Movement
BT   Physics
RT   Energy
     Force
     Horology
     Kinetic Molecular Theory
     Kinetics
     Quantum Mechanics
     Relativity

Motion Pictures
USE FILMS

MOTIVATION 040
UF   Achievement Incentives
     Achievement Motivation
     Incentives
     Motivation Factors
NT   Learning Motivation
     Low Motivation
     Student Motivation
     Teacher Motivation
RT   Academic Aspiration
     Attention Control
     Attention Span
     Behavior
     Bibliotherapy
     Educational Interest
     Morale
     Motivation Techniques

     Positive Reinforcement
     Professional Recognition
     Readiness (Mental)
     Reinforcement
     Rewards
     Self Reward
     Social Reinforcement
     Sportsmanship

Motivation Factors
USE MOTIVATION

MOTIVATION TECHNIQUES 510
BT   Techniques
RT   Educational Strategies
     Motivation
     Persuasive Discourse
     Self Actualization

Motor Ability
USE PSYCHOMOTOR SKILLS

Motorboat Operators
USE BOATMEN

MOTOR DEVELOPMENT 130
BT   Development
RT   Child Development
     Developmental Tasks
     Eye Hand Coordination
     Human Development
     Individual Development
     Maturation
     Motor Reactions
     Perceptual Motor Coordination
     Perceptual Motor Learning
     Physical Development
     Psychomotor Objectives
     Psychomotor Skills
     Skill Development
     Vocational Development

Motor Planning Techniques
USE PSYCHOMOTOR SKILLS

MOTOR REACTIONS 070
UF   Muscular Activities
     Muscular Extensions
     Muscular Flexions
BT   Physical Activities
RT   Motor Development
     Muscular Strength
     Physiology
     Psychomotor Skills
     Reaction Time

Motor Skills
USE PSYCHOMOTOR SKILLS

MOTOR VEHICLES 170
NT   Bookmobiles
     School Buses
     Service Vehicles
     Tractors
RT   Auto Body Repairmen
     Auto Mechanics
     Auto Mechanics (Occupation)

Auto Parts Men
Bus Garages
Diesel Engines
Fuels
Parking Controls
Parking Facilities
Traffic Circulation
Traffic Control
Traffic Patterns
Traffic Safety
Traffic Signs
Transportation
Vehicular Traffic

MOVABLE PARTITIONS 210
SN Interior walls that can be readily moved
UF Folding Partitions
BT Space Dividers
RT Flexible Classrooms
Flexible Facilities
Prefabrication
Space Utilization

Movement
USE MOTION

Mucilages
USE ADHESIVES

MULTICAMPUS DISTRICTS 020
BT School Districts
RT School Location
School Redistricting
Schools
School Systems
Zoning

MULTICHANNEL PROGRAMING 050
BT Programing
RT Educational Television
Televised Instruction
Viewing Time

MULTICULTURAL TEXTBOOKS 050
UF Interracial Primers
Multiethnic Primers
BT Textbooks
RT Cultural Interrelationships
Integration Methods
Textbook Bias
Textbook Content

Multiethnic Primers
USE MULTICULTURAL TEXTBOOKS

MULTIGRADED CLASSES 280
BT Classes (Groups Of Students)
RT Instructional Program Divisions

MULTILINGUALISM 290
BT Sociolinguistics
RT Bilingual Education
Bilingual Teacher Aides
Bilingual Teachers
English (Second Language)
Languages

Language Standardization
Modern Languages

MULTIMEDIA INSTRUCTION 270
BT Instruction
RT Individual Instruction
Instructional Design
Instructional Innovation
Instructional Materials
Instructional Technology
Programed Instruction
Teaching Machines
Teaching Methods
Teaching Procedures

Multimedia Materials
USE INSTRUCTIONAL MATERIALS

MULTIPLE CHOICE TESTS 520
BT Objective Tests
RT Test Construction
Testing

MULTIPLE EMPLOYMENT 150
UF Double Employment
Moonlighting
Multiple Jobholding
Secondary Employment
BT Employment
RT Jobs
Seasonal Employment

Multiple Jobholding
USE MULTIPLE EMPLOYMENT

MULTIPLICATION 340
BT Arithmetic
RT Addition
Division
Subtraction

MULTIPLY HANDICAPPED 240
NT Deaf Blind
BT Handicapped
RT Exceptional (Atypical)
Handicapped Children

MULTIPURPOSE CLASSROOMS 210
BT Classrooms
RT Classroom Design
Flexible Classrooms
Flexible Facilities
Flexible Lighting Design
Stages

MULTISENSORY LEARNING 310
BT Learning

Multivariate Analysis
USE STATISTICAL ANALYSIS

MUNICIPALITIES 230
BT Community
RT Collective Settlements
Metropolitan Areas
Urban Areas

Munukutaba
USE KITUBA

Muscle Sense
USE KINESTHETIC PERCEPTION

Muscular Activities
USE MOTOR REACTIONS

Muscular Exercise
USE EXERCISE (PHYSIOLOGY)

Muscular Extensions
USE MOTOR REACTIONS

Muscular Flexions
USE MOTOR REACTIONS

MUSCULAR STRENGTH 070
UF Physical Strength
   Strength (Biology)
BT Physical Characteristics
RT Calisthenics
   Exercise (Physiology)
   Motor Reactions
   Physical Development
   Physical Education
   Physical Fitness

MUSEUMS 210
BT Educational Facilities
RT Anthropology
   Arts Centers
   History
   Resource Centers
   Sciences

MUSIC 030
NT Applied Music
   Concerts
   Jazz
   Musical Composition
   Music Theory
   Oriental Music
   Singing
   Vocal Music
BT Fine Arts
RT Bands (Music)
   Dance
   Expressionism
   Musical Instruments
   Music Appreciation
   Music Education
   Music Facilities
   Musicians
   Music Reading
   Music Techniques
   Nineteenth Century Literature
   Opera
   Orchestras
   Outdoor Drama
   Recreational Activities

MUSIC ACTIVITIES 030
BT Activities
RT Applied Music
   Bands (Music)
   Choral Music
   Choruses
   Musical Composition
   Music Appreciation
   Music Education
   Music Facilities
   Music Techniques
   Orchestras
   Vocal Music

MUSICAL COMPOSITION 030
UF Composition (Music)
BT Music
RT Choral Music
   Jazz
   Music Activities
   Music Techniques
   Music Theory
   Opera
   Oriental Music
   Vocal Music

MUSICAL INSTRUMENTS 170
RT Bands (Music)
   Music
   Musicians
   Music Techniques
   Orchestras

MUSIC APPRECIATION 030
RT Music
   Music Activities
   Music Education

MUSIC EDUCATION 140
BT Education
RT Applied Music
   Choral Music
   Choruses
   Music
   Music Activities
   Music Appreciation
   Musicians
   Music Teachers
   Music Techniques
   Orchestras
   Vocal Music

MUSIC FACILITIES 210
BT Facilities
RT Auditoriums
   Classrooms
   Educational Facilities
   Music
   Music Activities
   Stages
   Theaters

MUSICIANS 380
RT Bands (Music)
     Concerts
     Fine Arts
     Music
     Musical Instruments
     Music Education
     Music Techniques
     Orchestras

MUSIC READING 030
UF Score Reading
     Sight Playing
     Sight Singing
BT Reading
RT Music

MUSIC TEACHERS 380
BT Teachers
RT Music Education

MUSIC TECHNIQUES 510
BT Techniques
RT Bands (Music)
     Choral Music
     Choruses
     Jazz
     Music
     Music Activities
     Musical Composition
     Musical Instruments
     Music Education
     Musicians
     Orchestras
     Vocal Music

MUSIC THEORY 030
BT Music
RT Musical Composition

MUTUAL INTELLIGIBILITY 290
BT Verbal Communication
RT Bilingualism
     Contrastive Linguistics
     Dialects
     Diglossia
     Language Classification
     Languages
     Sociolinguistics

MYOPIA 240
UF Miosis
     Myosis
     Nearsightedness
BT Ametropia
RT Hyperopia

Myosis
USE MYOPIA

MYTHIC CRITICISM 260
BT Literature
RT Drama
     Fiction
     Literary Analysis
     Literary Criticism
     Literary Influences
     Novels
     Poetry
     Prose

MYTHOLOGY 260
UF Myths
BT Literature
RT Biblical Literature
     Classical Literature
     Epics
     Fables
     Folk Culture
     German Literature
     Legends
     Medieval Literature
     Medieval Romance
     Metaphors
     Old English Literature
     Symbols (Literary)

Myths
USE MYTHOLOGY

NARCOTICS 250
NT Marihuana
     Sedatives
RT Drug Abuse
     Drug Addiction
     Drug Legislation
     Stimulants

Narcotics Addiction
USE DRUG ADDICTION

NARRATION 260
RT Drama
     Essays
     Fiction
     Literature
     Novels
     Poetry
     Prose
     Short Stories
     Tales
     Writing

NATIONAL COMPETENCY TESTS 520
BT Tests
RT Evaluation
     Measurement Instruments
     National Intelligence Norm
     National Surveys
     Performance
     Standardized Tests

NATIONAL DEFENSE 230
RT   Armed Forces
     Civil Defense
     Immigration Inspectors
     Military Organizations
     Military Personnel
     Military Science
     Military Training
     National Programs

NATIONAL DEMOGRAPHY 120
UF   United States Demography
BT   Demography

NATIONAL INTELLIGENCE NORM 180
BT   Measurement
RT   Intelligence Quotient
     National Competency Tests

NATIONALISM 040
RT   Black Power
     Colonialism
     Cultural Awareness
     Developing Nations
     Ethnic Groups
     Group Unity
     Imperialism
     National Programs
     Political Attitudes
     Political Divisions (Geographic)

NATIONAL LIBRARIES 210
BT   Libraries
RT   Archives
     Federal Government
     Government Libraries

NATIONAL NORMS 500
BT   Measurement
RT   Comparative Analysis
     Comparative Testing
     Group Norms
     Language Planning
     Language Standardization
     Statistical Analysis
     Statistical Data

NATIONAL ORGANIZATIONS 370
BT   Organizations (Groups)
RT   Community Organizations
     Dental Associations
     Honor Societies
     International Organizations
     Library Associations
     Medical Associations
     Professional Associations

NATIONAL PROGRAMS 230
BT   Programs
RT   Developing Nations
     Language Planning
     Language Standardization
     National Defense
     Nationalism
     Speeches

NATIONAL SURVEYS 180
BT   Surveys
RT   National Competency Tests

Native Informants
USE NATIVE SPEAKERS

Native Migrants
USE MIGRANTS

NATIVE SPEAKERS 380
UF   Foreign Language Speakers
     Native Informants
NT   Spanish Speaking
BT   Ethnic Groups
RT   Bilingualism
     Cultural Environment
     Dialects
     Dravidian Languages
     Foreign Culture
     Indo European Languages
     Language Patterns
     Language Styles
     Language Usage
     Malayo Polynesian Languages
     Official Languages
     Psycholinguistics
     Regional Dialects
     Second Languages
     Sino Tibetan Languages
     Slavic Languages
     Sociolinguistics
     Speech Habits
     Uto Aztecan Languages
     Verbal Communication

Natural Gases
USE FUELS

NATURALISM 260
BT   Literature
RT   American Literature
     Art
     English Literature
     Fiction
     Literary Analysis
     Literary Criticism
     Literary Genres
     Novels
     Philosophy
     Prose
     Religion
     Short Stories
     Twentieth Century Literature

Natural Light
USE DAYLIGHT

NATURAL RESOURCES 460
NT   Water Resources
BT   Resources
RT   Conservation Education
     Depleted Resources
     Environmental Education

Forestry
Soil Conservation

NATURAL SCIENCES 110
NT   Biological Sciences
     Physical Sciences
BT   Sciences
RT   Marine Biology
     Meteorology
     Nature Centers
     Radiation Biology
     Radioisotopes
     Scientific Enterprise

NATURE CENTERS 210
RT   Education Service Centers
     Natural Sciences
     Science Teaching Centers

Nature Trails
USE   TRAILS

NAVAHO 300
UF   Navajo
BT   American Indian Languages

Navajo
USE   NAVAHO

Naval Air Stations
USE   MILITARY AIR FACILITIES

NAVIGATION 400
RT   Astronomy
     Boatmen
     Radar
     Radio

N C Systems
USE   NUMERICAL CONTROL

Near Eastern History
USE   MIDDLE EASTERN HISTORY

Nearsightedness
USE   MYOPIA

NEED GRATIFICATION 420
SN   Satisfaction of basic needs
UF   Need Reduction
RT   Goal Orientation
     Job Satisfaction
     Morale
     Needs
     Psychological Needs
     Self Actualization

NEEDLE TRADES 350
RT   Clothing
     Clothing Design
     Clothing Instruction
     Industry
     Patternmaking
     Sewing Machine Operators

Need Reduction
USE   NEED GRATIFICATION

NEEDS 420
NT   Construction Needs
     Design Needs
     Educational Needs
     Evaluation Needs
     Facility Requirements
     Financial Needs
     Health Needs
     Housing Needs
     Individual Needs
     Information Needs
     Personnel Needs
     Psychological Needs
     Research Needs
     Student Needs
RT   Need Gratification

NEGATIVE ATTITUDES 040
BT   Attitudes

NEGATIVE FORMS (LANGUAGE) 290
BT   Language Patterns
RT   Grammar
     Language Universals
     Morphophonemics
     Semantics
     Tagmemic Analysis
     Transformation Theory (Language)

Negative Income Tax
USE   GUARANTEED INCOME

NEGATIVE PRACTICE 310
SN   Systematic repetition of erroneous
     responses to emphasize differences
     between appropriate and inappropriate
     performance
BT   Transfer Of Training
RT   Negative Reinforcement
     Teaching Techniques

NEGATIVE REINFORCEMENT 310
UF   Massed Negative Reinforcement
     Spaced Negative Reinforcement
BT   Reinforcement
RT   Negative Practice
     Positive Reinforcement
     Social Reinforcement

Neglected Languages
USE   UNCOMMONLY TAUGHT LANGUAGES

NEGOTIATION AGREEMENTS 220
SN   Documents containing a clause which
     recognizes one or more organizations as
     representative of employees on
     employment issues
RT   Arbitration
     Board Of Education Policy
     Collective Negotiation
     Contracts
     Negotiation Impasses
     Public School Teachers
     Teacher Associations

Teacher Strikes
Teacher Welfare

NEGOTIATION IMPASSES 150
UF Impasse Resolution
RT Arbitration
Board Of Education Policy
Collective Bargaining
Collective Negotiation
Employment Problems
Grievance Procedures
Labor Demands
Labor Economics
Labor Legislation
Labor Problems
Negotiation Agreements
Sanctions
Strikes
Teacher Associations
Teacher Militancy
Teacher Strikes
Unions

NEGRO ACHIEVEMENT 010
BT Achievement
RT Negroes

NEGRO ATTITUDES 040
BT Attitudes
RT Black Community
Black Power
Negroes

NEGRO BUSINESSES 370
RT Careers
Negroes
Occupations

Negro Children
USE NEGRO YOUTH

NEGRO COLLEGES 470
UF Negro Universities
BT Colleges
RT Higher Education
Negro Education
Negroes
Negro Institutions
Negro Students
Negro Teachers

Negro Community
USE BLACK COMMUNITY

NEGRO CULTURE 100
UF Negro Subculture
BT Culture
RT African American Studies
African Culture
African History
Negroes
Negro History
Negro Institutions
Negro Literature
Negro Role

NEGRO DIALECTS 290
BT Nonstandard Dialects
RT Negroes

Negro Discrimination (Racial)
USE RACIAL DISCRIMINATION

NEGRO EDUCATION 140
BT Education
RT African American Studies
Negro Colleges
Negroes
Negro Students

NEGRO EMPLOYMENT 150
BT Employment
RT Negroes

NEGROES 380
UF American Negroes
NT Negro Mothers
Negro Students
Negro Teachers
Negro Youth
RT African American Studies
Black Community
Ethnic Groups
Negro Achievement
Negro Attitudes
Negro Businesses
Negro Colleges
Negro Culture
Negro Dialects
Negro Education
Negro Employment
Negro History
Negro Housing
Negro Institutions
Negro Leadership
Negro Literature
Negro Organizations
Negro Population Trends
Negro Role
Negro Stereotypes
Racial Discrimination

NEGRO HISTORY 260
BT History
RT African American Studies
African History
Negro Culture
Negroes
Negro Literature
Slavery

NEGRO HOUSING 210
BT Housing
RT Negroes

NEGRO INSTITUTIONS 210
BT Institutions
RT African American Studies
Negro Colleges
Negro Culture
Negroes

NEGRO LEADERSHIP 060
BT Leadership
RT Black Power
Civil Rights
Negroes
Negro Organizations
Negro Role
Racial Integration

NEGRO LITERATURE 260
SN Literary works by or about Negroes
UF Black Literature
BT Literature
RT African American Studies
African History
African Literature
Negro Culture
Negroes
Negro History
World Literature

NEGRO MOTHERS 380
BT Mothers
Negroes

NEGRO ORGANIZATIONS 370
BT Organizations (Groups)
RT Black Power
Civil Rights
Negroes
Negro Leadership
Negro Role
Racial Integration

NEGRO POPULATION TRENDS 120
BT Population Trends
RT Negroes

NEGRO ROLE 490
RT African American Studies
Black Power
Negro Culture
Negroes
Negro Leadership
Negro Organizations

Negro Schools
USE SCHOOL SEGREGATION

NEGRO STEREOTYPES 100
BT Stereotypes
RT Negroes

NEGRO STUDENTS 380
BT Negroes
Students
RT Negro Colleges
Negro Education
Negro Youth

Negro Studies
USE AFRICAN AMERICAN STUDIES

Negro Subculture
USE NEGRO CULTURE

NEGRO TEACHERS 380
BT Minority Group Teachers
Negroes
RT Negro Colleges

Negro Universities
USE NEGRO COLLEGES

Negro White Relations
USE RACE RELATIONS

NEGRO YOUTH 380
UF Negro Children
BT Negroes
Youth
RT Negro Students

NEIGHBORHOOD 490
BT Community
RT Collective Settlements
Metropolitan Areas
Neighborhood Improvement
Neighborhood Schools

NEIGHBORHOOD CENTERS 210
RT Community Services
Settlement Houses

NEIGHBORHOOD IMPROVEMENT 160
BT Improvement
RT City Improvement
Community Responsibility
Neighborhood
Social Responsibility
Urban Renewal

NEIGHBORHOOD INTEGRATION 430
UF Integrated Neighborhoods
Residential Desegregation
RT Racial Integration
Social Integration

NEIGHBORHOOD SCHOOL POLICY 020
BT School Policy
RT Neighborhood Schools

NEIGHBORHOOD SCHOOLS 470
BT Schools
RT Compensatory Education
Neighborhood
Neighborhood School Policy

Neighborhood Settlements
USE SETTLEMENT HOUSES

NEMBE 300
BT African Languages

Neoclassic English Literary Period
USE ENGLISH NEOCLASSIC LITERARY PERIOD

Neopsychoanalysis
USE PSYCHIATRY

NEPALI 300
BT Indo European Languages

NETWORKS 080
NT Information Networks
    Library Networks
RT Communication Satellites
    Critical Path Method
    Interagency Cooperation
    Interagency Coordination
    Intercommunication
    Telephone Communication Systems
    Topology

NEUROLOGICAL DEFECTS 240
RT Neurologically Handicapped
    Neurological Organization
    Neurology
    Seizures

NEUROLOGICALLY HANDICAPPED 240
NT Cerebral Palsy
BT Handicapped
RT Auditory Agnosia
    Epilepsy
    Hyperactivity
    Language Handicapped
    Learning Disabilities
    Mentally Handicapped
    Minimally Brain Injured
    Neurological Defects
    Neurological Organization
    Neurology
    Seizures

NEUROLOGICAL ORGANIZATION 070
BT Neurology
RT Cerebral Dominance
    Child Development
    Growth Patterns
    Human Development
    Lateral Dominance
    Neurological Defects
    Neurologically Handicapped
    Physical Development
    Physiology
    Psychomotor Skills

NEUROLOGY 070
NT Neurological Organization
BT Medicine
RT Anatomy
    Electroencephalography
    Neurological Defects
    Neurologically Handicapped
    Pathology
    Physiology

Neuromuscular Relaxation
USE PROGRESSIVE RELAXATION

NEUROSIS 250
BT Mental Illness
RT Neurotic Children
    School Phobia

NEUROTIC CHILDREN 380
BT Children
RT Neurosis

NEWSLETTERS 080
BT Serials
RT Books
    Bulletins

NEWS MEDIA 080
UF Press
BT Mass Media
RT Newspapers
    Press Opinion
    Radio

NEWSPAPERS 080
BT Serials
RT Bulletins
    News Media

NIGHT SCHOOLS 470
BT Schools
RT Evening Colleges
    Evening Programs
    Evening Students
    Extension Education
    Part Time Students

NINETEENTH CENTURY LITERATURE 260
BT Literature
RT American Literature
    Art
    Autobiographies
    Biographies
    Culture
    Drama
    English Literature
    Humanities
    Letters (Correspondence)
    Literary Analysis
    Literary Criticism
    Literary Genres
    Literature Appreciation
    Music
    Novels
    Philosophy
    Poetry
    Prose
    Religion
    Romanticism
    Satire
    Short Stories
    Social Sciences
    Symbolism
    Symbols (Literary)
    World Literature

NOMADS 380
UF   Pastoral Peoples
     Transhumance
BT   Migrants
RT   Land Settlement
     Migration
     Migration Patterns
     Mobility
     Transient Children
     Tribes

NOMINALS 290
UF   Noun Phrases
     Nouns
BT   Form Classes (Languages)
RT   Language Patterns
     Morphology (Languages)
     Phrase Structure
     Plurals
     Sentence Structure
     Syntax

NONAUTHORITARIAN CLASSES 280
BT   Classes (Groups Of Students)
RT   Leadership
     Permissive Environment

NONCOLLEGE PREPARATORY STUDENTS
380
BT   Secondary School Students

NONCREDIT COURSES 110
BT   Courses
RT   Credit Courses
     Short Courses
     Ungraded Classes
     Ungraded Programs

NONDIRECTIVE COUNSELING 090
UF   Client Centered Counseling
BT   Counseling
RT   Behavior Change
     Client Caseworkers
     Counseling Theories

NONDISCRIMINATORY EDUCATION 140
BT   Education

Non Discursive Measures
USE VISUAL MEASURES

NON ENGLISH SPEAKING 380
UF   Non English Speaking Children
     Non English Speaking Students
     Non English Speaking Youth
RT   Bilingual Education
     Bilingual Teacher Aides
     Bilingual Teachers
     Language Handicaps
     Spanish Speaking

Non English Speaking Children
USE NON ENGLISH SPEAKING

Non English Speaking Students
USE NON ENGLISH SPEAKING

Non English Speaking Youth
USE NON ENGLISH SPEAKING

Nonfarm Agricultural Occupations
USE OFF FARM AGRICULTURAL
     OCCUPATIONS

NONFARM YOUTH 380
BT   Youth

Nongraded Approach
USE NONGRADED SYSTEM

NONGRADED CLASSES 280
BT   Classes (Groups Of Students)
     Nongraded System

NONGRADED PRIMARY SYSTEM 280
BT   Nongraded System
RT   Primary Education

NONGRADED SYSTEM 280
UF   Nongraded Approach
NT   Nongraded Classes
     Nongraded Primary System
RT   Continuous Progress Plan

NONINSTRUCTIONAL RESPONSIBILITY 020
UF   Extrainstructional Duties
     Extrateaching Duties
     Nonteaching Duties
BT   Teacher Responsibility
RT   Educational Responsibility
     School Responsibility
     Teacher Role
     Teachers
     Teaching
     Teaching Load

NONPROFESSIONAL PERSONNEL 380
NT   Clerical Workers
     Merchants
     Sales Workers
     Semiskilled Workers
     Service Workers
     Skilled Workers
     Unskilled Workers
BT   Personnel
RT   Bilingual Teacher Aides
     Medical Assistants
     Paraprofessional School Personnel
     Personnel Needs
     Practical Nurses
     Professional Personnel

Nonprofit Organizations
USE VOLUNTARY AGENCIES

Nonpublic Agencies
USE PRIVATE AGENCIES

Nonresident Farmers
USE PART TIME FARMERS

NONRESIDENTIAL SCHOOLS 470
UF Commuter Schools
BT Schools
RT Commuting Students
    Day Schools

NONRESIDENT STUDENTS 380
UF Out Of State Students
BT Students
RT Admission Criteria
    Residence Requirements

NONSTANDARD DIALECTS 290
NT Negro Dialects
BT Dialects
RT Diglossia
    Regional Dialects
    Social Dialects
    Sociolinguistics
    Standard Spoken Usage
    TENL
    Urban Language

Nonteaching Duties
USE NONINSTRUCTIONAL RESPONSIBILITY

NONVERBAL ABILITY 010
BT Ability
RT Nonverbal Learning
    Nonverbal Tests
    Verbal Ability
    Visual Learning

NONVERBAL COMMUNICATION 080
BT Communication (Thought Transfer)
RT Classroom Communication
    Communication Problems
    Communication Skills
    Verbal Communication

NONVERBAL LEARNING 310
BT Learning
RT Associative Learning
    Learning Difficulties
    Nonverbal Ability
    Performance
    Psychomotor Skills
    Visual Learning

NONVERBAL TESTS 520
BT Performance Tests
RT Nonverbal Ability

NON WESTERN CIVILIZATION 100
SN Includes Asia and Africa
UF Eastern Civilization
    Oriental Civilization
    South Asian Civilization
RT African Culture
    African History
    Arabs
    Area Studies
    Asian History
    Burmese Culture
    Chinese Culture
    Cultural Background

Cultural Environment
Cultural Factors
Culture
History
Korean Culture
Middle Eastern History
Religious Cultural Groups
Social Environment
Social Influences
Sociocultural Patterns
World History

NORTHERN ATTITUDES 040
BT Attitudes
RT Geographic Concepts
    Racial Attitudes
    Social Attitudes
    Southern Attitudes

NORTHERN SCHOOLS 470
BT School Location
    Schools

Northward Movement
USE MIGRATION

NORWEGIAN 300
BT Indo European Languages

Noun Phrases
USE NOMINALS

Nouns
USE NOMINALS

Novella
USE NOVELS

Novelle
USE NOVELS

NOVELS 260
UF Novella
    Novelle
NT Sociological Novels
BT Literary Genres
    Literature
RT Ambiguity
    Aristotelian Criticism
    Books
    Characterization (Literature)
    Composition (Literary)
    Czech Literature
    English Neoclassic Literary Period
    Existentialism
    Expressionism
    French Literature
    German Literature
    Humor
    Impressionistic Criticism
    Literary Influences
    Literary Perspective
    Local Color Writing
    Metaphors
    Mythic Criticism
    Narration
    Naturalism

Nineteenth Century Literature
Polish Literature
Prose
Realism
Renaissance Literature
Russian Literature
Spanish American Literature
Spanish Literature
Surrealism
Tales
Theoretical Criticism

Nuclear Medicine Technologists
USE   RADIOLOGIC TECHNOLOGISTS

NUCLEAR PHYSICS 400
UF   Atomic Physics
BT   Physics
RT   Atomic Structure
Atomic Theory
Force
Matter
Nuclear Warfare
Quantum Mechanics
Radiation
Radiation Biology
Radiation Effects
Radioisotopes
Scientific Research

NUCLEAR WARFARE 400
UF   Atomic Warfare
RT   Atomic Theory
Civil Defense
Military Science
Modern History
Nuclear Physics
Radiation Effects
United States History
World Problems

NUCLEATION (LANGUAGE LEARNING) 310
RT   Applied Linguistics
Creative Thinking
Language
Language Development
Language Proficiency
Language Skills
Linguistic Theory
Psycholinguistics
Second Language Learning

Number Concept Development
USE   CONCEPT FORMATION

NUMBER CONCEPTS 340
BT   Mathematical Concepts
RT   Congruence

NUMBERS 340
UF   Number Use
NT   Fractions
Rational Numbers
Reciprocals (Mathematics)
Whole Numbers
RT   Mathematics
Number Systems
Statistics

NUMBER SYSTEMS 340
UF   Arithmetic Systems
RT   Mathematics
Numbers

Number Use
USE   NUMBERS

NUMERICAL CONTROL 510
UF   N C Systems
RT   Automation
Computer Programs
Cybernetics
Electronic Control
Machine Tools
Mathematical Applications
Production Techniques
Systems Concepts

Numeric Filing
USE   FILING

NUNS 380
NT   Nun Teachers
RT   Catholics
Church Workers
Religion

NUN TEACHERS 380
BT   Nuns
Teachers
RT   Catholic Educators
Catholic Schools
Parochial Schools
Religious Education
Women Teachers

NURSERIES (HORTICULTURE) 210
UF   Nursery Operation
BT   Facilities
RT   Forestry
Greenhouses
Horticulture
Nursery Workers (Horticulture)
Ornamental Horticulture

Nursery Operation
USE   NURSERIES (HORTICULTURE)

NURSERY SCHOOLS 470
BT   Schools
RT   Child Care Workers
Preschool Education

NURSERY WORKERS (HORTICULTURE)
380
SN Unskilled or semiskilled persons working in a greenhouse or nursery
UF Greenhouse Workers
BT Ornamental Horticulture Occupation
RT Nurseries (Horticulture)
   Ornamental Horticulture
   Plant Propagation
   Vocational Agriculture

NURSES 380
NT Practical Nurses
   School Nurses
   Teacher Nurses
BT Health Personnel
RT Clinic Personnel (School)
   Companions (Occupation)
   Health Occupations
   Health Services
   Hospital Personnel
   Nurses Aides
   Nursing
   Professional Occupations
   Professional Personnel

NURSES AIDES 380
UF Hospital Attendants
   Nursing Aides
   Nursing Assistants
   Rest Home Aides
BT Health Personnel
RT Attendants
   Companions (Occupation)
   Health Occupations
   Health Occupations Education
   Medical Assistants
   Nurses
   Nursing
   Psychiatric Aides

NURSING 250
NT Practical Nursing
BT Medical Services
RT Medical Education
   Nurses
   Nurses Aides
   Nursing Homes
   Psychiatric Aides
   Teacher Nurses

Nursing Aides
USE NURSES AIDES

Nursing Assistants
USE NURSES AIDES

NURSING HOMES 210
SN Resident facilities providing skilled nursing care as their primary and predominant function
UF Convalescent Homes
BT Health Facilities
RT Foster Homes
   Hospitals

   Institution Libraries
   Medical Services
   Medical Treatment
   Nursing
   Personal Care Homes
   Practical Nursing
   Residential Care

NUTRITION 250
BT Physiology
RT Breakfast Programs
   Dietetics
   Dietitians
   Eating Habits
   Food
   Food Standards
   Health
   Home Economics
   Hunger
   Lunch Programs
   Nutrition Instruction

NUTRITION INSTRUCTION 270
BT Instruction
RT Cooking Instruction
   Cooks
   Foods Instruction
   Health Education
   Home Economics Education
   Nutrition

Nyanja
USE CHINYANJA

OBJECTIVES 020
UF Goals
NT Educational Objectives
   Guidance Objectives
   Measurement Goals
   Training Objectives
RT Aspiration
   College Choice
   Goal Orientation
   Guidelines
   Institutional Role
   Personal Interests

OBJECTIVE TESTS 520
NT Multiple Choice Tests
BT Tests
RT Group Tests
   Standardized Tests

OBJECT MANIPULATION 010
BT Psychomotor Skills
RT Eye Hand Coordination
   Self Care Skills
   Skill Analysis
   Tracking

OBSERVATION 190
RT Classroom Observation Techniques
 Critical Incidents Method
 Evaluation
 Expectation
 Inspection
 Lesson Observation Criteria
 Performance
 School Visitation

Observed Classroom Behaviors
USE CLASSROOM OBSERVATION
 TECHNIQUES

OBSOLESCENCE 500
NT Building Obsolescence
 Skill Obsolescence
RT Maintenance
 Preservation
 Repair
 Time
 Use Studies

Occidental Civilization
USE WESTERN CIVILIZATION

OCCUPATIONAL ASPIRATION 010
UF Occupational Aspiration Level
 Vocational Aspiration
BT Aspiration
RT Career Choice
 Occupational Choice
 Promotion (Occupational)
 Self Concept
 Vocational Interests
 Work Attitudes

Occupational Aspiration Level
USE OCCUPATIONAL ASPIRATION

OCCUPATIONAL CHOICE 150
UF Career Objectives
 Vocational Choice
BT Vocational Development
RT Aspiration
 Career Change
 Career Choice
 Career Planning
 Employment Opportunities
 Occupational Aspiration
 Occupational Guidance
 Occupations
 Vocational Interests

OCCUPATIONAL CLUSTERS 350
UF Job Clusters
 Job Families
 Occupational Families
RT Cluster Grouping
 Occupations

Occupational Counseling
USE VOCATIONAL COUNSELING

Occupational Courses
USE VOCATIONAL EDUCATION

OCCUPATIONAL DISEASES 250
BT Diseases
RT Occupations

Occupational Families
USE OCCUPATIONAL CLUSTERS

Occupational Followup
USE VOCATIONAL FOLLOWUP

OCCUPATIONAL GUIDANCE 090
UF Vocational Guidance
BT Guidance
RT Employment Counselors
 Employment Opportunities
 Group Guidance
 Job Placement
 Occupational Choice
 Occupations
 Recruitment
 Vocational Counseling
 Vocational Development

OCCUPATIONAL HOME ECONOMICS 140
SN Preparation for gainful employment in
 occupations using home economics
 knowledges and skills
UF Home Economics Gainful Employment
 Home Economics Wage Earning
BT Home Economics Education
RT Child Care Occupations
 Clothing Maintenance Specialists
 Companions (Occupation)
 Cooks
 Dietitians
 Food Service Occupations
 Food Service Workers
 Home Economics Teachers
 Housing Management Aides
 Maids
 Seamstresses
 Visiting Homemakers

OCCUPATIONAL INFORMATION 350
UF Job Descriptions
RT Demand Occupations
 Employment Qualifications
 Job Analysis
 Jobs
 Occupations
 Personnel Data
 Post High School Guidance
 Task Analysis
 Vocational Development
 Work Simplification

OCCUPATIONAL MOBILITY 350
UF Job Mobility
 Labor Mobility
 Occupational Succession
BT Mobility
RT Career Change
 Employment Experience
 Employment Opportunities
 Faculty Mobility

Job Tenure
Migrants
Overseas Employment
Population Trends
Promotion (Occupational)
Relocation
Social Mobility
Vocational Adjustment

Occupational Persistence
USE PERSISTENCE

Occupational Satisfaction
USE JOB SATISFACTION

Occupational Succession
USE OCCUPATIONAL MOBILITY

OCCUPATIONAL SURVEYS 350
UF Employment Surveys
    Job Vacancy Surveys
    Labor Force Surveys
BT Surveys
RT Community Surveys
    Employment
    Employment Opportunities
    Employment Patterns
    Employment Trends
    Job Market
    Jobs
    Labor Force
    Labor Market
    Labor Supply
    Occupations

OCCUPATIONAL TESTS 520
BT Tests
RT Aptitude Tests
    Performance Tests
    Vocational Counseling

OCCUPATIONAL THERAPISTS 380
BT Therapists
RT Employment
    Health Personnel
    Occupational Therapy
    Occupational Therapy Assistants
    Occupations
    Rehabilitation
    Therapeutic Environment

OCCUPATIONAL THERAPY 420
BT Therapy
RT Handicapped
    Medical Services
    Medical Treatment
    Occupational Therapists
    Occupational Therapy Assistants
    Physical Therapy

OCCUPATIONAL THERAPY ASSISTANTS
380
BT Health Personnel
RT Health Occupations
    Health Occupations Education
    Occupational Therapists
    Occupational Therapy
    Rehabilitation

Occupational Training
USE VOCATIONAL EDUCATION

OCCUPATIONS 350
NT Agricultural Occupations
    Blue Collar Occupations
    Building Trades
    Clerical Occupations
    Data Processing Occupations
    Demand Occupations
    Electrical Occupations
    Finance Occupations
    Health Occupations
    Insurance Occupations
    Managerial Occupations
    Metal Working Occupations
    Office Occupations
    Professional Occupations
    Real Estate Occupations
    Sales Occupations
    Semiskilled Occupations
    Service Occupations
    Skilled Occupations
    Technical Occupations
    Unskilled Occupations
    White Collar Occupations
RT Career Choice
    Careers
    Employment
    Employment Opportunities
    Jobs
    Journalism
    Merchandising
    Negro Businesses
    Occupational Choice
    Occupational Clusters
    Occupational Diseases
    Occupational Guidance
    Occupational Information
    Occupational Surveys
    Occupational Therapists
    Retraining
    Salesmanship
    Specialization
    Vocational Counseling

OCEAN ENGINEERING 400
BT Engineering
RT Climatic Factors
    Ecology
    Marine Biology
    Oceanology
    Physical Environment

Oceanography
USE OCEANOLOGY

OCEANOLOGY 400
UF Oceanography
BT Earth Science
RT Geography
Geology
Marine Technicians
Ocean Engineering
Physical Geography

Ocular Refractive Errors
USE AMETROPIA

ODES 260
BT Lyric Poetry
RT Analytical Criticism
Ballads
Literature
Moral Criticism
Pastoral Literature
Poets
Sonnets

OFF CAMPUS FACILITIES 210
BT Educational Facilities

Off Campus Student Teaching
USE STUDENT TEACHING

OFF FARM AGRICULTURAL OCCUPATIONS
350
UF Farm Related Occupations
Nonfarm Agricultural Occupations
NT Agricultural Chemical Occupations
Agricultural Machinery Occupations
Agricultural Supply Occupations
Crop Processing Occupations
Food Processing Occupations
Forestry Occupations
Ornamental Horticulture Occupation
BT Agricultural Occupations
RT Agricultural Education
Agriculture
Animal Caretakers
Farm Occupations
Feed Industry
Forestry Aides
Vocational Agriculture

Office Education
USE OFFICE OCCUPATIONS EDUCATION

OFFICE MACHINES 170
UF Business Machines
RT Business
Computers
Industry
Office Management
Typewriting

OFFICE MANAGEMENT 020
BT Management
RT Data Processing
Office Machines
Office Occupations
Office Occupations Education
Office Practice
Personnel
Records (Forms)

OFFICE OCCUPATIONS 350
BT Occupations
RT Business
Business Education
Clerical Occupations
Clerical Workers
Data Processing Occupations
Distributive Education
Employment Qualifications
File Clerks
Finance Occupations
Job Training
Office Management
Office Occupations Education
Office Practice
Work Experience Programs

OFFICE OCCUPATIONS EDUCATION 140
UF Office Education
BT Business Education
RT Business Education Teachers
Business Subjects
Clerical Workers
File Clerks
Office Management
Office Occupations

OFFICE PRACTICE 110
BT Business Subjects
RT Business Education
Distributive Education
Office Management
Office Occupations
Secretaries
Stenographers
Stenography

OFFICER PERSONNEL 380
BT Military Personnel
RT Immigration Inspectors
Military Training

OFFICES (FACILITIES) 210
UF Faculty Offices
Staff Offices
BT Facilities
RT Interior Design
Interior Space
School Space
Space Classification

OFFICIAL LANGUAGES 290
BT Language
RT Administrative Policy
   Bilingual Education
   Diglossia
   Educational Policy
   Language Planning
   Language Standardization
   Native Speakers
   Sociolinguistics
   Standard Spoken Usage

Off Site Training
USE OFF THE JOB TRAINING

OFF THE JOB TRAINING 270
SN Conducted in a company school or
   arranged with technical schools,
   universities, or professional agencies
UF Away From The Job Training
   Off Site Training
BT Job Training
RT Cooperative Programs
   Industrial Training
   Inplant Programs
   Institutes (Training Programs)
   Job Skills
   Labor Education
   Management Development
   Manpower Development
   On The Job Training
   Released Time
   Residential Programs
   Skill Centers
   Supervisory Training
   Vocational Training Centers

Oil
USE LUBRICANTS

OKINAWAN 300
BT Japanese

Old Age
USE OLDER ADULTS

OLD ENGLISH 300
UF Anglo Saxon
BT English
RT Diachronic Linguistics
   Indo European Languages
   Languages
   Linguistics
   Old English Literature

OLD ENGLISH LITERATURE 260
BT English Literature
RT Allegory
   Chronicles
   Epics
   Legends
   Mythology
   Old English
   Poetry
   World Literature

OLDER ADULTS 380
SN Persons 65 and over
UF Aged
   Old Age
NT Senior Citizens
BT Adults
RT Companions (Occupation)
   Dependents
   Foster Homes
   Geriatrics
   Personal Care Homes
   Retirement

OMBUDSMEN 380
BT Faculty
RT Counseling
   Faculty Advisors
   Grievance Procedures
   Student College Relationship
   Student Personnel Services
   Student Welfare

ONE PARENT FAMILY 490
NT Fatherless Family
   Motherless Family
BT Family (Sociological Unit)
RT Family Characteristics
   Family Environment
   Family Influence
   Heads Of Households
   Illegitimate Births
   Marital Instability
   Parents

ONE TEACHER SCHOOLS 470
BT Schools
RT Small Schools
   Teachers

ONOMASTICS 290
UF Onomatology
BT Etymology
RT Diachronic Linguistics
   Language
   Language Research
   Lexicology
   Linguistics

Onomatology
USE ONOMASTICS

On Site Courses
USE STUDENT TEACHING

ON THE JOB TRAINING 270
BT Job Training
RT Apprenticeships
   Industrial Training
   Inplant Programs
   Off The Job Training
   Research Apprenticeships
   Trade And Industrial Education

OPAQUE PROJECTORS 170
BT Projection Equipment

Open Air Theaters
USE OUTDOOR THEATERS

Open Area Schools
USE OPEN PLAN SCHOOLS

OPEN CIRCUIT TELEVISION 050
BT Audiovisual Communication
Television
RT Audiovisual Aids
Audiovisual Instruction
Educational Television

OPEN ENROLLMENT 020
UF Open Enrollment Policy
BT Enrollment
RT Free Choice Transfer Programs
School Districts
Transfers

Open Enrollment Policy
USE OPEN ENROLLMENT

OPEN PLAN SCHOOLS 210
UF Open Area Schools
BT Schools
RT Building Design
Classroom Design
Flexible Classrooms
Flexible Facilities
Interior Space
School Architecture
School Buildings
School Design
School Space

OPERA 030
BT Theater Arts
RT Acting
Music
Musical Composition
Vocal Music

OPERANT CONDITIONING 420
UF Instrumental Conditioning
NT Verbal Operant Conditioning
BT Conditioned Response
RT Behavioral Sciences
Psychology

OPERATING ENGINEERING 400
BT Engineering
RT Equipment Utilization
Industrial Arts
School Construction

OPERATING EXPENSES 220
UF Minimum Operating Expenses
BT Expenditures

Operating Room Technicians
USE SURGICAL TECHNICIANS

Operations Analysis
USE OPERATIONS RESEARCH

OPERATIONS RESEARCH 340
UF Operations Analysis
NT Game Theory
BT Mathematics
RT Action Research
Administration
Cost Effectiveness
Critical Path Method
Information Theory
Management Systems
Mathematical Models
Measurement
Models
Planning
Research
Search Strategies

OPHTHALMOLOGY 070
BT Medicine
RT Eyes
Medical Consultants
Medical Services
Visually Handicapped

OPINIONS 040
NT Public Opinion
Student Opinion
RT Attitudes
Dogmatism
Political Attitudes
Q Sort

OPPORTUNITIES 360
NT Career Opportunities
Cultural Opportunities
Educational Opportunities
Employment Opportunities
Equal Opportunities (Jobs)
Housing Opportunities
Research Opportunities
Youth Opportunities
RT Background

Opportunities For Youth
USE YOUTH OPPORTUNITIES

OPPORTUNITY CLASSES 280
BT Classes (Groups Of Students)

Optical Masers
USE LASERS

OPTICAL SCANNERS 170
UF Document Readers
Page Readers
Visual Scanners
RT Computers
Electronic Data Processing
Electronic Equipment
Information Processing
Input Output
Input Output Devices
Pattern Recognition

Optical Spectrum
USE LIGHT

OPTICS 400
UF Geometrical Optics
    Physical Optics
NT Electrooptics
BT Physics
RT Electronics
    Energy
    Illumination Levels
    Lasers
    Light
    Lighting
    Radiation
    Relativity
    Spectrograms

OPTIONAL BRANCHING 510
BT Branching
RT Programed Instruction
    Programed Materials
    Programed Texts
    Programed Tutoring
    Programing

Optional Reading
USE ELECTIVE READING

OPTOMETRISTS 380
RT Eyes
    Professional Services
    Specialists
    Vision
    Vision Tests

ORAL COMMUNICATION 080
BT Verbal Communication
RT Acoustical Environment
    Conversational Language Courses
    Language Rhythm
    Language Usage
    Linguistic Performance
    Oral Expression
    Speech

ORAL ENGLISH 290
BT English
RT Speech
    TENL

ORAL EXPRESSION 080
RT Language Rhythm
    Linguistic Performance
    Oral Communication
    Speech Instruction

Oral Facility
USE SPEECH SKILLS

Oral Hygienists
USE DENTAL HYGIENISTS

Oral Interpretation
USE INTERPRETIVE READING

Oral Language Translators
USE INTERPRETERS

Oral Language Usage
USE STANDARD SPOKEN USAGE

ORAL READING 440
NT Eye Voice Span
BT Reading
RT Reading Instruction
    Reading Skills

Oral Skills
USE SPEECH SKILLS

ORCHESTRAS 370
UF Repertory Orchestras
    Symphony Orchestras
RT Applied Music
    Bands (Music)
    Concerts
    Music
    Music Activities
    Musical Instruments
    Music Education
    Musicians
    Music Techniques
    Theater Arts

ORGANIC CHEMISTRY 400
BT Chemistry
RT Atomic Structure
    Biochemistry
    Chemical Bonding
    Chemical Reactions
    Chemical Technicians
    Coordination Compounds
    Radiation Biology

ORGANIZATION 020
UF Hierarchy
    Organizational Structure
NT Administrative Organization
    Course Organization
    Grade Organization
    Horizontal Organization
    Informal Organization
    Power Structure
    Pyramid Organization
    School Organization
    Vertical Organization
RT Bureaucracy
    Centralization
    Consortia
    Coordination
    Coordinators
    Decentralization
    Mergers
    Organizational Change
    Organizations (Groups)

ORGANIZATIONAL CHANGE 020
RT Administration
    Mergers
    Organization

ORGANIZATIONAL CLIMATE 020
RT Attitudes
    Behavior
    Environment
    Informal Organization
    Job Satisfaction
    Teacher Morale

Organizational Outlines
USE TEACHING GUIDES

Organizational Plans
USE PLANNING

Organizational Structure
USE ORGANIZATION

ORGANIZATIONS (GROUPS) 370
UF Formal Organizations
NT Clubs
    Community Organizations
    Cooperatives
    Faculty Organizations
    Fraternities
    Freedom Organizations
    Human Relations Organizations
    International Organizations
    Military Organizations
    National Organizations
    Negro Organizations
    Parent Associations
    Religious Organizations
    Segregationist Organizations
    Social Organizations
    Student Organizations
RT Agencies
    Committees
    Groups
    Industry
    Informal Organization
    Mergers
    Organization
    Voluntary Agencies

ORGANIZATION SIZE (GROUPS) 370
SN Commercial, agency, industrial or
    institutional organizations
UF Company Size (Industry)
RT Business
    Capital
    Capital Outlay (For Fixed Assets)
    Industrial Structure
    Industry
    Labor Force
    Mergers
    Physical Facilities

Oriental Civilization
USE NON WESTERN CIVILIZATION

ORIENTAL MUSIC 030
SN Music of China, Japan, Indochina,
    Polynesia, India, Arabia, and North Africa
UF Asian Music
BT Music
RT Folk Culture
    Musical Composition

ORIENTATION 270
NT Goal Orientation
    School Orientation
    Space Orientation
    Staff Orientation
    Teacher Orientation
    Visually Handicapped Orientation
RT Instruction
    Orientation Materials

ORIENTATION MATERIALS 050
BT Instructional Materials
RT Orientation

ORIGINALITY 420
BT Creativity
RT Creative Ability

ORNAMENTAL HORTICULTURE 070
NT Floriculture
    Landscaping
    Turf Management
BT Horticulture
RT Greenhouses
    Grounds Keepers
    Nurseries (Horticulture)
    Nursery Workers (Horticulture)
    Ornamental Horticulture Occupation
    Plant Growth
    Plant Identification
    Planting
    Plant Propagation
    Transplanting
    Trees

**ORNAMENTAL HORTICULTURE
OCCUPATION** 350
NT Grounds Keepers
    Nursery Workers (Horticulture)
BT Off Farm Agricultural Occupations
RT Ornamental Horticulture

Orthodontics
USE DENTISTRY

Orthodontic Technicians
USE DENTAL TECHNICIANS

Orthodontists
USE DENTISTS

ORTHOGONAL PROJECTION 340
UF Descriptive Geometry
    Orthographic Projection
RT Drafting
    Industrial Arts

Orthographic Projection
USE ORTHOGONAL PROJECTION

ORTHOGRAPHIC SYMBOLS 290
NT Phonetic Transcription
RT Abbreviations
   Diacritical Marking
   Graphemes
   Initial Teaching Alphabet
   Romanization
   Spelling

ORTHOPEDICALLY HANDICAPPED 240
BT Physically Handicapped
RT Quadriplegia

OSSETIC 300
BT Indo European Languages

OSTYAK 300
BT Finno Ugric Languages
   Uralic Altaic Languages

Otological Tests
USE AUDITORY TESTS

OUTDOOR DRAMA 260
BT Dramatics
RT Acting
   Dance
   Drama
   Music
   Outdoor Theaters

OUTDOOR EDUCATION 140
BT Education
RT Airborne Field Trips
   Camp Counselors
   Camping
   Conservation Education
   Environmental Education
   Rural Education
   Science Education
   Summer Programs
   Trails
   Urban Education

OUTDOOR THEATERS 210
UF Amphitheaters
   Open Air Theaters
BT Theaters
RT Dramatics
   Outdoor Drama
   Stages
   Theater Arts

OUT OF SCHOOL YOUTH 380
SN A child of compulsory school age who
   has been excused from attending school,
   or a child over 16 years of age who is
   out of school legally
BT Youth
RT Dropouts
   Withdrawal

Out Of State Students
USE NONRESIDENT STUDENTS

Output Devices
USE INPUT OUTPUT DEVICES

OVERACHIEVERS 380
BT Students
RT Achievement
   High Achievers

OVERHEAD PROJECTORS 170
UF Overhead Transparency Projectors
   Transparency Projectors
BT Projection Equipment

OVERHEAD TELEVISION 050
UF Overhead Television Cameras
BT Audiovisual Aids
   Television

Overhead Television Cameras
USE OVERHEAD TELEVISION

Overhead Transparency Projectors
USE OVERHEAD PROJECTORS

OVERPOPULATION 120
RT Community Size
   Demography
   Population Trends

OVERSEAS EMPLOYMENT 150
UF Working Abroad
   Working Overseas
BT Employment
RT Foreign Countries
   Occupational Mobility
   Work Environment

OVERTIME 150
RT Income
   Payroll Records
   Premium Pay
   Salaries
   Wages
   Wage Statements
   Working Hours

OVERT RESPONSE 060
BT Behavior
RT Behavior Change

OXIDATION 400
BT Chemical Reactions
RT Chemistry

Oxygen Therapists
USE INHALATION THERAPISTS

Oxygen Therapy Technicians
USE INHALATION THERAPISTS

PACING 270
NT Interval Pacing
RT Programed Instruction
   Reading
   Time Factors (Learning)

Page Readers
USE OPTICAL SCANNERS

PAINTING 030
BT Art
RT Artists
    Building Trades
    Color
    Freehand Drawing
    Surrealism
    Visual Arts

PAIRED ASSOCIATE LEARNING 310
BT Associative Learning
RT Association (Psychological)
    Learning Theories
    Patterned Responses
    Perception
    Serial Learning

Palaeontology
USE PALEONTOLOGY

PALEONTOLOGY 400
UF Fossils
    Palaeontology
BT Geology
RT Archaeology
    Earth Science
    Evolution
    Scientific Research
    Zoology

PAMPHLETS 080
UF Leaflets
BT Publications

PANJABI 300
UF Punjabi
BT Indo European Languages

PAPAGO 300
BT American Indian Languages

PAPER (MATERIAL) 460
RT Art Materials
    Handwriting Materials
    Printing
    Publications

PAPERBACK BOOKS 320
UF Paperback Editions
    Paperbooks
    Paperbound Books
    Paper Cover Books
    Soft Cover Books
BT Books
RT Library Collections
    Literature
    Reading Materials

Paperback Editions
USE PAPERBACK BOOKS

Paperbooks
USE PAPERBACK BOOKS

Paperbound Books
USE PAPERBACK BOOKS

Paper Cover Books
USE PAPERBACK BOOKS

PARAGRAPH COMPOSITION 080
BT Composition (Literary)
RT Discourse Analysis
    Paragraphs
    Writing Skills

PARAGRAPHS 290
NT Sentences
BT Language Patterns
RT Connected Discourse
    Paragraph Composition
    Parallelism (Literary)
    Traditional Grammar
    Writing
    Written Language

PARALINGUISTICS 290
BT Linguistics
RT Communication (Thought Transfer)
    Expressive Language
    Kinesthetic Methods
    Linguistic Patterns
    Psychomotor Skills
    Speech Habits

PARALLELISM (LITERARY) 260
RT Composition (Literary)
    Literature
    Paragraphs
    Poetry
    Prose
    Sentence Structure
    Versification

PARAMEDICAL OCCUPATIONS 350
UF Health Related Professions
NT Dental Assistants
BT Health Occupations
RT Clinic Personnel (School)
    Dental Hygienists
    Dental Technicians
    Health Occupations Education
    Health Personnel
    Health Services
    Medical Services
    Veterinary Assistants

PARAPROFESSIONAL SCHOOL PERSONNEL
380
NT School Aides
    Teacher Aides
    Teaching Assistants
BT School Personnel
RT Auxiliary Laborers
    Differentiated Staffs
    Nonprofessional Personnel
    Student Teachers
    Subprofessionals
    Teacher Interns
    Volunteers

PARENTAL ASPIRATION 420
BT Aspiration
RT Family Influence
   Parental Background
   Parents

Parental Attitudes
USE PARENT ATTITUDES

PARENTAL BACKGROUND 200
BT Background
RT Parental Aspiration
   Parent Attitudes
   Parent Child Relationship
   Parent Education
   Parent Reaction
   Parents
   Parent School Relationship

PARENTAL GRIEVANCES 040
BT Parent Reaction
RT Family School Relationship
   Interpersonal Problems
   Parent School Relationship
   Problems

Parental Obligations
USE PARENT RESPONSIBILITY

PARENT ASSOCIATIONS 370
BT Organizations (Groups)
RT Fathers
   Mothers
   Parent Participation
   Parent Responsibility
   Parents

Parent Attitude Changes
USE PARENT ATTITUDES

PARENT ATTITUDES 040
UF Parental Attitudes
   Parent Attitude Changes
   Parent Opinion
BT Attitudes
RT Family Influence
   Parental Background
   Parent Counseling
   Parents

Parent Child Interaction
USE PARENT CHILD RELATIONSHIP

PARENT CHILD RELATIONSHIP 420
UF Child Parent Relationship
   Mother Child Interaction
   Parent Child Interaction
BT Family Relationship
RT Child Abuse
   Children
   Family Counseling
   Parental Background
   Parent Counseling
   Parents
   Parent Student Relationship

PARENT CONFERENCES 510
UF Parent Forums
   Parent Study Group
BT Conferences
RT Parent Participation
   Parent Responsibility
   Parents
   Parent Workshops

PARENT COUNSELING 090
SN Counseling of parents
BT Counseling
RT Counseling Services
   Individual Counseling
   Parent Attitudes
   Parent Child Relationship
   Parent Participation
   Parent School Relationship
   Parent Teacher Conferences
   Parent Teacher Cooperation

PARENT EDUCATION 140
BT Education
RT Adult Education
   Parental Background
   Parents
   Parent Workshops

Parent Forums
USE PARENT CONFERENCES

PARENT INFLUENCE 420
RT Parent Role
   Parents

Parent Involvement
USE PARENT PARTICIPATION

Parent Opinion
USE PARENT ATTITUDES

Parent Opposition
USE PARENT REACTION

PARENT PARTICIPATION 510
UF Parent Involvement
BT Participation
RT Family Influence
   Parent Associations
   Parent Conferences
   Parent Counseling
   Parents

PARENT REACTION 060
UF Parent Opposition
NT Parental Grievances
RT Family Influence
   Parental Background
   Parents

PARENT RESPONSIBILITY 040
UF Parental Obligations
BT Responsibility
RT Administrator Responsibility
    Child Responsibility
    Educational Responsibility
    Parent Associations
    Parent Conferences
    Parents
    Teacher Responsibility

PARENT ROLE 060
UF Father Role
    Mother Role
RT Family Influence
    Family Role
    Parent Influence
    Parents
    Student Role

PARENTS 380
NT Catholic Parents
    Fathers
    Lower Class Parents
    Middle Class Parents
    Mothers
    Working Parents
RT Family (Sociological Unit)
    Family Life
    Family Problems
    Heads Of Households
    Home Visits
    One Parent Family
    Parental Aspiration
    Parental Background
    Parent Associations
    Parent Attitudes
    Parent Child Relationship
    Parent Conferences
    Parent Education
    Parent Influence
    Parent Participation
    Parent Reaction
    Parent Responsibility
    Parent Role
    Parent School Relationship
    Parent Student Conferences
    Parent Student Relationship
    Parent Workshops

PARENT SCHOOL RELATIONSHIP 490
UF School Parent Relationship
RT Family School Relationship
    Home Visits
    Parental Background
    Parental Grievances
    Parent Counseling
    Parents
    Parent Student Conferences
    Parent Teacher Conferences
    Parent Teacher Cooperation
    Schools

PARENT STUDENT CONFERENCES 090
UF Student Parent Conferences
BT Conferences
RT Parents
    Parent School Relationship
    Students

PARENT STUDENT RELATIONSHIP 420
BT Family Relationship
RT Family School Relationship
    Parent Child Relationship
    Parents
    School Phobia
    Students

Parent Study Group
USE PARENT CONFERENCES

PARENT TEACHER CONFERENCES 510
UF Teacher Parent Conferences
RT Parent Counseling
    Parent School Relationship

PARENT TEACHER COOPERATION 510
UF Teacher Parent Cooperation
RT Home Visits
    Parent Counseling
    Parent School Relationship

PARENT WORKSHOPS 270
BT Workshops
RT Parent Conferences
    Parent Education
    Parents

Parish Workers
USE CHURCH WORKERS

PARK DESIGN 030
BT Design
RT Parks
    Trails

PARKING AREAS 210
SN Surface areas designated for vehicle
    storage along curbs or in specific
    delineated areas
UF Parking Lots
    Street Parking Areas
BT Facilities
RT Driveways
    Parking Controls
    Parking Meters
    Traffic Circulation
    Traffic Control
    Traffic Patterns
    Vehicular Traffic

PARKING CONTROLS 210
UF Parking Permits
    Parking Regulations
NT Parking Meters
RT Commuting Students
    Motor Vehicles
    Parking Areas
    Parking Facilities

Traffic Circulation
Traffic Control
Traffic Signs
Vehicular Traffic

PARKING FACILITIES 210
SN   Above and/or below ground structures
     for storage of vehicles
UF   Parking Garages
     Parking Ramps
     Underground Garages
NT   Bus Garages
BT   Facilities
RT   Campus Planning
     Driveways
     Motor Vehicles
     Parking Controls
     Vehicular Traffic

Parking Garages
USE   PARKING FACILITIES

Parking Lots
USE   PARKING AREAS

PARKING METERS 170
BT   Parking Controls
RT   Parking Areas

Parking Permits
USE   PARKING CONTROLS

Parking Ramps
USE   PARKING FACILITIES

Parking Regulations
USE   PARKING CONTROLS

PARKS 210
BT   Recreational Facilities
RT   Athletic Fields
     Park Design
     Physical Education Facilities
     Trails
     Zoos

PAROCHIAL SCHOOLS 470
NT   Catholic Schools
BT   Private Schools
RT   Church Related Colleges
     Nun Teachers
     Religious Education

PARODY 260
BT   Literature
RT   Ambiguity
     Essays
     Fiction
     Poetry
     Prose
     Short Stories

PAROLE OFFICERS 380
RT   Crime
     Police

Parsons
USE   CLERGYMEN

Partially Seeing
USE   PARTIALLY SIGHTED

PARTIALLY SIGHTED 240
UF   Partially Seeing
     Partial Sight
BT   Visually Handicapped
RT   Blind
     Blind Children
     Exceptional (Atypical)
     Large Type Materials
     Special Education
     Visual Perception

Partial Sight
USE   PARTIALLY SIGHTED

PARTICIPANT CHARACTERISTICS 490
BT   Adult Characteristics
RT   Educational Background
     Individual Characteristics
     Student Characteristics

PARTICIPANT INVOLVEMENT 270
SN   Active participation of learner in design,
     execution and evaluation of educational
     activities
UF   Participant Representation
RT   Participant Satisfaction
     Participation

Participant Representation
USE   PARTICIPANT INVOLVEMENT

PARTICIPANT SATISFACTION 420
SN   The students assessment of the degree
     to which a learning experience meets his
     needs
RT   Adult Dropouts
     Evaluation
     Measurement
     Participant Involvement

PARTICIPATION 510
NT   Audience Participation
     Classroom Participation
     Leader Participation
     Parent Participation
     Student Participation
RT   Participant Involvement

PARTNERSHIP TEACHERS 380
SN   Two half-time teachers hired as one
     full-time teacher
BT   Teachers
RT   Part Time Teaching

Parts Of Speech
USE   FORM CLASSES (LANGUAGES)

PART TIME FARMERS 380
UF   Nonresident Farmers
BT   Farmers
RT   Agricultural Occupations
     Farm Labor
     Farm Management
     Farm Occupations
     Part Time Jobs

PART TIME JOBS 150
UF   Part Time Work
BT   Jobs
RT   Part Time Farmers
     Student Employment
     Underemployed
     Working Hours
     Work Study Programs
     Youth Employment

PART TIME STUDENTS 380
BT   Students
RT   Continuation Students
     Correspondence Study
     Evening Classes
     Evening Colleges
     Evening Programs
     Evening Students
     Extension Education
     Night Schools
     Work Study Programs

PART TIME TEACHERS 380
BT   Teachers
RT   Substitute Teachers
     Teacher Employment

PART TIME TEACHING 270
BT   Teaching
RT   Partnership Teachers
     Teaching Assignment
     Teaching Load

Part Time Work
USE   PART TIME JOBS

PASHTO 300
UF   Pashtu
     Pushto
     Pushtu
BT   Indo European Languages

Pashtu
USE   PASHTO

PASS FAIL GRADING 180
BT   Grading
RT   Academic Standards
     Achievement Rating
     College Credits
     Grades (Scholastic)
     Scoring
     Student Evaluation

Pastes
USE   ADHESIVES

PASTORAL LITERATURE 260
UF   Bucolic Literature
BT   Literature
RT   Drama
     Fiction
     Literary Conventions
     Literary Criticism
     Odes
     Poetry
     Prose

Pastoral Peoples
USE   NOMADS

PATENTS 230
BT   Publications
RT   Federal Laws
     Technology

Path Analysis
USE   CRITICAL PATH METHOD

Pathogenesis
USE   PATHOLOGY

PATHOLOGY 070
UF   Pathogenesis
NT   Plant Pathology
BT   Medicine
RT   Anatomy
     Death
     Embryology
     Neurology
     Physiology
     Psychopathology
     Psychophysiology
     Zoology

Pathways
USE   TRAILS

PATIENTS (PERSONS) 380
UF   Invalids
RT   Companions (Occupation)
     Institutionalized (Persons)
     Medical Case Histories
     Medical Services
     Mentally Handicapped
     Physical Examinations
     Physical Health

PATTERN DRILLS (LANGUAGE) 270
NT   Substitution Drills
BT   Language Instruction
RT   Patterned Responses

Patterned Behavior
USE   BEHAVIOR PATTERNS

PATTERNED RESPONSES 060
SN   Using various organizations of stimuli to
     cue desired responses
UF   Stimulus Synthesis
BT   Performance
RT   Association Tests
     Paired Associate Learning

Pattern Drills (Language)
Perception
Stimulus Generalization

PATTERNMAKING 350
RT Clothing
    Clothing Design
    Clothing Instruction
    Needle Trades
    Woodworking

PATTERN RECOGNITION 080
NT Character Recognition
BT Recognition
RT Cybernetics
    Information Processing
    Optical Scanners
    Perception
    Reading

PAYROLL RECORDS 020
BT Records (Forms)
RT Overtime
    Premium Pay
    Wage Statements

Peak Viewing Time
USE VIEWING TIME

Peanut Inspectors
USE FOOD AND DRUG INSPECTORS

Pedagogy
USE TEACHING

Pedestrian Circulation
USE PEDESTRIAN TRAFFIC

PEDESTRIAN TRAFFIC 210
UF Pedestrian Circulation
RT Traffic Circulation
    Traffic Control
    Traffic Signs
    Vehicular Traffic

PEDIATRICS TRAINING 270
BT Training
RT Child Care
    Infancy

PEER ACCEPTANCE 420
UF Acceptance
RT Morale
    Peer Groups
    Peer Relationship

PEER GROUPS 490
BT Groups
RT Age Groups
    Conformity
    Peer Acceptance
    Peer Relationship
    Professional Recognition
    Social Values

PEER RELATIONSHIP 480
BT Relationship
RT Friendship
    Group Status
    Peer Acceptance
    Peer Groups
    Teamwork

PEER TEACHING 270
BT Teaching
RT Cross Age Teaching

Percent
USE PERCENTAGE

PERCENTAGE 340
UF Percent
BT Arithmetic
RT Mathematical Concepts

PERCEPTION 070
UF Awareness
NT Auditory Perception
    Haptic Perception
    Kinesthetic Perception
    Role Perception
    Tactual Perception
    Visual Perception
BT Physiology
RT Adaptation Level Theory
    Arousal Patterns
    Character Recognition
    Color
    Comprehension
    Cutaneous Sense
    Discrimination Learning
    Figural Aftereffects
    Paired Associate Learning
    Patterned Responses
    Pattern Recognition
    Perception Tests
    Perceptual Development
    Perceptually Handicapped
    Perceptual Motor Coordinatior
    Recognition
    Sensory Deprivation
    Sensory Integration
    Space Orientation
    Surrealism

Perception Of Depth
USE STEREOPSIS

PERCEPTION TESTS 520
BT Tests
RT Perception
    Visual Measures

Perceptual Deprivation
USE SENSORY DEPRIVATION

PERCEPTUAL DEVELOPMENT 130
BT Development
RT Cerebral Dominance
    Figural Aftereffects
    Perception
    Perceptually Handicapped
    Progressive Retardation
    Self Actualization
    Sensory Integration
    Sensory Training

PERCEPTUALLY HANDICAPPED 240
NT Aurally Handicapped
    Visually Handicapped
BT Handicapped
RT Auditory Agnosia
    Learning Disabilities
    Perception
    Perceptual Development
    Perceptual Motor Coordination
    Perceptual Motor Learning
    Physically Handicapped

PERCEPTUAL MOTOR COORDINATION 420
BT Coordination
RT Eye Voice Span
    Motor Development
    Perception
    Perceptually Handicapped
    Perceptual Motor Learning
    Psychomotor Skills
    Reaction Time
    Tracking

PERCEPTUAL MOTOR LEARNING 310
UF Sensory Motor Learning
BT Learning
RT Learning Processes
    Motor Development
    Perceptually Handicapped
    Perceptual Motor Coordination
    Sensory Training

PERFORMANCE 010
NT Academic Performance
    Counselor Performance
    Linguistic Performance
    Patterned Responses
    Task Performance
RT Ability
    Achievement
    Aptitude
    Aspiration
    Complexity Level
    Expectation
    National Competency Tests
    Nonverbal Learning
    Observation
    Performance Criteria
    Performance Factors
    Performance Specifications
    Relevance (Information Retrieval)
    Reliability
    School Visitation

    Symbolic Learning
    Tests
    Timed Tests
    Vocational Aptitude

PERFORMANCE CRITERIA 500
SN Standards by which the efficacy of a
    system may be judged
BT Criteria
RT Educational Specifications
    Evaluation
    Performance
    Performance Factors
    Performance Specifications
    Standards

PERFORMANCE FACTORS 180
RT Counselor Performance
    Performance
    Performance Criteria
    Performance Specifications
    Reliability
    Success Factors

PERFORMANCE SPECIFICATIONS 500
SN Statement of the operational
    characteristics of a system
BT Specifications
RT Construction Costs
    Contracts
    Criteria
    Educational Specifications
    Equipment Standards
    Evaluation
    Performance
    Performance Criteria
    Performance Factors
    Purchasing
    School Construction
    Standards

PERFORMANCE TESTS 520
NT Nonverbal Tests
BT Tests
RT Individual Tests
    Intelligence Tests
    Occupational Tests
    Psychological Tests
    Timed Tests
    Verbal Tests

Performing Arts
USE THEATER ARTS

Performing Arts Centers
USE THEATERS

PERIODICALS 320
UF Journals
    Magazines
NT Foreign Language Periodicals
    Scholarly Journals
BT Serials
RT Annual Reports
    Booklists
    Books

Bulletins
Library Collections

Permanent Education
USE CONTINUOUS LEARNING

Permanent Magnets
USE MAGNETS

Permissive Atmosphere
USE PERMISSIVE ENVIRONMENT

PERMISSIVE ENVIRONMENT 160
UF Permissive Atmosphere
BT Environment
RT Classroom Environment
Family Environment
Nonauthoritarian Classes

PERMUTED INDEXES 320
UF Key Word In Context
Kwic Indexes
Kwoc Indexes
BT Indexes (Locaters)
RT Coordinate Indexes
Documentation
Indexing
Information Retrieval
Reference Materials
Subject Index Terms

PERSIAN 300
BT Indo European Languages

PERSISTENCE 040
UF Occupational Persistence
RT Dropouts
Employment
Employment Problems
Manpower Utilization
Teacher Employment
Unemployment

PERSONAL ADJUSTMENT 420
BT Adjustment (To Environment)
RT Morale
Vocational Adjustment

PERSONAL CARE HOMES 210
SN Resident facilities providing personal
services such as assistance in
mobilization, bathing, dressing, etc. as
opposed to highly skilled care
UF Homes For The Aged
Rest Homes
BT Facilities
RT Foster Homes
Nursing Homes
Older Adults
Residential Care

Personal Development
USE INDIVIDUAL DEVELOPMENT

Personal Grooming
USE HYGIENE

PERSONAL GROWTH 130
SN Development of psychological maturity
RT Growth Patterns
Individual Development
Individual Power
Maturation
Personality Development
Self Actualization
Sensitivity Training
Social Maturity

Personal Health
USE HYGIENE

PERSONAL INTERESTS 040
BT Interests
RT Career Choice
College Choice
Hobbies
Objectives
Student Science Interests

PERSONALITY 420
UF Individuality
NT Behavior
RT Adaptation Level Theory
Curiosity
Habit Formation
Individual Characteristics
Individual Psychology
Personality Assessment
Personality Change
Personality Development
Personality Problems
Personality Studies
Personality Tests
Personality Theories
Personal Values
Self Concept

PERSONALITY ASSESSMENT 180
UF Personality Rating
RT Behavior Rating Scales
Goal Orientation
Personality
Personality Studies
Personality Tests
Projective Tests
Q Sort
Sociometric Techniques

PERSONALITY CHANGE 420
RT Behavior Change
Personality
Personality Development

PERSONALITY DEVELOPMENT 130
BT Development
RT Individual Development
Personal Growth
Personality
Personality Change
Personality Problems
Self Actualization

PERSONALITY PROBLEMS 420
BT Problems
RT Autism
    Personality
    Personality Development
    Psychopathology

Personality Rating
USE PERSONALITY ASSESSMENT

PERSONALITY STUDIES 420
BT Research
RT Exceptional Child Research
    Personality
    Personality Assessment
    Personality Tests
    Sociometric Techniques
    Teaching Styles

PERSONALITY TESTS 520
BT Tests
RT Behavior Rating Scales
    Individual Characteristics
    Personality
    Personality Assessment
    Personality Studies
    Projective Tests
    Psychological Evaluation
    Psychological Tests
    Psychometrics

PERSONALITY THEORIES 420
BT Theories
RT Behavior Theories
    Personality

Personality Traits
USE INDIVIDUAL CHARACTERISTICS

Personal Liberty
USE CIVIL LIBERTIES

PERSONAL RELATIONSHIP 480
BT Relationship
RT Teamwork

PERSONAL VALUES 040
BT Values
RT Goal Orientation
    Personality
    Political Attitudes
    Self Actualization

PERSONNEL 380
NT Administrative Personnel
    Agricultural Personnel
    Aircraft Pilots
    Attendants
    Aviation Mechanics
    Employees
    Engineers
    Examiners
    Guidance Personnel
    Health Personnel
    Hospital Personnel
    Indigenous Personnel
    Industrial Personnel
    Institutional Personnel
    Job Applicants
    Landlords
    Military Personnel
    Nonprofessional Personnel
    Professional Personnel
    Researchers
    School Personnel
    Scientific Personnel
    Scientists
RT Employment
    Employment Counselors
    Government Employees
    Office Management
    Personnel Evaluation
    Personnel Integration
    Personnel Needs
    Personnel Policy
    Personnel Selection
    Recruitment
    Working Women

Personnel Administrators
USE PERSONNEL DIRECTORS

PERSONNEL DATA 150
BT Data
RT Employment Experience
    Employment Qualifications
    Job Tenure
    Occupational Information

PERSONNEL DIRECTORS 380
UF Personnel Administrators
    Personnel Managers
    School Personnel Directors
BT Administrative Personnel
RT Employment
    Personnel Policy
    Personnel Selection
    School Personnel

PERSONNEL EVALUATION 180
UF Employee Evaluation
    Staff Evaluation
    Worker Evaluation
BT Evaluation
RT Administrator Evaluation
    Counselor Evaluation
    Employment Qualifications
    Faculty Evaluation
    Personnel
    Teacher Evaluation

PERSONNEL INTEGRATION 430
RT Personnel
    Personnel Policy
    Racial Integration
    Social Integration

PERSONNEL MANAGEMENT 020
BT Management

Personnel Managers
USE PERSONNEL DIRECTORS

PERSONNEL NEEDS 150
SN Requirements for staff
BT Needs
RT Administrative Personnel
    Employees
    Nonprofessional Personnel
    Personnel
    Personnel Policy
    Personnel Selection
    Professional Personnel
    Recruitment

PERSONNEL POLICY 020
BT Policy
RT Administrator Selection
    Job Layoff
    Leave Of Absence
    Personnel
    Personnel Directors
    Personnel Integration
    Personnel Needs
    Personnel Selection
    Salary Differentials

Personnel Recruitment
USE RECRUITMENT

Personnel Role
USE STAFF ROLE

PERSONNEL SELECTION 150
NT Administrator Selection
    Counselor Selection
    Teacher Selection
BT Selection
RT Admission (School)
    Competitive Selection
    Employment Interviews
    Interviews
    Labor Market
    Personnel
    Personnel Directors
    Personnel Needs
    Personnel Policy
    Recruitment

PERSUASIVE DISCOURSE 080
BT Rhetoric
RT Communication (Thought Transfer)
    Composition Skills (Literary)
    Debate
    Logic
    Motivation Techniques
    Public Speaking
    Speech Skills
    Verbal Communication

Pert
USE CRITICAL PATH METHOD

PESTICIDES 250
NT Herbicides
    Insecticides
    Rodenticides
RT Agricultural Chemical Occupations
    Agricultural Production
    Agricultural Supplies
    Agriculture
    Disease Control
    Pollution
    Public Health

PHARMACISTS 380
UF Druggists
BT Professional Personnel
RT Health Occupations
    Health Personnel
    Health Services
    Professional Occupations

Philanthropy
USE PRIVATE FINANCIAL SUPPORT

PHILOSOPHY 260
NT Educational Philosophy
    Existentialism
    Expressionism
    Humanism
    Individualism
    Platonism
BT Humanities
RT Antithesis
    Christianity
    Judaism
    Logic
    Naturalism
    Nineteenth Century Literature
    Realism

PHONEMES 290
NT Consonants
BT Morphemes
RT Allomorphs
    Distinctive Features
    Intonation
    Language Typology
    Morphemes
    Morphology (Languages)
    Morphophonemics
    Phonemic Alphabets
    Phonemics
    Phonics
    Speech
    Syllables
    Vowels

PHONEMIC ALPHABETS 290
BT Alphabets
RT Consonants
    Phonemes
    Phonemics
    Phonics
    Speech

PHONEMICS 290
BT Phonology
RT Contrastive Linguistics
Descriptive Linguistics
Diachronic Linguistics
Language Patterns
Linguistic Patterns
Linguistics
Morphology (Languages)
Morphophonemics
Phonemes
Phonemic Alphabets
Phonetics
Phonological Units
Speech
Synchronic Linguistics

PHONETIC ANALYSIS 290
RT Phonetics
Phonics

PHONETICS 290
NT Acoustic Phonetics
Diacritical Marking
Phonics
Vowels
BT Linguistics
RT Articulation (Speech)
Consonants
Distinctive Features
Graphemes
Morphophonemics
Phonemics
Phonetic Analysis
Phonetic Transcription
Speech

PHONETIC TRANSCRIPTION 290
SN Representation of speech sounds in phonetic symbols
BT Orthographic Symbols
RT Alphabets
Diacritical Marking
Phonetics
Phonology
Written Language

Phonic Method
USE PHONICS

PHONICS 510
UF Phonic Method
BT Phonetics
RT Aural Learning
Beginning Reading
Initial Teaching Alphabet
Phonemes
Phonemic Alphabets
Phonetic Analysis
Phonology
Reading Instruction
Reading Skills

PHONOGRAPH RECORDS 050
NT Language Records (Phonograph)
BT Phonotape Recordings

PHONOLOGICAL UNITS 290
RT Componential Analysis
Phonemics
Phonology

PHONOLOGY 290
NT Phonemics
BT Morphophonemics
RT Acoustic Phonetics
Artificial Speech
Componential Analysis
Diachronic Linguistics
Distinctive Features
Intonation
Kernel Sentences
Language Typology
Morphology (Languages)
Phonetic Transcription
Phonics
Phonological Units
Spectrograms
Speech
Suprasegmentals
Surface Structure
Synchronic Linguistics
Vowels

PHONOTAPE RECORDINGS 050
UF Audio Tape Recording
Language Tapes
Recordings (Phonotape)
NT Kinescope Recordings
Phonograph Records
Video Tape Recordings
BT Audiovisuals
Audiovisual Communication
Mass Media
Tape Recordings
RT Sound Effects
Sound Tracks

PHOTOCHEMICAL REACTIONS 400
UF Photochemistry
BT Chemical Reactions
RT Chemistry

Photochemistry
USE PHOTOCHEMICAL REACTIONS

PHOTOCOMPOSITION 030
RT Computer Graphics
Graphic Arts
Photography
Printing

PHOTOGRAPHS 050
BT Photography
RT Films

PHOTOGRAPHY 030
NT   Photographs
RT   Film Study
       Photocomposition

Photometric Brightness
USE LUMINESCENCE

PHRASE STRUCTURE 290
UF   Constituent Structure
BT   Syntax
RT   Context Free Grammar
       Deep Structure
       Form Classes (Languages)
       Kernel Sentences
       Nominals
       Pronouns
       Suprasegmentals
       Surface Structure
       Transformation Generative Grammar
       Transformations (Language)

PHYSICAL ACTIVITIES 390
NT   Athletic Activities
       Exercise (Physiology)
       Lifting
       Motor Reactions
       Running
BT   Activities
RT   Intramural Athletic Programs
       Physical Education
       Physical Recreation Programs
       Playground Activities
       Recreational Activities

PHYSICAL CHARACTERISTICS 070
NT   Age
       Body Height
       Body Weight
       Cerebral Dominance
       Lateral Dominance
       Muscular Strength
       Sex (Characteristics)
BT   Individual Characteristics
RT   Cardiac (Person)
       Mongolism
       Physical Development
       Physically Handicapped
       Racial Characteristics

Physical Conditioning
USE PHYSICAL FITNESS

PHYSICAL DESIGN NEEDS 500
BT   Design Needs
RT   Building Design
       Carpeting
       Cleaning
       Climate Control
       Design Preferences
       Furniture Design
       Human Engineering
       Humidity
       Interior Design
       Psychological Design Needs

       Safety
       Sanitation
       Storage

PHYSICAL DEVELOPMENT 130
BT   Development
RT   Body Height
       Body Weight
       Cardiac (Person)
       Lateral Dominance
       Maturation
       Motor Development
       Muscular Strength
       Neurological Organization
       Physical Characteristics
       Physical Health
       Physically Handicapped
       Prenatal Influences

PHYSICAL DIVISIONS (GEOGRAPHIC) 480
RT   Geography
       Physical Geography

PHYSICAL EDUCATION 140
BT   Education
RT   Athletic Activities
       Athletic Equipment
       Athletic Fields
       Athletic Programs
       Athletics
       Muscular Strength
       Physical Activities
       Physical Education Facilities
       Physical Fitness
       Physical Recreation Programs
       Recreational Activities
       Running
       School Health Services
       Sportsmanship
       Tumbling

PHYSICAL EDUCATION FACILITIES 210
NT   Athletic Fields
       Field Houses
       Gymnasiums
BT   Educational Facilities
RT   Athletic Equipment
       Athletics
       Locker Rooms
       Parks
       Physical Education
       Playgrounds
       Recreational Facilities
       Swimming Pools

PHYSICAL ENVIRONMENT 160
NT   Acoustical Environment
       Climatic Factors
       Thermal Environment
       Visual Environment
BT   Environment
RT   Architectural Research
       Classroom Environment
       Color Planning
       Design Preferences

Environmental Influences
Environmental Research
Heating
Human Engineering
Illumination Levels
Interior Design
Interior Space
Ocean Engineering
Physical Facilities
Pollution
Temperature
Ventilation

PHYSICAL EXAMINATIONS 180
BT Tests
RT Patients (Persons)
Physical Health

Physical Exercise
USE EXERCISE (PHYSIOLOGY)

PHYSICAL FACILITIES 210
BT Facilities
RT Military Air Facilities
Organization Size (Groups)
Physical Environment
Spatial Relationship

PHYSICAL FITNESS 250
UF Physical Conditioning
Physical Performance
RT Athletic Activities
Athletic Equipment
Athletic Programs
Athletics
Calisthenics
Exercise (Physiology)
Fatigue (Biology)
Heart Rate
Intramural Athletic Programs
Muscular Strength
Physical Education
Physical Health
Physical Recreation Programs

PHYSICAL GEOGRAPHY 110
BT Geography
RT Earth Science
Geographic Concepts
Geographic Distribution
Geographic Location
Geographic Regions
Geology
Oceanology
Physical Divisions (Geographic)
Seismology
Social Sciences
Social Studies

PHYSICAL HANDICAPS 240
NT Quadriplegia
RT Physically Handicapped

PHYSICAL HEALTH 250
BT Health
RT Allergy
Asthma
Diabetes
Heart Rate
Hygiene
Patients (Persons)
Physical Development
Physical Examinations
Physical Fitness
Psychosomatic Diseases
Sanitary Facilities

PHYSICALLY HANDICAPPED 240
UF Disabled
NT Amputees
Cardiac (Person)
Crippled Children
Orthopedically Handicapped
BT Handicapped
RT Cerebral Palsy
Cosmetic Prostheses
Epilepsy
Handicapped Students
Labor Force Nonparticipants
Perceptually Handicapped
Physical Characteristics
Physical Development
Physical Handicaps
Physical Therapy
Prostheses
Quadriplegia
Rehabilitation Counseling
Self Care Skills
Special Health Problems

Physical Optics
USE OPTICS

Physical Performance
USE PHYSICAL FITNESS

PHYSICAL RECREATION PROGRAMS 390
BT Recreational Programs
RT Athletic Activities
Athletic Equipment
Athletic Fields
Athletic Programs
Athletics
Physical Activities
Physical Education
Physical Fitness
Playground Activities
School Health Services
Tumbling

PHYSICAL SCIENCES 400
NT Astronomy
Chemistry
Earth Science
Fluid Power Education
Physics
BT Natural Sciences

RT   Aerospace Technology
      Atomic Structure
      Biochemistry
      Chemical Bonding
      Conservation Education
      Radiation Biology

Physical Scientists
USE SCIENTISTS

Physical Strength
USE MUSCULAR STRENGTH

PHYSICAL THERAPISTS 380
BT   Therapists
RT   Health Occupations
      Health Personnel
      Physical Therapy
      Physical Therapy Aides

PHYSICAL THERAPY 250
BT   Therapy
RT   Medical Services
      Medical Treatment
      Occupational Therapy
      Physically Handicapped
      Physical Therapists
      Physical Therapy Aides

PHYSICAL THERAPY AIDES 380
UF   Physical Therapy Attendants
BT   Health Personnel
RT   Health Occupations
      Physical Therapists
      Physical Therapy
      Rehabilitation

Physical Therapy Attendants
USE PHYSICAL THERAPY AIDES

PHYSICIANS 380
UF   Medical Doctors
NT   Psychiatrists
BT   Professional Personnel
RT   Health Occupations
      Health Personnel
      Hospital Personnel
      Medical Consultants
      Medical Vocabulary
      Professional Occupations

PHYSICS 400
NT   Acoustics
      Atomic Structure
      Atomic Theory
      Electricity
      Electronics
      Energy
      Force
      Kinetic Molecular Theory
      Kinetics
      Light
      Magnets
      Matter
      Motion
      Nuclear Physics

      Optics
      Pressure
      Quantum Mechanics
      Relativity
      Thermodynamics
BT   Physical Sciences
RT   Acoustic Phonetics
      Biophysics
      Distinctive Features
      Earth Science
      Geophysics
      Lasers
      Luminescence
      Metallurgical Technicians
      Metallurgy
      Meteorology
      Physics Curriculum
      Physics Experiments
      Physics Instruction
      Radiation
      Radiation Biology
      Radioisotopes
      Radiology
      Scientific Research
      Spectrograms

PHYSICS CURRICULUM 110
BT   Curriculum
      Science Curriculum
RT   Physics
      Physics Instruction

PHYSICS EXPERIMENTS 510
BT   Science Experiments
RT   Physics
      Spectrograms

PHYSICS INSTRUCTION 270
BT   Instruction
RT   Chemistry Instruction
      Physics
      Physics Curriculum

PHYSICS TEACHERS 380
BT   Science Teachers
RT   Chemistry
      Chemistry Teachers

Physiological Chemistry
USE BIOCHEMISTRY

Physiological Factors
USE PHYSIOLOGY

Physiological Psychology
USE PSYCHOPHYSIOLOGY

PHYSIOLOGY 070
UF   Physiological factors
NT   Blood Circulation
      Cardiovascular System
      Death
      Heart Rate
      Nutrition
      Perception
BT   Biology

312

RT   Allergy
      Anatomy
      Asthma
      Biochemistry
      Culturing Techniques
      Cutaneous Sense
      Cytology
      Diabetes
      Embryology
      Evolution
      Growth Patterns
      Medicine
      Metabolism
      Microbiology
      Motor Reactions
      Neurological Organization
      Neurology
      Pathology
      Psychophysiology
      Radiation Biology
      Rh Factors
      Scientific Research
      Sedatives
      Sensory Deprivation
      Stimulants
      Zoology

PICTORIAL STIMULI 050
BT Visual Stimuli
RT Color Television
      Electrical Stimuli
      Projective Tests
      Stimulus Behavior
      Tachistoscopes
      Visual Learning
      Visual Measures
      Visual Perception

Pictorial Tests
USE VISUAL MEASURES

Picture Frustration Studies
USE PROJECTIVE TESTS

PIDGINS 300
SN A form of speech which usually has a
     simplified grammar, limited vocabulary
     and no native speakers
BT Languages

Pilot Programs
USE PILOT PROJECTS

PILOT PROJECTS 450
UF Pilot Programs
BT Projects
RT Demonstration Projects
      Research
      Testing

Pilot Training
USE FLIGHT TRAINING

Pipe Fitting
USE PLUMBING

PLACEMENT 280
NT Advanced Placement
      Age Grade Placement
      College Placement
      Job Placement
      Regular Class Placement
      Student Placement
      Teacher Placement
RT Admission (School)

PLAGIARISM 060
RT Academic Standards
      Composition (Literary)
      Copyrights
      Discipline Policy
      Failure Factors
      Moral Issues

PLANE GEOMETRY 340
BT Geometry

PLANETARIUMS 210
RT Astronomy
      Earth Science
      Science Education
      Science Facilities
      Science Laboratories
      Science Teaching Centers
      Scientific Research

PLANNED COMMUNITY 490
BT Community
RT Housing
      Planning
      Planning Commissions
      Urban Renewal

PLANNING 020
UF Administrative Planning
      Organizational Plans
NT Campus Planning
      Career Planning
      City Planning
      College Planning
      Color Planning
      Community Planning
      Cooperative Planning
      Curriculum Planning
      Educational Planning
      Estate Planning
      Family Planning
      Interagency Planning
      Language Planning
      Library Planning
      Program Planning
      Regional Planning
      School Planning
      Social Planning
RT Administration
      Administrator Guides
      Building Plans
      Component Building Systems
      Critical Path Method
      Educational Administration

Educational Specifications
Lesson Plans
Master Plans
Operations Research
Planned Community
Planning Commissions
Planning Meetings

PLANNING COMMISSIONS 230
BT   Community Agencies (Public)
RT   Planned Community
     Planning

PLANNING MEETINGS 020
BT   Meetings
RT   Planning

Plant Diseases
USE   PLANT PATHOLOGY

PLANT GROWTH 070
RT   Agricultural Production
     Agriculture
     Biochemistry
     Botany
     Embryology
     Fertilizers
     Greenhouses
     Herbicides
     Horticulture
     Insecticides
     Ornamental Horticulture
     Planting
     Plant Pathology
     Plant Science
     Transplanting

PLANT IDENTIFICATION 070
RT   Botany
     Floriculture
     Horticulture
     Landscaping
     Ornamental Horticulture
     Plant Science

PLANTING 070
UF   Crop Planting
RT   Agricultural Production
     Agriculture
     Agronomy
     Field Crops
     Horticulture
     Ornamental Horticulture
     Plant Growth
     Plant Science
     Transplanting

PLANT PATHOLOGY 070
UF   Plant Diseases
BT   Pathology
RT   Agriculture
     Botany
     Herbicides
     Plant Growth
     Plant Science

PLANT PROPAGATION 070
RT   Botany
     Grounds Keepers
     Horticulture
     Nursery Workers (Horticulture)
     Ornamental Horticulture
     Plant Science
     Transplanting

PLANT SCIENCE 070
SN   Application of principles of biological and
     earth sciences to culture and production
     of agricultural plants
BT   Sciences
RT   Agriculture
     Biochemistry
     Botany
     Corn (Field Crop)
     Fertilizers
     Field Crops
     Forestry
     Harvesting
     Herbicides
     Horticulture
     Insecticides
     Landscaping
     Microbiology
     Plant Growth
     Plant Identification
     Planting
     Plant Pathology
     Plant Propagation
     Soil Science
     Transplanting
     Weeds

PLASTICS 400
RT   Industrial Arts

PLATONISM 260
BT   Philosophy
RT   Characterization (Literature)
     Classical Literature
     Drama
     Literary Criticism
     Literary Styles
     Literature
     Poetry
     Prose

PLAYGROUND ACTIVITIES 390
BT   Activities
RT   Athletic Activities
     Physical Activities
     Physical Recreation Programs
     Recreational Activities

PLAYGROUNDS 210
NT   Lighted Playgrounds
BT   Public Facilities
     Recreational Facilities
RT   Athletic Fields
     Physical Education Facilities
     Trails

PLAY THERAPY 420
BT Psychotherapy
RT Emotionally Disturbed
    Milieu Therapy

PLAYWRITING 260
BT Writing
RT Characterization (Literature)
    Creative Activities
    Creative Writing
    Dramatics
    Scripts
    Writing Skills

PLUMBING 350
UF Pipe Fitting
RT Building Trades
    Sanitary Facilities

Pluralization
USE PLURALS

PLURALS 290
SN Grammatical forms used to denote more
    than one
UF Pluralization
BT Language Patterns
RT Form Classes (Languages)
    Grammar
    Morphology (Languages)
    Nominals
    Spelling

POETRY 260
NT Ballads
    Epics
    Haiku
    Lyric Poetry
    Sonnets
    Versification
BT Literary Genres
    Literature
RT Allegory
    Ambiguity
    Antithesis
    Aristotelian Criticism
    Biblical Literature
    Characterization (Literature)
    Choral Speaking
    Chronicles
    Comedy
    Composition (Literary)
    Czech Literature
    Descriptive Writing
    Didacticism
    Drama
    English Neoclassic Literary Period
    Expressionism
    Figurative Language
    Folk Drama
    French Literature
    German Literature
    Humanism
    Humor

Imagery
Impressionistic Criticism
Irony
Italian Literature
Language Rhythm
Literary Conventions
Literary Influences
Literary Perspective
Literary Styles
Local Color Writing
Medieval Literature
Medieval Romance
Metaphors
Modernism
Mythic Criticism
Narration
Nineteenth Century Literature
Old English Literature
Parallelism (Literary)
Parody
Pastoral Literature
Platonism
Poets
Polish Literature
Realism
Renaissance Literature
Romanticism
Russian Literature
Satire
Seventeenth Century Literature
Sixteenth Century Literature
Spanish American Literature
Surrealism
Symbolism
Symbols (Literary)
Tales
Theoretical Criticism
Tragedy

POETS 380
UF Bards
    Lyric Poets
    Minnesingers
    Troubadours
BT Authors
RT Epics
    German Literature
    Literature
    Medieval Literature
    Medieval Romance
    Odes
    Poetry

Point Of View (Literature)
USE LITERARY PERSPECTIVE

POLICE 380
UF Law Enforcement Officers
NT State Police
RT Crime
    Emergency Squad Personnel
    Government (Administrative Body)
    Law Enforcement
    Parole Officers

Police Community Relationship
Police Costs
Police School Relationship
Police Seminars

POLICE ACTION 230
RT Police Community Relationship
   Police School Relationship

POLICE COMMUNITY RELATIONSHIP 480
UF Community Police Relationship
BT Relationship
RT Community
   Police
   Police Action
   Police Costs
   Police School Relationship

POLICE COSTS 220
BT Costs
RT Police
   Police Community Relationship
   Tax Allocation

Police Department Secretaries
USE SECRETARIES

Police School Liaison
USE POLICE SCHOOL RELATIONSHIP

POLICE SCHOOL RELATIONSHIP 480
UF Police School Liaison
   School Police Relationship
BT Relationship
RT Delinquency
   Police
   Police Action
   Police Community Relationship
   Schools

POLICE SEMINARS 510
BT Seminars
RT Police

Police Stenographers
USE STENOGRAPHERS

POLICY 020
NT Administrative Policy
   Board Of Education Policy
   Educational Policy
   Imperialism
   Interdistrict Policies
   Personnel Policy
   Public Policy
   School Policy
RT Foreign Policy
   Policy Formation

POLICY FORMATION 020
RT Governance
   Governing Boards
   Interdistrict Policies
   Language Planning
   Policy

POLISH 300
BT Slavic Languages

POLISH LITERATURE 260
BT Literature
RT Drama
   Essays
   Fiction
   Legends
   Novels
   Poetry
   Prose
   Short Stories
   World Literature

POLITICAL AFFILIATION 230
RT Government (Administrative Body)
   Political Attitudes
   Political Issues
   Political Socialization
   Refugees

POLITICAL ATTITUDES 040
BT Attitudes
RT Activism
   Authoritarianism
   Colonialism
   Democratic Values
   Imperialism
   Nationalism
   Opinions
   Personal Values
   Political Affiliation
   Political Socialization
   Public Opinion
   Refugees
   Social Attitudes
   Social Values
   Values

POLITICAL DIVISIONS (GEOGRAPHIC) 480
RT Colonialism
   Geography
   Imperialism
   Nationalism

POLITICAL INFLUENCES 230
RT Political Issues
   Political Socialization
   Socioeconomic Influences

POLITICAL ISSUES 480
RT Elections
   Legislation
   Political Affiliation
   Political Influences
   Political Power
   Voting

Politicalization
USE POLITICAL SOCIALIZATION

POLITICAL POWER 230
UF Political Pressures
RT Black Power
      Imperialism
      Political Issues
      Power Structure
      Refugees

Political Pressures
USE POLITICAL POWER

Political Reform
USE SOCIAL ACTION

Political Refugees
USE REFUGEES

POLITICAL SCIENCE 480
NT American Government (Course)
      Civics
      Elections
      Foreign Policy
      Foreign Relations
BT Social Sciences
      Social Studies
RT Activism
      Area Studies
      Authoritarianism
      Communism
      Constitutional History
      Military Science
      Political Socialization
      Public Administration Education
      Public Affairs Education

POLITICAL SOCIALIZATION 230
SN Process by which political norms are
      transmitted through various social
      agents, e.g., school, parents, peer group,
      mass media, etc.
UF Politicalization
BT Socialization
RT Political Affiliation
      Political Attitudes
      Political Influences
      Political Science
      Social Attitudes
      Social Change
      Social Influences

POLLUTION 250
RT Air Pollution Control
      Chimneys
      Diseases
      Ecological Factors
      Environment
      Environmental Education
      Herbicides
      Human Engineering
      Pesticides
      Physical Environment
      Sanitation Improvement
      Thermal Environment
      Water Pollution Control

POLYGRAPHS 170
BT Measurement Instruments
RT Instrumentation

POMO 300
BT American Indian Languages

Population Changes
USE POPULATION TRENDS

POPULATION DISTRIBUTION 120
NT Rural Population
      Urban Population
BT Demography
RT Community Size
      Incidence
      Population Growth
      Population Trends
      Relocation

Population Factors
USE POPULATION TRENDS

POPULATION GROWTH 120
BT Demography
      Social Influences
RT Community Size
      Population Distribution
      Population Trends
      Rural Population
      Urbanization
      Urban Population

Population Minorities
USE MINORITY GROUPS

Population Movement
USE POPULATION TRENDS

Population Shifts
USE POPULATION TRENDS

POPULATION TRENDS 120
UF Population Changes
      Population Factors
      Population Movement
      Population Shifts
NT Negro Population Trends
BT Demography
RT Family Planning
      Land Settlement
      Occupational Mobility
      Overpopulation
      Population Distribution
      Population Growth
      Relocation
      Residential Patterns
      Rural Population
      Urban Population

PORTUGUESE 300
BT Romance Languages

POSITIVE REINFORCEMENT 310
BT Reinforcement
RT Motivation
    Negative Reinforcement
    Self Reward
    Social Reinforcement

Post Coordinate Indexes
USE COORDINATE INDEXES

POST DOCTORAL EDUCATION 140
BT Higher Education
RT Institute Type Courses
    Research
    Seminars
    Symposia

Post High School Education
USE POST SECONDARY EDUCATION

POST HIGH SCHOOL GUIDANCE 090
BT Guidance
RT College Admission
    College Preparation
    High School Graduates
    High Schools
    Occupational Information

POST SECONDARY EDUCATION 140
SN Education beyond grade 12 and less
    than the baccalaureate level
UF Post High School Education
    Post Secondary Instructional Level
BT Education
RT Associate Degrees
    Community Colleges
    Junior Colleges
    Junior College Students
    Technical Education
    Technical Institutes
    Vocational Education
    Vocational Schools

Post Secondary Instructional Level
USE POST SECONDARY EDUCATION

Post Tensioned Concrete
USE PRESTRESSED CONCRETE

POST TESTING 190
BT Testing

Posture Development
USE HUMAN POSTURE

Posture Patterns
USE HUMAN POSTURE

Pot (Drug)
USE MARIHUANA

POTENTIAL DROPOUTS 380
BT Dropouts
RT Dropout Identification

POTENTIOMETERS (INSTRUMENTS) 170
BT Measurement Instruments
RT Electricity

Poverty
USE ECONOMIC DISADVANTAGEMENT

Poverty Areas
USE DEPRESSED AREAS (GEOGRAPHIC)

Poverty Conditions
USE ECONOMIC DISADVANTAGEMENT

Poverty Factors
USE ECONOMIC FACTORS

Poverty Pockets
USE DEPRESSED AREAS (GEOGRAPHIC)

POVERTY PROGRAMS 490
UF Anti Poverty Programs
BT Programs
RT Economic Disadvantagement
    Low Income

Poverty Stricken
USE ECONOMICALLY DISADVANTAGED

POWER MECHANICS 400
RT Auto Mechanics
    Fluid Power Education
    Industrial Arts

POWER STRUCTURE 490
UF Authority Structure
BT Organization
RT Black Power
    Culture
    Informal Organization
    Political Power

Power Transfer Systems
USE KINETICS

PRACTICAL ARTS 030
RT Homemaking Skills
    Industrial Arts
    Practical Nursing

PRACTICAL MATHEMATICS 340
BT Mathematics

PRACTICAL NURSES 380
UF Vocational Nurses
BT Nurses
RT Companions (Occupation)
    Nonprofessional Personnel
    Practical Nursing

PRACTICAL NURSING 350
BT Nursing
RT Medical Services
    Nursing Homes
    Practical Arts
    Practical Nurses

Practical Skills
USE INDUSTRIAL ARTS

Practice Teaching
USE STUDENT TEACHING

PRACTICUMS 270
RT Clinical Experience
Counselor Training
Field Experience Programs
Internship Programs
Laboratory Training
Microcounseling
Practicum Supervision
Student Teaching
Teacher Education

PRACTICUM SUPERVISION 020
BT Supervision
RT Clinical Experience
Clinical Professors
College Supervisors
Cooperating Teachers
Field Experience Programs
Internship Programs
Laboratory Training
Practicums
Student Teaching

Preachers
USE CLERGYMEN

Precollege Level
USE HIGH SCHOOLS

PREDICTION 190
NT Grade Prediction
RT Expectancy Tables
Expectation
Predictive Ability (Testing)
Predictive Measurement
Predictive Validity
Probability
Risk
Testing

PREDICTIVE ABILITY (TESTING) 190
BT Ability
RT Grade Prediction
Prediction
Prognostic Tests
Testing

PREDICTIVE MEASUREMENT 190
BT Measurement
RT Grade Prediction
Prediction
Probability Theory
Sampling
Statistics

PREDICTIVE VALIDITY 190
BT Validity
RT Expectation
Prediction
Testing

PREFABRICATION 210
RT Adhesives
Air Structures
Architectural Elements
Building Design
Building Materials
Buildings
Component Building Systems
Construction (Process)
Construction Costs
Construction Industry
Construction Needs
Masonry
Movable Partitions
Prestressed Concrete
School Construction
Structural Building Systems

PREGNANCY 070
UF Cyesis
Gestation
RT Anomalies
Biology
Contraception
Illegitimate Births
Premature Infants
Prenatal Influences
Rh Factors

Prejudice
USE BIAS

Prejudice (Social)
USE SOCIAL DISCRIMINATION

Prekindergarten
USE PRESCHOOL EDUCATION

Prekindergarten Classes
USE PRESCHOOL EDUCATION

Prekindergarten Programs
USE PRESCHOOL PROGRAMS

Prekindergarten Teachers
USE PRESCHOOL TEACHERS

Premature Birth
USE PREMATURE INFANTS

PREMATURE INFANTS 380
UF Premature Birth
BT Infants
RT Infancy
Pregnancy

PREMIUM PAY 220
BT Income
RT Overtime
Payroll Records
Salaries
Wages
Wage Statements

PRENATAL INFLUENCES 070
RT Anomalies
    Biological Influences
    Diseases
    Drug Abuse
    Environmental Influences
    Genetics
    Health
    Heredity
    Physical Development
    Pregnancy
    Rh Factors
    Rubella

PREREADING EXPERIENCE 200
BT Experience
RT Beginning Reading

PRESCHOOL CHILDREN 380
UF Preschoolers
BT Children
RT Child Development Centers
    Preschool Clinics
    Preschool Education
    Preschool Evaluation

PRESCHOOL CLINICS 210
BT Clinics
RT Preschool Children
    Preschool Education
    Preschool Programs
    Psychoeducational Clinics

PRESCHOOL CURRICULUM 110
BT Curriculum
RT Preschool Education

PRESCHOOL EDUCATION 140
UF Prekindergarten
    Prekindergarten Classes
BT Education
RT Child Development Centers
    Early Childhood Education
    Nursery Schools
    Preschool Children
    Preschool Clinics
    Preschool Curriculum
    Preschool Evaluation
    Preschool Learning
    Preschool Programs
    Preschool Teachers
    Preschool Tests
    Preschool Workshops

Preschoolers
USE PRESCHOOL CHILDREN

PRESCHOOL EVALUATION 180
BT Evaluation
RT Preschool Children
    Preschool Education

Preschool Experience
USE EARLY EXPERIENCE

PRESCHOOL LEARNING 310
BT Learning
RT Cognitive Development
    Preschool Education

PRESCHOOL PROGRAMS 410
UF Prekindergarten Programs
BT Educational Programs
RT Early Childhood Education
    Preschool Clinics
    Preschool Education

PRESCHOOL TEACHERS 380
UF Kindergarten Teachers
    Prekindergarten Teachers
BT Teachers
RT Preschool Education

PRESCHOOL TESTS 520
BT Tests
RT Preschool Education

PRESCHOOL WORKSHOPS 270
BT Workshops
RT Preschool Education

Prescriptive Teaching
USE DIAGNOSTIC TEACHING

Presentation Methods
USE TEACHING METHODS

PRESERVATION 510
SN Prevention of deterioration of stored
    commodities, structural members,
    materials, etc.
RT Cleaning
    Fire Protection
    Maintenance
    Obsolescence
    Prevention
    Repair

PRESERVICE EDUCATION 140
UF Preservice Teacher Education
BT Teacher Education
RT Affiliated Schools
    Cooperating Teachers
    Student Teachers
    Student Teaching
    Subprofessionals
    Teacher Education Curriculum
    Teacher Educator Education

Preservice Teacher Education
USE PRESERVICE EDUCATION

Preservice Teaching Experience
USE TEACHING EXPERIENCE

PRESIDENTS 380
BT Chief Administrators
RT Administration
    Administrator Responsibility
    Administrator Role

Press
USE NEWS MEDIA

PRESS OPINION 040
RT Attitudes
News Media
Public Opinion

PRESSURE 400
UF Absolute Pressure
Ambient Pressure
BT Physics
RT Environment
Force
Scientific Concepts
Weight

PRESTRESSED CONCRETE 210
UF Post Tensioned Concrete
Pretensioned Concrete
BT Building Materials
RT Architectural Elements
Cement Industry
Component Building Systems
Masonry
Prefabrication
Structural Building Systems

Prestudent Teaching Laboratories
USE TRAINING LABORATORIES

PRETECHNOLOGY PROGRAMS 110
SN Special curriculum to prepare individuals
for technical training
BT Science Programs
RT Secondary Education
Technical Education
Vocational Education

Pretensioned Concrete
USE PRESTRESSED CONCRETE

PRETESTING 180
BT Testing
RT Pretests
Test Construction
Tests

PRETESTS 520
BT Tests
RT Pretesting

PREVENTION 510
UF Preventive Measures
NT Accident Prevention
Delinquency Prevention
RT Fire Protection
Preservation
Preventive Medicine

Preventive Measures
USE PREVENTION

PREVENTIVE MEDICINE 250
BT Medicine
RT Community Health
Immunization Programs
Medical Services
Prevention

PREVOCATIONAL EDUCATION 140
UF Prevocational Training
BT Vocational Education
RT Educable Mentally Handicapped
Technical Education

Prevocational Training
USE PREVOCATIONAL EDUCATION

PRIESTS 380
RT Catholics
Churches
Church Workers
Clergymen
Religion

PRIMARY EDUCATION 140
BT Elementary Education
RT Nongraded Primary System
Primary Grades

PRIMARY GRADES 280
BT Instructional Program Divisions
RT Early Childhood Education
Middle Schools
Primary Education

PRIMATOLOGY 070
BT Zoology
RT Anthropology
Biology

PRIME NUMBERS 340
BT Integers

PRINCIPALS 380
UF School Principals
BT Chief Administrators

PRINTING 350
BT Graphic Arts
RT Copyrights
Industrial Arts
Paper (Material)
Photocomposition
Publishing Industry
Signs
Typewriting
Written Language

Printscript
USE MANUSCRIPT WRITING
(HANDLETTERING)

Prison Education
USE CORRECTIONAL EDUCATION

PRISONERS 380
UF Inmates
     Jail Inmates
BT Institutionalized (Persons)
RT Correctional Education
     Correctional Rehabilitation
     Corrective Institutions
     Criminals
     Criminology
     Delinquency
     Delinquents

Prison Libraries
USE INSTITUTION LIBRARIES

PRIVATE AGENCIES 370
UF Nonpublic Agencies
BT Agencies
RT Agency Role
     Voluntary Agencies

PRIVATE COLLEGES 470
BT Colleges
RT Church Related Colleges
     Governance
     Higher Education
     Private Financial Support
     Private Schools
     Undergraduate Study
     Universities

PRIVATE FINANCIAL SUPPORT 220
UF Philanthropy
NT Fellowships
     Scholarships
BT Financial Support
RT Capital
     Costs
     Educational Economics
     Foundation Programs
     Incentive Grants
     Private Colleges
     Proprietary Schools

PRIVATE SCHOOLS 470
NT Parochial Schools
     Proprietary Schools
BT Schools
RT Correspondence Schools
     Private Colleges
     Public School Teachers

Proactive Inhibition
USE INHIBITION

PROBABILITY 340
RT Expectancy Tables
     Expectation
     Prediction
     Probability Theory
     Risk
     Statistical Analysis
     Tests Of Significance

PROBABILITY THEORY 340
BT Theories
RT Expectation
     Game Theory
     Mathematical Concepts
     Predictive Measurement
     Probability
     Sampling
     Statistical Analysis

PROBATIONARY PERIOD 020
SN Period in which a person must prove his
     ability to fulfill certain conditions as to
     achievement, behavior, or job
     assignment
UF Probationary Teacher
RT Ability Identification
     Academic Probation
     Beginning Teachers
     Behavior Development
     Behavior Standards
     Contracts
     Correctional Rehabilitation
     Delinquent Rehabilitation
     Employee Responsibility
     Employer Employee Relationship
     Student School Relationship
     Teacher Employment
     Teacher Persistence
     Teacher Promotion
     Tenure

Probationary Teacher
USE PROBATIONARY PERIOD

PROBATION OFFICERS 380
RT Crime
     Delinquents
     Rehabilitation
     Social Workers

PROBLEM CHILDREN 380
BT Children
RT Behavior Problems
     Problems

PROBLEMS 490
NT Adjustment Problems
     Administrative Problems
     Behavior Problems
     City Problems
     Communication Problems
     Community Problems
     Curriculum Problems
     Discipline Problems
     Dropout Problems
     Educational Problems
     Emotional Problems
     Employment Problems
     Family Problems
     Financial Problems
     Interpersonal Problems
     Labor Problems
     Legal Problems

Migrant Problems
Personality Problems
Programing Problems
Research Problems
Social Problems
Special Health Problems
Student Problems
Suburban Problems
Testing Problems
Welfare Problems
World Problems
Youth Problems
RT Complexity Level
Parental Grievances
Problem Children
Problem Solving

PROBLEM SETS 520
RT Problem Solving
Testing

PROBLEM SOLVING 310
BT Productive Thinking
Teaching Techniques
Thought Processes
RT Conflict Resolution
Convergent Thinking
Critical Incidents Method
Decision Making
Decision Making Skills
Divergent Thinking
Game Theory
Information Seeking
Management Games
Management Systems
Problems
Problem Sets
Risk
Scientific Attitudes
Scientific Methodology

Procedures
USE TEACHING PROCEDURES

Processed Foods Inspectors
USE FOOD AND DRUG INSPECTORS

PROCTORING 020
RT Supervision
Testing

PRODUCER SERVICES 460
SN Business, professional, and government services provided to the business community rather than the individual consumer, including maintenance, administrative, policy making, regulatory, financial, etc.
BT Services
RT Business
Government (Administrative Body)
Industry
Institutions
Service Occupations
Service Workers

Product Information
USE MERCHANDISE INFORMATION

Production Machine Operators
USE MACHINE TOOL OPERATORS

PRODUCTION TECHNICIANS 380
BT Subprofessionals
RT Assembly (Manufacturing)
Engineering Technicians
Industrial Personnel
Manufacturing
Manufacturing Industry
Technical Education
Technical Occupations
Trade And Industrial Education

PRODUCTION TECHNIQUES 510
NT Sound Effects
Television Lighting
BT Techniques
RT Film Study
Numerical Control
Television
Theater Arts

PRODUCTIVE LIVING 490
SN A pattern of living, including work and leisure, which makes possible progress in human growth, capabilities, and knowledge
RT Social Environment
Social Values

PRODUCTIVE THINKING 310
NT Problem Solving
BT Thought Processes
RT Abstract Reasoning
Cognitive Ability
Creative Thinking
Critical Thinking
Decision Making
Divergent Thinking
Evaluative Thinking
Logic
Logical Thinking
Productivity

PRODUCTIVITY 010
RT Ability
Achievement
Developed Nations
Economics
Educational Economics
Human Capital
Interest
Investment
Productive Thinking

Product Labels
USE MERCHANDISE INFORMATION

Product Literature
USE MERCHANDISE INFORMATION

PROFESSIONAL ASSOCIATIONS 370
NT Dental Associations
    Library Associations
    Medical Associations
    Teacher Associations
RT National Organizations

PROFESSIONAL CONTINUING EDUCATION
140
BT Adult Education
RT Alumni Education
    Management Development
    Professional Education
    Refresher Courses
    Womens Education

PROFESSIONAL EDUCATION 140
NT Architectural Education
    Medical Education
    Theological Education
BT Education
RT Counselor Educators
    Dental Schools
    Graduate Study
    Land Grant Universities
    Library Education
    Library Schools
    Medical Schools
    Medical Students
    Professional Continuing Education
    Professional Occupations
    Professional Personnel
    Professional Training
    Public Administration Education
    Research Apprenticeships
    Sabbatical Leaves
    State Licensing Boards
    Urban Universities

Professional Laboratory Experience
USE TEACHER EXPERIENCE

Professional Negotiation
USE COLLECTIVE NEGOTIATION

PROFESSIONAL OCCUPATIONS 350
BT Occupations
RT Administrative Personnel
    Anesthesiology
    Architects
    Dentists
    Engineers
    Hospital Personnel
    Lawyers
    Librarians
    Mathematicians
    Nurses
    Pharmacists
    Physicians
    Professional Education
    Professional Personnel
    Professors
    Psychiatrists

    Scientific Personnel
    Teachers

PROFESSIONAL PERSONNEL 380
NT Architects
    Audiologists
    Clergymen
    Dentists
    Designers
    Food And Drug Inspectors
    Lawyers
    Librarians
    Pharmacists
    Physicians
    Psychologists
    Systems Analysts
    Teachers
BT Personnel
RT Acting
    Administrative Personnel
    Employees
    Nonprofessional Personnel
    Nurses
    Personnel Needs
    Professional Education
    Professional Occupations
    Professional Recognition
    Professional Training
    Pupil Personnel Workers

PROFESSIONAL RECOGNITION 150
UF Professional Status
BT Recognition
RT Educational Benefits
    Motivation
    Peer Groups
    Professional Personnel
    Rewards
    Social Values
    Status
    Status Need
    Teacher Militancy
    Teacher Morale
    Teacher Welfare

PROFESSIONAL SERVICES 020
BT Services
RT Child Development Specialists
    Consultants
    Exceptional Child Services
    Intermediate Administrative Units
    Interprofessional Relationship
    Optometrists
    Referral

Professional Staff
USE INSTRUCTIONAL STAFF

Professional Standards
USE STANDARDS

Professional Status
USE PROFESSIONAL RECOGNITION

PROFESSIONAL TRAINING 270
SN   Special instruction for those engaged in professions or high-level occupations
BT   Training
RT   Aviation Vocabulary
    Banking Vocabulary
    Business Administration
    Inservice Courses
    Inservice Education
    Inservice Teacher Education
    International Trade Vocabulary
    Management Development
    Medical Vocabulary
    Professional Education
    Professional Personnel

PROFESSORS 380
UF   Undergraduate Professors
NT   Clinical Professors
    Graduate Professors
    Women Professors
BT   Teachers
RT   Academic Rank (Professional)
    College Faculty
    College Teachers
    Counselor Educators
    Higher Education
    Professional Occupations
    Teacher Educators

Proficiency Examinations
USE EQUIVALENCY TESTS

PROFILE EVALUATION 180
BT   Evaluation
RT   Program Costs

Prognoses
USE PROGNOSTIC TESTS

PROGNOSTIC TESTS 520
UF   Prognoses
BT   Tests
RT   Diagnostic Tests
    Educational Testing
    Predictive Ability (Testing)
    Visual Measures

PROGRAM ADMINISTRATION 020
BT   Administration
RT   Articulation (Program)
    Program Coordination
    Program Development
    Program Evaluation
    Program Improvement
    Program Planning
    Programs

PROGRAM ATTITUDES 040
SN   Attitudes of persons toward programs or courses of study
BT   Attitudes
RT   Class Attitudes

PROGRAM BUDGETING 220
SN   Process that structures fiscal information to help decision makers relate activities to goals
BT   Budgeting
RT   Cost Effectiveness
    Educational Finance
    Program Costs

Program Construction
USE PROGRAM DEVELOPMENT

PROGRAM CONTENT 110
SN   Activities or subject matter of an educational program
RT   Adult Education Programs
    Compensatory Education Programs
    Course Content
    Educational Programs

PROGRAM COORDINATION 020
BT   Coordination
RT   Articulation (Program)
    Educational Coordination
    Instructor Coordinators
    Program Administration
    Programs

PROGRAM COSTS 220
BT   Costs
RT   Cost Effectiveness
    Profile Evaluation
    Program Budgeting
    Program Evaluation
    Program Planning
    Programs
    Unit Costs

PROGRAM DESCRIPTIONS 020
UF   Descriptive Reports
RT   Catalogs
    Program Guides
    Program Proposals
    Programs
    Reports

PROGRAM DESIGN 020
BT   Design
RT   Program Development
    Program Planning
    Systems Analysts

PROGRAM DEVELOPMENT 130
UF   Program Construction
BT   Development
RT   Articulation (Program)
    Educational Development
    Program Administration
    Program Design
    Program Length
    Program Planning
    Programs

PROGRAMED INSTRUCTION 270
UF Programed Learning
    Programed Self Instruction
NT Programed Tutoring
BT Instruction
RT Autoinstructional Aids
    Branching
    Computer Assisted Instruction
    Computer Oriented Programs
    Computers
    Constructed Response
    Educational Technology
    Feedback
    Intermode Differences
    Language Laboratories
    Multimedia Instruction
    Optional Branching
    Pacing
    Programed Materials
    Programed Texts
    Programing
    Prompting
    Redundancy
    Response Mode
    Sequential Programs
    Teaching Machines

Programed Learning
USE PROGRAMED INSTRUCTION

Programed Learning Material
USE PROGRAMED MATERIALS

PROGRAMED MATERIALS 050
UF Programed Learning Material
NT Programed Texts
    Programed Units
BT Instructional Materials
RT Autoinstructional Aids
    Computer Assisted Instruction
    Instructional Technology
    Optional Branching
    Programed Instruction
    Programed Tutoring
    Programing
    Science Materials

Programed Self Instruction
USE PROGRAMED INSTRUCTION

PROGRAMED TEXTS 050
UF Taped Texts
NT Horizontal Texts
    Vertical Texts
BT Programed Materials
    Textbooks
RT Optional Branching
    Programed Instruction
    Programers
    Programing

PROGRAMED TUTORING 270
BT Programed Instruction
RT Lay Teachers
    Optional Branching
    Programed Materials
    Reinforcement
    Remedial Instruction
    Teacher Aides
    Tutoring

PROGRAMED UNITS 110
BT Programed Materials
    Units Of Study (Subject Fields)
RT Programing
    Unit Plan

PROGRAM EFFECTIVENESS 180
RT Cost Effectiveness
    Educational Research
    Methods Research
    Programs
    Quality Control
    Relevance (Education)

PROGRAMERS 380
RT Computer Programs
    Instructional Materials
    Instructional Programs
    Instructional Technology
    Programed Texts
    Programing
    Programing Languages
    Systems Analysts

PROGRAM EVALUATION 180
BT Evaluation
RT Cost Effectiveness
    Course Evaluation
    Critical Path Method
    Curriculum Evaluation
    Faculty Evaluation
    Program Administration
    Program Costs
    Program Improvement
    Programs
    School Surveys

PROGRAM GUIDES 020
BT Guides
RT Program Descriptions
    Program Planning
    Programs

PROGRAM IMPROVEMENT 020
BT Improvement
RT Action Research
    Articulation (Program)
    Program Administration
    Program Evaluation
    Programs

PROGRAMING 020
UF Computer Programing
Programing Techniques
NT Architectural Programing
Linear Programing
Multichannel Programing
RT Computer Assisted Instruction
Computer Science
Computer Science Education
Data Processing
Electronic Data Processing
Optional Branching
Programed Instruction
Programed Materials
Programed Texts
Programed Units
Programers
Programing Languages
Programing Problems
Program Planning

PROGRAMING LANGUAGES 300
UF Computer Languages
BT Language
RT Computational Linguistics
Computer Programs
Computer Science
Electronic Data Processing
Information Processing
Information Retrieval
Information Storage
Programers
Programing

PROGRAMING PROBLEMS 080
BT Problems
RT Programing

Programing Techniques
USE PROGRAMING

PROGRAM LENGTH 110
SN Length or duration of an educational
program
RT Program Development
Program Planning
Scheduling
Time Factors (Learning)
Viewing Time

PROGRAM PLANNING 020
BT Planning
RT Articulation (Program)
Cost Effectiveness
Program Administration
Program Costs
Program Design
Program Development
Program Guides
Programing
Program Length
Program Proposals
Programs

Speeches
Viewing Time

PROGRAM PROPOSALS 020
RT Program Descriptions
Program Planning
Research Projects
Research Proposals

PROGRAMS 410
NT Accelerated Programs
Adult Programs
Advanced Programs
After School Programs
Anti Segregation Programs
Assembly Programs
Athletic Programs
Audiovisual Programs
Bracero Programs
Breakfast Programs
Church Programs
City Wide Programs
College Programs
Community Programs
Comprehensive Programs
Computer Programs
Construction Programs
Consultation Programs
Cooperative Programs
Counseling Instructional Programs
Counseling Programs
Day Camp Programs
Day Care Programs
Day Programs
Daytime Programs
Demonstration Programs
Developmental Programs
Discussion Programs
Doctoral Programs
Dropout Programs
Educational Programs
Emergency Programs
Employment Programs
English Programs
Enrichment Programs
Evening Programs
Exchange Programs
Experimental Programs
Family Programs
Federal Programs
Feeder Programs
Foundation Programs
Guidance Programs
Health Programs
Home Programs
Human Relations Programs
Improvement Programs
Individualized Programs
Inplant Programs
Inservice Programs
Instructional Programs
Insurance Programs
Intercultural Programs

Project Proposals
USE PROJECT APPLICATIONS

PROJECTS 410
NT Demonstration Projects
Family Projects
Legal Aid Projects
Migrant Worker Projects
Pilot Projects
Research Projects
Science Course Improvement Project
Science Projects
Student Projects
RT Project Applications

Project Schools
USE EXPERIMENTAL SCHOOLS

PROJECT TRAINING METHODS 270
SN Programs combining classroom
instruction or vocational instruction with
supervised and coordinated laboratory
activities
UF Project Method
Project Plan
BT Educational Methods
RT Cooperative Education
Learning Laboratories
Simulated Environment
Student Projects
Training Laboratories
Vocational Education

PROMOTION (OCCUPATIONAL) 150
UF Advancement
NT Faculty Promotion
RT Career Change
Employment Level
Employment Opportunities
Employment Qualifications
Job Development
Job Skills
Manpower Needs
Occupational Aspiration
Occupational Mobility

Promotion (Publicize)
USE PUBLICIZE

PROMPTING 270
UF Cueing
RT Cues
Dramatics
Programed Instruction

Prompts
USE CUES

Pronominals
USE PRONOUNS

PRONOUNS 290
UF Pronominals
BT Form Classes (Languages)
RT Language Patterns
Morphology (Languages)
Phrase Structure
Sentence Structure
Syntax

PRONUNCIATION 290
RT Child Language
Diacritical Marking
Diction
Pronunciation Instruction
Speech
Word Lists

PRONUNCIATION INSTRUCTION 290
BT Speech Instruction
RT Pronunciation

PROPAGANDA 420
RT Public Opinion

PROPERTY ACCOUNTING 220
UF Property Control
Property Control Systems
BT Accounting
RT Estate Planning
Facility Inventory
Trusts (Financial)
Wills

PROPERTY APPRAISAL 220
UF Real Estate Appraisal
BT Evaluation
RT Assessed Valuation
Building Obsolescence
Estate Planning
Insurance Programs
Real Estate
Taxes
Trusts (Financial)
Wills

Property Control
USE PROPERTY ACCOUNTING

Property Control Systems
USE PROPERTY ACCOUNTING

Property Inventory
USE FACILITY INVENTORY

Proportion (Mathematics)
USE RATIOS (MATHEMATICS)

PROPRIETARY SCHOOLS 470
SN Private schools conducted for profit
UF Specialty Schools
BT Private Schools
RT Certification
Correspondence Schools
Educational Finance
Private Financial Support
Student Costs

Propulsion Development Technicians
USE MECHANICAL DESIGN TECHNICIANS

PROSE 260
BT Literature
RT Allegory
    Ambiguity
    Antithesis
    Aristotelian Criticism
    Baroque Literature
    Biblical Literature
    Characterization (Literature)
    Chronicles
    Comedy
    Connected Discourse
    Czech Literature
    Descriptive Writing
    Diaries
    Didacticism
    Drama
    Dramatic Unities
    English Neoclassic Literary Period
    Existentialism
    Expository Writing
    Expressionism
    Fifteenth Century Literature
    Figurative Language
    Folk Drama
    French Literature
    German Literature
    Humanism
    Humor
    Imagery
    Impressionistic Criticism
    Irony
    Italian Literature
    Language Rhythm
    Literary Conventions
    Literary Influences
    Literary Perspective
    Literary Styles
    Local Color Writing
    Medieval Literature
    Metaphors
    Mythic Criticism
    Narration
    Naturalism
    Nineteenth Century Literature
    Novels
    Parallelism (Literary)
    Parody
    Pastoral Literature
    Platonism
    Polish Literature
    Proverbs
    Realism
    Renaissance Literature
    Romanticism
    Russian Literature
    Satire
    Seventeenth Century Literature
    Short Stories
    Sixteenth Century Literature
    Sociological Novels
    Spanish American Literature
    Spanish Literature
    Surrealism
    Symbolism
    Symbols (Literary)
    Tales
    Theoretical Criticism
    Tragedy
    Writing

Prosody
USE VERSIFICATION

PROSTHESES 250
NT Cosmetic Prostheses
RT Amputees
    Physically Handicapped
    Sensory Aids

PROTESTANTS 380
NT Amish
    Puritans
BT Religious Cultural Groups

PROTOCOL MATERIALS 050
SN Audio and video recordings of behavior
    which the preservice and inservice
    teacher education student can observe
    and analyze
UF Behavioral Situation Films
    Teacher Training Films
BT Audiovisual Aids
RT Audiovisual Instruction
    Behavior
    Behavioral Objectives
    Instructional Films
    Instructional Materials
    Laboratory Training
    Microteaching
    Sensitivity Training
    Teacher Behavior
    Teacher Education
    Video Tape Recordings

PROVERBS 260
UF Adages
RT Cultural Context
    Expressive Language
    Figurative Language
    Folk Culture
    Idioms
    Literature
    Prose

Provincial Government
USE STATE GOVERNMENT

Proximity
USE DISTANCE

PSYCHIATRIC AIDES 380
BT Health Personnel
RT Health Occupations
    Mental Illness
    Nurses Aides
    Nursing
    Psychiatric Hospitals

PSYCHIATRIC HOSPITALS 210
BT Hospitals
RT Health Services
    Institution Libraries
    Mental Health
    Mental Health Clinics
    Mental Illness
    Psychiatric Aides
    Psychiatrists

PSYCHIATRIC SERVICES 250
BT Medical Services
RT Counseling Services
    Crisis Therapy
    Mental Health
    Mental Health Programs
    Mental Illness
    Psychiatrists
    Psychiatry
    Psychological Services
    Psychotherapy
    Therapy

PSYCHIATRISTS 380
BT Physicians
RT Emotionally Disturbed
    Emotional Maladjustment
    Health Personnel
    Medical Consultants
    Medical Services
    Professional Occupations
    Psychiatric Hospitals
    Psychiatric Services
    Psychiatry

PSYCHIATRY 420
SN Prevention, diagnosis, and therapy of
    emotional illness
UF Neopsychoanalysis
    Psychoanalysis
BT Behavioral Sciences
RT Emotional Maladjustment
    Medical Treatment
    Mental Health
    Mental Illness
    Psychiatric Services
    Psychiatrists
    Psychology
    Psychotherapy
    Therapy

PSYCHOACOUSTICS 420
RT Acoustics
    Audition (Physiology)
    Auditory Discrimination
    Auditory Perception
    Auditory Training
    Auditory Visual Tests
    Aural Stimuli

Psychoanalysis
USE PSYCHIATRY

Psychocatharsis
USE CATHARSIS

Psychoeducational Appraisal
USE PSYCHOEDUCATIONAL PROCESSES

PSYCHOEDUCATIONAL CLINICS 210
SN Concerned primarily with behavior
    problems of school children related to
    the school environment
BT Clinics
RT Clinical Diagnosis
    Diagnostic Tests
    Educational Diagnosis
    Educational Therapy
    Medical Evaluation
    Mental Health Clinics
    Preschool Clinics

Psychoeducational Intervention
USE INTERVENTION

PSYCHOEDUCATIONAL PROCESSES 420
UF Psychoeducational Appraisal
RT Diagnostic Teaching
    Individual Psychology
    Intervention
    Psychological Patterns
    Psychological Services

PSYCHOLINGUISTICS 290
BT Linguistics
RT Child Language
    Connected Discourse
    Idioms
    Language Development
    Linguistic Theory
    Native Speakers
    Nucleation (Language Learning)
    Psychology
    Receptive Language
    Sociolinguistics
    Verbal Operant Conditioning

PSYCHOLOGICAL CHARACTERISTICS 420
RT Adult Characteristics
    Empathy
    Goal Orientation
    Identification (Psychological)
    Individual Characteristics
    Individual Psychology
    Learning Plateaus
    Role Conflict
    Self Congruence

Psychological Conditioning
USE CONDITIONED RESPONSE

Psychological Defects
USE MENTAL ILLNESS

PSYCHOLOGICAL DESIGN NEEDS 500
BT Design Needs
RT Building Design
    Carpeting
    Controlled Environment
    Design Preferences
    Furniture Design
    Grouping (Instructional Purposes)
    Human Engineering
    Interior Design
    Physical Design Needs
    Psychological Needs

PSYCHOLOGICAL EVALUATION 180
BT Evaluation
RT Association Tests
    Educational Diagnosis
    Personality Tests
    Projective Tests
    Psychological Services
    Psychological Testing
    School Psychologists

PSYCHOLOGICAL NEEDS 420
NT Achievement Need
    Affection
    Affiliation Need
    Security
    Status Need
BT Needs
RT Individual Needs
    Individual Psychology
    Need Gratification
    Psychological Design Needs
    Psychological Services
    Sociopsychological Services
    Spatial Relationship

PSYCHOLOGICAL PATTERNS 420
UF Emotional Patterns
NT Anxiety
    Fantasy
    Fear
    Hostility
    Identification (Psychological)
    Immaturity
    Insecurity
    Maladjustment
    Morale
    Rejection
    School Phobia
    Stress Variables
    Student Alienation
    Teacher Alienation
BT Individual Psychology
RT Behavior Patterns
    Catharsis
    Emotional Development

Emotional Experience
Emotional Problems
Inhibition
Psychoeducational Processes
Psychological Services
Psychosomatic Diseases
Role Conflict
Sleep
Teaching Styles

PSYCHOLOGICAL SERVICES 420
BT Human Services
RT Ancillary Services
    Psychiatric Services
    Psychoeducational Processes
    Psychological Evaluation
    Psychological Needs
    Psychological Patterns
    Psychological Studies
    Psychological Testing
    Psychological Tests
    Psychologists
    Psychometrics
    Psychometrists
    Psychotherapy
    School Services

PSYCHOLOGICAL STUDIES 420
BT Research
RT Exceptional Child Research
    Experimental Psychology
    Force Field Analysis
    Psychological Services
    Psychology

PSYCHOLOGICAL TESTING 190
BT Testing
RT Educational Testing
    Psychological Evaluation
    Psychological Services
    Psychological Tests
    Psychology
    School Psychologists
    Stimulus Devices

PSYCHOLOGICAL TESTS 520
NT Association Tests
    Projective Tests
BT Tests
RT Performance Tests
    Personality Tests
    Psychological Services
    Psychological Testing
    Psychometrics
    Psychometrists

PSYCHOLOGISTS 380
NT Psychometrists
    School Psychologists
BT Professional Personnel
RT Psychological Services
    Psychology

PSYCHOLOGY 420
NT   Conditioned Response
     Educational Psychology
     Experimental Psychology
     Individual Psychology
     Social Psychology
BT   Behavioral Sciences
     Social Sciences
RT   Animal Behavior
     Behavior
     Decision Making
     Intervention
     Mental Illness
     Operant Conditioning
     Psychiatry
     Psycholinguistics
     Psychological Studies
     Psychological Testing
     Psychologists
     Psychometrics
     Psychometrists
     Psychopathology
     Psychophysiology
     Psychosomatic Diseases
     Schizophrenia
     Sensory Deprivation
     Verbal Operant Conditioning

Psychology (Individual)
USE INDIVIDUAL PSYCHOLOGY

Psychometrician
USE PSYCHOMETRISTS

PSYCHOMETRICS 180
BT   Measurement
RT   Behavior
     Personality Tests
     Psychological Services
     Psychological Tests
     Psychology
     Psychometrists
     School Psychologists
     Statistical Data

PSYCHOMETRISTS 380
UF   Psychometrician
BT   Psychologists
RT   Behavior
     Psychological Services
     Psychological Tests
     Psychology
     Psychometrics

Psychomotor Behavioral Objectives
USE PSYCHOMOTOR OBJECTIVES

PSYCHOMOTOR OBJECTIVES 060
UF   Psychomotor Behavioral Objectives
BT   Educational Objectives
RT   Affective Objectives
     Behavioral Objectives
     Cognitive Objectives
     Guidance Objectives
     Motor Development

     Psychomotor Skills
     Training Objectives

PSYCHOMOTOR SKILLS 010
UF   Motor Ability
     Motor Planning Techniques
     Motor Skills
NT   Eye Hand Coordination
     Marksmanship
     Object Manipulation
     Serial Ordering
     Sorting Procedures
     Speech
BT   Ability
RT   Basic Skills
     Behavior
     Lateral Dominance
     Memorizing
     Motor Development
     Motor Reactions
     Neurological Organization
     Nonverbal Learning
     Paralinguistics
     Perceptual Motor Coordination
     Psychomotor Objectives
     Skill Analysis
     Symbolic Learning
     Tracking

PSYCHOPATHOLOGY 420
SN   Pathology of mental and emotional
     illness
UF   Abnormal Psychology
RT   Behavior
     Behavior Problems
     Mental Illness
     Pathology
     Personality Problems
     Psychology
     Psychophysiology
     Psychosomatic Diseases
     Suicide

PSYCHOPHYSIOLOGY 420
UF   Physiological Psychology
RT   Figural Aftereffects
     Pathology
     Physiology
     Psychology
     Psychopathology
     Psychosomatic Diseases
     Stimuli

PSYCHOSIS 250
NT   Schizophrenia
BT   Mental Illness
RT   Autism
     Psychotic Children

PSYCHOSOMATIC DISEASES 250
UF Psychosomatic Disorders
    Psychosomatic Illnesses
    Psychosomatics
BT Diseases
RT Health
    Physical Health
    Psychological Patterns
    Psychology
    Psychopathology
    Psychophysiology

Psychosomatic Disorders
USE PSYCHOSOMATIC DISEASES

Psychosomatic Illnesses
USE PSYCHOSOMATIC DISEASES

Psychosomatics
USE PSYCHOSOMATIC DISEASES

PSYCHOTHERAPY 250
NT Bibliotherapy
    Group Therapy
    Play Therapy
    Progressive Relaxation
    Rational Therapy
    Role Playing
    Sociodrama
BT Therapy
RT Adaptation Level Theory
    Catharsis
    Hypnosis
    Individual Psychology
    Psychiatric Services
    Psychiatry
    Psychological Services
    Self Congruence

PSYCHOTIC CHILDREN 380
BT Children
RT Autism
    Psychosis

Public Accommodations
USE PUBLIC FACILITIES

PUBLIC ADMINISTRATION EDUCATION
140
BT Education
RT Administration
    Business Administration
    Government (Administrative Body)
    Governmental Structure
    Political Science
    Professional Education
    Public Affairs Education

PUBLIC AFFAIRS EDUCATION 140
BT Education
RT Citizen Participation
    Citizenship
    Civics
    Community Organizations
    Political Science

Public Administration Education
    Public Opinion

Public Agencies
USE COMMUNITY AGENCIES (PUBLIC)

PUBLICATIONS 080
NT Atlases
    Bibliographies
    Booklists
    Book Reviews
    Books
    Catalogs
    Directories
    Doctoral Theses
    Government Publications
    Historical Reviews
    Masters Theses
    Pamphlets
    Patents
    Reports
    Research Reviews (Publications)
    School Publications
    Serials
    Textbook Publications
    Yearbooks
BT Mass Media
RT Annotated Bibliographies
    Annual Reports
    Authors
    Encyclopedias
    Indexes (Locaters)
    Laboratory Manuals
    Library Materials
    Microforms
    Paper (Material)
    Publishing Industry
    Reading Materials
    Resource Materials
    Technical Reports

Public Demonstrations
USE DEMONSTRATIONS (CIVIL)

Public Documents
USE GOVERNMENT PUBLICATIONS

PUBLIC EDUCATION 140
BT Education
RT Public School Adult Education
    Public Schools
    Public School Systems
    Public School Teachers
    State Boards Of Education

Public Employees
USE GOVERNMENT EMPLOYEES

PUBLIC FACILITIES 210
UF Public Accommodations
NT Integrated Public Facilities
    Playgrounds
    Public Libraries
    Segregated Public Facilities
BT Facilities
RT Equal Facilities

Rail Transportation
Toilet Facilities

PUBLIC HEALTH 250
NT   Community Health
Sanitation
BT   Health
RT   Cleaning
Community Services
Companions (Occupation)
Dishwashing
Pesticides
Public Health Laws

PUBLIC HEALTH LAWS 230
BT   Laws
RT   Public Health

PUBLIC HOUSING 210
BT   Housing
RT   Community Services
Housing Management Aides
Low Rent Housing
Public Housing Residents
Urban Renewal
Welfare

PUBLIC HOUSING RESIDENTS 380
RT   Housing Management Aides
Public Housing

Public Image
USE   PUBLIC OPINION

PUBLICIZE 510
UF   Advertising
Promotion (Publicize)
RT   Commercial Art
Communications
Information Dissemination
Mass Media
Public Relations

PUBLIC LIBRARIES 210
NT   County Libraries
BT   Community Resources
Libraries
Public Facilities
RT   Archives
Branch Libraries
Depository Libraries
Research Libraries

PUBLIC OFFICIALS 380
NT   County Officials
Legislators
RT   City Officials
Government Employees
Immigration Inspectors
State Officials

PUBLIC OPINION 040
UF   Public Image
BT   Opinions
RT   Majority Attitudes
Political Attitudes
Press Opinion
Propaganda
Public Affairs Education
Social Attitudes

PUBLIC POLICY 020
BT   Policy
RT   Language Planning

PUBLIC RELATIONS 020
BT   Relationship
RT   Human Services
Industrial Relations
Publicize
School Community Relationship

PUBLIC SCHOOL ADULT EDUCATION 140
BT   Adult Education
RT   Adult Education Programs
Community Schools
Public Education

PUBLIC SCHOOLS 470
BT   Schools
RT   Public Education
Public School Systems
Public School Teachers
State Schools

Public School Services
USE   SCHOOL SERVICES

PUBLIC SCHOOL SYSTEMS 470
BT   School Systems
RT   County School Systems
Public Education
Public Schools
Public School Teachers

PUBLIC SCHOOL TEACHERS 380
BT   Government Employees
Teachers
RT   Boards Of Education
Elementary School Teachers
Faculty
Negotiation Agreements
Private Schools
Public Education
Public Schools
Public School Systems
Secondary School Teachers

PUBLIC SPEAKING 110
BT   Speaking
RT   Debate
Persuasive Discourse
Speech

Public Stenographers
USE   STENOGRAPHERS

PUBLIC SUPPORT 040
RT   Community Support
    Financial Support

PUBLIC TELEVISION 050
SN   Educational television directed at the
    general public
BT   Educational Television
RT   Instructional Television
    Mass Instruction
    Viewing Time

Public Utilities
USE   UTILITIES

Public Welfare
USE   WELFARE

Public Welfare Assistance
USE   WELFARE AGENCIES

Publishing Houses
USE   PUBLISHING INDUSTRY

PUBLISHING INDUSTRY 370
UF   Book Industry
    Publishing Houses
BT   Industry
RT   Communications
    Copyrights
    Information Dissemination
    Mass Media
    Printing
    Publications
    Reading Materials

PUERTO RICAN CULTURE 100
BT   Latin American Culture
RT   Ethnic Groups
    Foreign Culture
    Puerto Ricans

PUERTO RICANS 380
RT   Ethnic Groups
    Puerto Rican Culture

Pulse Rate
USE   HEART RATE

Punch Presses
USE   MACHINE TOOLS

PUNCTUATION 290
RT   Capitalization (Alphabetic)
    Composition Skills (Literary)
    Sentence Structure
    Spelling
    Writing Skills

Punjabi
USE   PANJABI

Pupil Assignment
USE   STUDENT PLACEMENT

Pupil Attitudes
USE   STUDENT ATTITUDES

Pupil Distribution
USE   STUDENT DISTRIBUTION

PUPILLARY DILATION 070
UF   Iris Reflex
    Pupillary Reflex
    Pupillary Response
RT   Eye Movements
    Eyes
    Response Mode
    Stimulus Behavior

Pupillary Reflex
USE   PUPILLARY DILATION

Pupillary Response
USE   PUPILLARY DILATION

Pupil Personnel Programs
USE   STUDENT PERSONNEL PROGRAMS

PUPIL PERSONNEL SERVICES 090
SN   Supportive, non-instructional services to
    elementary and secondary pupils in a
    school setting
NT   Attendance Services
    Student Placement
BT   School Services
RT   Counseling
    Guidance Counseling
    Guidance Programs
    Guidance Services
    Pupil Personnel Workers
    Social Work
    Student Personnel Services

PUPIL PERSONNEL WORKERS 380
SN   Professional personnel who provide
    supportive, non-instructional services to
    elementary and secondary pupils in a
    school setting
NT   Elementary School Counselors
    School Psychologists
    School Social Workers
    Secondary School Counselors
BT   School Personnel
RT   Counseling
    Guidance Personnel
    Guidance Services
    Health Personnel
    Professional Personnel
    Pupil Personnel Services
    Student Personnel Services

Pupil Placement
USE   STUDENT PLACEMENT

Pupil Redistribution
USE   STUDENT DISTRIBUTION

Pupils
USE   STUDENTS

Pupil School Relationship
USE   STUDENT SCHOOL RELATIONSHIP

Pupil Teacher Interaction
USE STUDENT TEACHER RELATIONSHIP

Pupil Teacher Ratio
USE STUDENT TEACHER RATIO

Pupil Teacher Relationship
USE STUDENT TEACHER RELATIONSHIP

Puppetry
USE THEATER ARTS

Puppet Shows
USE THEATER ARTS

PURCHASING 020
UF Equipment Purchasing
RT Bids
  Consumer Economics
  Consumer Education
  Educational Finance
  Educational Specifications
  Equipment Standards
  Facility Expansion
  Financial Needs
  Library Acquisition
  Performance Specifications
  Specifications

PURITANS 380
BT Protestants
RT Colonial History (United States)
  Religious Cultural Groups
  Seventeenth Century Literature

Pursuit Tracking
USE TRACKING

Pushto
USE PASHTO

Pushtu
USE PASHTO

PUZZLES 520
RT Educational Games
  Games
  Tests
  Toys

PYRAMID ORGANIZATION 020
BT Organization
RT Horizontal Organization
  Vertical Organization

Q SORT 190
UF Q Technique
BT Measurement Techniques
RT Attitudes
  Data Processing
  Factor Analysis
  Opinions
  Personality Assessment
  Questionnaires
  Rating Scales
  Statistical Analysis
  Testing

Q Technique
USE Q SORT

QUADRIPLEGIA 240
UF Tetraplegia
BT Physical Handicaps
RT Orthopedically Handicapped
  Physically Handicapped

QUALIFICATIONS 500
NT Administrator Qualifications
  Counselor Qualifications
  Credentials
  Employment Qualifications
  Supervisor Qualifications
  Teacher Qualifications
RT Background
  Skills

QUALITY CONTROL 180
RT Analysis Of Variance
  Environmental Technicians
  Equipment Evaluation
  Evaluation Methods
  Program Effectiveness
  Statistical Studies

Quality Education
USE EDUCATIONAL QUALITY

Quality Point Ratio
USE GRADE POINT AVERAGE

QUANTUM MECHANICS 400
BT Physics
RT Energy
  Force
  Matter
  Motion
  Nuclear Physics
  Relativity
  Space

QUARTER SYSTEM 020
RT Continuous Progress Plan
  Extended School Year
  School Calendars
  School Organization
  School Planning
  School Schedules
  Semester Division
  Year Round Schools

QUECHUA 300
UF Kechua
BT American Indian Languages

Question Answer Forms
USE QUESTIONNAIRES

QUESTION ANSWER INTERVIEWS 190
BT Interviews

Racial Groups
USE ETHNIC GROUPS

Racial Imbalance
USE RACIAL BALANCE

RACIAL INTEGRATION 430
UF Desegregation
Integration (Racial)
Urban Desegregation
RT Anti Segregation Programs
Biracial Committees
Biracial Government
Civil Rights
Classroom Integration
College Integration
Faculty Integration
Grade A Year Integration
Integrated Public Facilities
Integration Effects
Integration Litigation
Integration Methods
Integration Plans
Integration Readiness
Integration Studies
Negro Leadership
Negro Organizations
Neighborhood Integration
Personnel Integration
Race Relations
Racially Balanced Schools
Racial Segregation
School Integration
Social Integration
Voluntary Integration

Racial Interaction
USE RACE RELATIONS

RACIALLY BALANCED SCHOOLS 470
BT Schools
RT Racial Balance
Racial Integration
Racial Segregation

Racial Prejudice
USE RACIAL DISCRIMINATION

RACIAL RECOGNITION 430
BT Recognition
RT Ethnology
Race

Racial Relations
USE RACE RELATIONS

RACIAL SEGREGATION 430
UF Segregation (Racial)
NT College Segregation
Defacto Segregation
Dejure Segregation
Legal Segregation
School Segregation
Token Integration
RT Anti Segregation Programs
Civil Rights

Race Relations
Racial Balance
Racial Integration
Racially Balanced Schools
Segregated Public Facilities
Segregationist Organizations
Social Discrimination

Racial Self Identification
USE SELF CONCEPT

RACISM 430
RT Black Power
Race
Racial Discrimination

RADAR 170
RT Communications
Electronic Equipment
Electronics
Navigation
Radio
Telecommunication
Tracking

RADIATION 400
SN Process of energy emission
NT Solar Radiation
RT Energy
Laboratory Safety
Lasers
Light
Luminescence
Nuclear Physics
Optics
Physics
Radiation Biology
Radiation Effects
Radiology
Safety

RADIATION BIOLOGY 070
BT Biology
RT Atomic Theory
Botany
Chemistry
Ecology
Genetics
Marine Biology
Medicine
Natural Sciences
Nuclear Physics
Organic Chemistry
Physical Sciences
Physics
Physiology
Radiation
Radiation Effects
Radiology

RADIATION EFFECTS 400
SN Effects on organisms, food, and
    materials of gamma rays, fission
    fragments, or neutrons
RT Laboratory Safety
    Nuclear Physics
    Nuclear Warfare
    Radiation
    Radiation Biology
    Radioisotopes
    Safety

Radiation Therapy Technologists
USE RADIOLOGIC TECHNOLOGISTS

RADIO 050
NT Educational Radio
BT Mass Media
    Telecommunication
RT Acting
    Audiences
    Broadcast Industry
    Journalism
    Navigation
    News Media
    Radar
    Television
    Television Repairmen
    Transistors

RADIOGRAPHERS 380
UF Industrial X Ray Operators
BT Subprofessionals
RT Inspection
    Metallurgical Technicians
    Radiologic Technologists
    Technical Occupations
    Trade And Industrial Education

RADIOISOTOPES 400
RT Atomic Structure
    Atomic Theory
    Biology
    Botany
    Chemistry
    Genetics
    Matter
    Natural Sciences
    Nuclear Physics
    Physics
    Radiation Effects
    Radiology

RADIOLOGIC TECHNOLOGISTS 380
UF Nuclear Medicine Technologists
    Radiation Therapy Technologists
    X Ray Technologists
BT Health Personnel
RT Radiographers

RADIOLOGY 400
RT Physics
    Radiation
    Radiation Biology
    Radioisotopes

Radio Operation
USE RADIO TECHNOLOGY

Radio Repair
USE RADIO TECHNOLOGY

Radio Repairmen
USE TELEVISION REPAIRMEN

RADIO TECHNOLOGY 110
UF Radio Operation
    Radio Repair
BT Technology
RT Educational Radio
    Media Technology

Ragtime Music
USE JAZZ

Railroads
USE RAIL TRANSPORTATION

Railroad Transportation
USE RAIL TRANSPORTATION

RAIL TRANSPORTATION 020
UF Railroads
    Railroad Transportation
    Railways
BT Transportation
RT Marketing
    Public Facilities
    Travel

Railways
USE RAIL TRANSPORTATION

Raised Line Diagrams
USE RAISED LINE DRAWINGS

RAISED LINE DRAWINGS 050
UF Raised Line Diagrams
RT Blind
    Braille
    Tactile Adaptation
    Visually Handicapped

Range (Distance)
USE DISTANCE

Rank Upgrading
USE FACULTY PROMOTION

RAPID READING 440
BT Reading
RT Reading Skills
    Reading Speed

RAPPORT 040
BT Interpersonal Relationship
RT Human Relations
    Social Relations

Rate Test
USE TIMED TESTS

RATING SCALES 180
NT   Behavior Rating Scales
     Interest Scales
RT   Achievement Rating
     Forced Choice Technique
     Grade Equivalent Scales
     Measurement
     Q Sort

RATIONAL NUMBERS 340
NT   Integers
BT   Numbers

RATIONAL THERAPY 420
BT   Psychotherapy
RT   Behavior Development
     Counseling
     Individual Psychology

RATIOS (MATHEMATICS) 340
UF   Proportion (Mathematics)
RT   Mathematical Concepts

RATS 070
RT   Animal Science
     Laboratory Experiments
     Rodenticides

REACTION TIME 420
UF   Response Latency
     Response Time
RT   Motor Reactions
     Perceptual Motor Coordination
     Reactive Behavior
     Response Mode
     Time
     Time Factors (Learning)

REACTIVE BEHAVIOR 060
SN   Behavior primarily determined by the
     external situation
BT   Behavior
RT   Behavior Change
     Behavior Patterns
     Catharsis
     Reaction Time
     Situational Tests

Reactive Inhibition
USE INHIBITION

READABILITY 440
BT   Instructional Materials
RT   Literacy
     Reading Comprehension
     Reading Development
     Reading Instruction
     Reading Interests
     Reading Level
     Reading Research
     Reading Speed
     Sequential Reading Programs
     Vocabulary

READINESS 010
SN   Preparedness to respond or react
NT   Handwriting Readiness
     Integration Readiness
     Learning Readiness
     Readiness (Mental)
     Reading Readiness
RT   Maturation
     Measurement

READINESS (MENTAL) 180
BT   Readiness
RT   Attitudes
     Learning Readiness
     Maturation
     Measurement
     Motivation
     Reading Readiness

READING 440
NT   Applied Reading
     Basic Reading
     Beginning Reading
     Braille
     Content Reading
     Creative Reading
     Developmental Reading
     Directed Reading Activity
     Early Reading
     Elective Reading
     Factual Reading
     Functional Reading
     Group Reading
     Independent Reading
     Individualized Reading
     Individual Reading
     Interpretive Reading
     Lipreading
     Music Reading
     Oral Reading
     Rapid Reading
     Recreational Reading
     Remedial Reading
     Silent Reading
     Speed Reading
     Story Reading
BT   Language Arts
     Literacy
RT   Character Recognition
     Cloze Procedure
     Context Clues
     Diacritical Marking
     Initial Teaching Alphabet
     Inner Speech (Subvocal)
     Pacing
     Pattern Recognition
     Reading Ability
     Reading Achievement
     Reading Assignments
     Reading Centers
     Reading Clinics
     Reading Comprehension
     Reading Consultants

Reading Development
Reading Diagnosis
Reading Difficulty
Reading Failure
Reading Games
Reading Improvement
Reading Instruction
Reading Interests
Reading Level
Reading Materials
Reading Processes
Reading Programs
Reading Readiness
Reading Readiness Tests
Reading Research
Reading Skills
Reading Speed
Reading Tests
Retarded Readers
Sequential Reading Programs
Telegraphic Materials
Vocabulary

READING ABILITY 440
BT   Ability
RT   Cloze Procedure
     Informal Reading Inventory
     Reading
     Reading Achievement
     Reading Comprehension
     Reading Development
     Reading Diagnosis
     Reading Level
     Reading Skills
     Reading Speed

READING ACHIEVEMENT 440
UF   Reading Gain
BT   Achievement
RT   Academic Achievement
     Early Reading
     Reading
     Reading Ability
     Reading Development
     Reading Level
     Reading Skills

READING ASSIGNMENTS 440
BT   Assignments
RT   Reading

READING CENTERS 210
BT   Educational Facilities
RT   Reading
     Remedial Reading

READING CLINICS 210
NT   Remedial Reading Clinics
BT   Clinics
RT   Reading

READING COMPREHENSION 440
BT   Comprehension
     Reading Skills
RT   Cloze Procedure
     Content Reading
     Context Clues
     Factual Reading
     Informal Reading Inventory
     Literary Discrimination
     Readability
     Reading
     Reading Ability
     Reading Development
     Reading Skills
     Word Recognition

READING CONSULTANTS 380
BT   Consultants
RT   Reading

READING DEVELOPMENT 130
NT   Reading Habits
BT   Development
RT   Adult Reading Programs
     Basic Reading
     Directed Reading Activity
     Factual Reading
     Readability
     Reading
     Reading Ability
     Reading Achievement
     Reading Comprehension
     Reading Processes
     Reading Skills
     Reading Speed
     Vocabulary Development

READING DIAGNOSIS 440
BT   Educational Diagnosis
RT   Etiology
     Reading
     Reading Ability
     Reading Tests

READING DIFFICULTY 440
UF   Reading Disability
RT   Dyslexia
     Learning Disabilities
     Reading
     Reading Failure

Reading Disability
USE   READING DIFFICULTY

Reading Enjoyment
USE   LITERATURE APPRECIATION

READING FAILURE 440
BT   Academic Failure
RT   Reading
     Reading Difficulty

Reading Gain
USE   READING ACHIEVEMENT

READING GAMES 510
BT   Educational Games
RT   Reading
      Reading Instruction
      Reading Materials

READING HABITS 440
BT   Reading Development
RT   Habit Formation
      Reading Skills
      Study Habits

READING IMPROVEMENT 440
BT   Improvement
RT   Reading

READING INSTRUCTION 270
UF   Teaching Reading
NT   Basic Reading
      Language Experience Approach
BT   Instruction
RT   Adult Reading Programs
      Braille
      Content Reading
      Directed Reading Activity
      Early Reading
      Experience Charts
      Individualized Reading
      Initial Teaching Alphabet
      Kinesthetic Methods
      Large Type Materials
      Oral Reading
      Phonics
      Readability
      Reading
      Reading Games
      Sight Method
      Silent Reading
      Structural Analysis
      Talking Books

READING INTERESTS 040
BT   Interests
RT   Readability
      Reading
      Recreational Reading

READING LEVEL 440
RT   Readability
      Reading
      Reading Ability
      Reading Achievement

READING MATERIALS 440
NT   Supplementary Reading Materials
BT   Instructional Materials
RT   Basic Reading
      High Interest Low Vocabulary Books
      Informal Reading Inventory
      Large Type Materials
      Paperback Books
      Publications
      Publishing Industry
      Reading
      Reading Games

      Reading Material Selection
      Science Materials
      Sight Method
      Student Developed Materials
      Teacher Developed Materials
      Telegraphic Materials
      Textbooks

READING MATERIAL SELECTION 440
BT   Selection
RT   Instructional Materials
      Library Material Selection
      Reading Materials
      Textbook Selection

READING PROCESSES 310
RT   Basic Reading
      Reading
      Reading Development

READING PROGRAMS 440
NT   Adult Reading Programs
      Sequential Reading Programs
BT   Programs
RT   Basic Reading
      Individualized Reading
      Language Experience Approach
      Reading

Reading Rate
USE   READING SPEED

READING READINESS 180
BT   Readiness
RT   Basic Vocabulary
      Beginning Reading
      Directed Reading Activity
      Readiness (Mental)
      Reading
      Reading Readiness Tests

READING READINESS TESTS 520
BT   Reading Tests
RT   Reading
      Reading Readiness

READING RESEARCH 450
BT   Educational Research
RT   Readability
      Reading

READING SKILLS 010
NT   Critical Reading
      Reading Comprehension
BT   Skills
RT   Cloze Procedure
      Directed Reading Activity
      Eye Movements
      Eye Voice Span
      Factual Reading
      Literary Discrimination
      Oral Reading
      Phonics
      Rapid Reading
      Reading
      Reading Ability

Reading Achievement
Reading Comprehension
Reading Development
Reading Habits
Reading Speed
Sight Method
Silent Reading
Speed Reading
Word Recognition
Word Study Skills

READING SPEED 440
UF Reading Rate
RT Rapid Reading
    Readability
    Reading
    Reading Ability
    Reading Development
    Reading Skills
    Speed Reading

READING TESTS 520
UF Reading Test Scores
NT Informal Reading Inventory
    Reading Readiness Tests
BT Tests
RT Reading
    Reading Diagnosis

Reading Test Scores
USE READING TESTS

Reading Texts
USE TEXTBOOKS

REAL ESTATE 210
RT Landlords
    Land Use
    Property Appraisal
    Real Estate Occupations
    School Location
    Site Selection
    Zoning

Real Estate Appraisal
USE PROPERTY APPRAISAL

REAL ESTATE OCCUPATIONS 350
BT Occupations
RT Buildings
    Housing
    Housing Industry
    Housing Management Aides
    Landlords
    Real Estate

REALIA 050
BT Audiovisual Aids
RT Exhibits

REALISM 260
NT Local Color Writing
BT Literature
RT American Literature
    Art
    Dialogue
    Drama
    English Literature
    Essays
    Fiction
    Literary Analysis
    Literary Criticism
    Literary Genres
    Novels
    Philosophy
    Poetry
    Prose
    Religion
    Short Stories
    Twentieth Century Literature

RECALL (PSYCHOLOGICAL) 310
RT Connected Discourse
    Cues
    Learning
    Learning Processes
    Mediation Theory
    Memorizing
    Memory
    Recognition
    Retention
    Surrealism
    Visualization

Recall Ratio
USE RELEVANCE (INFORMATION RETRIEVAL)

Receptive Communication
USE RECEPTIVE LANGUAGE

RECEPTIVE LANGUAGE 080
UF Receptive Communication
BT Language
RT Communication (Thought Transfer)
    Communication Skills
    Expressive Language
    Psycholinguistics

RECIPROCALS (MATHEMATICS) 340
BT Numbers
RT Mathematical Concepts

RECOGNITION 010
NT Pattern Recognition
    Professional Recognition
    Racial Recognition
    Word Recognition
RT Memory
    Perception
    Recall (Psychological)

RECONSTRUCTION ERA 260
RT American History
    Civil War (United States)
    United States History

Record Clerks
USE FILE CLERKS

Recordings (Phonotape)
USE PHONOTAPE RECORDINGS

RECORDKEEPING 020
RT Bookkeeping
    Business Education
    Business Subjects
    Data Collection
    Information Storage
    Medical Record Technicians
    Records (Forms)
    Reports

RECORDS (FORMS) 020
NT Academic Records
    Case Records
    Confidential Records
    Data Sheets
    Diaries
    Medical Case Histories
    Payroll Records
    Student Records
    Wage Statements
RT Archives
    Farm Accounts
    Microfiche
    Microfilm
    Office Management
    Recordkeeping
    Reports

RECREATION 390
RT Human Services
    Recreational Activities
    Recreational Facilities
    Recreational Programs
    Recreation Finances
    Recreation Legislation
    Wildlife Management

RECREATIONAL ACTIVITIES 390
NT Camping
    Hobbies
    Recreational Reading
BT Activities
RT Athletic Activities
    Athletic Fields
    Cocurricular Activities
    Correctional Education
    Games
    Leisure Time
    Music
    Physical Activities
    Physical Education
    Playground Activities
    Recreation
    Singing
    Swimming
    Tourism
    Travel
    Tumbling

RECREATIONAL FACILITIES 210
NT Community Rooms
    Parks
    Playgrounds
    Swimming Pools
    Zoos
BT Facilities
RT Community Resources
    Field Houses
    Physical Education Facilities
    Recreation
    Recreation Finances
    Student Unions
    Trails
    Windowless Rooms

RECREATIONAL PROGRAMS 390
NT Community Recreation Programs
    Day Camp Programs
    Physical Recreation Programs
    School Recreational Programs
    Social Recreation Programs
    Vacation Programs
    Weekend Programs
BT Programs
RT Camp Counselors
    Community Service Programs
    Exceptional Child Services
    Folk Schools
    Recreation
    Resident Camp Programs
    Summer Programs

RECREATIONAL READING 440
UF Leisure Time Reading
BT Reading
    Recreational Activities
RT Elective Reading
    Reading Interests

RECREATION FINANCES 220
BT Financial Support
RT Recreation
    Recreational Facilities

RECREATION LEGISLATION 230
NT Community Recreation Legislation
    Federal Recreation Legislation
    Local Recreation Legislation
    State Recreation Legislation
BT Legislation
RT Recreation

RECRUITMENT 150
UF Personnel Recruitment
NT Faculty Recruitment
RT Career Opportunities
    Employment Opportunities
    Occupational Guidance
    Personnel
    Personnel Needs
    Personnel Selection
    Salary Differentials
    Selection

Redevelopment Areas
USE URBAN RENEWAL

Reduction In Force
USE JOB LAYOFF

REDUNDANCY 510
RT Programed Instruction
Repetitive Film Showings

REFERENCE BOOKS 320
BT Books
Reference Materials
RT Encyclopedias
Glossaries
Library Reference Services

REFERENCE MATERIALS 320
NT Dictionaries
Encyclopedias
Glossaries
Indexes (Locaters)
Reference Books
Thesauri
Yearbooks
RT Citation Indexes
Directories
Library Collections
Library Materials
Library Reference Services
Permuted Indexes
Research Libraries

References (Bibliographic)
USE BIBLIOGRAPHIC CITATIONS

Reference Work
USE LIBRARY REFERENCE SERVICES

REFERRAL 090
SN One that is referred or the process of
referring to an appropriate agency or
specialist
RT Consultants
Consultation Programs
Professional Services
Specialists

Reformatory Libraries
USE INSTITUTION LIBRARIES

Refractive Errors
USE AMETROPIA

REFRESHER COURSES 270
BT Courses
RT Correspondence Courses
Improvement
Improvement Programs
Inservice Courses
Professional Continuing Education
Remedial Courses
Short Courses

Refresher Training
USE RETRAINING

REFRIGERATION 170
RT Air Conditioning
Air Flow
Refrigeration Mechanics
Temperature

REFRIGERATION MECHANICS 380
UF Air Conditioning Mechanics
BT Service Workers
RT Air Conditioning
Refrigeration
Service Occupations
Trade And Industrial Education

REFUGEES 380
UF Escapees
Exiles
Political Refugees
RT Immigrants
Land Settlement
Migrants
Political Affiliation
Political Attitudes
Political Power
Relocation
Safety
Security

Regents
USE TRUSTEES

REGIONAL COOPERATION 020
RT Interagency Cooperation
Intermediate Administrative Units
Regional Libraries
Regional Programs

REGIONAL DIALECTS 290
SN Special varieties within a language,
defined by the geographical origin of its
speakers
UF Geographical Dialects
BT Dialects
RT American English
Area Studies
Dialect Studies
Ethnic Origins
Geographic Regions
Idioms
Language Classification
Language Usage
Native Speakers
Nonstandard Dialects
Social Dialects
Sociolinguistics
Speech Habits

REGIONAL LABORATORIES 210
BT Laboratories
RT Learning Laboratories
Regional Programs

REGIONAL LIBRARIES 210
UF   District Libraries
BT   Libraries
RT   Branch Libraries
      County Libraries
      Library Cooperation
      Library Networks
      Regional Cooperation
      Regional Programs

REGIONAL PLANNING 020
BT   Planning
RT   City Planning
      Social Planning

REGIONAL PROGRAMS 410
BT   Programs
RT   Regional Cooperation
      Regional Laboratories
      Regional Libraries

REGIONAL SCHOOLS 470
BT   Schools
RT   Boarding Homes
      Consolidated Schools
      Special Education
      Special Schools

Registered Record Librarians
USE   MEDICAL RECORD LIBRARIANS

REGULAR CLASS PLACEMENT 280
SN   Placement of students identified as
      handicapped or gifted in regular classes
BT   Placement
RT   Gifted
      Handicapped Children
      Itinerant Teachers
      Resource Teachers
      Special Education

REHABILITATION 090
NT   Correctional Rehabilitation
      Dropout Rehabilitation
      Student Rehabilitation
      Vocational Rehabilitation
RT   Correctional Education
      Corrective Institutions
      Crisis Therapy
      Educationally Disadvantaged
      Educational Therapy
      Exceptional Child Services
      Human Services
      Mental Health Clinics
      Occupational Therapists
      Occupational Therapy Assistants
      Physical Therapy Aides
      Probation Officers
      Rehabilitation Centers
      Rehabilitation Counseling
      Rehabilitation Programs
      Social Work
      Social Workers
      Therapeutic Environment

      Therapy
      Vocational Training Centers

REHABILITATION CENTERS 210
UF   Halfway Houses
BT   Institutions
RT   Boarding Schools
      Institution Libraries
      Rehabilitation
      Residential Schools
      Therapeutic Environment

REHABILITATION COUNSELING 090
BT   Counseling
RT   Correctional Education
      Physically Handicapped
      Rehabilitation
      Sheltered Workshops
      Vocational Training Centers

REHABILITATION PROGRAMS 490
BT   Programs
RT   Continuation Education
      Correctional Education
      Correctional Rehabilitation
      Delinquent Rehabilitation
      Dropout Rehabilitation
      Rehabilitation
      Sheltered Workshops
      Vocational Training Centers

REINFORCEMENT 310
UF   Learning Reinforcement
      Reinforcement Theory
NT   Negative Reinforcement
      Positive Reinforcement
      Reinforcers
      Rewards
      Social Reinforcement
RT   Discrimination Learning
      Extinction (Psychology)
      Feedback
      Learning Theories
      Mnemonics
      Motivation
      Programed Tutoring
      Teaching Techniques

Reinforcement Theory
USE   REINFORCEMENT

REINFORCERS 310
BT   Reinforcement
RT   Rewards
      Social Reinforcement

REJECTION 420
BT   Psychological Patterns

RELATIONSHIP 490
UF   Compatibility
NT   Board Administrator Relationship
      Community Relations
      Cultural Interrelationships
      Employer Employee Relationship
      Ethnic Relations

Family Relationship
Family School Relationship
Federal State Relationship
Group Relations
Human Relations
Industrial Relations
Interaction
Interfaith Relations
Interpersonal Relationship
Interprofessional Relationship
Peer Relationship
Personal Relationship
Police Community Relationship
Police School Relationship
Public Relations
School Community Relationship
School Industry relationship
Social Relations
Spatial Relationship
State School District Relationship
Student School Relationship
Student Teacher Relationship
Teacher Administrator Relationship
RT Taxonomy
Teacher Alienation

Relative Humidity
USE HUMIDITY

RELATIVITY 400
UF Geometrodynamics
Space Time Continuum
BT Physics
Scientific Concepts
RT Energy
Kinetics
Light
Matter
Motion
Optics
Quantum Mechanics
Space
Time

RELEASED TIME 020
UF Day Release
BT Scheduling
RT Employer Employee Relationship
Industrial Training
Off The Job Training
Religious Education
School Industry Relationship
School Schedules
Time Blocks

RELEVANCE (EDUCATION) 180
UF Curriculum Relevance
Educational Relevance
BT Evaluation
RT Curriculum Development
Educational Development
Educational Improvement
Educational Research
Effective Teaching

Experimental Colleges
Program Effectiveness
Residential Colleges
Student Interests
Student Needs
Student School Relationship

RELEVANCE (INFORMATION RETRIEVAL)
180
UF Information Retrieval Precision
Recall Ratio
Relevance Ratio
BT Evaluation
RT Evaluation Methods
Information Retrieval
Information Systems
Performance
Reliability
Systems Analysis

Relevance Ratio
USE RELEVANCE (INFORMATION RETRIEVAL)

RELIABILITY 180
NT Test Reliability
RT Analysis Of Variance
Expectation
Lesson Observation Criteria
Performance
Performance Factors
Relevance (Information Retrieval)
Statistical Analysis
Statistical Data
Test Results
Validity

Relief Teachers
USE SUBSTITUTE TEACHERS

RELIGION 480
NT Christianity
Judaism
RT Biblical Literature
Churches
Church Programs
Church Role
Church Workers
Clergymen
Humanities
Interfaith Relations
Islamic Culture
Naturalism
Nineteenth Century Literature
Nuns
Priests
Realism
Religious Agencies
Religious Conflict
Religious Cultural Groups
Religious Differences
Religious Discrimination
Religious Education
Religious Factors
Religious Organizations

State Church Separation
Theological Education

RELIGIOUS AGENCIES 370
BT   Agencies
RT   Agency Role
      Religion
      Religious Organizations
      Voluntary Agencies
      Welfare Agencies

RELIGIOUS CONFLICT 480
BT   Religious Factors
RT   Religion
      Religious Cultural Groups
      Religious Discrimination

RELIGIOUS CULTURAL GROUPS 100
UF   Religious Groups
NT   Catholics
      Jews
      Protestants
BT   Groups
RT   Biblical Literature
      Christianity
      Culture
      Judaism
      Non Western Civilization
      Puritans
      Religion
      Religious Conflict
      Religious Organizations

RELIGIOUS DIFFERENCES 480
BT   Religious Factors
RT   Religion

RELIGIOUS DISCRIMINATION 490
BT   Religious Factors
      Social Discrimination
RT   Religion
      Religious Conflict

RELIGIOUS EDUCATION 140
BT   Education
RT   Catholic Educators
      Church Migrant Projects
      Church Programs
      Church Related Colleges
      Church Workers
      Clergymen
      Ethical Instruction
      Ethics
      Nun Teachers
      Parochial Schools
      Released Time
      Religion
      Theological Education

RELIGIOUS FACTORS 480
NT   Religious Conflict
      Religious Differences
      Religious Discrimination
RT   Religion

Religious Groups
USE   RELIGIOUS CULTURAL GROUPS

RELIGIOUS ORGANIZATIONS 370
BT   Organizations (Groups)
RT   Church Related Colleges
      Clergymen
      Religion
      Religious Agencies
      Religious Cultural Groups

RELOCATION 480
BT   Migration
RT   Area Studies
      Depressed Areas (Geographic)
      Geographic Location
      Labor Problems
      Labor Turnover
      Land Settlement
      Manpower Utilization
      Migrants
      Migration Patterns
      Mobility
      Occupational Mobility
      Population Distribution
      Population Trends
      Refugees
      Residential Patterns

REMEDIAL ARITHMETIC 340
BT   Arithmetic
      Remedial Mathematics
RT   Remedial Instruction
      Remedial Programs

REMEDIAL COURSES 110
NT   Remedial Mathematics
      Remedial Reading
BT   Courses
RT   Refresher Courses
      Remedial Instruction
      Remedial Programs

Remedial Education
USE   REMEDIAL INSTRUCTION

Remedial Education Programs
USE   REMEDIAL PROGRAMS

REMEDIAL INSTRUCTION 270
UF   Remedial Education
      Remediation
BT   Instruction
RT   Coaching Teachers
      Cross Age Teaching
      Diagnostic Teaching
      Learning Difficulties
      Programed Tutoring
      Remedial Arithmetic
      Remedial Courses
      Remedial Mathematics
      Remedial Programs
      Remedial Reading
      Remedial Teachers

REMEDIAL MATHEMATICS 340
NT   Remedial Arithmetic
BT   Mathematics
       Remedial Courses
RT   Remedial Instruction
       Remedial Programs

REMEDIAL PROGRAMS 270
UF   Remedial Education Programs
NT   Remedial Reading Programs
BT   Programs
RT   Coaching Teachers
       Compensatory Education
       Continuation Education
       Educationally Disadvantaged
       Educational Therapy
       Remedial Arithmetic
       Remedial Courses
       Remedial Instruction
       Remedial Mathematics

REMEDIAL READING 270
NT   Corrective Reading
BT   Reading
       Remedial Courses
RT   Reading Centers
       Remedial Instruction
       Remedial Reading Clinics
       Remedial Reading Programs
       Retarded Readers

REMEDIAL READING CLINICS 210
BT   Reading Clinics
RT   Remedial Reading
       Remedial Reading Programs

REMEDIAL READING PROGRAMS 440
BT   Remedial Programs
RT   Remedial Reading
       Remedial Reading Clinics

REMEDIAL TEACHERS 380
BT   Teachers
RT   Coaching Teachers
       Remedial Instruction

Remediation
USE   REMEDIAL INSTRUCTION

RENAISSANCE LITERATURE 260
BT   Literature
RT   Drama
       Essays
       Humanism
       Novels
       Poetry
       Prose
       Sixteenth Century Literature
       Sonnets
       World Literature

Renovations
USE   SCHOOL IMPROVEMENT

REPAIR 210
RT   Auto Body Repairmen
       Buildings
       Bus Garages
       Cleaning
       Consumer Science
       Electrical Appliance Servicemen
       Equipment
       Machine Repairmen
       Maintenance
       Obsolescence
       Preservation

Repair Mechanics
USE   MACHINE REPAIRMEN

Repertory Catalogs
USE   UNION CATALOGS

Repertory Orchestras
USE   ORCHESTRAS

REPETITIVE FILM SHOWINGS 510
BT   Teaching Techniques
RT   Audiovisual Instruction
       Films
       Film Study
       Redundancy

REPORT CARDS 180
BT   Academic Records
RT   Achievement
       Achievement Rating
       Grades (Scholastic)
       Student Evaluation

REPORTS 320
SN   Only when used as a subject concept in
       document
NT   Annual Reports
       Conference Reports
       Technical Reports
BT   Publications
RT   Data Collection
       Documentation
       Program Descriptions
       Recordkeeping
       Records (Forms)
       Statistical Data

Report Writing
USE   TECHNICAL WRITING

Representatives
USE   LEGISLATORS

Required Courses
USE   CORE COURSES

RESCUE 250
RT   Accidents
       Emergency Squad Personnel
       First Aid
       Medical Services

Rescue Squad Personnel
USE   EMERGENCY SQUAD PERSONNEL

RESEARCH 450
UF Applied Research
    Basic Research
    Experimental Studies
    Exploratory Studies
    Studies
NT Action Research
    Architectural Research
    Behavioral Science Research
    Case Studies
    Community Study
    Creativity Research
    Deaf Research
    Economic Research
    Educational Research
    Environmental Research
    Exceptional Child Research
    Facility Case Studies
    Feasibility Studies
    Field Studies
    Institutional Research
    Integration Studies
    Interest Research
    Language Research
    Library Research
    Media Research
    Medical Research
    Methods Research
    Personality studies
    Psychological Studies
    Schematic Studies
    Scientific Research
    Student Research
    Television Research
    Textbook Research
RT Case Studies (Education)
    Community Surveys
    Doctoral Theses
    Experimental Programs
    Experimental Psychology
    Experiments
    Innovation
    Institutional Role
    Investigations
    Literature Reviews
    Masters Theses
    Operations Research
    Pilot Projects
    Post Doctoral Education
    Questionnaires
    Research And Development Centers
    Research Committees
    Research Criteria
    Research Directors
    Researchers
    Research Libraries
    Research Methodology
    Research Opportunities
    Research Problems
    Research Projects
    Research Reviews (Publications)
    Research Skills
    Research Tools
    Research Utilization
    Statistical Analysis
    Technical Reports

RESEARCH AND DEVELOPMENT CENTERS 210
RT Curriculum Study Centers
    Development
    Educational Development
    Experiment Stations
    Facilities
    Research
    Research And Instruction Units

RESEARCH AND INSTRUCTION UNITS 270
SN An organization within a single school
    that is concerned with the improvement
    of teaching methods
RT Educational Improvement
    Educational Research
    Instructional Innovation
    Research And Development Centers
    Research Coordinating Units
    School Cadres

RESEARCH APPRENTICESHIPS 360
BT Apprenticeships
RT On The Job Training
    Professional Education

Research Approaches
USE RESEARCH METHODOLOGY

RESEARCH COMMITTEES 370
BT Committees
RT Research

RESEARCH COORDINATING UNITS 450
RT Coordination
    Educational Research
    Research And Instruction Units

RESEARCH CRITERIA 450
BT Criteria
RT Environmental Criteria
    Measurement
    Measurement Techniques
    Research
    Research Methodology
    Research Problems

RESEARCH DESIGN 450
BT Design
RT Instructional Design
    Research Methodology
    Research Tools

RESEARCH DIRECTORS 380
UF   Directors Of Research
BT   Administrative Personnel
RT   Research
       Researchers

RESEARCHERS 380
NT   Educational Researchers
BT   Personnel
RT   Educational Research
       Institutional Research
       Research
       Research Directors
       Research Methodology
       Research Skills
       Scientists

RESEARCH LIBRARIES 210
BT   Libraries
RT   Library Reference Services
       Public Libraries
       Reference Materials
       Research
       Special Libraries
       University Libraries

Research Limitations
USE   RESEARCH PROBLEMS

RESEARCH METHODOLOGY 450
UF   Research Approaches
RT   Control Groups
       Critical Incidents Method
       Experimental Groups
       Field Studies
       Force Field Analysis
       Models
       Research
       Research Criteria
       Research Design
       Researchers
       Research Problems
       Research Reviews (Publications)
       Sampling
       Scientific Research
       Statistical Analysis

RESEARCH NEEDS 450
BT   Needs
RT   Educational Needs
       Experimental Programs
       Research Problems

RESEARCH OPPORTUNITIES 360
BT   Opportunities
RT   Research

RESEARCH PROBLEMS 450
UF   Research Limitations
BT   Problems
RT   Evaluation Criteria
       Research
       Research Criteria
       Research Methodology
       Research Needs

RESEARCH PROJECTS 450
NT   Agricultural Research Projects
BT   Projects
RT   Program Proposals
       Research
       Research Proposals

RESEARCH PROPOSALS 450
RT   Program Proposals
       Project Applications
       Research Projects

RESEARCH REVIEWS (PUBLICATIONS) 320
BT   Publications
RT   Annotated Bibliographies
       Bibliographies
       Booklists
       Literature Reviews
       Research
       Research Methodology
       Technical Reports

RESEARCH SKILLS 010
BT   Skills
RT   Educational Researchers
       Research
       Researchers

Research Specialists (Education)
USE   EDUCATIONAL RESEARCHERS

RESEARCH TOOLS 450
RT   Models
       Research
       Research Design

RESEARCH UTILIZATION 450
RT   Educational Research
       Information Utilization
       Research
       Use Studies

RESENTMENT 040
BT   Attitudes

Resettlement
USE   LAND SETTLEMENT

Residence Factor
USE   RESIDENCE REQUIREMENTS

Residence Halls
USE   DORMITORIES

RESIDENCE REQUIREMENTS 500
UF   Residence Factor
RT   Nonresident Students
       Resident Students
       Voting
       Welfare

RESIDENT ASSISTANTS 380
RT   Dormitories
       Student Personnel Work

RESIDENT CAMP PROGRAMS 390
BT Programs
RT Camping
   Day Camp Programs
   Recreational Programs
   Summer Programs

RESIDENTIAL CARE 490
NT Foster Homes
RT Attendants
   Attendant Training
   Companions (Occupation)
   Custodial Mentally Handicapped
   Day Care Services
   Handicapped
   Homebound Children
   Institutional Schools
   Nursing Homes
   Personal Care Homes
   Residential Centers
   Residential Programs
   Residential Schools
   Student Placement

RESIDENTIAL CENTERS 210
BT Educational Facilities
RT Continuing Education Centers
   Folk Schools
   Residential Care
   Residential Colleges
   Residential Programs
   Settlement Houses
   University Extension

RESIDENTIAL COLLEGES 470
SN Higher education institutions in which
   academic activity takes place where
   students live with arrangement designed
   to foster learning through integration
   with ordinary living activities
BT Colleges
RT Academic Education
   Campus Planning
   College Environment
   College Housing
   College Planning
   Educational Facilities
   Educational Objectives
   Institutional Role
   Relevance (Education)
   Residential Centers
   Residential Programs

Residential Desegregation
USE NEIGHBORHOOD INTEGRATION

RESIDENTIAL PATTERNS 120
BT City Demography
RT Population Trends
   Relocation

RESIDENTIAL PROGRAMS 410
BT Programs
RT Off The Job Training
   Residential Care
   Residential Centers
   Residential Colleges
   Residential Schools

RESIDENTIAL SCHOOLS 470
SN Boarding schools for blind and/or other
   atypical children of school age
BT Schools
RT Boarding Schools
   College Housing
   Custodial Mentally Handicapped
   Institutional Schools
   Institution Libraries
   Rehabilitation Centers
   Residential Care
   Residential Programs

RESIDENT STUDENTS 380
UF In State Students
BT Students
RT Admission Criteria
   Residence Requirements

Resilient Floor Covering
USE FLOORING

RESOURCE ALLOCATIONS 020
UF Allocation Of Resources
RT Cost Effectiveness
   Equalization Aid
   Fiscal Capacity
   Resources
   Tax Allocation
   Trusts (Financial)
   Wills

RESOURCE CENTERS 210
BT Educational Facilities
RT Arts Centers
   Clearinghouses
   Museums
   Resource Materials
   Resources

RESOURCE GUIDES 460
BT Guides
RT Resource Materials
   Resource Units

RESOURCE MATERIALS 460
UF Material Sources
BT Instructional Materials
RT Classroom Materials
   Manipulative Materials
   Publications
   Resource Centers
   Resource Guides
   Resources
   Resource Units
   Student Developed Materials
   Teacher Developed Materials

RESOURCES 460
NT Community Resources
   Depleted Resources
   Educational Resources
   Family Resources
   Human Resources
   Natural Resources
RT Buildings
   Consortia
   Equipment
   Facilities
   Facility Inventory
   Information Sources
   Resource Allocations
   Resource Centers
   Resource Materials
   Resource Units
   Supplies
   Wills

RESOURCE STAFF ROLE 020
BT Staff Role

RESOURCE TEACHERS 380
BT Teachers
RT Consultants
   Human Resources
   Itinerant Teachers
   Mathematics Teachers
   Regular Class Placement
   Science Consultants
   Science Teachers

RESOURCE UNITS 460
RT Resource Guides
   Resource Materials
   Resources
   Unit Plan
   Units Of Study (Subject Fields)

Response
USE RESPONSE MODE

Response Latency
USE REACTION TIME

RESPONSE MODE 060
UF Response
NT Constructed Response
RT Intermode Differences
   Programed Instruction
   Pupillary Dilation
   Reaction Time
   Situational Tests

Response Time
USE REACTION TIME

RESPONSIBILITY 040
NT Administrator Responsibility
   Business Responsibility
   Child Responsibility
   Church Responsibility
   Employee Responsibility
   Legal Responsibility
   Parent Responsibility
   School Responsibility
   Social Responsibility
   Teacher Responsibility
RT Administrator Guides
   Institutional Role

Rest Home Aides
USE NURSES AIDES

Rest Homes
USE PERSONAL CARE HOMES

RESTRICTIVE TRANSFER PROGRAMS 020
BT Transfer Programs
RT School Segregation
   Token Integration

RETAILING 220
BT Marketing
RT Distributive Education
   Food Stores
   Merchandising
   Salesmanship
   Sales Occupations
   Wholesaling

Retail Training
USE DISTRIBUTIVE EDUCATION

RETARDATION 240
NT Educational Retardation
   Mental Retardation
RT Retarded Children
   Retarded Readers
   Time Factors (Learning)

RETARDED CHILDREN 380
BT Children
RT Exceptional (Atypical)
   Institutionalized (Persons)
   Low Ability Students
   Mentally Handicapped
   Retardation
   Slow Learners

RETARDED READERS 240
RT Reading
   Remedial Reading
   Retardation
   Slow Learners

RETARDED SPEECH DEVELOPMENT 130
UF Delayed Speech
BT Development
RT Child Development
   Language Development
   Maturation
   Speech
   Vocabulary Development

RETENTION 310
BT Learning Processes
RT Conservation (Concept)
   Cues
   Extinction (Psychology)
   Mediation Theory
   Memorizing

Memory
Mnemonics
Recall (Psychological)
Retention Studies
Rote Learning
Visualization

Retention (Of Students)
USE SCHOOL HOLDING POWER

RETENTION STUDIES 310
BT Educational Research
RT Mnemonics
Retention

Retired Teachers
USE TEACHER RETIREMENT

RETIREMENT 150
NT Teacher Retirement
RT Labor Force Nonparticipants
Older Adults
Senior Citizens

RETRAINING 270
UF Refresher Training
NT Vocational Retraining
BT Training
RT Dropouts
Occupations
Trade And Industrial Education
Work Simplification

Retroactive Inhibition
USE INHIBITION

Revenue
USE INCOME

REVIEW (REEXAMINATION) 310
BT Learning Processes
RT Literature Reviews
Study Skills

Reviews Of Literature
USE LITERATURE REVIEWS

REVOLUTIONARY WAR (UNITED STATES)
260
UF American Revolutionary War
RT American Culture
American History
Colonial History (United States)
Colonialism
United States History

REWARDS 420
NT Self Reward
BT Reinforcement
RT Educational Benefits
Merit Rating Programs
Morale
Motivation
Professional Recognition
Reinforcers
Sanctions
Social Reinforcement

REZONING 120
UF Rezoning Districts
BT Zoning
RT School Districts

Rezoning Districts
USE REZONING

RHETORIC 260
NT Persuasive Discourse
BT Language
RT Composition (Literary)
Expository Writing
Literary Conventions
Speaking
Speech
Speech Skills
Writing

RH FACTORS 070
RT Physiology
Pregnancy
Prenatal Influences

Richer Nations
USE DEVELOPED NATIONS

RIFF 300
BT Afro Asiatic Languages

RISK 420
RT Banking
Cognitive Processes
Decision Making
Fire Insurance
Game Theory
Indemnity Bonds
Insurance Programs
Prediction
Probability
Problem Solving

River Pollution Control
USE WATER POLLUTION CONTROL

ROAD CONSTRUCTION 210
UF Highway Construction
BT Construction (Process)
RT City Planning
Civil Engineering
Construction Costs
Construction Industry
Construction Needs
Construction Programs
Land Use
Traffic Circulation
Traffic Patterns
Transportation

Road Signs
USE SIGNS

RODENTICIDES 070
BT Pesticides
RT Agricultural Chemical Occupations
Agricultural Supplies
Agriculture
Insecticides
Rats

ROLE CONFLICT 420
SN Incompatibility between multiple roles
taken by an individual or between group
and individual roles
BT Conflict
RT Psychological Characteristics
Psychological Patterns
Role Theory
Socialization
Student Alienation
Teacher Alienation

ROLE PERCEPTION 490
SN Awareness of behavior patterns or
functions expected of persons
BT Perception
RT Identification (Psychological)
Role Theory
Self Actualization
Student Role

ROLE PLAYING 420
BT Psychotherapy
RT Therapy

ROLE THEORY 420
RT Counselor Functions
Counselor Role
Identification (Psychological)
Role Conflict
Role Perception
Self Actualization
Student School Relationship

Romance
USE MEDIEVAL ROMANCE

ROMANCE LANGUAGES 300
NT French
Italian
Latin
Portuguese
Romanian
Spanish
BT Indo European Languages

ROMANIAN 300
UF Roumanian
Rumanian
BT Romance Languages

ROMANIZATION 290
SN The transliteration of another system of
writing into the Roman alphabet
RT Alphabets
Graphemes
Language Standardization
Orthographic Symbols
Written Language

ROMANTICISM 260
BT Literature
RT Drama
Eighteenth Century Literature
Essays
Fiction
Nineteenth Century Literature
Poetry
Prose

Roof Covering
USE ROOFING

ROOFERS 380
BT Skilled Workers
RT Roofing
Skilled Occupations
Trade And Industrial Education

ROOFING 210
UF Roof Covering
Roof Installation
Roofs
RT Asphalts
Building Materials
Buildings
Building Trades
Construction (Process)
Roofers

Roof Installation
USE ROOFING

Roofs
USE ROOFING

Room Dividers
USE SPACE DIVIDERS

ROTATION PLANS 020
RT Team Teaching

ROTE LEARNING 310
BT Learning
RT Learning Activities
Learning Processes
Learning Theories
Memorizing
Retention

Roumanian
USE ROMANIAN

Row Boss
USE CREW LEADERS

RUBELLA 250
UF Epidemic Roseola
     German Measles
BT Infectious Diseases
RT Communicable Diseases
     Prenatal Influences

Rumanian
USE ROMANIAN

RUNNING 390
UF Jogging
BT Physical Activities
RT Exercise (Physiology)
     Physical Education

Running Writing
USE CURSIVE WRITING

RURAL AREAS 120
UF Rural South
RT Collective Settlements
     Rural Clinics
     Rural Economics
     Rural Education
     Rural Environment
     Rural Family
     Rural Farm Residents
     Rural Population
     Rural Resettlement
     Rural Schools
     Rural Urban Differences
     Rural Youth

RURAL CLINICS 210
BT Clinics
RT Rural Areas
     Rural Schools
     Rural Youth

RURAL DEVELOPMENT 130
BT Development
RT Community Development
     Rural Economics

RURAL DROPOUTS 380
BT Dropouts

RURAL ECONOMICS 480
BT Economics
RT Rural Areas
     Rural Development

RURAL EDUCATION 140
BT Education
RT Extension Education
     Outdoor Education
     Rural Areas
     Rural Extension
     Rural Schools
     Rural School Systems

RURAL ENVIRONMENT 160
BT Environment
RT Rural Areas
     Rural Farm Residents
     Rural Youth

RURAL EXTENSION 140
SN Extension work in rural settings
UF Agricultural Extension
BT Extension Education
RT Community Development
     Land Grant Universities
     Rural Education
     University Extension

RURAL FAMILY 490
BT Family (Sociological Unit)
RT Rural Areas

RURAL FARM RESIDENTS 380
RT Agricultural Laborers
     Farm Committees
     Farmers
     Rural Areas
     Rural Environment
     Rural Population

Rural Inhabitants
USE RURAL POPULATION

RURAL POPULATION 120
UF Rural Inhabitants
BT Population Distribution
RT Demography
     Population Growth
     Population Trends
     Rural Areas
     Rural Farm Residents
     Rural Resettlement
     Rural Urban Differences

Rural Poverty
USE ECONOMIC DISADVANTAGEMENT

RURAL RESETTLEMENT 120
RT Rural Areas
     Rural Population

RURAL SCHOOLS 470
BT Schools
RT Rural Areas
     Rural Clinics
     Rural Education
     Rural School Systems

RURAL SCHOOL SYSTEMS 230
BT School Systems
RT County School Systems
     Rural Education
     Rural Schools

Rural South
USE RURAL AREAS

RURAL URBAN DIFFERENCES 480
UF   Urban Rural Differences
BT   Social Influences
RT   Rural Areas
        Rural Population
        Urban Areas
        Urban Language
        Urban Population

RURAL YOUTH 380
UF   Farm Youth
BT   Youth
RT   Rural Areas
        Rural Clinics
        Rural Environment

RUSSIAN 300
BT   Slavic Languages

RUSSIAN LITERATURE 260
BT   Literature
RT   Drama
        Fables
        Fiction
        French Literature
        Legends
        Novels
        Poetry
        Prose
        Short Stories
        World Literature

SABBATICAL LEAVES 150
BT   Leave Of Absence
RT   College Teachers
        Professional Education
        Teacher Attendance
        Teacher Improvement
        Teaching Benefits
        Teaching Conditions

SAFETY 250
UF   Safety Provisions
NT   Agricultural Safety
        Fire Protection
        Laboratory Safety
        School Safety
        Traffic Safety
RT   Accident Prevention
        Accidents
        Fallout Shelters
        Injuries
        Physical Design Needs
        Radiation
        Radiation Effects
        Refugees
        Safety Education
        Safety Equipment
        Traffic Accidents
        Traffic Regulations

SAFETY EDUCATION 140
BT   Education
RT   Accident Prevention
        Accidents
        Agricultural Safety
        Fire Protection
        Fire Science Education
        Safety
        Safety Equipment
        School Safety
        Traffic Accidents
        Traffic Safety

SAFETY EQUIPMENT 250
UF   Safety Glasses
BT   Equipment
RT   Accident Prevention
        Safety
        Safety Education

Safety Glasses
USE   SAFETY EQUIPMENT

Safety Provisions
USE   SAFETY

SALARIES 220
NT   Contract Salaries
        Teacher Salaries
BT   Expenditures
        Income
RT   Faculty Promotion
        Fringe Benefits
        Guaranteed Income
        Overtime
        Premium Pay
        Salary Differentials
        Wages

SALARY DIFFERENTIALS 220
RT   Contract Salaries
        Educational Finance
        Personnel Policy
        Recruitment
        Salaries
        Teacher Salaries
        Wages

Salary Income
USE   INCOME

Salary Raise
USE   FACULTY PROMOTION

Sales Clerks
USE   SALES WORKERS

SALESMANSHIP 110
RT   Auto Parts Men
        Business Education
        Business Subjects
        Distributive Education
        Merchandise Information
        Merchandising
        Occupations
        Retailing

Sales Occupations
Sales Workers

SALES OCCUPATIONS 350
BT Occupations
RT Agricultural Supply Occupations
Auto Parts Men
Distributive Education
Merchandising
Merchants
Retailing
Salesmanship
Sales Workers
Service Occupations
Service Workers

Sales Promotion
USE MERCHANDISING

SALES WORKERS 380
UF Sales Clerks
BT Nonprofessional Personnel
RT Agricultural Supply Occupations
Auto Parts Men
Distributive Education
Employees
Merchants
Salesmanship
Sales Occupations
Service Workers

SAMOAN 300
BT Malayo Polynesian Languages

SAMOYED LANGUAGES 300
NT Yurak
BT Uralic Altaic Languages

SAMPLING 340
BT Statistical Analysis
RT Data Collection
Measurement Techniques
Predictive Measurement
Probability Theory
Research Methodology
Statistical Studies
Statistical Surveys
Testing

Sanatoriums
USE HOSPITALS

SANCTIONS 020
RT Arbitration
Censorship
Collective Negotiation
Labor Demands
Laws
Moral Values
Negotiation Impasses
Rewards
Standards
Teacher Militancy
Teacher Strikes

SANGO 300
BT African Languages

Sanitarian Technicians
USE ENVIRONMENTAL TECHNICIANS

Sanitary Engineering Technicians
USE ENVIRONMENTAL TECHNICIANS

SANITARY FACILITIES 210
SN Equipment and building areas for
keeping buildings clean and/or facilities
for personal cleanliness
NT Toilet Facilities
BT Facilities
RT Building Equipment
Dishwashing
Equipment
Health Conditions
Health Facilities
Hygiene
Locker Rooms
Physical Health
Plumbing
Sanitation
Sanitation Improvement
Utilities

Sanitary Inspectors
USE ENVIRONMENTAL TECHNICIANS

SANITATION 250
NT Cleaning
BT Public Health
RT Community Health
Disease Control
Dishwashing
Hygiene
Locker Rooms
Physical Design Needs
Sanitary Facilities
Sanitation Improvement
Utilities

SANITATION IMPROVEMENT 250
BT Improvement
RT Cleaning
Dishwashing
Environmental Technicians
Health
Health Conditions
Health Education
Health Services
Pollution
Sanitary Facilities
Sanitation

SANSKRIT 300
BT Indo European Languages

SARA 300
BT African Languages

Sarcasm
USE IRONY

SATELLITE LABORATORIES 210
BT Laboratories

SATIRE 260
BT Literary Genres
    Literature
RT Composition (Literary)
    Drama
    English Neoclassic Literary Period
    Essays
    Fables
    Fiction
    Figurative Language
    French Literature
    German Literature
    Literary Analysis
    Literary Conventions
    Metaphors
    Nineteenth Century Literature
    Poetry
    Prose
    Spanish American Literature
    Spanish Literature

SCHEDULE MODULES 020
UF Modular Scheduling
RT Flexible Schedules
    Flexible Scheduling
    Scheduling

SCHEDULING 020
NT Flexible Scheduling
    Released Time
BT School Administration
RT Critical Path Method
    Double Sessions
    Facility Utilization Research
    Intervals
    Program Length
    Schedule Modules
    School Schedules
    Semester Division
    Trimester Schedules
    Viewing Time

SCHEMATIC STUDIES 450
BT Research

SCHIZOPHRENIA 420
UF Dementia Praecox
BT Psychosis
RT Autism
    Behavior Patterns
    Emotionally Disturbed
    Mental Health
    Mental Illness
    Psychology

SCHOLARLY JOURNALS 320
BT Periodicals

SCHOLARSHIP FUNDS 220
BT Scholarships
RT Scholarship Loans

SCHOLARSHIP LOANS 220
BT Scholarships
RT Scholarship Funds
    Student Loan Programs

SCHOLARSHIPS 220
NT Scholarship Funds
    Scholarship Loans
BT Private Financial Support
RT Educational Finance
    Tuition Grants

Scholastic Ability
USE ACADEMIC ABILITY

Scholastic Achievement
USE ACADEMIC ACHIEVEMENT

Scholastic Aptitude
USE ACADEMIC APTITUDE

Scholastic Failure
USE ACADEMIC FAILURE

Scholastic Performance
USE ACADEMIC PERFORMANCE

SCHOOL ACCIDENTS 250
BT Accidents
RT School Safety

SCHOOL ACCOUNTING 220
BT Accounting
RT Educational Administration
    Educational Finance

School Achievement
USE ACADEMIC ACHIEVEMENT

SCHOOL ACTIVITIES 140
BT Activities
RT Curriculum

School Adjustment
USE STUDENT ADJUSTMENT

SCHOOL ADMINISTRATION 020
NT Scheduling
BT Administration
    Educational Administration
RT Administrative Personnel
    Boards Of Education
    Chief Administrators
    Consolidated Schools
    Double Sessions
    Elementary School Supervisors
    Governing Boards
    High School Supervisors
    School Policy
    Schools
    School Supervision
    Trustees
    University Administration

School Administrators
USE ADMINISTRATIVE PERSONNEL

School Admission
USE ADMISSION (SCHOOL)

SCHOOL AIDES 380
BT Paraprofessional School Personnel
RT Bilingual Teacher Aides
    Teacher Aides
    Volunteers

SCHOOL ARCHITECTURE 030
BT Architecture
RT Campus Planning
    Modular Building Design
    Open Plan Schools
    School Design
    Schools
    Structural Building Systems

School Atmosphere
USE SCHOOL ENVIRONMENT

School Attendance
USE ATTENDANCE

SCHOOL ATTENDANCE LAWS 230
BT School Policy
    State Laws
RT Admission Criteria
    Attendance
    Expulsion

SCHOOL ATTITUDES 040
BT Attitudes
RT Schools

School Board Policy
USE BOARD OF EDUCATION POLICY

School Board Role
USE BOARD OF EDUCATION ROLE

School Boards
USE BOARDS OF EDUCATION

School Boundaries
USE SCHOOL DISTRICTS

SCHOOL BOYCOTTS 490
RT Demonstrations (Civil)
    Schools
    School Segregation

SCHOOL BUDGET ELECTIONS 220
BT Elections
RT Budgets
    Educational Finance

SCHOOL BUILDINGS 210
BT Buildings
    Educational Facilities
RT Architectural Elements
    Building Design
    Campuses
    Campus Planning
    Educational Equipment
    Open Plan Schools
    School Design
    Schools

School Shops
Structural Building Systems

SCHOOL BUSES 170
BT Motor Vehicles
RT Bus Transportation
    Equipment
    Student Transportation

School Business Officials
USE ADMINISTRATIVE PERSONNEL

SCHOOL CADRES 380
SN A group of school personnel previously
    coordinated in training to work together
    and to train others
BT School Personnel
RT Research And Instruction Units
    Staff Utilization
    Team Teaching
    Team Training

SCHOOL CALENDARS 020
RT Extended School Year
    Quarter System
    School Schedules
    Semester Division
    Trimester Schedules

School Climate
USE EDUCATIONAL ENVIRONMENT

SCHOOL CLOSING 020
UF Closed Schools
RT Board Of Education Policy
    Schools

School College Cooperation
USE COLLEGE SCHOOL COOPERATION

School Community Communication
USE SCHOOL COMMUNITY RELATIONSHIP

SCHOOL COMMUNITY COOPERATION 480
UF School Community Coordination
RT Community
    Interagency Cooperation
    School Community Relationship
    Schools

School Community Coordination
USE SCHOOL COMMUNITY COOPERATION

School Community Interaction
USE SCHOOL COMMUNITY RELATIONSHIP

SCHOOL COMMUNITY PROGRAMS 490
UF Community School Programs
BT Programs
RT Community
    School Community Relationship
    Schools

SCHOOL COMMUNITY RELATIONSHIP 480
UF Community School Relationship
    School Community Communication
    School Community Interaction
BT Relationship
RT Community
    Community Control
    Educational Sociology
    Public Relations
    School Community Cooperation
    School Community Programs
    School Industry Relationship
    Schools
    School Support

SCHOOL CONDITIONS 160
BT School Environment
RT Schools

School Consolidation
USE CONSOLIDATED SCHOOLS

SCHOOL CONSTRUCTION 210
BT Construction (Process)
RT Architectural Elements
    Bids
    Buildings
    Component Building Systems
    Construction Industry
    Construction Needs
    Modular Building Design
    Operating Engineering
    Performance Specifications
    Prefabrication
    School Design
    School Expansion
    Schools
    Sheet Metal Work
    Specifications
    Structural Building Systems

SCHOOL DEMOGRAPHY 120
BT Demography
RT Schools

School Desegregation
USE SCHOOL INTEGRATION

SCHOOL DESIGN 030
NT Decentralized School Design
    High School Design
BT Design
RT Architectural Elements
    Building Design
    Building Plans
    College Buildings
    Component Building Systems
    Flexible Classrooms
    Glass Walls
    Mobile Classrooms
    Modular Building Design
    Open Plan Schools
    School Architecture
    School Buildings
    School Construction

    Schools
    School Size
    School Space
    Site Development
    Site Selection
    Structural Building Systems
    Studio Floor Plans

SCHOOL DISTRICT AUTONOMY 020
SN Area of control granted a school district
    or its officials through expressed or
    implied state authority
UF Local Autonomy
    Local Control
RT Board Of Education Policy
    Board Of Education Role
    Boards Of Education
    City Government
    Community Control
    Educational Policy
    Governmental Structure
    Local Issues
    School Districts
    State School District Relationship

School District Policy
USE BOARD OF EDUCATION POLICY

SCHOOL DISTRICTS 120
UF School Boundaries
NT Comprehensive Districts
    Multicampus Districts
RT Consolidated Schools
    County School Systems
    Intermediate Administrative Units
    Open Enrollment
    Rezoning
    School District Autonomy
    School District Spending
    School Location
    School Redistricting
    Schools
    School Systems
    Zoning

SCHOOL DISTRICT SPENDING 220
BT Expenditures
RT Educational Finance
    Expenditure Per Student
    School Districts

School Dropouts
USE DROPOUTS

School Enrollment
USE STUDENT ENROLLMENT

SCHOOL ENVIRONMENT 160
UF School Atmosphere
NT School Conditions
BT Educational Environment
RT Academic Freedom
    Acoustical Environment
    College Environment
    Schools

Site Selection
Thermal Environment

School Excursions
USE INSTRUCTIONAL TRIPS

SCHOOL EXPANSION 020
UF Expansion
RT Mobile Classrooms
School Construction
Schools
School Size
Site Development
Site Selection

School Experience
USE EDUCATIONAL EXPERIENCE

School Facilities
USE EDUCATIONAL FACILITIES

School Failure
USE ACADEMIC FAILURE

School Family Relationship
USE FAMILY SCHOOL RELATIONSHIP

School Finance
USE EDUCATIONAL FINANCE

SCHOOL FUNDS 220
BT Financial Support
RT Educational Finance
Project Applications
Schools
School Support
School Taxes

School Grade Average
USE GRADE POINT AVERAGE

SCHOOL HEALTH SERVICES 250
BT Health Services
RT Physical Education
Physical Recreation Programs
School Nurses
Student Personnel Services

SCHOOL HOLDING POWER 020
UF Holding Power (Of Schools)
Retention (Of Students)
RT Attendance
Dropouts
Transfers
Truancy

School Home Relationship
USE FAMILY.SCHOOL RELATIONSHIP

SCHOOL IMPROVEMENT 020
UF Renovations
School Renovation
BT Improvement
RT Schools

SCHOOL INDUSTRY RELATIONSHIP 020
UF Industry School Relationship
BT Relationship
RT Cooperative Planning
Cooperative Programs
Industry
Released Time
School Community Relationship
Schools

SCHOOL INTEGRATION 430
UF Desegregated Schools
Integrated Schools
School Desegregation
RT Biracial Schools
Classroom Integration
Feeder Programs
Racial Integration
Schools
Social Integration
Special Zoning

SCHOOL INVOLVEMENT 020
RT Schools

SCHOOL LAW 230
BT Law Instruction

SCHOOL LIBRARIES 210
NT Elementary School Libraries
BT Libraries
RT Instructional Materials Centers
Schools
School Study Centers

SCHOOL LOCATION 120
UF School Sites
NT Northern Schools
Southern Schools
RT Campus Planning
Distance
Multicampus Districts
Real Estate
School Districts
School Redistricting
Schools
School Zoning
Site Analysis

SCHOOL MAINTENANCE 210
BT Maintenance
RT Building Operation
Cleaning
Custodian Training
Equipment Maintenance
Schools

SCHOOL NEWSPAPERS 080
BT School Publications
RT Class Newspapers
Cocurricular Activities
Schools

SCHOOL NURSES 380
BT Nurses
RT School Health Services
Teacher Nurses

School Officials
USE SCHOOL PERSONNEL

SCHOOL ORGANIZATION 020
UF School Reorganization
NT Departments
High School Organization
House Plan
BT Organization
RT Centralization
Decentralization
Departmental Teaching Plans
Double Sessions
Quarter System
Schools

SCHOOL ORIENTATION 270
BT Orientation
RT Schools
Teacher Orientation

School Parent Relationship
USE PARENT SCHOOL RELATIONSHIP

School Parks
USE EDUCATIONAL PARKS

School Performance
USE ACADEMIC PERFORMANCE

SCHOOL PERSONNEL 380
UF School Officials
NT Attendance Officers
Audiovisual Directors
Clinic Personnel (School)
Faculty
Instructional Staff
Paraprofessional School Personnel
Pupil Personnel Workers
School Cadres
Student Personnel Workers
Supervisors
BT Personnel
RT Personnel Directors
Schools
School Secretaries

School Personnel Directors
USE PERSONNEL DIRECTORS

School Philosophy
USE EDUCATIONAL PHILOSOPHY

SCHOOL PHOBIA 420
UF Schoolsickness
BT Psychological Patterns
RT Anxiety
Emotionally Disturbed Children
Fear
Maladjustment
Neurosis

Parent Student Relationship
Student School Relationship

SCHOOL PLANNING 020
UF School Shop Planning
BT Planning
RT Building Plans
Business Education Facilities
Campus Planning
Color Planning
Component Building Systems
Construction Programs
Facility Guidelines
Facility Requirements
Flexible Classrooms
Flexible Facilities
Quarter System
Schools
School Schedules
Site Analysis
Site Development
Site Selection
Space Utilization
Spatial Relationship

School Plant
USE EDUCATIONAL FACILITIES

School Police Relationship
USE POLICE SCHOOL RELATIONSHIP

SCHOOL POLICY 020
NT Discipline Policy
Neighborhood School Policy
School Attendance Laws
Transfer Policy
BT Policy
RT Interdistrict Policies
School Administration
Schools
Suspension

School Principals
USE PRINCIPALS

SCHOOL PSYCHOLOGISTS 380
BT Psychologists
Pupil Personnel Workers
Student Personnel Workers
RT Consultants
Guidance Personnel
Psychological Evaluation
Psychological Testing
Psychometrics
Schools

SCHOOL PUBLICATIONS 080
NT Class Newspapers
School Newspapers
BT Publications
RT Schools

SCHOOL RECREATIONAL PROGRAMS 390
BT Recreational Programs
RT Schools

SCHOOL REDISTRICTING 120
RT Consolidated Schools
    Feeder Patterns
    Multicampus Districts
    School Districts
    School Location
    Schools
    School Zoning

SCHOOL REGISTRATION 020
RT Admission (School)
    Dual Enrollment
    Schools

School Related Activities
USE COCURRICULAR ACTIVITIES

School Renovation
USE SCHOOL IMPROVEMENT

School Reorganization
USE SCHOOL ORGANIZATION

SCHOOL RESPONSIBILITY 490
BT Responsibility
RT Noninstructional Responsibility
    School Role
    Schools

SCHOOL ROLE 140
NT Elementary School Role
    High School Role
BT Institutional Role
RT Culture Conflict
    School Responsibility
    Schools

SCHOOLS 470
NT Affiliated Schools
    Bilingual Schools
    Biracial Schools
    Boarding Schools
    Community Schools
    Consolidated Schools
    Correspondence Schools
    Day Schools
    Dental Schools
    Disadvantaged Schools
    Elementary Schools
    Experimental Schools
    Folk Schools
    Freedom Schools
    High Schools
    Hospital Schools
    Institutional Schools
    Laboratory Schools
    Law Schools
    Library Schools
    Medical Schools
    Middle Schools
    Migrant Schools
    Military Schools
    Neighborhood Schools
    Night Schools
    Nonresidential Schools
    Northern Schools
    Nursery Schools
    One Teacher Schools
    Open Plan Schools
    Private Schools
    Public Schools
    Racially Balanced Schools
    Regional Schools
    Residential Schools
    Rural Schools
    Secondary Schools
    Slum Schools
    Small Schools
    Southern Schools
    Special Schools
    State Schools
    Suburban Schools
    Summer Schools
    Technical Institutes
    Traditional Schools
    Transitional Schools
    Ungraded Schools
    Urban Schools
    Vocational Schools
    Year Round Schools
BT Institutions
RT College School Cooperation
    Family School Relationship
    Multicampus Districts
    Parent School Relationship
    Police School Relationship
    School Administration
    School Architecture
    School Attitudes
    School Boycotts
    School Buildings
    School Closing
    School Community Cooperation
    School Community Programs
    School Community Relationship
    School Conditions
    School Construction
    School Demography
    School Design
    School Districts
    School Environment
    School Expansion
    School Funds
    School Improvement
    School Industry Relationship
    School Integration
    School Involvement
    School Libraries
    School Location
    School Maintenance
    School Newspapers
    School Organization
    School Orientation

School Personnel
School Planning
School Policy
School Psychologists
School Publications
School Recreational Programs
School Redistricting
School Registration
School Responsibility
School Role
School Schedules
School Segregation
School Services
School Size
School Space
School Statistics
School Study Centers
School Superintendents
School Support
School Systems
School Taxes
School Vandalism
School Zoning

SCHOOL SAFETY 250
BT Safety
RT Cleaning
Emergency Programs
Fire Protection
Safety Education
School Accidents

SCHOOL SCHEDULES 020
NT Flexible Schedules
Time Blocks
RT Double Sessions
Extended School Year
Flexible Scheduling
Quarter System
Released Time
Scheduling
School Calendars
School Planning
Schools
Year Round Schools

SCHOOL SECRETARIES 380
BT Secretaries
RT School Personnel

SCHOOL SEGREGATION 430
UF Negro Schools
BT Racial Segregation
RT Restrictive Transfer Programs
School Boycotts
Schools

SCHOOL SERVICES 020
UF Public School Services
NT Ancillary Services
Pupil Personnel Services
Student Personnel Services
BT Human Services
RT Exceptional Child Services
Psychological Services

Schools
Vending Machines

School Shop Planning
USE SCHOOL PLANNING

SCHOOL SHOPS 210
UF Comprehensive General Shops
Farm Mechanics Shops
Farm Shops
General Unit Shops
Industrial Arts Laboratories
Industrial Arts Shops
Shop Rooms
Unit Shops
BT Educational Facilities
RT Classrooms
Crafts Rooms
Industrial Arts
School Buildings
Shop Curriculum
Technical Education
Trade And Industrial Education
Vocational Agriculture

Schoolsickness
USE SCHOOL PHOBIA

School Sites
USE SCHOOL LOCATION

SCHOOL SIZE 210
RT Interior Space
School Design
School Expansion
Schools
School Space
Small Schools
Space Utilization

SCHOOL SOCIAL WORKERS 380
UF Visiting Teachers
BT Pupil Personnel Workers
Social Workers
Student Personnel Workers
RT Adjustment Counselors
Caseworkers
Guidance Personnel
Social Services
Social Work
Student Personnel Workers

Schools Of Dentistry
USE DENTAL SCHOOLS

Schools Of Medicine
USE MEDICAL SCHOOLS

SCHOOL SPACE 210
RT Corridors
Flexible Classrooms
Interior Space
Offices (Facilities)
Open Plan Schools
School Design
Schools
School Size

Space Dividers
Space Utilization
Spatial Relationship

SCHOOL STATISTICS 340
BT Statistical Data
RT Schools
Statistical Analysis

School Student Relationship
USE STUDENT SCHOOL RELATIONSHIP

SCHOOL STUDY CENTERS 210
BT Study Centers
RT School Libraries
Schools

SCHOOL SUPERINTENDENTS 380
BT Superintendents
RT Schools

SCHOOL SUPERVISION 020
BT Supervision
RT Administrative Personnel
Instruction
School Administration
Science Supervision

SCHOOL SUPPORT 220
BT Financial Support
RT Educational Economics
School Community Relationship
School Funds
Schools
School Taxes

SCHOOL SURVEYS 180
UF Educational Surveys
BT Surveys
RT Educational Research
Graduate Surveys
Program Evaluation

SCHOOL SYSTEMS 470
NT County School Systems
Public School Systems
Rural School Systems
RT Consolidated Schools
Educational Complexes
Multicampus Districts
School Districts
Schools

SCHOOL TAXES 230
BT Financial Support
Taxes
RT Assessed Valuation
School Funds
Schools
School Support
Tax Support

School Transfers
USE TRANSFER STUDENTS

School Transportation
USE STUDENT TRANSPORTATION

School Truancy
USE TRUANCY

SCHOOL VANDALISM 060
BT Vandalism
RT Delinquents
Schools

SCHOOL VISITATION 140
SN Approved interschool visitation by
teachers or administrators to observe
teaching methods or equipment
UF Interschool Visits
School Visits
RT Equipment Evaluation
Evaluation
Inservice Teacher Education
Observation
Performance

School Visits
USE SCHOOL VISITATION

SCHOOL ZONING 120
BT Zoning
RT Consolidated Schools
School Location
School Redistricting
Schools
Site Selection

Science
USE SCIENCES

SCIENCE ACTIVITIES 140
NT Science Fairs
BT Activities
RT Laboratory Procedures
Science Education
Science Experiments
Science Projects
Sciences
Summer Science Programs

SCIENCE CAREERS 150
BT Careers
RT Sciences
Scientific Personnel

SCIENCE CLUBS 370
BT Clubs
RT Cocurricular Activities

SCIENCE CONSULTANTS 380
BT Consultants
RT Faculty
Resource Teachers
Specialists
Supervisors

SCIENCE COURSE IMPROVEMENT PROJECT
110
BT Projects
RT Curriculum
Curriculum Development

SCIENCE COURSES 110
BT Courses
RT Chemistry Instruction
Science Curriculum
Science Education
Science Instruction
Sciences
Summer Science Programs

SCIENCE CURRICULUM 110
NT Elementary Science
General Science
Modern Science
Physics Curriculum
BT Curriculum
RT Science Courses
Sciences
Summer Science Programs

SCIENCE DEPARTMENTS 370
BT Departments
RT Administrative Organization
English Departments
Universities

SCIENCE EDUCATION 140
NT College Science
Elementary School Science
Secondary School Science
BT Education
RT Chemistry Instruction
Engineering Education
Land Grant Universities
Outdoor Education
Planetariums
Science Activities
Science Courses
Science Education History
Science Experiments
Science Programs
Science Projects
Sciences
Science Teachers
Science Teaching Centers
Scientific Literacy
Scientific Methodology
Technical Education

SCIENCE EDUCATION HISTORY 260
BT Educational History
RT American History
Asian History
European History
Science Education
Science History
World History

SCIENCE EQUIPMENT 170
NT Science Laboratories
Semiconductor Devices
Superconductors
RT Demonstration Centers
Educational Equipment
Equipment Manufacturers

Lasers
Science Experiments
Science Facilities
Sciences

SCIENCE EXPERIMENTS 510
NT Physics Experiments
BT Experiments
RT Laboratory Procedures
Science Activities
Science Education
Science Equipment
Science Projects
Sciences

SCIENCE FACILITIES 210
BT Facilities
RT Educational Specifications
Planetariums
Science Equipment
Science Laboratories

SCIENCE FAIRS 410
BT Science Activities
RT Cocurricular Activities
Science Projects

SCIENCE FICTION 260
BT Fiction
RT Fantasy
Literature
Scientific Concepts

SCIENCE HISTORY 260
BT History
RT American History
Asian History
European History
Science Education History
Sciences
World History

SCIENCE INSTITUTES 410
BT Institutes (Training Programs)
RT Courses
Inservice Courses
Inservice Programs
Institute Type Courses
Programs
Seminars
Short Courses
Summer Science Programs
Symposia
Teacher Education
Teacher Workshops

SCIENCE INSTRUCTION 270
NT Chemistry Instruction
BT Instruction
RT Science Courses
Sciences
Science Teachers
Summer Science Programs

367

SCIENCE LABORATORIES 210
BT Laboratories
     Science Equipment
RT Planetariums
     Science Facilities
     Sciences

SCIENCE MATERIALS 460
BT Instructional Materials
RT Classroom Materials
     Instructional Aids
     Mathematics Materials
     Programed Materials
     Reading Materials
     Student Developed Materials
     Teacher Developed Materials

SCIENCE PROGRAMS 110
UF Technological Programs
NT Pretechnology Programs
     Summer Science Programs
BT Programs
RT Science Education
     Sciences
     Technological Advancement

SCIENCE PROJECTS 270
BT Projects
RT Laboratory Procedures
     Science Activities
     Science Education
     Science Experiments
     Science Fairs
     Sciences
     Summer Science Programs

SCIENCES 110
UF Science
NT Animal Science
     Computer Science
     Consumer Science
     Mathematics
     Military Science
     Natural Sciences
     Plant Science
     Social Sciences
     Technology
BT Liberal Arts
RT Engineering
     Museums
     Science Activities
     Science Careers
     Science Courses
     Science Curriculum
     Science Education
     Science Equipment
     Science Experiments
     Science History
     Science Instruction
     Science Laboratories
     Science Programs
     Science Projects
     Science Tests
     Science Units

Scientific Attitudes
Scientific Concepts
Scientific Enterprise
Scientific Methodology
Scientific Principles

SCIENCE SUPERVISION 020
BT Supervision
RT School Supervision
     Supervisors
     Supervisory Methods
     Teacher Supervision

SCIENCE TEACHERS 380
NT Physics Teachers
BT Teachers
RT Faculty
     Resource Teachers
     Science Education
     Science Instruction
     Specialists
     Student Teachers
     Teacher Aides

SCIENCE TEACHING CENTERS 210
RT Education Service Centers
     Nature Centers
     Planetariums
     Science Education

SCIENCE TESTS 520
BT Tests
RT Achievement Tests
     Cognitive Tests
     Interest Tests
     Sciences
     Verbal Tests

SCIENCE UNITS 110
BT Units Of Study (Subject Fields)
RT Sciences
     Unit Plan

SCIENTIFIC ATTITUDES 040
BT Attitudes
RT Problem Solving
     Sciences
     Scientific Concepts
     Scientific Enterprise
     Scientific Methodology

SCIENTIFIC CONCEPTS 310
UF Technological Concepts
NT Height
     Intervals
     Relativity
     Space
     Time
     Weight
RT Conservation (Concept)
     Developed Nations
     Pressure
     Science Fiction
     Sciences
     Scientific Attitudes
     Scientific Literacy

Scientific Methodology
Scientific Principles
Technological Advancement
Technology

SCIENTIFIC ENTERPRISE 450
SN Totality of systematic activity of the
    sciences as an institution involving
    processes, attitudes, ethics, and
    interrelationships of science with other
    institutions
RT Developed Nations
    Natural Sciences
    Sciences
    Scientific Attitudes
    Scientific Principles

SCIENTIFIC LITERACY 010
BT Literacy
RT Comprehension
    Science Education
    Scientific Concepts
    Scientific Principles

SCIENTIFIC MANPOWER 150
RT Manpower Development
    Manpower Utilization
    Scientific Personnel
    Scientists

SCIENTIFIC METHODOLOGY 510
UF Scientific Methods
BT Methodology
RT Componental Analysis
    Developed Nations
    Problem Solving
    Science Education
    Sciences
    Scientific Attitudes
    Scientific Concepts

Scientific Methods
USE SCIENTIFIC METHODOLOGY

SCIENTIFIC PERSONNEL 380
NT Engineers
    Mathematicians
BT Personnel
RT Professional Occupations
    Science Careers
    Scientific Manpower
    Scientists

SCIENTIFIC PRINCIPLES 450
RT Developed Nations
    Sciences
    Scientific Concepts
    Scientific Enterprise
    Scientific Literacy

Scientific Reports
USE TECHNICAL REPORTS

SCIENTIFIC RESEARCH 450
SN Research conducted to advance
    knowledge in a scientific field
BT Research
RT Anatomy
    Astronomy
    Biology
    Chemistry
    Developed Nations
    Ecology
    Experiment Stations
    Geology
    Nuclear Physics
    Paleontology
    Physics
    Physiology
    Planetariums
    Research Methodology

Scientific Secretaries
USE SECRETARIES

Scientific Stenographers
USE STENOGRAPHERS

SCIENTISTS 380
UF Physical Scientists
BT Personnel
RT Engineers
    Researchers
    Scientific Manpower
    Scientific Personnel

Score Reading
USE MUSIC READING

SCORING 190
RT Answer Keys
    Grades (Scholastic)
    Grading
    Measurement
    Pass Fail Grading
    Testing

Scoring Keys
USE ANSWER KEYS

Screen Education
USE FILM STUDY

SCREENING TESTS 520
BT Tests

SCRIPTS 260
BT Literature
RT Comedy
    Composition (Literary)
    Creative Writing
    Dialogue
    Drama
    Playwriting
    Writing

SCULPTURE 030
BT Art
    Art Products
RT Visual Arts
    Welding

SEAFOOD 250
BT Food
RT Fisheries
    Food Service
    Food Service Industry

Sealants
USE SEALERS

SEALERS 460
UF Sealants
BT Building Materials
RT Adhesives
    Building Design
    Construction (Process)

SEAMEN 380
BT Semiskilled Workers
RT Boatmen
    Engineering Technicians
    Marine Technicians
    Technical Occupations

SEAMSTRESSES 380
UF Clothing Service Workers
BT Semiskilled Workers
RT Clothing Instruction
    Occupational Home Economics
    Semiskilled Occupations
    Service Occupations
    Sewing Instruction
    Sewing Machine Operators

SEARCH STRATEGIES 330
UF Search Theories
BT Information Retrieval
RT Bibliographic Coupling
    Classification
    Indexing
    Information Science
    Information Seeking
    Information Storage
    Library Science
    Operations Research

Search Theories
USE SEARCH STRATEGIES

SEASONAL EMPLOYMENT 150
BT Employment
RT Agriculture
    Braceros
    Migrant Employment
    Multiple Employment
    Seasonal Labor
    Seasonal Laborers
    Student Employment
    Youth Employment

SEASONAL LABOR 150
BT Labor
RT Seasonal Employment
    Seasonal Laborers

SEASONAL LABORERS 380
BT Laborers
RT Agricultural Laborers
    Braceros
    Migrant Workers
    Seasonal Employment
    Seasonal Labor

SECONDARY EDUCATION 140
UF Secondary School Education
BT Education
RT Laboratory Schools
    Pretechnology Programs
    Secondary Grades
    Secondary Schools
    Secondary School Students

Secondary Employment
USE MULTIPLE EMPLOYMENT

SECONDARY GRADES 280
UF Secondary Instructional Level
BT Instructional Program Divisions
RT High Schools
    Secondary Education

Secondary Instructional Level
USE SECONDARY GRADES

SECONDARY SCHOOL COUNSELORS 380
BT Counselors
    Pupil Personnel Workers
RT Guidance Personnel
    Guidance Programs
    Guidance Services
    Secondary Schools

Secondary School Education
USE SECONDARY EDUCATION

SECONDARY SCHOOL MATHEMATICS 340
BT Mathematics
RT College Mathematics
    Elementary School Mathematics
    Mathematics Education
    Mathematics Instruction

SECONDARY SCHOOLS 470
NT Biracial Secondary Schools
BT Schools
RT Affiliated Schools
    Area Vocational Schools
    High Schools
    Secondary Education
    Secondary School Counselors
    Secondary School Students

SECONDARY SCHOOL SCIENCE 110
BT Science Education
RT College Science
    Elementary School Science

SECONDARY SCHOOL STUDENTS 380
NT College Bound Students
      High School Students
      Junior High School Students
      Noncollege Preparatory Students
BT Students
RT Advanced Placement Programs
      Secondary Education
      Secondary Schools

SECONDARY SCHOOL TEACHERS 380
UF High School Teachers
      Junior High School Teachers
BT Teachers
RT Mathematics Teachers
      Public School Teachers
      Teaching

SECOND LANGUAGE LEARNING 290
UF Foreign Language Learning
      Language Learning
BT Learning
RT Bilingual Education
      Contrastive Linguistics
      Cultural Awareness
      English (Second Language)
      Intensive Language Courses
      Interference (Language Learning)
      Language Ability
      Language Development
      Language Enrichment
      Language Fluency
      Language Instruction
      Language Proficiency
      Language Skills
      Modern Languages
      Nucleation (Language Learning)
      Second Languages
      Unwritten Language

SECOND LANGUAGES 290
BT Language
RT Bilingual Education
      Bilingualism
      Bilingual Teacher Aides
      Bilingual Teachers
      English (Second Language)
      Fles Programs
      Language Instruction
      Language Planning
      Language Programs
      Native Speakers
      Second Language Learning

SECRETARIES 380
UF Administrative Secretaries
      Engineering Secretaries
      Executive Secretaries
      Legal Secretaries
      Medical Secretaries
      Police Department Secretaries
      Scientific Secretaries
      Social Secretaries
      Technical Secretaries

NT School Secretaries
BT Clerical Workers
RT Clerical Occupations
      Medical Assistants
      Office Practice
      Stenographers
      Stenography
      Typewriting
      Typists

Sectarian Colleges
USE CHURCH RELATED COLLEGES

SECURITY 420
UF Security Needs
BT Psychological Needs
RT Guaranteed Income
      Refugees

Security Needs
USE SECURITY

SEDATIVES 250
UF Barbiturates
      Hypnotics
      Tranquilizing Drugs
BT Narcotics
RT Health
      Medical Treatment
      Physiology
      Sensory Experience

SEGREGATED PUBLIC FACILITIES 210
BT Public Facilities
RT Racial Segregation

Segregation (Racial)
USE RACIAL SEGREGATION

Segregationist Groups
USE SEGREGATIONIST ORGANIZATIONS

SEGREGATIONIST ORGANIZATIONS 370
UF Segregationist Groups
BT Organizations (Groups)
RT Civil Disobedience
      Civil Rights
      Racial Segregation
      Social Discrimination

SEISMOLOGY 400
BT Earth Science
RT Geology
      Geophysics
      Physical Geography
      Soil Science

SEIZURES 240
RT Epilepsy
      Neurological Defects
      Neurologically Handicapped

SELECTION 020
NT Competitive Selection
     Personnel Selection
     Reading Material Selection
     Site Selection
RT Recruitment

Selection Of Library Materials
USE LIBRARY MATERIAL SELECTION

SELF ACTUALIZATION 420
SN The belief in or the process of
     developing the actuality of ones idealized
     image
UF Growth Motivation
     Self Development
     Self Motivation
     Self Realization
     Self Utilization
BT Self Concept
RT Behavior Development
     Growth Patterns
     Human Development
     Identification (Psychological)
     Individual Development
     Individualism
     Individual Psychology
     Job Satisfaction
     Morale
     Motivation Techniques
     Need Gratification
     Perceptual Development
     Personal Growth
     Personality Development
     Personal Values
     Role Perception
     Role Theory
     Self Congruence
     Self Evaluation
     Social Psychology

Self Appraisal Growth
USE SELF EVALUATION

Self Bias
USE BIAS

SELF CARE SKILLS 010
BT Skills
RT Child Care
     Custodial Mentally Handicapped
     Exceptional Child Education
     Habit Formation
     Hygiene
     Institutionalized (Persons)
     Object Manipulation
     Physically Handicapped
     Trainable Mentally Handicapped

SELF CONCEPT 420
UF Ego Strength
     Racial Self Identification
     Self Image
     Self Knowledge
     Self Understanding
     Student Self Image
NT Body Image
     Self Actualization
     Self Congruence
     Self Esteem
RT Aspiration
     Black Power
     Identification (Psychological)
     Individual Power
     Job Satisfaction
     Morale
     Occupational Aspiration
     Personality
     Self Evaluation

SELF CONGRUENCE 420
BT Self Concept
RT Behavior
     Individual Development
     Psychological Characteristics
     Psychotherapy
     Self Actualization

SELF CONTAINED CLASSROOMS 210
BT Classrooms

SELF CONTROL 420
UF Impulse Control
     Self Discipline
NT Behavior Patterns
RT Discipline
     Individual Development
     Individual Power
     Sportsmanship

Self Determination
USE INDIVIDUAL POWER

Self Development
USE SELF ACTUALIZATION

SELF DIRECTED CLASSROOMS 210
BT Classrooms

SELF DIRECTED GROUPS 380
UF Self Guided Groups
BT Groups
RT Experimental Colleges
     Group Activities
     Group Dynamics
     Group Experience
     Group Relations
     Interaction Process Analysis
     Laboratory Training
     Training Laboratories

Self Discipline
USE SELF CONTROL

SELF ESTEEM 040
BT   Self Concept
RT   Human Dignity
     Self Evaluation

SELF EVALUATION 190
UF   Self Appraisal Growth
BT   Evaluation
RT   Action Research
     Self Actualization
     Self Concept
     Self Esteem

SELF EXPRESSION 420
RT   Catharsis
     Creativity
     Individualism

Self Growth
USE INDIVIDUAL DEVELOPMENT

Self Guided Groups
USE SELF DIRECTED GROUPS

SELF HELP PROGRAMS 410
BT   Improvement Programs
RT   Self Pacing Machines

Self Image
USE SELF CONCEPT

Self Instructional Aids
USE AUTOINSTRUCTIONAL AIDS

Self Instructional Materials
USE AUTOINSTRUCTIONAL AIDS

Self Knowledge
USE SELF CONCEPT

Self Motivation
USE SELF ACTUALIZATION

SELF PACING MACHINES 170
BT   Teaching Machines
RT   Self Help Programs

Self Realization
USE SELF ACTUALIZATION

SELF REWARD 040
BT   Rewards
RT   Motivation
     Positive Reinforcement

Self Teaching
USE INDEPENDENT STUDY

Self Understanding
USE SELF CONCEPT

Self Utilization
USE SELF ACTUALIZATION

SEMANTICS 290
BT   Linguistics
RT   Abstraction Levels
     Componential Analysis
     Computational Linguistics
     Connected Discourse
     Deep Structure
     Discourse Analysis
     Etymology
     Lexicology
     Negative Forms (Language)
     Semiotics
     Syntax
     Thesauri

SEMESTER DIVISION 020
NT   Trimester Schedules
RT   Extended School Year
     Intervals
     Quarter System
     Scheduling
     School Calendars

SEMICONDUCTOR DEVICES 170
BT   Science Equipment
RT   Lasers
     Superconductors
     Transistors

Seminaries
USE CHURCH RELATED COLLEGES

Seminar Programs
USE SEMINARS

SEMINARS 510
UF   Seminar Programs
NT   Police Seminars
     Student Seminars
     Teacher Seminars
RT   Institutes (Training Programs)
     Institute Type Courses
     Post Doctoral Education
     Science Institutes
     Short Courses
     Summer Institutes
     Symposia
     Teaching Techniques
     Workshops

SEMIOTICS 080
BT   Communication (Thought Transfer)
RT   Language
     Language Patterns
     Linguistics
     Semantics
     Sign Language
     Symbolic Language
     Syntax
     Verbal Communication

SEMISKILLED OCCUPATIONS 350
BT Occupations
RT Blue Collar Occupations
   Boatmen
   Building Trades
   Data Processing Occupations
   Electrical Occupations
   Machine Tool Operators
   Metal Working Occupations
   Seamstresses
   Semiskilled Workers
   Sewing Machine Operators
   Skilled Labor
   Skilled Occupations
   Skilled Workers
   Trade And Industrial Education
   Unskilled Labor
   Unskilled Workers

SEMISKILLED WORKERS 380
NT Boatmen
   Machine Tool Operators
   Seamen
   Seamstresses
   Sewing Machine Operators
BT Nonprofessional Personnel
RT Blue Collar Occupations
   Metal Working Occupations
   Semiskilled Occupations
   Skilled Labor
   Skilled Occupations
   Skilled Workers
   Unskilled Labor
   Unskilled Occupations
   Unskilled Workers
   Vocational Education

SEMITIC LANGUAGES 300
NT Amharic
   Arabic
   Hebrew
BT Afro Asiatic Languages

Senators
USE LEGISLATORS

SENIOR CITIZENS 380
BT Older Adults
RT Age
   Age Groups
   Citizen Role
   Geriatrics
   Retirement

Senior Colleges
USE COLLEGES

SENIOR HIGH SCHOOLS 470
BT High Schools
RT Junior High Schools

SENIORS 380
BT Students
RT College Students
   High School Students

SENIOR TEACHER ROLE 490
BT Teacher Role
RT Team Teaching

SENSITIVITY TRAINING 270
SN Method of increasing quality and skills of
   interpersonal interaction through the use
   of primary group processes as a means
   of learning and reeducation
UF Human Relations Training
BT Training
RT Group Discussion
   Group Therapy
   Interaction Process Analysis
   Interpersonal Competence
   Laboratory Training
   Personal Growth
   Protocol Materials
   T Groups
   Therapy
   Training Laboratories

SENSORY AIDS 080
SN Educational material adapted to meet
   primarily the needs of blind and partially
   seeing students
NT Mobility Aids
BT Instructional Aids
RT Blind
   Braille
   Cosmetic Prostheses
   Hearing Aids
   Prostheses
   Sensory Training
   Tactile Adaptation
   Visually Handicapped

SENSORY DEPRIVATION 160
UF Isolation (Perceptual)
   Perceptual Deprivation
RT Behavior Change
   Cognitive Processes
   Cultural Disadvantagement
   Fatigue (Biology)
   Handicapped
   Perception
   Physiology
   Psychology
   Sensory Experience

SENSORY EXPERIENCE 070
BT Experience
RT Cutaneous Sense
   Figural Aftereffects
   Haptic Perception
   Sedatives
   Sensory Deprivation
   Sensory Integration
   Sensory Training
   Stimulants
   Stimuli
   Surrealism
   Tactual Perception
   Visual Discrimination

SENSORY INTEGRATION 420
UF Intersensory Integration
RT Behavior Patterns
      Perception
      Perceptual Development
      Sensory Experience
      Sensory Training
      Stimulus Behavior

Sensory Motor Learning
USE PERCEPTUAL MOTOR LEARNING

SENSORY TRAINING 270
NT Auditory Training
BT Training
RT Auditory Discrimination
      Auditory Perception
      Discrimination Learning
      Haptic Perception
      Perceptual Development
      Perceptual Motor Learning
      Sensory Aids
      Sensory Experience
      Sensory Integration
      Tactual Perception
      Visual Discrimination
      Visual Perception

SENTENCE DIAGRAMING 270
RT Deep Structure
      Diagrams
      Grammar
      Language Patterns
      Linguistics
      Sentences
      Sentence Structure
      Structural Analysis
      Surface Structure
      Syntax

SENTENCES 290
BT Paragraphs
RT Discourse Analysis
      Grammar
      Intonation
      Sentence Diagraming
      Sentence Structure
      Structural Analysis
      Syntax

SENTENCE STRUCTURE 290
RT Adjectives
      Adverbs
      Capitalization (Alphabetic)
      Deep Structure
      Function Words
      Generative Grammar
      Grammar
      Kernel Sentences
      Nominals
      Parallelism (Literary)
      Pronouns
      Punctuation
      Sentence Diagraming

Sentences
Structural Analysis
Structural Grammar
Structural Linguistics
Suprasegmentals
Surface Structure
Traditional Grammar
Verbs

SEQUENTIAL APPROACH 510
RT Critical Path Method
      Sequential Learning
      Sequential Programs

SEQUENTIAL LEARNING 310
BT Learning
RT Sequential Approach
      Sequential Programs
      Serial Learning

SEQUENTIAL PROGRAMS 080
NT Fixed Sequence
      Sequential Reading Programs
BT Computer Programs
RT Programed Instruction
      Sequential Approach
      Sequential Learning
      Teaching Methods

SEQUENTIAL READING PROGRAMS 440
BT Reading Programs
      Sequential Programs
RT Adult Reading Programs
      Basic Reading
      Readability
      Reading

SERBOCROATIAN 300
BT Slavic Languages

Serial Association
USE SERIAL LEARNING

SERIAL LEARNING 310
UF Serial Association
      Serial Method
BT Learning
RT Association (Psychological)
      Associative Learning
      Learning Theories
      Paired Associate Learning
      Sequential Learning

Serial Method
USE SERIAL LEARNING

SERIAL ORDERING 010
BT Psychomotor Skills

SERIALS 320
NT Bulletins
      Newsletters
      Newspapers
      Periodicals
BT Publications
RT Annual Reports
      Books

Library Collections
Technical Reports

SERVICE EDUCATION 140
BT Education
RT Industrial Arts
Service Occupations

SERVICE OCCUPATIONS 350
NT Child Care Occupations
Food Service Occupations
BT Occupations
RT Agricultural Supply Occupations
Attendants
Barbers
Child Care Workers
Clothing Maintenance Specialists
Companions (Occupation)
Cosmetologists
Domestics
Electrical Appliance Servicemen
Emergency Squad Personnel
Fire Fighters
Food Service Industry
Industrial Arts
Maids
Producer Services
Refrigeration Mechanics
Sales Occupations
Seamstresses
Service Education
Service Workers
Television Repairmen
Visiting Homemakers

SERVICES 020
NT Community Services
Financial Services
Guidance Services
Human Services
Producer Services
Professional Services
Special Services
Utilities
RT Developed Nations

SERVICE VEHICLES 170
SN Vehicles used to provide transportation,
maintenance, or repair services
UF Buses
Contractor Vehicles
Maintenance Vehicles
BT Motor Vehicles
RT Traffic Circulation
Vehicular Traffic

SERVICE WORKERS 380
NT Barbers
Clothing Maintenance Specialists
Companions (Occupation)
Cooks
Cosmetologists
Domestics
Electrical Appliance Servicemen
Emergency Squad Personnel

Fire Fighters
Food Service Workers
Maids
Refrigeration Mechanics
Television Repairmen
Visiting Homemakers
BT Nonprofessional Personnel
RT Agricultural Supply Occupations
Employees
Producer Services
Sales Occupations
Sales Workers
Service Occupations
Vocational Education

SET THEORY 340
BT Algebra
Mathematics
Theories
RT Arithmetic

SETTLEMENT HOUSES 210
UF Neighborhood Settlements
University Settlements
RT Collective Settlements
Community Programs
Neighborhood Centers
Residential Centers
Welfare Services

Settlement Patterns
USE LAND SETTLEMENT

SEVENTEENTH CENTURY LITERATURE 260
BT Literature
RT Drama
Essays
Fables
Poetry
Prose
Puritans
World Literature

SEWING INSTRUCTION 270
BT Instruction
RT Home Economics Education
Seamstresses
Sewing Machine Operators

SEWING MACHINE OPERATORS 380
BT Semiskilled Workers
RT Needle Trades
Seamstresses
Semiskilled Occupations
Sewing Instruction
Trade And Industrial Education

SEX (CHARACTERISTICS) 070
NT Females
Males
BT Physical Characteristics
RT Sex Differences
Sex Education
Sexuality

SEX DIFFERENCES 070
BT Individual Differences
RT Sex (Characteristics)

SEX EDUCATION 140
BT Education
RT Contraception
    Ethical Instruction
    Ethics
    Sex (Characteristics)
    Sexuality

SEXUALITY 070
RT Sex (Characteristics)
    Sex Education

Shade Trees
USE TREES

Shadow Plays
USE THEATER ARTS

Shapers
USE MACHINE TOOLS

SHARECROPPERS 380
BT Agricultural Laborers
RT Agricultural Personnel

SHARED SERVICES 020
BT Special Services
RT Consortia
    Cooperative Planning
    Cooperative Programs
    Dual Enrollment
    Specialists

Shared Time
USE DUAL ENROLLMENT

Sheet Metal Machine Operators
USE SHEET METAL WORKERS

SHEET METAL WORK 350
BT Metal Working Occupations
RT Air Conditioning Equipment
    Assembly (Manufacturing)
    Building Equipment
    School Construction
    Sheet Metal Workers

SHEET METAL WORKERS 380
UF Sheet Metal Machine Operators
BT Skilled Workers
RT Machine Tool Operators
    Metal Working Occupations
    Sheet Metal Work
    Skilled Occupations
    Trade And Industrial Education

SHELTERED WORKSHOPS 270
BT Workshops
RT Rehabilitation Counseling
    Rehabilitation Programs
    Vocational Rehabilitation

SHONA 300
BT African Languages
    Bantu Languages

SHOP CURRICULUM 110
UF General Shop
BT Curriculum
RT Hand Tools
    Industrial Arts
    School Shops

Shop Mechanics
USE MACHINE REPAIRMEN

Shop Rooms
USE SCHOOL SHOPS

SHORT COURSES 110
BT Courses
RT Noncredit Courses
    Refresher Courses
    Science Institutes
    Seminars
    Summer Institutes

Shorthand
USE STENOGRAPHY

SHORT STORIES 260
BT Literary Genres
    Literature
RT Books
    Characterization (Literature)
    Composition (Literary)
    Didacticism
    Existentialism
    French Literature
    German Literature
    Local Color Writing
    Metaphors
    Narration
    Naturalism
    Nineteenth Century Literature
    Parody
    Polish Literature
    Prose
    Realism
    Russian Literature
    Spanish American Literature
    Spanish Literature
    Tales

SIBLINGS 380
RT Birth Order
    Children
    Family (Sociological Unit)
    Twins

Sick Leave
USE LEAVE OF ABSENCE

SIERRA LEONE CREOLE 300
UF Krio
    Sierra Leone Krio
BT Creoles

Sierra Leone Krio
USE SIERRA LEONE CREOLE

Sight
USE VISION

SIGHT METHOD 510
SN Method of teaching reading based on recognition and pronunciation of whole words
UF Look Guess Method
Look Say Method
BT Teaching Methods
RT Beginning Reading
Reading Instruction
Reading Materials
Reading Skills
Sight Vocabulary
Visual Learning
Word Recognition

Sight Playing
USE MUSIC READING

Sightseeing Industry
USE TOURISM

Sight Singing
USE MUSIC READING

SIGHT VOCABULARY 440
BT Vocabulary
RT Beginning Reading
Sight Method
Vocabulary Development
Word Recognition

Signal Services
USE TELECOMMUNICATION

Signboards
USE SIGNS

Significance Measures
USE TESTS OF SIGNIFICANCE

SIGN LANGUAGE 290
SN Communication by means of gesture
BT Manual Communication
RT Deaf Interpreting
Finger Spelling
Language
Semiotics

SIGN PAINTERS 380
UF Sign Writers
BT Skilled Workers
RT Design
Graphic Arts
Signs
Skilled Occupations
Trade And Industrial Education

SIGNS 170
UF Road Signs
Signboards
RT Engineering Graphics
Graphic Arts
Printing
Sign Painters
Traffic Regulations
Traffic Safety

Sign Writers
USE SIGN PAINTERS

SILENT READING 440
BT Reading
RT Reading Instruction
Reading Skills

Similarity Transformations
USE TRANSFORMATIONS (MATHEMATICS)

Simple Fractions
USE COMMON FRACTIONS

SIMULATED ENVIRONMENT 160
RT Management Games
Project Training Methods
Simulation
Simulators

Simulated Speech
USE ARTIFICIAL SPEECH

SIMULATION 510
SN Duplication of the essential characteristics of a task or situation
BT Techniques
RT Critical Incidents Method
Game Theory
Laboratory Training
Management Games
Simulated Environment
Simulators
Teaching Experience
Teaching Methods
Teaching Techniques

SIMULATORS 170
SN Devices which duplicate the essential characteristics of a task or situation
UF Simulator Training
Training Devices
RT Models
Simulated Environment
Simulation
Trainers

Simulator Training
USE SIMULATORS

SINGHALESE 300
UF Sinhalese
BT Indo European Languages

SINGING 030
BT   Music
RT   Applied Music
     Art Song
     Choral Music
     Choruses
     Concerts
     Recreational Activities
     Vocal Music

SINGLE CONCEPT FILMS 050
BT   Films
RT   Audiovisual Aids
     Filmstrips
     Film Study
     Instructional Films

SINGLE STUDENTS 380
UF   Unmarried Students
BT   Students
RT   Adult Students
     College Students
     Marital Status

Sinhalese
USE   SINGHALESE

SINO TIBETAN LANGUAGES 300
NT   Austro Asiatic Languages
     Burmese
     Cambodian
     Chinese
     Lao
     Thai
     Tibetan
     Vietnamese
BT   Languages
RT   Language Classification
     Native Speakers

SITE ANALYSIS 210
RT   Campus Planning
     Facility Case Studies
     Facility Expansion
     Facility Guidelines
     Geographic Location
     School Location
     School Planning
     Site Development
     Site Selection

SITE DEVELOPMENT 130
SN   Process of planning, engineering, and
     landscaping a plot of ground
BT   Development
RT   Construction Programs
     Engineering
     Landscaping
     School Design
     School Expansion
     School Planning
     Site Analysis
     Site Selection

SITE SELECTION 210
BT   Selection
RT   Real Estate
     School Design
     School Environment
     School Expansion
     School Planning
     School Zoning
     Site Analysis
     Site Development

SITUATIONAL TESTS 520
UF   Situation Reaction Tests
     Situation Response Tests
BT   Tests
RT   Reactive Behavior
     Response Mode

Situation Reaction Tests
USE   SITUATIONAL TESTS

Situation Response Tests
USE   SITUATIONAL TESTS

SIXTEEN MILLIMETER PROJECTORS 170
BT   Projection Equipment

SIXTEENTH CENTURY LITERATURE 260
BT   Literature
RT   Biblical Literature
     Drama
     Poetry
     Prose
     Renaissance Literature
     World Literature

Six Three Three Organization
USE   INSTRUCTIONAL PROGRAM DIVISIONS

SKILL ANALYSIS 150
SN   Breaking down manipulative skills into
     their components
RT   Critical Incidents Method
     Job Analysis
     Job Skills
     Object Manipulation
     Psychomotor Skills
     Skill Obsolescence
     Systems Analysis

SKILL CENTERS 210
BT   Educational Facilities
RT   Off The Job Training
     Skill Development
     Skills

SKILL DEVELOPMENT 130
BT   Development
RT   Complexity Level
     Motor Development
     Skill Centers
     Skills
     Transfer Of Training

SKILLED LABOR 150
UF   Journeymen
BT   Labor
RT   Semiskilled Occupations
     Semiskilled Workers
     Skilled Occupations
     Skilled Workers
     Skills

SKILLED OCCUPATIONS 350
NT   Appliance Repairing
BT   Occupations
RT   Auto Body Repairmen
     Auto Mechanics (Occupation)
     Bricklayers
     Bricklaying
     Building Trades
     Data Processing Occupations
     Electrical Occupations
     Electricians
     Employment
     Floor Layers
     Glaziers
     Job Skills
     Locomotive Engineers
     Machine Repairmen
     Machine Tool Operators
     Machinists
     Metal Working Occupations
     Roofers
     Semiskilled Occupations
     Semiskilled Workers
     Sheet Metal Workers
     Sign Painters
     Skilled Labor
     Skilled Workers
     Trade And Industrial Education
     Watchmakers
     Welders

SKILLED WORKERS 380
NT   Appliance Service Technicians
     Auto Body Repairmen
     Auto Mechanics (Occupation)
     Bricklayers
     Carpenters
     Electricians
     Farm Mechanics (Occupation)
     Floor Layers
     Glaziers
     Locomotive Engineers
     Machine Repairmen
     Machinists
     Roofers
     Sheet Metal Workers
     Sign Painters
     Tool And Die Makers
     Watchmakers
     Welders
BT   Nonprofessional Personnel
RT   Employees
     Machine Tool Operators
     Metal Working Occupations

     Semiskilled Occupations
     Semiskilled Workers
     Skilled Labor
     Skilled Occupations
     Vocational Education

SKILL OBSOLESCENCE 010
BT   Obsolescence
RT   Employment Potential
     Employment Qualifications
     Job Skills
     Skill Analysis
     Technological Advancement
     Vocational Adjustment
     Vocational Retraining

SKILLS 010
NT   Agricultural Skills
     Alphabetizing Skills
     Basic Skills
     Business Skills
     Communication Skills
     Decision Making Skills
     Handwriting Skills
     Home Economics Skills
     Homemaking Skills
     Interpersonal Competence
     Interpretive Skills
     Job Skills
     Language Skills
     Library Skills
     Locational Skills (Social Studies)
     Map Skills
     Mechanical Skills
     Reading Skills
     Research Skills
     Self Care Skills
     Study Skills
     Teaching Skills
     Vocabulary Skills
     Writing Skills
RT   Qualifications
     Skill Centers
     Skill Development
     Skilled Labor

SKITS 030
RT   Dramatics
     Theater Arts

SLAVERY 100
RT   American History
     Negro History

SLAVIC LANGUAGES 300
NT   Bielorussian
     Bulgarian
     Czech
     Polish
     Russian
     Serbocroatian
     Slovenian
     Ukrainian
BT   Languages
RT   Cyrillic Alphabet

Language Classification
Native Speakers

SLEEP 070
UF Drowsiness
RT Behavior
     Psychological Patterns

SLIDES 050
SN A mounted transparency, either film or
     glass, intended for projection or viewing
     by transmitted light
BT Audiovisual Aids
     Transparencies
RT Color Presentation
     Filmstrips
     Instructional Aids
     Teacher Developed Materials

Slovene
USE SLOVENIAN

SLOVENIAN 300
UF Slovene
BT Slavic Languages

SLOW LEARNERS 380
BT Students
RT Ability
     Educationally Disadvantaged
     Low Ability Students
     Mentally Handicapped
     Progressive Retardation
     Retarded Children
     Retarded Readers

Slum Children
USE DISADVANTAGED YOUTH

SLUM CONDITIONS 160
BT Slum Environment
RT Slums

SLUM ENVIRONMENT 160
NT Slum Conditions
BT Environment
RT Slums

SLUMS 490
NT Urban Slums
BT Depressed Areas (Geographic)
RT Cultural Disadvantagement
     Ghettos
     Inner City
     Slum Conditions
     Slum Environment
     Slum Schools
     Urban Environment
     Urban Renewal Agencies

SLUM SCHOOLS 470
BT Schools
RT Slums

SMALL CLASSES 280
BT Classes (Groups Of Students)
RT Class Size

Small Engine Mechanics
USE AUTO MECHANICS

SMALL GROUP INSTRUCTION 510
BT Instruction
     Teaching Techniques
RT Flexible Schedules
     Laboratory Procedures
     Large Group Instruction
     Team Training

SMALL SCHOOLS 470
BT Schools
RT One Teacher Schools
     School Size

Smokestacks
USE CHIMNEYS

SMOKING 250
RT Health
     Health Education
     Stimulants
     Tobacco

Snack Bars
USE DINING FACILITIES

Sociability
USE INTERPERSONAL COMPETENCE

SOCIAL ACTION 490
UF Political Reform
     Social Reform
NT Community Action
RT Action Programs (Community)
     Activism
     Citizen Participation
     Community Change
     Social Attitudes
     Social Change
     Social Responsibility
     Social Welfare

SOCIAL ADJUSTMENT 420
BT Adjustment (To Environment)
RT Interpersonal Competence
     Social Development
     Social Influences
     Social Isolation
     Socially Maladjusted
     Social Maturity
     Social Problems
     Vocational Adjustment

SOCIAL AGENCIES 370
BT Social Organizations
     Welfare Agencies
RT Agency Role
     Social Services
     Social Work
     Social Workers

SOCIAL ATTITUDES 040
BT Attitudes
RT Activism
    Bias
    Interpersonal Competence
    Northern Attitudes
    Political Attitudes
    Political Socialization
    Public Opinion
    Social Action
    Social Change
    Social Characteristics
    Social Development
    Social Differences
    Social Environment
    Social Influences
    Socially Maladjusted
    Social Problems
    Social Values
    Student Alienation
    Teacher Alienation

Social Awareness
USE INTERPERSONAL COMPETENCE

SOCIAL BACKGROUND 200
BT Cultural Background
RT Social Class
    Socioeconomic Background

SOCIAL CHANGE 480
UF Social Revolution
RT Change Agents
    Community Change
    Educational Sociology
    Political Socialization
    Social Action
    Social Attitudes
    Social Influences
    Social Integration
    Social Values
    Sociocultural Patterns

SOCIAL CHARACTERISTICS 490
SN Criteria used to rate members of a social
    class
RT Adult Characteristics
    Cultural Context
    Interpersonal Competence
    Social Attitudes
    Social Differences
    Social Environment
    Social Influences
    Social Relations
    Social Values

SOCIAL CLASS 490
NT Lower Class
    Middle Class
    Upper Class
RT Culture Conflict
    Social Background
    Social Dialects
    Social Integration

Social Relations
Social Status
Social Structure
Subculture

Social Class Differences
USE SOCIAL DIFFERENCES

Social Class Integration
USE SOCIAL INTEGRATION

Social Climate
USE SOCIAL ENVIRONMENT

Social Competence
USE INTERPERSONAL COMPETENCE

Social Deprivation
USE SOCIAL DISADVANTAGEMENT

SOCIAL DEVELOPMENT 480
NT Dating (Social)
    Friendship
    Marriage
    Social Maturity
BT Development
RT Empathy
    Individualism
    Interpersonal Competence
    Social Adjustment
    Social Attitudes
    Social Differences
    Social Environment
    Social Experience
    Social Immaturity
    Social Influences
    Socialization
    Social Life
    Social Relations
    Sociopsychological Services

SOCIAL DIALECTS 290
SN Special varieties within a language,
    defined by the social environment of its
    speakers
BT Dialects
RT Dialect Studies
    Diglossia
    Language
    Language Role
    Linguistics
    Nonstandard Dialects
    Regional Dialects
    Social Class
    Sociolinguistics
    Standard Spoken Usage
    Tenl

SOCIAL DIFFERENCES 480
UF Social Class Differences
RT Culture Conflict
    Individual Differences
    Social Attitudes
    Social Characteristics
    Social Development
    Social Environment

Social Integration
Social Values

SOCIAL DISADVANTAGEMENT 490
UF Social Deprivation
RT Cultural Disadvantagement
    Functional Illiteracy
    Socially Disadvantaged
    Social Work

SOCIAL DISCRIMINATION 480
UF Bigotry
    Discrimination (Social)
    Prejudice (Social)
NT Educational Discrimination
    Housing Discrimination
    Racial Discrimination
    Religious Discrimination
RT Bias
    Civil Rights
    Discriminatory Attitudes (Social)
    Discriminatory Legislation
    Intergroup Education
    Racial Segregation
    Segregationist Organizations
    Social Integration

SOCIAL DISTRIBUTION 120
RT Demography
    Incidence

SOCIAL ENVIRONMENT 160
UF Social Climate
BT Environment
RT Culture Conflict
    Non Western Civilization
    Productive Living
    Social Attitudes
    Social Characteristics
    Social Development
    Social Differences
    Social Influences
    Social Integration
    Social Opportunities
    Social Values
    Spatial Relationship
    Student Subcultures
    Subculture
    Western Civilization

SOCIAL EXCHANGE THEORY 480
BT Theories
RT Behavior Theories

SOCIAL EXPERIENCE 200
BT Experience
RT Cross Age Teaching
    Interpersonal Competence
    Social Development
    Social Influences
    Social Maturity

SOCIAL FACTORS 490
RT Community Influence
    Cultural Factors
    Environmental Influences
    Progressive Retardation
    Social Influences
    Socioeconomic Influences
    Sociology

SOCIAL IMMATURITY 060
BT Immaturity
RT Social Development
    Social Influences
    Social Maturity

SOCIAL INFLUENCES 480
NT Population Growth
    Rural Urban Differences
RT Cultural Factors
    Cultural Interrelationships
    Culture Conflict
    Educational Sociology
    Language Role
    Non Western Civilization
    Political Socialization
    Social Adjustment
    Social Attitudes
    Social Change
    Social Characteristics
    Social Development
    Social Environment
    Social Experience
    Social Factors
    Social Immaturity
    Social Integration
    Social Opportunities
    Social Reinforcement
    Social Relations
    Social Status
    Social Values
    Socioeconomic Influences
    Western Civilization

SOCIAL INTEGRATION 490
UF Integration (Social)
    Social Class Integration
RT Classroom Integration
    College Integration
    Cultural Interrelationships
    Faculty Integration
    Human Relations
    Integration Effects
    Interaction Process Analysis
    Intergroup Relations
    Interpersonal Relationship
    Neighborhood Integration
    Personnel Integration
    Racial Integration
    School Integration
    Social Change
    Social Class
    Social Differences
    Social Discrimination

Social Environment
Social Influences
Social Opportunities
Social Problems
Social Relations
Social Systems
Voluntary Integration

Social Interaction
USE SOCIAL RELATIONS

SOCIAL ISOLATION 490
RT Cultural Isolation
Maladjustment
Social Adjustment
Social Psychology
Sociocultural Patterns

Social Issues
USE SOCIAL PROBLEMS

SOCIALIZATION 230
UF Social Learning
NT Political Socialization
RT Cross Age Teaching
Imitation
Inhibition
Interpersonal Competence
Role Conflict
Social Development

Social Learning
USE SOCIALIZATION

SOCIAL LIFE 490
RT Dating (Social)
Interpersonal Relationship
Social Development
Social Relations

Socially Deprived
USE SOCIALLY DISADVANTAGED

SOCIALLY DEVIANT BEHAVIOR 060
NT Crime
Drug Abuse
BT Behavior
RT Alcoholism
Anti Social Behavior
Delinquency
Drug Addiction
Juvenile Courts
Socially Maladjusted
Vandalism

SOCIALLY DISADVANTAGED 380
UF Socially Deprived
BT Culturally Disadvantaged
RT Social Disadvantagement

SOCIALLY MALADJUSTED 490
RT Maladjustment
Social Adjustment
Social Attitudes
Socially Deviant Behavior
Social Values
Student Alienation

SOCIAL MATURITY 420
BT Social Development
RT Interpersonal Competence
Maturation
Personal Growth
Social Adjustment
Social Experience
Social Immaturity

SOCIAL MOBILITY 120
BT Mobility
RT Educational Benefits
Ghettos
Occupational Mobility
Social Opportunities
Socioeconomic Influences

SOCIAL OPPORTUNITIES 360
UF Social Restrictions
BT Cultural Opportunities
RT Educational Benefits
Social Environment
Social Influences
Social Integration
Social Mobility

SOCIAL ORGANIZATIONS 370
NT Social Agencies
BT Organizations (Groups)
RT Community Organizations
Social Systems
Student Unions

SOCIAL PLANNING 490
BT Planning
RT City Planning
Language Planning
Regional Planning

SOCIAL PROBLEMS 490
UF Social Issues
BT Problems
RT Child Abuse
Culture Conflict
Debate
Interpersonal Problems
Social Adjustment
Social Attitudes
Social Integration
Social Relations
Social Values
Unwed Mothers

Social Profile
USE SOCIAL VALUES

SOCIAL PSYCHOLOGY 490
NT Group Dynamics
BT Psychology
RT Educational Sociology
Groups
Self Actualization
Social Isolation
Social Reinforcement

Sociology
Sociopsychological Services

Social Reconstruction
USE SOCIAL RESPONSIBILITY

SOCIAL RECREATION PROGRAMS 390
BT Recreational Programs
RT Student Unions

Social Reform
USE SOCIAL ACTION

SOCIAL REINFORCEMENT 310
BT Reinforcement
RT Motivation
Negative Reinforcement
Positive Reinforcement
Reinforcers
Rewards
Social Influences
Social Psychology
Sociology

SOCIAL RELATIONS 480
UF Social Interaction
NT Dating (Social)
Friendship
Marriage
BT Relationship
RT Human Relations
Interaction Process Analysis
Intergroup Relations
Interpersonal Competence
Interpersonal Relationship
Rapport
Social Characteristics
Social Class
Social Development
Social Influences
Social Integration
Social Life
Social Problems
Student School Relationship

SOCIAL RESPONSIBILITY 490
UF Social Reconstruction
NT Citizenship Responsibility
Community Responsibility
Educational Responsibility
Leadership Responsibility
BT Responsibility
RT City Improvement
Community Programs
Community Service Programs
Community Services
Environmental Influences
Neighborhood Improvement
Social Action
Social Services
Social Welfare
Social Work
Welfare Services

Social Restrictions
USE SOCIAL OPPORTUNITIES

Social Revolution
USE SOCIAL CHANGE

SOCIAL SCIENCES 480
NT Anthropology
Archaeology
Economics
Geography
History
Political Science
Psychology
Social Studies
Sociology
BT Sciences
RT Area Studies
Foreign Policy
Language And Area Centers
Middle Eastern History
Nineteenth Century Literature
Physical Geography

Social Secretaries
USE SECRETARIES

SOCIAL SERVICES 490
BT Human Services
RT Community Services
School Social Workers
Social Agencies
Social Responsibility
Social Work
Sociopsychological Services
Visiting Homemakers
Welfare Services

Social Skills
USE INTERPERSONAL COMPETENCE

SOCIAL STATUS 480
UF Class Status
BT Status
RT Social Class
Social Influences
Social Structure
Socioeconomic Influences
Socioeconomic Status
Status Need

SOCIAL STRUCTURE 490
RT Cultural Context
Social Class
Social Status

SOCIAL STUDIES 110
SN Social studies consist of adaptations of
knowledge from the social sciences for
teaching purposes at the elementary and
secondary levels of education
NT Current Events
Economics
Geography
History
Political Science
World Affairs
BT Curriculum

Social Sciences
RT   Anthropology
     Ethnology
     Language And Area Centers
     Locational Skills (Social Studies)
     Physical Geography
     Social Studies Units

SOCIAL STUDIES UNITS 110
BT   Units Of Study (Subject Fields)
RT   Social Studies
     Unit Plan

SOCIAL SYSTEMS 490
RT   Group Structure
     Interaction Process Analysis
     Social Integration
     Social Organizations

Social Trends
USE SOCIOCULTURAL PATTERNS

SOCIAL VALUES 040
UF   Group Values
     Social Profile
BT   Values
RT   Cultural Context
     Group Norms
     Individualism
     Peer Groups
     Political Attitudes
     Productive Living
     Professional Recognition
     Social Attitudes
     Social Change
     Social Characteristics
     Social Differences
     Social Environment
     Social Influences
     Socially Maladjusted
     Social Problems
     Sociological Novels

SOCIAL WELFARE 480
BT   Welfare
RT   Social Action
     Social Responsibility
     Social Work
     Welfare Agencies

SOCIAL WORK 350
NT   Caseworker Approach
BT   Welfare
RT   Caseworkers
     Pupil Personnel Services
     Rehabilitation
     School Social Workers
     Social Agencies
     Social Disadvantagement
     Social Responsibility
     Social Services
     Social Welfare
     Social Workers
     Welfare Agencies
     Welfare Services

SOCIAL WORKERS 380
NT   Caseworkers
     School Social Workers
RT   Counseling
     Probation Officers
     Rehabilitation
     Social Agencies
     Social Work

SOCIOCULTURAL PATTERNS 100
UF   Social Trends
NT   Human Living
RT   Biculturalism
     Cross Cultural Studies
     Cultural Interrelationships
     Cultural Pluralism
     Culture
     Ethnology
     Language Planning
     Non Western Civilization
     Social Change
     Social Isolation
     Sociolinguistics
     Sociology
     Western Civilization

SOCIODRAMA 420
BT   Psychotherapy
RT   Sociometric Techniques
     Therapy

SOCIOECONOMIC BACKGROUND 200
BT   Background
RT   Social Background
     Socioeconomic Influences

SOCIOECONOMIC INFLUENCES 490
RT   Black Community
     Industrialization
     Political Influences
     Social Factors
     Social Influences
     Social Mobility
     Social Status
     Socioeconomic Background
     Socioeconomic Status

Socioeconomic Level
USE SOCIOECONOMIC STATUS

SOCIOECONOMIC STATUS 480
UF   Socioeconomic Level
BT   Status
RT   Affluent Youth
     Aspiration
     Depressed Areas (Geographic)
     Economics
     Economic Status
     Educational Benefits
     Income
     Lower Middle Class
     Social Status
     Socioeconomic Influences
     Sociolinguistics
     Upper Class

SOCIOLINGUISTICS 290
NT Bilingualism
     Language Planning
     Multilingualism
BT Linguistics
RT Dialect Studies
     Diglossia
     Idioms
     Language Role
     Language Standardization
     Linguistic Theory
     Mutual Intelligibility
     Native Speakers
     Nonstandard Dialects
     Official Languages
     Psycholinguistics
     Regional Dialects
     Social Dialects
     Sociocultural Patterns
     Socioeconomic Status
     Sociology
     Standard Spoken Usage
     TENL

SOCIOLOGICAL NOVELS 260
BT Novels
RT Fiction
     Literature
     Prose
     Social Values

SOCIOLOGY 490
NT Educational Sociology
     Human Dignity
BT Behavioral Sciences
     Social Sciences
RT Area Studies
     Authoritarianism
     Behavior
     Cross Cultural Studies
     Ethnology
     Social Factors
     Social Psychology
     Social Reinforcement
     Sociocultural Patterns
     Sociolinguistics

SOCIOMETRIC TECHNIQUES 190
BT Measurement Techniques
RT Behavior
     Group Dynamics
     Group Relations
     Group Status
     Group Structure
     Interpersonal Relationship
     Personality Assessment
     Personality Studies
     Sociodrama

SOCIOPSYCHOLOGICAL SERVICES 490
BT Human Services
RT Psychological Needs
     Social Development
     Social Psychology
     Social Services

Soft Cover Books
USE PAPERBACK BOOKS

SOIL CONSERVATION 460
RT Agriculture
     Conservation Education
     Depleted Resources
     Environmental Education
     Forestry
     Land Use
     Natural Resources
     Soil Science

SOIL SCIENCE 400
BT Earth Science
RT Agriculture
     Agronomy
     Biology
     Chemistry
     Fertilizers
     Geology
     Land Use
     Plant Science
     Seismology
     Soil Conservation

Solar Energy
USE SOLAR RADIATION

Solar Heating
USE SOLAR RADIATION

SOLAR RADIATION 400
UF Solar Energy
     Solar Heating
     Solar Radiation Energy
BT Radiation
RT Climate Control
     Climatic Factors
     Controlled Environment
     Daylight
     Environmental Influences
     Heat
     Lasers
     Light
     Lighting
     Temperature
     Thermal Environment

Solar Radiation Energy
USE SOLAR RADIATION

Solicitors
USE LAWYERS

SOLID GEOMETRY 340
BT Geometry

SOMALI 300
BT Languages

Sonic Environment
USE ACOUSTICAL ENVIRONMENT

SONNETS 260
BT Poetry
RT Ballads
    Epics
    Odes
    Renaissance Literature

SORTING PROCEDURES 010
BT Psychomotor Skills

Sound
USE ACOUSTICS

Sound Absorbing Materials
USE ACOUSTIC INSULATION

Sound Barriers
USE ACOUSTIC INSULATION

SOUND EFFECTS 050
BT Production Techniques
RT Acoustics
    Audio Equipment
    Film Study
    Phonotape Recordings
    Sound Tracks
    Television

Sound Equipment
USE AUDIO EQUIPMENT

SOUND FILMS 050
UF Sound Motion Pictures
BT Audio Equipment
    Films
RT Film Study
    Sound Tracks

Sound Insulation
USE ACOUSTIC INSULATION

Sound Motion Pictures
USE SOUND FILMS

Soundproofing
USE ACOUSTIC INSULATION

Sound Reflecting Materials
USE ACOUSTIC INSULATION

Sound Spectrograms
USE SPECTROGRAMS

SOUND TRACKS 050
RT Phonotape Recordings
    Sound Effects
    Sound Films
    Television

Sound Transmission
USE ACOUSTICS

Sound Waves
USE ACOUSTICS

South Asian Civilization
USE NON WESTERN CIVILIZATION

SOUTHERN ATTITUDES 040
BT Attitudes
RT Northern Attitudes
    Southern Citizens

SOUTHERN CITIZENS 380
RT Southern Attitudes
    Southern Community
    Southern States

SOUTHERN COMMUNITY 120
BT Community
RT Southern Citizens
    Southern Schools
    Southern States

SOUTHERN SCHOOLS 470
BT School Location
    Schools
RT Southern Community
    Southern States

SOUTHERN STATES 120
BT Geographic Regions
RT Southern Citizens
    Southern Community
    Southern Schools

SPACE 400
BT Scientific Concepts
RT Atomic Structure
    Atomic Theory
    Intervals
    Quantum Mechanics
    Relativity
    Space Orientation
    Time

SPACE CLASSIFICATION 210
SN Categorization of areas in a given facility
    generally by function or purpose
BT Classification
RT Building Plans
    College Planning
    Design Needs
    Facility Inventory
    Facility Utilization Research
    Interior Design
    Interior Space
    Offices (Facilities)
    Space Utilization
    Spatial Relationship

SPACE DIVIDERS 210
SN Vertical surface or structure used for
    separating areas within larger rooms
UF Room Dividers
NT Movable Partitions
RT Audiovisual Aids
    Classroom Arrangement
    Flexible Classrooms
    School Space
    Vertical Work Surfaces

Spaced Negative Reinforcement
USE NEGATIVE REINFORCEMENT

SPACE ORIENTATION 210
BT Orientation
RT Body Image
Human Body
Kinesthetic Perception
Perception
Space
Visually Handicapped Orientation

Space Sciences
USE AEROSPACE TECHNOLOGY

Space Time Continuum
USE RELATIVITY

SPACE UTILIZATION 210
RT Building Conversion
Building Design
Building Plans
Campus Planning
Classroom Arrangement
Classroom Design
Color Planning
Corridors
Design Needs
Equipment Storage
Facilities
Facility Expansion
Facility Guidelines
Facility Requirements
Facility Utilization Research
Flexible Classrooms
Flexible Facilities
Furniture Arrangement
Interior Design
Interior Space
Movable Partitions
School Planning
School Size
School Space
Space Classification
Spatial Relationship
Storage

SPANISH 300
UF Conversational Spanish
BT Romance Languages
RT Modernism

SPANISH AMERICAN LITERATURE 260
BT Literature
RT Anthologies
Comedy
Composition (Literary)
Drama
Epics
Essays
Fables
Fiction
Journalism
Latin American Culture
Legends

Letters (Correspondence)
Literary Analysis
Literary Conventions
Literary Criticism
Literary Genres
Novels
Poetry
Prose
Satire
Short Stories
Tragedy
Twentieth Century Literature
World Literature

SPANISH AMERICANS 380
BT Ethnic Groups
RT Mexican Americans
Spanish Culture

SPANISH CULTURE 100
BT Culture
RT Latin American Culture
Spanish Americans

SPANISH LITERATURE 260
BT Literature
RT Anthologies
Baroque Literature
Biblical Literature
Classical Literature
Comedy
Composition (Literary)
Drama
Eighteenth Century Literature
Epics
Essays
Fables
Fiction
Journalism
Legends
Letters (Correspondence)
Literary Analysis
Literary Conventions
Literary Criticism
Literary Genres
Novels
Prose
Satire
Short Stories
Symbolism
Tragedy
Twentieth Century Literature
World Literature

SPANISH SPEAKING 380
UF Spanish Speaking Children
Spanish Speaking Students
Spanish Speaking Youth
BT Native Speakers
RT Biculturalism
Bilingual Students
English (Second Language)
Non English Speaking

Spanish Speaking Children
USE   SPANISH SPEAKING

Spanish Speaking Students
USE   SPANISH SPEAKING

Spanish Speaking Youth
USE   SPANISH SPEAKING

SPATIAL RELATIONSHIP 210
SN   Functional interconnections between
       areas of a building
BT   Relationship
RT   Architecture
       Building Design
       Building Plans
       Design Needs
       Flexible Facilities
       Interior Design
       Intervals
       Physical Facilities
       Psychological Needs
       School Planning
       School Space
       Social Environment
       Space Classification
       Space Utilization

SPEAKING 080
NT   Choral Speaking
       Public Speaking
BT   Language Arts
RT   Diction
       Expressive Language
       Rhetoric
       Speaking Activities
       Speech Skills

SPEAKING ACTIVITIES 080
BT   Activities
RT   Speaking
       Speech

Speaking Skills
USE   SPEECH SKILLS

SPECIAL CLASSES 280
BT   Classes (Groups Of Students)
RT   Exceptional Child Education
       Special Education
       Special Education Teachers

SPECIAL COUNSELORS 380
BT   Counselors
RT   Instructor Coordinators
       Specialists

SPECIAL DEGREE PROGRAMS 410
SN   Programs geared to the needs of adult
       students admitted on the basis of
       previous experience or self education
       rather than college credits
BT   Special Programs
RT   Adult Education
       Adult Education Programs
       Adult Students

       Bachelors Degrees
       College Credits
       Credentials
       Degree Requirements
       Degrees (Titles)
       Equivalency Tests
       Liberal Arts
       Masters Degrees

SPECIAL EDUCATION 140
UF   Special Training
NT   Deaf Education
       Speech Education
BT   Education
RT   Boarding Homes
       Boarding Schools
       Braille
       Diagnostic Teaching
       Exceptional Child Education
       High Interest Low Vocabulary Books
       Homebound
       Individual Instruction
       Institutional Administration
       Institutional Personnel
       Intervention
       Itinerant Teachers
       Large Type Materials
       Mobile Educational Services
       Partially Sighted
       Regional Schools
       Regular Class Placement
       Special Classes
       Special Education Teachers
       Specialists
       Special Programs
       Special Schools
       Special Services
       Talking Books
       Teaching Methods
       Telephone Instruction

SPECIAL EDUCATION TEACHERS 380
NT   Homebound Teachers
BT   Teachers
RT   Exceptional (Atypical)
       Gifted
       Handicapped
       Itinerant Teachers
       Special Classes
       Special Education
       Special Schools
       Teaching

SPECIAL HEALTH PROBLEMS 250
UF   Chronically Ill
       Chronic Medical Problems
       Health Impaired
BT   Problems
RT   Asthma
       Diabetes
       Emotionally Disturbed
       Epilepsy
       Exceptional (Atypical)
       Health

Mentally Handicapped
Physically Handicapped

SPECIALIST IN EDUCATION DEGREES 140
SN Two year program at post baccalaureate
     level for purpose of training school
     administrators
BT Degrees (Titles)
RT Bachelors Degrees
     Doctoral Degrees
     Masters Degrees

SPECIALISTS 380
UF Special Personnel
     Special Teachers
NT Child Development Specialists
     Film Production Specialists
     Learning Specialists
     Media Specialists
RT Consultants
     Itinerant Teachers
     Optometrists
     Referral
     Science Consultants
     Science Teachers
     Shared Services
     Special Counselors
     Special Education
     Specialization
     Special Services
     Teachers

SPECIALIZATION 140
RT College Majors
     Curriculum
     Occupations
     Specialists

SPECIAL LIBRARIES 210
NT Government Libraries
     Institution Libraries
     Law Libraries
     Legislative Reference Libraries
     Medical Libraries
     State Libraries
BT Libraries
RT Depository Libraries
     Research Libraries

Special Materials
USE INSTRUCTIONAL MATERIALS

Special Methods Courses
USE METHODS COURSES

Special Personnel
USE SPECIALISTS

SPECIAL PROGRAMS 410
NT Special Degree Programs
BT Programs
RT Exceptional Child Education
     Special Education
     Special Services

SPECIAL SCHOOLS 470
UF Special Service Schools
BT Schools
RT Exceptional Child Education
     Regional Schools
     Special Education
     Special Education Teachers

SPECIAL SERVICES 020
NT Shared Services
BT Services
RT Ancillary Services
     Exceptional Child Education
     Exceptional Child Services
     Mobile Educational Services
     Special Education
     Specialists
     Special Programs

Special Service Schools
USE SPECIAL SCHOOLS

Special Teachers
USE SPECIALISTS

Special Training
USE SPECIAL EDUCATION

Specialty Schools
USE PROPRIETARY SCHOOLS

SPECIAL ZONING 120
BT Zoning
RT School Integration

SPECIFICATIONS 500
NT Educational Specifications
     Performance Specifications
RT Construction Costs
     Contracts
     Criteria
     Equipment Standards
     Purchasing
     School Construction
     Standards

Spectator Traffic Control
USE TRAFFIC CONTROL

SPECTROGRAMS 170
UF Sound Spectrograms
RT Acoustic Phonetics
     Artificial Speech
     Audio Equipment
     Optics
     Phonology
     Physics
     Physics Experiments
     Speech
     Visible Speech

SPEECH 290
NT   Articulation (Speech)
Artificial Speech
Coded Speech
Cued Speech
Diction
Inner Speech (Subvocal)
Speech Compression
Visible Speech
BT   Psychomotor Skills
RT   Acoustic Phonetics
Alphabets
Child Language
Choral Speaking
Cleft Lip
Cleft Palate
Language
Language Patterns
Language Rhythm
Language Usage
Linguistic Performance
Linguistics
Oral Communication
Oral English
Phonemes
Phonemic Alphabets
Phonemics
Phonetics
Phonology
Pronunciation
Public Speaking
Retarded Speech Development
Rhetoric
Speaking Activities
Spectrograms
Speech Curriculum
Speech Education
Speech Evaluation
Speech Habits
Speech Handicaps
Speech Improvement
Speech Instruction
Speech Pathology
Speech Skills
Speech Therapists
Verbal Communication
Word Frequency

SPEECH CLINICS 210
BT   Clinics
RT   Speech Evaluation
Speech Handicapped
Speech Handicaps
Speech Improvement
Speech Therapists
Speech Therapy

SPEECH COMPRESSION 290
SN   Separating and transmitting voice
communicated words at accelerated
rates
BT   Speech
RT   Information Theory
Language Research

SPEECH CURRICULUM 110
BT   Curriculum
RT   Language Arts
Speech

SPEECH EDUCATION 140
BT   Special Education
RT   Aphasia
Language Arts
Linguistics
Lipreading
Speech
Speech Handicaps
Speech Improvement
Speech Pathology
Speech Skills
Speech Tests
Speech Therapists

SPEECHES 080
UF   Addresses
Talks
RT   Assembly Programs
Conferences
Discussion Programs
Institutes (Training Programs)
Lecture
Meetings
National Programs
Program Planning
Symposia

SPEECH EVALUATION 180
BT   Evaluation
RT   Speech
Speech Clinics
Speech Handicapped
Speech Tests
Speech Therapy

SPEECH HABITS 290
RT   American English
Child Language
Habit Formation
Language Development
Language Patterns
Language Rhythm
Language Usage
Native Speakers
Paralinguistics
Regional Dialects
Speech
Speech Pathology

SPEECH HANDICAPPED 240
UF   Speech Impaired
BT   Handicapped
RT   Aphasia
     Cleft Lip
     Cleft Palate
     Speech Clinics
     Speech Evaluation
     Speech Handicaps
     Speech Improvement
     Speech Therapy
     Stuttering

SPEECH HANDICAPS 240
NT   Cleft Lip
     Cleft Palate
BT   Language Handicaps
RT   Cerebral Palsy
     Speech
     Speech Clinics
     Speech Education
     Speech Handicapped
     Speech Improvement
     Speech Instruction
     Speech Pathology
     Speech Tests
     Speech Therapy
     Stuttering
     Voice Disorders

Speech Impaired
USE   SPEECH HANDICAPPED

SPEECH IMPROVEMENT 290
RT   Enunciation Improvement
     Speech
     Speech Clinics
     Speech Education
     Speech Handicapped
     Speech Handicaps
     Speech Instruction
     Speech Pathology
     Speech Therapists
     Speech Therapy
     Stuttering

SPEECH INSTRUCTION 270
UF   Voice Instruction
NT   Pronunciation Instruction
BT   Instruction
RT   Kinesthetic Methods
     Language Instruction
     Oral Expression
     Speech
     Speech Handicaps
     Speech Improvement
     Speech Skills
     Speech Therapists
     Visible Speech

SPEECH PATHOLOGY 240
RT   Speech
     Speech Education
     Speech Habits
     Speech Handicaps
     Speech Improvement
     Speech Therapists
     Speech Therapy

Speech Reading
USE   LIPREADING

SPEECH SKILLS 010
UF   Oral Facility
     Oral Skills
     Speaking Skills
BT   Audiolingual Skills
RT   Basic Skills
     Eye Voice Span
     Interpreters
     Language Fluency
     Language Patterns
     Language Rhythm
     Language Skills
     Language Styles
     Persuasive Discourse
     Rhetoric
     Speaking
     Speech
     Speech Education
     Speech Instruction
     Speech Tests
     Speech Therapy
     Stuttering
     Verbal Ability

SPEECH TESTS 520
BT   Tests
RT   Speech Education
     Speech Evaluation
     Speech Handicaps
     Speech Skills
     Speech Therapy

SPEECH THERAPISTS 380
BT   Therapists
RT   Aphasia
     Hearing Therapists
     Speech
     Speech Clinics
     Speech Education
     Speech Improvement
     Speech Instruction
     Speech Pathology

SPEECH THERAPY 290
UF   Language Therapy
BT   Therapy
RT   Cleft Lip
     Cleft Palate
     Educational Therapy
     Medical Treatment
     Speech Clinics
     Speech Evaluation

Speech Handicapped
Speech Handicaps
Speech Improvement
Speech Pathology
Speech Skills
Speech Tests
Stuttering
Voice Disorders

SPEED READING 440
BT   Reading
RT   Reading Skills
      Reading Speed

SPELLING 010
NT   Finger Spelling
BT   Writing
RT   Capitalization (Alphabetic)
      Diacritical Marking
      Graphemes
      Orthographic Symbols
      Plurals
      Punctuation
      Spelling Instruction
      Word Lists

SPELLING INSTRUCTION 270
UF   Teaching Spelling
BT   Instruction
RT   Spelling
      Teaching

SPIRAL CURRICULUM 110
BT   Curriculum
RT   Curriculum Development
      Curriculum Planning

Split Time
USE   DUAL ENROLLMENT

SPONTANEOUS BEHAVIOR 060
BT   Behavior

Sports
USE   ATHLETICS

Sports Grounds Keepers
USE   GROUNDS KEEPERS

SPORTSMANSHIP 060
RT   Behavior
      Behavior Patterns
      Individual Development
      Morale
      Motivation
      Physical Education
      Self Control
      Teamwork
      Values

Stacks (Exhaust)
USE   CHIMNEYS

Staff (Instructional)
USE   INSTRUCTIONAL STAFF

Staff Evaluation
USE   PERSONNEL EVALUATION

STAFF IMPROVEMENT 020
BT   Improvement
RT   Instructional Staff
      Teacher Improvement

STAFF MEETINGS 020
BT   Meetings
RT   Instructional Staff

Staff Offices
USE   OFFICES (FACILITIES)

STAFF ORIENTATION 270
BT   Orientation
RT   Instructional Staff
      Teacher Orientation

STAFF ROLE 020
UF   Personnel Role
NT   Resource Staff Role
RT   Instructional Staff
      Teacher Role

STAFF UTILIZATION 020
RT   Differentiated Staffs
      Instructional Staff
      School Cadres

STAGES 210
SN   Platform raised above floor level in a
      theater, lecture hall, classroom, or the
      like
RT   Arts Centers
      Auditoriums
      Classrooms
      Demonstration Centers
      Multipurpose Classrooms
      Music Facilities
      Outdoor Theaters
      Theaters

STANDARDIZED TESTS 520
BT   Tests
RT   National Competency Tests
      Objective Tests

STANDARDS 500
UF   Professional Standards
NT   Academic Standards
      Behavior Standards
      Equipment Standards
      Food Standards
      Group Norms
      Labor Standards
      Library Standards
      Living Standards
      Middle Class Norm
      State Standards
      Textbook Standards
RT   Acoustical Environment
      Codification
      Component Building Systems
      Copyrights
      Counselor Certification
      Counselor Qualifications
      Credentials

Criteria
Environmental Criteria
Evaluation Criteria
Performance Criteria
Performance Specifications
Sanctions
Specifications
Teaching Models
Thermal Environment
Validity

STANDARD SPOKEN USAGE 290
SN Customary use or employment of
    language, words, expressions, etc.
UF Colloquial Standard Usage
    Educated Colloquial Usage
    Informal Conversational Usage
    Oral Language Usage
BT Language Usage
RT American English
    Conversational Language Courses
    Language Patterns
    Language Planning
    Language Standardization
    Language Styles
    Nonstandard Dialects
    Official Languages
    Social Dialects
    Sociolinguistics

State
USE STATE PROGRAMS

STATE ACTION 230
RT State Departments Of Education
    State Government
    State Legislation
    State Programs

STATE AGENCIES 230
BT Agencies
RT Agency Role
    State Departments Of Education
    State Government
    State Legislation
    State Libraries
    State Officials
    State Programs
    Urban Renewal Agencies
    Welfare Agencies

STATE AID 220
UF State Assistance
    State Financial Aid
    State Support
RT Educational Finance
    Equalization Aid
    Financial Support
    Foundation Programs
    State Federal Aid
    State Federal Support
    State Government
    State Programs
    State Standards

State Universities
Training Allowances

State Assistance
USE STATE AID

State Boards
USE STATE LICENSING BOARDS

STATE BOARDS OF EDUCATION 020
UF State Committees On Education
    State School Boards
BT Governing Boards
RT Boards Of Education
    Public Education
    State Departments Of Education
    State School District Relationship
    State Standards

STATE CHURCH SEPARATION 230
RT Churches
    Church Role
    Federal Government
    Religion
    State Government

STATE COLLEGES 470
BT Colleges
RT Community Colleges
    Educational Facilities
    Higher Education
    Junior Colleges
    State Universities
    Teachers Colleges

State Committees On Education
USE STATE BOARDS OF EDUCATION

State Curriculum Bulletins
USE STATE CURRICULUM GUIDES

STATE CURRICULUM GUIDES 110
UF State Curriculum Bulletins
    State Syllabi
BT Curriculum Guides
RT Curriculum
    Curriculum Development
    Curriculum Planning
    State Programs

STATE DEPARTMENTS OF EDUCATION 230
UF State Education Agencies
RT State Action
    State Agencies
    State Boards Of Education
    State Programs

State Education Agencies
USE STATE DEPARTMENTS OF EDUCATION

STATE FEDERAL AID 220
RT Equalization Aid
    Federal Aid
    State Aid
    State Federal Support
    Training Allowances

STATE FEDERAL SUPPORT 220
RT Equalization Aid
Federal Aid
State Aid
State Federal Aid
Training Allowances

State Financial Aid
USE STATE AID

STATE FOREIGN LANGUAGE SUPERVISORS 380
BT State Supervisors
RT Administrative Personnel
Supervision
Supervisor Qualifications
Supervisory Methods
Teacher Supervision

STATE GOVERNMENT 230
UF Provincial Government
NT State Officials
BT Government (Administrative Body)
RT Depository Libraries
Federal State Relationship
Government Publications
State Action
State Agencies
State Aid
State Church Separation
State Laws
State Legislation
State Programs
States Powers

STATE LAWS 230
NT School Attendance Laws
BT Laws
RT Legislators
Loyalty Oaths
State Government
State Legislation

STATE LEGISLATION 230
NT State Recreation Legislation
BT Legislation
RT Educational Legislation
Federal Legislation
Loyalty Oaths
State Action
State Agencies
State Government
State Laws
State Standards

STATE LIBRARIES 210
BT Special Libraries
RT Archives
Government Libraries
State Agencies

STATE LICENSING BOARDS 230
UF State Boards
BT Governing Boards
RT Certification
Professional Education
State Standards
Testing Programs

STATE OFFICIALS 380
NT State Police
BT State Government
RT County Officials
Immigration Inspectors
Legislators
Public Officials
State Agencies

STATE POLICE 380
BT Police
State Officials
RT Immigration Inspectors

STATE PROGRAMS 230
UF State
BT Programs
RT Action Programs (Community)
Interstate Programs
Legislation
State Action
State Agencies
State Aid
State Curriculum Guides
State Departments Of Education
State Government

STATE RECREATION LEGISLATION 230
BT Recreation Legislation
State Legislation

State School Boards
USE STATE BOARDS OF EDUCATION

STATE SCHOOL DISTRICT RELATIONSHIP 230
BT Relationship
RT Board Administrator Relationship
Federal State Relationship
Intermediate Administrative Units
School District Autonomy
State Boards Of Education
Student School Relationship
Teacher Administrator Relationship

STATE SCHOOLS 470
BT Schools
RT Public Schools

STATES POWERS 230
UF States Rights
RT Federal State Relationship
State Government

States Rights
USE STATES POWERS

STATE STANDARDS 500
BT   Standards
RT   Accreditation (Institutions)
     State Aid
     State Boards Of Education
     State Legislation
     State Licensing Boards

STATE SUPERVISORS 380
NT   State Foreign Language Supervisors
BT   Supervisors
RT   Administrative Personnel
     Supervision
     Supervisor Qualifications
     Teacher Supervision

State Support
USE   STATE AID

STATE SURVEYS 180
BT   Surveys
RT   Questionnaires
     Statistical Surveys

State Syllabi
USE   STATE CURRICULUM GUIDES

STATE UNIVERSITIES 470
BT   Universities
RT   Colleges
     Educational Facilities
     Higher Education
     State Aid
     State Colleges

Static Controls
USE   ELECTRONIC CONTROL

STATISTICAL ANALYSIS 340
UF   Mathematical Statistics
     Multivariate Analysis
     Statistical Methods
     Statistical Processes
     Statistical Theory
NT   Analysis Of Variance
     Correlation
     Discriminant Analysis
     Factor Analysis
     Hypothesis Testing
     Sampling
RT   Equated Scores
     Etymology
     Expectancy Tables
     Force Field Analysis
     Glottochronology
     Interaction
     National Norms
     Probability
     Probability Theory
     Q Sort
     Reliability
     Research
     Research Methodology
     School Statistics
     Statistical Data

     Statistical Studies
     Statistics
     Student Distribution
     Tests Of Significance

Statistical Association Methods
USE   CORRELATION

STATISTICAL DATA 340
NT   Census Figures
     Comparative Statistics
     Demography
     Disease Rate
     Dropout Rate
     Employment Statistics
     Equated Scores
     School Statistics
BT   Data
RT   Attendance Records
     Calculation
     Measurement
     National Norms
     Psychometrics
     Reliability
     Reports
     Statistical Analysis
     Statistical Studies
     Statistical Surveys
     Statistics
     Tables (Data)
     Test Results
     Tests

Statistical Methods
USE   STATISTICAL ANALYSIS

Statistical Processes
USE   STATISTICAL ANALYSIS

STATISTICAL STUDIES 340
NT   Statistical Surveys
RT   Quality Control
     Sampling
     Statistical Analysis
     Statistical Data

STATISTICAL SURVEYS 340
BT   Statistical Studies
     Surveys
RT   Sampling
     State Surveys
     Statistical Data

Statistical Theory
USE   STATISTICAL ANALYSIS

STATISTICS 340
SN   A branch of mathematics dealing with
     the collection of quantitative data
BT   Mathematics
RT   Calculation
     Computational Linguistics
     Expectancy Tables
     Hypothesis Testing
     Mathematical Logic
     Mathematical Models

Numbers
Predictive Measurement
Statistical Analysis
Statistical Data

STATUS 480
NT Economic Status
Family Status
Group Status
Marital Status
Social Status
Socioeconomic Status
RT Professional Recognition
Status Need

STATUS NEED 420
SN Psychological need for recognition
BT Psychological Needs
RT Achievement Need
Affiliation Need
Professional Recognition
Social Status
Status

STEALING 060
UF Thefts
NT Book Thefts
BT Misbehavior
RT Discipline Problems

Steel Foundries
USE FOUNDRIES

STEEL INDUSTRY 370
BT Metal Industry
RT Industrialization

STENOGRAPHERS 380
UF Clerk Stenographers
Engineering Stenographers
Foreign Language Stenographers
Legal Stenographers
Medical Stenographers
Police Stenographers
Public Stenographers
Scientific Stenographers
BT Clerical Workers
RT Clerical Occupations
Court Reporters
Office Practice
Secretaries
Stenography
Typewriting
Typists

STENOGRAPHY 350
UF Shorthand
BT Writing
RT Abbreviations
Business Subjects
Office Practice
Secretaries
Stenographers
Writing Skills

STEREOPSIS 240
UF Depth Perception
Perception Of Depth
Stereoscopic Vision
BT Vision
RT Visual Acuity

Stereoscopic Vision
USE STEREOPSIS

STEREOTYPES 490
NT Jewish Stereotypes
Negro Stereotypes
Teacher Stereotypes
RT Attitudes

Stickers
USE ADHESIVES

STIMULANTS 250
RT Health
Narcotics
Physiology
Sensory Experience
Smoking
Stimuli
Tobacco

STIMULI 070
NT Aural Stimuli
Electrical Stimuli
Verbal Stimuli
Visual Stimuli
RT Conditioned Stimulus
Psychophysiology
Sensory Experience
Stimulants
Stimulus Behavior
Stimulus Devices
Stimulus Generalization

STIMULUS BEHAVIOR 060
BT Behavior
RT Adaptation Level Theory
Animal Behavior
Arousal Patterns
Conditioned Response
Conditioned Stimulus
Extinction (Psychology)
Figural Aftereffects
Mediation Theory
Pictorial Stimuli
Pupillary Dilation
Sensory Integration
Stimuli
Stimulus Generalization
Verbal Operant Conditioning

STIMULUS DEVICES 170
RT Cues
Electrical Stimuli
Psychological Testing
Stimuli

STIMULUS GENERALIZATION 310
BT Generalization
    Learning Processes
RT Conditioned Response
    Learning Theories
    Mediation Theory
    Patterned Responses
    Stimuli
    Stimulus Behavior

Stimulus Synthesis
USE PATTERNED RESPONSES

Stockpiles
USE SUPPLIES

Stop Signs
USE TRAFFIC SIGNS

STORAGE 210
NT Equipment Storage
    Information Storage
RT Building Equipment
    Classroom Furniture
    Design Needs
    Design Preferences
    Equipment
    Facility Requirements
    Furniture
    Furniture Arrangement
    Furniture Design
    Home Furnishings
    Individual Needs
    Interior Space
    Physical Design Needs
    Space Utilization

Storage Batteries
USE ELECTRIC BATTERIES

STORY READING 440
BT Reading
RT Story Telling

STORY TELLING 080
RT Story Reading

Strabismus
USE HETEROTROPIA

Straw Boss
USE CREW LEADERS

Stream Pollution Control
USE WATER POLLUTION CONTROL

Street Layouts
USE TRAFFIC PATTERNS

Street Parking Areas
USE PARKING AREAS

Strength (Biology)
USE MUSCULAR STRENGTH

STRESS VARIABLES 420
BT Psychological Patterns

STRIKES 150
RT Arbitration
    Collective Bargaining
    Collective Negotiation
    Labor Demands
    Labor Force
    Labor Problems
    Negotiation Impasses
    Unions

STRUCTURAL ANALYSIS 290
UF Word Analysis
NT Discourse Analysis
    Tagmemic Analysis
RT Componential Analysis
    Concordances
    Context Clues
    Diachronic Linguistics
    Graphemes
    Idioms
    Language Universals
    Linguistics
    Reading Instruction
    Sentence Diagraming
    Sentences
    Sentence Structure
    Structural Linguistics
    Suffixes
    Suprasegmentals
    Syllables
    Synchronic Linguistics

STRUCTURAL BUILDING SYSTEMS 210
SN Combination of such structural member
    and methods as foundations, post and
    beam, vaults, or lift-slabs to form the
    structural frame or shell of a building
RT Architectural Research
    Architecture
    Building Design
    Buildings
    Civil Engineering
    Component Building Systems
    Construction (Process)
    Construction Costs
    Masonry
    Prefabrication
    Prestressed Concrete
    School Architecture
    School Buildings
    School Construction
    School Design

STRUCTURAL GRAMMAR 290
BT Grammar
RT Descriptive Linguistics
    Form Classes (Languages)
    Function Words
    Sentence Structure
    Structural Linguistics
    Syntax
    Tagmemic Analysis
    Traditional Grammar

STRUCTURAL LINGUISTICS 290
BT Linguistics
RT Applied Linguistics
     Diachronic Linguistics
     Sentence Structure
     Structural Analysis
     Structural Grammar
     Synchronic Linguistics

Structural Work Occupations
USE BUILDING TRADES

STUDENT ABILITY 010
BT Ability
RT Academic Ability
     Average Students
     Low Ability Students

Student Achievement
USE ACADEMIC ACHIEVEMENT

Student Activism
USE ACTIVISM

Student Activities (Not Classwork)
USE COCURRICULAR ACTIVITIES

STUDENT ADJUSTMENT 420
UF School Adjustment
BT Adjustment (To Environment)
RT Conduct
     Continuation Students
     Students

STUDENT ALIENATION 040
BT Psychological Patterns
RT Activism
     Dropout Attitudes
     Generation Gap
     Role Conflict
     Social Attitudes
     Socially Maladjusted
     Student Attitudes
     Student Behavior

STUDENT APPLICATION 020
RT Admission (School)
     Student Placement

Student Appraisal
USE STUDENT EVALUATION

Student Aptitude
USE ACADEMIC APTITUDE

Student Aspiration
USE ASPIRATION

STUDENT ATTITUDES 040
UF Pupil Attitudes
     Student Feelings
BT Attitudes
RT Activism
     Student Alienation
     Student Behavior
     Student Motivation
     Student Opinion

     Student Reaction
     Student Role
     Students

STUDENT BEHAVIOR 060
NT Conduct
BT Behavior
RT Activism
     Behavioral Objectives
     Classroom Observation Techniques
     Student Alienation
     Student Attitudes
     Student Reaction
     Student Role
     Students

Student Centers
USE STUDENT UNIONS

STUDENT CERTIFICATION 500
BT Certification
RT Credentials
     Educational Certificates
     Equivalency Tests
     Student Testing

STUDENT CHARACTERISTICS 380
RT Average Students
     Family Characteristics
     Individual Characteristics
     Low Ability Students
     Participant Characteristics
     Students
     Student Subcultures

STUDENT COLLEGE RELATIONSHIP 420
SN The relationship between a college and
     its students
UF College Student Relationship
BT Student School Relationship
RT Activism
     College Students
     Ombudsmen
     Student Needs
     Student Teacher Relationship
     Student Welfare

STUDENT COSTS 220
NT Tuition
BT Costs
RT Proprietary Schools
     Student Loan Programs
     Students
     Unit Costs

Student Creativity
USE CREATIVITY

Student Credit Hours
USE CREDITS

STUDENT DEVELOPED MATERIALS 050
SN Instructional materials prepared by
    students
NT Student Writing Models
BT Instructional Materials
RT Art Materials
    Classroom Materials
    Instructional Aids
    Manipulative Materials
    Material Development
    Mathematics Materials
    Reading Materials
    Resource Materials
    Science Materials
    Student Projects
    Three Dimensional Aids

STUDENT DEVELOPMENT 130
BT Development
RT Individual Development
    Student Records
    Students

Student Dissent
USE ACTIVISM

STUDENT DISTRIBUTION 120
UF Pupil Distribution
    Pupil Redistribution
RT Counselor Client Ratio
    Incidence
    Statistical Analysis
    Student Placement

STUDENT EMPLOYMENT 150
BT Employment
RT Part Time Jobs
    Seasonal Employment
    Student Personnel Work
    Student Placement
    Students
    Work Study Programs

STUDENT ENROLLMENT 020
UF School Enrollment
NT Dual Enrollment
BT Enrollment
RT Average Daily Enrollment
    Double Sessions
    Students

STUDENT EVALUATION 180
UF Student Appraisal
BT Evaluation
RT Academic Achievement
    Achievement Rating
    Average Students
    College Credits
    Course Evaluation
    Credentials
    Educational Diagnosis
    Equivalency Tests
    Grades (Scholastic)
    Pass Fail Grading
    Report Cards

Student Records
Students
Student Testing

STUDENT EXCHANGE PROGRAMS 490
BT Exchange Programs
RT Foreign Student Advisers
    Foreign Students
    Students
    Study Abroad

STUDENT EXPERIENCE 200
BT Experience
RT Clinical Experience
    Field Experience Programs
    Students
    Supervised Farm Practice

Student Feelings
USE STUDENT ATTITUDES

STUDENT GROUPING 280
NT Ability Grouping
    Heterogeneous Grouping
    Homogeneous Grouping
BT Grouping (Instructional Purposes)
RT Average Students
    Classes (Groups Of Students)
    Cluster Grouping
    Students

Student Housing
USE COLLEGE HOUSING

STUDENT IMPROVEMENT 270
BT Improvement
RT Achievement Gains
    Student Rehabilitation
    Students

STUDENT INTERESTS 040
NT Student Science Interests
BT Interests
RT Cocurricular Activities
    Curiosity
    Educational Interest
    Experimental Colleges
    Relevance (Education)
    Student Motivation
    Students

STUDENT LEADERSHIP 060
BT Leadership
RT Students

STUDENT LOADING AREAS 210
RT Bus Transportation
    Student Transportation
    Traffic Regulations
    Traffic Safety

STUDENT LOAN PROGRAMS 220
BT Programs
RT Banking
Educational Finance
Federal Programs
Financial Needs
Financial Support
Loyalty Oaths
Scholarship Loans
Student Costs
Tuition

Student Militancy
USE ACTIVISM

STUDENT MOBILITY 120
BT Mobility
RT Students
Transfers

STUDENT MOTIVATION 040
BT Motivation
RT Curiosity
Student Attitudes
Student Interests
Students
Teacher Influence

STUDENT NEEDS 420
BT Needs
RT Relevance (Education)
Student College Relationship
Students

STUDENT OPINION 040
BT Opinions
RT Student Attitudes
Student Reaction
Students

STUDENT ORGANIZATIONS 370
BT Organizations (Groups)
RT Cocurricular Activities
Student Participation
Students
Student Unions

Student Parent Conferences
USE PARENT STUDENT CONFERENCES

STUDENT PARTICIPATION 270
BT Participation
RT Activism
Experimental Colleges
Student Organizations
Students

Student Performance
USE ACADEMIC PERFORMANCE

STUDENT PERSONNEL PROGRAMS 410
UF Pupil Personnel Programs
BT Programs
RT Counseling Programs
Health Programs
Student Personnel Services
Student Personnel Work
Student Personnel Workers

STUDENT PERSONNEL SERVICES 090
SN Supportive, non-instructional services to
college or university students in a school
setting
NT Student Placement
BT School Services
RT Ancillary Services
Attendance Officers
College Deans
Counseling Services
Employment Services
Foreign Student Advisers
Guidance Programs
Guidance Services
Ombudsmen
Pupil Personnel Services
Pupil Personnel Workers
School Health Services
Student Personnel Programs
Student Personnel Workers
Student Welfare

STUDENT PERSONNEL WORK 090
SN Consultant services performed for the
welfare of students in higher education,
including counseling, student
employment, housing etc.
BT College Programs
RT Counseling Centers
Counseling Services
Foreign Student Advisers
Guidance Services
Resident Assistants
Student Employment
Student Personnel Programs

STUDENT PERSONNEL WORKERS 380
SN Professional personnel who provide
supportive, non-instructional services to
college or university students in a school
setting
NT College Deans
Foreign Student Advisers
School Psychologists
School Social Workers
BT School Personnel
RT Ancillary Services
College Programs
Counseling Services
Counselors
Guidance Personnel
School Social Workers
Student Personnel Programs

Student Personnel Services
Student Welfare

STUDENT PLACEMENT 090
UF Pupil Assignment
    Pupil Placement
BT Placement
    Pupil Personnel Services
    Student Personnel Services
RT College Choice
    Guidance Services
    Job Placement
    Residential Care
    Student Application
    Student Distribution
    Student Employment
    Students

STUDENT PROBLEMS 090
BT Problems
RT Student Rehabilitation
    Students

Student Progress
USE ACHIEVEMENT

STUDENT PROJECTS 270
UF Individual Projects
BT Projects
RT Cocurricular Activities
    Cross Age Teaching
    Field Experience Programs
    Project Training Methods
    Student Developed Materials
    Student Research
    Students
    Supervised Farm Practice

STUDENT PROMOTION 510
SN Process by which a student is passed to
    the next higher instruction or grade level
UF Academic Promotion
RT Academic Achievement
    Academic Failure
    Academic Performance
    Age Grade Placement
    Flexible Progression
    Grade Repetition
    Instructional Program Divisions

Student Protest
USE ACTIVISM

STUDENT REACTION 060
UF Student Responses
RT Student Attitudes
    Student Behavior
    Student Opinion
    Students

STUDENT RECORDS 020
UF Cumulative Records
    Individual Inventory
    Progress Scale
BT Records (Forms)
RT Academic Records
    Case Records
    Confidential Records
    Credentials
    Student Development
    Student Evaluation
    Students

STUDENT REHABILITATION 090
BT Rehabilitation
RT Continuation Students
    Student Improvement
    Student Problems
    Students

STUDENT RESEARCH 450
BT Research
RT Student Projects
    Students

Student Responses
USE STUDENT REACTION

STUDENT ROLE 490
RT Family Role
    Parent Role
    Role Perception
    Student Attitudes
    Student Behavior
    Students
    Student School Relationship
    Teacher Role

STUDENTS 380
UF Pupils
NT Able Students
    Adult Students
    Advanced Students
    Average Students
    Bilingual Students
    Caucasian Students
    College Students
    Commuting Students
    Continuation Students
    Day Students
    Elementary School Students
    Evening Students
    Exceptional Students
    Foreign Students
    Freshmen
    Graduate Students
    Handicapped Students
    High Achievers
    Low Ability Students
    Low Achievers
    Lower Class Students
    Medical Students
    Negro Students
    Nonresident Students

Overachievers
Part Time Students
Resident Students
Secondary School Students
Seniors
Single Students
Slow Learners
Student Teachers
Student Volunteers
Superior Students
Transfer Students
Underachievers
RT Academic Ability
Academic Achievement
Academic Rank (Professional)
Aptitude
Cocurricular Activities
College Choice
College Housing
Competitive Selection
Dropouts
Home Visits
Labor Force Nonparticipants
Parent Student Conferences
Parent Student Relationship
Student Adjustment
Student Attitudes
Student Behavior
Student Characteristics
Student Costs
Student Development
Student Employment
Student Enrollment
Student Evaluation
Student Exchange Programs
Student Experience
Student Grouping
Student Improvement
Student Interests
Student Leadership
Student Mobility
Student Motivation
Student Needs
Student Opinion
Student Organizations
Student Participation
Student Placement
Student Problems
Student Projects
Student Reaction
Student Records
Student Rehabilitation
Student Research
Student Role
Student Seminars
Student Teacher Ratio
Student Teacher Relationship
Student Teaching
Student Testing

Student Transportation
Student Welfare
Trainees
Transfers
Truancy

STUDENT SCHOOL RELATIONSHIP 420
UF Pupil School Relationship
School Student Relationship
NT Student College Relationship
BT Relationship
RT Activism
Board Administrator Relationship
Experimental Colleges
Family School Relationship
Probationary Period
Relevance (Education)
Role Theory
School Phobia
Social Relations
State School District Relationship
Student Role
Student Teacher Relationship

STUDENT SCIENCE INTERESTS 040
BT Student Interests
RT Interest Research
Interest Scales
Interest Tests
Personal Interests
Vocational Interests

Student Selection
USE ADMISSION CRITERIA

Student Self Image
USE SELF CONCEPT

STUDENT SEMINARS 510
BT Seminars
RT Students

STUDENT SUBCULTURES 100
BT Subculture
RT Cultural Factors
Cultural Traits
Social Environment
Student Characteristics

Student Teacher Behavior
USE TEACHER BEHAVIOR

Student Teacher Interaction
USE STUDENT TEACHER RELATIONSHIP

STUDENT TEACHER RATIO 020
UF Pupil Teacher Ratio
Teacher Pupil Ratio
Teacher Student Ratio
RT Class Size
Students
Teacher Distribution
Teachers

STUDENT TEACHER RELATIONSHIP 480
UF Pupil Teacher Interaction
    Pupil Teacher Relationship
    Student Teacher Interaction
    Teacher Pupil Interaction
    Teacher Pupil Relationship
    Teacher Student Interaction
    Teacher Student Relationship
BT Relationship
RT Activism
    Classroom Communication
    Home Visits
    Student College Relationship
    Students
    Student School Relationship
    Teacher Evaluation
    Teacher Influence
    Teachers

STUDENT TEACHERS 380
BT Students
    Subprofessionals
    Teachers
RT College Supervisors
    Cooperating Teachers
    Education Majors
    Episode Teaching
    Microteaching
    Paraprofessional School Personnel
    Preservice Education
    Science Teachers
    Student Teaching
    Teacher Interns

Student Teacher Supervisors
USE COLLEGE SUPERVISORS

STUDENT TEACHING 140
UF Off Campus Student Teaching
    On Site Courses
    Practice Teaching
    Student Teaching Program
NT Episode Teaching
BT Teacher Education
RT Affiliated Schools
    College Supervisors
    Cooperating Teachers
    Lesson Observation Criteria
    Methods Courses
    Microteaching
    Practicums
    Practicum Supervision
    Preservice Education
    Students
    Student Teachers
    Teaching Experience

Student Teaching Program
USE STUDENT TEACHING

STUDENT TESTING 180
BT Testing
RT Student Certification
    Student Evaluation
    Students

Student Transfers
USE TRANSFER STUDENTS

STUDENT TRANSPORTATION 020
UF School Transportation
BT Transportation
RT Commuting Students
    School Buses
    Student Loading Areas
    Students
    Traffic Circulation

Student Travel
USE TRAVEL

STUDENT UNIONS 210
SN Organizations, programs, and/or
    facilities planned for community life of
    students
UF College Unions
    Student Centers
BT Facilities
RT Cocurricular Activities
    Recreational Facilities
    Social Organizations
    Social Recreation Programs
    Student Organizations

Student Unrest
USE ACTIVISM

STUDENT VOLUNTEERS 380
BT Students
    Volunteers

STUDENT WELFARE 480
BT Welfare
RT Ombudsmen
    Student College Relationship
    Student Personnel Services
    Student Personnel Workers
    Students

STUDENT WRITING MODELS 050
SN Written work by students used in
    instruction to represent composition,
    rhetoric, grammar, or usage principles
BT Student Developed Materials
RT Composition (Literary)
    Creative Writing
    Descriptive Writing
    Direction Writing
    English Instruction
    Expository Writing
    Instructional Materials
    Models
    Technical Writing
    Writing
    Writing Exercises

Studies
USE RESEARCH

STUDIO FLOOR PLANS 210
BT Building Plans
RT Design
   Educational Facilities
   School Design

STUDY 510
UF Study Hours
NT Correspondence Study
   Facility Utilization Research
   Film Study
   Home Study
   Independent Study
   Individual Study
RT Study Centers
   Study Facilities
   Study Habits
   Study Skills

STUDY ABROAD 110
RT Student Exchange Programs
   Tourism
   Travel

Study Aids
USE STUDY FACILITIES

STUDY CENTERS 210
UF Youth Study Centers
NT Curriculum Study Centers
   School Study Centers
BT Study Facilities
RT After School Centers
   Compensatory Education
   Disadvantaged Youth
   Study
   Tutoring
   Youth

Study Circles
USE DISCUSSION GROUPS

STUDY FACILITIES 210
UF Study Aids
NT Carrels
   Study Centers
BT Educational Facilities
RT Libraries
   Study

STUDY GUIDES 110
BT Guides
RT Supplementary Textbooks

STUDY HABITS 060
RT Reading Habits
   Study
   Study Skills
   Word Study Skills

Study Hours
USE STUDY

STUDY SKILLS 010
NT Cloze Procedure
   Word Study Skills
BT Skills
RT Basic Skills
   Locational Skills (Social Studies)
   Review (Reexamination)
   Study
   Study Habits

Stunts And Tumbling
USE TUMBLING

STUTTERING 290
BT Articulation (Speech)
RT Speech Handicapped
   Speech Handicaps
   Speech Improvement
   Speech Skills
   Speech Therapy

SUBCULTURE 100
NT Student Subcultures
BT Culture
RT Cultural Factors
   Cultural Traits
   Ethnic Groups
   Social Class
   Social Environment

SUBEMPLOYMENT 150
SN A combined measure of unemployment
   and substandard wages
RT Disadvantaged Groups
   Economic Disadvantagement
   Employment Problems
   Low Income
   Manpower Utilization
   Underemployed
   Unemployment
   Wages

Subject Disciplines
USE INTELLECTUAL DISCIPLINES

Subject Headings
USE SUBJECT INDEX TERMS

SUBJECT INDEX TERMS 330
UF Descriptors
   Subject Headings
   Uniterms
RT Cataloging
   Catalogs
   Classification
   Coordinate Indexes
   Documentation
   Indexes (Locaters)
   Indexing
   Permuted Indexes
   Thesauri
   Vocabulary
   Word Lists

Subjunctive Mood
USE VERBS

SUBPROFESSIONALS 380
SN Below level of professional but above
clerical or labor levels
UF Technicians
NT Agricultural Technicians
Chemical Technicians
Draftsmen
Electronic Technicians
Engineering Technicians
Housing Management Aides
Instrumentation Technicians
Library Technicians
Marine Technicians
Mechanical Design Technicians
Metallurgical Technicians
Production Technicians
Radiographers
Student Teachers
RT Dental Technicians
Differentiated Staffs
Employees
Medical Laboratory Assistants
Medical Record Technicians
Paraprofessional School Personnel
Preservice Education
Surgical Technicians
Technical Occupations
Veterinary Assistants

SUBSTITUTE TEACHERS 380
UF Relief Teachers
BT Teachers
RT Former Teachers
Part Time Teachers
Teacher Attendance
Teacher Employment

SUBSTITUTION DRILLS 270
BT Pattern Drills (Language)
RT Applied Linguistics
Language Instruction

SUBTRACTION 340
BT Arithmetic
RT Addition
Calculation
Multiplication

SUBURBAN ENVIRONMENT 160
BT Environment
RT Metropolitan Areas
Suburban Housing
Suburban Problems
Suburban Schools
Suburban Youth
Suburbs

SUBURBAN HOUSING 210
BT Housing
RT Suburban Environment
Suburban Problems
Suburbs

SUBURBAN PROBLEMS 230
BT Problems
RT Suburban Environment
Suburban Housing
Suburban Youth
Suburbs

SUBURBAN SCHOOLS 470
BT Schools
RT Suburban Environment
Suburbs

SUBURBAN YOUTH 380
BT Youth
RT Suburban Environment
Suburban Problems
Suburbs

SUBURBS 120
RT Metropolitan Areas
Suburban Environment
Suburban Housing
Suburban Problems
Suburban Schools
Suburban Youth

Success
USE SUCCESS FACTORS

SUCCESS FACTORS 180
UF Success
RT Achievement
Evaluation
Failure Factors
Performance Factors

SUFFIXES 290
BT Morphemes
RT Form Classes (Languages)
Linguistic Patterns
Morphology (Languages)
Morphophonemics
Structural Analysis

SUICIDE 420
BT Death
RT Behavior Problems
Psychopathology

SUMMER INSTITUTES 410
BT Institutes (Training Programs)
RT Courses
Inservice Courses
Inservice Programs
Institute Type Courses
Programs
Seminars
Short Courses
Summer Science Programs
Symposia
Teacher Education
Teacher Workshops

SUMMER PROGRAMS 410
NT Day Camp Programs
BT Programs
RT Outdoor Education
    Recreational Programs
    Resident Camp Programs
    Summer Schools
    Summer Science Programs
    Summer Workshops
    Vacation Programs

SUMMER SCHOOLS 470
UF Summer Session
BT Schools
RT Extended School Year
    Summer Programs

SUMMER SCIENCE PROGRAMS 110
BT Science Programs
RT Science Activities
    Science Courses
    Science Curriculum
    Science Institutes
    Science Instruction
    Science Projects
    Summer Institutes
    Summer Programs

Summer Session
USE SUMMER SCHOOLS

SUMMER WORKSHOPS 270
BT Workshops
RT Summer Programs

Sunlight
USE DAYLIGHT

SUPERCONDUCTORS 170
BT Science Equipment
RT Semiconductor Devices

SUPERINTENDENT ROLE 020
NT Assistant Superintendent Role
RT Superintendents

SUPERINTENDENTS 380
NT School Superintendents
BT Chief Administrators
RT Superintendent Role

SUPERIOR STUDENTS 380
BT Students
RT Able Students
    Academic Achievement
    Advanced Students
    Gifted
    High Achievers
    Talented Students

Supermarkets
USE FOOD STORES

SUPERVISED FARM PRACTICE 270
SN Experience under school direction related
    to classroom instruction
RT Agriculture
    Farm Visits
    Field Experience Programs
    Student Experience
    Student Projects
    Vocational Agriculture
    Work Study Programs

Supervised Food Service Workers
USE FOOD SERVICE WORKERS

SUPERVISION 020
NT Practicum Supervision
    School Supervision
    Science Supervision
    Teacher Supervision
RT Proctoring
    State Foreign Language Supervisors
    State Supervisors
    Supervisors
    Supervisory Activities
    Supervisory Methods

SUPERVISOR QUALIFICATIONS 500
BT Qualifications
RT State Foreign Language Supervisors
    State Supervisors

SUPERVISORS 380
UF Foreman
NT College Supervisors
    Elementary School Supervisors
    High School Supervisors
    State Supervisors
BT Administrative Personnel
    School Personnel
RT Crew Leaders
    Industrial Personnel
    Instructor Coordinators
    Leadership
    Science Consultants
    Science Supervision
    Supervision
    Supervisory Activities

Supervisor Training
USE SUPERVISORY TRAINING

SUPERVISORY ACTIVITIES 020
BT Activities
RT Supervision
    Supervisors
    Supervisory Methods

SUPERVISORY METHODS 020
RT Leadership Training
    Science Supervision
    State Foreign Language Supervisors
    Supervision
    Supervisory Activities

SUPERVISORY TRAINING 270
UF   Supervisor Training
BT   Training
RT   Leadership Training
     Management Development
     Off The Job Training

SUPPLEMENTARY EDUCATION 140
BT   Education
RT   Supplementary Educational Centers

SUPPLEMENTARY EDUCATIONAL CENTERS
210
UF   Educational Service Centers
RT   Supplementary Education

SUPPLEMENTARY READING MATERIALS
440
BT   Reading Materials
RT   Supplementary Textbooks

SUPPLEMENTARY TEXTBOOKS 050
BT   Textbooks
RT   Instructional Materials
     Manuals
     Study Guides
     Supplementary Reading Materials
     Textbook Selection

SUPPLIES 460
UF   Stockpiles
NT   Agricultural Supplies
RT   Equipment
     Facility Inventory
     Instructional Materials
     Resources

Supply Of Education
USE EDUCATIONAL SUPPLY

Supply Of Labor
USE LABOR SUPPLY

Supporting Services
USE ANCILLARY SERVICES

SUPRASEGMENTALS 290
NT   Intonation
BT   Language Patterns
RT   Morphology (Languages)
     Phonology
     Phrase Structure
     Sentence Structure
     Structural Analysis

Supreme Court Action
USE SUPREME COURT LITIGATION

Supreme Court Decisions
USE SUPREME COURT LITIGATION

SUPREME COURT LITIGATION 230
UF   Supreme Court Action
     Supreme Court Decisions
BT   Court Litigation
RT   Supreme Courts

SUPREME COURTS 230
BT   Courts
RT   Supreme Court Litigation

Surface Finishing
USE FINISHING

SURFACE STRUCTURE 290
BT   Transformation Theory (Language)
RT   Deep Structure
     Function Words
     Generative Grammar
     Grammar
     Morphology (Languages)
     Morphophonemics
     Phonology
     Phrase Structure
     Sentence Diagraming
     Sentence Structure
     Syntax
     Transformation Generative Grammar
     Transformations (Language)

SURGICAL TECHNICIANS 380
UF   Operating Room Technicians
BT   Health Occupations
RT   Health Occupations Education
     Medical Services
     Subprofessionals
     Technical Occupations

SURREALISM 260
BT   Art
     Twentieth Century Literature
RT   Art Expression
     Artists
     Association (Psychological)
     Composition (Literary)
     Creative Activities
     Creative Art
     Creative Development
     Creative Expression
     Creative Thinking
     Creativity
     Fiction
     French
     Imagination
     Literature
     Novels
     Painting
     Perception
     Poetry
     Prose
     Recall (Psychological)
     Sensory Experience
     Symbols (Literary)
     Thought Processes
     Writing

SURVEYS 190
NT   Community Surveys
     Graduate Surveys
     Library Surveys
     Literature Reviews
     National Surveys
     Occupational Surveys
     School Surveys
     State Surveys
     Statistical Surveys
     Television Surveys
RT   Comparative Analysis
     Feasibility Studies
     Interviews
     Measurement
     Questionnaires

SUSPENSION 020
BT   Discipline
RT   Discipline Policy
     Discipline Problems
     Expulsion
     Misbehavior
     School Policy
     Withdrawal

SUSU 300
BT   African Languages

SWAHILI 300
BT   African Languages
     Bantu Languages

SWIMMING 390
RT   Athletic Activities
     Recreational Activities

SWIMMING POOLS 210
BT   Recreational Facilities
RT   Athletics
     Physical Education Facilities

Swing Music
USE   JAZZ

SYLLABLES 290
BT   Morphemes
RT   Articulation (Speech)
     Consonants
     Intonation
     Phonemes
     Structural Analysis
     Vowels

Syllabus
USE   CURRICULUM GUIDES

SYMBOLIC LANGUAGE 290
BT   Language
RT   Semiotics

SYMBOLIC LEARNING 310
BT   Learning
RT   Associative Learning
     Learning Difficulties
     Performance
     Psychomotor Skills
     Visual Learning
     Word Recognition

SYMBOLISM 260
BT   Literature
RT   French Literature
     Haiku
     Nineteenth Century Literature
     Poetry
     Prose
     Spanish Literature
     Twentieth Century Literature

SYMBOLS (LITERARY) 260
RT   Analytical Criticism
     Composition (Literary)
     Drama
     Fiction
     Figurative Language
     Formal Criticism
     Historical Criticism
     Imagery
     Literary Analysis
     Literary Conventions
     Literature
     Metaphors
     Modernism
     Motifs
     Mythology
     Nineteenth Century Literature
     Poetry
     Prose
     Surrealism

SYMBOLS (MATHEMATICS) 340
BT   Mathematics

SYMMETRY 030
RT   Art Expression
     Geometry

Symphony Orchestras
USE   ORCHESTRAS

SYMPOSIA 510
RT   Conference Reports
     Conferences
     Documentation
     Institute Type Courses
     Meetings
     Post Doctoral Education
     Science Institutes
     Seminars
     Speeches
     Summer Institutes
     Workshops

SYNCHRONIC LINGUISTICS 290
NT Contrastive Linguistics
    Descriptive Linguistics
BT Linguistics
RT Diachronic Linguistics
    Idioms
    Language Typology
    Language Universals
    Morphology (Languages)
    Phonemics
    Phonology
    Structural Analysis
    Structural Linguistics

SYNTAX 290
NT Phrase Structure
BT Linguistics
RT Adjectives
    Adverbs
    Case (Grammar)
    Connected Discourse
    Deep Structure
    Determiners (Languages)
    Dictionaries
    Discourse Analysis
    Form Classes (Languages)
    Function Words
    Generative Grammar
    Kernel Sentences
    Language Patterns
    Language Typology
    Morphemes
    Morphology (Languages)
    Nominals
    Pronouns
    Semantics
    Semiotics
    Sentence Diagraming
    Sentences
    Structural Grammar
    Surface Structure
    Thesauri
    Traditional Grammar
    Transformation Generative Grammar
    Transformations (Language)
    Transformation Theory (Language)
    Verbs

SYNTHESIS 190
RT Comparative Analysis
    Evaluation

Synthetic Speech
USE ARTIFICIAL SPEECH

System Components
USE COMPONENT BUILDING SYSTEMS

SYSTEMS ANALYSIS 450
UF Functional Systems Theory
RT Architectural Programing
    Cost Effectiveness
    Critical Path Method
    Input Output Analysis
    Management Systems
    Models
    Relevance (Information Retrieval)
    Skill Analysis
    Systems Analysts
    Systems Approach
    Systems Concepts
    Systems Development

SYSTEMS ANALYSTS 380
BT Professional Personnel
RT Program Design
    Programers
    Systems Analysis
    Systems Approach
    Systems Development

SYSTEMS APPROACH 450
RT Management Systems
    Models
    Systems Analysis
    Systems Analysts
    Systems Concepts

SYSTEMS CONCEPTS 310
RT Advanced Systems
    Management Systems
    Numerical Control
    Systems Analysis
    Systems Approach

SYSTEMS DEVELOPMENT 130
BT Development
RT Educational Development
    Management Systems
    Systems Analysis
    Systems Analysts

TABLES (DATA) 080
NT Expectancy Tables
BT Data
RT Statistical Data

TACHISTOSCOPES 170
BT Audiovisual Aids
RT Pictorial Stimuli
    Projection Equipment
    Visual Perception
    Visual Stimuli

Tackboards
USE BULLETIN BOARDS

TACTILE ADAPTATION 070
SN The conversion of educational materials for use with the instruction of the blind
RT Blind
Braille
Magnification Methods
Material Development
Raised Line Drawings
Sensory Aids
Tactual Perception
Tactual Visual Tests
Visually Handicapped

TACTUAL PERCEPTION 070
BT Perception
RT Cutaneous Sense
Figural Aftereffects
Haptic Perception
Kinesthetic Perception
Sensory Experience
Sensory Training
Tactile Adaptation

TACTUAL VISUAL TESTS 520
BT Tests
RT Auditory Visual Tests
Tactile Adaptation
Vision Tests
Visual Measures

Tadjik Persian
USE TAJIK

TAGALOG 300
BT Indonesian Languages

TAGMEMIC ANALYSIS 290
BT Structural Analysis
RT Function Words
Grammar
Language Patterns
Negative Forms (Language)
Structural Grammar
Transformation Theory (Language)

TAJIK 300
UF Tadjik Persian
BT Indo European Languages

TALENT 010
RT Ability
Aptitude
Exceptional (Atypical)
Talent Development
Talented Students
Talent Identification
Talent Utilization
Vocational Aptitude

TALENT DEVELOPMENT 130
UF Talent Preservation
BT Development
RT Creative Development
Talent
Talented Students

TALENTED STUDENTS 380
UF Academically Talented
BT Exceptional Students
RT Ability
Gifted
High Achievers
Superior Students
Talent
Talent Development
Talent Identification

TALENT IDENTIFICATION 520
BT Identification
RT Identification Tests
Talent
Talented Students

Talent Preservation
USE TALENT DEVELOPMENT

TALENT UTILIZATION 460
RT Talent

TALES 260
BT Literature
RT Ambiguity
Didacticism
Formal Criticism
Humor
Narration
Novels
Poetry
Prose
Short Stories

TALKING BOOKS 050
RT Audio Equipment
Braille
Instructional Aids
Instructional Materials
Reading Instruction
Special Education

Talks
USE SPEECHES

TAMIL 300
BT Dravidian Languages

Taped Texts
USE PROGRAMED TEXTS

TAPE RECORDERS 170
BT Audio Equipment
Audiovisual Aids
RT Audio Active Compare Laboratories
Dubbing
Magnetic Tapes
Master Tapes (Audio)
Tape Recordings

TAPE RECORDINGS 050
NT Master Tapes (Audio)
   Phonotape Recordings
RT Audio Active Compare Laboratories
   Audio Equipment
   Dubbing
   Magnetic Tapes
   Tape Recorders
   Unwritten Language

TASK ANALYSIS 150
BT Job Analysis
RT Behavior Problems
   Complexity Level
   Critical Incidents Method
   Employment Qualifications
   Intellectual Development
   Mental Development
   Occupational Information
   Task Performance
   Thought Processes
   Work Simplification

TASK PERFORMANCE 010
UF Job Performance
BT Performance
RT Glare
   Illumination Levels
   Job Analysis
   Job Skills
   Lifting
   Task Analysis

TATAR 300
BT Turkic Languages

TAX ALLOCATION 220
RT Financial Support
   Police Costs
   Resource Allocations
   Tax Effort
   Taxes
   Tax Rates
   Tax Support

TAX EFFORT 220
SN Extent to which a government makes
   use of its taxable capacity
RT Equalization Aid
   Fiscal Capacity
   Tax Allocation
   Taxes
   Tax Support

TAXES 230
NT School Taxes
RT Assessed Valuation
   Estate Planning
   Property Appraisal
   Tax Allocation
   Tax Effort
   Tax Rates
   Tax Support

TAXONOMY 080
BT Classification
RT Data
   Data Analysis
   Indexes (Locaters)
   Relationship
   Typology
   Zoology

TAX RATES 230
RT Estate Planning
   Expenditures
   Tax Allocation
   Taxes

TAX SUPPORT 220
BT Financial Support
RT Assessed Valuation
   School Taxes
   Tax Allocation
   Tax Effort
   Taxes

Teacher Absence
USE TEACHER ATTENDANCE

TEACHER ADMINISTRATOR RELATIONSHIP
020
UF Administrator Teacher Relationship
BT Relationship
RT Board Administrator Relationship
   Employer Employee Relationship
   State School District Relationship
   Teacher Militancy

Teacher Advancement
USE TEACHER PROMOTION

TEACHER AIDES 380
UF Teacher Assistants
NT Bilingual Teacher Aides
BT Paraprofessional School Personnel
RT Differentiated Staffs
   Programed Tutoring
   School Aides
   Science Teachers
   Teachers
   Volunteers

TEACHER ALIENATION 420
BT Psychological Patterns
RT Maladjustment
   Relationship
   Role Conflict
   Social Attitudes
   Teacher Attitudes
   Teacher Behavior

Teacher Assignment
USE TEACHER PLACEMENT

Teacher Assistants
USE TEACHER AIDES

TEACHER ASSOCIATIONS 370
UF Teacher Organizations
BT Professional Associations
RT Arbitration
    Negotiation Agreements
    Negotiation Impasses
    Teacher Militancy
    Teacher Welfare

TEACHER ATTENDANCE 020
UF Teacher Absence
BT Attendance
RT Attendance Patterns
    Sabbatical Leaves
    Substitute Teachers
    Teacher Behavior
    Teachers

TEACHER ATTITUDES 040
UF Teacher Opinion
    Teacher Reaction
NT Teacher Morale
BT Attitudes
RT Teacher Alienation
    Teacher Characteristics
    Teachers

TEACHER BACKGROUND 200
BT Background
RT Certification
    Teacher Education
    Teachers

TEACHER BEHAVIOR 060
UF Student Teacher Behavior
BT Behavior
RT Behavior Change
    Behavior Patterns
    Classroom Observation Techniques
    Protocol Materials
    Teacher Alienation
    Teacher Attendance
    Teacher Characteristics
    Teacher Evaluation
    Teaching Styles

TEACHER CERTIFICATES 500
UF Teaching Certificates
RT Certification
    Educational Certificates
    Teacher Certification
    Teacher Employment
    Teacher Qualifications
    Teaching

TEACHER CERTIFICATION 500
BT Certification
RT Beginning Teachers
    Credentials
    Teacher Certificates
    Teacher Education
    Teacher Education Curriculum
    Teacher Employment
    Teacher Qualifications

TEACHER CHARACTERISTICS 380
RT Individual Characteristics
    Teacher Attitudes
    Teacher Behavior
    Teachers
    Teaching Styles

Teacher Competencies
USE TEACHING SKILLS

Teacher Competency
USE TEACHER QUALIFICATIONS

Teacher Coordinators
USE INSTRUCTOR COORDINATORS

Teacher Desegregation
USE TEACHER INTEGRATION

TEACHER DEVELOPED MATERIALS 050
SN Instructional materials prepared by
    teachers
BT Instructional Materials
RT Art Materials
    Audiovisual Aids
    Classroom Materials
    Instructional Aids
    Manipulative Materials
    Material Development
    Mathematics Materials
    Reading Materials
    Resource Materials
    Science Materials
    Slides
    Three Dimensional Aids

Teacher Directed Practice
USE TEACHER GUIDANCE

TEACHER DISTRIBUTION 020
RT Incidence
    Racial Balance
    Student Teacher Ratio
    Teachers

TEACHER EDUCATION 140
UF Teacher Preparation
    Teacher Training
    Teacher Training Education
    University Training Centers
NT Inservice Teacher Education
    Preservice Education
    Student Teaching
    Teacher Educator Education
BT Education
RT Affiliated Schools
    Clinical Professors
    Cooperating Teachers
    Education Majors
    Institutes (Training Programs)
    Laboratory Schools
    Laboratory Training
    Methods Courses
    Methods Teachers
    Microteaching
    Practicums

Protocol Materials
Science Institutes
Summer Institutes
Teacher Background
Teacher Certification
Teacher Educators
Teachers
Teachers Colleges

TEACHER EDUCATION CURRICULUM 110
BT Curriculum
RT Education Courses
     Education Majors
     Preservice Education
     Teacher Certification
     Teacher Programs
     Teacher Qualifications
     Teachers Colleges

TEACHER EDUCATOR EDUCATION 140
BT Teacher Education
RT Clinical Professors
     College Supervisors
     Cooperating Teachers
     Doctoral Degrees
     Doctoral Programs
     Inservice Teacher Education
     Masters Degrees
     Preservice Education
     Teacher Educators

TEACHER EDUCATORS 380
UF Teacher Trainers
BT College Teachers
RT Clinical Professors
     College Faculty
     College Supervisors
     Professors
     Teacher Education
     Teacher Educator Education

Teacher Effectiveness
USE EFFECTIVE TEACHING

TEACHER EMPLOYMENT 150
BT Employment
RT Beginning Teachers
     Loyalty Oaths
     Part Time Teachers
     Persistence
     Probationary Period
     Substitute Teachers
     Teacher Certificates
     Teacher Certification
     Teacher Exchange Programs
     Teacher Persistence
     Teacher Placement
     Teacher Recruitment
     Teachers
     Teacher Salaries
     Teacher Shortage
     Teacher Supply And Demand
     Teaching Assignment
     Tenure

TEACHER EVALUATION 180
SN Judging teacher performance as related
     to established criteria
NT Teacher Rating
BT Evaluation
RT Course Evaluation
     Credentials
     Effective Teaching
     Lesson Observation Criteria
     Personnel Evaluation
     Student Teacher Relationship
     Teacher Behavior
     Teacher Improvement
     Teachers
     Teaching Quality

TEACHER EXCHANGE PROGRAMS 410
SN Includes domestic and international
     teacher exchange programs
BT Exchange Programs
RT Intercultural Programs
     Teacher Employment
     Teachers

TEACHER EXPERIENCE 200
UF Professional Laboratory Experience
BT Experience
RT Affiliated Schools
     Credentials
     Microteaching
     Teacher Qualifications
     Teachers

Teacher Growth
USE TEACHER IMPROVEMENT

TEACHER GUIDANCE 090
UF Teacher Directed Practice
BT Guidance
RT Teachers
     Teacher Supervision

Teacher Guides
USE TEACHING GUIDES

TEACHER HOUSING 210
BT Housing
RT Teachers

TEACHER IMPROVEMENT 140
UF Teacher Growth
BT Improvement
RT Sabbatical Leaves
     Staff Improvement
     Teacher Evaluation
     Teachers

TEACHER INFLUENCE 040
RT Achievement
     Student Motivation
     Student-Teacher Relationship

TEACHER INTEGRATION 430
UF Teacher Desegregation
BT Faculty Integration

TEACHER INTERNS 380
SN A trainee teacher under joint supervision
of his college or university and the
school system which employs him
UF Intern Teachers
Urban Teaching Interns
BT Teachers
RT Academic Rank (Professional)
Differentiated Staffs
Episode Teaching
Inservice Teacher Education
Paraprofessional School Personnel
Student Teachers

Teacher Load
USE TEACHING LOAD

TEACHER MILITANCY 040
RT Arbitration
Collective Bargaining
Collective Negotiation
Negotiation Impasses
Professional Recognition
Sanctions
Teacher Administrator Relationship
Teacher Associations
Teacher Morale
Teacher Strikes

TEACHER MORALE 040
BT Teacher Attitudes
RT Organizational Climate
Professional Recognition
Teacher Militancy
Teacher Motivation

TEACHER MOTIVATION 040
BT Motivation
RT Incentive Systems
Teacher Morale
Teachers

TEACHER NURSES 380
BT Nurses
Teachers
RT Health Services
Nursing
School Nurses

Teacher Opinion
USE TEACHER ATTITUDES

Teacher Organizations
USE TEACHER ASSOCIATIONS

TEACHER ORIENTATION 270
BT Orientation
RT School Orientation
Staff Orientation
Teachers
Teacher Supervision

Teacher Parent Conferences
USE PARENT TEACHER CONFERENCES

Teacher Parent Cooperation
USE PARENT TEACHER COOPERATION

TEACHER PARTICIPATION 270
RT Teachers

TEACHER PERSISTENCE 150
UF Teaching Persistance
RT Probationary Period
Teacher Employment
Teacher Recruitment
Teacher Shortage

TEACHER PLACEMENT 020
UF Teacher Assignment
BT Placement
RT Teacher Employment
Teacher Recruitment
Teachers
Teacher Selection
Teacher Supply And Demand

Teacher Preparation
USE TEACHER EDUCATION

TEACHER PROGRAMS 410
NT Teacher Seminars
Teacher Workshops
BT Programs
RT Methods Courses
Teacher Education Curriculum
Teachers

TEACHER PROMOTION 020
UF Teacher Advancement
BT Faculty Promotion
RT Probationary Period
Teachers

Teacher Pupil Interaction
USE STUDENT TEACHER RELATIONSHIP

Teacher Pupil Ratio
USE STUDENT TEACHER RATIO

Teacher Pupil Relationship
USE STUDENT TEACHER RELATIONSHIP

TEACHER QUALIFICATIONS 500
UF Teacher Competency
BT Qualifications
RT Certification
Credentials
Teacher Certificates
Teacher Certification
Teacher Education Curriculum
Teacher Experience
Teachers
Teaching Experience

Teacher Quality
USE TEACHING QUALITY

TEACHER RATING 180
BT Teacher Evaluation
RT Lesson Observation Criteria
Merit Rating Programs

Teacher Reaction
USE TEACHER ATTITUDES

TEACHER RECRUITMENT 150
BT Faculty Recruitment
RT Teacher Employment
Teacher Persistence
Teacher Placement
Teachers
Teacher Selection
Teacher Shortage
Teacher Supply And Demand

TEACHER RESPONSE 060
RT Teachers
Teaching Styles

TEACHER RESPONSIBILITY 040
NT Noninstructional Responsibility
BT Responsibility
RT Administrator Responsibility
Child Responsibility
Educational Responsibility
Leadership Responsibility
Parent Responsibility
Teachers

TEACHER RETIREMENT 150
UF Retired Teachers
BT Retirement
RT Teacher Welfare

TEACHER ROLE 490
UF Instructor Role
NT Senior Teacher Role
RT Noninstructional Responsibility
Staff Role
Student Role
Teachers
Teaching Styles

TEACHERS 380
UF Instructors
NT Art Teachers
Beginning Teachers
Bilingual Teachers
Chemistry Teachers
Coaching Teachers
College Teachers
Cooperating Teachers
Elementary School Teachers
Fles Teachers
Former Teachers
Homebound Teachers
Industrial Arts Teachers
Itinerant Teachers
Language Teachers
Lay Teachers
Master Teachers
Mathematics Teachers
Methods Teachers
Minority Group Teachers
Music Teachers
Nun Teachers
Partnership Teachers

Part Time Teachers
Preschool Teachers
Professors
Public School Teachers
Remedial Teachers
Resource Teachers
Science Teachers
Secondary School Teachers
Special Education Teachers
Student Teachers
Substitute Teachers
Teacher Interns
Teacher Nurses
Television Teachers
Vocational Education Teachers
Women Teachers
BT Instructional Staff
Professional Personnel
RT Academic Rank (Professional)
Adult Educators
Counselor Educators
Differentiated Staffs
Employees
Home Visits
Instructor Coordinators
Noninstructional Responsibility
One Teacher Schools
Professional Occupations
Specialists
Student Teacher Ratio
Student Teacher Relationship
Teacher Aides
Teacher Attendance
Teacher Attitudes
Teacher Background
Teacher Characteristics
Teacher Distribution
Teacher Education
Teacher Employment
Teacher Evaluation
Teacher Exchange Programs
Teacher Experience
Teacher Guidance
Teacher Housing
Teacher Improvement
Teacher Motivation
Teacher Orientation
Teacher Participation
Teacher Placement
Teacher Programs
Teacher Promotion
Teacher Qualifications
Teacher Recruitment
Teacher Response
Teacher Responsibility
Teacher Role
Teacher Salaries
Teachers Colleges
Teacher Selection

Teacher Seminars
Teacher Shortage
Teacher Stereotypes
Teacher Supervision
Teacher Transfer
Teacher Workshops
Teaching
Teaching Experience
Trainers

TEACHER SALARIES 220
BT Salaries
RT Salary Differentials
Teacher Employment
Teachers
Teacher Welfare

TEACHERS COLLEGES 470
BT Colleges
RT State Colleges
Teacher Education
Teacher Education Curriculum
Teachers
Undergraduate Study

TEACHER SELECTION 020
BT Personnel Selection
RT Teacher Placement
Teacher Recruitment
Teachers
Teacher Supply And Demand

TEACHER SEMINARS 270
BT Seminars
Teacher Programs
RT Teachers
Teacher Workshops

TEACHER SHORTAGE 020
BT Teacher Supply And Demand
RT Teacher Employment
Teacher Persistence
Teacher Recruitment
Teachers

Teacher Skills
USE TEACHING SKILLS

TEACHER STEREOTYPES 490
BT Stereotypes
RT Teachers

TEACHER STRIKES 150
RT Arbitration
Collective Bargaining
Collective Negotiation
Labor Problems
Negotiation Agreements
Negotiation Impasses
Sanctions
Teacher Militancy
Teacher Welfare

Teacher Student Interaction
USE STUDENT TEACHER RELATIONSHIP

Teacher Student Ratio
USE STUDENT TEACHER RATIO

Teacher Student Relationship
USE STUDENT TEACHER RELATIONSHIP

TEACHER SUPERVISION 020
BT Supervision
RT Science Supervision
State Foreign Language Supervisors
State Supervisors
Teacher Guidance
Teacher Orientation
Teachers

TEACHER SUPPLY AND DEMAND 150
NT Teacher Shortage
BT Labor Market
RT Teacher Employment
Teacher Placement
Teacher Recruitment
Teacher Selection

Teacher Trainers
USE TEACHER EDUCATORS

Teacher Training
USE TEACHER EDUCATION

Teacher Training Education
USE TEACHER EDUCATION

Teacher Training Films
USE PROTOCOL MATERIALS

TEACHER TRANSFER 020
BT Transfers
RT Teachers

Teacher Travel
USE TRAVEL

TEACHER WELFARE 150
BT Welfare
RT Academic Freedom
Classroom Environment
Leave Of Absence
Negotiation Agreements
Professional Recognition
Teacher Associations
Teacher Retirement
Teacher Salaries
Teacher Strikes
Teaching Conditions
Teaching Load
Tenure

TEACHER WORKSHOPS 270
BT Teacher Programs
Workshops
RT Inservice Teacher Education
Science Institutes
Summer Institutes
Teachers
Teacher Seminars

TEACHING 270
UF   Pedagogy
      Teaching Profession
NT   Concept Teaching
      Creative Teaching
      Diagnostic Teaching
      Dropout Teaching
      Effective Teaching
      Experimental Teaching
      Inservice Teaching
      Microteaching
      Part Time Teaching
      Peer Teaching
      Urban Teaching
RT   Institutional Role
      Instruction
      Learning
      Noninstructional Responsibility
      Secondary School Teachers
      Special Education Teachers
      Spelling Instruction
      Teacher Certificates
      Teachers
      Teaching Assignment
      Teaching Benefits
      Teaching Conditions
      Teaching Guides
      Teaching Load
      Teaching Machines
      Teaching Methods
      Teaching Procedures
      Teaching Programs
      Teaching Quality
      Teaching Skills
      Teaching Techniques

Teaching Aids
USE INSTRUCTIONAL AIDS

Teaching Areas
USE CURRICULUM

TEACHING ASSIGNMENT 020
RT   Part Time Teaching
      Teacher Employment
      Teaching
      Teaching Load

TEACHING ASSISTANTS 380
SN   Graduate students assisting as
      instructors
BT   Paraprofessional School Personnel
RT   College Faculty
      Graduate Students
      Universities

TEACHING BENEFITS 360
RT   Sabbatical Leaves
      Teaching

Teaching Certificates
USE TEACHER CERTIFICATES

Teaching Competencies
USE TEACHING SKILLS

TEACHING CONDITIONS 160
RT   Academic Freedom
      Classroom Environment
      Loyalty Oaths
      Sabbatical Leaves
      Teacher Welfare
      Teaching

Teaching Core
USE CORE CURRICULUM

TEACHING EXPERIENCE 200
SN   Actual and simulated experiences of
      preservice and inservice teachers
UF   Inservice Teaching Experience
      Preservice Teaching Experience
BT   Experience
RT   Affiliated Schools
      Beginning Teachers
      Classroom Observation Techniques
      Credentials
      Experimental Schools
      Field Experience Programs
      Inservice Teaching
      Internship Programs
      Laboratory Schools
      Laboratory Training
      Microteaching
      Simulation
      Student Teaching
      Teacher Qualifications
      Teachers
      Training Laboratories

Teaching Facilities
USE EDUCATIONAL FACILITIES

TEACHING GUIDES 110
UF   Organizational Outlines
      Teacher Guides
BT   Guides
RT   Curriculum Guides
      Teaching

TEACHING LOAD 500
UF   Faculty Load
      Teacher Load
RT   Contracts
      Noninstructional Responsibility
      Part Time Teaching
      Teacher Welfare
      Teaching
      Teaching Assignment
      Teaching Quality
      Working Hours

TEACHING MACHINES 050
NT   Self Pacing Machines
BT   Educational Equipment
      Instructional Aids
RT   Autoinstructional Aids
      Computer Assisted Instruction
      Multimedia Instruction
      Programed Instruction
      Teaching

Teaching Materials
USE INSTRUCTIONAL MATERIALS

TEACHING METHODS 510
SN Standard procedures in the presentation of instructional material and the content of activities
UF Presentation Methods
Teaching Practices
Teaching Systems
NT Autoinstructional Methods
Cooperative Teaching
Departmental Teaching Plans
Grammar Translation Method
Sight Method
Team Teaching
Thematic Approach
BT Educational Methods
RT Deductive Methods
English (Second Language)
Experimental Teaching
Field Instruction
Individualized Reading
Inductive Methods
Instruction
Intermode Differences
Laboratory Procedures
Multimedia Instruction
Sequential Programs
Simulation
Special Education
Teaching
Teaching Models
Teaching Procedures
Teaching Techniques
Telephone Instruction

TEACHING MODELS 270
SN Standard of teaching behaviors identified as desirable for given teaching situations
BT Models
RT Instruction
Standards
Teaching Methods
Teaching Procedures
Teaching Techniques

Teaching Persistance
USE TEACHER PERSISTENCE

Teaching Practices.
USE TEACHING METHODS

TEACHING PROCEDURES 270
UF Instructional Procedures
Procedures
NT Laboratory Procedures
RT Diagnostic Teaching
Educational Strategies
Multimedia Instruction
Teaching
Teaching Methods
Teaching Models
Teaching Techniques

Teaching Profession
USE TEACHING

TEACHING PROGRAMS 410
BT Programs
RT Curriculum
Education
Teaching
Tutorial Programs

TEACHING QUALITY 500
UF Teacher Quality
RT Incentive Systems
Teacher Evaluation
Teaching
Teaching Load

Teaching Reading
USE READING INSTRUCTION

Teaching Resources
USE EDUCATIONAL RESOURCES

TEACHING SKILLS 010
UF Teacher Competencies
Teacher Skills
Teaching Competencies
BT Skills
RT Communication Skills
Job Skills
Microteaching
Teaching

Teaching Spelling
USE SPELLING INSTRUCTION

Teaching Staff
USE INSTRUCTIONAL STAFF

TEACHING STYLES 510
RT Leadership Styles
Personality Studies
Psychological Patterns
Teacher Behavior
Teacher Characteristics
Teacher Response
Teacher Role
Teaching Techniques

Teaching Systems
USE TEACHING METHODS

TEACHING TECHNIQUES 510
SN Specific ways of presenting instructional material or conducting instructional activities--i.e., the teachers method of teaching
NT Centers Of Interest
Classroom Techniques
Cross Age Teaching
Demonstrations (Educational)
Discussion (Teaching Technique)
Experience Charts
Lead Lecture Plan
Lecture
Mass Instruction

Problem Solving
Repetitive Film Showings
Small Group Instruction
Tutoring
BT   Techniques
RT   Dramatic Play
     English (Second Language)
     Episode Teaching
     Inquiry Training
     Instruction
     Instructional Media
     Integrated Activities
     Interval Pacing
     Laboratory Techniques
     Microteaching
     Negative Practice
     Questioning Techniques
     Reinforcement
     Seminars
     Simulation
     Teaching
     Teaching Methods
     Teaching Models
     Teaching Procedures
     Teaching Styles
     Training Techniques
     Tutorial Programs

Teaching Units
USE   UNIT PLAN

TEAM ADMINISTRATION 020
UF   Teaming Of Principals
BT   Administration
RT   Cooperative Planning
     Team Teaching

Team Counseling
USE   COCOUNSELING

Teaming Of Principals
USE   TEAM ADMINISTRATION

TEAM LEADER (TEACHING) 380
RT   Team Teaching

TEAM TEACHING 510
BT   Teaching Methods
RT   Departmental Teaching Plans
     Episode Teaching
     Flexible Schedules
     Flexible Scheduling
     Lead Lecture Plan
     Rotation Plans
     School Cadres
     Senior Teacher Role
     Team Administration
     Team Leader (Teaching)
     Team Training
     Teamwork

TEAM TRAINING 270
SN   Training individuals in teams or to work
     as teams
BT   Training
RT   School Cadres
     Small Group Instruction
     Team Teaching
     Training Techniques

TEAMWORK 490
RT   Cocounseling
     Cooperative Planning
     Group Behavior
     Interpersonal Competence
     Interpersonal Relationship
     Morale
     Peer Relationship
     Personal Relationship
     Sportsmanship
     Team Teaching

TECHNICAL ASSISTANCE 130
RT   Community Development
     Consultants
     Developing Nations

TECHNICAL EDUCATION 140
SN   A type of preparation for occupations
     between the skilled trades and the
     professions
UF   Technical Instruction
NT   Fire Science Education
BT   Vocational Education
RT   Agricultural Technicians
     Appliance Service Technicians
     Architectural Education
     Associate Degrees
     Aviation Technology
     Chemical Technicians
     Computer Science Education
     Dental Technicians
     Electronic Technicians
     Engineering Education
     Engineering Technicians
     Engineering Technology
     Horology
     Industrial Technology
     Instrumentation Technicians
     Land Grant Universities
     Library Technicians
     Marine Technicians
     Mechanical Design Technicians
     Medical Laboratory Assistants
     Medical Record Technicians
     Metallurgical Technicians
     Post Secondary Education
     Pretechnology Programs
     Prevocational Education
     Production Technicians
     School Shops
     Science Education
     Technical Institutes
     Terminal Students

Technical Education Directors
USE VOCATIONAL DIRECTORS

Technical High Schools
USE VOCATIONAL HIGH SCHOOLS

TECHNICAL ILLUSTRATION 350
BT Drafting
   Graphic Arts
RT Illustrations
   Technical Writing

TECHNICAL INSTITUTES 410
SN Post secondary schools offering training
   in occupations at a level between the
   skilled trades and the professions
BT Schools
RT Community Colleges
   Junior Colleges
   Post Secondary Education
   Technical Education
   Vocational Education

Technical Instruction
USE TECHNICAL EDUCATION

TECHNICAL MATHEMATICS 340
BT Mathematics

TECHNICAL OCCUPATIONS 350
BT Occupations
RT Agricultural Education
   Agricultural Technicians
   Appliance Service Technicians
   Chemical Technicians
   Dental Technicians
   Draftsmen
   Electronic Technicians
   Engineering Technicians
   Highway Engineering Aides
   Instrumentation Technicians
   Library Technicians
   Marine Technicians
   Mechanical Design Technicians
   Medical Laboratory Assistants
   Medical Record Technicians
   Metallurgical Technicians
   Production Technicians
   Radiographers
   Seamen
   Subprofessionals
   Surgical Technicians
   Trade And Industrial Education
   Veterinary Assistants

Technical Processes (Libraries)
USE LIBRARY TECHNICAL PROCESSES

TECHNICAL REPORTS 320
SN Only when used as a subject concept in
   document
UF Scientific Reports
BT Reports
RT Publications
   Research
   Research Reviews (Publications)

Serials
Technical Writing

Technical Schools
USE VOCATIONAL SCHOOLS

Technical Secretaries
USE SECRETARIES

Technical Services (Libraries)
USE LIBRARY TECHNICAL PROCESSES

TECHNICAL WRITING 350
UF Report Writing
BT Writing
RT Composition Skills (Literary)
   Expository Writing
   Student Writing Models
   Technical Illustration
   Technical Reports
   Writing Skills

Technicians
USE SUBPROFESSIONALS

TECHNIQUES 510
NT Evaluation Techniques
   Laboratory Techniques
   Measurement Techniques
   Motivation Techniques
   Music Techniques
   Production Techniques
   Simulation
   Teaching Techniques
   Training Techniques
RT Forced Choice Technique
   Methodology

TECHNOLOGICAL ADVANCEMENT 450
RT Automation
   Building Obsolescence
   Computers
   Cybernetics
   Developed Nations
   Industrialization
   Science Programs
   Scientific Concepts
   Skill Obsolescence
   Technology

Technological Concepts
USE SCIENTIFIC CONCEPTS

Technological Programs
USE SCIENCE PROGRAMS

TECHNOLOGY 110
NT Aerospace Technology
   Aviation Technology
   Educational Technology
   Electromechanical Technology
   Engineering Technology
   Human Engineering
   Industrial Technology
   Instructional Technology
   Laboratory Technology
   Media Technology

Radio Technology
BT Sciences
RT Automation
Developed Nations
Engineering
Industrialization
Patents
Scientific Concepts
Technological Advancement

Teenage Boys
USE TEENAGERS

Teenage Girls
USE TEENAGERS

TEENAGERS 380
UF Teenage Boys
Teenage Girls
BT Adolescents

TEFL
USE ENGLISH (SECOND LANGUAGE)

TELECOMMUNICATION 080
UF Communication Networks
Communication Services
Communication Systems
Electrical Communication Systems
Electronic Communication Systems
Signal Services
Wire Communication
Wireless Communication
NT Closed Circuit Television
Facsimile Communication Systems
Radio
Telephone Communication Systems
Television
BT Communications
RT Broadcast Industry
Communication Satellites
Computers
Information Systems
Information Theory
Input Output Devices
Mass Media
Radar
Telephone Communications Industry

TELECOURSES 270
BT Televised Instruction
RT Educational Television

Telefacsimile
USE FACSIMILE TRANSMISSION

Telefax
USE FACSIMILE TRANSMISSION

TELEGRAPHIC MATERIALS 050
SN Highly abbreviated and condensed
textual materials retaining all essential
information
BT Instructional Materials
RT Reading
Reading Materials

Telegu
USE TELUGU

TELEPHONE COMMUNICATIONS INDUSTRY
370
BT Industry
RT Communications
Communication Satellites
Mass Media
Telecommunication
Telephone Communication Systems

TELEPHONE COMMUNICATION SYSTEMS
080
SN Includes hardware as well as techniques
used in applying a system
UF Telephone Systems
BT Telecommunication
RT Dial Access Information Systems
Facsimile Communication Systems
Facsimile Transmission
Information Networks
Instructional Media
Networks
Telephone Communications Industry
Telephone Instruction
Utilities

TELEPHONE INSTRUCTION 270
SN Special education by use of the
telephone
BT Instruction
RT Exceptional Child Education
Individual Instruction
Instructional Media
Special Education
Teaching Methods
Telephone Communication Systems

Telephone Systems
USE TELEPHONE COMMUNICATION
SYSTEMS

TELEVISED INSTRUCTION 270
UF Television Instruction
NT Telecourses
BT Instruction
RT Educational Television
Instructional Media
Multichannel Programing
Television
Television Curriculum
Television Teachers
Television Viewing

TELEVISION 050
NT Airborne Television
Broadcast Television
Cable Television
Closed Circuit Television
Color Television
Commercial Television
Educational Television
Instructional Television
Open Circuit Television

Overhead Television
BT Mass Media
     Telecommunication
RT Acting
     Broadcast Industry
     Community Antennas
     Electronic Equipment
     Journalism
     Kinescope Recordings
     Production Techniques
     Radio
     Sound Effects
     Sound Tracks
     Televised Instruction
     Television Commercials
     Television Curriculum
     Television Lighting
     Television Lights
     Television Repairmen
     Television Research
     Television Surveys
     Television Teachers
     Television Viewing
     Transistors
     Video Tape Recordings

TELEVISION COMMERCIALS 050
RT Commercial Television
     Television

TELEVISION CURRICULUM 110
BT Curriculum
RT Televised Instruction
     Television

Television Instruction
USE TELEVISED INSTRUCTION

Television Lecturers
USE TELEVISION TEACHERS

TELEVISION LIGHTING 210
BT Lighting
     Production Techniques
RT Color Television
     Television
     Television Lights

TELEVISION LIGHTS 170
BT Lights
RT Television
     Television Lighting

TELEVISION REPAIRMEN 380
UF Radio Repairmen
     TV Repairmen
BT Service Workers
RT Radio
     Service Occupations
     Television
     Trade And Industrial Education

TELEVISION RESEARCH 450
BT Research
RT Television
     Television Surveys

TELEVISION SURVEYS 180
BT Surveys
RT Television
     Television Research

TELEVISION TEACHERS 380
UF Television Lecturers
BT Teachers
RT Mathematics Teachers
     Televised Instruction
     Television

Television Technology
USE MEDIA TECHNOLOGY

TELEVISION VIEWING 050
RT Audiences
     Color Television
     Televised Instruction
     Television
     Viewing Time

TELUGU 300
UF Telegu
BT Dravidian Languages

TEMPERATURE 160
RT Air Conditioning
     Air Conditioning Equipment
     Air Flow
     Classroom Environment
     Climate Control
     Climatic Factors
     Environment
     Fuel Consumption
     Heat
     Heating
     Humidity
     Physical Environment
     Refrigeration
     Solar Radiation
     Thermal Environment
     Ventilation

Temporal Perspective
USE TIME PERSPECTIVE

TENES
USE ENGLISH (SECOND LANGUAGE)

TENL 290
SN Teaching English as a native language to
     speakers of nonstandard dialect
BT English Instruction
RT Applied Linguistics
     Bilingualism
     Culturally Disadvantaged
     Language Handicaps
     Language Instruction
     Language Skills
     Language Standardization
     Nonstandard Dialects
     Oral English
     Social Dialects
     Sociolinguistics

TENURE 150
SN Status granted to a person in a position, usually after serving a probationary period
NT Job Tenure
RT Contracts
   Contract Salaries
   Probationary Period
   Teacher Employment
   Teacher Welfare

TERMINAL EDUCATION 140
BT Education
RT Continuation Education
   Terminal Students

TERMINAL STUDENTS 380
BT College Students
RT Technical Education
   Terminal Education
   Transfer Programs
   Transfer Students

Terminology
USE VOCABULARY

TESL
USE ENGLISH (SECOND LANGUAGE)

TESOL
USE ENGLISH (SECOND LANGUAGE)

Test Administration
USE TESTING

Test Booklets
USE TESTS

Test Books
USE TESTS

TEST CONSTRUCTION 520
UF Test Design
NT Internal Scaling
   Item Analysis
BT Construction (Process)
RT Essay Tests
   Multiple Choice Tests
   Pretesting
   Testing
   Tests

Test Design
USE TEST CONSTRUCTION

Test Examiners
USE EXAMINERS

TESTING 180
UF Test Administration
   Testing Methods
   Testing Techniques
NT Comparative Testing
   Educational Testing
   Group Intelligence Testing
   Post Testing
   Pretesting

   Psychological Testing
   Student Testing
RT Equated Scores
   Error Patterns
   Evaluation
   Examiners
   Factor Analysis
   Grade Equivalent Scales
   Instrumentation
   Item Analysis
   Matched Groups
   Measurement
   Measurement Techniques
   Multiple Choice Tests
   Pilot Projects
   Prediction
   Predictive Ability (Testing)
   Predictive Validity
   Problem Sets
   Proctoring
   Q Sort
   Sampling
   Scoring
   Test Construction
   Testing Problems
   Testing Programs
   Tests
   Test Scoring Machines

Testing Methods
USE TESTING

TESTING PROBLEMS 520
BT Problems
RT Testing

TESTING PROGRAMS 520
BT Programs
RT State Licensing Boards
   Testing

Testing Techniques
USE TESTING

TEST INTERPRETATION 180
RT Equated Scores
   Grade Equivalent Scales
   Test Results
   Tests
   Test Validity

TEST RELIABILITY 180
BT Reliability
RT Tests
   Test Validity

TEST RESULTS 180
RT Equated Scores
   Evaluation
   Reliability
   Statistical Data
   Test Interpretation
   Tests
   Test Validity

TESTS 520
UF   Examinations
      Quizzes
      Test Booklets
      Test Books
NT   Abstraction Tests
      Achievement Tests
      Aptitude Tests
      Attitude Tests
      Auditory Tests
      Auditory Visual Tests
      Cognitive Tests
      College Entrance Examinations
      Culture Free Tests
      Diagnostic Tests
      Equivalency Tests
      Essay Tests
      group Tests
      Identification Tests
      Individual Tests
      Intelligence Tests
      Interest Tests
      Language Tests
      Maturity Tests
      Mental Tests
      National Competency Tests
      Objective Tests
      Occupational Tests
      Perception Tests
      Performance Tests
      Personality Tests
      Physical Examinations
      Preschool Tests
      Pretests
      Prognostic Tests
      Psychological Tests
      Reading Tests
      Science Tests
      Screening Tests
      Situational Tests
      Speech Tests
      Standardized Tests
      Tactual Visual Tests
      Timed Tests
      Verbal Tests
      Visual Measures
RT   Answer Keys
      Clinical Diagnosis
      Evaluation
      Examiners
      Group Norms
      Item Analysis
      Measurement Instruments
      Performance
      Pretesting
      Puzzles
      Statistical Data

      Test Construction
      Testing
      Test Interpretation
      Test Reliability
      Test Results
      Test Selection
      Test Validity

TEST SCORING MACHINES 170
RT   Answer Keys
      Instrumentation
      Testing

TEST SELECTION 520
RT   Tests

TESTS OF SIGNIFICANCE 520
SN   Determination of the probability of
      rejecting a hypothesis when it is actually
      true
UF   Significance Measures
RT   Calculation
      Hypothesis Testing
      Measurement
      Probability
      Statistical Analysis

TEST VALIDITY 520
UF   Concurrent Validity
NT   Item Analysis
BT   Validity
RT   Test Interpretation
      Test Reliability
      Test Results
      Tests

Tetraplegia
USE   QUADRIPLEGIA

TEXTBOOK ASSIGNMENTS 270
BT   Assignments
RT   Textbooks

TEXTBOOK BIAS 040
BT   Bias
RT   Attitudes
      Multicultural Textbooks
      Textbook Content
      Textbook Preparation
      Textbook Research
      Textbooks
      Textbook Selection

TEXTBOOK CONTENT 110
RT   Content Analysis
      Multicultural Textbooks
      Textbook Bias
      Textbooks

TEXTBOOK EVALUATION 180
BT   Evaluation
RT   Course Evaluation
      Textbook Research
      Textbooks

TEXTBOOK PREPARATION 080
UF Textbook Writing
RT Textbook Bias
      Textbooks
      Textbook Standards
      Writing

Textbook Production
USE TEXTBOOK PUBLICATIONS

TEXTBOOK PUBLICATIONS 080
UF Textbook Production
BT Publications
RT Copyrights
      Textbooks

TEXTBOOK RESEARCH 450
BT Research
RT Textbook Bias
      Textbook Evaluation
      Textbooks

TEXTBOOKS 050
UF Reading Texts
NT High Interest Low Vocabulary Books
      History Textbooks
      Multicultural Textbooks
      Programed Texts
      Supplementary Textbooks
BT Books
RT Instructional Materials
      Reading Materials
      Textbook Assignments
      Textbook Bias
      Textbook Content
      Textbook Evaluation
      Textbook Preparation
      Textbook Publications
      Textbook Research
      Textbook Selection
      Textbook Standards

TEXTBOOK SELECTION 020
RT Reading Material Selection
      Supplementary Textbooks
      Textbook Bias
      Textbooks
      Textbook Standards

TEXTBOOK STANDARDS 500
BT Standards
RT Textbook Preparation
      Textbooks
      Textbook Selection

Textbook Writing
USE TEXTBOOK PREPARATION

Textile Finishing
USE FINISHING

TEXTILES INSTRUCTION 270
BT Instruction
RT Clothing Instruction
      Clothing Maintenance Specialists
      Home Economics Education

TEXTUAL CRITICISM 260
BT Literary Criticism
RT Analytical Criticism
      Chronicles
      Formal Criticism
      Historical Criticism
      Italian Literature
      Literary Analysis
      Literary Conventions
      Literary Genres
      Literature

T GROUPS 490
SN Unstructured heterogeneous groups of learners used to examine interpersonal relations and group dynamics
UF Training Groups
BT Groups
RT Discussion Groups
      Group Dynamics
      Heterogeneous Grouping
      Interaction Process Analysis
      Laboratory Training
      Sensitivity Training
      Trainers
      Training Laboratories

THAI 300
BT Sino Tibetan Languages

Theater
USE THEATER ARTS

THEATER ARTS 030
UF Childrens Theater
      Performing Arts
      Puppetry
      Puppet Shows
      Shadow Plays
      Theater
NT Acting
      Dramatics
      Opera
BT Fine Arts
RT Acoustical Environment
      Ballet
      Czech Literature
      Dance
      Dramatic Unities
      Orchestras
      Outdoor Theaters
      Production Techniques
      Skits
      Theaters

THEATERS 210
UF Performing Arts Centers
NT Outdoor Theaters
BT Facilities
RT Arts Centers
      Auditoriums
      Demonstration Centers
      Dramatics
      Drama Workshops

Music Facilities
Stages
Theater Arts

Thefts
USE STEALING

THEMATIC APPROACH 510
SN Teaching approach which organizes
   subject matter around broad themes
BT Teaching Methods
RT Interdisciplinary Approach
   Literature

Theme Writing
USE COMPOSITION (LITERARY)

THEOLOGICAL EDUCATION 140
BT Professional Education
RT Churches
   Church Related Colleges
   Religion
   Religious Education

THEORETICAL CRITICISM 260
BT Literary Criticism
RT Drama
   Essays
   Fiction
   Novels
   Poetry
   Prose

Theoretical Models
USE MODELS

THEORIES 450
NT Adaptation Level Theory
   Behavior Theories
   Counseling Theories
   Educational Theories
   Information Theory
   Learning Theories
   Linguistic Theory
   Mediation Theory
   Personality Theories
   Probability Theory
   Set Theory
   Social Exchange Theory
RT Conceptual Schemes
   Models

THERAPEUTIC ENVIRONMENT 160
BT Environment
RT Counselor Acceptance
   Educational Therapy
   Milieu Therapy
   Occupational Therapists
   Rehabilitation
   Rehabilitation Centers
   Therapy

Therapeutics
USE THERAPY

THERAPISTS 380
NT Hearing Therapists
   Occupational Therapists
   Physical Therapists
   Speech Therapists
RT Milieu Therapy
   Therapy

THERAPY 250
UF Therapeutics
NT Crisis Therapy
   Drug Therapy
   Educational Therapy
   Hearing Therapy
   Milieu Therapy
   Occupational Therapy
   Physical Therapy
   Psychotherapy
   Speech Therapy
RT Cocounseling
   Family Counseling
   Medical Services
   Progressive Relaxation
   Psychiatric Services
   Psychiatry
   Rehabilitation
   Role Playing
   Sensitivity Training
   Sociodrama
   Therapeutic Environment
   Therapists

THERMAL ENVIRONMENT 160
SN Related to the combined effects of
   radiant temperature, air temperature,
   humidity, and air velocity
BT Physical Environment
RT Air Conditioning
   Air Conditioning Equipment
   Building Design
   Climate Control
   Climatic Factors
   Controlled Environment
   Environmental Influences
   Fuel Consumption
   Heating
   Human Engineering
   Humidity
   Interior Design
   Pollution
   School Environment
   Solar Radiation
   Standards
   Temperature
   Ventilation

THERMODYNAMICS 400
UF Heat Equations
   Thermomechanics
   Thermophysics
   Thermoscience
BT Physics

RT Chemical Equilibrium
    Heat

Thermomechanics
USE THERMODYNAMICS

Thermophysics
USE THERMODYNAMICS

Thermoscience
USE THERMODYNAMICS

THESAURI 320
BT Reference Materials
RT Coordinate Indexes
    Dictionaries
    Glossaries
    Indexes (Locaters)
    Information Retrieval
    Lexicography
    Semantics
    Subject Index Terms
    Syntax
    Vocabulary
    Word Lists

THOUGHT PROCESSES 310
NT Abstract Reasoning
    Creative Thinking
    Critical Thinking
    Logical Thinking
    Problem Solving
    Productive Thinking
RT Association (Psychological)
    Cognitive Processes
    Deductive Methods
    Eidetic Images
    Imagination
    Inductive Methods
    Intellectualization
    Intelligence
    Learning Processes
    Logic
    Mediation Theory
    Surrealism
    Task Analysis

THREE DIMENSIONAL AIDS 050
BT Instructional Aids
RT Audiovisual Aids
    Display Panels
    Student Developed Materials
    Teacher Developed Materials

TIBETAN 300
BT Sino Tibetan Languages

Timber Based Industry
USE LUMBER INDUSTRY

TIME 400
BT Scientific Concepts
RT Horology
    Obsolescence
    Reaction Time
    Relativity
    Space

TIME BLOCKS 020
UF Block Time Teaching
BT School Schedules
RT Flexible Schedules
    Flexible Scheduling
    Man Days
    Released Time

TIMED TESTS 520
UF Rate Test
BT Tests
RT Achievement Tests
    Measurement Instruments
    Performance
    Performance Tests

TIME FACTORS (LEARNING) 310
RT Acceleration
    Interval Pacing
    Learning
    Pacing
    Program Length
    Reaction Time
    Retardation
    Time Perspective

TIME PERSPECTIVE 310
UF Temporal Perspective
RT Time Factors (Learning)

TIME SHARING 080
SN Use of a device for two or more
    purposes during same time interval with
    interspersing component actions in time
RT Computer Assisted Instruction
    Computer Oriented Programs
    Computers

TOBACCO 250
RT Health
    Health Education
    Smoking
    Stimulants

TOILET FACILITIES 210
BT Sanitary Facilities
RT Health Facilities
    Public Facilities

TOKEN INTEGRATION 430
BT Racial Segregation
RT Defacto Segregation
    Restrictive Transfer Programs

TONE LANGUAGES 290
SN A language having lexically significant,
    contrastive, but relative pitch on each
    syllable. See African languages and Sino
    Tibetan language families for specific
    languages
BT Language
RT Descriptive Linguistics
    Language Typology
    Morphophonemics

TOOL AND DIE MAKERS 380
BT Skilled Workers
RT Machinery Industry
    Machine Tool Operators
    Machine Tools
    Machinists
    Metal Working Occupations

TOPOLOGY 340
BT Geometry
RT Algebra
    Distance
    Graphs
    Networks

TOURISM 370
UF Sightseeing Industry
    Tourist Industry
BT Industry
RT Camping
    Hotels
    Instructional Trips
    Recreational Activities
    Study Abroad
    Transportation
    Travel

Tourist Courts
USE HOTELS

Tourist Industry
USE TOURISM

TOYS 050
RT Games
    Instructional Materials
    Puzzles

TRACKING 400
SN Adjustment of an instrument to maintain
    a normal or desired value or to follow a
    moving reference marker
UF Automatic Tracking
    Compensatory Tracking
    Pursuit Tracking
    Tracking Systems
RT Aviation Technology
    Electronic Equipment
    Eye Hand Coordination
    Object Manipulation
    Perceptual Motor Coordination
    Psychomotor Skills
    Radar

Tracking Systems
USE TRACKING

Track System
USE FLEXIBLE PROGRESSION

TRACTORS 170
BT Motor Vehicles
RT Agricultural Machinery
    Agriculture

TRADE AND INDUSTRIAL EDUCATION 140
SN Vocational education programs for a
    wide range of trades and occupations in
    industry at the semiskilled, skilled or
    supervisory levels
UF Trade Instruction
    Vocational Industrial Education
BT Vocational Education
RT Apprenticeships
    Auto Body Repairmen
    Auto Mechanics (Occupation)
    Auto Parts Men
    Barbers
    Boatmen
    Bricklayers
    Building Trades
    Carpenters
    Cooks
    Cosmetologists
    Data Processing Occupations
    Draftsmen
    Electrical Appliance Servicemen
    Electrical Occupations
    Electricians
    Electronics
    Electronic Technicians
    Fire Fighters
    Floor Layers
    Food Service Occupations
    Glaziers
    Industrial Arts
    Industrial Education
    Industrial Training
    Machine Repairmen
    Machine Tool Operators
    Machinists
    Manpower Development
    Mechanical Design Technicians
    Mechanical Skills
    Metal Working Occupations
    On The Job Training
    Production Technicians
    Radiographers
    Refrigeration Mechanics
    Retraining
    Roofers
    School Shops
    Semiskilled Occupations
    Sewing Machine Operators
    Sheet Metal Workers
    Sign Painters
    Skilled Occupations
    Technical Occupations
    Television Repairmen
    Trade And Industrial Teachers
    Vocational Education Teachers
    Welders

TRADE AND INDUSTRIAL TEACHERS 380
BT Vocational Education Teachers
RT Industrial Education
    Trade And Industrial Education

Trade Instruction
USE TRADE AND INDUSTRIAL EDUCATION

Trade Unions
USE LABOR UNIONS

Traditional Classrooms
USE TRADITIONAL SCHOOLS

TRADITIONAL GRAMMAR 290
BT Grammar
RT Form Classes (Languages)
Linguistics
Morphology (Languages)
Paragraphs
Sentence Structure
Structural Grammar
Syntax
Transformation Generative Grammar

TRADITIONAL SCHOOLS 470
UF Traditional Classrooms
BT Schools
RT Conventional Instruction
Transitional Schools

TRAFFIC ACCIDENTS 250
BT Accidents
RT Safety
Safety Education
Traffic Regulations
Traffic Safety

TRAFFIC CIRCULATION 210
UF Traffic Flow
RT Commuting Students
Driveways
Motor Vehicles
Parking Areas
Parking Controls
Pedestrian Traffic
Road Construction
Service Vehicles
Student Transportation
Traffic Control
Traffic Patterns
Traffic Signs
Vehicular Traffic

TRAFFIC CONTROL 210
UF Spectator Traffic Control
RT Motor Vehicles
Parking Areas
Parking Controls
Pedestrian Traffic
Traffic Circulation
Traffic Patterns
Traffic Signs
Vehicular Traffic

Traffic Flow
USE TRAFFIC CIRCULATION

TRAFFIC PATTERNS 210
UF Circulation Patterns
Street Layouts
RT Motor Vehicles
Parking Areas
Road Construction
Traffic Circulation
Traffic Control
Traffic Signs
Vehicular Traffic

TRAFFIC REGULATIONS 230
RT Safety
Signs
Student Loading Areas
Traffic Accidents
Traffic Safety
Vehicular Traffic

TRAFFIC SAFETY 250
BT Safety
RT Driver Education
Motor Vehicles
Safety Education
Signs
Student Loading Areas
Traffic Accidents
Traffic Regulations

Traffic Signals
USE TRAFFIC SIGNS

TRAFFIC SIGNS 170
UF Stop Signs
Traffic Signals
RT Motor Vehicles
Parking Controls
Pedestrian Traffic
Traffic Circulation
Traffic Control
Traffic Patterns
Vehicular Traffic

TRAGEDY 260
BT Drama
RT Characterization (Literature)
Composition (Literary)
English Neoclassic Literary Period
French Literature
Literary Analysis
Literary Conventions
Poetry
Prose
Spanish American Literature
Spanish Literature

TRAILS 210
UF Nature Trails
Pathways
RT Camping
Conservation Education
Landscaping
Outdoor Education
Park Design
Parks

Playgrounds
Recreational Facilities

TRAINABLE MENTALLY HANDICAPPED 240
BT   Mentally Handicapped
RT   Educable Mentally Handicapped
      Mental Retardation
      Self Care Skills

TRAINEES 380
SN   Participants in vocational, administrative,
      or technical training programs for
      purpose of developing job related skills
RT   Apprenticeships
      Industrial Training
      Internship Programs
      Job Training
      Students
      Work Experience Programs

TRAINERS 380
SN   Persons who direct the practice of skills
      toward immediate improvement in some
      art or task
BT   Instructional Staff
RT   Adult Educators
      Industrial Training
      Laboratory Training
      Leadership Training
      Simulators
      Teachers
      T Groups
      Training
      Training Techniques

TRAINING 270
SN   Systematic educative process by which
      one learns new skills
NT   Attendant Training
      Counselor Training
      Cross Cultural Training
      Flight Training
      Industrial Training
      Inquiry Training
      Job Training
      Laboratory Training
      Leadership Training
      Military Training
      Pediatrics Training
      Professional Training
      Retraining
      Sensitivity Training
      Sensory Training
      Supervisory Training
      Team Training
      Travel Training
      Volunteer Training
RT   Education
      Institutional Role
      Manpower Development
      Trainers
      Training Objectives
      Transfer Of Training
      Vocational Training Centers

TRAINING ALLOWANCES 220
RT   Federal Aid
      Financial Support
      State Aid
      State Federal Aid
      State Federal Support
      Tuition Grants

Training Devices
USE   SIMULATORS

Training Goals
USE   TRAINING OBJECTIVES

Training Groups
USE   T GROUPS

TRAINING LABORATORIES 210
UF   Instrumented Laboratories
      Prestudent Teaching Laboratories
BT   Laboratories
RT   Group Dynamics
      Laboratory Training
      Learning Laboratories
      Project Training Methods
      Self Directed Groups
      Sensitivity Training
      Teaching Experience
      T Groups

Training Needs
USE   EDUCATIONAL NEEDS

TRAINING OBJECTIVES 270
UF   Training Goals
BT   Objectives
RT   Affective Objectives
      Cognitive Objectives
      College Role
      Educational Objectives
      Institutional Role
      Psychomotor Objectives
      Training

Training Opportunities
USE   EDUCATIONAL OPPORTUNITIES

Training Programs
USE   EDUCATIONAL PROGRAMS

TRAINING TECHNIQUES 510
SN   Specific teaching formats designed for
      learning new skills
NT   Microteaching
BT   Techniques
RT   Management Games
      Teaching Techniques
      Team Training
      Trainers

Tranquilizing Drugs
USE   SEDATIVES

Transfer Of Learning
USE   TRANSFER OF TRAINING

TRANSFER OF TRAINING 310
UF Transfer Of Learning
NT Negative Practice
BT Learning Theories
RT Diffusion
   Learning Processes
   Skill Development
   Training
   Visualization

TRANSFER POLICY 020
BT School Policy
RT College Credits
   Free Choice Transfer Programs
   Transfer Programs
   Transfers

TRANSFER PROGRAMS 410
NT Free Choice Transfer Programs
   Restrictive Transfer Programs
BT Programs
RT Terminal Students
   Transfer Policy
   Transfers

TRANSFERS 020
NT Teacher Transfer
RT Credits
   Educational Mobility
   Free Choice Transfer Programs
   Open Enrollment
   School Holding Power
   Student Mobility
   Students
   Transfer Policy
   Transfer Programs
   Transfer Students
   Transient Children

TRANSFER STUDENTS 380
UF Incoming Transfer Students
   School Transfers
   Student Transfers
BT Students
RT Free Choice Transfer Programs
   Terminal Students
   Transfers

Transformational Grammar
USE TRANSFORMATION GENERATIVE
   GRAMMAR

TRANSFORMATION GENERATIVE GRAMMAR
290
UF Generative Transformation Grammar
   Transformational Grammar
BT Generative Grammar
RT Context Free Grammar
   Deep Structure
   Phrase Structure
   Surface Structure
   Syntax
   Traditional Grammar
   Transformations (Language)
   Transformation Theory (Language)

TRANSFORMATIONS (LANGUAGE) 290
BT Transformation Theory (Language)
RT Context Free Grammar
   Deep Structure
   Kernel Sentences
   Phrase Structure
   Surface Structure
   Syntax
   Transformation Generative Grammar

TRANSFORMATIONS (MATHEMATICS) 340
UF Similarity Transformations

TRANSFORMATION THEORY (LANGUAGE)
290
NT Context Free Grammar
   Deep Structure
   Kernel Sentences
   Surface Structure
   Transformations (Language)
BT Linguistic Theory
RT Grammar
   Negative Forms (Language)
   Syntax
   Tagmemic Analysis
   Transformation Generative Grammar

Transhumance
USE NOMADS

TRANSIENT CHILDREN 380
UF Transient Students
BT Children
RT Immigrants
   Migrants
   Migration
   Mobility
   Nomads
   Transfers

Transient Students
USE TRANSIENT CHILDREN

TRANSISTORS 170
RT Electricity
   Electronics
   Instrumentation
   Radio
   Semiconductor Devices
   Television

TRANSITIONAL CLASSES 280
BT Classes (Groups Of Students)

TRANSITIONAL SCHOOLS 470
BT Schools
RT Traditional Schools

TRANSLATION 290
SN One language to another
NT Machine Translation
BT Language Arts
RT Grammar Translation Method
   Interpreters
   Language Ability
   Language Skills

TRANSPARENCIES 050
NT   Slides
BT   Audiovisual Aids
     Audiovisual Communication
RT   Color Presentation

Transparency Projectors
USE OVERHEAD PROJECTORS

TRANSPLANTING 070
SN   The process of removing botanical plants
     from one place and resetting elsewhere
RT   Agricultural Production
     Agriculture
     Agronomy
     Field Crops
     Forestry
     Horticulture
     Ornamental Horticulture
     Plant Growth
     Planting
     Plant Propagation
     Plant Science

TRANSPORTATION 020
NT   Bus Transportation
     Migrant Transportation
     Rail Transportation
     Student Transportation
RT   Distance
     Instructional Trips
     Mobile Classrooms
     Motor Vehicles
     Road Construction
     Tourism
     Travel
     Vehicular Traffic

TRAVEL 260
UF   Student Travel
     Teacher Travel
RT   Instructional Trips
     Rail Transportation
     Recreational Activities
     Study Abroad
     Tourism
     Transportation

Traveling Teachers
USE ITINERANT TEACHERS

TRAVEL TRAINING 270
SN   Process of teaching a handicapped
     person to move freely in his environment
BT   Training
RT   Blind
     Echolocation
     Mobility Aids
     Visually Handicapped
     Visually Handicapped Mobility
     Visually Handicapped Orientation

Treatment Centers
USE CLINICS

TREES 070
UF   Shade Trees
RT   Forestry
     Forestry Aides
     Ornamental Horticulture

Tribal Societies
USE TRIBES

TRIBES 380
UF   Tribal Societies
BT   Groups
RT   African Culture
     American Indians
     Ethnic Groups
     Minority Groups
     Nomads

TRIGONOMETRY 340
BT   Mathematics
RT   Mathematical Applications
     Mathematical Concepts
     Mathematical Enrichment
     Mathematical Experience
     Mathematical Vocabulary

Trimester Plan
USE TRIMESTER SCHEDULES

TRIMESTER SCHEDULES 020
UF   Trimester Plan
BT   Semester Division
RT   Extended School Year
     Scheduling
     School Calendars
     Year Round Schools

Troubadours
USE POETS

TRUANCY 060
UF   School Truancy
RT   Attendance
     Attendance Patterns
     Attendance Services
     Continuation Students
     School Holding Power
     Students

Truck Mechanics
USE AUTO MECHANICS (OCCUPATION)

TRUSTEES 380
SN   Members of governing boards
UF   Regents
RT   Administrative Personnel
     Board Candidates
     Board Of Education Role
     Estate Planning
     Governance
     Governing Boards
     School Administration
     Trusts (Financial)

TRUSTS (FINANCIAL) 220
RT   Capital
Estate Planning
Finance Occupations
Financial Services
Foundation Programs
Income
Investment
Property Accounting
Property Appraisal
Resource Allocations
Trustees
Wills

TUITION 220
UF   Tuition Fee
BT   Fees
Student Costs
RT   Student Loan Programs
Tuition Grants

Tuition Fee
USE   TUITION

TUITION GRANTS 220
BT   Grants
RT   Scholarships
Training Allowances
Tuition
Veterans Education

TUMBLING 390
UF   Stunts And Tumbling
BT   Athletic Activities
RT   Exercise (Physiology)
Physical Education
Physical Recreation Programs
Recreational Activities

TURF MANAGEMENT 070
UF   Lawn Maintenance
BT   Ornamental Horticulture
RT   Grounds Keepers
Landscaping
Land Use

TURKIC LANGUAGES 300
NT   Azerbaijani
Bashkir
Chuvash
Kirghiz
Tatar
Turkish
Uzbek
Yakut
BT   Uralic Altaic Languages

TURKISH 300
BT   Turkic Languages

Tutorial Instruction
USE   TUTORING

Tutorial Plan
USE   TUTORIAL PROGRAMS

TUTORIAL PROGRAMS 270
UF   Tutorial Plan
BT   Programs
RT   Coaching Teachers
Grouping (Instructional Purposes)
Individual Instruction
Individualized Programs
Teaching Programs
Teaching Techniques
Tutoring

Tutorial Services
USE   TUTORING

TUTORING 510
UF   Tutorial Instruction
Tutorial Services
NT   After School Tutoring
BT   Teaching Techniques
RT   Coaching Teachers
Cross Age Teaching
Individual Instruction
Programed Tutoring
Study Centers
Tutorial Programs

Tv Repairmen
USE   TELEVISION REPAIRMEN

TWENTIETH CENTURY LITERATURE 260
UF   Midtwentieth Century Literature
NT   Surrealism
BT   Literature
RT   American Literature
Characterization (Literature)
English Literature
Existentialism
Expressionism
French Literature
German Literature
Local Color Writing
Metaphors
Modernism
Naturalism
Realism
Spanish American Literature
Spanish Literature
Symbolism
World Literature

Twi
USE   AKAN

TWINS 380
RT   Children
Family (Sociological Unit)
Siblings

TYPEWRITING 080
UF   Typing
BT   Business Subjects
Writing
RT   Office Machines
Printing
Secretaries

Stenographers
Typists

Typing
USE TYPEWRITING

TYPISTS 380
UF Clerk Typists
BT Clerical Workers
RT Clerical Occupations
Court Reporters
Secretaries
Stenographers
Typewriting

TYPOLOGY 290
NT Language Typology
BT Classification
RT Literary Genres
Taxonomy

TZELTAL 300
UF Tzendal
BT American Indian Languages

Tzendal
USE TZELTAL

TZOTZIL 300
BT American Indian Languages

UKRAINIAN 300
BT Slavic Languages

Uncial Script
USE MANUSCRIPT WRITING
(HANDLETTERING)

UNCOMMONLY TAUGHT LANGUAGES 290
SN Languages not generally offered for
instruction in the united states
educational system. Also see the specific
language, e.g., Turkish, or the language
family, e.g., Uralic Altaic languages
UF Less Commonly Taught Languages
Neglected Languages
BT Language
RT Unwritten Language

UNDERACHIEVERS 380
BT Students
RT Academic Achievement
Achievement
Continuation Students
Learning Disabilities
Low Ability Students

Underdeveloped Nations
USE DEVELOPING NATIONS

UNDEREMPLOYED 380
SN Persons employed part-time, part-year,
or below their demonstrated skill or
earning level
RT Job Applicants
Part Time Jobs
Subemployment

Unemployed
Unemployment

Undergraduate Education
USE UNDERGRADUATE STUDY

Undergraduate Professors
USE PROFESSORS

UNDERGRADUATE STUDY 140
UF Undergraduate Education
Undergraduate Training
RT Colleges
Community Colleges
Higher Education
Junior Colleges
Private Colleges
Teachers Colleges
Universities
Urban Universities

Undergraduate Training
USE UNDERGRADUATE STUDY

Underground Garages
USE PARKING FACILITIES

Underprivileged
USE CULTURALLY DISADVANTAGED

UNEMPLOYED 150
NT Labor Force Nonparticipants
RT Dropouts
Employment
Employment Problems
Job Applicants
Job Layoff
Laborers
Underemployed

UNEMPLOYMENT 150
RT Dropouts
Employment
Employment Level
Job Applicants
Job Layoff
Job Market
Labor Economics
Labor Market
Manpower Utilization
Persistence
Subemployment
Underemployed
Unemployment Insurance

UNEMPLOYMENT INSURANCE 150
RT Fringe Benefits
Health Insurance
Insurance Occupations
Insurance Programs
Unemployment
Workmans Compensation

Unequal Education
USE EDUCATIONAL DISADVANTAGEMENT

UNGRADED CLASSES 280
BT   Classes (Groups Of Students)
RT   Flexible Progression
     Noncredit Courses
     Ungraded Curriculum
     Ungraded Elementary Programs
     Ungraded Programs
     Ungraded Schools

UNGRADED CURRICULUM 110
BT   Curriculum
RT   Elementary School Curriculum
     Ungraded Classes
     Ungraded Programs
     Ungraded Schools

UNGRADED ELEMENTARY PROGRAMS 140
NT   Ungraded Primary Programs
BT   Ungraded Programs
RT   Ungraded Classes
     Ungraded Schools

UNGRADED PRIMARY PROGRAMS 140
BT   Ungraded Elementary Programs

UNGRADED PROGRAMS 140
NT   Ungraded Elementary Programs
BT   Programs
RT   Noncredit Courses
     Ungraded Classes
     Ungraded Curriculum
     Ungraded Schools

UNGRADED SCHOOLS 470
BT   Schools
RT   Ungraded Classes
     Ungraded Curriculum
     Ungraded Elementary Programs
     Ungraded Programs

Unification
USE   GROUP UNITY

UNIFIED STUDIES PROGRAMS 140
BT   Educational Programs
RT   Curriculum Development
     Fused Curriculum

UNION CATALOGS 320
UF   Repertory Catalogs
BT   Catalogs
RT   Bibliographies
     Booklists
     Cataloging
     Indexes (Locaters)
     Information Storage
     Interlibrary Loans
     Libraries
     Library Cooperation

UNION MEMBERS 380
RT   Unions

UNIONS 150
NT   Labor Unions
     Local Unions
RT   Arbitration
     Collective Bargaining
     Negotiation Impasses
     Strikes
     Union Members

UNIT COSTS 220
BT   Costs
RT   Estimated Costs
     Program Costs
     Student Costs

United States Demography
USE   NATIONAL DEMOGRAPHY

UNITED STATES HISTORY 260
NT   Colonial History (United States)
BT   American History
RT   Civil Liberties
     Civil War (United States)
     Nuclear Warfare
     Reconstruction Era
     Revolutionary War (United States)

Uniterm Indexes
USE   COORDINATE INDEXES

Uniterms
USE   SUBJECT INDEX TERMS

UNIT PLAN 110
UF   Teaching Units
RT   Programed Units
     Resource Units
     Science Units
     Social Studies Units
     Units Of Study (Subject Fields)

Unit Shops
USE   SCHOOL SHOPS

UNITS OF STUDY (SUBJECT FIELDS) 110
NT   Activity Units
     Business Subjects
     Human Relations Units
     Programed Units
     Science Units
     Social Studies Units
BT   Courses
     Intellectual Disciplines
RT   College Majors
     Course Organization
     Departments
     Resource Units
     Unit Plan

UNIVERSAL EDUCATION 140
SN   System of education extending
     opportunities to all youth regardless of
     race, color, creed, sex, or ability
BT   Education
RT   Educational Equality
     Educational Opportunities

UNIVERSITIES 470
NT Land Grant Universities
    State Universities
    Urban Universities
BT Institutions
RT College Buildings
    Colleges
    English Departments
    Experimental Colleges
    Extension Education
    Graduate Study
    Higher Education
    Private Colleges
    Science Departments
    Teaching Assistants
    Undergraduate Study
    University Libraries

UNIVERSITY ADMINISTRATION 020
BT Educational Administration
RT College Administration
    College Deans
    Governance
    Governing Boards
    School Administration

UNIVERSITY EXTENSION 140
SN Extension activity of universities
    including agricultural and cooperative
    extension
UF Extramural Departments
BT Extension Education
RT Continuing Education Centers
    Evening Colleges
    Residential Centers
    Rural Extension
    Urban Extension
    Urban Universities

UNIVERSITY LIBRARIES 210
BT Libraries
RT College Libraries
    Depository Libraries
    Research Libraries
    Universities

University Policy
USE ADMINISTRATIVE POLICY

University Schools
USE LABORATORY SCHOOLS

University Settlements
USE SETTLEMENT HOUSES

University Training Centers
USE TEACHER EDUCATION

Unmarried Students
USE SINGLE STUDENTS

UNSKILLED LABOR 150
BT Labor
RT Blue Collar Occupations
    Semiskilled Occupations
    Semiskilled Workers
    Unskilled Occupations
    Unskilled Workers

UNSKILLED OCCUPATIONS 350
BT Occupations
RT Blue Collar Occupations
    Semiskilled Workers
    Unskilled Labor
    Unskilled Workers

UNSKILLED WORKERS 380
BT Nonprofessional Personnel
RT Blue Collar Occupations
    Employees
    Semiskilled Occupations
    Semiskilled Workers
    Unskilled Labor
    Unskilled Occupations

UNWED MOTHERS 380
BT Mothers
RT Social Problems

UNWRITTEN LANGUAGE 290
BT Language
RT Applied Linguistics
    Field Instruction
    Instructional Materials
    Language Instruction
    Language Research
    Second Language Learning
    Tape Recordings
    Uncommonly Taught Languages

Upgrading
USE IMPROVEMENT

UPPER CLASS 490
BT Social Class
RT Culturally Advantaged
    Lower Middle Class
    Socioeconomic Status

URALIC ALTAIC LANGUAGES 300
UF Altaic Languages
NT Buriat
    Cheremis
    Finno Ugric Languages
    Mongolian Languages
    Ostyak
    Samoyed Languages
    Turkic Languages
    Vogul
BT Languages

URBAN AREAS 120
UF Large Cities
NT Metropolitan Areas
RT Municipalities
    Rural Urban Differences
    Urban Culture
    Urban Education
    Urban Environment
    Urban Immigration
    Urbanization
    Urban Language
    Urban Population
    Urban Renewal
    Urban Renewal Agencies
    Urban Schools
    Urban Slums
    Urban Teaching
    Urban Universities
    Urban Youth

URBAN CULTURE 100
UF Urban Life
BT Culture
RT Urban Areas
    Urban Environment
    Urban Language

Urban Desegregation
USE RACIAL INTEGRATION

URBAN DROPOUTS 380
BT Dropouts
RT Urban Youth

URBAN EDUCATION 140
UF Inner City Education
BT Education
RT Extension Education
    Outdoor Education
    Urban Areas
    Urban Teaching

URBAN ENVIRONMENT 160
BT Environment
RT Air Pollution Control
    Community Characteristics
    Ghettos
    Inner City
    Slums
    Urban Areas
    Urban Culture
    Urban Language
    Urban Slums
    Urban Youth

URBAN EXTENSION 140
SN Extension work in urban settings
BT Extension Education
RT University Extension
    Urban Universities

URBAN IMMIGRATION 120
RT Urban Areas
    Urban Population

URBANIZATION 490
RT Population Growth
    Urban Areas
    Urban Population
    Urban Universities

URBAN LANGUAGE 290
BT Language
RT Cultural Factors
    Language Classification
    Language Patterns
    Language Research
    Nonstandard Dialects
    Rural Urban Differences
    Urban Areas
    Urban Culture
    Urban Environment

Urban Life
USE URBAN CULTURE

Urban Planning
USE CITY PLANNING

URBAN POPULATION 120
BT Population Distribution
RT Community Size
    Demography
    Population Growth
    Population Trends
    Rural Urban Differences
    Urban Areas
    Urban Immigration
    Urbanization
    Urban Population

Urban Poverty
USE ECONOMIC DISADVANTAGEMENT

Urban Problems
USE CITY PROBLEMS

URBAN RENEWAL 490
UF Redevelopment Areas
RT City Improvement
    City Planning
    Community Change
    Neighborhood Improvement
    Planned Community
    Public Housing
    Urban Areas
    Urban Renewal Agencies

URBAN RENEWAL AGENCIES 230
BT Agencies
RT Agency Role
    Housing
    Inner City
    Slums
    State Agencies
    Urban Areas
    Urban Renewal
    Welfare Agencies

Urban Rural Differences
USE RURAL URBAN DIFFERENCES

URBAN SCHOOLS 470
UF   City Schools
BT   Schools
RT   Urban Areas

URBAN SLUMS 490
BT   Slums
RT   Urban Areas
     Urban Environment

URBAN TEACHING 270
BT   Teaching
RT   Urban Areas
     Urban Education

Urban Teaching Interns
USE TEACHER INTERNS

URBAN UNIVERSITIES 210
BT   Universities
RT   Colleges
     Graduate Study
     Higher Education
     Professional Education
     Undergraduate Study
     University Extension
     Urban Areas
     Urban Extension
     Urbanization

URBAN YOUTH 380
BT   Youth
RT   Urban Areas
     Urban Dropouts
     Urban Environment

URDU 300
BT   Indo European Languages
RT   Hindi

User Studies
USE USE STUDIES

USE STUDIES 180
SN   Studies of the use of information,
     information sources, and libraries
UF   User Studies
RT   Documentation
     Information Needs
     Information Science
     Information Seeking
     Information Sources
     Information Utilization
     Libraries
     Library Research
     Library Science
     Library Surveys
     Obsolescence
     Research Utilization

UTILITIES 210
UF   Electric Utilities
     Gas Utilities
     Public Utilities
     Water Utilities
BT   Services
RT   Communications
     Electrical Systems
     Fuels
     Heating
     Kinetics
     Lighting
     Sanitary Facilities
     Sanitation
     Telephone Communication Systems

UTO AZTECAN LANGUAGES 300
BT   American Indian Languages
RT   Language Classification
     Native Speakers

UZBEK 300
BT   Turkic Languages

VACATION PROGRAMS 410
BT   Recreational Programs
RT   Summer Programs

Vacations
USE LEAVE OF ABSENCE

VALIDITY 500
NT   Predictive Validity
     Test Validity
RT   Correlation
     Evaluation
     Evaluative Thinking
     Logic
     Reliability
     Standards

VALUES 040
NT   Democratic Values
     Ethical Values
     Middle Class Values
     Moral Values
     Personal Values
     Social Values
RT   Affective Behavior
     Beliefs
     Culture Conflict
     Group Norms
     Political Attitudes
     Sportsmanship

VANDALISM 060
NT   School Vandalism
BT   Delinquency
RT   Anti Social Behavior
     Crime
     Misbehavior
     Socially Deviant Behavior

Vascular System
USE CARDIOVASCULAR SYSTEM

Vehicular Circulation
USE   VEHICULAR TRAFFIC

VEHICULAR TRAFFIC 210
UF   Vehicular Circulation
RT   Campus Planning
     Driveways
     Master Plans
     Motor Vehicles
     Parking Areas
     Parking Controls
     Parking Facilities
     Pedestrian Traffic
     Service Vehicles
     Traffic Circulation
     Traffic Control
     Traffic Patterns
     Traffic Regulations
     Traffic Signs
     Transportation

VENDING MACHINES 170
BT   Mechanical Equipment
RT   School Services

VENTILATION 170
RT   Air Conditioning
     Air Conditioning Equipment
     Air Flow
     Chimneys
     Climate Control
     Controlled Environment
     Design Needs
     Exhausting
     Fuel Consumption
     Heating
     Lighting
     Mechanical Equipment
     Physical Environment
     Temperature
     Thermal Environment
     Windowless Rooms
     Windows

VERBAL ABILITY 010
BT   Ability
RT   Academic Ability
     Basic Skills
     Communication Skills
     Language Skills
     Nonverbal Ability
     Speech Skills
     Verbal Development
     Verbal Learning
     Verbal Operant Conditioning
     Verbal Tests

VERBAL COMMUNICATION 080
UF   Verbal Interaction
NT   Mutual Intelligibility
     Oral Communication
BT   Communication (Thought Transfer)
RT   Child Language
     Classroom Communication

     Idioms
     Interpreters
     Language Uságe
     Native Speakers
     Nonverbal Communication
     Persuasive Discourse
     Semiotics
     Speech

VERBAL DEVELOPMENT 130
BT   Development
RT   Child Language
     Language Development
     Verbal Ability
     Verbal Learning
     Verbal Stimuli
     Vocabulary Development

Verbal Interaction
USE   VERBAL COMMUNICATION

VERBAL LEARNING 310
BT   Learning
RT   Mediation Theory
     Memorizing
     Verbal Ability
     Verbal Development

VERBAL OPERANT CONDITIONING 420
BT   Operant Conditioning
RT   Conditioned Response
     Psycholinguistics
     Psychology
     Stimulus Behavior
     Verbal Ability

VERBAL STIMULI 420
BT   Stimuli
RT   Association Tests
     Electrical Stimuli
     Verbal Development
     Visual Stimuli
     Word Recognition

VERBAL TESTS 520
BT   Tests
RT   Essay Tests
     Performance Tests
     Science Tests
     Verbal Ability

VERBS 290
UF   Imperative Mood
     Indicative Mood
     Subjunctive Mood
BT   Form Classes (Languages)
RT   Adverbs
     Morphology (Languages)
     Sentence Structure
     Syntax
     Vocabulary

VERSIFICATION 260
UF   Prosody
BT   Poetry
RT   Allegory
        Ballads
        Epics
        Fables
        Literature
        Lyric Poetry
        Parallelism (Literary)

VERTICAL ORGANIZATION 020
BT   Organization
RT   Horizontal Organization
        Pyramid Organization

VERTICAL TEXTS 050
BT   Programed Texts

VERTICAL WORK SURFACES 170
NT   Chalkboards
BT   Audiovisual Aids
RT   Bulletin Boards
        Display Panels
        Space Dividers

VETERANS 380
RT   Enlisted Men
        Military Personnel
        Military Service
        Veterans Education

VETERANS EDUCATION 140
BT   Education
RT   Federal Aid
        Military Personnel
        Tuition Grants
        Veterans

VETERINARY ASSISTANTS 380
UF   Veterinary Hospital Attendants
NT   Animal Caretakers
BT   Health Personnel
RT   Animal Science
        Paramedical Occupations
        Subprofessionals
        Technical Occupations
        Veterinary Medicine

Veterinary Hospital Attendants
USE   VETERINARY ASSISTANTS

VETERINARY MEDICINE 250
BT   Medicine
RT   Agriculture
        Animal Caretakers
        Animal Science
        Horses
        Medical Services
        Veterinary Assistants

VICTORIAN LITERATURE 260
BT   Literature
RT   Literary Analysis
        Literary Conventions
        Literary Criticism
        Literary Genres
        World Literature

VIDEO TAPE RECORDINGS 050
BT   Phonotape Recordings
RT   Audio Video Laboratories
        Color Television
        Microcounseling
        Microteaching
        Protocol Materials
        Television

VIETNAMESE 300
BT   Sino Tibetan Languages

Viewing Hours
USE   VIEWING TIME

VIEWING TIME 080
SN   Scheduled time of television broadcasts
UF   Peak Viewing Time
        Viewing Hours
RT   Broadcast Television
        Closed Circuit Television
        Commercial Television
        Educational Television
        Multichannel Programing
        Program Length
        Program Planning
        Public Television
        Scheduling
        Television Viewing

Village Workers
USE   CHANGE AGENTS

VIOLENCE 060
RT   Aggression
        Crime
        Delinquency
        Demonstrations (Civil)

VISAYAN 300
NT   Cebuano
BT   Indonesian Languages

Visible Radiation
USE   LIGHT

Visible Spectrum
USE   LIGHT

VISIBLE SPEECH 290
BT   Speech
RT   Articulation (Speech)
        Aurally Handicapped
        Communication (Thought Transfer)
        Deaf Education
        Electronic Equipment
        Spectrograms

Speech Instruction
Visual Learning

VISION 070
UF Sight
NT Stereopsis
BT Visual Perception
RT Auditory Visual Tests
Eidetic Images
Eyes
Figural Aftereffects
Optometrists
Vision Tests
Visual Discrimination
Visual Environment
Visual Learning
Visually Handicapped
Visual Stimuli

VISION TESTS 520
BT Auditory Visual Tests
RT Optometrists
Tactual Visual Tests
Vision
Visual Acuity
Visual Discrimination
Visual Perception

VISITING HOMEMAKERS 380
BT Service Workers
RT Family Problems
Home Management
Maids
Occupational Home Economics
Service Occupations
Social Services

Visiting Teachers
USE SCHOOL SOCIAL WORKERS

VISUAL ACUITY 010
BT Visual Perception
RT Ametropia
Aniseikonia
Glare
Heterophoria
Heterotropia
Stereopsis
Vision Tests
Visual Discrimination

Visual Aids
USE AUDIOVISUAL AIDS

VISUAL ARTS 030
BT Art
RT Buildings
Color Planning
Freehand Drawing
Painting
Sculpture

VISUAL DISCRIMINATION 070
RT Contrast
Eyes
Glare
Illumination Levels
Sensory Experience
Sensory Training
Vision
Vision Tests
Visual Acuity
Visual Environment
Visual Learning
Visual Perception
Visual Stimuli

VISUAL ENVIRONMENT 160
BT Physical Environment
RT Glare
Vision
Visual Discrimination

Visual Handicaps
USE VISUALLY HANDICAPPED

VISUALIZATION 310
SN Act or power of forming mentally visual
images of objects not present to the eye
RT Cognitive Processes
Memorizing
Memory
Recall (Psychological)
Retention
Transfer Of Training
Visual Perception

Visual Language Learning
USE VISUAL LEARNING

VISUAL LEARNING 310
UF Visual Language Learning
BT Learning
RT Associative Learning
Nonverbal Ability
Nonverbal Learning
Pictorial Stimuli
Sight Method
Symbolic Learning
Visible Speech
Vision
Visual Discrimination
Visual Perception
Visual Stimuli

VISUALLY HANDICAPPED 240
UF Visual Handicaps
NT Blind
Partially Sighted
BT Perceptually Handicapped
RT Ametropia
Aniseikonia
Echolocation
Eyes
Heterotropia
Large Type Materials
Mobility Aids

Ophthalmology
Raised Line Drawings
Sensory Aids
Tactile Adaptation
Travel Training
Vision
Visually Handicapped Mobility
Visually Handicapped Orientation

VISUALLY HANDICAPPED MOBILITY 240
BT Mobility
RT Blind
Echolocation
Mobility Aids
Travel Training
Visually Handicapped
Visually Handicapped Orientation

VISUALLY HANDICAPPED ORIENTATION 240
BT Orientation
RT Blind
Echolocation
Mobility Aids
Space Orientation
Travel Training
Visually Handicapped
Visually Handicapped Mobility

Visual Materials
USE AUDIOVISUAL AIDS

VISUAL MEASURES 190
SN Test items presented in picture form only
UF Non Discursive Measures
Pictorial Tests
BT Tests
RT Audiovisual Aids
Perception Tests
Pictorial Stimuli
Prognostic Tests
Projective Tests
Tactual Visual Tests

VISUAL PERCEPTION 070
NT Vision
Visual Acuity
BT Perception
RT Color
Color Planning
Eyes
Eye Voice Span
Figural Aftereffects
Glare
Illumination Levels
Partially Sighted
Pictorial Stimuli
Sensory Training
Tachistoscopes
Vision Tests
Visual Discrimination
Visualization
Visual Learning
Visual Stimuli

Visual Scanners
USE OPTICAL SCANNERS

VISUAL STIMULI 070
NT Pictorial Stimuli
BT Stimuli
RT Association Tests
Electrical Stimuli
Tachistoscopes
Verbal Stimuli
Vision
Visual Discrimination
Visual Learning
Visual Perception

VOCABULARY 080
UF Terminology
NT Aviation Vocabulary
Banking Vocabulary
Developmental Vocabulary
International Trade Vocabulary
Mathematical Vocabulary
Medical Vocabulary
Sight Vocabulary
RT Adjectives
Adverbs
Definitions
Glossaries
Glottochronology
Language Arts
Lexicology
Readability
Reading
Subject Index Terms
Thesauri
Verbs
Vocabulary Development
Vocabulary Skills
Word Frequency

Vocabulary Building
USE VOCABULARY DEVELOPMENT

VOCABULARY DEVELOPMENT 130
UF Vocabulary Building
BT Development
RT Developmental Vocabulary
Reading Development
Retarded Speech Development
Sight Vocabulary
Verbal Development
Vocabulary

VOCABULARY SKILLS 010
BT Skills
RT Context Clues
Vocabulary

Vocal Ensembles
USE CHORUSES

VOCAL MUSIC 030
SN Musical compositions written for voices, either solo or chorus
NT Art Song
    Choral Music
BT Music
RT Choruses
    Music Activities
    Musical Composition
    Music Education
    Music Techniques
    Opera
    Singing

VOCATIONAL ADJUSTMENT 090
UF Employment Adjustment
    Job Adjustment
    Work Adjustment
BT Adjustment (To Environment)
RT Adjustment Problems
    Career Change
    Emotional Adjustment
    Employer Employee Relationship
    Job Satisfaction
    Occupational Mobility
    Personal Adjustment
    Skill Obsolescence
    Social Adjustment
    Vocational Counseling
    Vocational Education
    Vocational Training Centers
    Work Attitudes
    Work Study Programs

VOCATIONAL AGRICULTURE 110
BT Agricultural Education
RT Agricultural Chemical Occupations
    Agricultural Occupations
    Agricultural Supply Occupations
    Agriculture
    Crop Processing Occupations
    Farm Occupations
    Forestry Aides
    Forestry Occupations
    Grounds Keepers
    Nursery Workers (Horticulture)
    Off Farm Agricultural Occupations
    School Shops
    Supervised Farm Practice
    Vocational Agriculture Teachers

VOCATIONAL AGRICULTURE TEACHERS 380
BT Vocational Education Teachers
RT Agricultural Education
    Vocational Agriculture

VOCATIONAL APTITUDE 010
UF Vocational Talents
BT Aptitude
RT Ability
    Academic Aptitude
    Employment Qualifications
    Performance
    Talent

Vocational Aspiration
USE OCCUPATIONAL ASPIRATION

Vocational Change
USE CAREER CHANGE

Vocational Choice
USE OCCUPATIONAL CHOICE

Vocational Competencies
USE JOB SKILLS

VOCATIONAL COUNSELING 090
UF Occupational Counseling
BT Counseling
RT Adult Counseling
    Career Planning
    Job Placement
    Occupational Guidance
    Occupational Tests
    Occupations
    Vocational Adjustment
    Vocational Development
    Vocational Education
    Vocational Interests
    Vocational Training Centers

VOCATIONAL DEVELOPMENT 130
NT Occupational Choice
BT Development
RT Career Opportunities
    Career Planning
    Developmental Tasks
    Motor Development
    Occupational Guidance
    Occupational Information
    Vocational Counseling
    Vocational Interests
    Vocational Training Centers

VOCATIONAL DIRECTORS 380
UF Technical Education Directors
    Vocational Education Directors
BT Administrative Personnel

VOCATIONAL EDUCATION 140
SN Formal preparation for an occupation below the bacculaureate degree
UF Occupational Courses
    Occupational Training
    Vocational Training
NT Adult Vocational Education
    Agricultural Education
    Business Education
    Distributive Education
    Health Occupations Education
    Home Economics Education

Prevocational Education
Technical Education
Trade And Industrial Education
BT Education
RT Apprenticeships
Commercial Art
Consumer Education
Continuation Education
Cooperative Education
Cosmetologists
Custodian Training
Engineering Education
Fluid Power Education
Hand Tools
Industrial Arts
Industrial Education
Job Training
Manpower Development
Post Secondary Education
Pretechnology Programs
Project Training Methods
Semiskilled Workers
Service Workers
Skilled Workers
Technical Institutes
Vocational Adjustment
Vocational Counseling
Vocational Education Teachers
Vocational Interests
Vocational Rehabilitation
Vocational Retraining
Vocational Schools
Vocational Training Centers

Vocational Education Directors
USE VOCATIONAL DIRECTORS

VOCATIONAL EDUCATION TEACHERS 380
NT Business Education Teachers
Distributive Education Teachers
Home Economics Teachers
Trade And Industrial Teachers
Vocational Agriculture Teachers
BT Teachers
RT Agricultural Education
Business Education
Distributive Education
Trade And Industrial Education
Vocational Education

VOCATIONAL FOLLOWUP 150
UF Occupational Followup
RT Followup Studies
Graduate Surveys

Vocational Guidance
USE OCCUPATIONAL GUIDANCE

VOCATIONAL HIGH SCHOOLS 470
UF Technical High Schools
BT High Schools
Vocational Schools
RT Area Vocational Schools
Continuation High Schools

Vocational Industrial Education
USE TRADE AND INDUSTRIAL EDUCATION

VOCATIONAL INTERESTS 040
BT Interests
RT Career Choice
Occupational Aspiration
Occupational Choice
Student Science Interests
Vocational Counseling
Vocational Development
Vocational Education

Vocational Nurses
USE PRACTICAL NURSES

Vocational Placement
USE JOB PLACEMENT

VOCATIONAL REHABILITATION 140
BT Rehabilitation
RT Correctional Education
Sheltered Workshops
Vocational Education
Vocational Retraining
Vocational Training Centers

VOCATIONAL RETRAINING 270
BT Retraining
RT Skill Obsolescence
Vocational Education
Vocational Rehabilitation

Vocational Satisfaction
USE JOB SATISFACTION

VOCATIONAL SCHOOLS 470
UF Technical Schools
NT Area Vocational Schools
Vocational High Schools
BT Schools
RT Industrial Education
Post Secondary Education
Vocational Education
Vocational Training Centers

Vocational Skills
USE JOB SKILLS

Vocational Talents
USE VOCATIONAL APTITUDE

Vocational Training
USE VOCATIONAL EDUCATION

VOCATIONAL TRAINING CENTERS 210
RT Off The Job Training
Rehabilitation
Rehabilitation Counseling
Rehabilitation Programs
Training
Vocational Adjustment
Vocational Counseling
Vocational Development
Vocational Education
Vocational Rehabilitation
Vocational Schools

Vocational Work Experience
USE COOPERATIVE EDUCATION

Vocoids
USE VOWELS

VOGUL 300
BT Uralic Altaic Languages

VOICE DISORDERS 240
RT Speech Handicaps
Speech Therapy

Voice Instruction
USE SPEECH INSTRUCTION

Volition
USE INDIVIDUAL POWER

Voluntarily Idle
USE LABOR FORCE NONPARTICIPANTS

VOLUNTARY AGENCIES 370
UF Nonprofit Organizations
Voluntary Associations
Voluntary Organizations
Volunteer Organizations
BT Agencies
RT Administrative Agencies
Agency Role
Organizations (Groups)
Private Agencies
Religious Agencies
Youth Agencies

Voluntary Associations
USE VOLUNTARY AGENCIES

VOLUNTARY INTEGRATION 430
RT Racial Integration
Social Integration

Voluntary Organizations
USE VOLUNTARY AGENCIES

Volunteer Organizations
USE VOLUNTARY AGENCIES

VOLUNTEERS 380
NT Student Volunteers
RT Paraprofessional School Personnel
School Aides
Teacher Aides
Volunteer Training

VOLUNTEER TRAINING 270
BT Training
RT Volunteers

VOTER REGISTRATION 230
RT Elections
Voting
Voting Rights

VOTING 230
RT Citizenship Responsibility
Elections
Political Issues
Residence Requirements
Voter Registration
Voting Rights

VOTING RIGHTS 230
BT Civil Rights
RT Civil Liberties
Elections
Voter Registration
Voting

VOWELS 290
UF Vocoids
BT Phonetics
RT Articulation (Speech)
Consonants
Phonemes
Phonology
Syllables

Vulgar Fractions
USE COMMON FRACTIONS

Vulgate Romance
USE MEDIEVAL ROMANCE

WAGES 220
NT Minimum Wage
BT Income
RT Collective Bargaining
Fringe Benefits
Guaranteed Income
Overtime
Premium Pay
Salaries
Salary Differentials
Subemployment
Wage Statements

WAGE STATEMENTS 150
BT Records (Forms)
RT Overtime
Payroll Records
Premium Pay
Wages

Walleyes
USE HETEROTROPIA

WAREHOUSES 210
BT Facilities
RT Equipment Storage

WATCHMAKERS 380
UF Clockmakers
Horologists
Watch Repairmen
BT Skilled Workers
RT Horology
Skilled Occupations

Watch Repairmen
USE WATCHMAKERS

WATER POLLUTION CONTROL 250
UF River Pollution Control
    Stream Pollution Control
RT Environmental Education
    Pollution
    Water Resources

WATER RESOURCES 460
BT Natural Resources
RT Water Pollution Control

Water Utilities
USE UTILITIES

Weariness
USE FATIGUE (BIOLOGY)

Weed (Drug)
USE MARIHUANA

WEEDS 070
RT Agriculture
    Botany
    Herbicides
    Plant Science

WEEKEND PROGRAMS 410
BT Recreational Programs

WEIGHT 400
BT Scientific Concepts
RT Force
    Matter
    Pressure

WELDERS 380
UF Acetylene Welders
    Arc Welders
    Gas Welders
BT Skilled Workers
RT Skilled Occupations
    Trade And Industrial Education
    Welding

WELDING 350
UF Arc Welding
    Gas Welding
RT Finishing
    Metal Working Occupations
    Sculpture
    Welders

WELFARE 220
UF Public Welfare
NT Child Welfare
    Social Welfare
    Social Work
    Student Welfare
    Teacher Welfare
RT Public Housing
    Residence Requirements
    Welfare Agencies
    Welfare Problems
    Welfare Services

WELFARE AGENCIES 230
UF Public Welfare Assistance
NT Social Agencies
BT Agencies
RT Agency Role
    Community Agencies (Public)
    Religious Agencies
    Social Welfare
    Social Work
    State Agencies
    Urban Renewal Agencies
    Welfare
    Welfare Services
    Youth Agencies

WELFARE PROBLEMS 490
UF Medical Disadvantagement
BT Problems
RT Child Abuse
    Hunger
    Welfare

WELFARE RECIPIENTS 490
BT Dependents
RT Economically Disadvantaged
    Low Income Groups
    Welfare Services

WELFARE SERVICES 230
NT Migrant Welfare Services
BT Human Services
RT Child Care Centers
    Housing Management Aides
    Settlement Houses
    Social Responsibility
    Social Services
    Social Work
    Welfare
    Welfare Agencies
    Welfare Recipients

WESTERN CIVILIZATION 100
SN Includes Europe and the Western
    Hemisphere from the time of the Roman
    Empire through the present.
UF Occidental Civilization
RT American Culture
    American History
    Area Studies
    Cultural Background
    Cultural Environment
    Cultural Factors
    Culture
    European History
    Greek Civilization
    History
    Latin American Culture
    Social Environment
    Social Influences
    Sociocultural Patterns

WHEEL CHAIRS 170
BT Mobility Aids
RT Biomedical Equipment
     Educational Equipment
     Equipment
     Handicapped
     Mechanical Equipment
     Mobility

WHITE COLLAR OCCUPATIONS 350
BT Occupations
RT Managerial Occupations

White Race
USE CAUCASIAN RACE

Whites
USE CAUCASIANS

White Students
USE CAUCASIAN STUDENTS

WHOLE NUMBERS 340
BT Numbers

WHOLESALING 220
BT Marketing
RT Distributive Education
     Retailing

WILDLIFE MANAGEMENT 020
UF Gamekeeping
RT Animal Science
     Forestry
     Recreation

WILLS 220
RT Estate Planning
     Property Accounting
     Property Appraisal
     Resource Allocations
     Resources
     Trusts (Financial)

WINDOWLESS ROOMS 210
SN Any area in a building closed to exterior
     environment
BT Facilities
RT Air Conditioning
     Auditoriums
     Climate Control
     Corridors
     Fallout Shelters
     Lighting
     Lighting Design
     Recreational Facilities
     Ventilation

WINDOWS 210
UF Fenestration
RT Building Design
     Climate Control
     Daylight
     Glare
     Glass Walls
     Illumination Levels
     Lighting
     Ventilation

Window Walls
USE GLASS WALLS

Wire Communication
USE TELECOMMUNICATION

Wireless Communication
USE TELECOMMUNICATION

WITHDRAWAL 060
SN Act of leaving school permanently
RT Disqualification
     Expulsion
     Out Of School Youth
     Suspension

WITHDRAWAL TENDENCIES (PSYCHOLOGY)
420
BT Behavior Patterns
RT Autism

WOLOF 300
BT African Languages

Women
USE FEMALES

WOMEN PROFESSORS 380
BT Professors
RT Women Teachers
     Working Women

WOMENS EDUCATION 140
BT Education
RT Adult Education
     Alumni Education
     Coeducation
     Higher Education
     Professional Continuing Education

WOMEN TEACHERS 380
BT Teachers
RT Females
     Nun Teachers
     Women Professors
     Working Women

Women Workers
USE WORKING WOMEN

Wood Finishing
USE FINISHING

WOODWORKING 350
RT Building Trades
     Cabinetmaking
     Carpenters
     Finishing
     Hand Tools
     Industrial Arts
     Lumber Industry
     Patternmaking

Word Analysis
USE STRUCTURAL ANALYSIS

Word Associations (Reading)
USE ASSOCIATIVE LEARNING

WORD FREQUENCY 290
RT   Computational Linguistics
     Connected Discourse
     Language
     Languages
     Speech
     Vocabulary
     Word Recognition
     Written Language

WORD LISTS 290
RT   Basic Reading
     Dictionaries
     Glossaries
     Pronunciation
     Spelling
     Subject Index Terms
     Thesauri

WORD RECOGNITION 010
BT   Recognition
RT   Associative Learning
     Context Clues
     Informal Reading Inventory
     Reading Comprehension
     Reading Skills
     Sight Method
     Sight Vocabulary
     Symbolic Learning
     Verbal Stimuli
     Word Frequency
     Word Study Skills

WORD STUDY SKILLS 010
BT   Study Skills
RT   Language Skills
     Reading Skills
     Study Habits
     Word Recognition

Work
USE EMPLOYMENT

Work Adjustment
USE VOCATIONAL ADJUSTMENT

WORK ATTITUDES 040
SN   Attitude of persons who are either
     employed, unemployed, or preparing for
     employment toward a particular job,
     employment in general, or a particular
     aspect of employment
BT   Attitudes
RT   Employee Attitudes
     Job Satisfaction
     Labor Force Nonparticipants
     Occupational Aspiration
     Vocational Adjustment
     Work Experience

WORKBOOKS 270
BT   Instructional Materials
RT   Worksheets

Work Change
USE CAREER CHANGE

Workday
USE WORKING HOURS

Work Education Programs
USE WORK STUDY PROGRAMS

WORK ENVIRONMENT 160
BT   Environment
RT   Employment
     Human Engineering
     Job Satisfaction
     Overseas Employment

Worker Evaluation
USE PERSONNEL EVALUATION

Workers Education
USE LABOR EDUCATION

WORK EXPERIENCE 200
UF   Job Experience
BT   Experience
RT   Employment Experience
     Employment Qualifications
     Work Attitudes
     Work Experience Programs

WORK EXPERIENCE PROGRAMS 410
UF   Work Training Programs
BT   Programs
RT   Activity Learning
     Apprenticeships
     Cooperative Education
     Jobs
     Job Training
     Office Occupations
     Trainees
     Work Experience
     Work Study Programs

Work Force
USE LABORERS

Working Abroad
USE OVERSEAS EMPLOYMENT

WORKING HOURS 150
UF   Hours Of Work
     Workday
     Workweek
RT   Employment
     Man Days
     Overtime
     Part Time Jobs
     Teaching Load

Working Overseas
USE OVERSEAS EMPLOYMENT

WORKING PARENTS 380
BT   Parents
RT   Working Women

WORKING WOMEN 380
UF Women Workers
BT Females
RT Employment
    Labor Force
    Personnel
    Women Professors
    Women Teachers
    Working Parents

WORK LIFE EXPECTANCY 150
BT Expectation
RT Job Tenure
    Occupations

WORKMANS COMPENSATION 220
RT Health Insurance
    Insurance Programs
    Unemployment Insurance

Work Satisfaction
USE JOB SATISFACTION

WORKSHEETS 270
BT Instructional Materials
RT Workbooks

WORKSHOPS 270
NT Drama Workshops
    Parent Workshops
    Preschool Workshops
    Sheltered Workshops
    Summer Workshops
    Teacher Workshops
RT Seminars
    Symposia

WORK SIMPLIFICATION 150
UF Job Redesign
RT Job Analysis
    Job Development
    Jobs
    Manpower Utilization
    Occupational Information
    Occupations
    Retraining
    Task Analysis

Work Study
USE WORK STUDY PROGRAMS

WORK STUDY PROGRAMS 410
SN Programs providing part time
    employment to students who need
    financial aid in order to commence or
    continue their education
UF Work Education Programs
    Work Study
BT Programs
RT Cooperative Education
    Cooperative Programs
    Jobs
    Part Time Jobs
    Part Time Students
    Student Employment
    Supervised Farm Practice

    Vocational Adjustment
    Work Experience Programs

Work Training Programs
USE WORK EXPERIENCE PROGRAMS

Workweek
USE WORKING HOURS

WORLD AFFAIRS 480
BT Social Studies
    World History
RT Current Events
    Developing Nations
    Foreign Policy
    Foreign Relations
    World Problems

WORLD GEOGRAPHY 480
BT Geography

WORLD HISTORY 260
NT World Affairs
BT History
RT Constitutional History
    Middle Eastern History
    Non Western Civilization
    Science Education History
    Science History

WORLD LITERATURE 260
BT Literature
RT African Literature
    American Literature
    Biblical Literature
    Classical Literature
    Czech Literature
    Eighteenth Century Literature
    English Literature
    Fifteenth Century Literature
    French Literature
    German Literature
    Italian Literature
    Medieval Literature
    Negro Literature
    Nineteenth Century Literature
    Old English Literature
    Polish Literature
    Renaissance Literature
    Russian Literature
    Seventeenth Century Literature
    Sixteenth Century Literature
    Spanish American Literature
    Spanish Literature
    Twentieth Century Literature
    Victorian Literature

WORLD PROBLEMS 490
BT Problems
RT Developing Nations
    Imperialism
    Nuclear Warfare
    World Affairs

Writers
USE AUTHORS

WRITING 080
UF   Writing Systems
NT   Abstracting
     Braille
     Composition (Literary)
     Creative Writing
     Descriptive Writing
     Direction Writing
     Expository Writing
     Handwriting
     Playwriting
     Spelling
     Stenography
     Technical Writing
     Typewriting
     Writing Exercises
BT   Language Arts
     Literacy
RT   Abbreviations
     Business Correspondence
     Diaries
     Journalism
     Letters (Correspondence)
     Narration
     Paragraphs
     Prose
     Rhetoric
     Scripts
     Student Writing Models
     Surrealism
     Textbook Preparation
     Writing Skills
     Written Language

WRITING EXERCISES 510
BT   Writing
RT   Cursive Writing
     Descriptive Writing
     Expository Writing
     Manuscript Writing (Handlettering)
     Student Writing Models
     Writing Skills

WRITING SKILLS 010
NT   Composition Skills (Literary)
BT   Skills
RT   Basic Skills
     Capitalization (Alphabetic)
     Cloze Procedure
     Descriptive Writing
     Expository Writing
     Language Styles
     Paragraph Composition
     Playwriting
     Punctuation
     Stenography
     Technical Writing
     Writing
     Writing Exercises

Writing Systems
USE   WRITING

Written Expression
USE   COMPOSITION (LITERARY)

WRITTEN LANGUAGE 290
BT   Language
RT   Alphabets
     Composition (Literary)
     Cyrillic Alphabet
     Language Rhythm
     Language Usage
     Paragraphs
     Phonetic Transcription
     Printing
     Romanization
     Word Frequency
     Writing

X Ray Technologists
USE   RADIOLOGIC TECHNOLOGISTS

YAKUT 300
BT   Turkic Languages

Yard Laborers
USE   GROUNDS KEEPERS

YEARBOOKS 320
UF   Annuals
BT   Publications
     Reference Materials
RT   Annual Reports

YEAR ROUND SCHOOLS 470
BT   Schools
RT   Extended School Year
     Quarter System
     School Schedules
     Trimester Schedules

YIDDISH 300
BT   German

YORUBA 300
BT   African Languages

YOUNG ADULTS 380
SN   Adults aged 18 to 30
BT   Adults
RT   Youth

YOUNG FARMER EDUCATION 140
SN   Education for young men not more than
     25 years of age, who have not yet
     become established as farm operators
UF   Beginning Farmer Education
BT   Agricultural Education
RT   Adult Farmer Education
     Adult Vocational Education
     Farmers
     Farm Visits

YOUTH 380
NT Affluent Youth
Disadvantaged Youth
Migrant Youth
Negro Youth
Nonfarm Youth
Out Of School Youth
Rural Youth
Suburban Youth
Urban Youth
RT Dropouts
Study Centers
Young Adults
Youth Agencies
Youth Clubs
Youth Employment
Youth Leaders
Youth Opportunities
Youth Problems
Youth Programs

YOUTH AGENCIES 230
BT Agencies
RT Agency Role
Community Agencies (Public)
Voluntary Agencies
Welfare Agencies
Youth

YOUTH CLUBS 370
BT Youth Programs
RT Youth
Youth Leaders

YOUTH EMPLOYMENT 150
UF Youth Mobilization
BT Employment
RT Part Time Jobs
Seasonal Employment
Youth
Youth Programs

YOUTH LEADERS 380
RT Adult Leaders
Leadership
Leadership Training
Youth
Youth Clubs

Youth Mobilization
USE YOUTH EMPLOYMENT

YOUTH OPPORTUNITIES 360
UF Opportunities For Youth
BT Opportunities
RT Youth
Youth Programs

YOUTH PROBLEMS 090
BT Problems
RT Generation Gap
Juvenile Courts
Youth

YOUTH PROGRAMS 410
NT Youth Clubs
BT Programs
RT Community Programs
Youth
Youth Employment
Youth Opportunities

Youth Study Centers
USE STUDY CENTERS

Youth Work Opportunities
USE EMPLOYMENT OPPORTUNITIES

YURAK 300
BT Samoyed Languages

ZONING 120
NT Community Zoning
Rezoning
School Zoning
Special Zoning
RT Multicampus Districts
Real Estate
School Districts

ZOOLOGY 070
NT Primatology
BT Biology
RT Anatomy
Animal Science
Anthropology
Cardiovascular System
Culturing Techniques
Ecology
Embryology
Evolution
Genetics
Microbiology
Paleontology
Pathology
Physiology
Taxonomy

ZOOS 210
BT Community Resources
Recreational Facilities
RT Parks

ROTATED DESCRIPTOR DISPLAY

ABBREVIATIONS
PREDICTIVE ABILITY (TESTING)
ABILITY
ACADEMIC ABILITY
COGNITIVE ABILITY
CREATIVE ABILITY
LANGUAGE ABILITY
NONVERBAL ABILITY
READING ABILITY
STUDENT ABILITY
VERBAL ABILITY
ABILITY GROUPING
ABILITY IDENTIFICATION
LOW ABILITY STUDENTS
ABLE STUDENTS
AUSTRALIAN ABORIGINAL LANGUAGES
STUDY ABROAD
ABSENCE
LEAVE OF ABSENCE
ABSTRACT REASONING
ABSTRACTING
ABSTRACTION LEVELS
ABSTRACTION TESTS
ABSTRACTS
CHILD ABUSE
DRUG ABUSE
ACADEMIC ABILITY
ACADEMIC ACHIEVEMENT
ACADEMIC APTITUDE
ACADEMIC ASPIRATION
ACADEMIC EDUCATION
ACADEMIC ENRICHMENT
ACADEMIC FAILURE
ACADEMIC FREEDOM
ACADEMIC PERFORMANCE
ACADEMIC PROBATION
ACADEMIC RANK (PROFESSIONAL)
ACADEMIC RECORDS
ACADEMIC STANDARDS
ACADEMICALLY HANDICAPPED
ACCELERATED COURSES
ACCELERATED PROGRAMS
ACCELERATION
COUNSELOR ACCEPTANCE
PEER ACCEPTANCE
DIAL ACCESS INFORMATION SYSTEMS
ACCIDENT PREVENTION
ACCIDENTS
SCHOOL ACCIDENTS
TRAFFIC ACCIDENTS
ACCOUNTANTS
CERTIFIED PUBLIC ACCOUNTANTS
ACCOUNTING
PROPERTY ACCOUNTING
SCHOOL ACCOUNTING
FARM ACCOUNTS
ACCREDITATION (INSTITUTIONS)
ACCULTURATION
ACADEMIC ACHIEVEMENT
ACHIEVEMENT
NEGRO ACHIEVEMENT
READING ACHIEVEMENT
LOW ACHIEVEMENT FACTORS
ACHIEVEMENT GAINS
ACHIEVEMENT NEED
ACHIEVEMENT RATING
ACHIEVEMENT TESTS
HIGH ACHIEVERS
LOW ACHIEVERS
LYSERGIC ACID DIETHYLAMIDE
ACOUSTIC INSULATION
ACOUSTIC PHONETICS
ACOUSTICAL ENVIRONMENT
ACOUSTICS
LIBRARY ACQUISITION
ACTING
COMMUNITY ACTION
POLICE ACTION
SOCIAL ACTION
STATE ACTION
ACTION PROGRAMS (COMMUNITY)
ACTION RESEARCH
AUDIO ACTIVE COMPARE LABORATORIES
AUDIO ACTIVE LABORATORIES
ACTIVISM
ACTIVITIES
AFTER SCHOOL ACTIVITIES
ART ACTIVITIES
ATHLETIC ACTIVITIES
CLASS ACTIVITIES
COCURRICULAR ACTIVITIES
CREATIVE ACTIVITIES
CULTURAL ACTIVITIES
ENRICHMENT ACTIVITIES
GROUP ACTIVITIES
HEALTH ACTIVITIES
INDIVIDUAL ACTIVITIES
INTEGRATED ACTIVITIES
LEARNING ACTIVITIES
MUSIC ACTIVITIES
PHYSICAL ACTIVITIES

PLAYGROUND ACTIVITIES
RECREATIONAL ACTIVITIES
SCHOOL ACTIVITIES
SCIENCE ACTIVITIES
SPEAKING ACTIVITIES
SUPERVISORY ACTIVITIES
HEALTH ACTIVITIES HANDBOOKS
DIRECTED READING ACTIVITY
ACTIVITY LEARNING
ACTIVITY UNITS
SELF ACTUALIZATION
VISUAL ACUITY
TACTILE ADAPTATION
ADAPTATION LEVEL THEORY
DRUG ADDICTION
ADDITION
ADHESIVES
ADJECTIVES
ADJUSTMENT (TO ENVIRONMENT)
EMOTIONAL ADJUSTMENT
PERSONAL ADJUSTMENT
SOCIAL ADJUSTMENT
STUDENT ADJUSTMENT
VOCATIONAL ADJUSTMENT
ADJUSTMENT COUNSELORS
ADJUSTMENT PROBLEMS
ADMINISTRATION
BUSINESS ADMINISTRATION
COLLEGE ADMINISTRATION
EDUCATIONAL ADMINISTRATION
INSTITUTIONAL ADMINISTRATION
PROGRAM ADMINISTRATION
SCHOOL ADMINISTRATION
TEAM ADMINISTRATION
UNIVERSITY ADMINISTRATION
PUBLIC ADMINISTRATION EDUCATION
ADMINISTRATIVE AGENCIES
GOVERNMENT (ADMINISTRATIVE BODY)
ADMINISTRATIVE CHANGE
ADMINISTRATIVE ORGANIZATION
ADMINISTRATIVE PERSONNEL
ADMINISTRATIVE POLICY
ADMINISTRATIVE PRINCIPLES
ADMINISTRATIVE PROBLEMS
INTERMEDIATE ADMINISTRATIVE UNITS
ADMINISTRATOR ATTITUDES
ADMINISTRATOR BACKGROUND
ADMINISTRATOR CHARACTERISTICS
ADMINISTRATOR EVALUATION
ADMINISTRATOR GUIDES
ADMINISTRATOR QUALIFICATIONS
BOARD ADMINISTRATOR RELATIONSHIP
TEACHER ADMINISTRATOR RELATIONSHIP
ADMINISTRATOR RESPONSIBILITY
ADMINISTRATOR ROLE
ADMINISTRATOR SELECTION
CHIEF ADMINISTRATORS
ADMISSION (SCHOOL)
COLLEGE ADMISSION
EARLY ADMISSION
ADMISSION CRITERIA
ADOLESCENCE
ADOLESCENTS
ADOPTED CHILDREN
ADOPTION (IDEAS)
ADOPTION
ADULT BASIC EDUCATION
ADULT CHARACTERISTICS
ADULT COUNSELING
ADULT DEVELOPMENT
ADULT DROPOUTS
ADULT EDUCATION
MIGRANT ADULT EDUCATION
PUBLIC SCHOOL ADULT EDUCATION
ADULT EDUCATION PROGRAMS
ADULT EDUCATORS
ADULT FARMER EDUCATION
ADULT LEADERS
ADULT LEARNING
ADULT PROGRAMS
ADULT READING PROGRAMS
ADULT STUDENTS
ADULT VOCATIONAL EDUCATION
ADULTS
ILLITERATE ADULTS
OLDER ADULTS
YOUNG ADULTS
ADVANCED PLACEMENT
ADVANCED PLACEMENT PROGRAMS
ADVANCED PROGRAMS
ADVANCED STUDENTS
ADVANCED SYSTEMS
TECHNOLOGICAL ADVANCEMENT
CULTURALLY ADVANTAGED
ADVERBS
FOREIGN STUDENT ADVISERS
FACULTY ADVISORS
ADVISORY COMMITTEES
AEROSPACE INDUSTRY
AEROSPACE TECHNOLOGY

INDIVIDUALIZED INSTRUCTION
INSTRUCTION
LANGUAGE INSTRUCTION
LARGE GROUP INSTRUCTION
LAW INSTRUCTION
LIBRARY INSTRUCTION
MASS INSTRUCTION
MATHEMATICS INSTRUCTION
MULTIMEDIA INSTRUCTION
NUTRITION INSTRUCTION
PHYSICS INSTRUCTION
PROGRAMED INSTRUCTION
PRONUNCIATION INSTRUCTION
READING INSTRUCTION
REMEDIAL INSTRUCTION
SCIENCE INSTRUCTION
SEWING INSTRUCTION
SMALL GROUP INSTRUCTION
SPEECH INSTRUCTION
SPELLING INSTRUCTION
TELEPHONE INSTRUCTION
TELEVISED INSTRUCTION
TEXTILES INSTRUCTION
RESEARCH AND INSTRUCTION UNITS
INSTRUCTIONAL AIDS
INSTRUCTIONAL DESIGN
INSTRUCTIONAL FILMS
INSTRUCTIONAL IMPROVEMENT
INSTRUCTIONAL INNOVATION
INSTRUCTIONAL MATERIALS
INSTRUCTIONAL MATERIALS CENTERS
INSTRUCTIONAL MEDIA
INSTRUCTIONAL PROGRAM DIVISIONS
COUNSELING INSTRUCTIONAL PROGRAMS
INSTRUCTIONAL PROGRAMS
GROUPING (INSTRUCTIONAL PURPOSES)
INSTRUCTIONAL STAFF
INSTRUCTIONAL TECHNOLOGY
INSTRUCTIONAL TELEVISION
INSTRUCTIONAL TRIPS
INSTRUCTOR CENTERED TELEVISION
INSTRUCTOR COORDINATORS
INSTRUMENTATION
INSTRUMENTATION TECHNICIANS
MEASUREMENT INSTRUMENTS
MUSICAL INSTRUMENTS
POTENTIOMETERS (INSTRUMENTS)
ACOUSTIC INSULATION
FIRE INSURANCE
HEALTH INSURANCE
UNEMPLOYMENT INSURANCE
INSURANCE COMPANIES
INSURANCE OCCUPATIONS
INSURANCE PROGRAMS
INTEGERS
INTEGRATED ACTIVITIES
INTEGRATED CURRICULUM
INTEGRATED PUBLIC FACILITIES
CLASSROOM INTEGRATION
COLLEGE INTEGRATION
FACULTY INTEGRATION
GRADE A YEAR INTEGRATION
NEIGHBORHOOD INTEGRATION
PERSONNEL INTEGRATION
RACIAL INTEGRATION
SCHOOL INTEGRATION
SENSORY INTEGRATION
SOCIAL INTEGRATION
TEACHER INTEGRATION
TOKEN INTEGRATION
VOLUNTARY INTEGRATION
INTEGRATION EFFECTS
INTEGRATION LITIGATION
INTEGRATION METHODS
INTEGRATION PLANS
INTEGRATION READINESS
INTEGRATION STUDIES
INTEGRITY
INTELLECTUAL DEVELOPMENT
INTELLECTUAL DISCIPLINES
INTELLECTUAL EXPERIENCE
ANTI INTELLECTUALISM
INTELLECTUALIZATION
INTELLIGENCE
INTELLIGENCE DIFFERENCES
INTELLIGENCE FACTORS
INTELLIGENCE LEVEL
NATIONAL INTELLIGENCE NORM
INTELLIGENCE QUOTIENT
GROUP INTELLIGENCE TESTING
GROUP INTELLIGENCE TESTS
INTELLIGENCE TESTS
MUTUAL INTELLIGIBILITY
INTENSIVE LANGUAGE COURSES
INTERACTION
INTERACTION PROCESS ANALYSIS
INTERAGENCY COOPERATION
INTERAGENCY COORDINATION
INTERAGENCY PLANNING
INTERCOLLEGIATE PROGRAMS
INTERCOMMUNICATION
INTERCULTURAL PROGRAMS
INTERDISCIPLINARY APPROACH
INTERDISTRICT POLICIES
CENTERS OF INTEREST
EDUCATIONAL INTEREST
HIGH INTEREST LOW VOCABULARY BOOKS
INTEREST RESEARCH
INTEREST SCALES
INTEREST TESTS
CHILDHOOD INTERESTS
INTERESTS
PERSONAL INTERESTS
READING INTERESTS
STUDENT INTERESTS
STUDENT SCIENCE INTERESTS
VOCATIONAL INTERESTS
INTERFAITH RELATIONS
INTERFERENCE (LANGUAGE LEARNING)
INTERGROUP EDUCATION
INTERGROUP RELATIONS
INTERINSTITUTIONAL COOPERATION
INTERIOR DESIGN

INTERIOR SPACE
INTERLIBRARY LOANS
INTERMARRIAGE
INTERMEDIATE ADMINISTRATIVE UNITS
INTERMEDIATE GRADES
INTERMODE DIFFERENCES
INTERNAL SCALING
INTERNATIONAL EDUCATION
INTERNATIONAL ORGANIZATIONS
INTERNATIONAL PROGRAMS
INTERNATIONAL TRADE VOCABULARY
TEACHER INTERNS
INTERNSHIP PROGRAMS
INTERPERSONAL COMPETENCE
INTERPERSONAL PROBLEMS
INTERPERSONAL RELATIONSHIP
TEST INTERPRETATION
INTERPRETERS
DEAF INTERPRETING
INTERPRETIVE READING
INTERPRETIVE SKILLS
INTERPROFESSIONAL RELATIONSHIP
CULTURAL INTERRELATIONSHIPS
INTERSCHOOL COMMUNICATION
INTERSTATE PROGRAMS
INTERSTATE WORKERS
INTERVAL PACING
INTERVALS
INTERVENTION
EMPLOYMENT INTERVIEWS
FIELD INTERVIEWS
INTERVIEWS
QUESTION ANSWER INTERVIEWS
INTONATION
INTRAMURAL ATHLETIC PROGRAMS
FACILITY INVENTORY
INFORMAL READING INVENTORY
INVESTIGATIONS
INVESTMENT
COMMUNITY INVOLVEMENT
FAMILY INVOLVEMENT
PARTICIPANT INVOLVEMENT
SCHOOL INVOLVEMENT
IRONY
ISLAMIC CULTURE
CULTURAL ISOLATION
SOCIAL ISOLATION
BOND ISSUES
LOCAL ISSUES
MORAL ISSUES
POLITICAL ISSUES
ITALIAN
ITALIAN AMERICANS
ITALIAN LITERATURE
ITEM ANALYSIS
ITINERANT CLINICS
ITINERANT TEACHERS
JAPANESE
JAPANESE AMERICAN CULTURE
JAPANESE AMERICANS
JAVANESE
JAZZ
JEWISH STEREOTYPES
JEWS
JOB ANALYSIS
JOB APPLICANTS
JOB APPLICATION
JOB DEVELOPMENT
JOB LAYOFF
JOB MARKET
JOB PLACEMENT
JOB SATISFACTION
JOB SKILLS
JOB TENURE
JOB TRAINING
OFF THE JOB TRAINING
ON THE JOB TRAINING
JOBS
PART TIME JOBS
EQUAL OPPORTUNITIES (JOBS)
JOURNALISM
SCHOLARLY JOURNALS
JUDAISM
JUNIOR COLLEGE LIBRARIES
JUNIOR COLLEGE STUDENTS
JUNIOR COLLEGES
JUNIOR HIGH SCHOOL ROLE
JUNIOR HIGH SCHOOL STUDENTS
JUNIOR HIGH SCHOOLS
JUVENILE COURTS
JUVENILE GANGS
KABYLE
KANNADA
KASHMIRI
GROUNDS KEEPERS
KERNEL SENTENCES
ANSWER KEYS
KINDERGARTEN
KINDERGARTEN CHILDREN
KINESCOPE RECORDINGS
KINESTHETIC METHODS
KINESTHETIC PERCEPTION
KINETIC MOLECULAR THEORY
KINETICS
KINYARWANDA
KIRGHIZ
KIRUNDI
KITUBA
KNOWLEDGE LEVEL
KOREAN
KOREAN AMERICANS
KOREAN CULTURE
KURDISH
CHILD LABOR
FARM LABOR
LABOR
SEASONAL LABOR
SKILLED LABOR
UNSKILLED LABOR
LABOR CAMP COMMISSARIES
LABOR CAMPS
LABOR CONDITIONS
LABOR DEMANDS
AGRICULTURAL LABOR DISPUTES

FACULTY ORGANIZATIONS
FREEDOM ORGANIZATIONS
HUMAN RELATIONS ORGANIZATIONS
INTERNATIONAL ORGANIZATIONS
MILITARY ORGANIZATIONS
NATIONAL ORGANIZATIONS
NEGRO ORGANIZATIONS
RELIGIOUS ORGANIZATIONS
SEGREGATIONIST ORGANIZATIONS
SOCIAL ORGANIZATIONS
STUDENT ORGANIZATIONS
ORIENTAL MUSIC
GOAL ORIENTATION
ORIENTATION
SCHOOL ORIENTATION
SPACE ORIENTATION
STAFF ORIENTATION
TEACHER ORIENTATION
VISUALLY HANDICAPPED ORIENTATION
ORIENTATION MATERIALS
COMPUTER ORIENTED PROGRAMS
ORIGINALITY
ETHNIC ORIGINS
ORNAMENTAL HORTICULTURE
ORNAMENTAL HORTICULTURE OCCUPATION
ORTHOGONAL PROJECTION
ORTHOGRAPHIC SYMBOLS
ORTHOPEDICALLY HANDICAPPED
OSSETIC
OSTYAK
OUT OF SCHOOL YOUTH
OUTDOOR DRAMA
OUTDOOR EDUCATION
OUTDOOR THEATERS
CAPITAL OUTLAY (FOR FIXED ASSETS)
INPUT OUTPUT
INPUT OUTPUT ANALYSIS
INPUT OUTPUT DEVICES
COMPUTER OUTPUT MICROFILM
OVERACHIEVERS
OVERHEAD PROJECTORS
OVERHEAD TELEVISION
OVERPOPULATION
OVERSEAS EMPLOYMENT
OVERT RESPONSE
OVERTIME
OXIDATION
INTERVAL PACING
PACING
SELF PACING
MEAT PACKING MACHINES
PACKING INDUSTRY
SIGN PAINTERS
PAINTING
PAIRED ASSOCIATE LEARNING
CLEFT PALATE
PALEONTOLOGY
CEREBRAL PALSY
PAMPHLETS
DISPLAY PANELS
PANELS
PANJABI
PAPAGO
PAPER (MATERIAL)
PAPERBACK BOOKS
PARAGRAPH COMPOSITION
PARAGRAPHS
PARALINGUISTICS
PARALLELISM (LITERARY)
PARAMEDICAL OCCUPATIONS
PARAPROFESSIONAL SCHOOL PERSONNEL
PARENT ASSOCIATIONS
PARENT ATTITUDES
PARENT CHILD RELATIONSHIP
PARENT CONFERENCES
PARENT COUNSELING
PARENT EDUCATION
ONE PARENT FAMILY
PARENT INFLUENCE
PARENT PARTICIPATION
PARENT REACTION
PARENT RESPONSIBILITY
PARENT ROLE
PARENT SCHOOL RELATIONSHIP
PARENT STUDENT CONFERENCES
PARENT STUDENT RELATIONSHIP
PARENT TEACHER CONFERENCES
PARENT TEACHER COOPERATION
PARENT WORKSHOPS
PARENTAL ASPIRATION
PARENTAL BACKGROUND
PARENTAL GRIEVANCES
CATHOLIC PARENTS
LOWER CLASS PARENTS
MIDDLE CLASS PARENTS
PARENTS
WORKING PARENTS
PARK DESIGN
PARKING AREAS
PARKING CONTROLS
PARKING FACILITIES
PARKING METERS
EDUCATIONAL PARKS
PARKS
PAROCHIAL SCHOOLS
PARODY
PAROLE OFFICERS
PART TIME FARMERS
PART TIME JOBS
PART TIME STUDENTS
PART TIME TEACHERS
PART TIME TEACHING
PARTIALLY SIGHTED
PARTICIPANT CHARACTERISTICS
PARTICIPANT INVOLVEMENT
PARTICIPANT SATISFACTION
AUDIENCE PARTICIPATION
CITIZEN PARTICIPATION
CLASSROOM PARTICIPATION
LEADER PARTICIPATION
PARENT PARTICIPATION
PARTICIPATION
STUDENT PARTICIPATION
TEACHER PARTICIPATION
MOVABLE PARTITIONS
PARTITIONS
PARTNERSHIP TEACHERS

AUTO PARTS MEN
PASHTO
PASS FAIL GRADING
AUDIO PASSIVE LABORATORIES
PASTORAL LITERATURE
PATENTS
CRITICAL PATH METHOD
PATHOLOGY
PLANT PATHOLOGY
SPEECH PATHOLOGY
PATIENTS (PERSONS)
PATTERN DRILLS (LANGUAGE)
PATTERN RECOGNITION
PATTERNED RESPONSES
PATTERNMAKING
AROUSAL PATTERNS
ATTENDANCE PATTERNS
BEHAVIOR PATTERNS
EMPLOYMENT PATTERNS
ERROR PATTERNS
FEEDER PATTERNS
GROWTH PATTERNS
HOUSING PATTERNS
LANGUAGE PATTERNS
LINGUISTIC PATTERNS
MIGRATION PATTERNS
PSYCHOLOGICAL PATTERNS
RESIDENTIAL PATTERNS
SOCIOCULTURAL PATTERNS
TRAFFIC PATTERNS
PREMIUM PAY
PAYROLL RECORDS
PEDESTRIAN TRAFFIC
PEDIATRICS TRAINING
PEER ACCEPTANCE
PEER GROUPS
PEER RELATIONSHIP
PEER TEACHING
FINES (PENALTIES)
EXPENDITURE PER STUDENT
PERCENTAGE
AUDITORY PERCEPTION
HAPTIC PERCEPTION
KINESTHETIC PERCEPTION
PERCEPTION
ROLE PERCEPTION
TACTUAL PERCEPTION
VISUAL PERCEPTION
PERCEPTION TESTS
PERCEPTUAL DEVELOPMENT
PERCEPTUAL MOTOR COORDINATION
PERCEPTUAL MOTOR LEARNING
PERCEPTUALLY HANDICAPPED
ACADEMIC PERFORMANCE
COUNSELOR PERFORMANCE
LINGUISTIC PERFORMANCE
TASK PERFORMANCE
PERFORMANCE CRITERIA
PERFORMANCE FACTORS
PERFORMANCE SPECIFICATIONS
PERFORMANCE TESTS
ENGLISH NEOCLASSIC LITERARY PERIOD
PROBATIONARY PERIOD
FOREIGN LANGUAGE PERIODICALS
PERIODICALS
PERMISSIVE ENVIRONMENT
PERMUTED INDEXES
PERSIAN
PERSISTENCE
TEACHER PERSISTENCE
CARDIAC (PERSON)
PERSONAL ADJUSTMENT
PERSONAL CARE HOMES
PERSONAL GROWTH
PERSONAL INTERESTS
PERSONAL RELATIONSHIP
PERSONAL VALUES
PERSONALITY
PERSONALITY ASSESSMENT
PERSONALITY CHANGE
PERSONALITY DEVELOPMENT
PERSONALITY PROBLEMS
PERSONALITY STUDIES
PERSONALITY TESTS
PERSONALITY THEORIES
CLINIC PERSONNEL (SCHOOL)
ADMINISTRATIVE PERSONNEL
AGRICULTURAL PERSONNEL
EMERGENCY SQUAD PERSONNEL
GUIDANCE PERSONNEL
HEALTH PERSONNEL
HOSPITAL PERSONNEL
INDIGENOUS PERSONNEL
INDUSTRIAL PERSONNEL
INSTITUTIONAL PERSONNEL
MILITARY PERSONNEL
NONPROFESSIONAL PERSONNEL
OFFICER PERSONNEL
PARAPROFESSIONAL SCHOOL PERSONNEL
PERSONNEL
PROFESSIONAL PERSONNEL
SCHOOL PERSONNEL
SCIENTIFIC PERSONNEL
PERSONNEL DATA
PERSONNEL DIRECTORS
PERSONNEL EVALUATION
PERSONNEL INTEGRATION
PERSONNEL MANAGEMENT
PERSONNEL NEEDS
PERSONNEL POLICY
STUDENT PERSONNEL PROGRAMS
PERSONNEL SELECTION
PUPIL PERSONNEL SERVICES
STUDENT PERSONNEL SERVICES
STUDENT PERSONNEL WORK
PUPIL PERSONNEL WORKERS
STUDENT PERSONNEL WORKERS
INSTITUTIONALIZED (PERSONS)
PATIENTS (PERSONS)
LITERARY PERSPECTIVE
TIME PERSPECTIVE
PERSUASIVE DISCOURSE
PESTICIDES

ORAL READING
RAPID READING
READING
RECREATIONAL READING
REMEDIAL READING
SILENT READING
SPEED READING
STORY READING
READING ABILITY
READING ACHIEVEMENT
DIRECTED READING ACTIVITY
READING ASSIGNMENTS
READING CENTERS
READING CLINICS
REMEDIAL READING CLINICS
READING COMPREHENSION
READING CONSULTANTS
READING DEVELOPMENT
READING DIAGNOSIS
READING DIFFICULTY
READING FAILURE
READING GAMES
READING HABITS
READING IMPROVEMENT
READING INSTRUCTION
READING INTERESTS
INFORMAL READING INVENTORY
READING LEVEL
READING MATERIAL SELECTION
READING MATERIALS
SUPPLEMENTARY READING MATERIALS
READING PROCESSES
ADULT READING PROGRAMS
READING PROGRAMS
REMEDIAL READING PROGRAMS
SEQUENTIAL READING PROGRAMS
READING READINESS
READING READINESS TESTS
READING RESEARCH
READING SKILLS
READING SPEED
READING TESTS
REAL ESTATE
REAL ESTATE OCCUPATIONS
REALIA
REALISM
CHILD REARING
ABSTRACT REASONING
RECALL (PSYCHOLOGICAL)
BROADCAST RECEPTION EQUIPMENT
RECEPTIVE LANGUAGE
WELFARE RECIPIENTS
RECIPROCALS (MATHEMATICS)
CHARACTER RECOGNITION
PATTERN RECOGNITION
PROFESSIONAL RECOGNITION
RACIAL RECOGNITION
RECOGNITION
WORD RECOGNITION
RECONSTRUCTION ERA
MEDICAL RECORD LIBRARIANS
MEDICAL RECORD TECHNICIANS
TAPE RECORDERS
KINESCOPE RECORDINGS
PHONOTAPE RECORDINGS
TAPE RECORDINGS
VIDEO TAPE RECORDINGS
RECORDKEEPING
RECORDS (FORMS)
LANGUAGE RECORDS (PHONOGRAPH)
ACADEMIC RECORDS
ATTENDANCE RECORDS
CASE RECORDS
CONFIDENTIAL RECORDS
PAYROLL RECORDS
PHONOGRAPH RECORDS
STUDENT RECORDS
RECREATION
RECREATION FINANCES
COMMUNITY RECREATION LEGISLATION
FEDERAL RECREATION LEGISLATION
LOCAL RECREATION LEGISLATION
STATE RECREATION LEGISLATION
COMMUNITY RECREATION PROGRAMS
PHYSICAL RECREATION PROGRAMS
SOCIAL RECREATION PROGRAMS
RECREATIONAL ACTIVITIES
RECREATIONAL FACILITIES
RECREATIONAL PROGRAMS
SCHOOL RECREATIONAL PROGRAMS
RECREATIONAL READING
FACULTY RECRUITMENT
RECRUITMENT
TEACHER RECRUITMENT
SCHOOL REDISTRICTING
REDUNDANCY
REVIEW (REEXAMINATION)
REFERENCE BOOKS
LEGISLATIVE REFERENCE LIBRARIES
REFERENCE MATERIALS
LIBRARY REFERENCE SERVICES
REFERRAL
REFRESHER COURSES
REFRIGERATION
REFRIGERATION MECHANICS
REFUGEES
REGIONAL COOPERATION
REGIONAL DIALECTS
REGIONAL LABORATORIES
REGIONAL LIBRARIES
REGIONAL PLANNING
REGIONAL PROGRAMS
REGIONAL SCHOOLS
GEOGRAPHIC REGIONS
SCHOOL REGISTRATION
VOTER REGISTRATION
EYE REGRESSIONS
REGULAR CLASS PLACEMENT
TRAFFIC REGULATIONS
CORRECTIONAL REHABILITATION
DELINQUENT REHABILITATION
DROPOUT REHABILITATION
REHABILITATION

STUDENT REHABILITATION
VOCATIONAL REHABILITATION
REHABILITATION CENTERS
REHABILITATION COUNSELING
REHABILITATION PROGRAMS
NEGATIVE REINFORCEMENT
POSITIVE REINFORCEMENT
REINFORCEMENT
SOCIAL REINFORCEMENT
REINFORCERS
REJECTION
CHURCH RELATED COLLEGES
COMMUNITY RELATIONS
ETHNIC RELATIONS
FOREIGN RELATIONS
GROUP RELATIONS
HUMAN RELATIONS
INDUSTRIAL RELATIONS
INTERFAITH RELATIONS
INTERGROUP RELATIONS
PUBLIC RELATIONS
RACE RELATIONS
SOCIAL RELATIONS
HUMAN RELATIONS ORGANIZATIONS
HUMAN RELATIONS PROGRAMS
HUMAN RELATIONS UNITS
BOARD ADMINISTRATOR RELATIONSHIP
EMPLOYER EMPLOYEE RELATIONSHIP
FAMILY RELATIONSHIP
FAMILY SCHOOL RELATIONSHIP
FEDERAL STATE RELATIONSHIP
INTERPERSONAL RELATIONSHIP
INTERPROFESSIONAL RELATIONSHIP
PARENT CHILD RELATIONSHIP
PARENT SCHOOL RELATIONSHIP
PARENT STUDENT RELATIONSHIP
PEER RELATIONSHIP
PERSONAL RELATIONSHIP
POLICE COMMUNITY RELATIONSHIP
POLICE SCHOOL RELATIONSHIP
RELATIONSHIP
SCHOOL COMMUNITY RELATIONSHIP
SCHOOL INDUSTRY RELATIONSHIP
SPATIAL RELATIONSHIP
STATE SCHOOL DISTRICT RELATIONSHIP
STUDENT COLLEGE RELATIONSHIP
STUDENT SCHOOL RELATIONSHIP
STUDENT TEACHER RELATIONSHIP
TEACHER ADMINISTRATOR RELATIONSHIP
RELATIVITY
PROGRESSIVE RELAXATION
RELEASED TIME
RELEVANCE (EDUCATION)
RELEVANCE (INFORMATION RETRIEVAL)
RELIABILITY
TEST RELIABILITY
RELIGION
RELIGIOUS AGENCIES
RELIGIOUS CONFLICT
RELIGIOUS CULTURAL GROUPS
RELIGIOUS DIFFERENCES
RELIGIOUS DISCRIMINATION
RELIGIOUS EDUCATION
RELIGIOUS FACTORS
RELIGIOUS ORGANIZATIONS
RELOCATION
REMEDIAL ARITHMETIC
REMEDIAL COURSES
REMEDIAL INSTRUCTION
REMEDIAL MATHEMATICS
REMEDIAL PROGRAMS
REMEDIAL READING
REMEDIAL READING CLINICS
REMEDIAL READING PROGRAMS
REMEDIAL TEACHERS
RENAISSANCE LITERATURE
URBAN RENEWAL
URBAN RENEWAL AGENCIES
LOW RENT HOUSING
REPAIR
APPLIANCE REPAIRING
AUTO BODY REPAIRMEN
MACHINE REPAIRMEN
TELEVISION REPAIRMEN
GRADE REPETITION
REPETITIVE FILM SHOWINGS
REPORT CARDS
COURT REPORTERS
ANNUAL REPORTS
CONFERENCE REPORTS
REPORTS
TECHNICAL REPORTS
DEGREE REQUIREMENTS
FACILITY REQUIREMENTS
GRADUATION REQUIREMENTS
RESIDENCE REQUIREMENTS
RESCUE
ACTION RESEARCH
ARCHITECTURAL RESEARCH
BEHAVIORAL SCIENCE RESEARCH
CLASSROOM RESEARCH
CREATIVITY RESEARCH
CURRICULUM RESEARCH
DEAF RESEARCH
DROPOUT RESEARCH
ECONOMIC RESEARCH
EDUCATIONAL RESEARCH
ENVIRONMENTAL RESEARCH
EXCEPTIONAL CHILD RESEARCH
FACILITY UTILIZATION RESEARCH
INSTITUTIONAL RESEARCH
INTEREST RESEARCH
LANGUAGE RESEARCH
LIBRARY RESEARCH
MEDIA RESEARCH
MEDICAL RESEARCH
METHODS RESEARCH
OPERATIONS RESEARCH
READING RESEARCH
RESEARCH
SCIENTIFIC RESEARCH
STUDENT RESEARCH
TELEVISION RESEARCH
TEXTBOOK RESEARCH

```
               SCHOOL CALENDARS
         AFTER SCHOOL CENTERS
               SCHOOL CLOSING
               SCHOOL COMMUNITY COOPERATION
               SCHOOL COMMUNITY PROGRAMS
               SCHOOL COMMUNITY RELATIONSHIP
               SCHOOL CONDITIONS
               SCHOOL CONSTRUCTION
  COLLEGE HIGH SCHOOL COOPERATION
       COLLEGE SCHOOL COOPERATION
    ELEMENTARY SCHOOL COUNSELING
    ELEMENTARY SCHOOL COUNSELORS
     SECONDARY SCHOOL COUNSELORS
    ELEMENTARY SCHOOL CURRICULUM
          HIGH SCHOOL CURRICULUM
      EXTENDED SCHOOL DAY
               SCHOOL DEMOGRAPHY
 DECENTRALIZED SCHOOL DESIGN
          HIGH SCHOOL DESIGN
               SCHOOL DESIGN
     COMMUNITY SCHOOL DIRECTORS
               SCHOOL DISTRICT AUTONOMY
         STATE SCHOOL DISTRICT RELATIONSHIP
               SCHOOL DISTRICT SPENDING
               SCHOOL DISTRICTS
         AFTER SCHOOL EDUCATION
          LATE SCHOOL ENTRANCE
               SCHOOL ENVIRONMENT
               SCHOOL EXPANSION
               SCHOOL FUNDS
          HIGH SCHOOL GRADUATES
    ELEMENTARY SCHOOL GUIDANCE
     POST HIGH SCHOOL GUIDANCE
               SCHOOL HEALTH SERVICES
               SCHOOL HOLDING POWER
               SCHOOL IMPROVEMENT
               SCHOOL INDUSTRY RELATIONSHIP
               SCHOOL INTEGRATION
               SCHOOL INVOLVEMENT
               SCHOOL LAW
    ELEMENTARY SCHOOL LIBRARIES
               SCHOOL LIBRARIES
               SCHOOL LOCATION
               SCHOOL MAINTENANCE
    ELEMENTARY SCHOOL MATHEMATICS
     SECONDARY SCHOOL MATHEMATICS
               SCHOOL NEWSPAPERS
               SCHOOL NURSES
          HIGH SCHOOL ORGANIZATION
               SCHOOL ORGANIZATION
               SCHOOL ORIENTATION
 PARAPROFESSIONAL SCHOOL PERSONNEL
               SCHOOL PERSONNEL
               SCHOOL PHOBIA
               SCHOOL PLANNING
  NEIGHBORHOOD SCHOOL POLICY
               SCHOOL POLICY
         AFTER SCHOOL PROGRAMS
               SCHOOL PSYCHOLOGISTS
               SCHOOL PUBLICATIONS
               SCHOOL RECREATIONAL PROGRAMS
               SCHOOL REDISTRICTING
               SCHOOL REGISTRATION
        FAMILY SCHOOL RELATIONSHIP
        PARENT SCHOOL RELATIONSHIP
        POLICE SCHOOL RELATIONSHIP
       STUDENT SCHOOL RELATIONSHIP
               SCHOOL RESPONSIBILITY
    ELEMENTARY SCHOOL ROLE
          HIGH SCHOOL ROLE
   JUNIOR HIGH SCHOOL ROLE
               SCHOOL ROLE
               SCHOOL SAFETY
               SCHOOL SCHEDULES
    ELEMENTARY SCHOOL SCIENCE
     SECONDARY SCHOOL SCIENCE
               SCHOOL SECRETARIES
               SCHOOL SEGREGATION
               SCHOOL SERVICES
               SCHOOL SHOPS
               SCHOOL SIZE
               SCHOOL SOCIAL WORKERS
               SCHOOL SPACE
               SCHOOL STATISTICS
    ELEMENTARY SCHOOL STUDENTS
          HIGH SCHOOL STUDENTS
   JUNIOR HIGH SCHOOL STUDENTS
     SECONDARY SCHOOL STUDENTS
               SCHOOL STUDY CENTERS
               SCHOOL SUPERINTENDENTS
    ELEMENTARY SCHOOL SUPERVISION
          HIGH SCHOOL SUPERVISORS
               SCHOOL SUPERVISORS
               SCHOOL SUPPORT
               SCHOOL SURVEYS
        COUNTY SCHOOL SYSTEMS
        PUBLIC SCHOOL SYSTEMS
         RURAL SCHOOL SYSTEMS
               SCHOOL SYSTEMS
               SCHOOL TAXES
    ELEMENTARY SCHOOL TEACHERS
        PUBLIC SCHOOL TEACHERS
     SECONDARY SCHOOL TEACHERS
         AFTER SCHOOL TUTORING
               SCHOOL VANDALISM
               SCHOOL VISITATION
      EXTENDED SCHOOL YEAR
        OUT OF SCHOOL YOUTH
               SCHOOL ZONING
      ADMISSION (SCHOOL)
 CLINIC PERSONNEL (SCHOOL)
DEPARTMENT DIRECTORS (SCHOOL)
      AFFILIATED SCHOOLS
 AREA VOCATIONAL SCHOOLS
       BILINGUAL SCHOOLS
BIRACIAL ELEMENTARY SCHOOLS
        BIRACIAL SCHOOLS
BIRACIAL SECONDARY SCHOOLS
        BOARDING SCHOOLS
CATHOLIC ELEMENTARY SCHOOLS
   CATHOLIC HIGH SCHOOLS
        CATHOLIC SCHOOLS
       COMMUNITY SCHOOLS
COMPREHENSIVE HIGH SCHOOLS


   CONSOLIDATED SCHOOLS
CONTINUATION HIGH SCHOOLS
  CORRESPONDENCE SCHOOLS
             DAY SCHOOLS
          DENTAL SCHOOLS
   DISADVANTAGED SCHOOLS
      ELEMENTARY SCHOOLS
    EXPERIMENTAL SCHOOLS
            FOLK SCHOOLS
         FREEDOM SCHOOLS
    GENERAL HIGH SCHOOLS
            HIGH SCHOOLS
        HOSPITAL SCHOOLS
   INSTITUTIONAL SCHOOLS
     JUNIOR HIGH SCHOOLS
      LABORATORY SCHOOLS
             LAW SCHOOLS
         LIBRARY SCHOOLS
         MEDICAL SCHOOLS
          MIDDLE SCHOOLS
         MIGRANT SCHOOLS
        MILITARY SCHOOLS
    NEIGHBORHOOD SCHOOLS
           NIGHT SCHOOLS
  NONRESIDENTIAL SCHOOLS
        NORTHERN SCHOOLS
         NURSERY SCHOOLS
     ONE TEACHER SCHOOLS
       OPEN PLAN SCHOOLS
       PAROCHIAL SCHOOLS
         PRIVATE SCHOOLS
     PROPRIETARY SCHOOLS
RACIALLY BALANCED SCHOOLS
        REGIONAL SCHOOLS
     RESIDENTIAL SCHOOLS
           RURAL SCHOOLS
                 SCHOOLS
       SECONDARY SCHOOLS
     SENIOR HIGH SCHOOLS
            SLUM SCHOOLS
           SMALL SCHOOLS
        SOUTHERN SCHOOLS
         SPECIAL SCHOOLS
           STATE SCHOOLS
        SUBURBAN SCHOOLS
          SUMMER SCHOOLS
     TRADITIONAL SCHOOLS
    TRANSITIONAL SCHOOLS
        UNGRADED SCHOOLS
           URBAN SCHOOLS
 VOCATIONAL HIGH SCHOOLS
      VOCATIONAL SCHOOLS
      YEAR ROUND SCHOOLS
          ANIMAL SCIENCE
         COLLEGE SCIENCE
        COMPUTER SCIENCE
        CONSUMER SCIENCE
           EARTH SCIENCE
ELEMENTARY SCHOOL SCIENCE
      ELEMENTARY SCIENCE
         GENERAL SCIENCE
     INFORMATION SCIENCE
         LIBRARY SCIENCE
        MILITARY SCIENCE
          MODERN SCIENCE
           PLANT SCIENCE
       POLITICAL SCIENCE
SECONDARY SCHOOL SCIENCE
            SOIL SCIENCE
                 SCIENCE ACTIVITIES
                 SCIENCE CAREERS
                 SCIENCE CLUBS
                 SCIENCE CONSULTANTS
                 SCIENCE COURSE IMPROVEMENT PROJECT
                 SCIENCE COURSES
                 SCIENCE CURRICULUM
                 SCIENCE DEPARTMENTS
        COMPUTER SCIENCE EDUCATION
            FIRE SCIENCE EDUCATION
                 SCIENCE EDUCATION
                 SCIENCE EDUCATION HISTORY
                 SCIENCE EQUIPMENT
                 SCIENCE EXPERIMENTS
                 SCIENCE FACILITIES
                 SCIENCE FAIRS
                 SCIENCE FICTION
                 SCIENCE HISTORY
                 SCIENCE INSTITUTES
                 SCIENCE INSTRUCTION
         STUDENT SCIENCE INTERESTS
                 SCIENCE LABORATORIES
                 SCIENCE MATERIALS
                 SCIENCE PROGRAMS
          SUMMER SCIENCE PROGRAMS
                 SCIENCE PROJECTS
      BEHAVIORAL SCIENCE RESEARCH
                 SCIENCE SUPERVISION
                 SCIENCE TEACHERS
                 SCIENCE TEACHING CENTERS
                 SCIENCE TESTS
                 SCIENCE UNITS
      BEHAVIORAL SCIENCES
      BIOLOGICAL SCIENCES
         NATURAL SCIENCES
        PHYSICAL SCIENCES
          SOCIAL SCIENCES
                 SCIENTIFIC ATTITUDES
                 SCIENTIFIC CONCEPTS
                 SCIENTIFIC ENTERPRISE
                 SCIENTIFIC LITERACY
                 SCIENTIFIC MANPOWER
                 SCIENTIFIC METHODOLOGY
                 SCIENTIFIC PERSONNEL
                 SCIENTIFIC PRINCIPLES
                 SCIENTIFIC RESEARCH
                 SCIENTISTS
         EQUATED SCORES
                 SCORING
            TEST SCORING MACHINES
                 SCREENING TESTS
                 SCRIPTS
                 SCULPTURE
```

DESCRIPTOR GROUPS

010 Abilities
Intelligence and performance of individuals, e.g., Academic Aptitude, etc. Also contained herein are specific skills as they relate to the ability for acquiring and performing given skills, knowledge of the means or methods for accomplishing a task. For skill-related occupations, *see* OCCUPATIONS.

020 Administration
Management and management-related processes in administering various types of school plants and educational organizations. For different types of administrative personnel, *see* PERSONNEL AND GROUPS. For program development, *see* FINANCE. For financial factors, *see* FINANCE. *See also* PROGRAMS.

030 Arts
Fine Arts, Theater Arts, Painting, Freehand Drawing, Sculpture, Music, Ceramics, Graphic Arts, Dramatics, etc. *See also* HUMANITIES.

040 Attitudes
Attitudes of individuals or groups toward a given object or condition, e.g., Student Attitudes, Class Attitudes, Personal Interests, Values, etc.

050 Audiovisual Materials and Methods
Audiovisual materials and methods used for instructional purposes, e.g., Closed Circuit Television, Mass Media. *See also* COMMUNICATION, EQUIPMENT.

060 Behavior
Kinds and types of human behavior and factors related to the study of behavior, e.g., Violence, Socially Deviant Behavior, Conditioned Response, Overt Response, etc. *See also* LEARNING AND COGNITION, PSYCHOLOGY, SOCIOLOGY.

070 Biology
Study of life including Zoology and Botany, e.g., Ecology, Heredity, Plant Science, Animal Science, Physiology, Neurology, etc. *See also* HEALTH AND SAFETY.

080 Communication
Methods and characteristics of communication, e.g., Oral Expression, Verbal Communication, etc. For types of communication equipment, *see also* EQUIPMENT.

090 Counseling
Counseling Programs, Counseling Services, Guidance Programs, Guidance Services, Individual Counseling, Group Counseling, Vocational Counseling, etc. *See also* ADMINISTRATION, ATTITUDES, BEHAVIOR, PSYCHOLOGY.

100 Culture
Specific cultures, e.g., African Culture, and culture-related factors, e.g., Cultural Differences, Ethnic Grouping, Urban Culture, etc. *See also* RACE RELATIONS.

110 Curriculum
Specific types of curriculum and specific types of courses, e.g., Business English, Elementary Science, Fused Curriculum, Correspondence Courses, In-service Courses, etc.

120 Demography
Studies related to population including statistical, social and economic factors, e.g., Census Figures, Geographic Distribution, Migration, Population Trends, Student Distribution, Urban Population, etc.

130 Development
Includes stages of growth, the development of specific materials, and the development of education programs, e.g., Childhood Material Development, Program Development, etc. *See also* ADMINISTRATION, BIOLOGY.

140 Education
General education concepts, specific types of education, e.g., Cooperative Education, Educational Improvement, Art Education, Mathematics Education, Music Education, Vocational Education, etc.

150 Employment
Employment, job processes and labor, e.g., Youth Employment, Employment Practices, Job Analysis, Labor Conditions, Labor Unions, Personnel Data, Unemployment, etc. For specific occupations, *see* OCCUPATIONS. *See also* PERSONNEL AND GROUPS.

160 Environment
Aggregate of conditions or influences on communities, schools, culture, and social factors, e.g., Community Influence, Classroom Environment, Cultural Environment, Social Environment, etc. *See also* CULTURE, SOCIOLOGY.

170 Equipment
Instructional equipment and general school and classroom equipment, e.g., Filmstrip Projectors, Tape Recorders, Building Equipment, Classroom Furniture, Vending Machines, etc. *See also* AUDIOVISUAL MATERIALS AND METHODS, FACILITIES.

180 Evaluation
Judgment of processes and people in the education system, e.g., Counseling Effectiveness, Cognitive Measurement, Educational Testing, Student Evaluation, Teacher Evaluation, Test Interpretation. Descriptors that describe the products of evaluation techniques should be applied to the group EVALUATION TECHNIQUES.

190 Evaluation Techniques
Specific techniques or methods used in educational processes for evaluation and comparison of the effectiveness of the education system, e.g., Comparative

Testing, Forced Choice Technique, Q Sort, Self Evaluation, etc. *See also* EVALUATION, PSYCHOLOGY, TESTS.

200   Experience
Knowledge or acquired skills, e.g., Emotional Experience, Learning Experience, Social Experience, Teacher Experience, etc. *See also* ABILITIES, ATTITUDES, DEVELOPMENT.

210   Facilities
Buildings, installations, and appendages designed to serve a specific function, e.g., Art Centers, Auditoriums, Crafts Rooms, Dormitories, Lighting, Parks, Public Facilities, Rural Clinics, School Space, Self Contained Classrooms, etc. *See also* EQUIPMENT.

220   Finance
Relating or pertaining to money matters and transaction, e.g., Bond Issues, Expenditures, Fiscal Capacity, Minimum Wage, Salaries, Scholarships, State Aid, Tax Allocation, Welfare, etc. *See also* ADMINISTRATION, GOVERNMENT.

230   Government
Executive, legislative, and judicial aspects of federal, state, and local government, e.g., Federal Government, Federal Legislation, Federal Courts, State Government, State Legislation, City Government, Community Agencies (Public), Taxes, etc. *See also* ADMINISTRATION, FINANCE.

240   Handicapped
Limited to persons with or conditions related to physiological or psychological impairments such as Blind, Aurally Handicapped, Partially Sighted, etc.

250   Health and Safety
The physical condition, preservation, or control of an organism or its parts such as Accident Prevention, Family Health, Medical Service, Traffic Safety, and Diseases. *See also* BIOLOGY.

260   Humanities
Branches of learning having primarily a cultural character usually including Literature, History, and Philosophy. *See also* ARTS, CULTURE, LANGUAGE AND SPEECH.

270   Instruction
Activities, materials, and guidance that facilitate learning in either formal or informal situations such as Academic Enrichment, Assignments, Computer Oriented Programs, Correspondence Study, Workshops, etc. *See also* CURRICULUM, EDUCATION, AUDIOVISUAL MATERIALS AND METHODS.

280   Instructional Program Divisions
Any segment of or grouping of students such as Ability Grouping, Age Grade Placement, Non-graded Classes, Grade 1, Grade 2, Grade 3, etc. *See also* ADMINISTRATION.

290 Language and Speech
The study of language includes Morphology (Languages), Phonology, and Syntax. *See also* HUMANITIES. Includes also oral communication such as speech sounds and gesture, e.g., Diction, Phonetic Analysis, Pronunciation, Speech Habits, Speech Therapy, Vowels, etc. *See also* LANGUAGES.

300 Languages
For specific languages and language groups, e.g., Czech, African Languages, English, etc. *See also* COMMUNICATION.

310 Learning and Cognition
The process of acquiring knowledge or skills through study, instruction, or experience such as in Creative Thinking, Discovery Processes, Through Processes, etc.

320 Library Materials
Includes library collections such as Books, Annotated Bibliographies, Historical Reviews, etc. *See also* AUDIOVISUAL MATERIALS AND METHODS, COMMUNICATION.

330 Library Science
The principles and practices related to processing conducted in the library as well as related user requirements and services, e.g., Abstracting, Information Dissemination, Library Services, etc.

340 Mathematics
Operation and processes involved in the solution of mathematical problems such as Operations Research, Statistics, Algebra, etc.

350 Occupations
One's usual or principal work especially as a means of earning a living, e.g., Farm Occupations, Office Occupations, etc., as well as any study or result of that study, e.g., Occupational Clusters, Occupational Surveys, etc. *See also* EMPLOYMENT, and PERSONNEL AND GROUPS.

360 Opportunities
Advantageous circumstance or combination of circumstances when effecting security, wealth, education, or freedom. Specific opportunities would include Career Opportunities, Teaching Benefits, Housing Opportunities, etc.

370 Organizations (Groups)
A group of persons that has more or less a constant membership, a body of officers, a purpose, and usually a set of regulations such as Advisory Committees, Citizens Councils, Clubs, Housing Industry, etc. *See also* PERSONNEL AND GROUPS.

380 Personnel and Groups
Persons considered together as being related in some manner or having some common characteristics, Accountants, Advanced Students, etc. Also includes a number of things or persons ranged or considered together as being related in some manner having common bonds, e.g., Age Groups, Deliquents, Anglo

Americans, Middle Aged, Young Adults, Senior Citizens, College Freshmen, etc. *See also* EMPLOYMENT and SOCIOLOGY. For specific occupations, *see* OCCUPATIONS.

390   Physical Education and Recreation
Activity in which persons refresh themselves mentally or physically, such as in Community Recreation Programs, Social Recreation Programs, etc.

400   Physical Sciences
Study of nonliving materials, e.g., Electricity, Matter, Space, Time, Physics, etc.

410   Programs
A plan or procedure: a schedule or system under which action may be taken towards a desired goal such as After School Programs, College Programs, Work Experience Programs, Youth Programs, etc. *See also* ADMINISTRATION.

420   Psychology
The study of mental phenomena, activities, and processes, e.g., Aggression, Conflict, Fear, Intelligence Factors, Student Adjustment, etc. Also includes psychological forms of treatment, e.g., Role Playing, Sociodrama, etc.

430   Race Relations
Relations among members of different races and methods of affecting such relations, e.g., Classroom Integration, Integration Methods, Racial Balance, Racism, etc. *See also* CULTURE, SOCIOLOGY.

440   Reading
The action or practice of one who reads or the oral Reading, Reading Assignments, Elective Reading, Group Reading, Readability, etc. Also includes reading facility, e.g., Reading Ability, Reading Failure, Illiteracy, etc. *See also* ABILITIES, COMMUNICATION, and INSTRUCTION.

450   Research
Areas and methods of investigation or experimentation having for its aim the discovery of new facts, e.g., Area Studies, Deaf Research, Experimental Programs, Research Methodology, etc.

460   Resources
Source of supply, support or aid, such as Community Resources, Educational Resources, Natural Resources, etc.

470   Schools
Institutions offering defined studies at defined levels, e.g., Catholic Elementary Schools, Day Schools, High Schools, etc.

480   Social Sciences
Study of the functioning of human society and with the inter-personal relationships of individuals as members of society such as Behavioral Sciences, Communism, Economic Progress, Social Relations. *See also* BEHAVIOR, SOCIOLOGY, RACE RELATIONS.

498

490 Sociology
A broad Social Science which deals with the study of the structure of society, its groups, institutions, and culture, primarily interested in the way people organize themselves into groups, social classes, and institutions such as Anti Segregation Programs, Church Role, Deliquency Causes, Family Characteristics, etc. *See also* SOCIAL SCIENCES, ORGANIZATIONS (GROUPS), RACE RELATIONS.

500 Standards
Morals, ethics, habits, requirements, etc., established by authority, custom, or an individual as acceptable, e.g., Academic Standards, Behavior Standards, Certification, Educational Specifications, Graduation Requirements, Living Standards, State Standards, Teacher Certification, etc.

510 Techniques
Processes, manipulations, or procedures required in any art, study activity, or production, e.g., Classroom Games, Classroom Techniques, Creative Teaching, Educational Methods, Field Trips, Lesson Plans, Methodology, Optional Branching, Production Techniques, Tutoring, etc.

520 Tests
Devices or procedures for measuring ability, achievement, interest, etc., e.g., Achievement Tests, Aptitude Tests, Cognitive Tests, Interest Tests, Language Tests, Multiple Choice Tests, Problem Tests, Reading Tests, Talent Identification, Test Validity, etc.

DESCRIPTOR GROUP DISPLAY

010 Abilities

ABILITY
ABILITY IDENTIFICATION
ACADEMIC ABILITY
ACADEMIC ACHIEVEMENT
ACADEMIC APTITUDE
ACADEMIC FAILURE
ACADEMIC PERFORMANCE
ACHIEVEMENT
AGRICULTURAL SKILLS
ALPHABETIZING SKILLS
APTITUDE
AUDIOLINGUAL SKILLS
BASIC SKILLS
BUSINESS SKILLS
COGNITIVE ABILITY
COMMUNICATION SKILLS
COMPOSITION SKILLS (LITERARY)
COMPREHENSION
CREATIVE ABILITY
DECISION MAKING SKILLS
EYE VOICE SPAN
HANDWRITING SKILLS
HOME ECONOMICS SKILLS
HOMEMAKING SKILLS
INDIVIDUAL POWER
INTELLIGENCE
INTELLIGENCE DIFFERENCES
INTELLIGENCE LEVEL
INTELLIGENCE QUOTIENT
INTERPERSONAL COMPETENCE
INTERPRETIVE SKILLS
JOB SKILLS
KNOWLEDGE LEVEL
LANGUAGE SKILLS
LEADERSHIP QUALITIES
LIBRARY SKILLS
LISTENING SKILLS
LOCATIONAL SKILLS (SOCIAL STUDIES)
LOW ACHIEVEMENT FACTORS
MAP SKILLS
MARKSMANSHIP
MECHANICAL SKILLS
NEGRO ACHIEVEMENT
NONVERBAL ABILITY
OBJECT MANIPULATION
OCCUPATIONAL ASPIRATION
PERFORMANCE
PRODUCTIVITY
PSYCHOMOTOR SKILLS

READINESS
READING SKILLS
RECOGNITION
RESEARCH SKILLS
SCIENTIFIC LITERACY
SELF CARE SKILLS
SERIAL ORDERING
SKILL OBSOLESCENCE
SKILLS
SORTING PROCEDURES
SPEECH SKILLS
SPELLING
STUDENT ABILITY
STUDY SKILLS
TALENT
TASK PERFORMANCE
TEACHING SKILLS
VERBAL ABILITY
VISUAL ACUITY
VOCABULARY SKILLS
VOCATIONAL APTITUDE
WORD RECOGNITION
WORD STUDY SKILLS
WRITING SKILLS

020 Administration

ACADEMIC RECORDS
ADMINISTRATION
ADMINISTRATIVE CHANGE
ADMINISTRATIVE ORGANIZATION
ADMINISTRATIVE POLICY
ADMINISTRATIVE PRINCIPLES
ADMINISTRATIVE PROBLEMS
ADMINISTRATOR CHARACTERISTICS
ADMINISTRATOR GUIDES
ADMINISTRATOR ROLE
ADMINISTRATOR SELECTION
ADMISSION (SCHOOL)
ADOPTION (IDEAS)
ANCILLARY SERVICES
ANNUAL REPORTS
ASSISTANT SUPERINTENDENT ROLE
ATTENDANCE
ATTENDANCE RECORDS
ATTENDANCE SERVICES
AVERAGE DAILY ATTENDANCE
AVERAGE DAILY ENROLLMENT
BOARD ADMINISTRATOR RELATIONSHIP
BOARD OF EDUCATION POLICY
BOARD OF EDUCATION ROLE
BOARDS OF EDUCATION

SCHOOL INDUSTRY RELATIONSHIP
SCHOOL INVOLVEMENT
SCHOOL ORGANIZATION
SCHOOL PLANNING
SCHOOL POLICY
SCHOOL REGISTRATION
SCHOOL SCHEDULES
SCHOOL SERVICES
SCHOOL SUPERVISION
SCIENCE SUPERVISION
SELECTION
SEMESTER DIVISION
SERVICES
SHARED SERVICES
SPECIAL SERVICES
STAFF IMPROVEMENT
STAFF MEETINGS
STAFF ROLE
STAFF UTILIZATION
STATE BOARDS OF EDUCATION
STUDENT APPLICATION
STUDENT ENROLLMENT
STUDENT RECORDS
STUDENT TEACHER RATIO
STUDENT TRANSPORTATION
SUPERINTENDENT ROLE
SUPERVISION
SUPERVISORY ACTIVITIES
SUPERVISORY METHODS
SUSPENSION
TEACHER ADMINISTRATOR RELATIONSHIP
TEACHER ATTENDANCE
TEACHER DISTRIBUTION
TEACHER PLACEMENT
TEACHER PROMOTION
TEACHER SELECTION
TEACHER SHORTAGE
TEACHER SUPERVISION
TEACHER TRANSFER
TEACHING ASSIGNMENT
TEAM ADMINISTRATION
TEXTBOOK SELECTION
TIME BLOCKS
TRANSFER POLICY
TRANSFERS
TRANSPORTATION
TRIMESTER SCHEDULES
UNIVERSITY ADMINISTRATION
VERTICAL ORGANIZATION
WILDLIFE MANAGEMENT

030 Arts

ACTING
APPLIED MUSIC
ART
ART ACTIVITIES
ART APPRECIATION
ART EXPRESSION
ART MATERIALS
ART PRODUCTS
ART SONG
BALLET
BANDS (MUSIC)

BUILDING DESIGN
CERAMICS
CHORAL MUSIC
CHORAL SPEAKING
CLASSROOM DESIGN
COLOR
COLOR PLANNING
COMMERCIAL ART
COMPONENT BUILDING SYSTEMS
CONCERTS
CONTRAST
CREATIVE ART
CREATIVE DRAMATICS
DANCE
DECENTRALIZED SCHOOL DESIGN
DESIGN
DESIGN CRAFTS
DRAMATIC PLAY
DRAMATICS
FINE ARTS
FREEHAND DRAWING
FURNITURE DESIGN
GRAPHIC ARTS
HANDICRAFTS
HIGH SCHOOL DESIGN
INDUSTRIAL ARTS
INTERIOR DESIGN
JAZZ
MODULAR BUILDING DESIGN
MUSIC
MUSIC ACTIVITIES
MUSIC APPRECIATION
MUSIC READING
MUSIC THEORY
MUSICAL COMPOSITION
OPERA
ORIENTAL MUSIC
PAINTING
PARK DESIGN
PHOTOCOMPOSITION
PHOTOGRAPHY
PRACTICAL ARTS
SCHOOL ARCHITECTURE
SCHOOL DESIGN
SCULPTURE
SINGING
SKITS
SYMMETRY
THEATER ARTS
VISUAL ARTS
VOCAL MUSIC

040 Attitudes

ACADEMIC ASPIRATION
ADMINISTRATOR ATTITUDES
ADMINISTRATOR RESPONSIBILITY
ANTI INTELLECTUALISM
ATTENTION CONTROL
ATTITUDES
BELIEFS
BIAS
BUSINESS RESPONSIBILITY
CHANGING ATTITUDES

CHILD RESPONSIBILITY
CHILDHOOD ATTITUDES
CHILDHOOD INTERESTS
CHURCH RESPONSIBILITY
CIVIC BELIEF
CLASS ATTITUDES
COMMUNITY ATTITUDES
COUNSELOR ATTITUDES
CULTURAL AWARENESS
DEMOCRATIC VALUES
DESIGN PREFERENCES
DISCRIMINATORY ATTITUDES (SOCIAL)
DOGMATISM
DROPOUT ATTITUDES
EDUCATIONAL ATTITUDES
EDUCATIONAL INTEREST
EMPATHY
EMPLOYEE ATTITUDES
EMPLOYEE RESPONSIBILITY
EMPLOYER ATTITUDES
ETHICAL VALUES
FAMILY ATTITUDES
GENERATION GAP
INTERESTS
LEARNING MOTIVATION
LOW MOTIVATION
MAJORITY ATTITUDES
MIDDLE CLASS VALUES
MORAL VALUES
MORALE
MOTHER ATTITUDES
MOTIVATION
NATIONALISM
NEGATIVE ATTITUDES
NEGRO ATTITUDES
NORTHERN ATTITUDES
OPINIONS
PARENT ATTITUDES
PARENT RESPONSIBILITY
PARENTAL GRIEVANCES
PERSISTENCE
PERSONAL INTERESTS
PERSONAL VALUES
POLITICAL ATTITUDES
PRESS OPINION
PROGRAM ATTITUDES
PUBLIC OPINION
PUBLIC SUPPORT
RACIAL ATTITUDES
RAPPORT
READING INTERESTS
RESENTMENT
RESPONSIBILITY
SCHOOL ATTITUDES
SCIENTIFIC ATTITUDES
SELF ESTEEM
SELF REWARD
SOCIAL ATTITUDES
SOCIAL VALUES
SOUTHERN ATTITUDES
STUDENT ALIENATION
STUDENT ATTITUDES
STUDENT INTERESTS

STUDENT MOTIVATION
STUDENT OPINION
STUDENT SCIENCE INTERESTS
TEACHER ATTITUDES
TEACHER INFLUENCE
TEACHER MILITANCY
TEACHER MORALE
TEACHER MOTIVATION
TEACHER RESPONSIBILITY
TEXTBOOK BIAS
VALUES
VOCATIONAL INTERESTS
WORK ATTITUDES

050 Audiovisual Materials and Methods

AIRBORNE TELEVISION
AUDIOVISUAL AIDS
AUDIOVISUAL COMMUNICATION
AUDIOVISUAL PROGRAMS
AUTOINSTRUCTIONAL AIDS
BROADCAST TELEVISION
CARTOONS
CHARTS
CLASSROOM MATERIALS
CLOSED CIRCUIT TELEVISION
COLOR PRESENTATION
COLOR TELEVISION
COMMERCIAL TELEVISION
COMPUTER OUTPUT MICROFILM
DIAGRAMS
DIAL ACCESS INFORMATION SYSTEMS
DISPLAY SYSTEMS
DUBBING
EDUCATIONAL RADIO
EDUCATIONAL TELEVISION
ELECTROMECHANICAL AIDS
EXHIBITS
FACSIMILE TRANSMISSION
FILM PRODUCTION
FILM STUDY
FILMS
FILMSTRIPS
FIXED SERVICE TELEVISION
FLES MATERIALS
FOREIGN LANGUAGE FILMS
GRAPHS
HANDWRITING MATERIALS
HEALTH ACTIVITIES HANDBOOKS
HEALTH BOOKS
HIGH INTEREST LOW VOCABULARY BOOKS
HISTORY TEXTBOOKS
HORIZONTAL TEXTS
ILLUSTRATIONS
INSTRUCTIONAL AIDS
INSTRUCTIONAL FILMS
INSTRUCTIONAL MATERIALS
INSTRUCTIONAL MEDIA
INSTRUCTIONAL TELEVISION
INSTRUCTOR CENTERED TELEVISION
KINESCOPE RECORDINGS
LABORATORY MANUALS
LANGUAGE AIDS
LANGUAGE RECORDS (PHONOGRAPH)

LARGE TYPE MATERIALS
MANIPULATIVE MATERIALS
MAPS
MASS MEDIA
MASTER TAPES (AUDIO)
MATHEMATICS MATERIALS
MECHANICAL TEACHING AIDS
MICROFICHE
MICROFILM
MICROFORMS
MULTICHANNEL PROGRAMING
MULTICULTURAL TEXTBOOKS
OPEN CIRCUIT TELEVISION
ORIENTATION MATERIALS
OVERHEAD TELEVISION
PHONOGRAPH RECORDS
PHONOTAPE RECORDINGS
PHOTOGRAPHS
PICTORIAL STIMULI
PROGRAMED MATERIALS
PROGRAMED TEXTS
PROTOCOL MATERIALS
PUBLIC TELEVISION
RADIO
RAISED LINE DRAWINGS
REALIA
SINGLE CONCEPT FILMS
SLIDES
SOUND EFFECTS
SOUND FILMS
SOUND TRACKS
STUDENT DEVELOPED MATERIALS
STUDENT WRITING MODELS
SUPPLEMENTARY TEXTBOOKS
TALKING BOOKS
TAPE RECORDINGS
TEACHER DEVELOPED MATERIALS
TEACHING MACHINES
TELEGRAPHIC MATERIALS
TELEVISION
TELEVISION COMMERCIALS
TELEVISION VIEWING
TEXTBOOKS
THREE DIMENSIONAL AIDS
TOYS
TRANSPARENCIES
VERTICAL TEXTS
VIDEO TAPE RECORDINGS

060 Behavior

AFFECTIVE BEHAVIOR
AFFECTIVE OBJECTIVES
ANIMAL BEHAVIOR
ANTI SOCIAL BEHAVIOR
ATTENDANCE PATTERNS
ATTENTION
ATTENTION SPAN
BEHAVIOR
BEHAVIOR CHANGE
BEHAVIOR PATTERNS
BEHAVIOR PROBLEMS
BEHAVIOR THEORIES
BEHAVIORAL OBJECTIVES

BOOK THEFTS
CATHARSIS
CHEATING
COGNITIVE OBJECTIVES
CONDITIONED RESPONSE
CONDITIONED STIMULUS
CONDUCT
CONFORMITY
CONSTRUCTED RESPONSE
COVERT RESPONSE
CRIME
DELINQUENCY
DELINQUENT BEHAVIOR
DISCIPLINE
DISCIPLINE PROBLEMS
DRUG ABUSE
DRUG ADDICTION
EATING HABITS
ECHOLALIA
GROUP BEHAVIOR
HYPERACTIVITY
IMMATURITY
INFANT BEHAVIOR
INFORMAL LEADERSHIP
INTEGRITY
LEADER PARTICIPATION
LEADERSHIP
MISBEHAVIOR
NEGRO LEADERSHIP
OVERT RESPONSE
PARENT REACTION
PARENT ROLE
PATTERNED RESPONSES
PLAGIARISM
PSYCHOMOTOR OBJECTIVES
REACTIVE BEHAVIOR
RESPONSE MODE
SCHOOL VANDALISM
SOCIAL IMMATURITY
SOCIALLY DEVIANT BEHAVIOR
SPONTANEOUS BEHAVIOR
SPORTSMANSHIP
STEALING
STIMULUS BEHAVIOR
STUDENT BEHAVIOR
STUDENT LEADERSHIP
STUDENT REACTION
STUDY HABITS
TEACHER BEHAVIOR
TEACHER RESPONSE
TRUANCY
VANDALISM
VIOLENCE
WITHDRAWAL

070 Biology

AGE
AGE DIFFERENCES
AGRICULTURAL PRODUCTION
AGRICULTURAL TRENDS
AGRICULTURE
AGRONOMY
ANATOMY

ANIMAL SCIENCE
ANOMALIES
AUDIOLOGY
AUDITION (PHYSIOLOGY)
AUDITORY DISCRIMINATION
AUDITORY PERCEPTION
AURAL STIMULI
BIOCHEMISTRY
BIOLOGICAL INFLUENCES
BIOLOGICAL SCIENCES
BIOLOGY
BIOPHYSICS
BIRTH ORDER
BLOOD CIRCULATION
BODY HEIGHT
BODY WEIGHT
BOTANY
CARDIOVASCULAR SYSTEM
CELL THEORY
CORN (FIELD CROP)
CUTANEOUS SENSE
CYTOLOGY
DEATH
EARS
ECHOLOCATION
ECOLOGICAL FACTORS
ECOLOGY
EIDETIC IMAGES
ELECTRICAL STIMULI
EMBRYOLOGY
ENTOMOLOGY
EYE FIXATIONS
EYE HAND COORDINATION
EYE MOVEMENTS
EYE REGRESSIONS
EYES
FEMALES
FERTILIZERS
FIELD CROPS
FIGURAL AFTEREFFECTS
FLORICULTURE
FORESTRY
GENETICS
HAPTIC PERCEPTION
HEART RATE
HERBICIDES
HEREDITY
HORSES
HORTICULTURE
HUMAN BODY
INSECTICIDES
KINESTHETIC PERCEPTION
LIVESTOCK
MALES
MARINE BIOLOGY
MEDICINE
METABOLISM
MICROBIOLOGY
MOTOR REACTIONS
MUSCULAR STRENGTH
NEUROLOGICAL ORGANIZATION
NEUROLOGY
OPHTHALMOLOGY

ORNAMENTAL HORTICULTURE
PATHOLOGY
PERCEPTION
PHYSICAL CHARACTERISTICS
PHYSIOLOGY
PLANT GROWTH
PLANT IDENTIFICATION
PLANT PATHOLOGY
PLANT PROPAGATION
PLANT SCIENCE
PLANTING
PREGNANCY
PRENATAL INFLUENCES
PRIMATOLOGY
PUPILLARY DILATION
RADIATION BIOLOGY
RATS
RH FACTORS
RODENTICIDES
SENSORY EXPERIENCE
SEX (CHARACTERISTICS)
SEX DIFFERENCES
SEXUALITY
SLEEP
STIMULI
TACTILE ADAPTATION
TACTUAL PERCEPTION
TRANSPLANTING
TREES
TURF MANAGEMENT
VISION
VISUAL DISCRIMINATION
VISUAL PERCEPTION
VISUAL STIMULI
WEEDS
ZOOLOGY

080 Communication
ABBREVIATIONS
BASIC VOCABULARY
BRAILLE
BUSINESS CORRESPONDENCE
CABLE TELEVISION
CHARACTER RECOGNITION
CLASS NEWSPAPERS
CLASSROOM COMMUNICATION
COMMUNICATION (THOUGHT TRANSFER)
COMMUNICATION PROBLEMS
COMMUNICATION SATELLITES
COMMUNICATIONS
COMPOSITION (LITERARY)
COMPUTER PROGRAMS
COMPUTER SCIENCE
CONFERENCE REPORTS
CREATIVE EXPRESSION
CREATIVE WRITING
CURSIVE WRITING
CYBERNETICS
DATA
DATA PROCESSING
DATA SHEETS
DEAF INTERPRETING
DEBATE

DEFINITIONS
DESCRIPTIVE WRITING
DEVELOPMENTAL VOCABULARY
DIRECTION WRITING
ELECTRONIC DATA PROCESSING
EXPOSITORY WRITING
FACSIMILE COMMUNICATION SYSTEMS
FEEDBACK
GROUP DISCUSSION
HANDWRITING
INFORMATION NETWORKS
INFORMATION PROCESSING
INFORMATION THEORY
INPUT OUTPUT
INPUT OUTPUT ANALYSIS
INTERCOMMUNICATION
INTERSCHOOL COMMUNICATION
LETTERS (CORRESPONDENCE)
LIPREADING
LISTENING
LITERARY CONVENTIONS
MAN MACHINE SYSTEMS
MANUAL COMMUNICATION
MANUSCRIPT WRITING (HANDLETTERING)
MEDIA TECHNOLOGY
MERCHANDISE INFORMATION
NETWORKS
NEWS MEDIA
NEWSLETTERS
NEWSPAPERS
NONVERBAL COMMUNICATION
ORAL COMMUNICATION
ORAL EXPRESSION
PAMPHLETS
PARAGRAPH COMPOSITION
PATTERN RECOGNITION
PERSUASIVE DISCOURSE
PROGRAMING PROBLEMS
PUBLICATIONS
RECEPTIVE LANGUAGE
SCHOOL NEWSPAPERS
SCHOOL PUBLICATIONS
SEMIOTICS
SENSORY AIDS
SEQUENTIAL PROGRAMS
SPEAKING
SPEAKING ACTIVITIES
SPEECHES
STORY TELLING
TABLES (DATA)
TAXONOMY
TELECOMMUNICATION
TELEPHONE COMMUNICATION SYSTEMS
TEXTBOOK PREPARATION
TEXTBOOK PUBLICATIONS
TIME SHARING
TYPEWRITING
VERBAL COMMUNICATION
VIEWING TIME
VOCABULARY
WRITING

090 Counseling

ADULT COUNSELING
BEHAVIORAL COUNSELING
CAREER PLANNING
COCOUNSELING
COLLEGE DAY
COLLEGE HIGH SCHOOL COOPERATION
COLLEGE PLACEMENT
COMMUNITY CONSULTANT PROGRAMS
CONSULTATION PROGRAMS
CONTINUOUS GUIDANCE
CORRECTIONAL REHABILITATION
COUNSELING
COUNSELING GOALS
COUNSELING PROGRAMS
COUNSELING SERVICES
COUNSELING THEORIES
COUNSELOR CHARACTERISTICS
COUNSELOR FUNCTIONS
COUNSELOR PERFORMANCE
DELINQUENT REHABILITATION
DEVELOPMENTAL GUIDANCE
DROPOUT REHABILITATION
EDUCATIONAL COUNSELING
EDUCATIONAL GUIDANCE
EDUCATIONAL THERAPY
ELEMENTARY SCHOOL COUNSELING
ELEMENTARY SCHOOL GUIDANCE
EVENING COUNSELING PROGRAMS
EXCEPTIONAL CHILD SERVICES
FAMILY COUNSELING
GROUP COUNSELING
GROUP GUIDANCE
GUIDANCE
GUIDANCE COUNSELING
GUIDANCE FUNCTIONS
GUIDANCE OBJECTIVES
GUIDANCE PROGRAMS
GUIDANCE SERVICES
INDIVIDUAL COUNSELING
INTERVENTION
MARRIAGE COUNSELING
MICROCOUNSELING
NONDIRECTIVE COUNSELING
OCCUPATIONAL GUIDANCE
PARENT COUNSELING
PARENT STUDENT CONFERENCES
POST HIGH SCHOOL GUIDANCE
PUPIL PERSONNEL SERVICES
REFERRAL
REHABILITATION
REHABILITATION COUNSELING
STUDENT PERSONNEL SERVICES
STUDENT PERSONNEL WORK
STUDENT PLACEMENT
STUDENT PROBLEMS
STUDENT REHABILITATION
TEACHER GUIDANCE
VOCATIONAL ADJUSTMENT
VOCATIONAL COUNSELING
YOUTH PROBLEMS

100 **Culture**

ACCULTURATION
AFRICAN CULTURE
AMERICAN CULTURE
AMERICAN INDIAN CULTURE
BICULTURALISM
BURMESE CULTURE
CHINESE CULTURE
CROSS CULTURAL STUDIES
CULTURAL ACTIVITIES
CULTURAL BACKGROUND
CULTURAL CONTEXT
CULTURAL DIFFERENCES
CULTURAL DISADVANTAGEMENT
CULTURAL ENRICHMENT
CULTURAL EVENTS
CULTURAL EXCHANGE
CULTURAL FACTORS
CULTURAL IMAGES
CULTURAL INTERRELATIONSHIPS
CULTURAL ISOLATION
CULTURAL PLURALISM
CULTURAL TRAITS
CULTURE
CULTURE CONFLICT
CULTURE CONTACT
CULTURE LAG
DUTCH CULTURE
ETHNIC GROUPING
ETHNIC GROUPS
ETHNIC ORIGINS
ETHNIC STATUS
ETHNIC STEREOTYPES
FOLK CULTURE
FOREIGN CULTURE
INTERCULTURAL PROGRAMS
ISLAMIC CULTURE
JAPANESE AMERICAN CULTURE
JEWISH STEREOTYPES
KOREAN CULTURE
LATIN AMERICAN CULTURE
LUSO BRAZILIAN CULTURE
MIDDLE CLASS CULTURE
NEGRO CULTURE
NEGRO STEREOTYPES
NON WESTERN CIVILIZATION
PUERTO RICAN CULTURE
RELIGIOUS CULTURAL GROUPS
SLAVERY
SOCIOCULTURAL PATTERNS
SPANISH CULTURE
STUDENT SUBCULTURES
SUBCULTURE
URBAN CULTURE
WESTERN CIVILIZATION

110 **Curriculum**

ACCELERATED COURSES
ACTIVITY UNITS
AFRICAN AMERICAN STUDIES
AMERICAN GOVERNMENT (COURSE)
ARITHMETIC CURRICULUM

BOOKKEEPING
BUSINESS ADMINISTRATION
BUSINESS ENGLISH
BUSINESS SUBJECTS
COLLEGE CURRICULUM
COLLEGE SCIENCE
CONSUMER EDUCATION
CONSUMER SCIENCE
CONVERSATIONAL LANGUAGE COURSES
CORE COURSES
CORE CURRICULUM
CORRESPONDENCE COURSES
COURSE CONTENT
COURSE DESCRIPTIONS
COURSE OBJECTIVES
COURSES
CREDIT COURSES
CURRICULUM
CURRICULUM DESIGN
CURRICULUM ENRICHMENT
CURRICULUM GUIDES
CURRICULUM PROBLEMS
EDUCATION COURSES
ELECTIVE SUBJECTS
ELEMENTARY SCHOOL CURRICULUM
ELEMENTARY SCHOOL SCIENCE
ELEMENTARY SCIENCE
ENGLISH CURRICULUM
ENRICHMENT PROGRAMS
ETHNIC STUDIES
EXPERIMENTAL CURRICULUM
FELLOWSHIPS
FLES
FLIGHT TRAINING
FUSED CURRICULUM
GENERAL SCIENCE
HIGH SCHOOL CURRICULUM
HOME ECONOMICS
HONORS CURRICULUM
HUMAN RELATIONS UNITS
INDIVIDUALIZED CURRICULUM
INSERVICE COURSES
INSTITUTE TYPE COURSES
INTEGRATED CURRICULUM
INTELLECTUAL DISCIPLINES
INTENSIVE LANGUAGE COURSES
LABORATORY TECHNOLOGY
LANGUAGE PROGRAMS
LIBERAL ARTS
MARKETING
MATHEMATICS CURRICULUM
MERCHANDISING
MILITARY SCIENCE
MILITARY TRAINING
MODERN LANGUAGE CURRICULUM
MODERN SCIENCE
NATURAL SCIENCES
NONCREDIT COURSES
OFFICE PRACTICE
PHYSICAL GEOGRAPHY
PHYSICS CURRICULUM
PRESCHOOL CURRICULUM
PRETECHNOLOGY PROGRAMS

PROGRAM CONTENT
PROGRAM LENGTH
PROGRAMED UNITS
PUBLIC SPEAKING
RADIO TECHNOLOGY
REMEDIAL COURSES
SALESMANSHIP
SCIENCE COURSE IMPROVEMENT PROJECT
SCIENCE COURSES
SCIENCE CURRICULUM
SCIENCE PROGRAMS
SCIENCE UNITS
SCIENCES
SECONDARY SCHOOL SCIENCE
SHOP CURRICULUM
SHORT COURSES
SOCIAL STUDIES
SOCIAL STUDIES UNITS
SPEECH CURRICULUM
SPIRAL CURRICULUM
STATE CURRICULUM GUIDES
STUDY ABROAD
STUDY GUIDES
SUMMER SCIENCE PROGRAMS
TEACHER EDUCATION CURRICULUM
TEACHING GUIDES
TECHNOLOGY
TELEVISION CURRICULUM
TEXTBOOK CONTENT
UNGRADED CURRICULUM
UNIT PLAN
UNITS OF STUDY (SUBJECT FIELDS)
VOCATIONAL AGRICULTURE

120 Demography

CENSUS FIGURES
CITY DEMOGRAPHY
COMMUNITY SIZE
COMMUNITY ZONING
COMPREHENSIVE DISTRICTS
DEMOGRAPHY
DEPRESSED AREAS (GEOGRAPHIC)
DEVELOPED NATIONS
DEVELOPING NATIONS
DROPOUT RATE
EDUCATIONAL MOBILITY
ETHNIC DISTRIBUTION
FACULTY MOBILITY
FAMILY MOBILITY
FEEDER PATTERNS
GEOGRAPHIC DISTRIBUTION
GEOGRAPHIC LOCATION
GEOGRAPHIC REGIONS
HOUSING PATTERNS
INCIDENCE
METROPOLITAN AREAS
MIGRATION
MIGRATION PATTERNS
MOBILITY
NATIONAL DEMOGRAPHY
NEGRO POPULATION TRENDS
OVERPOPULATION

POPULATION DISTRIBUTION
POPULATION GROWTH
POPULATION TRENDS
RESIDENTIAL PATTERNS
REZONING
RURAL AREAS
RURAL POPULATION
RURAL RESETTLEMENT
SCHOOL DEMOGRAPHY
SCHOOL DISTRICTS
SCHOOL LOCATION
SCHOOL REDISTRICTING
SCHOOL ZONING
SOCIAL DISTRIBUTION
SOCIAL MOBILITY
SOUTHERN COMMUNITY
SOUTHERN STATES
SPECIAL ZONING
STUDENT DISTRIBUTION
STUDENT MOBILITY
SUBURBS
URBAN AREAS
URBAN IMMIGRATION
URBAN POPULATION
ZONING

130 Development

ADOLESCENCE
ADULT CHARACTERISTICS
ADULT DEVELOPMENT
BEHAVIOR DEVELOPMENT
CHILD DEVELOPMENT
CHILD REARING
CHILDHOOD
COGNITIVE DEVELOPMENT
COMMUNITY DEVELOPMENT
COMPREHENSION DEVELOPMENT
CREATIVE DEVELOPMENT
CURRICULUM DEVELOPMENT
DEVELOPMENT
DEVELOPMENTAL TASKS
EARLY CHILDHOOD
ECONOMIC DEVELOPMENT
EDUCATIONAL CHANGE
EDUCATIONAL DEVELOPMENT
EMOTIONAL DEVELOPMENT
EVOLUTION
GROWTH PATTERNS
HANDWRITING DEVELOPMENT
HUMAN DEVELOPMENT
IMPROVEMENT
INDIVIDUAL DEVELOPMENT
INFANCY
INTELLECTUAL DEVELOPMENT
LANGUAGE DEVELOPMENT
LIGHTING DESIGN
MANAGEMENT DEVELOPMENT
MANPOWER DEVELOPMENT
MATERIAL DEVELOPMENT
MATURATION
MOTOR DEVELOPMENT
PERCEPTUAL DEVELOPMENT
PERSONAL GROWTH

PERSONALITY DEVELOPMENT
PHYSICAL DEVELOPMENT
PROGRAM DEVELOPMENT
READING DEVELOPMENT
RETARDED SPEECH DEVELOPMENT
RURAL DEVELOPMENT
SITE DEVELOPMENT
SKILL DEVELOPMENT
STUDENT DEVELOPMENT
SYSTEMS DEVELOPMENT
TALENT DEVELOPMENT
TECHNICAL ASSISTANCE
VERBAL DEVELOPMENT
VOCABULARY DEVELOPMENT
VOCATIONAL DEVELOPMENT

140 Education

ACADEMIC EDUCATION
ACADEMIC FREEDOM
ADULT BASIC EDUCATION
ADULT EDUCATION
ADULT EDUCATION PROGRAMS
ADULT FARMER EDUCATION
ADULT VOCATIONAL EDUCATION
AFTER SCHOOL EDUCATION
AGRICULTURAL EDUCATION
ALCOHOL EDUCATION
ALUMNI EDUCATION
ARCHITECTURAL EDUCATION
ART EDUCATION
ASSOCIATE DEGREES
BACHELORS DEGREES
BUSINESS EDUCATION
CLASS ACTIVITIES
COEDUCATION
COLLEGE CHOICE
COLLEGE MAJORS
COLLEGE PREPARATION
COMMUNITY EDUCATION
COMPARATIVE EDUCATION
COMPENSATORY EDUCATION
COMPENSATORY EDUCATION PROGRAMS
COMPUTER SCIENCE EDUCATION
CONSERVATION EDUCATION
CONTINUATION EDUCATION
COOPERATIVE EDUCATION
CORRECTIONAL EDUCATION
CULTURAL EDUCATION
DEAF EDUCATION
DEGREES (TITLES)
DIFFUSION
DISTRIBUTIVE EDUCATION
DOCTORAL DEGREES
DRIVER EDUCATION
EARLY CHILDHOOD EDUCATION
EDUCATION MAJORS
EDUCATIONAL BENEFITS
EDUCATIONAL DEMAND
EDUCATIONAL EQUALITY
EDUCATIONAL HISTORY
EDUCATIONAL IMPROVEMENT
EDUCATIONAL INNOVATION
EDUCATIONAL NEEDS

EDUCATIONAL OBJECTIVES
EDUCATIONAL PHILOSOPHY
EDUCATIONAL PRACTICE
EDUCATIONAL PRINCIPLES
EDUCATIONAL PROBLEMS
EDUCATIONAL PROGRAMS
EDUCATIONAL QUALITY
EDUCATIONAL STRATEGIES
EDUCATIONAL SUPPLY
EDUCATIONAL TECHNOLOGY
EDUCATIONAL THEORIES
EDUCATIONAL TRENDS
ELEMENTARY EDUCATION
ELEMENTARY SCHOOL ROLE
ENGINEERING EDUCATION
ENGLISH EDUCATION
ENVIRONMENTAL EDUCATION
EXCEPTIONAL CHILD EDUCATION
EXTENSION EDUCATION
FAMILY LIFE EDUCATION
FIRE SCIENCE EDUCATION
GENERAL EDUCATION
GRADUATE STUDY
GRADUATION
GROUP ACTIVITIES
HEALTH EDUCATION
HEALTH OCCUPATIONS EDUCATION
HIGHER EDUCATION
HOME ECONOMICS EDUCATION
HOMEMAKING EDUCATION
INDUSTRIAL EDUCATION
INNOVATION
INSERVICE EDUCATION
INSERVICE TEACHER EDUCATION
INTEGRATED ACTIVITIES
INTERGROUP EDUCATION
INTERNATIONAL EDUCATION
JUNIOR HIGH SCHOOL ROLE
LABOR EDUCATION
LIBERAL ARTS MAJORS
LIBRARY EDUCATION
LITERACY EDUCATION
MANAGEMENT EDUCATION
MASTERS DEGREES
MATHEMATICS EDUCATION
MEDICAL EDUCATION
MIGRANT ADULT EDUCATION
MIGRANT CHILD EDUCATION
MIGRANT EDUCATION
MOBILE EDUCATIONAL SERVICES
MUSIC EDUCATION
NEGRO EDUCATION
NONDISCRIMINATORY EDUCATION
OCCUPATIONAL HOME ECONOMICS
OFFICE OCCUPATIONS EDUCATION
OUTDOOR EDUCATION
PARENT EDUCATION
PHYSICAL EDUCATION
POST DOCTORAL EDUCATION
POST SECONDARY EDUCATION
PRESCHOOL EDUCATION
PRESERVICE EDUCATION
PREVOCATIONAL EDUCATION

PRIMARY EDUCATION
PROFESSIONAL CONTINUING EDUCATION
PROFESSIONAL EDUCATION
PROGRESSIVE EDUCATION
PUBLIC ADMINISTRATION EDUCATION
PUBLIC AFFAIRS EDUCATION
PUBLIC EDUCATION
PUBLIC SCHOOL ADULT EDUCATION
RELIGIOUS EDUCATION
RURAL EDUCATION
RURAL EXTENSION
SAFETY EDUCATION
SCHOOL ACTIVITIES
SCHOOL ROLE
SCHOOL VISITATION
SCIENCE ACTIVITIES
SCIENCE EDUCATION
SECONDARY EDUCATION
SERVICE EDUCATION
SEX EDUCATION
SPECIAL EDUCATION
SPECIALIST IN EDUCATION DEGREES
SPECIALIZATION
SPEECH EDUCATION
STUDENT TEACHING
SUPPLEMENTARY EDUCATION
TEACHER EDUCATION
TEACHER EDUCATOR EDUCATION
TEACHER IMPROVEMENT
TECHNICAL EDUCATION
TERMINAL EDUCATION
THEOLOGICAL EDUCATION
TRADE AND INDUSTRIAL EDUCATION
UNDERGRADUATE STUDY
UNGRADED ELEMENTARY PROGRAMS
UNGRADED PRIMARY PROGRAMS
UNGRADED PROGRAMS
UNIFIED STUDIES PROGRAMS
UNIVERSAL EDUCATION
UNIVERSITY EXTENSION
URBAN EDUCATION
URBAN EXTENSION
VETERANS EDUCATION
VOCATIONAL EDUCATION
VOCATIONAL REHABILITATION
WOMENS EDUCATION
YOUNG FARMER EDUCATION

150 Employment

AGRICULTURAL LABOR DISPUTES
ARBITRATION
CAREER CHANGE
CAREER CHOICE
CAREERS
CHILD LABOR
COLLECTIVE BARGAINING
COLLECTIVE NEGOTIATION
COUNSELOR SELECTION
EMPLOYER EMPLOYEE RELATIONSHIP
EMPLOYMENT
EMPLOYMENT INTERVIEWS
EMPLOYMENT LEVEL
EMPLOYMENT PATTERNS

EMPLOYMENT POTENTIAL
EMPLOYMENT PRACTICES
EMPLOYMENT PROBLEMS
EMPLOYMENT PROJECTIONS
EMPLOYMENT SERVICES
EMPLOYMENT STATISTICS
EMPLOYMENT TRENDS
FACULTY RECRUITMENT
FARM LABOR
FARM LABOR PROBLEMS
FARM LABOR SUPPLY
FRINGE BENEFITS
GRIEVANCE PROCEDURES
INDUSTRIAL RELATIONS
INTERPROFESSIONAL RELATIONSHIP
INTERVIEWS
JOB ANALYSIS
JOB APPLICATION
JOB DEVELOPMENT
JOB LAYOFF
JOB MARKET
JOB PLACEMENT
JOB SATISFACTION
JOB TENURE
JOBS
LABOR
LABOR CONDITIONS
LABOR DEMANDS
LABOR FORCE
LABOR MARKET
LABOR PROBLEMS
LABOR SUPPLY
LABOR TURNOVER
LABOR UNIONS
LEAVE OF ABSENCE
LOCAL UNIONS
MAN DAYS
MANPOWER NEEDS
MANPOWER UTILIZATION
MIGRANT EMPLOYMENT
MULTIPLE EMPLOYMENT
NEGOTIATION IMPASSES
NEGRO EMPLOYMENT
OCCUPATIONAL CHOICE
OVERSEAS EMPLOYMENT
OVERTIME
PART TIME JOBS
PERSONNEL DATA
PERSONNEL NEEDS
PERSONNEL SELECTION
PROFESSIONAL RECOGNITION
PROMOTION (OCCUPATIONAL)
RECRUITMENT
RETIREMENT
SABBATICAL LEAVES
SCIENCE CAREERS
SCIENTIFIC MANPOWER
SEASONAL EMPLOYMENT
SEASONAL LABOR
SKILL ANALYSIS
SKILLED LABOR
STRIKES
STUDENT EMPLOYMENT

SUBEMPLOYMENT
TASK ANALYSIS
TEACHER EMPLOYMENT
TEACHER PERSISTENCE
TEACHER RECRUITMENT
TEACHER RETIREMENT
TEACHER STRIKES
TEACHER SUPPLY AND DEMAND
TEACHER WELFARE
TENURE
UNEMPLOYED
UNEMPLOYMENT
UNEMPLOYMENT INSURANCE
UNIONS
UNSKILLED LABOR
VOCATIONAL FOLLOWUP
WAGE STATEMENTS
WORK LIFE EXPECTANCY
WORK SIMPLIFICATION
WORKING HOURS
YOUTH EMPLOYMENT

160 Environment

ACOUSTICAL ENVIRONMENT
CITY IMPROVEMENT
CLASSROOM ARRANGEMENT
CLASSROOM ENVIRONMENT
CLIMATE CONTROL
CLIMATIC FACTORS
COLLEGE ENVIRONMENT
COMMUNITY ACTION
COMMUNITY CHANGE
COMMUNITY COOPERATION
COMMUNITY COORDINATION
COMMUNITY INFLUENCE
COMMUNITY INVOLVEMENT
COMMUNITY SUPPORT
CONTROLLED ENVIRONMENT
CULTURAL ENVIRONMENT
DISADVANTAGED ENVIRONMENT
DISTANCE
EDUCATIONAL ENVIRONMENT
ENVIRONMENT
ENVIRONMENTAL INFLUENCES
FAMILY ENVIRONMENT
HUMIDITY
INSTITUTIONAL ENVIRONMENT
NEIGHBORHOOD IMPROVEMENT
PERMISSIVE ENVIRONMENT
PHYSICAL ENVIRONMENT
RURAL ENVIRONMENT
SCHOOL CONDITIONS
SCHOOL ENVIRONMENT
SENSORY DEPRIVATION
SIMULATED ENVIRONMENT
SLUM CONDITIONS
SLUM ENVIRONMENT
SOCIAL ENVIRONMENT
SUBURBAN ENVIRONMENT
TEACHING CONDITIONS
TEMPERATURE
THERAPEUTIC ENVIRONMENT
THERMAL ENVIRONMENT

URBAN ENVIRONMENT
VISUAL ENVIRONMENT
WORK ENVIRONMENT

170 Equipment

AGRICULTURAL MACHINERY
AIR CONDITIONING
AIR CONDITIONING EQUIPMENT
ANALOG COMPUTERS
ATHLETIC EQUIPMENT
AUDIO EQUIPMENT
BIOMEDICAL EQUIPMENT
BOOKMOBILES
BROADCAST RECEPTION EQUIPMENT
BUILDING EQUIPMENT
BULLETIN BOARDS
CABINET TYPE PROJECTORS
CALORIMETERS
CARRELS
CENTRAL SOUND SYSTEMS
CHALKBOARDS
CLASSROOM FURNITURE
COMMUNITY ANTENNAS
COMPUTER STORAGE DEVICES
COMPUTERS
DIESEL ENGINES
DIGITAL COMPUTERS
DISPLAY PANELS
EDUCATIONAL EQUIPMENT
ELECTRIC BATTERIES
ELECTRIC CIRCUITS
ELECTRIC MOTORS
ELECTRICAL APPLIANCES
ELECTRONIC CONTROL
ELECTRONIC EQUIPMENT
ENGINES
EQUIPMENT
EQUIPMENT MAINTENANCE
EQUIPMENT UTILIZATION
EXPERIENCE CHARTS
FILMSTRIP PROJECTORS
FURNITURE
GLASS
GRADE CHARTS
HAND TOOLS
HEATING
HOME FURNISHINGS
INPUT OUTPUT DEVICES
INSTRUMENTATION
LABORATORY EQUIPMENT
LANGUAGE LABORATORY EQUIPMENT
LIBRARY EQUIPMENT
LIGHTS
LOOP INDUCTION SYSTEMS
MACHINE TOOLS
MAGNETIC TAPES
MEASUREMENT INSTRUMENTS
MECHANICAL EQUIPMENT
MICROPHONES
MICROSCOPES
MOTOR VEHICLES
MUSICAL INSTRUMENTS
OFFICE MACHINES

OPAQUE PROJECTORS
OPTICAL SCANNERS
OVERHEAD PROJECTORS
PARKING METERS
POLYGRAPHS
POTENTIOMETERS (INSTRUMENTS)
PROJECTION EQUIPMENT
RADAR
REFRIGERATION
SCHOOL BUSES
SCIENCE EQUIPMENT
SELF PACING MACHINES
SEMICONDUCTOR DEVICES
SERVICE VEHICLES
SIGNS
SIMULATORS
SIXTEEN MILLIMETER PROJECTORS
SPECTROGRAMS
STIMULUS DEVICES
SUPERCONDUCTORS
TACHISTOSCOPES
TAPE RECORDERS
TELEVISION LIGHTS
TEST SCORING MACHINES
TRACTORS
TRAFFIC SIGNS
TRANSISTORS
VENDING MACHINES
VENTILATION
VERTICAL WORK SURFACES
WHEEL CHAIRS

180 Evaluation
ACHIEVEMENT GAINS
ACHIEVEMENT RATING
ADMINISTRATOR EVALUATION
AUDITORY EVALUATION
BEHAVIOR RATING SCALES
CLINICAL DIAGNOSIS
COGNITIVE MEASUREMENT
COLLEGE CREDITS
COMMUNITY SURVEYS
COUNSELING EFFECTIVENESS
COUNSELOR EVALUATION
COURSE EVALUATION
CREDITS
CRITICAL INCIDENTS METHOD
CURRICULUM EVALUATION
DATA ANALYSIS
DENTAL EVALUATION
EDUCATIONAL DIAGNOSIS
EDUCATIONAL TESTING
EQUIPMENT EVALUATION
EVALUATION
EVALUATION NEEDS
EXPECTATION
FACULTY EVALUATION
FAILURE FACTORS
FIELD CHECK
GRADE POINT AVERAGE
GRADES (SCHOLASTIC)
GRADUATE SURVEYS
HANDWRITING READINESS

HYPOTHESIS TESTING
IDENTIFICATION
INSPECTION
INTEREST SCALES
INVESTIGATIONS
LEARNING READINESS
MEASUREMENT
MEASUREMENT GOALS
MEDICAL EVALUATION
MERIT RATING PROGRAMS
NATIONAL INTELLIGENCE NORM
NATIONAL SURVEYS
PASS FAIL GRADING
PERFORMANCE FACTORS
PERSONALITY ASSESSMENT
PERSONNEL EVALUATION
PHYSICAL EXAMINATIONS
PRESCHOOL EVALUATION
PRETESTING
PROFILE EVALUATION
PROGRAM EFFECTIVENESS
PROGRAM EVALUATION
PSYCHOLOGICAL EVALUATION
PSYCHOMETRICS
QUALITY CONTROL
RATING SCALES
READINESS (MENTAL)
READING READINESS
RELEVANCE (EDUCATION)
RELEVANCE (INFORMATION RETRIEVAL)
RELIABILITY
REPORT CARDS
SCHOOL SURVEYS
SPEECH EVALUATION
STATE SURVEYS
STUDENT EVALUATION
STUDENT TESTING
SUCCESS FACTORS
TEACHER EVALUATION
TEACHER RATING
TELEVISION SURVEYS
TEST INTERPRETATION
TEST RELIABILITY
TEST RESULTS
TESTING
TEXTBOOK EVALUATION
USE STUDIES

190 Evaluation Techniques
ACADEMIC PROBATION
CHECK LISTS
COMPARATIVE TESTING
CONTENT ANALYSIS
COST EFFECTIVENESS
EDUCATIONAL STATUS COMPARISON
EQUATED SCORES
ERROR PATTERNS
EVALUATION METHODS
EVALUATION TECHNIQUES
FIELD INTERVIEWS
FOLLOWUP STUDIES
FORCED CHOICE TECHNIQUE
GRADE EQUIVALENT SCALES

GRADE PREDICTION
GRADING
GROUP INTELLIGENCE TESTING
INTERNAL SCALING
ITEM ANALYSIS
LONGITUDINAL STUDIES
MATCHED GROUPS
MEASUREMENT TECHNIQUES
OBSERVATION
POST TESTING
PREDICTION
PREDICTIVE ABILITY (TESTING)
PREDICTIVE MEASUREMENT
PREDICTIVE VALIDITY
PSYCHOLOGICAL TESTING
Q SORT
QUESTION ANSWER INTERVIEWS
QUESTIONING TECHNIQUES
SCORING
SELF EVALUATION
SOCIOMETRIC TECHNIQUES
SURVEYS
SYNTHESIS
VISUAL MEASURES

200 Experience

ADMINISTRATOR BACKGROUND
BACKGROUND
CLINICAL EXPERIENCE
DISCUSSION EXPERIENCE
EARLY EXPERIENCE
ECONOMIC DISADVANTAGEMENT
EDUCATIONAL BACKGROUND
EDUCATIONAL DISADVANTAGEMENT
EDUCATIONAL EXPERIENCE
EMOTIONAL EXPERIENCE
EMPLOYMENT EXPERIENCE
ENRICHMENT EXPERIENCE
EXPERIENCE
FAMILY BACKGROUND
GROUP EXPERIENCE
INTELLECTUAL EXPERIENCE
LEARNING EXPERIENCE
LIMITED EXPERIENCE
MATHEMATICAL EXPERIENCE
PARENTAL BACKGROUND
PREREADING EXPERIENCE
SOCIAL BACKGROUND
SOCIAL EXPERIENCE
SOCIOECONOMIC BACKGROUND
STUDENT EXPERIENCE
TEACHER BACKGROUND
TEACHER EXPERIENCE
TEACHING EXPERIENCE
WORK EXPERIENCE

210 Facilities

ACOUSTIC INSULATION
AFTER SCHOOL CENTERS
AIR STRUCTURES
ANIMAL FACILITIES
ARCHITECTURAL BARRIERS
ARCHITECTURAL CHARACTER

ARCHITECTURAL ELEMENTS
ARCHITECTURAL PROGRAMING
ARCHITECTURE
ARCHIVES
ARTS CENTERS
ASPHALTS
ATHLETIC FIELDS
AUDIO ACTIVE COMPARE LABORATORIES
AUDIO ACTIVE LABORATORIES
AUDIO PASSIVE LABORATORIES
AUDIO VIDEO LABORATORIES
AUDIOVISUAL CENTERS
AUDITORIUMS
AUTOINSTRUCTIONAL LABORATORIES
BLUEPRINTS
BOARDING HOMES
BRANCH LIBRARIES
BUILDING CONVERSION
BUILDING IMPROVEMENT
BUILDING INNOVATION
BUILDING OBSOLESCENCE
BUILDING OPERATION
BUILDING PLANS
BUILDINGS
BUS GARAGES
BUSINESS EDUCATION FACILITIES
CAMPUS PLANNING
CAMPUSES
CARPETING
CEILINGS
CHILD CARE CENTERS
CHILD DEVELOPMENT CENTERS
CHIMNEYS
CHURCHES
CLASSROOM LIBRARIES
CLASSROOMS
CLEARINGHOUSES
CLINICS
COLLEGE BUILDINGS
COLLEGE HOUSING
COLLEGE LIBRARIES
COMMUNITY ROOMS
COMPUTER BASED LABORATORIES
CONSTRUCTION (PROCESS)
CONSTRUCTION NEEDS
CONSTRUCTION PROGRAMS
CONTINUING EDUCATION CENTERS
CORRECTIVE INSTITUTIONS
CORRIDORS
COUNSELING CENTERS
COUNTY LIBRARIES
CRAFTS ROOMS
CULTURAL CENTERS
CURRICULUM STUDY CENTERS
DAYLIGHT
DEMONSTRATION CENTERS
DENTAL CLINICS
DEPOSITORY LIBRARIES
DINING FACILITIES
DOORS
DORMITORIES
DRIVEWAYS
EDUCATION SERVICE CENTERS

EDUCATIONAL COMPLEXES
EDUCATIONAL FACILITIES
EDUCATIONAL PARKS
ELECTRICAL SYSTEMS
ELECTRONIC CLASSROOM USE
ELECTRONIC CLASSROOMS
ELEMENTARY SCHOOL LIBRARIES
EQUAL FACILITIES
EQUIPMENT STORAGE
EXHAUSTING
EXPERIMENT STATIONS
FACILITIES
FACILITY EXPANSION
FACILITY GUIDELINES
FACILITY IMPROVEMENT
FACILITY INVENTORY
FACILITY UTILIZATION RESEARCH
FALLOUT SHELTERS
FEED STORES
FIELD HOUSES
FISHERIES
FLEXIBLE CLASSROOMS
FLEXIBLE FACILITIES
FLEXIBLE LIGHTING DESIGN
FLOORING
FOOD HANDLING FACILITIES
FOOD STORES
FOSTER HOMES
FOUNDRIES
FUEL CONSUMPTION
FURNITURE ARRANGEMENT
GLARE
GLASS WALLS
GOVERNMENT LIBRARIES
GREENHOUSES
GUIDANCE CENTERS
GUIDANCE FACILITIES
GYMNASIUMS
HEALTH FACILITIES
HEALTH OCCUPATIONS CENTERS
HEARING CLINICS
HOSPITALS
HOTELS
HOUSE PLAN
HOUSING
HOUSING NEEDS
INFORMATION CENTERS
INSTITUTION LIBRARIES
INSTITUTIONAL FACILITIES
INSTITUTIONS
INSTRUCTIONAL MATERIALS CENTERS
INTEGRATED PUBLIC FACILITIES
INTERIOR SPACE
ITINERANT CLINICS
JUNIOR COLLEGE LIBRARIES
LABOR CAMP COMMISSARIES
LABOR CAMPS
LABORATORIES
LANGUAGE AND AREA CENTERS
LANGUAGE LABORATORIES
LAW LIBRARIES
LEARNING LABORATORIES
LEGISLATIVE REFERENCE LIBRARIES

LIBRARIES
LIBRARY FACILITIES
LIGHTED PLAYGROUNDS
LIGHTING
LOCKER ROOMS
LOW RENT HOUSING
MASONRY
MEDICAL LIBRARIES
MENTAL HEALTH CLINICS
MIDDLE INCOME HOUSING
MIGRANT CHILD CARE CENTERS
MIGRANT HOUSING
MILITARY AIR FACILITIES
MOBILE CLASSROOMS
MOBILE LABORATORIES
MOVABLE PARTITIONS
MULTIPURPOSE CLASSROOMS
MUSEUMS
MUSIC FACILITIES
NATIONAL LIBRARIES
NATURE CENTERS
NEGRO HOUSING
NEGRO INSTITUTIONS
NEIGHBORHOOD CENTERS
NURSERIES (HORTICULTURE)
NURSING HOMES
OFF CAMPUS FACILITIES
OFFICES (FACILITIES)
OPEN PLAN SCHOOLS
OUTDOOR THEATERS
PARKING AREAS
PARKING CONTROLS
PARKING FACILITIES
PARKS
PEDESTRIAN TRAFFIC
PERSONAL CARE HOMES
PHYSICAL EDUCATION FACILITIES
PHYSICAL FACILITIES
PLANETARIUMS
PLAYGROUNDS
PREFABRICATION
PRESCHOOL CLINICS
PRESTRESSED CONCRETE
PSYCHIATRIC HOSPITALS
PSYCHOEDUCATIONAL CLINICS
PUBLIC FACILITIES
PUBLIC HOUSING
PUBLIC LIBRARIES
READING CENTERS
READING CLINICS
REAL ESTATE
RECREATIONAL FACILITIES
REGIONAL LABORATORIES
REGIONAL LIBRARIES
REHABILITATION CENTERS
REMEDIAL READING CLINICS
REPAIR
RESEARCH AND DEVELOPMENT CENTERS
RESEARCH LIBRARIES
RESIDENTIAL CENTERS
RESOURCE CENTERS
ROAD CONSTRUCTION
ROOFING

RURAL CLINICS
SANITARY FACILITIES
SATELLITE LABORATORIES
SCHOOL BUILDINGS
SCHOOL CONSTRUCTION
SCHOOL LIBRARIES
SCHOOL MAINTENANCE
SCHOOL SHOPS
SCHOOL SIZE
SCHOOL SPACE
SCHOOL STUDY CENTERS
SCIENCE FACILITIES
SCIENCE LABORATORIES
SCIENCE TEACHING CENTERS
SEGREGATED PUBLIC FACILITIES
SELF CONTAINED CLASSROOMS
SELF DIRECTED CLASSROOMS
SETTLEMENT HOUSES
SITE ANALYSIS
SITE SELECTION
SKILL CENTERS
SPACE CLASSIFICATION
SPACE DIVIDERS
SPACE ORIENTATION
SPACE UTILIZATION
SPATIAL RELATIONSHIP
SPECIAL LIBRARIES
SPEECH CLINICS
STAGES
STATE LIBRARIES
STORAGE
STRUCTURAL BUILDING SYSTEMS
STUDENT LOADING AREAS
STUDENT UNIONS
STUDIO FLOOR PLANS
STUDY CENTERS
STUDY FACILITIES
SUBURBAN HOUSING
SUPPLEMENTARY EDUCATIONAL CENTERS
SWIMMING POOLS
TEACHER HOUSING
TELEVISION LIGHTING
THEATERS
TOILET FACILITIES
TRAFFIC CIRCULATION
TRAFFIC CONTROL
TRAFFIC PATTERNS
TRAILS
TRAINING LABORATORIES
UNIVERSITY LIBRARIES
URBAN UNIVERSITIES
UTILITIES
VEHICULAR TRAFFIC
VOCATIONAL TRAINING CENTERS
WAREHOUSES
WINDOWLESS ROOMS
WINDOWS
ZOOS

220 Finance
ACCOUNTING
ASSESSED VALUATION
BANKING

BIDS
BOND ISSUES
BUDGETING
BUDGETS
BUSINESS CYCLES
CAPITAL
CAPITAL OUTLAY (FOR FIXED ASSETS)
CONSTRUCTION COSTS
CONTRACT SALARIES
CONTRACTS
COSTS
CREDIT (FINANCE)
ECONOMIC CHANGE
ECONOMIC CLIMATE
EDUCATIONAL FINANCE
EQUALIZATION AID
ESTATE PLANNING
ESTIMATED COSTS
EXPENDITURE PER STUDENT
EXPENDITURES
FACULTY FELLOWSHIPS
FAMILY INCOME
FEDERAL AID
FEES
FINANCIAL NEEDS
FINANCIAL POLICY
FINANCIAL PROBLEMS
FINANCIAL SERVICES
FINANCIAL SUPPORT
FINES (PENALTIES)
FIRE INSURANCE
FISCAL CAPACITY
GRANTS
GUARANTEED INCOME
INCENTIVE GRANTS
INCOME
INDEMNITY BONDS
INITIAL EXPENSES
INTEREST
INVESTMENT
LEGAL COSTS
LIBRARY EXPENDITURES
LOW INCOME
MINIMUM WAGE
MONEY MANAGEMENT
MONEY SYSTEMS
NEGOTIATION AGREEMENTS
OPERATING EXPENSES
POLICE COSTS
PREMIUM PAY
PRIVATE FINANCIAL SUPPORT
PROGRAM BUDGETING
PROGRAM COSTS
PROPERTY ACCOUNTING
PROPERTY APPRAISAL
RECREATION FINANCES
RETAILING
SALARIES
SALARY DIFFERENTIALS
SCHOLARSHIP FUNDS
SCHOLARSHIP LOANS
SCHOLARSHIPS
SCHOOL.ACCOUNTING

SCHOOL BUDGET ELECTIONS
SCHOOL DISTRICT SPENDING
SCHOOL FUNDS
SCHOOL SUPPORT
STATE AID
STATE FEDERAL AID
STATE FEDERAL SUPPORT
STUDENT COSTS
STUDENT LOAN PROGRAMS
TAX ALLOCATION
TAX EFFORT
TAX SUPPORT
TEACHER SALARIES
TRAINING ALLOWANCES
TRUSTS (FINANCIAL)
TUITION
TUITION GRANTS
UNIT COSTS
WAGES
WELFARE
WHOLESALING
WILLS
WORKMANS COMPENSATION

230 Government

ADMINISTRATIVE AGENCIES
AGENCIES
BIRACIAL GOVERNMENT
BUREAUCRACY
CHILD LABOR LAWS
CITIZENSHIP
CITY GOVERNMENT
CITY PLANNING
CITY PROBLEMS
CITY WIDE COMMISSIONS
CIVIL LIBERTIES
CIVIL RIGHTS
CIVIL RIGHTS LEGISLATION
COLONIALISM
COMMUNITY
COMMUNITY AGENCIES (PUBLIC)
COMMUNITY PLANNING
COMMUNITY PROBLEMS
COMMUNITY RECREATION LEGISLATION
COMMUNITY SERVICES
COPYRIGHTS
COUNTY SCHOOL SYSTEMS
COURT CASES
COURT DOCTRINE
COURT LITIGATION
COURT ROLE
COURTS
DEMOCRACY
DISCRIMINATORY LEGISLATION
DRUG LEGISLATION
EDUCATIONAL LEGISLATION
ELECTIONS
EQUAL EDUCATION
EQUAL OPPORTUNITIES (JOBS)
EQUAL PROTECTION
FARM LABOR LEGISLATION
FEDERAL COURT LITIGATION
FEDERAL COURTS

FEDERAL GOVERNMENT
FEDERAL LAWS
FEDERAL LEGISLATION
FEDERAL PROGRAMS
FEDERAL RECREATION LEGISLATION
FEDERAL STATE RELATIONSHIP
FOREIGN COUNTRIES
FOREIGN POLICY
FREEDOM OF SPEECH
GOVERNMENT (ADMINISTRATIVE BODY)
GOVERNMENT ROLE
GOVERNMENTAL STRUCTURE
IMPERIALISM
JUVENILE COURTS
LABOR LAWS
LABOR LEGISLATION
LAW ENFORCEMENT
LAWS
LEGAL AID
LEGAL AID PROJECTS
LEGAL PROBLEMS
LEGISLATION
LOCAL HOUSING AUTHORITIES
LOCAL ISSUES
LOCAL RECREATION LEGISLATION
LOW INCOME COUNTIES
LOW INCOME STATES
LOYALTY OATHS
MIGRANT WELFARE SERVICES
MINIMUM WAGE LAWS
MINIMUM WAGE LEGISLATION
MUNICIPALITIES
NATIONAL DEFENSE
NATIONAL PROGRAMS
PATENTS
PLANNING COMMISSIONS
POLICE ACTION
POLITICAL AFFILIATION
POLITICAL INFLUENCES
POLITICAL POWER
POLITICAL SOCIALIZATION
PUBLIC HEALTH LAWS
RECREATION LEGISLATION
RURAL SCHOOL SYSTEMS
SCHOOL ATTENDANCE LAWS
SCHOOL LAW
SCHOOL TAXES
SOCIALIZATION
STATE ACTION
STATE AGENCIES
STATE CHURCH SEPARATION
STATE DEPARTMENTS OF EDUCATION
STATE GOVERNMENT
STATE LAWS
STATE LEGISLATION
STATE LICENSING BOARDS
STATE PROGRAMS
STATE RECREATION LEGISLATION
STATE SCHOOL DISTRICT RELATIONSHIP
STATES POWERS
SUBURBAN PROBLEMS
SUPREME COURT LITIGATION
SUPREME COURTS

TAX RATES
TAXES
TRAFFIC REGULATIONS
URBAN RENEWAL AGENCIES
VOTER REGISTRATION
VOTING
VOTING RIGHTS
WELFARE AGENCIES
WELFARE SERVICES
YOUTH AGENCIES

240 Handicapped

ACADEMICALLY HANDICAPPED
AMETROPIA
ANISEIKONIA
APHASIA
AUDITORY AGNOSIA
AURALLY HANDICAPPED
AUTISM
BLIND
CEREBRAL PALSY
CLEFT LIP
CLEFT PALATE
CRIPPLED CHILDREN
CUSTODIAL MENTALLY HANDICAPPED
DEAF
DEAF BLIND
EDUCABLE MENTALLY HANDICAPPED
EPILEPSY
HANDICAP DETECTION
HANDICAPPED
HANDICAPPED CHILDREN
HANDICAPPED STUDENTS
HARD OF HEARING
HEARING LOSS
HETEROPHORIA
HETEROTROPIA
HOMEBOUND
HYPEROPIA
LANGUAGE HANDICAPPED
LANGUAGE HANDICAPS
LEARNING DISABILITIES
MENTAL RETARDATION
MENTALLY HANDICAPPED
MINIMALLY BRAIN INJURED
MOBILITY AIDS
MONGOLISM
MULTIPLY HANDICAPPED
MYOPIA
NEUROLOGICAL DEFECTS
NEUROLOGICALLY HANDICAPPED
ORTHOPEDICALLY HANDICAPPED
PARTIALLY SIGHTED
PERCEPTUALLY HANDICAPPED
PHYSICAL HANDICAPS
PHYSICALLY HANDICAPPED
QUADRIPLEGIA
RETARDATION
RETARDED READERS
SEIZURES
SPEECH HANDICAPPED
SPEECH HANDICAPS
SPEECH PATHOLOGY

STEREOPSIS
TRAINABLE MENTALLY HANDICAPPED
VISUALLY HANDICAPPED
VISUALLY HANDICAPPED MOBILITY
VISUALLY HANDICAPPED ORIENTATION
VOICE DISORDERS

250 Health and Safety

ACCIDENT PREVENTION
ACCIDENTS
AGRICULTURAL SAFETY
AIR POLLUTION CONTROL
ALCOHOLISM
ALLERGY
ASTHMA
BREAKFAST PROGRAMS
CLEANING
CLOTHING
COMMUNICABLE DISEASES
COMMUNITY HEALTH
COMMUNITY HEALTH SERVICES
CONTRACEPTION
COSMETIC PROSTHESES
DENTAL HEALTH
DIABETES
DIETETICS
DISEASE CONTROL
DISEASE RATE
DISEASES
DISHWASHING
DRUG THERAPY
ETIOLOGY
FAMILY HEALTH
FATIGUE (BIOLOGY)
FIRE PROTECTION
FIRST AID
FOOD
FOOD SERVICE
GERIATRICS
HEALTH
HEALTH ACTIVITIES
HEALTH CONDITIONS
HEALTH GUIDES
HEALTH INSURANCE
HEALTH NEEDS
HEALTH PROGRAMS
HEALTH SERVICES
HEARING AIDS
HEARING CONSERVATION
HEARING THERAPY
HUMAN POSTURE
HUNGER
HYGIENE
IMMUNIZATION PROGRAMS
INFECTIOUS DISEASES
INJURIES
LABORATORY SAFETY
LUNCH PROGRAMS
LYSERGIC ACID DIETHYLAMIDE
MARIHUANA
MEDICAL CASE HISTORIES
MEDICAL SERVICES
MEDICAL TREATMENT

MENTAL HEALTH
MENTAL HEALTH PROGRAMS
MENTAL ILLNESS
MIGRANT HEALTH SERVICES
NARCOTICS
NEUROSIS
NURSING
NUTRITION
OCCUPATIONAL DISEASES
PESTICIDES
PHYSICAL FITNESS
PHYSICAL HEALTH
PHYSICAL THERAPY
POLLUTION
PREVENTIVE MEDICINE
PROSTHESES
PSYCHIATRIC SERVICES
PSYCHOSIS
PSYCHOSOMATIC DISEASES
PSYCHOTHERAPY
PUBLIC HEALTH
RESCUE
RUBELLA
SAFETY
SAFETY EQUIPMENT
SANITATION
SANITATION IMPROVEMENT
SCHOOL ACCIDENTS
SCHOOL HEALTH SERVICES
SCHOOL SAFETY
SEAFOOD
SEDATIVES
SMOKING
SPECIAL HEALTH PROBLEMS
STIMULANTS
THERAPY
TOBACCO
TRAFFIC ACCIDENTS
TRAFFIC SAFETY
VETERINARY MEDICINE
WATER POLLUTION CONTROL

260 Humanities

AFRICAN HISTORY
AFRICAN LITERATURE
ALLEGORY
AMBIGUITY
AMERICAN HISTORY
AMERICAN LITERATURE
ANALYTICAL CRITICISM
ANCIENT HISTORY
ANTHOLOGIES
ANTITHESIS
ARISTOTELIAN CRITICISM
ASIAN HISTORY
AUTOBIOGRAPHIES
BALLADS
BAROQUE LITERATURE
BIBLICAL LITERATURE
BIOGRAPHIES
CHARACTERIZATION (LITERATURE)
CHRONICLES
CIVIL WAR (UNITED STATES)

CLASSICAL LITERATURE
COLONIAL HISTORY (UNITED STATES)
COMEDY
CONSTITUTIONAL HISTORY
CZECH LITERATURE
DIALOGUE
DIARIES
DIDACTICISM
DRAMA
DRAMATIC UNITIES
EIGHTEENTH CENTURY LITERATURE
ENGLISH LITERATURE
ENGLISH NEOCLASSIC LITERARY PERIOD
ENGLISH PROGRAMS
EPICS
ESSAYS
EUROPEAN HISTORY
EXISTENTIALISM
EXPRESSIONISM
FABLES
FICTION
FIFTEENTH CENTURY LITERATURE
FIGURATIVE LANGUAGE
FOLK DRAMA
FORMAL CRITICISM
FRENCH LITERATURE
GERMAN LITERATURE
GREEK CIVILIZATION
HAIKU
HISTORICAL CRITICISM
HISTORY
HUMANISM
HUMANITIES
HUMOR
IMAGERY
IMPRESSIONISTIC CRITICISM
INDIVIDUALISM
IRONY
ITALIAN LITERATURE
JOURNALISM
LEGENDS
LITERARY ANALYSIS
LITERARY CRITICISM
LITERARY GENRES
LITERARY HISTORY
LITERARY INFLUENCES
LITERARY PERSPECTIVE
LITERARY STYLES
LITERATURE
LITERATURE APPRECIATION
LOCAL COLOR WRITING
LYRIC POETRY
MEDIEVAL HISTORY
MEDIEVAL LITERATURE
MEDIEVAL ROMANCE
METAPHORS
MEXICAN AMERICAN HISTORY
MIDDLE EASTERN HISTORY
MODERN HISTORY
MODERNISM
MORAL CRITICISM
MOTIFS
MYTHIC CRITICISM

MYTHOLOGY
NARRATION
NATURALISM
NEGRO HISTORY
NEGRO LITERATURE
NINETEENTH CENTURY LITERATURE
NOVELS
ODES
OLD ENGLISH LITERATURE
OUTDOOR DRAMA
PARALLELISM (LITERARY)
PARODY
PASTORAL LITERATURE
PHILOSOPHY
PLATONISM
PLAYWRITING
POETRY
POLISH LITERATURE
PROSE
PROVERBS
REALISM
RECONSTRUCTION ERA
RENAISSANCE LITERATURE
REVOLUTIONARY WAR (UNITED STATES)
RHETORIC
ROMANTICISM
RUSSIAN LITERATURE
SATIRE
SCIENCE EDUCATION HISTORY
SCIENCE FICTION
SCIENCE HISTORY
SCRIPTS
SEVENTEENTH CENTURY LITERATURE
SHORT STORIES
SIXTEENTH CENTURY LITERATURE
SOCIOLOGICAL NOVELS
SONNETS
SPANISH AMERICAN LITERATURE
SPANISH LITERATURE
SURREALISM
SYMBOLISM
SYMBOLS (LITERARY)
TALES
TEXTUAL CRITICISM
THEORETICAL CRITICISM
TRAGEDY
TRAVEL
TWENTIETH CENTURY LITERATURE
UNITED STATES HISTORY
VERSIFICATION
VICTORIAN LITERATURE
WORLD HISTORY
WORLD LITERATURE

270 Instruction

ACADEMIC ENRICHMENT
ACCELERATED PROGRAMS
AIRBORNE FIELD TRIPS
APPRENTICESHIPS
ARTICULATION (PROGRAM)
ASSIGNMENTS
ATTENDANT TRAINING
AUDIOVISUAL INSTRUCTION

AUDITORY TRAINING
AUTOINSTRUCTIONAL PROGRAMS
BIOLOGY INSTRUCTION
BRANCHING
CHAUTAUQUAS
CHEMISTRY INSTRUCTION
CLASS MANAGEMENT
CLASSROOM PARTICIPATION
CLOTHING INSTRUCTION
COLLEGE INSTRUCTION
COMPUTER ASSISTED INSTRUCTION
COMPUTER ORIENTED PROGRAMS
CONTINUOUS PROGRESS PLAN
CONVENTIONAL INSTRUCTION
COOKING INSTRUCTION
CORRESPONDENCE STUDY
COUNSELOR TRAINING
CROSS AGE TEACHING
CROSS CULTURAL TRAINING
CUSTODIAN TRAINING
DEDUCTIVE METHODS
DEMONSTRATION PROGRAMS
DEMONSTRATION PROJECTS
DEVELOPMENTAL PROGRAMS
DIAGNOSTIC TEACHING
DISCUSSION PROGRAMS
DRAMA WORKSHOPS
DROPOUT TEACHING
EDUCATIONAL GAMES
EFFECTIVE TEACHING
ENGLISH INSTRUCTION
EPISODE TEACHING
ETHICAL INSTRUCTION
EXPERIMENTAL TEACHING
FIELD INSTRUCTION
FOODS INSTRUCTION
GEOGRAPHY INSTRUCTION
GOAL ORIENTATION
GRAMMAR TRANSLATION METHOD
GROUP INSTRUCTION
HANDWRITING INSTRUCTION
HISTORY INSTRUCTION
HOME INSTRUCTION
HOME STUDY
HOME VISITS
HOMEWORK
HUMANITIES INSTRUCTION
INDIVIDUAL INSTRUCTION
INDIVIDUALIZED INSTRUCTION
INDUSTRIAL TRAINING
INQUIRY TRAINING
INSERVICE TEACHING
INSTRUCTION
INSTRUCTIONAL DESIGN
INSTRUCTIONAL IMPROVEMENT
INSTRUCTIONAL INNOVATION
INSTRUCTIONAL PROGRAMS
INSTRUCTIONAL TECHNOLOGY
JOB TRAINING
LABORATORY TRAINING
LANGUAGE EXPERIENCE APPROACH
LANGUAGE INSTRUCTION
LARGE GROUP INSTRUCTION

LAW INSTRUCTION
LEADERSHIP TRAINING
LIBRARY INSTRUCTION
LITERATURE PROGRAMS
MANAGEMENT GAMES
MASS INSTRUCTION
MATHEMATICS INSTRUCTION
METHODS COURSES
MICROTEACHING
MULTIMEDIA INSTRUCTION
NUTRITION INSTRUCTION
OFF THE JOB TRAINING
ON THE JOB TRAINING
ORIENTATION
PACING
PARENT WORKSHOPS
PART TIME TEACHING
PARTICIPANT INVOLVEMENT
PATTERN DRILLS (LANGUAGE)
PEDIATRICS TRAINING
PEER TEACHING
PHYSICS INSTRUCTION
PRACTICUMS
PRESCHOOL WORKSHOPS
PROFESSIONAL TRAINING
PROGRAMED INSTRUCTION
PROGRAMED TUTORING
PROJECT TRAINING METHODS
PROMPTING
READING INSTRUCTION
REFRESHER COURSES
REMEDIAL INSTRUCTION
REMEDIAL PROGRAMS
REMEDIAL READING
RESEARCH AND INSTRUCTION UNITS
RETRAINING
SCHOOL ORIENTATION
SCIENCE INSTRUCTION
SCIENCE PROJECTS
SENSITIVITY TRAINING
SENSORY TRAINING
SENTENCE DIAGRAMING
SEWING INSTRUCTION
SHELTERED WORKSHOPS
SPEECH INSTRUCTION
SPELLING INSTRUCTION
STAFF ORIENTATION
STUDENT IMPROVEMENT
STUDENT PARTICIPATION
STUDENT PROJECTS
SUBSTITUTION DRILLS
SUMMER WORKSHOPS
SUPERVISED FARM PRACTICE
SUPERVISORY TRAINING
TEACHER ORIENTATION
TEACHER PARTICIPATION
TEACHER SEMINARS
TEACHER WORKSHOPS
TEACHING
TEACHING MODELS
TEACHING PROCEDURES
TEAM TRAINING
TELECOURSES

TELEPHONE INSTRUCTION
TELEVISED INSTRUCTION
TEXTBOOK ASSIGNMENTS
TEXTILES INSTRUCTION
TRAINING
TRAINING OBJECTIVES
TRAVEL TRAINING
TUTORIAL PROGRAMS
URBAN TEACHING
VOCATIONAL RETRAINING
VOLUNTEER TRAINING
WORKBOOKS
WORKSHEETS
WORKSHOPS

280 Instructional Program Divisions
ABILITY GROUPING
ADVANCED PLACEMENT
AGE GRADE PLACEMENT
CLASS SIZE
CLASSES (GROUPS OF STUDENTS)
CLUSTER GROUPING
COURSE ORGANIZATION
DISCUSSION GROUPS
ELEMENTARY GRADES
EVENING CLASSES
GRADE ORGANIZATION
GRADE 1
GRADE 2
GRADE 3
GRADE 4
GRADE 5
GRADE 6
GRADE 7
GRADE 8
GRADE 9
GRADE 10
GRADE 11
GRADE 12
GRADE 13
GRADE 14
GROUPING (INSTRUCTIONAL PURPOSES)
HETEROGENEOUS GROUPING
HOMOGENEOUS GROUPING
HONORS CLASSES
INSTRUCTIONAL PROGRAM DIVISIONS
INTERMEDIATE GRADES
KINDERGARTEN
MULTIGRADED CLASSES
NONAUTHORITARIAN CLASSES
NONGRADED CLASSES
NONGRADED PRIMARY SYSTEM
NONGRADED SYSTEM
OPPORTUNITY CLASSES
PLACEMENT
PRIMARY GRADES
REGULAR CLASS PLACEMENT
SECONDARY GRADES
SMALL CLASSES
SPECIAL CLASSES
STUDENT GROUPING
TRANSITIONAL CLASSES
UNGRADED CLASSES

290 Language and Speech

ACOUSTIC PHONETICS
ADJECTIVES
ADVERBS
ALLOMORPHS
ALPHABETS
AMERICAN ENGLISH
APPLIED LINGUISTICS
ARTICULATION (SPEECH)
ARTIFICIAL SPEECH
AVIATION VOCABULARY
BANKING VOCABULARY
BILINGUAL EDUCATION
BILINGUALISM
CAPITALIZATION (ALPHABETIC)
CASE (GRAMMAR)
CHILD LANGUAGE
CODED SPEECH
COLLEGE LANGUAGE PROGRAMS
COMPONENTIAL ANALYSIS
COMPUTATIONAL LINGUISTICS
CONNECTED DISCOURSE
CONSONANTS
CONTEXT FREE GRAMMAR
CONTRASTIVE LINGUISTICS
CUED SPEECH
CYRILLIC ALPHABET
DEEP STRUCTURE
DESCRIPTIVE LINGUISTICS
DETERMINERS (LANGUAGES)
DIACHRONIC LINGUISTICS
DIACRITICAL MARKING
DIALECT STUDIES
DIALECTS
DICTION
DIGLOSSIA
DISCOURSE ANALYSIS
DISTINCTIVE FEATURES
ENUNCIATION IMPROVEMENT
ETYMOLOGY
EXPRESSIVE LANGUAGE
FINGER SPELLING
FLES GUIDES
FLES PROGRAMS
FORM CLASSES (LANGUAGES)
FUNCTION WORDS
GENERATIVE GRAMMAR
GLOTTOCHRONOLOGY
GRAMMAR
GRAPHEMES
IDIOMS
INNER SPEECH (SUBVOCAL)
INTERNATIONAL TRADE VOCABULARY
INTONATION
KERNEL SENTENCES
LANGUAGE
LANGUAGE ABILITY
LANGUAGE ARTS
LANGUAGE CLASSIFICATION
LANGUAGE ENRICHMENT
LANGUAGE ENROLLMENT
LANGUAGE FLUENCY

LANGUAGE GUIDES
LANGUAGE LABORATORY USE
LANGUAGE PATTERNS
LANGUAGE PLANNING
LANGUAGE PROFICIENCY
LANGUAGE RHYTHM
LANGUAGE ROLE
LANGUAGE STYLES
LANGUAGE TYPOLOGY
LANGUAGE UNIVERSALS
LANGUAGE USAGE
LEXICOGRAPHY
LEXICOLOGY
LINGUISTIC COMPETENCE
LINGUISTIC PATTERNS
LINGUISTIC PERFORMANCE
LINGUISTIC THEORY
LINGUISTICS
MACHINE TRANSLATION
MATHEMATICAL LINGUISTICS
MEDICAL VOCABULARY
MORPHEMES
MORPHOLOGY (LANGUAGES)
MORPHOPHONEMICS
MULTILINGUALISM
MUTUAL INTELLIGIBILITY
NEGATIVE FORMS (LANGUAGE)
NEGRO DIALECTS
NOMINALS
NONSTANDARD DIALECTS
OFFICIAL LANGUAGES
ONOMASTICS
ORAL ENGLISH
ORTHOGRAPHIC SYMBOLS
PARAGRAPHS
PARALINGUISTICS
PHONEMES
PHONEMIC ALPHABETS
PHONEMICS
PHONETIC ANALYSIS
PHONETIC TRANSCRIPTION
PHONETICS
PHONOLOGICAL UNITS
PHONOLOGY
PHRASE STRUCTURE
PLURALS
PRONOUNS
PRONUNCIATION
PRONUNCIATION INSTRUCTION
PSYCHOLINGUISTICS
PUNCTUATION
REGIONAL DIALECTS
ROMANIZATION
SECOND LANGUAGE LEARNING
SECOND LANGUAGES
SEMANTICS
SENTENCE STRUCTURE
SENTENCES
SIGN LANGUAGE
SOCIAL DIALECTS
SOCIOLINGUISTICS
SPEECH
SPEECH COMPRESSION

SPEECH HABITS
SPEECH IMPROVEMENT
SPEECH THERAPY
STANDARD SPOKEN USAGE
STRUCTURAL ANALYSIS
STRUCTURAL GRAMMAR
STRUCTURAL LINGUISTICS
STUTTERING
SUFFIXES
SUPRASEGMENTALS
SURFACE STRUCTURE
SYLLABLES
SYMBOLIC LANGUAGE
SYNCHRONIC LINGUISTICS
SYNTAX
TAGMEMIC ANALYSIS
TENL
TONE LANGUAGES
TRADITIONAL GRAMMAR
TRANSFORMATION GENERATIVE
    GRAMMAR
TRANSFORMATION THEORY (LANGUAGE)
TRANSFORMATIONS (LANGUAGE)
TRANSLATION
TYPOLOGY
UNCOMMONLY TAUGHT LANGUAGES
UNWRITTEN LANGUAGE
URBAN LANGUAGE
VERBS
VISIBLE SPEECH
VOWELS
WORD FREQUENCY
WORD LISTS
WRITTEN LANGUAGE

300 Languages

AFRICAN LANGUAGES
AFRIKAANS
AFRO ASIATIC LANGUAGES
AKAN
ALBANIAN
AMERICAN INDIAN LANGUAGES
AMHARIC
APACHE
ARABIC
ARMENIAN
AUSTRALIAN ABORIGINAL LANGUAGES
AUSTRO ASIATIC LANGUAGES
AYMARA
AZERBAIJANI
BALUCHI
BANTU LANGUAGES
BASHKIR
BASQUE
BEMBA
BENGALI
BERBER LANGUAGES
BIELORUSSIAN
BIKOL
BINI
BRAHMINS
BULGARIAN
BURIAT

BURMESE
BURUSHASKI
CAKCHIQUEL
CAMBODIAN
CANTONESE
CAUCASIAN LANGUAGES
CEBUANO
CHAD LANGUAGES
CHEREMIS
CHEROKEE
CHILUBA
CHINESE
CHINYANJA
CHOCTAW
CHUVASH
CLASSICAL LANGUAGES
CREE
CREOLES
CZECH
DAGUR
DRAVIDIAN LANGUAGES
DUSUN
DUTCH
DYULA
ENGLISH
ENGLISH (SECOND LANGUAGE)
ESTONIAN
EWE
FINNISH
FINNO UGRIC LANGUAGES
FOOCHOW
FRENCH
FULANI
GA
GANDA
GBAYA
GERMAN
GREEK
GUJARATI
GULLAH
HAITIAN CREOLE
HAUSA
HAWAIIAN
HEBREW
HINDI
HUNGARIAN
IBO
IGBO
INDO EUROPEAN LANGUAGES
INDONESIAN
INDONESIAN LANGUAGES
ITALIAN
JAPANESE
JAVANESE
KABYLE
KANNADA
KASHMIRI
KINYARUANDA
KIRGHIZ
KIRUNDI
KITUBA
KOREAN
KURDISH

LANGUAGES
LAO
LATIN
LINGALA
MALAGASY
MALAY
MALAYALAM
MALAYO POLYNESIAN LANGUAGES
MANDARIN CHINESE
MANDINGO
MARANAO
MARATHI
MELANESIAN LANGUAGES
MENDE
MIDDLE ENGLISH
MODERN LANGUAGES
MONGOLIAN
MONGOLIAN LANGUAGES
MOSSI
NAVAHO
NEMBE
NEPALI
NORWEGIAN
OKINAWAN
OLD ENGLISH
OSSETIC
OSTYAK
PANJABI
PAPAGO
PASHTO
PERSIAN
PIDGINS
POLISH
POMO
PORTUGUESE
PROGRAMING LANGUAGES
QUECHUA
RIFF
ROMANCE LANGUAGES
ROMANIAN
RUSSIAN
SAMOAN
SAMOYED LANGUAGES
SANGO
SANSKRIT
SARA
SEMITIC LANGUAGES
SERBOCROATIAN
SHONA
SIERRA LEONE CREOLE
SINGHALESE
SINO TIBETAN LANGUAGES
SLAVIC LANGUAGES
SLOVENIAN
SOMALI
SPANISH
SUSU
SWAHILI
TAGALOG
TAJIK
TAMIL
TATAR
TELUGU

THAI
TIBETAN
TURKIC LANGUAGES
TURKISH
TZELTAL
TZOTZIL
UKRAINIAN
URALIC ALTAIC LANGUAGES
URDU
UTO AZTECAN LANGUAGES
UZBEK
VIETNAMESE
VISAYAN
VOGUL
WOLOF
YAKUT
YIDDISH
YORUBA
YURAK

310 Learning and Cognition

ACCELERATION
ACTIVITY LEARNING
ADULT LEARNING
ASSOCIATIVE LEARNING
AURAL LEARNING
COGNITIVE PROCESSES
COMPLEXITY LEVEL
CONCEPT FORMATION
CONCEPTUAL SCHEMES
CONSERVATION (CONCEPT)
CONTEXT CLUES
CONTINUOUS LEARNING
CONVERGENT THINKING
CREATIVE THINKING
CREATIVITY
CRITICAL THINKING
CUES
DECISION MAKING
DISCOVERY LEARNING
DISCOVERY PROCESSES
DISCRIMINATION LEARNING
DIVERGENT THINKING
EDUCATIONAL RETARDATION
EVALUATIVE THINKING
FUNDAMENTAL CONCEPTS
GENERALIZATION
INCIDENTAL LEARNING
INFORMATION SEEKING
INTERFERENCE (LANGUAGE LEARNING)
LANGUAGE LEARNING LEVELS
LEARNING
LEARNING ACTIVITIES
LEARNING CHARACTERISTICS
LEARNING DIFFICULTIES
LEARNING PLATEAUS
LEARNING PROCESSES
LEARNING THEORIES
LISTENING COMPREHENSION
LITERARY DISCRIMINATION
LOGIC
LOGICAL THINKING
MEMORIZING

MEMORY
MENTAL DEVELOPMENT
MNEMONICS
MULTISENSORY LEARNING
NEGATIVE PRACTICE
NEGATIVE REINFORCEMENT
NONVERBAL LEARNING
NUCLEATION (LANGUAGE LEARNING)
PAIRED ASSOCIATE LEARNING
PERCEPTUAL MOTOR LEARNING
POSITIVE REINFORCEMENT
PRESCHOOL LEARNING
PROBLEM SOLVING
PRODUCTIVE THINKING
PROGRESSIVE RETARDATION
READING PROCESSES
RECALL (PSYCHOLOGICAL)
REINFORCEMENT
REINFORCERS
RETENTION
RETENTION STUDIES
REVIEW (REEXAMINATION)
ROTE LEARNING
SCIENTIFIC CONCEPTS
SEQUENTIAL LEARNING
SERIAL LEARNING
SOCIAL REINFORCEMENT
STIMULUS GENERALIZATION
SYMBOLIC LEARNING
SYSTEMS CONCEPTS
THOUGHT PROCESSES
TIME FACTORS (LEARNING)
TIME PERSPECTIVE
TRANSFER OF TRAINING
VERBAL LEARNING
VISUAL LEARNING
VISUALIZATION

320 Library Materials

ABSTRACTS
ANNOTATED BIBLIOGRAPHIES
ATLASES
BIBLIOGRAPHIC CITATIONS
BIBLIOGRAPHIES
BOOK CATALOGS
BOOK REVIEWS
BOOKLISTS
BOOKS
BULLETINS
CATALOGS
CHILDRENS BOOKS
CITATION INDEXES
CONCORDANCES
COORDINATE INDEXES
DICTIONARIES
DICTIONARY CATALOGS
DIRECTORIES
DIVIDED CATALOGS
ENCYCLOPEDIAS
FOLKLORE BOOKS
FOREIGN LANGUAGE BOOKS
FOREIGN LANGUAGE PERIODICALS
GLOSSARIES

GOVERNMENT PUBLICATIONS
GUIDES
HISTORICAL REVIEWS
LIBRARY COLLECTIONS
LIBRARY GUIDES
LIBRARY MATERIALS
LITERATURE GUIDES
LITERATURE REVIEWS
MANUALS
PAPERBACK BOOKS
PERIODICALS
PERMUTED INDEXES
REFERENCE BOOKS
REFERENCE MATERIALS
REPORTS
RESEARCH REVIEWS (PUBLICATIONS)
SCHOLARLY JOURNALS
SERIALS
TECHNICAL REPORTS
THESAURI
UNION CATALOGS
YEARBOOKS

330 Library Science

ABSTRACTING
BIBLIOGRAPHIC COUPLING
CATALOGING
CLASSIFICATION
CODIFICATION
DATA BASES
DECENTRALIZED LIBRARY SYSTEMS
DOCUMENTATION
FILING
INDEXING
INFORMATION DISSEMINATION
INFORMATION NEEDS
INFORMATION RETRIEVAL
INFORMATION SCIENCE
INFORMATION SERVICES
INFORMATION STORAGE
INFORMATION SYSTEMS
INFORMATION UTILIZATION
INTERLIBRARY LOANS
LIBRARY ACQUISITION
LIBRARY CIRCULATION
LIBRARY EXTENSION
LIBRARY MATERIAL SELECTION
LIBRARY NETWORKS
LIBRARY PROGRAMS
LIBRARY REFERENCE SERVICES
LIBRARY SCIENCE
LIBRARY SERVICES
LIBRARY SURVEYS
LIBRARY TECHNICAL PROCESSES
SEARCH STRATEGIES
SUBJECT INDEX TERMS

340 Mathematics

ADDITION
ALGEBRA
ALGORITHMS
ANALYSIS OF VARIANCE
ANALYTIC GEOMETRY

ARITHMETIC
CALCULATION
CALCULUS
COLLEGE MATHEMATICS
COMMON FRACTIONS
COMPARATIVE STATISTICS
CONGRUENCE
CORRELATION
DECIMAL FRACTIONS
DISCRIMINANT ANALYSIS
DIVISION
ELEMENTARY SCHOOL MATHEMATICS
EXPECTANCY TABLES
FACTOR ANALYSIS
FRACTIONS
GEOMETRIC CONCEPTS
GEOMETRY
INEQUALITIES
INTEGERS
LINEAR PROGRAMING
MATHEMATICAL APPLICATIONS
MATHEMATICAL CONCEPTS
MATHEMATICAL ENRICHMENT
MATHEMATICAL LOGIC
MATHEMATICAL MODELS
MATHEMATICAL VOCABULARY
MATHEMATICS
MODERN MATHEMATICS
MULTIPLICATION
NUMBER CONCEPTS
NUMBER SYSTEMS
NUMBERS
OPERATIONS RESEARCH
ORTHOGONAL PROJECTION
PERCENTAGE
PLANE GEOMETRY
PRACTICAL MATHEMATICS
PRIME NUMBERS
PROBABILITY
PROBABILITY THEORY
RATIONAL NUMBERS
RATIOS (MATHEMATICS)
RECIPROCALS (MATHEMATICS)
REMEDIAL ARITHMETIC
REMEDIAL MATHEMATICS
SAMPLING
SCHOOL STATISTICS
SECONDARY SCHOOL MATHEMATICS
SET THEORY
SOLID GEOMETRY
STATISTICAL ANALYSIS
STATISTICAL DATA
STATISTICAL STUDIES
STATISTICAL SURVEYS
STATISTICS
SUBTRACTION
SYMBOLS (MATHEMATICS)
TECHNICAL MATHEMATICS
TOPOLOGY
TRANSFORMATIONS (MATHEMATICS)
TRIGONOMETRY
WHOLE NUMBERS

350 Occupations

AGRICULTURAL CHEMICAL OCCUPATIONS
AGRICULTURAL MACHINERY OCCUPATIONS
AGRICULTURAL OCCUPATIONS
AGRICULTURAL SUPPLY OCCUPATIONS
ANESTHESIOLOGY
APPLIANCE REPAIRING
ARCHITECTURAL DRAFTING
ASSEMBLY (MANUFACTURING)
AUTO MECHANICS (OCCUPATION)
BLUE COLLAR OCCUPATIONS
BRICKLAYING
BUILDING TRADES
CABINETMAKING
CHILD CARE OCCUPATIONS
CLERICAL OCCUPATIONS
CLOTHING DESIGN
COSMETOLOGY
CROP PROCESSING OCCUPATIONS
DATA PROCESSING OCCUPATIONS
DEMAND OCCUPATIONS
DENTISTRY
DRAFTING
ELECTRICAL OCCUPATIONS
ENGINEERING DRAWING
ENGINEERING GRAPHICS
FARM OCCUPATIONS
FINANCE OCCUPATIONS
FINISHING
FOOD PROCESSING OCCUPATIONS
FOOD SERVICE OCCUPATIONS
FORESTRY OCCUPATIONS
HARVESTING
HEALTH OCCUPATIONS
HOROLOGY
INSURANCE OCCUPATIONS
LANDSCAPING
MANAGERIAL OCCUPATIONS
METAL WORKING OCCUPATIONS
MILITARY SERVICE
NEEDLE TRADES
OCCUPATIONAL CLUSTERS
OCCUPATIONAL INFORMATION
OCCUPATIONAL MOBILITY
OCCUPATIONAL SURVEYS
OCCUPATIONS
OFF FARM AGRICULTURAL OCCUPATIONS
OFFICE OCCUPATIONS
ORNAMENTAL HORTICULTURE OCCUPATION
PARAMEDICAL OCCUPATIONS
PATTERNMAKING
PLUMBING
PRACTICAL NURSING
PRINTING
PROFESSIONAL OCCUPATIONS
REAL ESTATE OCCUPATIONS
SALES OCCUPATIONS
SEMISKILLED OCCUPATIONS
SERVICE OCCUPATIONS
SHEET METAL WORK

SKILLED OCCUPATIONS
SOCIAL WORK
STENOGRAPHY
TECHNICAL ILLUSTRATION
TECHNICAL OCCUPATIONS
TECHNICAL WRITING
UNSKILLED OCCUPATIONS
WELDING
WHITE COLLAR OCCUPATIONS
WOODWORKING

360 Opportunities

CAREER OPPORTUNITIES
COMMUNITY BENEFITS
CULTURAL OPPORTUNITIES
ECONOMIC OPPORTUNITIES
EDUCATIONAL OPPORTUNITIES
EMPLOYMENT OPPORTUNITIES
HOUSING OPPORTUNITIES
OPPORTUNITIES
RESEARCH APPRENTICESHIPS
RESEARCH OPPORTUNITIES
SOCIAL OPPORTUNITIES
TEACHING BENEFITS
YOUTH OPPORTUNITIES

370 Organizations (Groups)

ADVISORY COMMITTEES
AEROSPACE INDUSTRY
ARMED FORCES
BIRACIAL COMMITTEES
BROADCAST INDUSTRY
BUSINESS
CEMENT INDUSTRY
CHEMICAL INDUSTRY
CITIZENS COUNCILS
CLASS ORGANIZATION
CLUBS
COLLECTIVE SETTLEMENTS
COMMITTEES
COMMUNITY ORGANIZATIONS
CONSTRUCTION INDUSTRY
COOPERATIVES
DENTAL ASSOCIATIONS
ELECTRONICS INDUSTRY
ENGLISH DEPARTMENTS
EQUIPMENT MANUFACTURERS
FACULTY ORGANIZATIONS
FARM COMMITTEES
FEDERAL TROOPS
FEED INDUSTRY
FOOD SERVICE INDUSTRY
FRATERNITIES
FREEDOM ORGANIZATIONS
FURNITURE INDUSTRY
GIRLS CLUBS
HOMEMAKERS CLUBS
HONOR SOCIETIES
HOUSING INDUSTRY
HUMAN RELATIONS ORGANIZATIONS
INDEXES (LOCATERS)
INDUSTRY
INSURANCE COMPANIES

INTERNATIONAL ORGANIZATIONS
LIBRARY ASSOCIATIONS
LUMBER INDUSTRY
MACHINERY INDUSTRY
MANUFACTURING INDUSTRY
MEAT PACKING INDUSTRY
MEDICAL ASSOCIATIONS
METAL INDUSTRY
MILITARY ORGANIZATIONS
NATIONAL ORGANIZATIONS
NEGRO BUSINESSES
NEGRO ORGANIZATIONS
ORCHESTRAS
ORGANIZATION SIZE (GROUPS)
ORGANIZATIONS (GROUPS)
PARENT ASSOCIATIONS
PRIVATE AGENCIES
PROFESSIONAL ASSOCIATIONS
PUBLISHING INDUSTRY
RELIGIOUS AGENCIES
RELIGIOUS ORGANIZATIONS
RESEARCH COMMITTEES
SCIENCE CLUBS
SCIENCE DEPARTMENTS
SEGREGATIONIST ORGANIZATIONS
SOCIAL AGENCIES
SOCIAL ORGANIZATIONS
STEEL INDUSTRY
STUDENT ORGANIZATIONS
TEACHER ASSOCIATIONS
TELEPHONE COMMUNICATIONS INDUSTRY
TOURISM
VOLUNTARY AGENCIES
YOUTH CLUBS

380 Personnel and Groups

ABLE STUDENTS
ACCOUNTANTS
ADJUSTMENT COUNSELORS
ADMINISTRATIVE PERSONNEL
ADOLESCENTS
ADOPTED CHILDREN
ADULT DROPOUTS
ADULT EDUCATORS
ADULT LEADERS
ADULT STUDENTS
ADULTS
ADVANCED STUDENTS
AFFLUENT YOUTH
AGE GROUPS
AGRICULTURAL LABORERS
AGRICULTURAL PERSONNEL
AGRICULTURAL TECHNICIANS
AIRCRAFT PILOTS
ALUMNI
AMERICAN INDIANS
AMISH
AMPUTEES
ANGLO AMERICANS
ANIMAL CARETAKERS
APPLIANCE SERVICE TECHNICIANS
ARABS
ARCHITECTS

ART TEACHERS
ARTISTS
ATHLETES
ATTENDANCE OFFICERS
ATTENDANTS
AUDIENCES
AUDIOLOGISTS
AUDIOMETRISTS
AUDIOVISUAL COORDINATORS
AUDIOVISUAL DIRECTORS
AUTHORS
AUTO BODY REPAIRMEN
AUTO PARTS MEN
AUXILIARY LABORERS
AVERAGE STUDENTS
AVIATION MECHANICS
BARBERS
BEGINNING TEACHERS
BILINGUAL STUDENTS
BILINGUAL TEACHER AIDES
BILINGUAL TEACHERS
BLIND CHILDREN
BOARD CANDIDATES
BOATMEN
BRACEROS
BRICKLAYERS
BUSINESS EDUCATION TEACHERS
CAMP COUNSELORS
CARDIAC (PERSON)
CARPENTERS
CASEWORKERS
CATHOLIC EDUCATORS
CATHOLIC PARENTS
CATHOLICS
CAUCASIAN RACE
CAUCASIAN STUDENTS
CAUCASIANS
CERTIFIED PUBLIC ACCOUNTANTS
CHEMICAL TECHNICIANS
CHEMISTRY TEACHERS
CHIEF ADMINISTRATORS
CHILD CARE WORKERS
CHILD DEVELOPMENT SPECIALISTS
CHILDREN
CHINESE AMERICANS
CHORUSES
CHURCH WORKERS
CITY OFFICIALS
CLERGYMEN
CLERICAL WORKERS
CLIENT CASEWORKERS
CLINIC PERSONNEL (SCHOOL)
CLINICAL PROFESSORS
CLOTHING MAINTENANCE SPECIALISTS
COACHING TEACHERS
COLLEGE BOUND STUDENTS
COLLEGE DEANS
COLLEGE FACULTY
COLLEGE FRESHMEN
COLLEGE GRADUATES
COLLEGE STUDENTS
COLLEGE SUPERVISORS
COLLEGE TEACHERS

COMMUNITY CONSULTANTS
COMMUNITY COORDINATORS
COMMUNITY LEADERS
COMMUNITY SCHOOL DIRECTORS
COMMUTING STUDENTS
COMPANIONS (OCCUPATION)
CONSULTANTS
CONTINUATION STUDENTS
COOKS
COOPERATING TEACHERS
COORDINATORS
COSMETOLOGISTS
COUNSELOR EDUCATORS
COUNSELORS
COUNTY OFFICIALS
COURT REPORTERS
CREW LEADERS
CRIMINALS
CULTURALLY ADVANTAGED
CULTURALLY DISADVANTAGED
DAIRYMEN
DAY STUDENTS
DEAF CHILDREN
DELINQUENTS
DENTAL ASSISTANTS
DENTAL HYGIENISTS
DENTAL TECHNICIANS
DENTISTS
DEPARTMENT DIRECTORS (SCHOOL)
DEPENDENTS
DESIGNERS
DIETITIANS
DIFFERENTIATED STAFFS
DISADVANTAGED GROUPS
DISADVANTAGED YOUTH
DISTRIBUTIVE EDUCATION TEACHERS
DOMESTICS
DRAFTSMEN
DROPOUTS
EDUCATIONAL RESEARCHERS
EDUCATIONALLY DISADVANTAGED
ELECTRICAL APPLIANCE SERVICEMEN
ELECTRICIANS
ELECTRONIC TECHNICIANS
ELEMENTARY SCHOOL COUNSELORS
ELEMENTARY SCHOOL STUDENTS
ELEMENTARY SCHOOL SUPERVISORS
ELEMENTARY SCHOOL TEACHERS
EMERGENCY SQUAD PERSONNEL
EMOTIONALLY DISTURBED CHILDREN
EMPLOYEES
EMPLOYERS
EMPLOYMENT COUNSELORS
ENGINEERING TECHNICIANS
ENGINEERS
ENLISTED MEN
ENTRY WORKERS
ENVIRONMENTAL TECHNICIANS
ESKIMOS
EVENING STUDENTS
EXAMINERS
EXCEPTIONAL (ATYPICAL)
EXCEPTIONAL CHILDREN

EXCEPTIONAL STUDENTS
EXPERIENCED LABORERS
EXTENSION AGENTS
FACULTY
FACULTY ADVISORS
FARM MECHANICS (OCCUPATION)
FARMERS
FATHERS
FILE CLERKS
FILIPINO AMERICANS
FILM PRODUCTION SPECIALISTS
FIRE FIGHTERS
FLES TEACHERS
FLOOR LAYERS
FOOD AND DRUG INSPECTORS
FOOD SERVICE WORKERS
FOREIGN DIPLOMATS
FOREIGN STUDENT ADVISERS
FOREIGN STUDENTS
FOREIGN WORKERS
FORESTRY AIDES
FORMER TEACHERS
FOSTER CHILDREN
FRESHMEN
GIFTED
GLAZIERS
GOVERNMENT EMPLOYEES
GRADUATE PROFESSORS
GRADUATE STUDENTS
GRADUATES
GROUNDS KEEPERS
GROUPS
GUIDANCE PERSONNEL
HEADS OF HOUSEHOLDS
HEALTH PERSONNEL
HEARING THERAPISTS
HIGH ACHIEVERS
HIGH SCHOOL GRADUATES
HIGH SCHOOL STUDENTS
HIGH SCHOOL SUPERVISORS
HIGHWAY ENGINEERING AIDES
HOME ECONOMICS TEACHERS
HOMEBOUND CHILDREN
HOMEBOUND TEACHERS
HOSPITAL PERSONNEL
HOSPITALIZED CHILDREN
HOUSEWIVES
HOUSING MANAGEMENT AIDES
ILLITERATE ADULTS
IMMIGRANTS
IMMIGRATION INSPECTORS
INDIANS
INDIGENOUS PERSONNEL
INDIVIDUAL CHARACTERISTICS
INDUSTRIAL ARTS TEACHERS
INDUSTRIAL PERSONNEL
INFANTS
INHALATION THERAPISTS
INSTITUTIONAL PERSONNEL
INSTITUTIONALIZED (PERSONS)
INSTRUCTIONAL STAFF
INSTRUCTOR COORDINATORS
INSTRUMENTATION TECHNICIANS

INTERPRETERS
INTERSTATE WORKERS
ITALIAN AMERICANS
ITINERANT TEACHERS
JAPANESE AMERICANS
JEWS
JOB APPLICANTS
JUNIOR COLLEGE STUDENTS
JUNIOR HIGH SCHOOL STUDENTS
JUVENILE GANGS
KINDERGARTEN CHILDREN
KOREAN AMERICANS
LABOR FORCE NONPARTICIPANTS
LABORERS
LANDLORDS
LANGUAGE TEACHERS
LAWYERS
LAY TEACHERS
LAYMEN
LEARNING SPECIALISTS
LEFT HANDED WRITER
LEGISLATORS
LIBRARIANS
LIBRARY TECHNICIANS
LISTENING GROUPS
LOCOMOTIVE ENGINEERS
LOW ABILITY STUDENTS
LOW ACHIEVERS
LOW INCOME GROUPS
LOWER CLASS MALES
LOWER CLASS PARENTS
LOWER CLASS STUDENTS
LOWER MIDDLE CLASS
MACHINE REPAIRMEN
MACHINE TOOL OPERATORS
MACHINISTS
MAIDS
MARINE TECHNICIANS
MASTER TEACHERS
MATHEMATICIANS
MATHEMATICS TEACHERS
MECHANICAL DESIGN TECHNICIANS
MEDIA SPECIALISTS
MEDICAL ASSISTANTS
MEDICAL CONSULTANTS
MEDICAL LABORATORY ASSISTANTS
MEDICAL RECORD LIBRARIANS
MEDICAL RECORD TECHNICIANS
MEDICAL STUDENTS
MEDICAL TECHNOLOGISTS
MERCHANTS
METALLURGICAL TECHNICIANS
METHODS TEACHERS
MEXICAN AMERICANS
MIDDLE AGED
MIDDLE CLASS COLLEGE STUDENTS
MIDDLE CLASS FATHERS
MIDDLE CLASS MOTHERS
MIDDLE CLASS PARENTS
MIGRANT CHILDREN
MIGRANT WORKERS
MIGRANT YOUTH
MIGRANTS

MILITARY PERSONNEL
MINORITY GROUP CHILDREN
MINORITY GROUP TEACHERS
MINORITY GROUPS
MOTHERS
MUSIC TEACHERS
MUSICIANS
NATIVE SPEAKERS
NEGRO MOTHERS
NEGRO STUDENTS
NEGRO TEACHERS
NEGRO YOUTH
NEGROES
NEUROTIC CHILDREN
NOMADS
NON ENGLISH SPEAKING
NONCOLLEGE PREPARATORY STUDENTS
NONFARM YOUTH
NONPROFESSIONAL PERSONNEL
NONRESIDENT STUDENTS
NUN TEACHERS
NUNS
NURSERY WORKERS (HORTICULTURE)
NURSES
NURSES AIDES
OCCUPATIONAL THERAPISTS
OCCUPATIONAL THERAPY ASSISTANTS
OFFICER PERSONNEL
OLDER ADULTS
OMBUDSMEN
OPTOMETRISTS
OUT OF SCHOOL YOUTH
OVERACHIEVERS
PARAPROFESSIONAL SCHOOL PERSONNEL
PARENTS
PAROLE OFFICERS
PART TIME FARMERS
PART TIME STUDENTS
PART TIME TEACHERS
PARTNERSHIP TEACHERS
PATIENTS (PERSONS)
PERSONNEL
PERSONNEL DIRECTORS
PHARMACISTS
PHYSICAL THERAPISTS
PHYSICAL THERAPY AIDES
PHYSICIANS
PHYSICS TEACHERS
POETS
POLICE
POTENTIAL DROPOUTS
PRACTICAL NURSES
PREMATURE INFANTS
PRESCHOOL CHILDREN
PRESCHOOL TEACHERS
PRESIDENTS
PRIESTS
PRINCIPALS
PRISONERS
PROBATION OFFICERS
PROBLEM CHILDREN
PRODUCTION TECHNICIANS
PROFESSIONAL PERSONNEL

PROFESSORS
PROGRAMERS
PROTESTANTS
PSYCHIATRIC AIDES
PSYCHIATRISTS
PSYCHOLOGISTS
PSYCHOMETRISTS
PSYCHOTIC CHILDREN
PUBLIC HOUSING RESIDENTS
PUBLIC OFFICIALS
PUBLIC SCHOOL TEACHERS
PUERTO RICANS
PUPIL PERSONNEL WORKERS
PURITANS
RADIOGRAPHERS
RADIOLOGIC TECHNOLOGISTS
READING CONSULTANTS
REFRIGERATION MECHANICS
REFUGEES
REMEDIAL TEACHERS
RESEARCH DIRECTORS
RESEARCHERS
RESIDENT ASSISTANTS
RESIDENT STUDENTS
RESOURCE TEACHERS
RETARDED CHILDREN
ROOFERS
RURAL DROPOUTS
RURAL FARM RESIDENTS
RURAL YOUTH
SALES WORKERS
SCHOOL AIDES
SCHOOL CADRES
SCHOOL NURSES
SCHOOL PERSONNEL
SCHOOL PSYCHOLOGISTS
SCHOOL SECRETARIES
SCHOOL SOCIAL WORKERS
SCHOOL SUPERINTENDENTS
SCIENCE CONSULTANTS
SCIENCE TEACHERS
SCIENTIFIC PERSONNEL
SCIENTISTS
SEAMEN
SEAMSTRESSES
SEASONAL LABORERS
SECONDARY SCHOOL COUNSELORS
SECONDARY SCHOOL STUDENTS
SECONDARY SCHOOL TEACHERS
SECRETARIES
SELF DIRECTED GROUPS
SEMISKILLED WORKERS
SENIOR CITIZENS
SENIORS
SERVICE WORKERS
SEWING MACHINE OPERATORS
SHARECROPPERS
SHEET METAL WORKERS
SIBLINGS
SIGN PAINTERS
SINGLE STUDENTS
SKILLED WORKERS
SLOW LEARNERS

SOCIAL WORKERS
SOCIALLY DISADVANTAGED
SOUTHERN CITIZENS
SPANISH AMERICANS
SPANISH SPEAKING
SPECIAL COUNSELORS
SPECIAL EDUCATION TEACHERS
SPECIALISTS
SPEECH THERAPISTS
STATE FOREIGN LANGUAGE SUPERVISORS
STATE OFFICIALS
STATE POLICE
STATE SUPERVISORS
STENOGRAPHERS
STUDENT CHARACTERISTICS
STUDENT PERSONNEL WORKERS
STUDENT TEACHERS
STUDENT VOLUNTEERS
STUDENTS
SUBPROFESSIONALS
SUBSTITUTE TEACHERS
SUBURBAN YOUTH
SUPERINTENDENTS
SUPERIOR STUDENTS
SUPERVISORS
SURGICAL TECHNICIANS
SYSTEMS ANALYSTS
TALENTED STUDENTS
TEACHER AIDES
TEACHER CHARACTERISTICS
TEACHER EDUCATORS
TEACHER INTERNS
TEACHER NURSES
TEACHERS
TEACHING ASSISTANTS
TEAM LEADER (TEACHING)
TEENAGERS
TELEVISION REPAIRMEN
TELEVISION TEACHERS
TERMINAL STUDENTS
THERAPISTS
TOOL AND DIE MAKERS
TRADE AND INDUSTRIAL TEACHERS
TRAINEES
TRAINERS
TRANSFER STUDENTS
TRANSIENT CHILDREN
TRIBES
TRUSTEES
TWINS
TYPISTS
UNDERACHIEVERS
UNDEREMPLOYED
UNION MEMBERS
UNSKILLED WORKERS
UNWED MOTHERS
URBAN DROPOUTS
URBAN YOUTH
VETERANS
VETERINARY ASSISTANTS
VISITING HOMEMAKERS
VOCATIONAL AGRICULTURE TEACHERS
VOCATIONAL DIRECTORS

VOCATIONAL EDUCATION TEACHERS
VOLUNTEERS
WATCHMAKERS
WELDERS
WOMEN PROFESSORS
WOMEN TEACHERS
WORKING PARENTS
WORKING WOMEN
YOUNG ADULTS
YOUTH
YOUTH LEADERS

390 Physical Education and Recreation

AFTER SCHOOL ACTIVITIES
ATHLETIC ACTIVITIES
ATHLETIC PROGRAMS
ATHLETICS
CALISTHENICS
CAMPING
CHILDRENS GAMES
COCURRICULAR ACTIVITIES
COMMUNITY RECREATION PROGRAMS
DAY CAMP PROGRAMS
EXERCISE (PHYSIOLOGY)
EXTRAMURAL ATHLETIC PROGRAMS
GAMES
HOBBIES
INTRAMURAL ATHLETIC PROGRAMS
LEISURE TIME
LIFTING
PHYSICAL ACTIVITIES
PHYSICAL RECREATION PROGRAMS
PLAYGROUND ACTIVITIES
RECREATION
RECREATIONAL ACTIVITIES
RECREATIONAL PROGRAMS
RESIDENT CAMP PROGRAMS
RUNNING
SCHOOL RECREATIONAL PROGRAMS
SOCIAL RECREATION PROGRAMS
SWIMMING
TUMBLING

400 Physical Sciences

ACOUSTICS
AEROSPACE TECHNOLOGY
AGRICULTURAL ENGINEERING
AIR FLOW
ASTRONOMY
ATOMIC STRUCTURE
ATOMIC THEORY
AUTO MECHANICS
AVIATION TECHNOLOGY
CHEMICAL ANALYSIS
CHEMICAL BONDING
CHEMICAL EQUILIBRIUM
CHEMICAL REACTIONS
CHEMISTRY
CHROMATOGRAPHY
CIVIL ENGINEERING
COORDINATION COMPOUNDS
EARTH SCIENCE
ELECTRICITY

ELECTROMECHANICAL TECHNOLOGY
ELECTRONICS
ELECTROOPTICS
ENERGY
ENGINEERING
ENGINEERING TECHNOLOGY
FLUID POWER EDUCATION
FORCE
GEOLOGY
GEOPHYSICS
HEAT
HEIGHT
HYDRAULICS
INDUSTRIAL TECHNOLOGY
INTERVALS
KINETIC MOLECULAR THEORY
KINETICS
LASERS
LIGHT
LUMINESCENCE
MAGNETS
MATTER
MECHANICS (PROCESS)
METALLURGY
METEOROLOGY
MOTION
NAVIGATION
NUCLEAR PHYSICS
NUCLEAR WARFARE
OCEANOLOGY
OPERATING ENGINEERING
OPTICS
ORGANIC CHEMISTRY
OXIDATION
PALEONTOLOGY
PHOTOCHEMICAL REACTIONS
PHYSICAL SCIENCES
PHYSICS
PLASTICS`
POWER MECHANICS
PRESSURE
QUANTUM MECHANICS
RADIATION
RADIATION EFFECTS
RADIOISOTOPES
RADIOLOGY
RELATIVITY
SEISMOLOGY
SOIL SCIENCE
SOLAR RADIATION
SPACE
THERMODYNAMICS
TIME
TRACKING
WEIGHT

410 Programs
ACTIVITIES
ADULT PROGRAMS
ADVANCED PLACEMENT PROGRAMS
ADVANCED PROGRAMS
AFTER SCHOOL PROGRAMS
ASSEMBLY PROGRAMS

CLASSROOM GUIDANCE PROGRAMS
COLLEGE PROGRAMS
COMPREHENSIVE PROGRAMS
COOPERATIVE PROGRAMS
COUNSELING INSTRUCTIONAL PROGRAMS
DAY PROGRAMS
DAYTIME PROGRAMS
DOCTORAL PROGRAMS
EVENING PROGRAMS
FAMILY PROGRAMS
FEEDER PROGRAMS
FIELD EXPERIENCE PROGRAMS
FOUNDATION PROGRAMS
HOME PROGRAMS
IMPROVEMENT PROGRAMS
INDIVIDUALIZED PROGRAMS
INPLANT PROGRAMS
INSTITUTES (TRAINING PROGRAMS)
INSURANCE PROGRAMS
INTERCOLLEGIATE PROGRAMS
INTERNATIONAL PROGRAMS
INTERNSHIP PROGRAMS
INTERSTATE PROGRAMS
PRESCHOOL PROGRAMS
PROGRAMS
PROJECTS
REGIONAL PROGRAMS
RESIDENTIAL PROGRAMS
SCIENCE FAIRS
SCIENCE INSTITUTES
SELF HELP PROGRAMS
SPECIAL DEGREE PROGRAMS
SPECIAL PROGRAMS
STUDENT PERSONNEL PROGRAMS
SUMMER INSTITUTES
SUMMER PROGRAMS
TEACHER EXCHANGE PROGRAMS
TEACHER PROGRAMS
TEACHING PROGRAMS
TECHNICAL INSTITUTES
TRANSFER PROGRAMS
VACATION PROGRAMS
WEEKEND PROGRAMS
WORK EXPERIENCE PROGRAMS
WORK STUDY PROGRAMS
YOUTH PROGRAMS

420 Psychology
ABSTRACT REASONING
ABSTRACTION LEVELS
ACHIEVEMENT NEED
ADAPTATION LEVEL THEORY
ADJUSTMENT (TO ENVIRONMENT)
ADJUSTMENT PROBLEMS
AFFECTION
AFFILIATION NEED
AGGRESSION
ANXIETY
AROUSAL PATTERNS
ASPIRATION
ASSOCIATION (PSYCHOLOGICAL)
BIBLIOTHERAPY
BODY IMAGE

CEREBRAL DOMINANCE
CHILD PSYCHOLOGY
CHILDHOOD NEEDS
CONFLICT
CONFLICT RESOLUTION
COUNSELOR ACCEPTANCE
COUNSELOR CLIENT RATIO
CRISIS THERAPY
CURIOSITY
DELINQUENT IDENTIFICATION
DEVELOPMENTAL PSYCHOLOGY
EDUCATIONAL PSYCHOLOGY
EMOTIONAL ADJUSTMENT
EMOTIONAL MALADJUSTMENT
EMOTIONAL PROBLEMS
EMOTIONALLY DISTURBED
EXPERIMENTAL PSYCHOLOGY
EXTINCTION (PSYCHOLOGY)
FANTASY
FEAR
FORCE FIELD ANALYSIS
GROUP THERAPY
HABIT FORMATION
HOSTILITY
HUMAN ENGINEERING
HYPNOSIS
IDENTIFICATION (PSYCHOLOGICAL)
IMAGINATION
IMITATION
INDIVIDUAL DIFFERENCES
INDIVIDUAL NEEDS
INDIVIDUAL PSYCHOLOGY
INHIBITION
INSECURITY
INTELLIGENCE FACTORS
INTERPERSONAL PROBLEMS
LATERAL DOMINANCE
LISTENING HABITS
LOW LEVEL ASPIRATION
MALADJUSTMENT
MEDIATION THEORY
MENTAL RIGIDITY
MILIEU THERAPY
NEED GRATIFICATION
NEEDS
OCCUPATIONAL THERAPY
OPERANT CONDITIONING
ORIGINALITY
PARENT CHILD RELATIONSHIP
PARENT INFLUENCE
PARENT STUDENT RELATIONSHIP
PARENTAL ASPIRATION
PARTICIPANT SATISFACTION
PEER ACCEPTANCE
PERCEPTUAL MOTOR COORDINATION
PERSONAL ADJUSTMENT
PERSONALITY
PERSONALITY CHANGE
PERSONALITY PROBLEMS
PERSONALITY STUDIES
PERSONALITY THEORIES
PLAY THERAPY
PROGRESSIVE RELAXATION

PROPAGANDA
PSYCHIATRY
PSYCHOACOUSTICS
PSYCHOEDUCATIONAL PROCESSES
PSYCHOLOGICAL CHARACTERISTICS
PSYCHOLOGICAL NEEDS
PSYCHOLOGICAL PATTERNS
PSYCHOLOGICAL SERVICES
PSYCHOLOGICAL STUDIES
PSYCHOLOGY
PSYCHOPATHOLOGY
PSYCHOPHYSIOLOGY
RATIONAL THERAPY
REACTION TIME
REJECTION
REWARDS
RISK
ROLE CONFLICT
ROLE PLAYING
ROLE THEORY
SCHIZOPHRENIA
SCHOOL PHOBIA
SECURITY
SELF ACTUALIZATION
SELF CONCEPT
SELF CONGRUENCE
SELF CONTROL
SELF EXPRESSION
SENSORY INTEGRATION
SOCIAL ADJUSTMENT
SOCIAL MATURITY
SOCIODRAMA
STATUS NEED
STRESS VARIABLES
STUDENT ADJUSTMENT
STUDENT COLLEGE RELATIONSHIP
STUDENT NEEDS
STUDENT SCHOOL RELATIONSHIP
SUICIDE
TEACHER ALIENATION
VERBAL OPERANT CONDITIONING
VERBAL STIMULI
WITHDRAWAL TENDENCIES
(PSYCHOLOGY)

430 Race Relations
ANTI SEMITISM
BLACK POWER
CLASSROOM INTEGRATION
COLLEGE INTEGRATION
COLLEGE SEGREGATION
DEFACTO SEGREGATION
DEJURE SEGREGATION
FACULTY INTEGRATION
GRADE A YEAR INTEGRATION
INTEGRATION EFFECTS
INTEGRATION LITIGATION
INTEGRATION METHODS
INTEGRATION PLANS
INTEGRATION READINESS
INTEGRATION STUDIES
LEGAL SEGREGATION
NEIGHBORHOOD INTEGRATION

PERSONNEL INTEGRATION
RACE
RACE INFLUENCES
RACE RELATIONS
RACIAL BALANCE
RACIAL CHARACTERISTICS
RACIAL COMPOSITION
RACIAL DIFFERENCES
RACIAL DISCRIMINATION
RACIAL DISTRIBUTION
RACIAL FACTORS
RACIAL INTEGRATION
RACIAL RECOGNITION
RACIAL SEGREGATION
RACISM
SCHOOL INTEGRATION
SCHOOL SEGREGATION
TEACHER INTEGRATION
TOKEN INTEGRATION
VOLUNTARY INTEGRATION

440 Reading

ADULT READING PROGRAMS
APPLIED READING
BASIC READING
BEGINNING READING
CONTENT READING
CORRECTIVE READING
CRITICAL READING
DEVELOPMENTAL READING
DIRECTED READING ACTIVITY
DYSLEXIA
EARLY READING
ELECTIVE READING
FACTUAL READING
FUNCTIONAL ILLITERACY
FUNCTIONAL READING
GROUP READING
ILLITERACY
INDEPENDENT READING
INDIVIDUAL READING
INDIVIDUALIZED READING
INITIAL TEACHING ALPHABET
INTERPRETIVE READING
LITERACY
LITERACY CLASSES
ORAL READING
RAPID READING
READABILITY
READING
READING ABILITY
READING ACHIEVEMENT
READING ASSIGNMENTS
READING COMPREHENSION
READING DIAGNOSIS
READING DIFFICULTY
READING FAILURE
READING HABITS
READING IMPROVEMENT
READING LEVEL
READING MATERIAL SELECTION
READING MATERIALS
READING PROGRAMS

READING SPEED
RECREATIONAL READING
REMEDIAL READING PROGRAMS
SEQUENTIAL READING PROGRAMS
SIGHT VOCABULARY
SILENT READING
SPEED READING
STORY READING
SUPPLEMENTARY READING MATERIALS

450 Research

ACTION RESEARCH
ADVANCED SYSTEMS
AGRICULTURAL RESEARCH PROJECTS
ARCHITECTURAL RESEARCH
AREA STUDIES
BEHAVIORAL SCIENCE RESEARCH
CASE STUDIES
CASE STUDIES (EDUCATION)
CLASSROOM RESEARCH
CONTROL GROUPS
CREATIVITY RESEARCH
CROSS SECTIONAL STUDIES
CURRICULUM RESEARCH
DATA COLLECTION
DEAF RESEARCH
DROPOUT RESEARCH
ECONOMIC RESEARCH
EDUCATIONAL EXPERIMENTS
EDUCATIONAL RESEARCH
ENVIRONMENTAL RESEARCH
EXCEPTIONAL CHILD RESEARCH
EXPERIMENTAL GROUPS
EXPERIMENTAL PROGRAMS
FACILITY CASE STUDIES
FACTOR STRUCTURE
FEASIBILITY STUDIES
FIELD STUDIES
INSTITUTIONAL RESEARCH
INTEREST RESEARCH
LANGUAGE RESEARCH
LIBRARY RESEARCH
MEDIA RESEARCH
MEDICAL RESEARCH
METHODS RESEARCH
PILOT PROJECTS
READING RESEARCH
RESEARCH
RESEARCH COORDINATING UNITS
RESEARCH CRITERIA
RESEARCH DESIGN
RESEARCH METHODOLOGY
RESEARCH NEEDS
RESEARCH PROBLEMS
RESEARCH PROJECTS
RESEARCH PROPOSALS
RESEARCH TOOLS
RESEARCH UTILIZATION
SCHEMATIC STUDIES
SCIENTIFIC ENTERPRISE
SCIENTIFIC PRINCIPLES
SCIENTIFIC RESEARCH
STUDENT RESEARCH

SYSTEMS ANALYSIS
SYSTEMS APPROACH
TECHNOLOGICAL ADVANCEMENT
TELEVISION RESEARCH
TEXTBOOK RESEARCH
THEORIES

460 Resources

ADHESIVES
AGRICULTURAL SUPPLIES
BUILDING MATERIALS
COMMUNITY RESOURCES
DEPLETED RESOURCES
DOCTORAL THESES
EDUCATIONAL RESOURCES
EXPORTS
FAMILY RESOURCES
FUELS
GRAINS (FOOD)
HUMAN CAPITAL
HUMAN RESOURCES
INFORMATION SOURCES
LAND SETTLEMENT
LAND USE
LUBRICANTS
MASTERS THESES
MEAT
METALS
NATURAL RESOURCES
PAPER (MATERIAL)
PRODUCER SERVICES
RESOURCE GUIDES
RESOURCE MATERIALS
RESOURCE UNITS
RESOURCES
SCIENCE MATERIALS
SEALERS
SOIL CONSERVATION
SUPPLIES
TALENT UTILIZATION
WATER RESOURCES

470 Schools

AFFILIATED SCHOOLS
AGRICULTURAL COLLEGES
AREA VOCATIONAL SCHOOLS
BILINGUAL SCHOOLS
BIRACIAL ELEMENTARY SCHOOLS
BIRACIAL SCHOOLS
BIRACIAL SECONDARY SCHOOLS
BOARDING SCHOOLS
CATHOLIC ELEMENTARY SCHOOLS
CATHOLIC HIGH SCHOOLS
CATHOLIC SCHOOLS
CHURCH RELATED COLLEGES
COLLEGE ROLE
COLLEGES
COMMUNITY COLLEGES
COMMUNITY SCHOOLS
COMPREHENSIVE HIGH SCHOOLS
CONSOLIDATED SCHOOLS
CONTINUATION HIGH SCHOOLS
CORRESPONDENCE SCHOOLS

DAY SCHOOLS
DENTAL SCHOOLS
DISADVANTAGED SCHOOLS
ELEMENTARY SCHOOLS
EVENING COLLEGES
EXPERIMENTAL COLLEGES
EXPERIMENTAL SCHOOLS
FOLK SCHOOLS
FREEDOM SCHOOLS
GENERAL HIGH SCHOOLS
HIGH SCHOOLS
HOSPITAL SCHOOLS
INSTITUTIONAL SCHOOLS
JUNIOR COLLEGES
JUNIOR HIGH SCHOOLS
LABORATORY SCHOOLS
LAND GRANT UNIVERSITIES
LAW SCHOOLS
LIBRARY SCHOOLS
MEDICAL SCHOOLS
MIDDLE SCHOOLS
MIGRANT SCHOOLS
MILITARY SCHOOLS
NEGRO COLLEGES
NEIGHBORHOOD SCHOOLS
NIGHT SCHOOLS
NONRESIDENTIAL SCHOOLS
NORTHERN SCHOOLS
NURSERY SCHOOLS
ONE TEACHER SCHOOLS
PAROCHIAL SCHOOLS
PRIVATE COLLEGES
PRIVATE SCHOOLS
PROPRIETARY SCHOOLS
PUBLIC SCHOOL SYSTEMS
PUBLIC SCHOOLS
RACIALLY BALANCED SCHOOLS
REGIONAL SCHOOLS
RESIDENTIAL COLLEGES
RESIDENTIAL SCHOOLS
RURAL SCHOOLS
SCHOOL SYSTEMS
SCHOOLS
SECONDARY SCHOOLS
SENIOR HIGH SCHOOLS
SLUM SCHOOLS
SMALL SCHOOLS
SOUTHERN SCHOOLS
SPECIAL SCHOOLS
STATE COLLEGES
STATE SCHOOLS
STATE UNIVERSITIES
SUBURBAN SCHOOLS
SUMMER SCHOOLS
TEACHERS COLLEGES
TRADITIONAL SCHOOLS
TRANSITIONAL SCHOOLS
UNGRADED SCHOOLS
UNIVERSITIES
URBAN SCHOOLS
VOCATIONAL HIGH SCHOOLS
VOCATIONAL SCHOOLS
YEAR ROUND SCHOOLS

480 Social Sciences

ACTIVISM
ANTHROPOLOGY
ARCHAEOLOGY
AUTHORITARIANISM
BEHAVIORAL SCIENCES
CHILD WELFARE
CHRISTIANITY
CIVICS
COMMUNISM
CONSUMER ECONOMICS
CURRENT EVENTS
ECONOMIC FACTORS
ECONOMIC PROGRESS
ECONOMIC STATUS
ECONOMICS
EDUCATIONAL ECONOMICS
ETHNOLOGY
FOREIGN RELATIONS
GEOGRAPHIC CONCEPTS
GEOGRAPHY
INTERFAITH RELATIONS
INTERPERSONAL RELATIONSHIP
JUDAISM
LABOR ECONOMICS
PEER RELATIONSHIP
PERSONAL RELATIONSHIP
PHYSICAL DIVISIONS (GEOGRAPHIC)
POLICE COMMUNITY RELATIONSHIP
POLICE SCHOOL RELATIONSHIP
POLITICAL DIVISIONS (GEOGRAPHIC)
POLITICAL ISSUES
POLITICAL SCIENCE
RELIGION
RELIGIOUS CONFLICT
RELIGIOUS DIFFERENCES
RELIGIOUS FACTORS
RELOCATION
RURAL ECONOMICS
RURAL URBAN DIFFERENCES
SCHOOL COMMUNITY COOPERATION
SCHOOL COMMUNITY RELATIONSHIP
SOCIAL CHANGE
SOCIAL DEVELOPMENT
SOCIAL DIFFERENCES
SOCIAL DISCRIMINATION
SOCIAL EXCHANGE THEORY
SOCIAL INFLUENCES
SOCIAL RELATIONS
SOCIAL SCIENCES
SOCIAL STATUS
SOCIAL WELFARE
SOCIOECONOMIC STATUS
STATUS
STUDENT TEACHER RELATIONSHIP
STUDENT WELFARE
WORLD AFFAIRS
WORLD GEOGRAPHY

490 Sociology

ACTION PROGRAMS (COMMUNITY)
ADOPTION

AGENCY ROLE
ANTI SEGREGATION PROGRAMS
BLACK COMMUNITY
BRACERO PROGRAMS
CASEWORKER APPROACH
CHANGE AGENTS
CHILD ABUSE
CHILD CARE
CHILD ROLE
CHILDHOOD FRIENDSHIP
CHURCH MIGRANT PROJECTS
CHURCH PROGRAMS
CHURCH ROLE
CITIZEN PARTICIPATION
CITIZEN ROLE
CITIZENSHIP RESPONSIBILITY
CITY WIDE PROGRAMS
CIVIL DEFENSE
CIVIL DISOBEDIENCE
COMMUNITY CHARACTERISTICS
COMMUNITY MIGRANT PROJECTS
COMMUNITY PROGRAMS
COMMUNITY RELATIONS
COMMUNITY RESPONSIBILITY
COMMUNITY ROLE
COMMUNITY SERVICE PROGRAMS
COMMUNITY STUDY
COUNSELOR ROLE
CRIMINOLOGY
DATING (SOCIAL)
DAY CARE PROGRAMS
DAY CARE SERVICES
DELINQUENCY CAUSES
DELINQUENCY PREVENTION
DELINQUENT ROLE
DEMONSTRATIONS (CIVIL)
DROPOUT CHARACTERISTICS
DROPOUT PROBLEMS
DROPOUT PROGRAMS
DROPOUT ROLE
ECONOMICALLY DISADVANTAGED
EDUCATIONAL DISCRIMINATION
EDUCATIONAL RESPONSIBILITY
EDUCATIONAL SOCIOLOGY
EMPLOYMENT PROGRAMS
ENROLLMENT INFLUENCES
ETHICS
ETHNIC RELATIONS
EXCHANGE PROGRAMS
FAMILY (SOCIOLOGICAL UNIT)
FAMILY CHARACTERISTICS
FAMILY INFLUENCE
FAMILY INVOLVEMENT
FAMILY LIFE
FAMILY MANAGEMENT
FAMILY PLANNING
FAMILY PROBLEMS
FAMILY PROJECTS
FAMILY RELATIONSHIP
FAMILY ROLE
FAMILY SCHOOL RELATIONSHIP
FAMILY STATUS
FAMILY STRUCTURE

FATHERLESS FAMILY
FOSTER FAMILY
FRIENDSHIP
GHETTOS
GROUP DYNAMICS
GROUP LIVING
GROUP MEMBERSHIP
GROUP RELATIONS
GROUP STATUS
GROUP STRUCTURE
GROUP UNITY
HIGH SCHOOL ROLE
HOME MANAGEMENT
HOUSING DEFICIENCIES
HOUSING DISCRIMINATION
HUMAN DIGNITY
HUMAN LIVING
HUMAN RELATIONS
HUMAN RELATIONS PROGRAMS
HUMAN SERVICES
ILLEGITIMATE BIRTHS
INDUSTRIAL STRUCTURE
INDUSTRIALIZATION
INNER CITY
INSTITUTIONAL ROLE
INTERACTION
INTERGROUP RELATIONS
INTERMARRIAGE
LOWER CLASS
MARITAL INSTABILITY
MARITAL STATUS
MARRIAGE
MIDDLE CLASS
MIGRANT PROBLEMS
MIGRANT WORKER PROJECTS
MINORITY ROLE
MORAL ISSUES
MOTHERLESS FAMILY
NEGRO ROLE
NEIGHBORHOOD
ONE PARENT FAMILY
PARENT SCHOOL RELATIONSHIP
PARTICIPANT CHARACTERISTICS
PEER GROUPS
PLANNED COMMUNITY
POVERTY PROGRAMS
POWER STRUCTURE
PROBLEMS
PRODUCTIVE LIVING
REHABILITATION PROGRAMS
RELATIONSHIP
RELIGIOUS DISCRIMINATION
RESIDENTIAL CARE
ROLE PERCEPTION
RURAL FAMILY
SCHOOL BOYCOTTS
SCHOOL COMMUNITY PROGRAMS
SCHOOL RESPONSIBILITY
SENIOR TEACHER ROLE
SLUMS
SOCIAL ACTION
SOCIAL CHARACTERISTICS
SOCIAL CLASS

SOCIAL DISADVANTAGEMENT
SOCIAL FACTORS
SOCIAL INTEGRATION
SOCIAL ISOLATION
SOCIAL LIFE
SOCIAL PLANNING
SOCIAL PROBLEMS
SOCIAL PSYCHOLOGY
SOCIAL RESPONSIBILITY
SOCIAL SERVICES
SOCIAL STRUCTURE
SOCIAL SYSTEMS
SOCIALLY MALADJUSTED
SOCIOECONOMIC INFLUENCES
SOCIOLOGY
SOCIOPSYCHOLOGICAL SERVICES
STEREOTYPES
STUDENT EXCHANGE PROGRAMS
STUDENT ROLE
T GROUPS
TEACHER ROLE
TEACHER STEREOTYPES
TEAMWORK
UPPER CLASS
URBAN RENEWAL
URBAN SLUMS
URBANIZATION
WELFARE PROBLEMS
WELFARE RECIPIENTS
WORLD PROBLEMS

500 Standards
ACADEMIC RANK (PROFESSIONAL)
ACADEMIC STANDARDS
ACCREDITATION (INSTITUTIONS)
ADMINISTRATOR QUALIFICATIONS
ADMISSION CRITERIA
BEHAVIOR STANDARDS
CENSORSHIP
CERTIFICATION
CLASS AVERAGE
COUNSELOR CERTIFICATION
COUNSELOR QUALIFICATIONS
CREDENTIALS
CRITERIA
DEGREE REQUIREMENTS
DESIGN NEEDS
DISQUALIFICATION
DROPOUT IDENTIFICATION
EDUCATIONAL CERTIFICATES
EDUCATIONAL SPECIFICATIONS
EMPLOYMENT QUALIFICATIONS
ENVIRONMENTAL CRITERIA
EQUIPMENT STANDARDS
EVALUATION CRITERIA
FACILITY REQUIREMENTS
FOOD STANDARDS
GRADUATION REQUIREMENTS
GROUP NORMS
ILLUMINATION LEVELS
LABOR STANDARDS
LANGUAGE STANDARDIZATION
LESSON OBSERVATION CRITERIA

LIBRARY STANDARDS
LIVING STANDARDS
MIDDLE CLASS NORM
NATIONAL NORMS
OBSOLESCENCE
PERFORMANCE CRITERIA
PERFORMANCE SPECIFICATIONS
PHYSICAL DESIGN NEEDS
PSYCHOLOGICAL DESIGN NEEDS
QUALIFICATIONS
RESIDENCE REQUIREMENTS
SPECIFICATIONS
STANDARDS
STATE STANDARDS
STUDENT CERTIFICATION
SUPERVISOR QUALIFICATIONS
TEACHER CERTIFICATES
TEACHER CERTIFICATION
TEACHER QUALIFICATIONS
TEACHING LOAD
TEACHING QUALITY
TEXTBOOK STANDARDS
VALIDITY

510 Techniques

AFTER SCHOOL TUTORING
AUDIENCE PARTICIPATION
AUDIOLINGUAL METHODS
AUTOINSTRUCTIONAL METHODS
AUTOMATION
CENTERS OF INTEREST
CLASSROOM GAMES
CLASSROOM OBSERVATION TECHNIQUES
CLASSROOM TECHNIQUES
COMPARATIVE ANALYSIS
COMPUTER GRAPHICS
CONCEPT TEACHING
CONFERENCES
COOPERATIVE TEACHING
CREATIVE ACTIVITIES
CREATIVE READING
CREATIVE TEACHING
CULTURING TECHNIQUES
DEMONSTRATIONS (EDUCATIONAL)
DISCUSSION (TEACHING TECHNIQUE)
DROPOUT PREVENTION
EDUCATIONAL METHODS
ELECTROENCEPHALOGRAPHY
ENRICHMENT
ENRICHMENT ACTIVITIES
EXPERIMENTS
FARM VISITS
FIELD TRIPS
FLEXIBLE PROGRESSION
GAME THEORY
GRADE REPETITION
GROUPING PROCEDURES
INDEPENDENT STUDY
INDIVIDUAL ACTIVITIES
INDIVIDUAL STUDY
INDUCTIVE METHODS
INSTRUCTIONAL TRIPS
INTELLECTUALIZATION

INTERACTION PROCESS ANALYSIS
INTERDISCIPLINARY APPROACH
INTERMODE DIFFERENCES
INTERVAL PACING
KINESTHETIC METHODS
LABORATORY EXPERIMENTS
LABORATORY PROCEDURES
LABORATORY TECHNIQUES
LEAD LECTURE PLAN
LEADERSHIP STYLES
LECTURE
LESSON PLANS
MAGNIFICATION METHODS
MANUFACTURING
MASS PRODUCTION
MEETINGS
METHODOLOGY
METHODS
MODELS
MOTIVATION TECHNIQUES
MUSIC TECHNIQUES
NUMERICAL CONTROL
OPTIONAL BRANCHING
PARENT CONFERENCES
PARENT PARTICIPATION
PARENT TEACHER CONFERENCES
PARENT TEACHER COOPERATION
PARTICIPATION
PHONICS
PHYSICS EXPERIMENTS
POLICE SEMINARS
PRESERVATION
PREVENTION
PRODUCTION TECHNIQUES
PUBLICIZE
QUESTIONNAIRES
READING GAMES
REDUNDANCY
REPETITIVE FILM SHOWINGS
SCIENCE EXPERIMENTS
SCIENTIFIC METHODOLOGY
SEMINARS
SEQUENTIAL APPROACH
SIGHT METHOD
SIMULATION
SMALL GROUP INSTRUCTION
STUDENT PROMOTION
STUDENT SEMINARS
STUDY
SYMPOSIA
TEACHING METHODS
TEACHING STYLES
TEACHING TECHNIQUES
TEAM TEACHING
TECHNIQUES
THEMATIC APPROACH
TRAINING TECHNIQUES
TUTORING
WRITING EXERCISES

520 Tests

ABSTRACTION TESTS
ACHIEVEMENT TESTS

ANSWER KEYS
APTITUDE TESTS
ASSOCIATION TESTS
ATTITUDE TESTS
AUDIOMETRIC TESTS
AUDITORY TESTS
AUDITORY VISUAL TESTS
CLOZE PROCEDURE
COGNITIVE TESTS
COLLEGE ENTRANCE EXAMINATIONS
CULTURE FREE TESTS
DIAGNOSTIC TESTS
EQUIVALENCY TESTS
ESSAY TESTS
GROUP INTELLIGENCE TESTS
GROUP TESTS
IDENTIFICATION TESTS
INDIVIDUAL TESTS
INFORMAL READING INVENTORY
INTELLIGENCE TESTS
INTEREST TESTS
LANGUAGE TESTS
MATURITY TESTS
MENTAL TESTS
MULTIPLE CHOICE TESTS
NATIONAL COMPETENCY TESTS
NONVERBAL TESTS
OBJECTIVE TESTS
OCCUPATIONAL TESTS

PERCEPTION TESTS
PERFORMANCE TESTS
PERSONALITY TESTS
PRESCHOOL TESTS
PRETESTS
PROBLEM SETS
PROGNOSTIC TESTS
PROJECTIVE TESTS
PSYCHOLOGICAL TESTS
PUZZLES
READING READINESS TESTS
READING TESTS
SCIENCE TESTS
SCREENING TESTS
SITUATIONAL TESTS
SPEECH TESTS
STANDARDIZED TESTS
TACTUAL VISUAL TESTS
TALENT IDENTIFICATION
TEST CONSTRUCTION
TEST SELECTION
TEST VALIDITY
TESTING PROBLEMS
TESTING PROGRAMS
TESTS
TESTS OF SIGNIFICANCE
TIMED TESTS
VERBAL TESTS
VISION TESTS

BIBLIOGRAPHY

Alexander, Carter, and Arvid J. Burke. *How to Locate Educational Information and Data*. 4th ed., rev. New York: Teachers College Press, 1958. 417 p.

Allen, William H., ed. *Dictionary of Technical Terms for Aerospace Use*. 1st ed. Washington: National Aeronautics and Space Administration, 1965. 314 p.

American Association of Collegiate Registrars and Admissions Officers. *Handbook of Data and Definitions in Higher Education*. Washington: The Association, American Council on Education, 1962. 132 p.

American Library Association. *ALA Glossary of Library Terms*. Chicago: American Library Association, 1943. 159 p.

Anthropological Linguistics. *Index to Languages of the World:* A-L. Florence M. Voegelin, and C. F. Voegelin, comps. Bloomington, Ind., Anthropological linguistics, Archives of languages of the world, Indiana University, 1966. 222 p. (Vol. 8, No. 6)

------. *Index to Languages of the World:* M-Z. Florence M. Voegelin, and C. F. Voegelin, comps. Bloomington, Ind., Anthropological linguistics, Archives of languages of the world, Indiana University. 1966. 202 p. (Vol. 8, No. 7)

Apel, Willi. *Harvard Dictionary of Music*. Cambridge, Mass.: Harvard University Press, 1944. 833 p.

Asimov, Isaac, and others, eds. *Stedman's Medical Dictionary; A Vocabulary of Medicine and Its Allied Sciences, With Pronunciations and Derivations*. 21st ed. Baltimore, Md.: Williams & Wilkins, 1966. 1,836 p.

Beam, Robert E. *A Dictionary of Electronic Terms*. 7th ed. Chicago: Allied Radio, 1963. 88 p.

Berrey, Lester V., and Gorton Carruth, eds. *Roget's International Thesaurus*. 3d ed. New York: Thomas Y. Crowell, 1962. 1,258 p.

Bloom, Benjamin S., ed. *Taxonomy of Educational Objectives*. Handbook I: *Cognitive Domain*. New York: McKay, 1956. 207 p.

Camp, Ruth D., comp. *Bureau of Ships Technical Library Thesaurus of Descriptive Terms and Code Book*. 1st ed. Washington: U.S. Bureau of Ships, Navy Department, 1963.

Center for Studies in Vocational and Technical Education. *Center Uniterm Vocabulary: A Coordinated Listing*. Madison, Wis.: The Center, University of Wisconsin. 1966. 65 pp.

Cochran, William G., and Gertrude M. Cox. *Experimental Designs*. 2d ed. New York: John Wiley & Sons, 1957. 611 p.

Coulson, John E., ed. *Programmed Learning and Computer-Based Instruction*. New York: John Wiley & Sons, 1962. 291 p.

Cronbach, Lee J., *Educational Psychology*. 2d ed. New York: Harcourt, 1963, 706 p.

Dawson, Mildred A., and others. *Guiding Language Learning*. 2d ed. New York: Harcourt, 1963. 430 p.

Defense Documentation Center. *ASTIA Chemical Thesaurus*. Alexandria, Va.: The Center, 1962. 34 p.

------. *COSATI Subject Category List; DOD Extended*. Alexandria, Va.; The Center, 1965. 69 p.

DeYoung, Cris A., and Richard Wynn. *American Education*. 5th ed. New York: McGraw-Hill, 1964. 538 p.

Dorland's Illustrated Medical Dictionary. 24th ed. Philadelphia, Pa.: Saunders, 1965. 1,724 p.

The Encyclopedia of Electronics. Charles Susskind, ed. New York: Reinhold, 1962. 974 p.

Engineers Joint Council. *Thesaurus of Engineering Terms*. 1st ed. New York: The Council, 1964. 302 p.

------. *Thesaurus Rules and Conventions*. New York: The Council, 1966. 7 p.

English, Horace B., and Ava C. English. *A Comprehensive Dictionary of Psychological and Psychoanalytical Terms*. New York: McKay, 1958. 594 p.

Federal Aviation Agency. *Thesaurus of FAA Descriptors*. 2d ed. Washington: The Agency, 1965. 232 p.

Ferguson, Charles A. *Glossary of Terms Relating to Languages of the Middle East*. 2d ed. Washington: Modern Language Association of America, 1964. 11 p.

Freiberger, Walter F., editor in chief. *International Dictionary of Applied Mathematics*. Princeton, N. J.: Van Nostrand, 1960. 1,173 p.

Freyer, Douglas H., and Edwin R. Henry, eds. *Handbook of Applied Psychology*. Vols. I and II. New York: Rinehart, 1950. Vol. I, 380 p.; Vol. II, 462 p.

Galanter, Eugene, ed. *Automatic Teaching*. New York: John Wiley & Sons, 1959. 198 p.

Ghiselli, Edwin E. *Theory of Psychological Measurements*. New York: McGraw-Hill, 1964. 408 p.

Glaser, Robert, ed. *Training Research and Education*. Pittsburgh, Pa.: University of Pittsburgh Press, 1962. 596 p.

Goldwyn, A.J., and others. *The Preparation of a Thesaurus of Educational Terms, Final Report.* Cleveland, Ohio: Western Reserve University, 1966. 98 p. (ED 010 239 from EDRS, 4936 Farimount Ave., Bethesda, Maryland 20014.)

Good, Carter V. *Dictionary of Education.* 2d ed. New York: McGraw-Hill, 1959. 676 p.

Goodman, Edith H., ed. *Automated Education Handbook.* Detroit, Mich.: Automated Education Center, 1965.

Gove, Philip B., and others, eds. *Webster's Third New International Dictionary.* Springfield, Mass.: Merriam, 1966. 2,622 p.

Graf, Rudolf F., comp. *Modern Dictionary of Electronics.* 2d ed. Indianapolis, Ind.: Howard W. Sams, 1962. 370 p.

Handel, S. *A Dictionary of Electronics.* Baltimore, Md.: Penguin Books, 1962. 384 p.

Hanson, J. L. *A Dictionary of Economics and Commerce.* 2d ed. London: MacDonald and Evans, Ltd., 1967. 432 p.

Harris, Chester W., ed. *Encyclopedia of Educational Research.* 3d ed. New York: Macmillan, 1960. 1,564 p.

Hilgard, Ernest R., and G. H. Bower. *Theories of Learning.* 3d ed. New York: Appleton-Century-Crofts, 1948. 563 p.

Hill, Winfred F. *Learning; A Survey of Psychological Interpretations.* San Francisco, Calif.: Chandler, 1963. 227 p.

Hinsie, Leland E., and Robert J. Campbell. *Psychiatric Dictionary.* 3d ed. New York: Oxford University Press, 1960. 788 p.

Hoerr, Normand L., and Arthur Osol, eds. *Blakiston's New Gould Medical Dictionary.* 2d ed. New York: McGraw-Hill, 1956. 1,463 p.

Horn, Jack. *Computer and Data Processing Dictionary and Guide.* Englewood Cliffs, N.J.: Prentice-Hall, 1966. 200 p.

Hunt, Joseph McV. *Intelligence and Experience.* New York: Ronald Press, 1961. 416 p.

The International Dictionary of Physics and Electronics. Edited by Walter C. Michels. Princeton, New Jersey, D. Van Nostrand Company, 1961. 1,355 p.

James, Glenn, and Robert C. James, eds. *Mathematics Dictionary; Multilingual.* 2d ed. Princeton, N. J.: Van Nostrand, 1959. 546 p.

Jarolimek, John. *Social Studies in Elementary Education.* 2d ed. New York: Macmillan, 1963. 418 p.

Kausler, Donald H. *Readings in Verbal Learning; Contemporary Theory and Research*. New York: John Wiley & Sons, 1966. 578 p.

Kendall, Maurice G., and William R. Buckland, eds. *Dictionary of Statistical Terms*; with a combined glossary in English, French, German, Italian and Spanish. 2d ed. New York: Hafner, 1960. 575 p.

Kimble, Gregory A., and Norman Garmezy. *Principles of General Psychology*. 2d ed. New York: Ronald Press, 1963. 655 p.

Library of Congress. *Subject Headings*. Used in the dictionary catalog of the Library of Congress. Edited by Marguerite V. Quattlebaum. 7th ed. Washington, D.C., Library of Congress, 1966. 1,432 p.

Lindgren, Bernard W., and G. W. McElrath. *Introduction to Probability and Statistics*. 2d ed. New York: Macmillan, 1966. 288 p.

Lindquist, Everet F., ed. *Educational Measurement*. Washington: American Council on Education, 1951. 819 p.

Lindzey, Gardner, ed. *Handbook of Social Psychology*: Vol I. *Theory and Method*; Vol. II. *Special Fields and Applications*. Reading, Mass.: Addison-Wesley, 1954. Vol. I, 588 p.; Vol. II, 639 p.

Markus, John. *Electronics and Nucleonics Dictionary*. 3d ed. New York: McGraw-Hill, 1965. 743 p.

Melton, Arthur W., ed. *Categories of Human Learning*. Report on a Symposium on the Psychology of Human Learning, University of Michigan, 1962. New York: Academic Press, 1962. 356 p.

Mesics, Emil A. *Training and Education for Manpower Development; An Annotated Bibliography on Education and Training in Organizations*. Ithaca, N. Y.: New York State School of Industrial and Labor Relations, Cornell University, 1964. 99 p.

Modern Language Association of America. *Foreign Language Codes for the 1966 National Register of Scientific and Technical Personnel*. Washington: The Association, 1966. 39 p.

Morgan, Clifford T., and R. A. King. *Introduction to Psychology*. 3d ed. New York: McGraw-Hill, 1966. 816 p.

Morse, William C., and Glenn M. Wingo. *Psychology and Teaching*. Rev. ed. Glenview, Ill.: Scott, Foresman, 1962. 816 p.

Mowrer, O. Hobart. *Learning Theory and Behavior*. New York: John Wiley & Sons, 1960. 555 p.

National Aeronautics and Space Administration. *NASA Thesaurus*: Vol I. Alphabetical Listing A-L. Prelim. ed. Washington, 1967. 433 p. (NASA SP-7030)

———. *NASA Thesaurus*: Vol. II. Alphabetical Listing M-Z. Prelim. ed. Washington, 1967. 425 p. (NASA SP-7030)

———. *NASA Thesaurus*: Vol. III. Appendixes. Prelim. ed. Washington, 1967. 643 p. (NASA SP-7030)

National Education Association. *Changing Role of the Audiovisual Process in Education; A Definition and a Glossary of Related Terms*. Washington: Audio-Visual Instruction Department, National Education Association, 1963. 148 p.

National Referral Center for Science and Technology. *A Directory of Information Resources in the United States*. Washington, National Referral Center for Science and Technology, Library of Congress, 1965. 352 p.

Ofiesh, Gabriel D. *Programmed Instruction; a Guide for Management*. New York: American Management Association, 1965. 416 p.

Parke, Nathan G. *Guide to the Literature of Mathematics and Physics; Including Related Works on Engineering Science*. 2d ed., rev. New York: Dover, 1959. 436 p.

Pei, Mario. *Glossary of Linguistic Terminology*. New York: Columbia University Press, 1966. 299 p.

Perrin, Porter G., and others. *Writer's Guide and Index to English*. 4th ed. Glenview, Ill.: Scott, Foresman, 1965. 833 p.

Rigney, Joseph W., and Edward B. Fry. "Current Teaching-Machine Programs and Programming Techniques," *Audio Visual Communication Review*. Supplement 3, Vol. 9, No. 3. Washington: National Education Association, 1961. 122 p.

Samuelson, Paul A. *Economics; an Introductory Analysis*. 7th ed. New York: McGraw-Hill, 1967. 821 p.

Sarbacker, Robert I. *Encyclopedic Dictionary of Electronics and Nuclear Engineering*. New York: Prentice-Hall, 1959. 1,417 p.

Saylor, Henry H. *Dictionary of Architecture*. New York: Science Editions, John Wiley & Sons, 1952. 219 p.

Schneider, Erwin H., and Henry L. Cady. *Evaluation and Synthesis of Research Studies Related to Music Education*. Columbus, Ohio: Ohio State University, 1965. 651 p.

Sippl, Charles J. *Computerman's Dictionary; A Glossary of Computer Definitions and Concepts*. Los Angeles: Trio Management Science Publication, 1965. 271 p.

———. *Computer Dictionary and Handbook*. Indianapolis, Ind.: Howard W. Sams, 1966. 766 p.

Stein, Jess, editor in chief. *Random House Dictionary of the English Language*: Unabridged edition. New York: Random House, 1966. 2,059 p.

Stevens, Stanley S., ed. *Handbook of Experimental Psychology*. New York: John Wiley & Sons, 1951. 1,436 p.

Thrall, William Flint, and Addison A. Hibbard, *Handbook to Literature*, revised and enlarged by C. Hugh Holman. New York: Odyssey Press, 1960. 595 p.

Trent, Horace M., and Betty Anderson, comps. *Glossary of Terms Frequently Used in Acoustics*. New York: American Institute of Physics, 1960. 44 p.

Uhr, Leonard, ed. *Pattern Recognition; Theory, Experiment, Computer Simulations, and Dynamic Models of Form Perception and Discovery*. New York: John Wiley & Sons, 1965. 393 p.

Underwood, Benton J. *Experimental Psychology*. 2d ed. New York: Appleton-Century-Crofts, 1966. 678 p.

U. S. Air Force, Educational Requirements Board Secretariat. *Educational Terms by General Areas of Study, Major Academic Fields, Specializations, and Subspecializations*. Montgomery, Ala.: Air Force Base, 1963. 69 p.

U. S. Air Force. *The United States Air Force Dictionary*, edited by Woodford A. Heflin. Princeton, N.J.: Van Nostrand, 578 p.

U. S. Department of Health, Education, and Welfare. *Medical Subject Headings*. Index Medicus, Vol. 8, No. 1, Pt. 2. Washington: The Department, 1967. 385 p.

——, Office of Education, Washington, D. C.

Combined Glossary of Standarized Items and Terms Presented in the Handbooks in the State Educational Records and Reports Series, 1966. 165 p.

Lichtenberger, Allan R., and Richard J. Penrod, comps. *Staff Accounting for Local and State School Systems*. 1965. 174 p.

Putnam, John F., and George G. Tankard, comps. *Pupil Accounting for Local and State School Systems*. 1964. 133 p.

Putnam, John F., and W. Dale Chismore, comps. *Standard Terminology for Instruction in Local and State School Systems; An Analysis of Instructional Content, Resources, and Processes* (Third draft - for selected distribution). 1967. 690 p.

Reason, Paul L., and Alpheus L. White, comps. *Financial Accounting for Local and State School Systems; Standard Receipt and Expenditure Accounts*. 1957. 235 p.

Reason, Paul L., and George G. Tankard, comps. *Property Accounting for Local and State School Systems*. 1959. 194 p.

Roberts, Charles T. *Guide for Implementing Handbook III, Property Accounting for Local and State School Systems*. 1966. 54 p.

Rules for Thesaurus Preparation. 1966. 9 p.

Samuelson, Everett V., George G. Tankard, and Hoyt W. Poe, comps. *Financial Accounting for School Activities.* 1959. 109 p.

U. S. Department of the Interior. *Water Resources Thesaurus;* A Vocabulary for Indexing and Retrieving the Literature of Water Resources Research and Development. Washington: The Department, 1966. 237 p.

U. S. Department of Labor. *Dictionary of Occupational Titles.* Vol. I: *Definitions of Titles.* 3d ed. Washington: U. S. Government Printing Office, 1965. 809 p.

------. *Dictionary of Occupational Titles.* Vol. II: *Occupational Classification.* 3d ed. Washington: U. S. Government Printing Office, 1965. 656 p.

U. S. Government Printing Office. *Style Manual.* Rev. ed. Washington: The Office, 1967. 512 p.

U. S. Office of Naval Research. *Thesaurus of Engineering and Scientific Terms.* Washington. 1967. 690 p.

Van Nostrand's Scientific Encyclopedia. 3d ed. Princeton, N. J.: Van Nostrand, 1958. 1,839 p.

Verplank, Williams S. "A glossary of some terms used in the objective science of behavior," Supplement to the *Psychological Review*, Vol. 64, No. 6, Pt. 2, Washington: American Psychological Association, 1957. 42 p.

Walsh, Donald D., comp. *What's What; A list of Useful Terms for the Teacher of Modern Languages.* 3d ed. New York: Modern Language Association, 1965. 34 p.

Wasserman, Morton N., comp. *Thesaurus of Communication Descriptors; A List of Terms Used in the ICS Information Center.* 1st ed. Paramus, N. J.: ITT Communication Systems, 1964. 127 p.

Weik, Martin H., comp. *A Glossary of Computer Engineering and Programming Terminology.* Aberdeen Proving Ground, Md.: U. S. Army, Ballistic Research Laboratory, 1958. 24 p.

Whitford, Harold C. *A Dictionary of American Homophones and Homographs.* New York: Teachers College Press, 1966. 83 p.

Whittaker, Kenneth. *Dictionaries.* New York: Philosophical Library, 1966. 88 p.

Wilson, Louis R. *Education and Libraries.* Hamden, Conn.: Shoe String Press, 1966. 344 p.

Woodworth, Robert S., and Harold Schlosberg. *Experimental Psychology.* Rev. New York: Holt, 1954. 948 p.

Zadrozny, John T. *Dictionary of Social Sciences*. Washington: Public Affairs Press, 1959. 367 p.

Zisa, Charles A., comp. *A Preliminary Directory of Language Names*. Washington, D.C.: Center for Applied Linguistics, 1968. 112 p.